VINTAGE CHART

S0-BZR-572

77	76	75	74	73	72	71	70	69	68	67	66	65	64	63	62	61	60
14	16	17	15	14	12	18	19	10	6	16	19	6	17	9	18	20	14
14	17	11	15	14	17	19	17	18	6	15	16	5	17	7	17	19	9
14	19	13	14	13	15	17	17	18	5	16	16	4	16	6	18	18	8
15	18	14	16	16	18	16	18	18	7	16	17	5	18	7	17	19	20
14	17	17	15	11	12	19	18	15	2	18	13	6	10	8	19	18	12
12	20	18	14	17	12	19	16	17	9	17	16	5	16	6	10	16	7
12	20	18	14	17	12	19	16	17	8	16	15	3	16	6	10	15	7
16	14	18	19	16	14	17	14	18	17	16	16	13	20	14	17	16	12
11	15	10	18	12	0	19	17	14	14	16	7	17	20	10	16	19	8
18	12	18	18	13	10	20	18	17	18	17	13	12	19	8	12	17	10
6	10	13	10	14	8	17	17	16	9	15	9	6	19	10	10	17	8
13	15	17	16	15	12	16	19	15	17	15	15	12	18	15	17	16	9
16	15	17	19	16	12	14	19	17	18	X	X	X	X	X	X	X	X
17	18	15	18	16	14	15	18	15	18	X	X	X	X	X	X	X	X
16	16	15	18	15	10	15	18	17	17	X	X	X	X	X	X	X	X
17	19	16	18	16	13	15	18	16	18	X	X	X	X	X	X	X	X
17	15	16	17	15	12	14	16	16	15	X	X	X	X	X	X	X	X
16	17	15	17	15	14	15	16	15	17	X	X	X	X	X	X	X	X
16	17	18	16	11	9	17	17	16	14	18	18	12	15	10	10	15	16
16	16	18	15	14	18	13	13	14	17	13	X	X	X	X	X	X	X

Scale: 19–20 = Best; 16–18 = Very Good; 13–15 = Good; 10–12 = Fair; –9 = Poor. X = Unlikely to be found or too variable to evaluate accurately.

Vintage Wine Merchants of San Francisco for California vintages, James Gifford and Guy Devaux for New York, and Château Ste. Michelle for Washington.

TERRY ROBARDS'
NEW BOOK OF
W·I·N·E

To Nicky,

on your birthday –
a vintage year and
many more !!

Love,
The Blakes
3 / 9 / 85

TERRY ROBARDS'
NEW BOOK OF
W·I·N·E

The Ultimate Guide to Wines
Throughout the World

TERRY ROBARDS

G. P. PUTNAM'S SONS / NEW YORK

To Margaret Maurice Robards, my most enthusiastic editor-in-chief,
to Joan Stewart, who manned the battlements,
and to Winston, who would still rather be in Hyde Park.

Copyright © by Sherman M. Robards
All rights reserved. This book, or parts thereof, must not be reproduced in any form
without permission. Published simultaneously in Canada by
General Publishing Co. Limited, Toronto.

Designed by Richard Oriolo

Library of Congress Cataloging in Publication Data

Robards, Terry.
  Terry Robards' New book of wine.

  Rev. and updated ed. of: The New York times book of
wine. c1976.
  Includes index.
  1. Wine and wine making. I. Robards, Terry. New York
times book of wine. II. Title. III. Title: New book of
wine.
TP548.R63 1984   641.2′22   83–19129
ISBN 0-399-12909-X

Printed in the United States of America

Contents

Preface

The original version of this work was *The New York Times Book of Wine,* conceived and planned in 1972 and published by Quadrangle/The New York Times Book Company in 1976. A paperback edition was published the following year by Avon Books. Since then a great deal of change has occurred in the wine world. Wineries and vineyards that did not exist when I researched and wrote the original edition have now achieved prominence. The public's desire for wine knowledge has grown enormously, and a broad revision and updating of the original work were necessary. This new edition, containing vast quantities of new information, especially on the exciting wines of California and the increasingly respected wines of Italy, bears only a passing resemblance to the original book. The resources of G. P. Putnam's Sons, a different publisher, are now behind it, and the work has a new title, *Terry Robards' New Book of Wine.*

T.R.
March 1984

Introduction

The wine boom that began in the early 1970s has gathered momentum, and American consumers are now confronted with an enormous array of wines from all over the world. Wine producers abroad are trying to capitalize on our thirst for wine by sending an ever-widening range of products across the oceans to these shores. American producers, especially in California and New York, have grown far more adept at making wines of charm and complexity which contrast with the dull, one-dimensional wines of yesteryear. Restaurants and retailers have expanded their lists and inventories. The bottom line is that although consumers have grown far more sophisticated, the wine universe has expanded, and there is much more to know today than there was a decade ago.

This book now contains full descriptions of more than 200 *more* California wineries and their products than when the first text was completed in 1975, when most of these wineries did not even exist. The number of European wines now deserving entries in the encyclopedic section has risen sharply; the entries from Italy alone have grown by more than a hundred, and there are many more entries for French, Spanish, and other regions as well.

For any expert, must less a typical consumer, to have complete knowledge of today's wine spectrum is probably impossible, yet the purpose of this book is to lay out the information necessary—and, most important, in simple, readable form. This book is intended to be the most nearly complete work on wine written to date; at the same time it is meant to be entirely comprehensible to the lay person, a source of information and ideas on the total wine experience. This is obviously an ambitious undertaking, and there may be areas in which the text falls short in terms of comprehensiveness.

It is also true that much information on wine is best left to the individual palate to discover or is perhaps best presented in more scholarly, specialized texts that focus on specific wine regions or varieties. After all, there is only so much that can be conveyed within the confines of a manageable, readable work that attempts to cover every facet of a subject.

I acknowledge with high respect the pioneering books of my friend Alexis Lichine, who has probably conveyed more information in book form to wine consumers than any other writer. I acknowledge equally the works of the late Frank Schoonmaker, the late André Simon, the late Harold Grossman, the excellent revision of Simon by Serena Suttcliff, Julius Wile's updating of Schoonmaker's encyclopedia, Peter M. F. Sichel's expert revision of Schoonmaker on German wines, Harriet Lembeck's updating of Grossman, and Hugh Johnson's unique wine atlas. I have attempted to take the subject one small but important step farther, into the realm of the lay reader who may lack any familiarity with wine, who may want to start from the beginning, who may want to make a stab at putting together the complex jigsaw puzzle that wine has become in the modern era.

In sixteen years of writing for *The New York Times,* in treating the complex subjects of business and finance as well as wine, my goal was always to render the subject matter totally comprehensible to any reader. I consider my audience so broad that it encompasses all people who can read, and I have written this book with that concept uppermost. Wine is one of the more important amenities of civilized people, but an aura of mystery has grown up around this intoxicating product of the grape, inspiring awe if not outright fear in otherwise sensible human beings. The connoisseur, unfortunately, has become a person to be held in reverence, and the sommelier in a restaurant has become an authority figure, even though his knowledge may often be inadequate.

Too often forgotten is the simple fact that wine is an agricultural product, little more than fermented grape juice, and the people who profess to know about it and purvey it are no more special than those involved with any other commercial product. Anyone can become just as knowledgeable simply by applying himself, by taking the time and trouble to taste and learn about what he is tasting, although the task is far more daunting today than it was only a decade ago. Because wine has no ultimate purpose other than to please and divert the people who drink it, it is prudent to learn how best to assure that this purpose is accomplished, and here is where a good book on the subject can be useful.

The goal of this book is not to dictate taste but to lead the consumer in the right directions as he experiments and explores and to provide the answers to his questions. It does not attempt to set out a rigid route that will brook no deviation, for wine is meant to be fun, not a chore or a duty. The goal is to be a helpful reference, a guide that can be used easily, for, like wine itself, reading about it should be pleasing and diverting.

P·A·R·T I

BASICS

The Grape and the Vine: A Natural History

The Making of Wine

Although wine seems to be a complex substance, with many facets and personalities, it is really very simple. Wine is an agricultural product, the beverage that results from the fermentation of grape juice. Despite centuries of experimentation, despite huge changes in the technology of picking, crushing, and vinifying grapes, despite quantum advances in the knowledge of viticulture, wine is really the same beverage it has always been. At the same time, the volume of wine produced to satisfy the demands of consumers all over the world has expanded vastly, and much of this increase in volume is the result of changing technology. It is now much easier to make good wine than it was even a decade ago, and it is also true that humans have learned better how to cope with the unpredictability of the weather, which plays an important role in the ripening of grapes. Yet the product that ends up in the glass is still red, white, rosé, or sparkling, and it still tastes pretty much the same as it did long ago.

If the identity of the man who made the first wine were known, there would be statues in his honor all over the civilized world. But the discovery of how to make wine, the process known as vinification, probably occurred long before the beginning of recorded history and no doubt happened by sheer accident, for the transformation of grape juice into wine is a purely natural process. The vine acts as a conduit between the soil and the grape, carrying nutrients and moisture to the fruit. If the soil contains the proper nutrients in good balance and there is adequate moisture from rainfall or irrigation, and if there is sufficient sunshine to stimulate growth and photosynthesis, then the vine will thrive and produce grapes that fill with juice in the growing season prior to the autumn harvest.

Wine is the product of fermented grape juice. It is not a mixture of alcohol and grape juice or grape juice with anything else. The process of fermentation occurs naturally, requiring no artificial stimulus. Ripe grapes contain, among other things, natural sugar. During fermentation the sugar is converted through decomposition into two principal byproducts: alcohol and carbon dioxide gas. Yeasts are the agents of fermentation. They are microscopic plants found naturally in the air and on the skins of grapes; they contain enzymes, which decompose the sugar. During the early stages of fermentation, the grape juice, pulps, skins, and seeds—a mixture called the "must"—react furiously. The must heaves, gurgles, and bubbles, and probably would cause explosions if permitted to occur in a tightly closed container. Later in the process, if the carbon dioxide gas is not allowed to escape into the atmosphere and is partially contained in a sufficiently strong bottle, a sparkling wine results.

It is the grape skins that hold the pigment that imparts color to wine. If the skins are removed from the juice after the grapes are crushed, white wine will be produced. Thus, a great deal of French Champagne is produced from black grapes. If dark-colored skins are allowed to remain through part of the fermentation, a pink, or *rosé*, wine will be produced. The longer the dark skins remain with the fermenting juice, the darker the wine will be. Of course, the skins of white grapes do not yield dark pigment, but all grape skins add certain extra properties to the wine. One of these is tannin, an astringent element also found in tree bark and tea leaves, which also exists in the grape stems. Its presence gives a wine backbone and hardness during its youth, but this hardness will soften later on. The longer the skins and stems are left in the fermenting must, the more tannic the resulting wine will be. This tannic quality is one of the elements of longevity, whereby most good red wines need several years or more of bottle-age before reaching a supple maturity.

In France, since the late 1960s, and in Italy, since the mid-1970s, a so-called "new vinification" has been practiced, involving the removal of the skins and other grape residue at a very early stage in the fermentation. The resultant wines are ready for drinking at a much younger age but uncertainty exists as to their longevity. Lovers of Bordeaux red wines and of certain reds from northern Italy ask, moreover, whether a wine can ever achieve the same exquisite balance and character with the new vinification, since some of the basic ingredients are present in only modest amounts. Only time will tell, but no one questions that most of the vintages since 1966 in Burgundy and 1967 in Bordeaux, and since about 1975 in northern Italy, have been extraordinarily drinkable within four to six years of the harvest—compared to a minimum of ten and more likely 15 years for the earlier vintages of good quality.

During fermentation, as the grape sugar is converted to alcohol and carbon dioxide, the alcohol level of the wine gradually rises until it reaches around 11 or 12 percent. In extraordinary vintages, when the weather conditions have been ideal and the grapes are fairly bursting with ripeness and have a very high natural sugar content, the percentage of natural alcohol may climb to 16 percent or even more. In poor vintages, when the grapes have not achieved the proper ripeness due to poor weather, the alcohol level may be less than 10 percent. As the yeasts do their work and the sugar is gradually consumed, a point is reached at which they become exhausted and are killed off by the alcohol they helped create. The consumption of the sugar can be halted at any point by the addition of distilled alcohol, which kills the yeast outright. Thus, to make a fairly sweet Port or Sherry, grape brandy is added when plenty of sugar remains in the juice. The fermentation stops, the resulting wine is sweet, and it has a higher alcoholic level due to the addition of the brandy. A completely dry wine is made when all of the sugar is allowed to ferment out. Fermentation can also be slowed or halted by temperature control, and many modern wineries are able to monitor closely the rate of fermentation by altering the temperature.

Acids are also contained naturally in wine and are considered necessary ingredients for a wine to be balanced. Yet an overly acidic wine is unpleasant. Under natural conditions, the first and most violent fermentation in the autumn immediately after the harvest is followed by a dormant period during the winter and then by a second fermentation in the following spring. This is often called the malolactic fermentation, because it involves the transformation of natural malic acid, through the action of bacteria, into lactic acid, which renders the wine less tart.

At various stages during vinification, the wine may be racked. This involves drawing the young wine off the grape residue and sediment, or lees, in an effort to capture only the purest, clearest juice. It is always practiced at large, efficient wineries attempting to produce the best possible product. But peasant farmers producing wine for their own consumption are inclined simply to let everything ferment together. This explains the coarseness of some of the peasant wines found in out-of-the-way places all over Europe. In producing red wines, the skins and other residue are naturally left in contact with the juice for more time. With white wines, the skins must be removed much sooner, even if they are white, because greater delicacy is usually desired.

After the period of fermentation, which generally occurs in fairly large vats, some with capacities in the thousands of gallons, the young wine is transferred to casks or barrels for its initial aging. The wood imparts additional taste to both red wines and white, and the amount of time spent in wood will vary according to the wishes of the producer. Racking may occur several times during the stay in wood; the wine

is pumped from one barrel to another, leaving behind the residue that has settled out in the bottom of the first. Fining is also accomplished at this stage. It involves clarification of the young wine through the addition of colloidal agents (e.g., gelatin and egg white have been commonly used for many years) that cause suspended matter to precipitate out and fall to the bottom. In recent years some California wineries have bottled "unfined" wines in the effort to achieve what they regard as greater character. The time spent in barrels or casks may be only a matter of weeks with a fresh Beaujolais or it may be a decade or more with some of the robust wines of Spain and Italy. Years spent in casks or barrels can impart additional tannin to a young wine and often will produce a woody taste. Some wines benefit from this sort of treatment, while others become overwhelmingly astringent. Local custom and the whim of the winemaker dictate the handling.

Bottling may take place within fewer than two months of the completion of the harvest in the case of Beaujolais Nouveau, when the producers are striving to present the youngest, freshest possible wine to a thirsty public desirous of sampling the new vintage. But such early bottling is the exception, rather than the rule. A fine château-bottled Bordeaux will spend at least two years in wood, and some wines from northern Italy and northern Spain may lie in casks for a decade or more. Generally, the closer a wine is bottled to the vineyard where it was produced, the better it is likely to be. That is why the terms "estate-bottled" and "château-bottled" on labels are important. They indicate that the wine has remained under the control of the producer, instead of being sold to a shipper, who may blend it with other wines. Of course, wines bottled by shippers may be the best available, especially in parts of the Burgundy country of France, as well as in Portugal, Spain, Italy, and Germany, but their high standards often arise from the fact that the estate-bottling function probably does not exist in their areas.

The treatment that a wine receives, from the moment the grapes are picked to the point when it is bottled, will determine its quality and its style. The more the consumer knows about that treatment, the more prudent he can be in selecting his wines. But such knowledge with respect to individual producers or vineyards is hard to come by. So the best alternative is to experiment with the wines of reputable producers or shippers, no matter the country of origin, and then continue to seek out the wines that merit their reputations. (*See also* Labels and Wine Laws, Storage, Aging.)

Fortified Wines

Some wines are fortified with raw alcohol or grape brandy to raise their alcohol level beyond the 12 to 14 percent that would be achieved through normal fermentation. In this category are Sherry, Port, Madeira and Marsala, to name some of the best known. Often these wines are sweet, because the raw alcohol is added before the fermentation of the grape sugar is complete. The added alcohol kills the yeasts that cause the fermentation, and residual sugar is left behind. Fortified wines normally are 18 to 20 percent alcohol. They are drunk as aperitifs or as postprandials—after a meal. Normally they are not consumed during a meal and thus are not usually called table wines. The alcohol for fortification may be purchased from a government agency or it may be distilled from grape wine on the premises of the winery itself. Brandy, after all, is merely distilled wine—or wine that has been vaporized through boiling until only the alcohol is captured through the distillation process.

Making Champagne and Sparkling Wines

The two chief by-products of fermentation are alcohol and carbon dioxide gas. In making nonsparkling, or still, wines, the carbon dioxide gas is allowed to flow off into the atmosphere. No effort is made to capture it. But in making Champagne and the other sparkling wines of the world, capturing the carbon dioxide gas is crucial.

Under the classic *méthode champenoise* there is an initial fermentation in the autumn immediately after the harvest. Then the wine goes through a dormant period in the winter. In the spring and early summer bottling takes place, and in each bottle a small amount of wine mixed with sugar is inserted. This triggers a second fermentation in the bottle, and this time the bubbles of carbon dioxide gas are not allowed to escape. They are retained inside the bottles— thus, a sparkling wine. This explanation is perhaps an oversimplification, and a more detailed discussion can be found under the "Champagne" entry in the alphabetical section.

Grape Varieties

Wines from different parts of the world tend to have differing flavors and characteristics, usually because they are made from different kinds of grapes. Sometimes their flavors will be similar because they are made with the same kinds of grapes, as with the Cabernet Sauvignons of California and the Bordeaux of France. But in general the different flavors and styles can be attributed to the cultivation of different varieties, and a knowledge of these varieties will provide a foundation for a broad knowledge of wine.

The Principal Grape Varieties of the World

Alicante Bouschet: Red grape used extensively by home winemakers and occasionally bottled as a varietal by commercial producers, including Papagni Vineyards of California.

Aligoté: White grape cultivated in the Burgundy country of France and used for the lesser wines of the region. Tends to be acidic and is best used for the aperitif known as the Kir, a mixture of white Burgundy and Cassis liqueur.

Aurora: White French-American hybrid grape cultivated mostly in the eastern United States and sometimes bottled as a varietal by New York State producers.

Baco Noir: European-American hybrid named after Maurice Baco, a French hybridizer. The wines made from this grape in New York and other northeastern states are among the best reds made in the region, although they rarely measure up to the European varietals grown in the same area when the weather conditions permit. The Baco Noir, however, tends to be a more durable grape and is more successful in adverse weather.

Barbera: Member of the *Vitis vinifera* species, originally cultivated in Italy but now extensively grown in California as well. Often used in blending for jug wines, it is also bottled as a varietal by some producers, notably Sebastiani Vineyards and the Louis M. Martini Winery.

Cabernet Franc: One of the important red grapes of Bordeaux, one that imparts texture to the wine, although not as important as the Cabernet Sauvignon, which is the mainstay of red Bordeaux.

Cabernet Sauvignon: The most important red grape of Bordeaux and of California, producing wines of great longevity, elegance and finesse. Often blended with Merlot, Cabernet Franc, and other grapes to achieve flavor nuances.

Canaiolo: Red grape of Italy often used in making Chianti, usually imparting softness and an early-maturing quality, and usually blended with the Sangiovese.

Carignan: Grape of warm climates in France, Algeria, and California (where it is spelled Carignane). Produces intensely flavored reds not highly regarded for their finesse.

Catawba: Pink grape cultivated widely in the southern United States as well as in New York State and the Niagara Peninsula of Canada. Noted for its native "foxy" taste.

Cayuga: White hybrid grape cultivated in New York State and bottled as a varietal by several wineries.

Chancellor: Red French hybrid grape cultivated extensively in the eastern United States and responsible for perhaps the best red varietal wines of the area. Also cultivated extensively in France.

Charbono: An intensely dark and robust wine that is made in California from the Charbono grape; it has enough followers that a Charbono Society has been formed. However, the wines, made by only a handful of producers, are not very stylish and tend to be heavy and awkward.

Chardonnay: One of the great white grapes of the world, the basis for all of the best white Burgundies of France and of the best dry white table wines of California. Also used extensively in making Champagne.

Chasselas: White grape cultivated in Switzerland and Alsace, where it yields crisp, clean-tasting wines. Grown in many other parts of the world but with less success.

Chelois: French-American hybrid grape grown mostly in the eastern United States and used for dry red wines.

Chenin Blanc: Well known white grape of the Loire Valley of France, where it is responsible for Vouvray, among other wines. It can be vinified dry or sweet, but many of its devotees contend that it is best when made sweet and used as an aperitif or dessert wine. Also widely cultivated in California, where it is a principal varietal. Sometimes called Pinot de la Loire, especially in the Loire Valley areas around Tours and Anjou.

Cinsault: A principal red grape of the Rhône Valley of France, where it is an ingredient in most blends of Châteauneuf-du-Pape. It is also widely cultivated in South Africa, where it is called the Hermitage, after the Rhône wine of the same name.

Concord: One of the most widely cultivated labrusca grapes of the American East Coast, where it makes red wines that epitomize the "foxy" taste that is so readily identifiable. But it is a durable grape that is able to survive difficult winters, which helps explain its popularity among farmers.

De Chaunac: French-American hybrid grape cultivated in the eastern United States and some other parts of the country, yielding red wines of moderate quality.

Delaware: A popular white native grape in the American East Coast and Middle West, responsible for slightly sweet, "foxy"-tasting wines that lack finesse.

Diamond: Native American grape variety yielding fruity, grapey wines, mostly in the eastern United States.

Dutchess: Hybrid American grape named after Dutchess County, New York, where it was developed and is still cultivated for the white wines it yields. Not taken seriously by connoisseurs.

Emerald Riesling: Grape variety resulting from a cross between the Johannisberg Riesling and the Muscadelle. Often vinified slightly sweet and bottled as a varietal by a number of California producers.

Foch, Maréchal Foch: Popular French-American red hybrid grape grown extensively in the eastern United States and bottled as a varietal wine.

Folle Blanche: Once the principal grape that was the basis for Cognac brandy, now more widely used to produce the ordinary whites grown near Nantes in the western Loire Valley.

French Colombard: Widely cultivated Vinifera grape variety in California, yielding undistinguished wines used mostly for blending in the jug-wine industry and for making low-priced champagne. Some California producers have tried barrel-fermenting and oak-aging it with interesting results.

Fumé Blanc: Term for Sauvignon Blanc that is vinified dry in California. Originated by Robert Mondavi and now widely emulated.

Furmint: The basic grape of Tokay of Hungary and of some other eastern European wines. Also produced in parts of Germany and Italy; identifiable by its distinctive bouquet.

Gamay: The basic grape of Beaujolais in France, where it produces red wines of freshness and zest that should usually be drunk young and well chilled. Cultivated less successfully in California, where it is called the Napa Gamay (not to be confused with the Gamay Beaujolais of California, which is really a clone of Pinot Noir).

Gamay Beaujolais: A clone, or offshoot, of the Pinot Noir family responsible for red Burgundy in France, it was mistakenly identified for many years as the Gamay of the Beaujolais district of France. The Napa Gamay is now believed to be the American version of the true Gamay of Beaujolais.

Gewürztraminer: The word literally means "spicy traminer," and wines made from this white grape tend to be spicy indeed. It is one of the basic grapes of Alsace but is also widely grown in Germany and California.

Grenache: Important grape of the Rhône Valley of France, where it is responsible for the high alcohol level in such robust reds as Châteauneuf-du-Pape. It is also cultivated in the Roussillon region of France and is sometimes called the Alicante. In Spain it is called the Alicantina, and in California it is used for Grenache Rosés.

Grey Riesling: Not a true Riesling but a relative of the Chauché Gris of France. It is sometimes vinified sweet and is bottled as a varietal by a number of California wineries.

Johannisberg Riesling: Also known as White Riesling, this is the basic premium grape of the best German white wines and takes its name from the famous Schloss Johannisberger of the Rheingau. Most often called Johannisberg Riesling in California (rarely in Germany), it is vinified both dry and sweet and is responsible for the best California dessert wines.

Léon Millot: French-American red hybrid grape variety grown in some eastern states and bottled by just a few wineries. It is medium in body and sometimes resembles light red Burgundies.

Malbec: Red Vinifera grape that is often included in red Bordeaux and sometimes blended with Cabernet Sauvignon in California. Also an important variety in Argentina, where it is bottled as a varietal wine.

Malmsey: Best known nowadays as a type of Madeira from the island of that name; also known in Italy as Malvasia, in Spain as Malvagia, and in France as Malvoisie. Usually slightly sweet.

Maurisco: One of the grapes that goes into the Port blends of northern Portugal.

Melon de Bourgogne: The grape of Muscadet, extensively produced in the western Loire Valley, where it makes crisp, dry, often elegant wines that have become increasingly popular alternatives to Chablis. As the name implies, the grape originated in Burgundy. Also produced in small quantities in California, specifically by Beaulieu Vineyards in the Napa Valley.

Mission: White grape variety introduced in California by the Spanish missionaries in the eighteenth century and still fairly widely cultivated, although few wineries bottle any as a varietal and most of the production goes into jug wines.

Merlot: Important grape of Bordeaux, where it imparts softness and mellowness when blended with the more robust Cabernet Sauvignon. Most extensively planted in the Pomerol and Saint-Emilion subregions of Bordeaux but found to some extent in the Médoc and Graves as well. Château Lafite, for example, tends to be about 20 percent Merlot blended with Cabernet Sauvignon. Also grown in California and bottled as a varietal wine.

Moscato, Muscat: White Vinifera grape variety produced in many versions in a number of countries—e.g., Moscato Amabile, Moscato di Canelli, Muscat Blanc, Muscat de Frontignan, etc. Often spicy in aroma and flavor, the wines from Muscat grapes are sometimes vinified sweet and can be high in alcohol. The best version is probably the Muscat de Beaumes-de-Venise produced in the Rhône Valley of France, a slightly sweet wine, high in alcohol and best used as an aperitif or with dessert.

Müller-Thurgau: Cross-breed of the German Riesling and Sylvaner grape varieties that is thought to be more durable than either of its components. Increasingly popular.

Muscadet: Muscadet is basically the crisp, dry, white wine produced from the Melon de Bourgogne grape in the western Loire Valley, but the term is increasingly being used to refer to the grape variety itself, and the use of the term "Melon de Bourgogne" is dying out.

Muscadine: A type of native American vine cultivated in the South and used to make such wines as Scuppernong, which has never been a favorite of connoisseurs.

Nebbiolo: One of Italy's noblest grapes, used to make the great Barolo, Barbaresco, Gattinara, Ghemme, Sassella, Inferno, and many other fine red wines of great style and longevity. Often called the Spanna grape in the area around Gattinara, where it is bottled as a varietal.

Niagara: American hybrid grape yielding wines of "foxy" flavor generally lacking in elegance. Widely produced in New York State.

Palomino: Dominant grape of dry Sherry in Spain, where it is widely cultivated in the region around Jerez. Also grown in other parts of the world producing Sherry-style wines, where it goes by the name Chasselas Doré and Golden Chasselas.

Pedro Ximenez: Sweet grape widely cultivated in the Sherry country of Spain, where it is blended with the Palomino grape to produce cream Sherries. It is usually vinified quite sweet and is sometimes bottled unblended and used after a meal in lieu of Port. Often abbreviated simply as P.X.

Petit Verdot: Ingredient grape in many Bordeaux red wines but not noted for its finesse or elegance.

Petite Sirah: California red grape said to be descended from the Syrah of France. Produces wines of less elegance and balance than the Cabernet Sauvignon or Zinfandel.

Pinot Blanc: White member of the celebrated Pinot family of grapes, used in blending white Burgundies and in Champagne. Not to be confused with the Pinot Chardonnay, which is not really a member of the Pinot family.

Pinot Chardonnay: See Chardonnay.

Pinot Gris: Member of the Pinot family in Alsace, where it is also called Tokay d'Alsace. In Germany it is the Ruländer.

Pinot Meunier: Red member of the noble Pinot family, cultivated extensively in the Champagne district of France and blended with Chardonnay and Pinot Noir to make Champagne.

Pinot Noir: Basic grape of red Burgundy in France, responsible for all of the greats but cultivated with less success in other parts of the world, including California, where it tends to yield awkward, heavy wines lacking in finesse.

Pinot St. George: Red grape variety unrelated to the Pinot Noir and cultivated in small amounts in California. Bottled as a varietal by only a few producers, including Christian Brothers.

Rabigato: White grape used to make white Port, which has a limited market.

Ravat: White French-American hybrid grape grown mainly in the eastern states and bottled as a varietal by several producers. It yields a fruity, spicy flavor and is sometimes vinified sweet.

Riesling: The noble grape of Germany, used to make the best Mosels, Rheingaus, Rheinhessens, etc. Also cultivated extensively in Alsace, northern Italy, and California as well as South Africa, Austria, Switzerland, and various countries in South America. It is often described as having a "peachy" flavor, and displays a flowery bouquet at its best.

Ruby Cabernet: Popular red Vinifera grape variety resulting from a cross between Cabernet Sauvignon and Carignane. It has never achieved the finesse of Cabernet Sauvignon but is bottled as a varietal by a number of California producers.

Ruländer: German version of the Pinot Gris of Alsace; also grown in Switzerland.

Sangiovese: Basic red grape of Chianti, the grape that provides its texture and internal structure, although several other grapes go into the Chianti blend under the Italian wine law. Also used in Brunello di Montalcino and Vino Nobile di Montepulciano.

Sauvignon Blanc: The leading white grape of Bordeaux, used to make the sweetest Sauternes and Barsacs as well as the driest white Graves. Also used in the Loire Valley to make Sancerre and Fumé Blanc. It is also widely cultivated in

California, where it is the basis for Fumé Blanc as well.

Savagnin: Important grape in the yellow wines of the Jura Mountains, especially Château-Châlon.

Scheurebe: Newly developed German hybrid especially popular in the Rheinpfalz.

Scuppernong: Native American grape belonging to the Muscadine family that thrives in the southern United States. It is usually vinified sweet.

Sémillon: White grape often blended with the Sauvignon Blanc in Bordeaux to make both sweet and dry wines. Occasionally bottled as a varietal under its own name in California.

Sercial: White grape cultivated on the island of Madeira and used to make some of the better Madeiras known for their special bouquet.

Seyval Blanc: Highly successful French-American hybrid grown extensively in the eastern United States. Makes crisp, dry wines similar to Muscadet and Chablis in style.

Steen: South African version of Chenin Blanc.

Sylvaner: Important German grape that is very prolific and therefore popular in a number of other countries, including Austria, Switzerland, and Alsace. Sometimes called Österreicher. Not considered in the same exalted class as the Riesling, which is cultivated in the same areas.

Syrah: Important grape of the French Rhône Valley and the primary grape of the great Hermitage wines. Also used in many other Rhône wines, including Châteauneuf-du-Pape. Relationship to the Petite Sirah of California remains unproven.

Tempranillo: The most important red grape of the Rioja region of northern Spain. It gives depth and texture to the best red wines produced there.

Thompson Seedless: The nation's most popular table grape; also used extensively for raisins. It is produced in vast quantities and is blended widely for use in white jug wines.

Trebbiano: A white grape widely cultivated in Italy and often blended into Soave. Also known in France as Ugni Blanc. Grown in the Charentes area of France, where it is called the Saint-Emilion and is used in making Cognac brandy.

Ugni Blanc: French name for the Trebbiano of Italy.

Vidal Blanc: White French-American hybrid grape variety found in the eastern states, characterized by fruity flavors that often convey hints of Labrusca, the native American grape species.

Villard Blanc: White French-American hybrid cultivated mainly in the eastern states but also extensively in France.

Viognier: White grape of the northern Rhône Valley of France, blended in small amounts to make Côte-Rôtie. Also the basic grape of Château Grillet, which produces only white wines.

Zinfandel: One of the most widely cultivated red grapes of California, with origins unproven. Known to have come originally from somewhere in Europe and to be a member of the European *Vitis vinifera* group. Makes intensely flavored, robust wines, often of great character.

The Vine and How It Produces Grapes

In most northern-hemisphere vineyards the so-called "set" in June is the moment of truth for the year's crop of grapes. The set is the fertilizing of the flowers on the vines. Grapes, after all, are simply pregnant flowers from the vines. Rain could interfere by diluting the stigmatic fluid of fertilization, or hail could knock the flowers off the vines, or cold weather could retard the flowering.

The set occurs when the flowers on the vines are properly fertilized and begin to turn into berries. Not all of the flowers are fertilized, and as many as 80 percent simply drop off the vines. The remaining 20 percent set is normal. The vine naturally sheds the flowers it does not need in a process called "shatter." If the normal 20 percent of the flowers are not retained to develop into grapes over the summer growing season, the crop is said to suffer from shatter.

Sunlight is the key to making fruitful buds. Next year's bud actually begins to develop microscopically in the vegetation of the vine. These embryonic buds can be dissected and seen with a microscope later in the year. At the time of the set the berries are the size of BB shot. Later in June or in early July there is cell division in the berries, and then cell expansion and growth into full-sized grapes takes place, assuming sufficient sunlight and just the right amount of moisture. But the whole process can be spoiled by bad weather, which is why some vintages are held in higher regard than others.

The leaves on the vines also play a crucial role. They are solar panels that enable both the grapes and the wood of the vines to ripen properly. There thus must be a balance of vegetative growth and ripening growth in the fruit. Assuming all goes well with the weather,

the grapes will ripen properly, the vines will develop properly, and the grapes will develop sufficiently high levels of natural grape sugars to make good wine after the harvest in the autumn, which may occur in September or October in most regions of the northern hemisphere.

The vines become dormant in the late fall, although there is still considerable risk if the weather remains too warm too late. For example, if sap is still running in the vines in December and there is a sudden freeze, the vines can be split and in some cases killed. But normally the season of dormancy is entered without such problems. During the dormant season, carbohydrates are stored in the roots and trunk of the vine.

When growth renews in the spring, the stored energy of the carbohydrates is drawn on. It is at this point that the pruners, who are important and skilled vineyard workers, try to evaluate each vine and try to calculate from the color of the wood and the size of the vine's trunk just how much carbohydrate energy is stored there. The vines cannot be allowed to grow at will. Too much leaf growth may mean a diminished crop size. Prolonged vegetative growth may mean late ripening of the grapes. Without pruning of the vines, overcropping will occur, and more growth energy will flow into the fruit and less into the leaves, which may mean a longer ripening period because the solar panels, the leaves, are too sparse. The result could be unripe grapes at the harvest.

Thus the pruners try to match the capacity of the vine with the vigor of the vine. For each bud (which began to develop the previous June) there is normally one vine shoot, and for each shoot there may be two clusters of grapes, although customs vary in different parts of the world. Under normal conditions the budbreak occurs in March, and the vegetation begins to grow. The flowers begin forming in April and May, when strong growth occurs in the vines. Then the bloom occurs in early June, and the growth of the vines slows. And now we are back at the point where we started—in June, the crucial month when the flowering and the set occur.

Starting from scratch—that is, planting a vine and waiting for it to produce a commercial crop—normally takes at least three years and often four. There are exceptions, but usually three to four years must pass while a vineyard matures. At the opposite end of the growth curve, when vines become 30 and 40 years old, they tend to yield fewer grapes, so replanting of vineyards is common after the vines reach a certain age. Nevertheless some growers intentionally maintain plots of old vines because they feel they obtain superior wines from them, although in smaller amounts. But if they are indeed superior wines, higher prices can be charged, so there may be some economic justification in maintaining elderly vineyards.

Tending the Vines

Grapevines would grow indiscriminately if not trained and cut back, or pruned. If left to their own devices, they would keep yielding more and more grapes, and the wines from those grapes would be thin and dull and uninteresting. Vineyard managers try to strike a balance between the tonnage of grapes they need from an acre of vines to make wine growing economical and to make the best possible wines.

In some areas a yield of perhaps four tons of Cabernet Sauvignon grapes per acre would produce excellent wines. In other areas two tons per acre are all that can be produced to make the best wines. To strike the proper balance the vines are pruned each winter, or cut back, to assure that the production the next summer will be the desired amount. At the same time the vines may be trained along wires attached to stakes in the ground, so that they will achieve the maximum exposure to the sun during the growing season.

The vines are dormant from late November until about mid-March. So in March the soil is generally ploughed to aerate it and facilitate growth of the vines. Frost danger is ever present at this time of year, even into April and early May, and kerosene-fueled smudge pots are evident in many vineyards to ward off a killing frost that might damage the tender young buds. The flowering of the vines usually occurs in June, and it is these flowers that eventually become the grapes. Spraying with powdered sulphur at this time of year can prevent certain diseases, and the spraying often goes on through July, and the soil is continually cultivated against weeds.

Some pruning may still go on in June and July to assure that overcropping will not occur. In August everyone prays for good weather to ripen the grapes in preparation for the harvest, which will occur in September or perhaps October. Ideally the grapes will be ripe and ready for picking in early September, but if the weather has not been ideal, it may be prudent to wait longer, in the hope of more sun for further ripening in September. Then an October harvest may be necessary. But this is risky, for the longer the wait, the greater the danger of hail or a killing frost or heavy rains that might knock the grapes from the vines.

Assuming favorable conditions, the harvest occurs in September, and the grapes are carried into the winery and are crushed and dumped into fermenting tanks. Now the yeasts go to work and trigger the chemical reaction that creates alcohol and carbon dioxide gas from the grape juice, which has developed a natural sugar content through the ripening process during the growing season. The fermentation often is violent, accompanied by gurgling and heaving within the tanks.

The Climate

Climate is a key element in the growth and development of grapes. The number of days of sunshine, the dates of the last frost of spring and the first frost of autumn, the amount of rainfall all make up the complex formula that decides whether vines will thrive and what kind of grapes will do best. Changes in weather conditions dictate the characteristics of the wines of each year. In California, where the weather tends to be fairly constant, the differences among vintages are not as great as they are in France, where the weather tends to be more variable.

Certain grapes thrive in certain types of weather. The Syrah and the Grenache do well in the heat of the Rhône Valley of France but are not seen in Bordeaux. Some degree of dampness is desirable for certain types of grapes at certain times of the year. Sauternes needs to be attacked by the disease caused by the mold *Botrytis cinerea,* a condition also called *pourriture noble,* the noble rot, late in the growing season to impart that honeylike quality that makes Sauternes special. Damp, misty weather is needed to encourage the noble rot in this part of Bordeaux, but the same kind of weather is unwelcome in the nearby red-wine areas of the Médoc, Graves, Saint-Emilion, and Pomerol.

Temperature is important too. Most of the best wines are made in temperate climates. Too much heat and too much sun can create heavy, awkward wines that are not pleasing on the palate. That is one reason why the grapes are harvested early in some parts of the world and late in other areas.

The Soil

It is said that the sparsest, least fertile soil is the best for growing grapes, that the grapes must work hard to extract minerals and nutrients from the soil in order to produce the best wines. It has been proven time and again that the rich soil near the bed of a river yields wines of less elegance and finesse than the rockier, sparser soil farther away from the riverbank.

Drainage is the key factor. Soil that is rocky, chalky, filled with loam and lacking in clay, soil that drains easily when rain falls, has been shown to be best for growing grapevines. Sloping vineyards that catch the sun also are advantageously situated, partly because the slopes themselves also aid in the drainage. In addition, the sloping land creates air currents that help dry off the grapes and the vines after rainfall, thereby helping to prevent mildew and other diseases of the vine. All vines are subject to diseases, and these can be prevented by a sunny climate that forestalls the growth of undesirable organisms.

Wine Tasting

A certain ritual is necessary to perceive all of the characteristics of a wine. Oenophiles soon learn that the ritual adds to the tasting experience and enables them to identify individual traits more readily. It also enables them to differentiate more effectively among similar wines by permitting their qualities to become more evident. Unfortunately the tasting ritual has given rise to wine snobbery. Those who observe the ritual for any reason other than to taste the wine are guilty of limiting their own enjoyment and perhaps impinging on the enjoyment of others. But those who follow the proper wine-tasting procedure strictly to maximize their own experience are creating the conditions that reveal the wine at its best.

The ritual should begin long before you actually start tasting. To assure that your taste buds are properly prepared, avoid food or drink that might impair your ability to taste. Raw onion, garlic, mustard, hot peppers, and vinegar can have a deadening impact on the taste buds. The same is true of cocktails. Next, you must be sure that the wine is able to perform well. Remember that red wines should be permitted to "breathe," with the corks removed from the bottles for a period of time before tasting. White wines must be chilled. But once your taste buds are ready and the wine itself is ready, the tasting ritual can begin.

What to Look For

Wines have four principal characteristics: appearance, bouquet, taste, and aftertaste. Each should be considered as a quality unto itself, even if they tend to mingle. Try to separate the qualities in your mind by concentrating on them individually.

APPEARANCE

Your first clue about a wine will come from its visual aspects—color and clarity. A white background, ideally a white tablecloth, will be helpful. Pour no more than a half ounce into a clear glass and tip the glass on its side, being careful to hold it by the stem and not by the bowl. Is the wine crystal-clear? Is it free of sediment or floating particles? Is it slightly cloudy? A sound wine should be limpid, without a hint of cloudiness. Red wines, of course, may throw off sediment as a natural part of their development, but the sediment should be collected in the bottom of the bottle and should not be permitted to enter your tasting glass. To assure that a red wine will be clear, decant it first. White wines generally do not throw off sediment. Those that do are questionable.

Color is a very important aspect and it will provide you with a great deal of information about the age and manner in which a wine has been matured and stored. All wines—whether red, rosé, or white—tend to turn brown as they mature. Very old wines may have a very brown color, whereas very young wines may contain not even a hint of brownness. A properly mature red wine should have a deep ruby color, perhaps with tinges of brown evident only around the edges when you tip your glass on its side. A sound white wine may have golden highlights but will not exhibit any brown color. Obviously a wine that has turned brown after only a few years in the bottle may have something wrong with it. It may have been improperly made or improperly stored.

On the other hand, a wine that is supposed to be very old but that shows no signs of turning brown may also be open to suspicion. If it has the hue of a young wine, then perhaps it really is younger than the label indicates. It will take practice and refinement for you to identify such subtleties, but your reward will be the ability to know a great deal about a wine merely from its appearance.

Of course, you must beware of condemning a wine merely on the basis of its appearance. For example, a Sauternes with 20 years in the bottle is likely to display a deep caramel color, but it probably will still be sound. Sauternes is a naturally sweet wine whose sugar content helps to preserve it. On the other hand, a white Burgundy, Rhine or Mosel with an obvious brown tinge may have begun to deteriorate. You may

discover also that you prefer your white wines to be more mature. The decision must be your own, so learn to be subjective and follow your own instincts.

Red table wines tend to change color less readily than whites, mainly because they contain larger amounts of tannin, a substance imparted to them by the skins, stems, and seeds of grapes during the fermenting process. Red wines that are coarse and harsh due to an abundance of tannin at a young age may live for decades, slowly improving in the bottle. Even now, some of the great Bordeaux from the magnificent 1928 vintage display a deep ruby color, with only a hint of mahogany around the edges. Red Burgundies tend to mature sooner, but they too can last for decades when properly stored. At some point, of course, all wines reach their peak and then recede into old age, some more or less gracefully than others. Beware of those ancient bottles from the last century that are sold at auctions in England and the United States for fabulous sums. They often contain brown wine of very doubtful quality.

Old white wines that are far past their prime are subject to maderization. This is a process whereby the wine deteriorates and actually takes on some of the less desirable characteristics of Madeira, the fortified Portuguese red wine. Maderized whites even produce a slightly rotten odor and tend to be rather dark brown in color. Beware of them.

BOUQUET

The aroma, or bouquet, of a wine is one of its most important traits and is a vital part of the tasting experience. Like most other plants, grapevines go through a flowering process, usually in late spring. The grapes begin growing only after the plant has flowered, and, by a quirk of nature, the aroma of the flower seems to remain in the fermented grape juice that becomes wine. At its peak a fine table wine will exude an aroma that can be described only as a bouquet. If the bouquet is very strong and especially flowery, as sometimes happens in a well made red Burgundy, the wine is said to have a "nose." In a great wine the bouquet will be complex and challenging, sometimes evoking images of herbs, spices, violets, or lilacs. As time passes, the bouquet of a great wine may grow ever more complex. Gradually it will lose its intensity, but it should remain balanced, so that the wine will not be overwhelmed by a single obvious characteristic.

Because the bouquet of a great wine tends to ebb with age, however, the lack of a pronounced aroma should not be used as a determinant of quality. Often when very mature bottles are uncorked, the bouquet will be full and elegant—for perhaps five minutes. Then it will begin to disappear, and after another five or ten minutes have passed, it may be entirely gone, having expired after waiting for decades, trapped like a genie inside the bottle. It is well to remember this when deciding how long to let an old wine breathe before drinking it. By waiting you may lose much of what the wine has left to offer.

Some wines have aromas that are odd or distasteful, and usually such wines are inferior. Experience will help to identify these negative characteristics. Remember that the bouquet of a great wine is always either very pleasant or very subtle. If it is neither, you may have reason to question the wine's condition or authenticity.

TASTE

Is a wine supposed to taste a certain way? This question is perhaps the most frequently asked and the most difficult to answer. Tasting is a completely sub-jective experience, and each person will react differently to a particular wine. Some wine lovers think red Burgundy tastes better than red Bordeaux. Some people think California Chardonnays taste better than white Burgundies. Others think a big, strong Barolo from Italy has much more character than the best red Burgundies. All of these people are correct; nobody has the right to dictate how you should react to a taste sensation.

Naturally, wines have individual characteristics, just as people do, and the fact that some wines are more popular with connoisseurs than others would imply that some do taste better to people with highly trained palates. So it is true that a great red Bordeaux from a good vintage can be expected to taste a certain way. A great Bordeaux from a mediocre vintage will not taste as good, but it should still taste like a Bordeaux, and it might very well taste better than most other wines produced that year. A great red Burgundy may be big and robust, with many complexities in its taste. Yet some of the best Burgundies are very subtle wines. With experience, you will learn to expect certain wines to taste a certain way, and then you must decide for yourself which you prefer.

Many experienced wine drinkers discover that their tasting ability and their preferences evolve over a period of years. The neophyte often becomes enamored of Bordeaux, partly because Bordeaux wine production is so great that many good examples are available and partly because of the system of classification that has existed for these wines since 1855 which makes selecting a good Bordeaux relatively simple. But as he gains in experience and sophistication and learns how to select good Burgundies, a developing oenophile often will move on to Burgundy as his favorite type of wine. The depth and character of a fine

Burgundy, after all, are difficult to match. Later, as he reaches the expert category, a wine lover may return to Bordeaux because of its elegance and subtlety. The evolution of an oenophile does not always occur this way. But it often seems to.

At a very special dinner of the International Wine and Food Society in New York some years ago the members were asked to try something new: to select a bottle or two from their own cellars to contribute to the dinner. It may have been the first "B.Y.O.B." (Bring Your Own Bottle) party held by such an august group. Not surprisingly, most of the members who participated in the event volunteered bottles of very old and very fine Bordeaux. In a truly majestic array of oenological nobility, the Château Lafite-Rothschild 1928 and 1929 were present, along with the Château Latour, Château Margaux, Château Haut-Brion and Château Mouton-Rothschild of the same vintages. These great châteaux also were represented in several other rare and well known vintages, and the evening was an extraordinary and wonderful event. At its conclusion the members were asked to vote for the one wine that they had preferred above all others. The winner in a virtually unanimous ballot was none of the noble Bordeaux but a Burgundy—the Musigny Comte de Vogüé 1934. Which demonstrates that the celebrated châteaux of Bordeaux may occasionally be vanquished in a tasting contest and that the experts who *think* they prefer Bordeaux may sometimes prefer Burgundy.

If any rule is worth following in evaluating the taste of a wine, it is to follow your own instincts. Taste is highly subjective and based on personal experience. But the same standards that apply for bouquet are useful for taste: it should be complex without being mysterious, and it should be challenging without

being overwhelming. A good table wine is light but not thin, full-bodied but not heavy, and, above all, balanced. Only experience will enable you to make judgments on these characteristics.

To help make decisions, a frame of reference must exist. Unless you are very experienced, it will be useless to taste one wine without comparing it with another. No truly successful tasting can involve only a single wine. You must have a basis for comparison, and under ideal conditions you will be able to compare several different wines. Progress from one to another in individual tastings. Open two bottles with dinner each evening, even if you do not consume all of each. Gradually your sophistication will increase and you will be able to return to the wines that please you most.

To assure that your taste buds will be fully exposed to the wine, you must learn to hold it in your mouth for a few seconds, swishing it around, drawing air in and almost gargling it. The process is difficult to describe and comical to watch, but expert tasters can be seen tilting their heads back slightly and making gurgling sounds as they aerate the wine in their mouths. Drawing air in seems to accentuate the taste and permits you to identify characteristics more readily. Learning to do this will take practice, but once you have learned you will never forget. Some wine lovers are sometimes perceived gurgling such other drinks as milk or water in an almost reflexive reaction to the passage of a liquid between their lips.

How should a wine taste? The question remains unanswered, because the taster must make his own judgments. Many experts will tell you that a Beaujolais tastes fruity, a young Bordeaux tastes hard or tannic, a big and noble white Burgundy may taste of almonds, a mature red Bordeaux may offer a hint of blackberries, and a big red Amarone from Italy may have a texture that you can almost chew and a taste reminiscent of figs or freshly cut cedar. The trouble with describing taste is that only four entirely distinct words exist in the English language for the purpose: sweet, sour, salt, bitter. If any of these words is useful for discussing wine, it must be sweet, because all wine has a natural sugar content. Yet who would call a steely Chablis sweet? Over the centuries the vocabulary that has evolved for wine tasting has become largely metaphorical, reflecting the paucity of actual tastewords in the language. Thus an elegant red Burgundy may suggest violets or lilacs or even mint, while a rich Pomerol produced mostly from the Merlot grape may remind the taster of the smell of fresh road tar. The best taste words, it seems, are often olfactory, relating as much to the sense of smell as to taste.

Because wine tends to lubricate the vocabulary, the best discussions of its merits usually take place during or after a dinner at which great wines have been served. The rhetoric becomes flowery indeed under such circumstances, and whole new sections of the language may be employed by imaginative speakers to describe their reactions. Under these circumstances it is not difficult to appreciate Thurber's classic: "It's only a naïve little domestic Burgundy without any breeding, but I think you'll be amused by its presumption." Absurd? Certainly not, when the words are uttered at the appropriate moment.

AFTERTASTE

The impression that remains after you have swallowed the wine is the aftertaste. Commercial wine buyers always spit out the wine they sample when they are trying to decide on their purchases. The main reason is to avoid the buildup of alcohol in their systems that will hinder their ability to make wise investment decisions. It is said in the wine trade that the worst investment decisions usually involve the last wine tasted, assuming the buyer is swallowing. Somehow, the more wine you drink, the better each successive wine tastes. But the commercial buyers who do not swallow are robbing themselves of one of the most important elements in the tasting experience. The aftertaste can differ substantially from the impressions given by the bouquet and the taste itself. A wine's acidity, for example, tends to be more evident in the aftertaste. Other subtleties will become apparent as well, partly because your intake of air after swallowing accentuates the characteristics of the small amount of wine that remains in your mouth.

"How *should* you react to aftertaste? The same rule applies here that applies to taste itself. You must be subjective and decide for yourself. The important thing is to try to identify the aftertaste and remember that the tasting experience is not complete until you have swallowed the wine and studied the impressions it has left behind. Some very fine wines leave little or no impression, while poor ones may yield an unpleasant aftertaste. Immature wines may leave an acid or tannic impression in your mouth that does not necessarily mean they are inferior. The aftertaste of a big red wine probably will be more pronounced than that of a subtle and balanced white. It will take some practice to perceive all of the traits that exist in the aftertaste, but your perception will broaden your whole tasting experience.

Clearing the Palate

Wise men in the wine trade have a saying: Sell on cheese and buy on bread. It means that you should use bread to clear your palate to perceive all the aspects of a wine if you are considering buying some, while if you are in the business of selling wine, offer your potential customers cheese. Although cheese is a traditional accompaniment to wine, it does not enhance your ability to taste. In fact, one reason for cheese's popularity with wine is that sometimes it can mask the objectionable characteristics of a wine. No one would argue that a ripe Brie or Camembert can make an excellent taste combination with a good wine. But it probably will not enable you to appreciate the wine at its best.

Many experts have found that bread is much better for freshening the palate between wines. It has a much more subtle taste than cheese, does not linger on the palate and tends actually to absorb any residue of wine that may be left in your mouth. The knowledgeable host at a wine tasting will set out baskets with chunks of Italian or French loaves, so that his guests can easily munch on a bite or two as they progress from one wine to the next. The cheese can come later, after the serious part of the tasting is finished.

Another way to clear the palate is with water. Simply take a mouthful, swish it around and spit it out. This will effectively clear out the wine taste, but works best only if the water has not been heavily treated with chlorine or other chemicals. Ideally, use bottled spring water if you are willing to bear the added expense.

Recording Your Impressions

If you wish to be serious about your tasting sessions and keep a longer-term account of your impressions, it would be wise to record them. A simple loose-leaf notebook can suffice, or a spiral notebook. Many professional tasters keep stacks of spiral notebooks, each containing notes from a number of tastings. The dates and types of wines can be noted on the front or the inside cover.

When recording your impressions, be sure to be disciplined about writing basic information concerning each wine—its full name, producer, vintage, origin, etc., before writing your tasting notes. It will be a disappointment to find any of this data missing when you return to your notes later. Moreover, you may wish to keep track of the development of a particular wine that you have bought in quantity. In this case,

set aside a separate page for each wine, so that your impressions can be recorded each time you taste it over a period of time, which could well run into years.

A number of so-called "cellar books" have been published over the years, providing the means for recording tasting notes and consumption and inventory levels in your own cellar, whether it is a simple closet with racks or a full-fledged basement room for large quantities. These can also be useful even without a cellar, if you wish to write down your impressions each time you buy and taste a wine. Such books can be found in any well stocked bookstore or can be ordered through it. But for everyday tasting, your own spiral notebook probably will be more useful.

The Language of Wine: A Glossary

ACID, ACIDITY: Acids are a natural by-product of wine, and most wines contain them. They provide the backbone of a good wine, and a certain amount of acidity is needed to provide firmness on the palate. Wines lacking in acid tend to be soft and lacking in character, but too much acidity can provide a bitter and harsh flavor. Acidity is never obvious in a balanced wine.

AROMA: The scent or bouquet of a wine as it relates to the level of alcohol and other constituents. Some wines are described as aromatic. "Aroma" is used to connote a pleasant bouquet and is not ordinarily used in a negative sense.

BALANCE: The proper harmony of acidity, sugar level, tannin, fruit, alcohol level, and all the other components. A wine may display many favorable characteristics, but it will not be complete unless balanced.

BIG: Full-bodied, strong, intensely flavored, robust, assertive. Some oenophiles prefer their wines big, others prefer them more subtle and delicate. The choice is subjective.

BODY: Depth and substance underlying the taste. The opposite of thin or watery. Relates to the level of texture and flavor intensity that can be sensed in the mouth. A full body is an important component in good wines and connotes the presence of glycerin and other natural elements that add to complexity.

BOTRYTISED: Containing evidence of *Botrytis cinerea*, the so-called noble rot that is a favorable component of late-harvested wines from Sauternes and certain parts of Germany, California, Hungary, and elsewhere. A botrytised wine has a honeylike quality that is identifiable in the bouquet and flavor. Such wines normally are fairly sweet, containing unfermented sugar, and are best with dessert or *foie gras*.

BOUQUET: The smell or scent that is one of the most important characteristics of the tasting experience. Similar to aroma. Sometimes it is pronounced, sometimes subtle. The bouquet should be pleasant, and, if it is very pronounced and complex, it may properly be called a "nose."

BOUTIQUE: In French the term literally means "shop" or "small store." In the United States it refers to a small winery with modest production levels, one that sometimes specializes in only a few varieties of wine.

BRAMBLE: Term popularized by the Sebastiani wine family of California to connote the prickly, peppery texture, bouquet, and flavor of certain Zinfandel wines.

BREED: Character and complexity, usually meaning high quality and often used to refer to wines that have a long track record of superiority. A wine of great breeding will be like a prize-winning racehorse—sleek, strong, properly reared, and graceful.

BRUT: Dry; usually applied to Champagne and other sparkling wines; indicates less than 1.5 percent of residual sugar by volume in Champagne and connotes greater dryness than the term "extra dry," which leads to some confusion among consumers. The term "extra dry" actually means "slightly sweet" in Champagne parlance.

BUTTERY: The rich, creamy, butterlike flavor evident in some wines made from the Chardonnay grape, suggesting a combination of intense fruit taste with nuances of oak from the aging barrels.

CHARACTER: Balance, assertiveness, finesse, grace. The combination of favorable qualities that come together in a good wine. The term is most often used in a favorable context. Sometimes it is intended to suggest that a wine is true to the best form of its type or variety, as in a Zinfandel of "true varietal character."

CHEWY: Descriptive of the texture, body, and intensity of a good red wine, suggesting an ability to sense tiny solids in the wine on the palate. A chewy wine will be mouth-filling and complex, with a full body and intense flavor.

CHOCOLATY: Implying the flavor of chocolate, as in some Zinfandels and occasionally in other red wines.

COCONUTTY: Nuances of coconuts that can be detected in the flavor of some reds and whites. Also suggestive of texture.

COFFEE-BOX: Some red wines from California, France, and Italy are said to display a coffee-box or coffee-grinder bouquet, which implies the scent of coffee. The aroma probably comes from the wood in which the wine was aged.

COMPLEX: Having a broad range of qualities that are challenging and interesting to the taster. Many-faceted, in contrast to simple wines that lack character.

CORKED, CORKY: Tasting of the cork stopper and suggesting that the taste of the cork has entered the wine due to the cork's deterioration. The taste is slightly musty and unpleasant. The French term is *bouchonné*.

CREAMY: Similar to "buttery" and typical of some Chardonnay wines aged in oak barrels. The impression is of rich cream, just short of buttery but nevertheless a favorable trait.

DEMI-SEC: Literally, "half-dry"; used to indicate a sweet Champagne with at least 4 percent residual sugar by volume but less than 8 percent. Sometimes also applied to sweet nonsparkling wines.

DEPTH: Similar to "character," "complexity," and "body." A wine of depth will have great texture and body.

DOUX: Sweet or very sweet. Applied to Champagne with 8 to 10 percent residual sugar by volume, best used as a dessert wine. Also sometimes applied to other sweet wines.

DRY: The absence of residual sugar or sweetness. An overused term that should imply no positive or negative evaluation. Often misused when applied to slightly sweet American jug wines.

DUSTY: Having great texture, usually applied only to reds and creating the impression that dustlike particles of flavor can be detected on the palate. Similar to "chewy," although in a more subtle sense.

EARTHY: Tasting of the soil in which the grapes were grown. Sometimes a negative quality if the earthiness is especially pronounced and masks the other attributes of the wine.

ELEGANT: Fine, balanced, subtle, at the summit of maturity, true to form, engaging and challenging. Not chewy or full-boded.

FAT: Heavy, sweetish, insipid, obvious, unsubtle, lacking in acidity and complexity. Sometimes (rarely) used in a favorable context with certain sweet dessert wines.

FINED: Having been treated to cause the solids in a wine to precipitate out and sink to the bottom of the barrel. Egg whites or gelatin or other substances are dropped into the barrels, causing the particulate matter to sink to the bottom. This is the process of clarifying. Some California wineries bottle "unfined" wines in an effort to achieve greater texture and body.

FINESSE: High quality, showing great harmony among the various characteristics of a good wine; balance as well. That extra "something" that sets a wine apart from others.

FINISH: Aftertaste. The residue of flavor left in the mouth after the wine has been swallowed. Good wines have a long, pleasing aftertaste that lingers on the palate.

FLINTY: Slightly metallic taste that can be detected in certain dry white wines, especially Chablis. A favorable trait.

FLORAL: Flowery. Usually applied to the bouquet and suggestive of the scent of flowers.

FLOWERY: Displaying an intense bouquet that reminds the taster of flowers—sometimes jasmine, lilacs, honeysuckle. Sometimes the fruity bouquet of the grape itself.

FORWARD: Maturing early. Lacking in tannin and hardness at an unexpectedly young age. Usually applied to red wines and hinting at a lack of longevity.

FOXY: Term used for the flavor of native grapes, usually grown in New York and other northeastern and central states, although sometimes applied to inferior European wines. Sometimes associated with the Concord grape variety widely cultivated in New York.

FRUITY: Having a pronounced taste of the grape. Sometimes suggestive of other fruits as well, including raspberries, cranberries, or black currants. Often mistakenly used to mean sweet. The term should not have a negative connotation.

GRAPEY: Very similar to "fruity," although implying more directly the taste of the grape itself. Often used to describe very young or immature wines.

GRASSY: Smelling of freshly mown grass or hay and tasting of vegetation. Similar to "vegetal" and "herbaceous." Not necessarily a negative quality if not too pronounced.

GREEN: Young, immature, not ready for drinking, sometimes suggestive of wine made from grapes that did not achieve full ripeness.

HARD: Immature, lacking in fruit, undeveloped, tannic, needing somewhat more bottle-age.

HERBACEOUS: Grassy, vegetal, somewhat awkward, lacking in proper fruit balance.

HOT: High in alcohol, above the 12 to 13 percent that is considered normal. Suggestive of lack of balance between the alcohol and the other constituents of a wine, especially the fruit.

HYBRID: Crossbreeds between European and American grape varieties are called hybrids and are produced mostly in the eastern and central states of America. Usually lacking the high quality of the better European varietals but cultivated extensively because of their resistance to adverse weather conditions.

LEATHERY: Suggesting the scent of rawhide or the odor of a tackroom in a stable. Probably attributable to the wood used for barrel-aging.

LEGS: These are the narrow rivulets of wine that run down the inside of the glass when the wine is swirled around inside. Their presence implies the presence of good quantities of glycerin, a natural constituent of wine, and suggests that the wine is full-bodied. When the legs are broad and wide and cling to the glass, they are called sheets.

LIGHT: Lacking in alcoholic strength. Unassertive, shallow.

MELLOW: Soft and smooth texture, mature and pleasant, but sometimes lacking in complexity and body. Some wines that are past their peaks are described as mellow if they remain pleasing.

MINTY: Suggestive of fresh green mint. Quality found in some Cabernet Sauvignons and Zinfandels from California. Some oenophiles find it a rare and flavorful quality; others contend it obscures some of the other traits of the wine.

MUSCULAR: Full-bodied and big. Robust, textured, and assertive. Usually applied to red wines from California and Italy but occasionally to some California Chardonnays and other whites.

NEEDLES: Sharp taste in some wines, suggesting high acidity or imbalanced spiciness. A negative characteristic if found in wines that should have achieved maturity, such as red Bordeaux or California Cabernet Sauvignons more than six or eight years of age.

NOBLE: Wine produced from noble grape varieties or those that traditionally make the best wines in a specific region, e.g., the Pinot Noir in red Burgundy and the Cabernet Sauvignon in red Bordeaux. Almost always used in a favorable context, although the presence of noble grapes does not necessarily mean a fine wine has been made.

NOSE: Intense bouquet and aroma, highly suggestive of freshly blooming flowers and other pleasant scents. Often used in place of "bouquet" or "aroma," which traditionally have not connoted the same degree of intensity. In California, "nose" has virtually replaced "bouquet" as a descriptive word, and such phrases as "a small nose" are now heard, when once they would have been self-contradictory.

NUTTY: Spicy taste evocative of walnuts and other types of nuts. Often associated with certain Burgundies, Sherries from Spain, and some California wines.

OAKY: Conveying the bouquet and flavor of oak from the barrels in which the wine has been aged. A negative trait if too intense, for it can hide the fruit and other components of a wine's flavor.

OEIL DE PERDRIX: Literally, "eye of the partridge," referring to the pinkish brown tinge visible at the rim or edge of the surface of the wine in a glass when viewed against a white background.

OFF: Having deteriorated in the bottle, or turned bad, probably due to improper storage or an inferior cork.

OXIDIZED: Having reacted with oxygen in the air, resulting in deterioration of the wine. Characterized by a brownish color in both reds and whites and often found in wines that are past their peak ages for drinking. With very young wines, some oxidation may be helpful in softening them for current drinking.

PELURE D'OIGNON: Literally, "onion skin," referring to the golden or slightly brownish hue at the surface edges or rim of a mature red wine when viewed against a white background.

PEPPERY: Spicy in flavor, suggesting complexity in a Zinfandel and an oaky or tannic quality in other red wines. A positive characteristic in moderation.

PÉTILLANT: Lightly sparkling or bubbling, but with smaller, more subtle bubbles than a sparkling wine. Sometimes the bubbles are detectable only as a very slight prickle on the tongue. Some German whites as well as some Johannisberg Rieslings from California are expected to display a *pétillant* quality occasionally, but when it appears in older wines it can be a sign of secondary fermentation in the bottle and perhaps deterioration.

RACE: Elegance; finesse and style; with distinctive flavor and an additional quality that eludes description but that demonstrates complexity.

RAWHIDE: Leathery bouquet and flavor indicative of too much aging in oak barrels, although not unpleasant when found in moderation in full-bodied, robust reds.

REEDY: Tasting of wood and vegetation, lacking in fruit, suggestive of unripe grapes or too much contact between the wine and the stems and seeds of the grapes during fermentation and aging.

RESIDUAL SUGAR: Sugar that has not fermented and remains in the wine, providing a sweet flavor. A favorable characteristic in some German wines and American Johannisberg Rieslings, as well as in some fortified wines, including Ports and Sherries. Generally not looked upon favorably in other wines, although some high-alcohol Zinfandels with residual sugar have their devotees.

RESTAURANT WINE: Red or white that is early-maturing, mellow, and not in need of years of bottle-aging prior to service. Its value is that it can be offered for immediate drinking in restaurants, even at a young age.

RIM: The edge of the surface of the wine in the glass. Its appearance when tipped against a white background can provide clues about the wine's stage of development and quality. A brownish hue in the rim of either a red or white suggests maturity. A dark brown rim suggests that the wine itself may be turning tawny and deteriorating.

ROBUST: Assertive, full-bodied and characterful. Similar in meaning to "big." Typical of many young red wines that eventually will evolve into more subtle potions.

RUM POT: Modern term for wines that are fruity and aromatic and perhaps slightly sweet, conveying an impression of rum punch. Not necessarily a negative trait when found in certain Zinfandels and other typically spicy wines.

SEC: Dry. In Champagne, the term refers to an unfermented sugar content of 1.5 to 4 percent by volume, which is slightly sweet. But the meaning is "dry" when applied to other wines.

SHEETS: Wide rivulets of wine that cling to the sides of the glass and slide down slowly after the wine has been swirled around inside. Sheets indicate a fairly high glycerine content and good texture. Sheets are wider than legs, which are narrower rivulets on the inside of the glass.

SHELLFISH WINE: Extremely crisp and dry white wine, usually with fairly high acidity, that is appropriate with such shellfish as raw clams and oysters on the half shell or with cold shrimp. More austere in style than the whites described as buttery or creamy.

SHORT: Lacking in aftertaste and texture, suggesting low acidity and small character. A dull wine.

SOFT: Lacking firmness or crispness, suggesting low acidity. Not robust or textured but sometimes pleasing in a simple way. The term is also used in modern California winemaking to connote low alcohol levels.

SPICY: Conveying an impression of spices and herbs, suggesting complexity and flavor intensity. A favorable trait if in balance with the fruit, body, and other characteristics.

SPRITZ: Shortened form of the German term spritzig, which means "lightly sparkling"; pétillant—connoting effervescence but not the full-sized bubbles of a sparkling wine. Expected in some German wines and some Johannisberg Rieslings from California, but should not be present in most red table wines.

STEMMY: Suggestive of the stems of the grapes. Similar to "reedy" and "woody" and indicating a lack of fruit flavor.

TANNIC: The presence of tannic acid that comes mainly from the skins, seeds, and stems of the grapes, as well as from the wooden barrels in which the wine is aged. A necessary constituent of good red wines and of some whites, most evident during a wine's first few years of age. Eventually it subsides during the process of maturing.

TAR: Some devotees perceive the aroma of melting road tar on a hot summer's day in certain Cabernet Sauvignons and Zinfandels. Not a negative trait and suggestive of a fairly high level of fruit.

TERROIR, GOÛT DE TERROIR: Having the taste of the earth or soil. Similar to "earthy." Pleasant in modest amounts in some wines, but sometimes overwhelming, especially in whites that lack other redeeming features.

TEXTURE: The feel of the wine, as opposed to its flavor, although a textured wine will have readily identifiable flavor characteristics. A wine of great texture creates an impression of tiny solid particles on the palate. It may not be robust, but it will have character.

TIGHT: Immature and undeveloped, with the fruit hidden and other characteristics difficult to identify, sometimes because of high levels of tannin. Typical of many young reds that may ultimately evolve into rich and balanced wines.

VANILLA, VANILLAN: Creamy or buttery white wines, especially Chardonnays from Burgundy or California, are sometimes described as having a vanilla quality. This is derived mainly from the oak barrels used for aging and is a favorable trait in moderation.

VARIETAL: Wine named after the grape used to make it, as in Cabernet Sauvignon, Chardonnay, Chenin Blanc, Nebbiolo, etc., as opposed to generically named wines that use names borrowed from other countries, for example, "Chablis," "Rhine," or "Burgundy" from American vineyards. Varietals are almost always superior to generics, and they are honest names that convey more information to the consumer.

VEGETAL: Tasting of vegetation rather than the ripe fruit of the grape. Sometimes synonymous with "grassy" or "herbaceous." Generally a negative quality that suggests poor growing conditions or immature grapes.

VELOUTÉ: Literally means "velvety" in French, referring to the smoothness and balance of a mature wine. Also connotes a certain fullness of flavor and elegance.

WOODY: Tasting of wood, usually due to extended aging in wooden casks or barrels prior to bottling. Especially evident in some California wines, reflecting the efforts of producers to add complexity to the flavor. The aroma and flavor of the wood should be in harmony with the fruit. When the woodiness is too obvious, the wine is imbalanced, although some enthusiasts like the taste.

Classic Wine and Food Combinations

"A meal without wine is like a day without sunshine." This is perhaps the most frequently quoted maxim in French gastronomic literature and is possibly one of the most quoted sayings to which the French lay claim. Whether it is true is another question, for a rainy Sunday afternoon in Paris in April can indeed be a splendid experience that no meal without wine could match. But the essence of the maxim cannot be refuted: food and wine go together. The one enhances the other, and the combination is the reason that gastronomy is so important to the French that at times it even surpasses another most popular pastime, which also has to do with pleasing the senses.

The French are not the only ones who hold gastronomy in high regard, of course, and it is true that all over the world people who revere wine also worship food and rarely experience one without the other. Wherever people passionate about wine meet, they are likely to do so over food, and the experimentation with gastronomic combinations goes on without cessation. Yet it is also probable that most of the food-and-wine combinations have already been discovered and that the French are responsible for many of them. As a result,

the classic marriages of food and wine that follow may appear to be largely French-influenced. Yet they are all basically simple, for complexity in food is not a prerequisite to achieve a wondrous taste sensation with wine. What is vital is the basic harmony that should exist throughout the gastronomic experience. So what we will be discussing will be harmony, even if this harmony will at times involve contrasts or counterpoints.

Another popular maxim related to gastronomy needs debunking, the saying that white wine should be consumed with white meat and red wine only with red meat. How this concept originated is uncertain, but it clearly violates the essence of gastronomy: that the individual should do whatever pleases his palate. The person who prefers red wine with shellfish may be odd, but he has the right to enjoy that combination if it pleases him. Moreover, anybody who has tasted a mature Chianti with chicken or other types of poultry knows that red wine with white meat can indeed be an exquisite gastronomic experience. Most sophisticated palates also prefer red wines with pasta, pork, and game birds of all kinds. In fact, the rule about red wine with red meat only is so often violated by knowledgeable gastronomes that it might as well not even exist.

What follows is an array of classic wine-and-food combinations. These are not meant to be totally comprehensive nor to be slavishly followed, for people who like to eat and drink well are also likely to be experimental. Gastronomy is constantly evolving, thanks to human creativity, and new and exciting combinations are probably being discovered even as this is being written. In setting out an array of classic combinations, moreover, there is the risk of failing to be comprehensive enough, of omitting some that should be included or of seeming to be idiosyncratic with others. Still, these combinations should be comfortable to all and are intended to be a useful guide that will enhance the wine experience. They are arranged according to the type of food to be consumed, starting with foods likely to be served as first courses and concluding with desserts and cheeses.

Shellfish (shrimp, lobster, crab, clams, oysters, mussels, etc.)
Chablis
Muscadet
Alsatian Riesling
White Graves
American Sauvignon Blanc
American Seyval Blanc
Champagne
Mâcon Blanc
Dry eastern American Riesling
Dry California Johannisberg Riesling
Galestro
Gavi
Pinot Grigio
Soave
Trebbiano
Frascati
Verdicchio
Dry Rhines and Mosels
Fino Sherry

The point to remember in combining white wine with shellfish is that the flavor of shellfish is fairly subtle, so the wine must be crisp and dry. The classic combination is Chablis with oysters, but there are many others. Gavi or Pinot Grigio with lobster can be splendid, and Muscadet with clams or oysters is another excellent combination.

Smoked Salmon and Smoked Poultry
Rhines or Mosels of Cabinet or
    Spätlese sweetness
New York Riesling
California semi-dry Riesling
California semi-dry Chenin Blanc
White Burgundy
Gavi
Pinot Grigio
Orvieto
Beaujolais
Valpolicella
Bardolino

The flavor of smoked fish or meat demands a slightly sweet white wine or a light red wine. The Rieslings produced in the Rhine and Mosel valleys of Germany are especially suitable. Moreover, they tend to be low in alcohol and are ideal lead-ins to a feast that may involve heavier wines with meat courses that come later.

Broiled or Sautéed Fish
White Burgundy
Mâcon Blanc
American Chardonnay
American Seyval Blanc
Muscadet
White Graves
Gavi
Pinot Grigio
Frascati
Est! Est! Est!
Rhines or Mosels of Cabinet or drier
    degree of sweetness

How fish is cooked and served has an important bearing on the wine that will taste best with it. Fish with complex cream sauces require a fairly robust white, perhaps a California Chardonnay that has been aged in oak or a rich and creamy Meursault, Corton-Charlemagne, or other white Burgundy. More simply prepared fish—for example, broiled sole with only subtle seasoning—requires a more austere wine, perhaps a Mâcon Blanc or white Graves. More strongly flavored fish—turbot or shad, for example—marry well with the full-bodied Gavi or Pinot Grigio from Italy. Experimentation will be rewarded.

Pasta with Clam Sauce or Seafood Sauce
Galestro
Gavi
Pinot Grigio
Pinot Bianco
Orvieto
Soave
Trebbiano
Garganega
Bardolino
Valpolicella

All pasta dishes not only are flavorful but have wonderful texture as well. They demand a textured wine, a wine of body and defined flavor. Red wines normally fit this category, but pasta served with a seafood sauce—for example, linguini with clam sauce—is more subtly flavored and requires a white wine, ideally a Gavi or Pinot Grigio, although Soave or Trebbiano, made from the same grape as Soave, are also suitable. Two light reds, Bardolino and Valpolicella, can also be used with pasta prepared in this way.

Pasta with Cream, Cheese, or Meat Sauce
Chianti Classico
Barolo
Gattinara
Spanna
Barbaresco
Grumello
Inferno
Amarone
Corvo Rosso
California Zinfandel
Brunello di Montalcino

The classic Italian pasta dish, fettucini Alfredo, with its creamy sauce and marvelous texture, is superb with any robust Italian red, and individual taste preferences will dictate the choice. Devotees of Chianti will insist on a mature example of this excellent Tuscan wine with their pasta, while followers of the fleshy reds of the Piedmont District will opt for a Barolo, Gattinara, Spanna, or Barbaresco. If the sauce used on the pasta is heavily garlicked, as it often is, the younger, less mature vintages of these wines can be used, for the garlic flavor would overwhelm the flavor of a mature red of this type, no matter how robust, whereas the tannins and chewy structure of an immature Chianti or Grumello or Spanna would create a viable flavor combination. If the goal is to experience a great and mature Italian red—perhaps a Brunello di Montalcino at least a decade old—more subtle seasoning is in order.

Poultry (chicken, turkey, squab, pigeon, etc.)
Bordeaux red
Chianti Classico
Rioja red
California Cabernet Sauvignon or Merlot
New York Baco Noir
New York Chancellor

Although poultry is mostly white meat, its flavor and texture demand a red wine, and the best are the great reds of Bordeaux. These wines display extraordinary finesse and complexity when at their best, and they show their best personality in the company of poultry, although the poultry should not be so heavily seasoned as to threaten the flavor of the wine. The Cabernet Sauvignons of California, made from the same basic grape as the reds of Bordeaux, also marry well with chicken and other poultry, as do mature Chianti Classicos and Riojas and some wines from the eastern United States, notably the Baco Noir and Chancellor.

Lamb
Burgundy red
Bordeaux red
California Cabernet Sauvignon or
    Merlot
California Zinfandel
Rioja red
Portuguese red
Brunello di Montalcino

Lamb is perhaps the ideal meat to serve with good red wine. Its slightly pungent quality when not overcooked, plus its texture, are perfect with all mature, balanced reds, even the spicy Zinfandels of California when properly mature after at least five or six years. Every wine devotee has his favorite red for lamb, and the choice will depend on one's mood as well as his budget and access to mature vintages. The reds of Rioja are especially suitable for the budget-conscious because they tend to mature earlier and are not expensive. If cost is no object, a château-bottled Bordeaux or estate-bottled Burgundy from a good vintage at least ten years old can be superb with lamb. Italy's greatest red, Brunello di Montalcino, also is perfect with lamb, but most Brunellos need extended bottle-aging to reach maturity. The heralded 1970 vintage was still not mature enough by the mid-1980s and was becoming very expensive. One of the best ways to enjoy a fully mature Brunello is with a butterflied, or deboned, leg of lamb grilled

open and flat over a hardwood fire and taken from the flames while the meat remains pink and juicy.

Beef
Bordeaux red
American Cabernet Sauvignon or
    Merlot
Chianti Classico
Rioja red
Portuguese red
Argentine Cabernet Sauvignon or
    Malbec
Châteauneuf-du-Pape
Hermitage
Côte Rôtie

The American infatuation with beef of all kinds and this country's enormous beef production have meant that more red wines have been tried with beef than with any other meat. To list all of the reds appropriate with beef would be an enormous undertaking, so the list has been restricted to those that happen to be the author's favorites. The maturity of these wines is important, for young and tannic wines should be used with more intensely flavored meats or cheeses. The best values tend to be the reds of Rioja in Spain or of northern Portugal, although the better Portuguese reds need at least a decade to reach maturity, whereas Rioja reds mature somewhat earlier. If a young wine is the only choice, a Rioja will be the most appropriate, especially if veal is being served, for veal is more subtly flavored than fully mature beef.

Pork
Beaujolais
California Pinot Noir
Corvo Rosso
Portuguese rosé
White Burgundy
California Chardonnay
California Sauvignon Blanc

Pork is prepared in so many ways that it is difficult to be specific in choosing a wine to go with it unless the exact preparation is known. Ham is quite salty, and Beaujolais is especially appropriate with it because of its fruity quality and relatively high acidity. Ham is also one of the few meats that seems to go well with rosés. Pork other than ham often is heavily seasoned and requires a more robust red, such as a California Pinot Noir. Pork that is not heavily seasoned and not served with a strongly flavored sauce or gravy can be excellent with fully flavored white wines, including white Burgundies, American Chardonnays that have been oak-aged, and American Sauvignon Blancs. Flexibility is the rule of thumb when serving pork.

Game Birds
Burgundy red
Bordeaux red
Portuguese red
Barolo
Gattinara
Spanna
Barbaresco
Brunello di Montalcino
Chianti Classico
Rioja red
Rubesco Riserva
Sassicaia
Tignanello
Taurasi
Vino Nobile di Montepulciano

Game birds such as pheasant, grouse, partridge, quail, wild ducks, and geese are at the heart of many classic feasts. A host serving such fare often will serve his best wines, for the complexity of the birds and the sauces and stuffings served with them demand complex, mature red wines. A game feast presents an opportunity to dig into the cellar and come up with a red that has been lying in wait for a special occasion, a red not to be taken casually, perhaps a

Burgundy such as Bonnes-Mares or Musigny, or any of those very special reds of Italy that are not well known in other countries but that achieve high levels of quality.

In this category are the Rubesco Riserva of Lungarotti, the Sassicaia bottled and distributed by Antinori, the Tignanello of Antinori, the Taurasi of Mastroberardino, the Vino Nobile di Montepulciano of a number of producers in Tuscany. None of these should be served before age ten, and many connoisseurs would advise waiting until at least age 20. Maturity is crucial with the reds to be served with game birds because of the complexity of the flavor of the birds. Coarsely tannic young reds render the complexity difficult to perceive, whereas silky-textured mature reds help bring out the birds' flavor and contribute to a complete gastronomic experience.

Game Meat (venison, boar, etc.)
Barolo
Barbaresco
Gattinara
Spanna
Brunello di Montalcino
Amarone
Portuguese red
California Zinfandel
Châteauneuf-du-Pape
Hermitage
Côte Rôtie

One characteristic shared by most game meats is toughness. Although it is true that one sometimes encounters tender venison, most chefs cook game meats in such a way as to minimize the anticipated toughness that results from existence in the wild. This often means lengthy hanging in cold storage while the fibers break down and the meat becomes "ripe," long soaking in marinades to achieve a similar purpose, and the use of sauces or gravies made from berries and other fruits to offset the gamy flavor of the meat. As a result, game meats are almost never subtly flavored, and they demand robust red wines of pronounced texture and character. The reds of northern Italy and of the Rhône Valley of France are especially useful in this category of cuisine, even when less than fully mature. Portuguese reds from the northern part of the country often display similar traits, as do California Zinfandels made in the "old" style, meaning with the intense flavor and texture that result from lengthy skin contact and late harvesting.

Foie Gras
Sauternes or Barsac
Trockenbeerenauslese Rhine or Mosel
Late-harvested California Johannisberg
   Riesling

Foie gras, the fattened liver of force-fed geese, is presented with Sauternes or its close neighbor Barsac in one of the most revered food-and-wine combinations in French gastronomy. In France the dish is always served at the outset of a meal, even though Sauternes is regarded as a dessert wine, but in America it is often served at the conclusion of a feast, lest the palate be shocked by such richness prior to dining on other dishes. The flavor combination of the foie gras, cooked only until pink, with chilled Sauternes, a wine of intense sweetness, defies description. Suffice it to say that this is the quintessence of richness and that no other food-and-wine combination is in any way similar, although duck liver is sometimes substituted for goose.

In Germany the intensely sweet Trockenbeerenauslese, made from grapes that have turned into raisins in the late autumn sun with the help of *Edelfäule,* the noble rot, is naturally used in place of Sauternes and is arguably just as exquisite. Wines equivalent to these are

vinified from the Johannisberg Riesling in California and perhaps marry better with foie gras than with any other food. This is not a combination for the shy or the hesitant. In fact, it goes beyond mere eating and drinking. No one who has the opportunity to sample it should miss the chance.

Desserts
Sauternes or Barsac
Rhine or Mosel of Auslese or greater
   degree of sweetness
Late-harvested Johannisberg Riesling
   from California
Late-harvested Alsatian Riesling or
   Gewürztraminer
Botrytised California Sauvignon Blanc
   or Semillon

Dessert wines, in contrast to desserts, are a misunderstood phenomenon in the United States, perhaps because of a misconception that their sweetness is somehow unnatural and similar to the sweetness of the cheap, high-alcohol wines consumed by hoboes and derelicts. The fact is that dessert wines are made from late-harvested grapes that achieve a high level of natural sugar because of their ripeness. Some of this grape sugar is left in the wines after most of it has been converted to alcohol through fermentation, so it is entirely natural. Additional flavor complexity is derived from *Botrytis cinerea,* a mold that attacks the grapes only under the right conditions of humidity. It is called *pourriture noble* in French, for "noble rot," and *Edelfäule* in German, meaning the same thing. The result is intense natural sweetness in combination with a honeylike flavor partly due to the Botrytis. Some connoisseurs prefer such wines with foie gras, some with sweet desserts, some with sharp cheeses. For use with such desserts as pastries, tarts, mousses, caramel custards, soufflées, and the like, a dessert wine is entirely appropriate. But it should be served in small quantities, well chilled.

Bland Cheeses (Brie, Camembert, Muenster, etc.)
American Chardonnay
American Sauvignon Blanc
Mâcon Blanc
Burgundy white
Rhine or Mosel Riesling
Gewürztraminer
Soave
Gavi
Pinot Grigio
Galestro
Traminer Aromatico

Almost any wine, red or white, can be served with bland cheeses, for this kind of cheese is complementary to a broad range of flavors. But the author's preference is fully flavored dry whites, so that red wines can be reserved for sharper cheeses.

Sharp Cheeses (blue, Roquefort, Stilton, Gorgonzola, Cheddar, etc.)
Vintage Port
Cream Sherry
Amontillado Sherry
Madeira
Marsala
Rhine or Mosel of at least Spätlese sweetness
Late-harvested Johannisberg Riesling from California
Sauternes or Barsac
Amarone

The flavor counterpoint delivered by a relatively sweet wine when tasted with a sharp cheese can be exquisite. The sharpness of a Stilton accentuates the sweetness of an old Port, and the almost astringent quality of a Roquefort brings out many nuances in a well chilled Sauternes or Barsac. Some hosts substitute this for the dessert course, some serve it in addition to dessert. Some people make an entire meal of the combination.

Best Buys

The best buys in wine are nearly always secondary wines of major producers, primary wines of minor producers, or wines that are unfashionable or obscure and therefore do not benefit from the demand that tends to drive up prices and curtail value. The key to finding a best buy is the balance, or perhaps imbalance, of supply and demand. Wines in heavy supply and moderate demand tend to be good values. Wines in restricted supply and heavy demand tend to be the worst values. The notion of value, of course, will often depend on the means of the buyer, but even the most affluent consumer is likely to be appreciative of value.

The best buys in imported red wines through the late 1970s and well into the 1980s were from Italy, Spain, and Portugal. Italy, as the largest wine-producing nation in the world (possibly excepting the Soviet Union, for which statistics are not disclosed), keeps pumping out fine reds at moderate prices year after year. It will behoove any value-conscious consumer to experiment with unfamiliar names from Italy in order to identify the values, but connoisseurs know that many good buys are in the Chiantis and Chianti Classicos of Tuscany. Hundreds of different brands exist,

creating a large supply of often excellent wine, and new producers are sending their wines to the export markets frequently.

The supply side of the supply-demand equation favors consumers of Chianti, so long as they are willing to experiment. When a wine of high quality at a moderate price is found, moreover, it should be bought in case lots, for the chances are good that other consumers are discovering it at the same time, and the oversupply soon will disappear. Many excellent Chiantis are available for less than $5 a bottle, and there are some to be found for under $4 or $3. In 1982 and 1983 the Chianti Classico 1979 from an unheralded producer named Cellole was selling at $2.59 a bottle at many East Coast stores. It was full-bodied, fruity, spicy, and aromatic, a good buy at $6, an extraordinary buy at $2.59. In the same period the Chianti Classico 1977 of Poggio al Sole, another obscure producer, was selling for less than $4 a bottle. This wine was so high in quality that it challenged Chiantis costing three times as much. It was low-priced because Poggio al Sole had a reputation that scarcely stretched to Florence, much less across the Atlantic.

As a category, no group of reds could

be deemed better value than the Riojas of northern Spain. The production standards there are high, and the level of quality is almost uniformly good. The wines are mellow yet full-bodied, charming, and accessible at a fairly young age, after five or six years. Consistently one of the best was the Marqués de Cáceres, selling at between $3 and $4 a bottle, a wine of elegance. For some implausible reason Riojas are not considered fashionable, so the demand for them is smaller than it should be. The result is that high quality in the bottle can be obtained for modest sums. But, again, it pays to experiment, because some Riojas are better values than others. Numerous examples are on the market, and smart consumers will identify the values and cart home cases before they are discovered by others.

The reds of northern Portugal are perhaps even higher in quality than the Spanish Riojas, for they tend to have better internal structure and are longer-lived. Yet most consumers seem to believe that not much comes out of Portugal other than Lancers and Mateus rosés or that the only red wines worth considering from Portugal are vintage Ports. Because of these misconceptions there is a paucity of demand for the very good full-bodied red table wines of Portugal, and many sell for less than $5 a bottle. Like the Riojas, they suffer from not being fashionable. Yet the quality of the product inside the bottle is what should count, and consumers who prefer tasting wines to labels should experiment with the Portuguese reds.

The most expensive wines in the world come from France, as nearly everyone knows, but does this mean there are no best buys from Burgundy, Bordeaux, or elsewhere in that large country? Consistently one of the best buys in any and all markets is Beaujolais, which is produced in huge quantities each year in the southern part of the Burgundy country. Somehow, no matter what the economic conditions, good Beaujolais can always be found for less than $5 a bottle. Moreover, good Beaujolais is not unfashionable, for it is French and often high in quality. What benefits consumers here is that the supply of Beaujolais is so enormous year after year and the competition among exporters and importers so great that prices tend to remain low. Moreover, most Beaujolais does not benefit from extended bottle-aging, so it does not increase in value beyond about two years of age, which means there is no economic incentive for importers and exporters to hold onto their inventories. This year's Beaujolais *must* be sold before next year's hits the market, and one result is that prices are kept low so that the wine keeps moving. The ultimate beneficiary is the consumer.

Is Beaujolais the only best buy among French reds? Hardly. For example, there is Cahors, from the rugged country inland from Bordeaux. Cahors tends to be inky dark in color, fragrant with the scent of berries, and chewy with fruit in the mouth. It is a wine of considerable longevity, capable of lasting two and three decades while retaining its vigor, yet it is also charming in its youth, often displaying good drinkability by age five. Because it is little known in the United States, it can often be found for less than $5 a bottle, a price that does not reflect its level of quality. Rather, it reflects only the demand, which is very low because of a lack of recognition.

No discussion of best buys could fail to omit the so-called *petits châteaux* of Bordeaux, the ones that were not classified according to quality at the Paris Exposition of 1855. Because they are not automatically listed in every comprehensive wine book, as are the classified growths, they tend to be much less known. Yet only some 65 châteaux were classified in 1855 in the Médoc, followed by some more in Graves and Saint-Emilion in the 1950s, but the total amounts to only a fraction of the châteaux or wine estates in the Bordeaux District. The number runs into the thousands, and many of them make good wine. Again, consumers must experiment, for the quality can be variable and the supply in one city or market may be entirely different from the availability in another area. Yet in the early 1980s many very good small Bordeaux reds could be found from the excellent 1979 vintage for $5 a bottle or less— a fraction of the cost of most classified growths.

White wines have been in far greater demand than reds for the last decade, for the wine boom seems to have largely bypassed the reds, and best buys among whites are harder to find. Yet from France there are the Mâcon Blancs, produced in the same region that gives us Pouilly-Fuissé yet lacking the recognition of the Burgundy country's most famous white on this side of the Atlantic. A simple Mâcon Blanc from an obscure producer may turn out to be a fine wine—crisp and dry, cleanly made, showing a bit of character—yet lack of consumer recognition can mean it fetches only a modest sum in the American retail market, perhaps as little as $4 a bottle.

Among secondary wines of major producers, there is the Moreau Blanc of Jean Jacques Moreau, the leading producer of genuine Chablis in France. Moreau's Chablis Grand Cru from the Hospices des Clos vineyard runs $20 or more a bottle at retail. It is an excellent Chablis, recognized by many connoisseurs who are willing to pay its exalted price. On the other hand, the same producer's Moreau Blanc, a simple white wine not entitled to the Chablis appellation because it is not made from grapes grown in the Chablis District, was selling for less than $3 a bottle through the early 1980s. It was a crisp, clean white, benefiting from the know-how of Jean Jacques Moreau yet lacking wide public recognition and available in good supply, for production was not restricted by the French *appellation contrôlée* laws.

Many consumers regard American jug wines as good buys, and it is probable that Ernest and Julio Gallo alone have given more values to American consumers than all of the other American producers combined. American jug wines, such as the so-called Chablis Blanc of Gallo, tend to taste like what they are—American wines. But they are very well made, will not readily deteriorate and are inexpensive. Do they fall into the best buy category? That is up to the individual consumer to decide, but the point to remember is that there are many low-priced wines on the shelves, and, if they taste good, they are good value.

Jug Wines

The concept of jug wines was pioneered in the United States by California and New York State producers who carried wines around in bulk-sized wooden tanks on carts drawn by horses. They would pull up in front of a general store in a village and wait for local citizens to approach with their own jugs, which would be filled from spigots on the tanks. One California producer is fond of telling the story of how his grandfather carted his tank of wine from village to village and offered Zinfandel from the spigot on one side and Burgundy from the spigot on the other. Actually, it was the same wine, but his customers had set ideas about what they wanted to drink and insisted on calling their wines by certain names.

The jug has evolved a great deal since those days around the turn of the century, and now only consumers in rural parts of Europe take their own jugs to local wineries for refills. The Gallo Brothers, with their huge winery in Modesto, California, have become one of the largest manufacturers of glass in the world. Rather than buy bottles, they make their own, right there in their own bottle factory in Modesto. Many of those bottles are jug-shaped, reflecting the Gallo product mix, and the chances are that nearly all are used only once.

Nowadays the definition of a jug wine goes beyond the shape of the bottle. It is more accurately defined as a wine with a brand name, rather than a geographical or varietal name, which is sold for low prices, a wine that is durable, perhaps very slightly sweet, pleasant to drink and lacking in complexity. There are jug wines from dozens of American producers besides Gallo, and now there are dozens being imported from other countries as foreign producers try to capitalize on the American wine boom by grabbing a piece of the market from Gallo, Taylor, Carlo Rossi, Almadén, Los Hermanos, Paul Masson, Louis Martini, Sebastiani, Christian Brothers, Charles Krug, Robert Mondavi, and all the others.

Villa Banfi was an early purveyor of blended wines called Roman red and Roman white, providing a European taste at California jug prices. Many Soaves suddenly began crossing the Atlantic in large, jug-shaped bottles, attractively priced. Even the French, who took such pride in their dominant position in the premium end of the market, watched enviously as the Italians captured 60 percent of the import market in the United States largely because of the success of a cheap, lightly sparkling, slightly sweet concoction called Lambrusco.

With Riunite, the leading brand of Lambrusco, making sales of millions of cases a year in the U.S., many French, Spanish, German, and Austrian producers realized that the brand allegiance of American consumers was not strong and that their affections could be captured with the right products. The list of French jug wines selling in numerous American population centers is now enormous, and some of these wines are directly competitive on a price basis with Gallo and the other high-volume California producers.

In 1982 the staff of the International Wine Center, an educational enterprise in New York, undertook to comparison-taste all of the jug wines on the American market, a monumental task. Nobody even knew precisely how many were available, much less where all of them could be found. They amassed 220 in all in what was perhaps the largest jug tasting ever undertaken. To qualify, a wine had to be priced at less than $6 per 1.5-liter container, the equivalent of two single bottles of 750-milliliter capacity. Virtually all jug wines fell into this category and so did some that never saw the inside of a jug container. The evaluation was made in two phases. The first called for dividing the wines into three categories according to price. Each group was blind-tasted separately a week apart. The wines that received ratings of good, as opposed to acceptable or flawed, totaled 38 whites and 26 reds.

All of these were retasted on yet another occasion to identify those that could be called superior. Seventeen whites and 15 reds were placed in this category. They were as follows:

Whites: Alexis Lichine White Table Wine of France, Almadén Mountain Chablis, Boucheron Blanc de Blancs, Concha y Toro Sauvignon Blanc/Sémillon 1981, Cuvée Saint Pierre Blanc, Della Scala Soave, Gallo Chablis Blanc, Gallo Sauvignon Blanc, Klosterkeller

Siegendorf Grüner Veltliner 1980, L'Epayrié Blanc de Blancs, Los Hermanos Chablis, Parducci Vintage White 1980, Paul Masson Chablis, Petternella Soave, Sebastiani Mountain Chablis, Sommelière Blanc de Blancs, Villa Carasol Bianco Fino.

Reds: Beaudet Rouge, Concannon Burgundy 1979, Cuvée Saint Pierre Rouge, Jean Boulaine Cuvée Rouge, L'Epayrié Rouge, Louis Martini Burgundy, Monterey Vineyard Classic Red 1979, Moreau Rouge, Parducci Vintage Red 1978, Partager Vin Rouge, Robert Mondavi Red 1980, San Martin Burgundy 1977, Sebastiani Country Cabernet, Sebastiani Mountain Burgundy, Villa Banfi Roman Red.

The tasters rated 21 other whites as good and 11 reds as good. As for those that failed to make the "superior" or "good" categories, the Wine Center declined to disclose their names publicly because of the real possibility of errors in a tasting of 220 wines in all, regardless of how much care was taken and how scientific the conditions. The point was that so many of these jug wines were indeed pleasant to drink—not complex, not connoisseurs' wines, not wines for laying away in cellars. It was evident that the jug wine had come of age and that the chief problem confronting consumers was to find the best one, for so many are available.

Serving Wine

A great mystique has grown up over the years surrounding the way in which wine is served. Indeed, a certain ritual is often involved, and it is understandable that people who are unfamiliar with the ritual may be not only confused but repelled by it. Nevertheless many of the procedures used in serving wine exist for sound reasons, and a thorough understanding of them will add to the total experience and make the difference between a routine occasion and an event of rich enjoyment.

Temperature

Your preparations must begin long before the moment when you begin filling the glasses at your dining table. If you plan to serve a white wine or a rosé, you must place the bottles in your refrigerator at least 90 minutes in advance so that they can be well chilled when they are served. If you forget, 20 or 30 minutes in the deep freeze can be a substitute, but don't leave a bottle of wine in a freezer for too long. Eventually it will freeze and crack or perhaps push its cork out, due to the expansion that accompanies freezing.

The most elegant method of chilling is to use a silver ice bucket expressly designed for the purpose. Place the bottle inside the bucket first, then add ice cubes. Finally, fill up the bucket with water. The last requirement is often overlooked, but it is vital. Merely adding ice is not enough, because the warm air from the surrounding atmosphere will prevent the bottle from cooling efficiently. When water is added, its temperature will drop sharply, due to the ice, and the frigid liquid will surround the bottle, drawing out the warmth much more rapidly. This method is even quicker than the deep freeze. Remember to place a rubber band around the bottle to hold the label in place so that it will not float off after it has become soaked. Some of your guests will want to inspect the label, and using the rubber band will save you the trouble of fishing it out of the ice bucket after it has come loose. Remove the cork from the bottle before you place it in the bucket; even a white wine often will benefit from a few minutes of breathing before it is served. Use a white towel to prevent water from dripping when the wine is being poured.

As nearly everybody knows, red wines—most of them, that is—should be served at "room" temperature. But what does this mean? Obviously the meaning must vary with the temperature of the room, so it is hardly satisfactory to suggest that red wine should be served at whatever temperature happens to prevail in a particular room. Because the practice has its roots in Europe, where central heating is not nearly as common as in the United States and where, as a consequence, rooms tend to be cooler, the best temperature for serving red wines is not quite as high as you might think. Whereas American rooms tend to be kept between 70° and 72° Fahrenheit, a better temperature for serving most red wines would be around 68° or perhaps even a bit lower. If you are fortunate enough to have a cool cellar for storing your wine, then no special preparation is necessary, except to make sure your bottles have ample time to warm up from cellar temperature to the ideal serving temperature. But remember also that the wine will warm up in the glass after it is poured. If you store your bottles in a dining room cupboard or comparable location, however, you may wish to chill them briefly in the refrigerator before serving. This procedure is not vital, but it does enhance the tasting experience.

Some red wines require just as much chilling as whites. The best known of these is Beaujolais, which has a freshness and fruitiness that is similar in many ways to the characteristics of a white wine. Connoisseurs know that the best-tasting Beaujolais comes directly out of the wooden casks stored deep in the frigid cellars among the Beaujolais hillsides in eastern France. Naturally it is impossible to duplicate this atmosphere in your own home, but you can serve the wine at the same temperature by chilling it yourself. The practice is common in France and is followed to a lesser extent in other European countries. It is almost unheard of in the United States, but presumably its popularity will spread as Americans learn how much the taste of Beaujolais improves with chilling. Wines produced in California from the principal grape of Beaujolais—the Gamay—also benefit from chilling.

Breathing

Nearly all wines benefit from a certain amount of breathing, or being exposed to the atmosphere prior to being drunk. Just how much breathing is necessary or advisable will depend on the type of wine and on its age. Whites and rosés generally require very little breathing before you drink them. But permitting the bottle to stand for five or ten minutes with the cork extracted can be helpful in enabling the wine to become softer and mellower. This is especially true of the youthful whites that exhibit a high level of acidity after spending only a year or two in the bottle.

The amount of breathing required for red wines is an entirely different matter and involves a considerable amount of care and skill. As a rule, the younger the wine, the more breathing it will need to soften its backbone of tannin and acidity. Moreover, a red that is being drunk before it has reached proper maturity will tend to age a little if exposed to the air for a period of time. But it is also possible to permit a wine to breathe too much and lose its character and vitality. There are few greater disappointments than to discover that a fine wine has been ruined because it has been uncorked too far in advance of being consumed.

Very old wines—those dating back a quarter century or more—can be spoiled if permitted to undergo the assault of the atmosphere for more than a few moments, for they will quickly oxidize. Yet even these will benefit from some breathing, and experienced connoisseurs occasionally discover a Bordeaux of the 1926 or 1928 vintage that is able to reach its peak only after being exposed to the air for at least an hour. The best procedure is to taste the wine immediately after opening the bottle. If it is hard and ungenerous, it may need at least 30 minutes of breathing and perhaps an hour or more to become soft and mellow. But if it exhibits a great deal of fruit and is already soft and rounded when you taste it, then immediate consumption is probably in order to prevent it from deteriorating, or going "over the hill." Obviously it helps to have sampled a particular type of wine from a particular vintage before uncorking a fresh bottle if you wish to time it for a special moment during your meal.

Generally, red Bordeaux, certain red Chiantis, and other robust reds from northern Italy as well as other wines made of similar grapes in a similar fashion require the most breathing. Included in this category would be American wines made from the Cabernet Sauvignon grape and certain Spanish and South American wines. A Bordeaux from a good vintage with less than a decade in the bottle should ideally be permitted to breathe for at least an hour. If the Bordeaux is under five years of age, breathing for two hours may be in order, although some châteaux have changed their production methods to the extent that their wines become surprisingly soft within only a few years. Some vintages also are more "forward" than others, achieving a great deal of maturity in a short time. The 1970 Bordeaux are an example; many of them tasted splendid by late 1973.

Burgundies from the Côte d'Or in France and Burgundy-type wines need less breathing. Those with less than ten years of bottle age need 30 minutes to an hour, although methods of vinification vary greatly in the Burgundy country and some producers are still making wines of great longevity. The Pinot Noirs of California, made from the basic Burgundy grape, should be treated similarly. Older Burgundies, dating from prewar vintages, were made differently and often require as much breathing today as young wines from the same vineyards. In general, though, no Burgundy needs to breathe for more than an hour to reach its summit.

Most Beaujolais and other wines made from the Gamay grape require much less breathing, although there are exceptions. Some of the better *grand cru* Beaujolais—for example, Morgon and Moulin-à-Vent—can be treated similarly to a full-blooded Burgundy from the Côte d'Or to the north. The lighter Beaujolais and Rhône wines, with the important exceptions of Côte-Rôtie, Hermitage, and Châteauneuf-du-Pape, can be treated almost like white wines; lengthy breathing improves them little. Hermitage and Châteauneuf should be treated in the same way as Burgundies from the Côte d'Or.

All the rules about breathing are, of course, based on the assumption of proper storage. The maturing of a wine can be hastened drastically by sharp and rapid temperature fluctuations and by excessive heat, which may even destroy it. Wines exposed to such conditions require much less breathing than their vintages might indicate, assuming they are drinkable at all.

Decanting

One way to hasten the breathing process of a good red wine is to decant it, or pour it from its original bottle into another container. Not only does the resultant aeration help the wine to become soft and mellow but decanting also enables you to separate the clear wine from whatever sediment there may be in the bottom of the bottle. (Decanting is generally not practiced for white wines because most of them do not throw off any sediment.) Fine crystal decanters of antique heritage can also be used to add luster to your dining table.

The process itself should be a highlight of your meal. Because one of the goals of decanting is to eliminate the sediment, be sure not to shake the bottle. If the bottle has been properly stored lying on its side, the sediment will be collected in a line along the side of the bottle. If you stand the bottle upright an hour or so before decanting, the sediment will settle in the bottom, rendering the decanting process easier.

The best method devised so far is the oldest. It involves the use of a lighted candle. As you pour the wine from its bottle into the decanter, look through the neck of the bottle at the flame as the wine flows past. When tiny grains of sediment appear against the bright background, stop pouring. The purpose of the candle is to enable you to perceive the sediment as soon as it starts flowing. When the process is done properly, only about a half inch of wine will remain in the bottom of the bottle. Even some of this can be salvaged if you permit the bottle to sit upright and undisturbed through your meal and then carefully pour off the clear remainder.

In England many restaurants automatically decant all red wines as a matter of habit. In the United States wines are rarely decanted. Perhaps the best practice lies somewhere in between. Older wines that have produced sediment should be decanted. Young wines that have thrown off no sediment need not be decanted unless aeration is the primary purpose. Any clean container can be used as a decanter—even another wine bottle that has been rinsed thoroughly. But connoisseurs and collectors of wine paraphernalia are likely to use elegant crystal to enhance the experience of drinking an elegant wine.

Uncorking

Removing the cork from a bottle of wine is usually a rather simple process that requires very little skill or effort, but it is wise to keep a few principles in mind when approaching the task, especially if a mature wine and an aged cork are involved. Generally, the more expensive wines of greater breeding will have longer corks—in fact, sometimes double the length of the cork in a cheap bottle of wine. To prevent the cork from breaking while you are trying to extract it, you must insert the corkscrew far enough so that the point pierces the end of the cork next to the wine.

If the point does not penetrate sufficiently, the cork may break. The purpose of the coils in the screw is to grip the cork; if the device is not inserted far enough, only part of the cork will be gripped. If the cork is strong, this will make no difference. But if it is weak, it may break, complicating the task. The best insurance against broken corks is to make sure the coil penetrates far enough and to insert it carefully down the middle, so that it does not touch the neck of the bottle.

Innumerable designs exist for corkscrews, and some of them are so complex and unusual that they cost fabulous sums. Collectors pay fortunes for some of the older models at the London auction houses. But the simple device used by the wine waiters in most restaurants remains one of the best money can buy. It involves a basic principle of leverage that assists in extracting the cork. Vastly more complicated devices are available and some of them work quite nicely. One very efficient extractor, called the Screwpull, has recently developed a devoted following, largely because it includes a guide that centers the screw in the cork. Each wine lover will have his own favorite, and it probably will not be much more or less efficient than some other kind.

The important part of the device is the one that seems to get the least attention. This is the screw itself, known as the "worm." It should look like a spring, or coil, with a hollow interior, rather than like a straight piece of metal with threads attached. The latter kind often merely drills a hole in the cork and is useless in extracting the more stubborn ones. The former is much more efficient because its coils grip the cork more securely.

CHAMPAGNE CORKS

Champagne and other sparkling wines require special handling because their corks are under a great deal of pressure. They should be treated with great care and respect, lest they become dangerous missiles propelled through the air with surprising force. Doctors report a regular and predictable increase in eye injuries on January 1 of each year—reflecting the increased consumption of Champagne on New Year's Eve the night before. Although the popping of Champagne corks helps create a festive atmosphere, it is the wrong way to open a bottle of sparkling wine for two basic reasons.

First, it is dangerous and, second, it is harmful to the wine itself. Most of the danger will be experienced by the person who is trying to uncork the bottle. Inevitably, it seems, the cork is directed toward his face as he wrestles with the foil and the wire straps that hold the cork secure. Then, with sudden force, the cork is expelled, the person is caught by surprise and loses his grip, and the damage is done. Even if the cork misses the holder of the bottle, it may bounce off the ceiling, leaving a dent in the plaster, or strike a lampshade or perhaps a painting or objet d'art, inflicting minor but significant damage.

Almost as important, the effect on the wine will be negative. The reason that Champagne and other sparkling wines are special is their bubbles. The complex process that produces the bubbles is one reason why sparkling wines are more costly. Because the bubbles provide the unique character of such wines, it is foolish to do anything that might reduce or impair them. Yet this is precisely what the popping of a Champagne cork accomplishes. It causes the cork to be expelled in a rush of gas that often carries a portion of the wine with it. The more gas that is lost, the fewer the bubbles in the wine. And if you are going to reduce or eliminate the bubbles in your Champagne, you might as well save yourself some money and drink a still wine.

To avoid the loss of bubbles and to escape any danger from flying corks, you must follow a simple but important procedure in opening a bottle of sparkling wine. First, peel off all of the metal foil or paper surrounding the cork and neck of the bottle, so that you will not have to wrestle with the foil at the moment when the cork is about to fly out. Then carefully loosen the metal straps holding the cork in place, all the while keeping the palm of one hand resting flat on the top of the cork. You will experience a tricky moment when you attempt to remove the metal straps without removing your hand from the top of the cork, but a little practice will enable you to discern whether the cork is ready to fly at that point. After the straps are out of the way, gently twist the bottle—not the cork. You may suddenly feel the cork pressing against your palm due to the force of the gas, or you may discover that it is stubborn and requires forceful twisting, perhaps even with a pair of pliers or with the help of a towel. (Champagne pliers are available from most shops that offer other items of wine paraphernalia.) The crucial moment comes when you hear the gas begin to escape around the edges of the cork. Your goal here is to permit the gas to hiss out gently without letting the cork escape your grip. That gentle hissing sound followed by a "pop" that is just barely audible will indicate that you've done the job properly. The wine itself will not suddenly foam over the lip of the bottle and the bubbles will have been preserved.

Baskets and Cradles

A very elegant sight on the sideboard in your dining room or in a good restaurant is an array of bottles nestled in wicker baskets or in cradles made of silver or some other bright metal. These holders display the bottles in such a way that the labels are readily visible, and they give you the impression that special care has been devoted to the bottles, perhaps so that the sediment within will have remained undisturbed while the bottle was transferred from its rack in the cellar to its resting place whence it will be served. The theory is that keeping the bottle on its side will preserve the wine in the same position as when it was in storage and prevent the sediment from becoming roiled.

The trouble with the theory is that it defies logic. Despite the care that may be devoted to keeping a bottle undisturbed while it is being brought from the cellar, the sediment inevitably becomes stirred up and remains stirred up unless hours pass before the wine is served. In fact, leaving the bottle on its side actually will mean that the sediment will take longer to settle. Standing the bottle upright will enable the sediment to sink to the bottom much more effectively, because gravity will be on your side. Some wine waiters will insist that resting the bottle in a basket will even eliminate the necessity of decanting, but this too is nonsense.

Each time the bottle is tipped to pour, the sediment will be disturbed. Keeping the bottle on its side in a basket will prevent the sediment from settling out, and you will discover that a deposit of vinous mud will have collected in your glass as a result. Baskets and cradles are excellent devices for displaying bottles, but they should not be used for serving wines. If the bottle contains sediment, the wine should be decanted after the bottle has been permitted to stand upright. If the wine contains no sediment, the basket becomes merely an affectation that takes up additional space on your table and adds nothing to the tasting experience. Waiters will even admit that using a basket renders it more—not less—difficult to pour the wine. Proof of this fact is that many waiters in restaurants that insist on using such holders will avoid using the handle on the basket and will grip the basket around its middle when pouring the wine.

For purposes of display, baskets and cradles are useful gadgets. But display should be their only function. Insist that bottles be stood upright as a general practice, and you will save yourself and your waiter some trouble.

There is one exception to this rule. That is when the entire contents of the bottle are to be poured into glasses all at once or into a decanter, and only if the bottle does not have to undergo a journey from the cellar. In this case the wine can be poured off the sediment in one motion, so that the sediment does not become agitated. But this will be effective only when the bottle has been lying in the basket or cradle near your table for several hours.

Glassware

It should be obvious that the glass used for drinking wine plays a crucial role and therefore merits considerable attention, yet many wine drinkers seem to forget about it or take it for granted. Highly polished crystalware not only has its own inherent beauty but also enables you to appreciate fully the appearance of the wine. Clusters of glasses set out beside each place at your dining table will add to the total experience of a fine meal and enhance the ability of your guests to appreciate the wines that you serve them.

There are many different kinds of glasses, some dictated by convenience, some by national custom, and some by function. The best tend to be those that display the wine most effectively. For serious tasting, colored glasses are inappropriate, for they mask the true appearance of the wine. Such glasses may add to the beauty of your table setting, but they prevent you and your guests from accurately judging the color and clarity of the wine inside them. Similarly, cut or etched glasses also hinder your ability to perceive the wine's appearance. There is no denying that they add to the elegance of your table, but they detract from your perception of the wine. The best glasses are absolutely clear.

The size of your glassware is also crucially important. All too often wine glasses simply are too small to permit complete enjoyment of the tasting experience. A proper glass should be large enough to enable you to swirl the wine around inside and force out its bouquet. This means a size of at least eight ounces. Many knowledgeable tasters prefer glasses twice that size, and some glasses are available that are capable of holding an entire bottle of wine, although they are meant to be filled only partly. Sadly, many restaurants, confronted with the task of keeping their glassware clean, opt for small goblets that can be accommodated in commercial dishwashers. The result is that their customers are prevented from fully enjoying their wines. Any serious restaurant should have adequately sized glasses to give customers the full benefit of the wine they purchase. The same goes for the host serving wine in his own home. An investment in proper glassware provides many long-term benefits.

The shape of wine glasses is equally critical. The sides should curve in at the top, so that wine will not spill out when being swirled around to develop the bouquet. The classic shape is the tulip—similar to the shape of the flower. The tulip may have a chimney on its top, so that the bouquet of the wine will be thrust upward into the nostrils of the taster. The Burgundy glass, sometimes called a *balon* or a *bourgogne,* is rounder and more closely resembles a sphere with its top cut off. Glasses for dessert wines, such as Sauternes or Rhines or Mosels, tend to be round also but are smaller, reflecting the more modest quantities of such wines consumed at the conclusion of a meal.

Champagne glasses come in three basic varieties: the flute, the tulip, and the *coupe,* or cup. For some unexplained reason the *coupe* is used often in the United States, despite its many basic shortcomings. Because it is wide and shallow, the Champagne bubbles are dissipated into the atmosphere more quickly. This violates the essence of Champagne, which after all is a sparkling wine. It is more difficult to produce and costs more because of the bubbles, so it is a shame to drink it from a glass that does not preserve the bubbles. According to legend, the first *coupe* was fashioned from the breast of Helen of Troy, using a wax mould to create an exact replica, so that the gods henceforth would be able to experience the illusion that they were drinking from the breast of Jupiter's daughter. Another tale has it that the *coupe* was designed from the breasts of Marie Antoinette. In any case, the *coupe* is highly distinctive and is used almost exclusively for Champagne. It is readily identifiable as a Champagne glass, which may explain part of its popularity.

In the Champagne country around Reims and Epernay, however, the *coupe* is rarely used. The Champenois go to great lengths to create the bubbles in their unique wine, and they bend every effort to preserve them while they are drinking it. Thus the tulip is more common here. Unlike the tulip used for other wines, however, the Champagne tulip is taller and narrower, with a basically more graceful design. Its shape enables the drinker to perceive a string of bubbles rising from the point at which the bowl joins the stem. At the same time, the tulip is less likely to overflow and better able to retain the sparkle of the wine.

The Champagne flute is equally elegant. The difference between it and the tulip is that its sides do not curve in at the top but are straight. Generally, you should not swirl Champagne around in the glass to develop its bouquet in the way you would swirl a still wine, so the flute shape is not a handicap in this context. The constant rising of the bubbles to the surface tends to force up the bouquet without swirling. Moreover, swirling Champagne tends to dissipate the bubbles—which you want to avoid. Some people prefer the flute because of its different shape. It is just as appropriate for Champagne as the tulip.

The best all-purpose glass is what the British refer to as the claret shape, often used for serving Bordeaux. It is the classic tulip, slightly wider than the long, narrow Champagne tulip but not as broad as the *balon,* or Burgundy glass. You may properly serve any wine in the standard claret glass, from Champagne to dessert wines, without violating any customs or principles. But your table setting will be enhanced if you are able to provide a different style of glass for each different type of wine that you serve. The tulip for the white wine you would serve with your appetizer or fish course should be slightly smaller than the tulip for your red Bordeaux or Chianti or California Cabernet Sauvignon. The *balon,* or *bourgogne,* for serving red Burgundy or perhaps for Barolo or Gattinara should have a larger capacity but might not be as tall as the claret glass. Glasses for sweet dessert wines tend to have longer stems and smaller bowls.

Be sure that all of your glasses are highly polished. It is disconcerting to discover fingerprints, a lipstick smear, or residue from the dishwasher on an otherwise elegant glass just at the moment when you are examining a lovely, deep-colored wine. Also remember why wine glasses have stems—for holding, so that you will not have to mar the beauty of the bowl with your fingerprints. In addition, the stem keeps the natural warmth of your hand away from the wine. If you ever take part in or observe a professional tasting, you will note that nobody grips his glass by the bowl. Glasses covered with fingerprints are ugly and detract from the tasting experience by preventing you from accurately judging the appearance of the wine.

The Tastevin

Although the French wine-tasting cup, known as the *tastevin,* is not made of glass, it is a device commonly used for examining and otherwise testing wine. It is most often made of silver or silver plate, so that the shiny surfaces can reflect light through the wine to demonstrate its appearance. Many different designs exist, but the standard *tastevin* is shallow—no more than an inch deep—and has a maximum diameter of perhaps three inches. Along its bottom and sides are dimples and striations whose purpose is to reflect the light in varying ways and enable the taster to examine a wine's every facet, as well as to taste.

The cup is most often used in Burgundy, where it is the emblem of the Confrérie des Chevaliers du Tastevin, the world's most renowned wine society. Each *vigneron* carries one in his pocket, often wrapped in a kerchief which he uses to wipe it clean after a tasting session. The *tastevin* has a ring on its side through which one's forefinger is hooked. Atop the ring is a flat thumb-rest, so that the taster can hold the cup steady. Some of the more elaborate *tastevins*—those designed by jewelers rather than wine growers—have fancy silver displays around their sides and rings fashioned from tiny silver grape roots. Any visitor to Beaune, in the heart of the Burgundy country, will see thousands on display in the shops around the town's main square. Prices range from a few francs—less than a dollar—to fifty dollars or more.

Some *tastevins* are made of pewter rather than silver, and these are less useful for reflecting the light through the wine. But the pewter ones do make handsome ashtrays for your dining table. If you should use your own personal *tastevin* at your dining table, be wary of resting it on the tabletop. Smokers will invariably assume it is an ashtray, and you are likely to discover a bed of wine-soaked ashes in the bottom after your meal. Such a sight is especially revolting to a true wine lover, who will always shun tobacco when he is drinking even the most pedestrian wine. A true silver *tastevin* should be used only for the purpose for which it was designed.

Storage of Wine

Wine is a living, changing substance. Its development reflects the manner in which it is handled throughout its life, from the moment when the grapes are picked to the point at which it passes the drinker's lips. There is little that you can do about how a wine is handled before it comes into your possession. Dealing with a reliable merchant and reliable shippers or importers can help assure that the wine will reach you in good condition. But once you have acquired it, you can have an important influence on its life. Even older wines that you plan to drink shortly rather than store will benefit from whatever tender loving care you bestow on them, so it behooves you to know how to create the best conditions.

That is where wine cellars come in. Every oenophile at some time wants his own cellar, not only because cellars usu-

ally are the best places to store wine but also because they are part of the total experience of wine. Descending into a subterranean vault or unlocking the door to a closet-sized cache to select a bottle or two is, after all, part of the ritual of serving wine. But leaving ritual aside, it is highly practical to keep a cellar of your own, for it enables you to buy wines when they are young and inexpensive rather than after their cost has been marked up by a retailer or importer to reflect their increased maturity and greater scarcity. Because wine is constantly being consumed, the supply of any vintage is forever decreasing. Yet as it approaches maturity, it becomes more desirable than ever. It does not take a degree in economics to recognize the advantages of buying young and storing during the period of development.

Temperature

But why are cellars the traditional storage places for wines? The answer is simple: because of temperature. Cellars are by definition underground or partially underground structures. The earth surrounding the walls and the existence of

a house or other building above act as insulation against heat and against sudden temperature fluctuations. It is said that heat is the greatest enemy of wine. Surely it is true that more wine is spoiled due to excessive heat than to any other factor. A wine should be permitted to develop slowly in a cool environment where any temperature changes occur very gradually, over a period of months, and never exceed perhaps 10° Fahrenheit. Ideally, there should be no fluctuations at all, but who can create ideal conditions in this era of central heating?

The perfect temperature for wine storage is widely agreed to be about 55° Fahrenheit, although some experts are inclined to argue in favor of a slightly colder cellar. Maintaining a cellar at 55° may prove to be extremely difficult, especially in warm climates, but this does not mean that you cannot safely store wine in these areas. An expensive solution is air-conditioning through the use of an electrically powered cooling unit. But not even this measure is strictly necessary.

A valid rule of thumb is that a high temperature of around 70° Fahrenheit in summer is permissible, so long as it is reached slowly, as the seasons change. Sudden temperature fluctuations can have almost as devastating an impact on wine as prolonged exposure to heat, so the key factor in wine storage at your home is to avoid those rapid changes. Even if the temperature in your cellar pushes toward 80° in the depths of the summer, the consequences may not be really bad if the change is gradual. It is certainly true that wines exposed to temperatures above 55° will not age as gracefully as those kept at the ideal. The life span will be shortened, but who is to say that such wines cannot at least approach the peaks of perfection which properly stored wines attain? Instead of lasting 40 years, your good château-bottled red Bordeaux or California Cabernet Sauvignon or Brunello may last only 20. Does this really make a difference? The purist will say it does, but the pragmatist will come to the conclusion that it is still useful to keep a wine cellar even under less than ideal temperature conditions.

Of course, there are precautions you can take to insure against rapid temperature changes in your cellar even if you are unable to keep the temperature near 55°. Presumably you will not devote your entire basement area to wine storage. You will want to select a corner or separate room and seal it off from the rest of the cellar. This is especially important in cases where the central heating unit of the house is located in the cellar. You may have to erect a partition and fully insulate your wine against whatever heat may be present in other parts of your cellar. The crucial factor will be the insulation; one method is to use glass fiber inside whatever partitions you build. Another method is to make partitions out of cement blocks that are so thick they act as insulation themselves. You should also consider sealing off any windows opening into your wine storage area, because glass provides virtually no barrier against heat conduction. Some purists contend that closing off the windows is equally important to keep light away from your wine, but this theory is probably based on the practice of keeping European cellars dark rather than on any scientific evidence. Since light traditionally has meant sun and sun has meant heat, it was considered wise to keep the light away. Besides, European cellars are dark mainly because many of them are so old that they were never adequately wired for electricity, not because there has been any real effort to keep them dark.

If after building partitions and providing insulation, you find that the temperature rises too high in the summer months and you are determined to create better conditions, then artificial cooling may be the only answer. But it can be expensive to install as well as to operate. Moreover, another factor must be kept in mind in this time of fuel shortages and occasional power failures. A sudden loss of power will prevent your cooling unit from functioning. Blackouts tend to occur during the summer months when power usage is at its peak—just when you want most to protect your wine from exposure to excessive heat. If your cooling system suddenly becomes nonfunctional at this time of year, you run the risk of a rather substantial change in temperature. Such a fluctuation, occurring over a period of hours or a day or so, can do much greater harm to your wine than the gradual, seasonal changes that would occur naturally. A possible alternative is to install your own private source of electrical power which would be triggered into action by any interruptions in conventional power sources. But here again you must decide whether the benefit will justify the costs.

Humidity

Once you have resolved the temperature problem, you can go on to another important consideration—humidity. Wine bottles are always stored lying on their sides, so that the inner surface of the cork remains wet. A properly moist cork helps keep your wine from deteriorating by preventing oxygen from entering the bottle. Corks that are permitted to dry out will shrink and admit air. The result is oxidation. Storing bottles upright prevents the corks from coming into contact with the wine and hastens the drying process. If upright storage occurs over a long enough period of time, the result will be almost the same as if you were storing your wine in the open air. It would age prematurely and undergo chemical changes rendering it undesirable to drink.

For the same reason that you must store wine bottles lying on their sides, you must assure that the proper humidity exists throughout your cellar, so that the ends of the corks exposed to the air will not become excessively dry. But in 99 out of 100 cellars you will not have to be concerned. The normal prevailing humidity should be more than adequate, especially if you maintain proper temperatures. Cooler air tends to be moister.

But if you are determined to create ideal conditions, you may want to increase the humidity of your cellar artificially. One method adopted by serious wine lovers is to build up the floor of the cellar with small pebbles or crushed gravel and then irrigate it with a constant flow of water. The evaporation from the moist gravel will keep the atmosphere fairly damp—comparable to the conditions that exist in many European cellars, where water actually drips through the walls naturally and the bottles soon become covered with mold. But here again, you must consider whether the benefits justify the costs, because the logistics of creating such a system are considerable. A drainage system and a method to monitor the flow of water are prerequisites. Are such perfect conditions necessary? Certainly not, unless your goal is to create the ideal wine cellar, in which the best bottles will have every chance of reaching perfection. Obviously you can compromise without sacrificing a great deal, and the best compromise in this instance is to assume that the natural humidity in your cellar will be adequate or that you will drink the contents before inadequate humidity can seriously do any damage.

Vibration

Another important consideration, especially for city dwellers, is vibration. Wine should be permitted to sleep peacefully, without agitation. If your cellar is situated near a railway line, either subway or surface, or if it is near a heavy trucking route, the constant vibration will tend to keep your wine stirred up. The sediment normally thrown off by maturing red wines will be prevented from settling out, and it is possible that the corks will be loosened. Elaborate precautions against vibrations have been taken—even to the extent that wine racks have been positioned on springs or foam rubber padding to assure that all the bottles are cushioned in a completely vibration-free environment. It is probably safe to say that most wine lovers need not be concerned with such measures.

A rather simple test can be used to determine whether your cellar is subject to vibrations. Place a full glass of wine on a flat surface in the cellar, preferably on a wine rack if you have already installed them. Examine the surface of the wine in the glass very carefully. If you are able to observe concentric rings, vibrations exist. This does not mean, of course, that you should not store wine in that location. But it may mean that the life span of some of your wine will be reduced, just as it will by excessive temperatures or inadequate humidity. Constant, rapid vibrations may suggest that you consider another location for storing your wine. But in most cases it is safe to assume that the problems in wine maturation attributable to vibrations are exaggerated.

Closet Cellars

Many wine lovers live in apartments rather than private houses and therefore do not have access to actual cellars for storage purposes, but this does not mean they cannot create suitable storage conditions elsewhere. In fact, most of the conditions that exist in a subterranean vault can be closely approximated in a storage room far above ground—for example, in a closet. If you happen to live in a modern apartment building with central heating and cooling, the temperature may be beyond your control. But it will also probably be steady— around 72° Fahrenheit all year round. Much worse things can happen to wine than storing it at an unwavering 72°. Some apartment dwellers simply select a closet near the kitchen or dining area and install racks. Such closets may be devoted entirely to wine or may be used to store other items of food or drink. They are best when used exclusively for

wine, because the bottles will not be disturbed by rummaging on nearby shelves for other things. It is important to remember, however, that closets often are not exposed to the same temperatures as the other rooms in an apartment. Thus, they should be ventilated, either by cutting sections off the tops and bottoms of the doors or by drilling one-inch holes through the doors themselves. Without some kind of ventilation the closet may not benefit from the cooling system in your building and may react instead to the presence of pipes hidden inside the walls.

An alternative for apartment dwellers is to acquire one of the special cold-storage units commercially manufactured for wine. They are available in various capacities and can be built into a closet or hallway, so that they remain completely hidden until the moment when you select a bottle to accompany a meal. The initial cost of such a unit can be substantial, however, and you must also consider the cost of having it installed. And then there is the operating cost, for such coolers use compressors that eat up electricity constantly.

You must also consider the consequences if a power failure prevents your cooler from operating for a sufficiently long period of time: the temperature inside will fluctuate sharply.

Bottle Turning

Many people with a superficial knowledge of wine and its storage are under the impression that the keeper of a cellar must periodically descend to his subterranean vault and methodically turn each bottle of wine in its rack. The theory apparently is that wine needs such attention so that it can develop properly. The theory is a complete myth that probably grew out of the process known as *rémuage* in producing Champagne. An important stage in the *méthode champenoise* involves the turning and shaking of the upended bottles to permit the sediment to settle in the necks in preparation for disgorging. But this is accomplished by the Champagne producers—never by the consumer, who receives it years later after all the sediment has been cleared and when turning the bottle is no longer necessary or appropriate.

For the same reasons that vibrations should be avoided in wine storage, turning the bottles should also not be practiced. It will merely stir up the wine inside, preventing it from benefiting from the peaceful slumber that is so important to its development. Turning the bottles actually is harmful, and the true connoisseur will do his utmost to assure that his wines are left untouched until just before they are to be consumed. Visitors to the cellar also should not be encouraged to handle the bottles. Rather, if they want to take a closer look, they can do so without touching. Some cellar-keepers place a few interesting bottles in strategic positions so that visitors can easily see them and need not go probing into racks and bins to satisfy their curiosity. One of the main reasons to have a cellar is to give your wine the opportunity to sleep undisturbed while it matures, and anything that prevents this from happening violates the purpose.

Racks and Bins

After you have decided where to locate your cellar, secured it from the outside world, and created the appropriate temperature and humidity conditions, you must decide how to rack your bottles. There are a number of different ways. The simplest is to purchase ready-made racks from a store. Generally, the same companies that produce those dozen-bottle racks made of steel and wood for your table top will turn out larger ones to order. Stores that carry the small racks can either order the large ones for you or can furnish you with the name and address of the man-

ufacturer. Measure the area you wish to fill with racks and order according to that measurement. If you want to cover an entire wall, you should consider breaking up the area into several medium-sized racks rather than one large one. This will simplify transporting them and setting them up. Once a ready-made rack gets larger than about six feet by four feet, it becomes fairly difficult to handle. Keep in mind also that your racks may have to fit through some narrow doorways and hallways when being carried into your storage area. If your "cellar" is to be located inside a closet, you can order racks to fit on the shelves, making sure that the shelves are adequately supported, or you can simply eliminate the shelves and cover a wall or two with racks.

A cellar with custom-made racks filled with slumbering bottles awaiting consumption can be handsome indeed, but it has one major disadvantage. Racks made to cradle each bottle individually take up much more space than bins, in which bottles are stacked one on top of another. The amount of space devoted to individual-bottle racks will have a capacity about one-third less than the same amount of space devoted to bins. The principal disadvantage of bins is that they cannot usually be ordered from a store or a manufacturer; they have to be hand-built in your cellar—by you if you are skillful in carpentry or by a hired carpenter. The basic design is simple, however, and the home handyman with only a modicum of skill should be able to construct his own wine bins without much trouble. Because the bins are meant to be functional rather than beautiful, it makes little difference that a corner may not be precisely square or an edge may be uneven or rough. Moreover, minor errors in construction tend to disappear after the bins are stained a deep walnut or mahogany and are filled with bottles.

The most important consideration in building bins is strength. Several hundred bottles of wine will be quite heavy, and your bins must be made to bear the weight without cracking or bending. Therefore it is best to use one-inch boards that are ten inches wide as your basic material. This width not only will provide the needed strength but also will permit the necks of wine bottles to protrude, offering better visibility for the labels. Visualize your wall of bins as a huge bookcase and construct it in pretty much the same way, except with more uprights for strength. Each bin should

be roughly 14 by 16 inches to hold about a case of wine. But you should make some bins larger than others, so that your uprights can be spaced irregularly. Not only will this provide more strength, but it will also permit you to nail the uprights securely into place from both the top and bottom. Some bins can be designed to hold half bottles and some to hold magnums.

After you have constructed your wine "bookcase," anchor it to the wall with metal "L" braces available at any hardware store. Two braces on each side should be adequate if they are secured to the wall with one-inch screws. If the wall is made of plaster, the screws should be sunk into lead cores that will expand to grip the plaster when the screws enter them. If the wall is made of concrete building blocks or cement, as most cellar walls are, you will need to use an electric drill with a tungsten-carbide bit to make the holes for the lead cores. Such equipment is available for rent in most communities. The cores are simply tapped into the holes with a hammer in preparation for receiving the screws.

Another method of racking wine bottles involves the use of clay pipes of the variety used in building water and sewer lines or drainage ducts. These pipes come in sections about a foot long and just wide enough to hold a wine bottle. Their external surfaces usually are flat, in the form of a hexagon, which is ideal for stacking. An entire wall of pipe racks can be built up simply by stacking the pipes one on top of another. They can be cemented together for added security, but the shape of the pipes and the weight of the wine bottles inside them should be sufficient to keep a stack of them quite stable. It is said that pipe racks are more resistant to sudden temperature changes than other kinds, but no scientific evidence in support of the theory seems to exist.

Decor

If you have established your cellar in a room of its own, you will have an opportunity to make it a handsome addition to your home with a little tasteful decoration. Ideally, your racks or bins will cover only three walls, leaving the fourth free for a tasting table to hold corkscrews, wine glasses, tasting cups, perhaps a collection of labels and a cellar book in which to record the bottles you are storing. You may also want to have a candle in readiness for use in decanting, so that the sediment in a properly mature red will not become stirred up when the bottle is carried from the cellar to the dining room. You can hang framed vineyard maps, vintage charts, or wine-oriented prints on the wall. A copy of a menu or wine list from your favorite restaurant can also add to the gastronomic atmosphere of your cellar.

Your storage area need not be elaborately or brightly lit, but Tiffany-style lamps hung from the ceiling can provide an elegant touch. The floor can be just plain earth or cement, although the ambiance can be improved with a layer of crushed gravel or with colorful rugs or carpeting—whose motif, of course, will be Burgundy or claret-colored. Use your imagination and let your wine cellar reflect your own tastes and personality. Make it as elaborate as you can or keep it strictly functional, but remember to leave plenty of room for adding future vintages so that it will not soon overflow.

Tasting Parties

Wine is the most festive drink ever known to humans. For many centuries it has been the potion of revelry and of celebration, evoking gaiety, warmth, even love. It loosens the tongue, calms the nerves, stimulates the appetite and brings people together. It can be an accompaniment to another event—for example, Champagne at a wedding or a classic dinner with red Burgundy and roast duckling. Or wine can be an event in itself when it is the centerpiece of a party. What better reason to call one's friends together than to sample a range of red Bordeaux, compare Beaujolais of several different vintages, demonstrate the superiority of a Chardonnay from California to an elegant white Burgundy or prove that a properly mature Barolo from Italy's Piedmont District has more depth and intensity than the best Châteauneuf-du-Pape from the Rhône Valley of France?

Because of wine's festive nature, tasting parties are splendid social events. Yet they need to be properly organized so that the wines have an optimum chance to be tasted and your friends are best able to appreciate what you are offering. Each tasting party should have a theme, and it is well to remember that the theme should be educational. The greatest connoisseurs never stop learning by comparison tasting, and it is imperative for neophytes to refine and educate their palates by comparing one wine with another. Even individuals with little interest in wine will appreciate knowing that the inexpensive Chianti Classico from a shop around the corner represents much better value for dinner parties than the more costly red Bordeaux they have become accustomed to serving.

Red, White, or Rosé?

First decide whether you wish to focus on red wines, white wines, or both. As a rule, it makes more sense to restrict your tastings to red or white, or perhaps rosé. Because you will want to compare several different wines of each type, it is simpler to present a grouping of one type. Moreover, it leads to less confusion of the taste buds, and, because of its simplicity, its goal will not be lost on your guests.

Next, decide where you will hold your

tasting. The ideal room should be sufficiently large so that participants can move along a sideboard or long table from one wine to the next, with sufficient space between each wine to permit pauses for conversation without blocking other tasters from proceeding to the next wine. As a practical matter, most houses or apartments do not have dining rooms or living rooms sufficiently large to do this. One good alternative is to set up your tasting on your dining table, so that guests are able to progress from one wine to another around the table. If the living room is

nearby, you may want to set up a tasting table there as well, to minimize traffic in the dining room and to keep your guests moving.

Wherever your table is located, be sure to cover it with a white tablecloth. Since color is one of the principal aspects of wine, your guests should be able to tilt their glasses against a white background to perceive all the facets. Some hosts purchase tablecloths made of synthetic materials especially for wine tastings because they are inexpensive and easy to clean.

Number the Bottles

Your bottles should be numbered to give your guests a simple method of identifying each wine. And if you want to avoid the possibility that some participants may be prejudiced by the labels, cover them up by placing a blank sheet of paper around the bottle and securing it with tape or a rubber band. Then write the number of the wine on the paper. Later, when you disclose the identity of each bottle, your guests may be surprised to learn that an Italian or California wine tasted better than a French one—a fact they might not have fully appreciated if they had seen the labels first.

Tasting sheets and pens or pencils should be provided to permit your guests to note their reactions to each bottle. You may wish to purchase small, inexpensive note pads to hand to each taster when he arrives at your door. Or you may wish to design a tasting sheet of your own, with sections blocked out for your guests to comment on the principal aspects of each wine: appearance, bouquet, taste, and aftertaste. You need only to design one sheet and then reproduce as many as you feel you may need on an office copier. Divide your tasting sheet into as many sections as

the number of bottles you will serve and number each section down the left-hand column. As a rule, a sheet of regular typing paper can be divided easily into eight sections, with plenty of space in each section to permit your guests to write their comments. A tasting involving eight different wines will stimulate the participants and permit their host to produce a fairly broad range of tastes.

Professional tasters who must make important investment decisions based on their reactions to wines rarely swallow when they are sampling. Obviously, swallowing great quantities of wine will eventually render the tastebuds as dull as overimbibing will fog the brain. Of course, if you are planning a tasting party, your guests probably will not be making investment decisions. Nevertheless, depending on how serious an event you want to stage, you may wish to offer the opportunity to spit out the wines being tasted. Several plastic wastebaskets placed at strategic locations around your tasting room and partly filled with sawdust to absorb the wine and prevent splashing may be appropriate. You may also wish to place empty wine bottles equipped with funnels on or near the tasting table to enable your guests to pour off any excess wine from their glasses.

The logistics are different if your tasting is to involve white or rosé wines, because these wines should be served chilled. It is a simple matter to place the bottles in the refrigerator several hours before the start of your party, assuming your refrigerator has the capacity. But this will not prevent the wines from warming up to room temperature during the party. The most elegant tastings involve the use of silver ice buckets for each wine, but most hosts will not have more than one or two of these. Additional buckets can be borrowed, of course, and they need not be silver. Remember also that the buckets should contain not only ice but water as well. Placing a bottle in a bucket containing ice alone is virtually useless for chilling, whereas ice water will bring the temperature down rapidly.

In Germany and France, where a hundred or more white wines may be set out for sampling by professionals, the wines are generally not chilled, partly because some of their characteristics are more obvious when at room temperature. But the guests at your tasting party will want their whites or rosés well below room temperature, which is the proper way to serve them at the dining table anyway. Moreover, sweet wines such as Sauternes or German Rhines and Mosels of at least the Spätlese degree of sweetness cry out for chilling. The coldness seems to add to their luster and eliminates part of the cloying taste that some people consider objectionable in dessert wines.

One problem with tasting parties involving white or rosé wines is that it is almost impossible to cover the labels effectively after they become wet in an ice bucket. This problem sometimes resolves itself when the labels become sufficiently soaked to peel off. When this happens, be sure to remove them from the ice buckets so as to preserve the mystery around each wine. On the other hand, if you want your guests to see and recognize the labels on each bottle, you have another problem: preventing the labels from peeling off and floating. This can be remedied by simply placing a rubber band around each bottle at mid-label before putting the bottle in the ice bucket. Remember also that you must keep several bottles of each wine chilled if you plan to entertain more than just a few guests. To do this, you may wish to fill a large galvanized or plastic tub or trash can partly with ice water and keep it in your kitchen or on your porch or balcony for the bottles to be held in reserve.

For blind tastings, when you wish to preserve the anonymity of each wine until after all your guests have had an opportunity to guess its identity, you must be careful not to leave any of the corks lying around. The corks are often branded not only with the name of the producer, the estate or château, but with the vintage as well. Even the lack of a brand may provide valuable information to an astute taster. Since most of the leading estates and châteaux in France and Germany as well as some in Italy and Spain use branded corks, the appearance of an unbranded cork may confirm that the wine is of less than noble heritage.

Tales of Prowess

Many oenophiles have heard those tales of tasting prowess wherein certain gifted experts have been able to identify not only the château and vintage of a particular wine but also the portion of the hillside from which the grapes were picked during the harvest, even though the tasting was blind and no bottles or labels were in sight. It would be no exaggeration to describe most of these tales as apocryphal and to suggest that such tastings were hardly "blind."

Experts participating in blind tastings use a broad range of clues to identify the wines. Moreover, virtually all tastings involve a specific type of wine—for example, red wines from Bordeaux or wines made from the Cabernet Sauvignon grape or the Pinot Noir grape, or white wines made from the Riesling grape and so on. When the expert is able to identify the general source of the wines, he can proceed to pick out specific characteristics that should lead to a closer identification. The author once participated in a tasting in New York in which he was able to identify correctly the Château Cos d'Estournel of the 1949, 1959, 1964, 1967, and 1969 vintages. His tasting notes provide an insight:

1. Aged aroma—an old or improperly stored wine. Brown around the edges. Mature aftertaste. Definitely the 1949.
2. Light, mature, deep Cabernet. Deep ruby color. Full-bodied dusty taste. Good depth. Plenty left, but this is the '59. The best wine—balanced, full, and mature.
3. Lacking in bouquet—but some youth

possible. Some lightness at the edges. A bit thin on the palate. The 1967.
4. Full and mature aroma, but not old—strong Cabernet. Deep claret color. Just a tinge of *pelure* at the edges. The 1964.
5. Very young and grapey bouquet. Young, astringent taste—the '69.

The tasting, which took place in the spring of 1973, was "blind" to the extent that the participants sampled from unmarked glasses and no bottles or corks were in sight. But all of us knew in advance that we would be tasting the Cos d'Estournel from five different vintages, so our task merely involved sorting out the vintages. A knowledge of the characteristics of each vintage was necessary of course, but all of the participants started with the basic information that the wines came from a specific château in Bordeaux. Almost all of the tales of brilliant tasting coups neglect to mention that certain vital information was provided in advance. All the expert needs is this slight edge, and he can go on with the identification process. It is safe to say that no connoisseur can single out the Château Giscours 1953, for example, from a group of unmarked glasses or decanters unless he starts with the knowledge that the Giscours '53 is one of the wines in the tasting.

Tasting Glasses

An important aspect of any tasting party, one that many people tend to overlook, is the glassware. Because the color and general appearance of wine are highly important to the complete tasting experience, the glassware you use must be free of water spots and polished, just as you would expect it to be in a good restaurant, so that every visible facet of the wine inside can be perceived. Moreover, clusters of brightly polished glasses on your tasting table

will add a visual highlight to the setting.

The size of the glassware is also important. Each glass should be large enough so that the wine can be swirled around inside to force out the bouquet. Some experts feel that the larger the glasses, the better. But for practical reasons, a six- to eight-ounce glass is appropriate for tasting parties. The sides should curve gently inward toward the top, so that the wine will not slop over the edges when swirled around. Surprisingly inexpensive glasses can be obtained at department stores or discount houses; they may not be elegant, but they serve the purpose well. Tasting glasses also should be free of etching and color. Tinted cut glass may be very attractive, but it is not appropriate for tasting wine properly.

Ideally, each guest should be able to use a different, clean glass for each wine. Obviously this will be impractical unless you plan to entertain a very small number of guests with only a few wines. If you plan to serve a half dozen wines to a dozen guests, simple arithmetic tells you that 72 glasses will be required. But you do have alternatives. Perhaps the most realistic is to provide each guest with his or her own glass, to be used for all the wines. Although some residue from each wine will remain to mix with

the next, the impact on the taste will be minimal if noticeable at all. And to obviate the problem entirely, you need merely swirl a small amount of each new wine around in your glass and pour it out before pouring in the wine to be tasted. Another alternative is to set one glass out in front of each bottle of wine, for everybody to use. This is done occasionally at professional tastings, but for hygienic reasons you may prefer to provide each guest with his own glass. If your tasting is to involve both red and white wines, each guest will need two glasses, because it is not appropriate to use one for both types. Water can also be used for rinsing glasses, but it involves additional bottles or carafes plus receptacles to pour it into after the glasses have been rinsed.

Breathing

Part of your advance preparation must involve deciding whether or how long to let your wines breathe. Generally, young red wines—those less than a decade old—need more breathing than older ones. If you are planning a tasting of the 1979 red Bordeaux in 1985 or '86, each bottle should be opened at least an hour before your guests arrive. On the other hand, if an older wine is to be a highlight of your tasting, you may want to open it in the presence of your guests. Since older red wines also tend to produce sediment, decanting may be advisable as well. The ceremonial uncorking and decanting of a bottle of great heritage can be a memorable experience. Moreover, old wines tend to lose what remaining fruit they have within a matter of moments. It is possible to miss everything that a noble old bottle has to offer by waiting too long to drink it after uncorking it. Generally, white wines need not breathe for long periods ahead of tasting. Ten or

fifteen minutes before the arrival of your guests should suffice.

If your tasting party is to be a festive occasion, you may want to plan for the moment when all of your guests have gone through the tasting ritual and are relaxing in conversation about subjects other than wine. At this point, the thoughtful host will be aware that his guests will want to continue imbibing. Placing additional bottles on the tasting table will permit them to do so. Or an entirely different wine can be served, perhaps a young Beaujolais or a Mâcon or a California jug wine of good quality. Keep in mind that one bottle per person is not too much wine to have available for a tasting party—a fact to remember if budget considerations are important.

Hors d'oeuvres may also be set out, although you should take care not to serve anything that will interfere with the tasting. Highly spiced foods will hamper the ability to taste wine. Small pieces of bread and cheese, on the other hand, can be complementary to wine, although purists maintain that even cheese hampers one's ability to taste. Certainly bland cheeses should not have a significant impact on the taste buds, and, since one goal of your tasting party should be to have fun, providing an assortment of good food will add to the occasion.

The Tasting Theme

Perhaps your most important preparation will be to decide on the theme of your tasting. Not only should you serve wines that your guests will enjoy but you also should educate them. A very popular tasting in recent years, when French wine prices have been soaring into the stratosphere, has been the one centered on value. Its goal is to demonstrate that good wines can be found at reasonable prices and that expensive wines are not necessarily better wines. You will need to undertake some homework yourself to set up this kind of tasting. You will want to offer several wines that you consider exceptional value. You will also want to serve an expensive wine that seems not to be worth its cost, as well as an inexpensive one that may be almost undrinkable. Concealing the identity of each during the tasting will be important, so that your guests will not be prejudiced by a wine's reputation. Then, at the conclusion of the formal part of your tasting, the disclosure of each wine's cost may surprise your guests. As a host, you should also be prepared to inform your guests of the shop where each wine was purchased, so that they can take advantage of the knowledge they have just gained from your tasting party. A space for this information can be blocked out on the tasting sheets that you give to your guests when they arrive.

Beaujolais Tastings

The wines of the Beaujolais District of France are ideally suited for tasting parties. They are easy to obtain and they vary widely according to the particular part of the district they come from and the classification that they merit. Basically, there are four grades, or levels, of quality: Beaujolais, Beaujolais Supérieur, Beaujolais-Villages, and grand cru. The last category is entitled to any of nine village names within the district, depending on where the grapes were grown: Brouilly, Côte de Brouilly, Chénas, Chiroubles, Fleurie, Juliénas, Morgon, Moulin-à-Vent and Saint-Amour. Each has its own style. A Fleurie will be light and flowery; a Morgon will be bigger and heavier.

For your Beaujolais tasting you may wish to demonstrate the differences among the four basic categories. Serve an ordinary Beaujolais, a Beaujolais Supérieur, a Beaujolais-Villages, and one of the nine grands crus. Decide which you and your guests prefer and then determine whether it is the best value. (Beaujolais should not be expensive, so value judgments must be based mostly on straight personal preference.)

Or you may wish to compare among some or all of the nine grands crus. Few shops will stock all nine, but any serious wine merchant should carry four or five and should be able to order the others for you. A comparison tasting among the nine grands crus can be a fascinating experience, especially when you realize that although the entire Beaujolais District is only about 45 miles long and nine or ten miles wide, strong taste variations occur among the wines.

In the late fall or early winter of each

year the Beaujolais Nouveau or Beaujolais Primeur or Beaujolais de l'Année
becomes available. This is the product
of the first fermentation of the newly
harvested grapes, and it is fresh, young,
and zesty. It can be an intriguing experience to sample several different
bottlings of the new Beaujolais, because
the methods used by each vintner at
this time of year may vary greatly. Much
fanfare and plenty of promotional effort
are devoted to the introduction of the

new Beaujolais, so you will have no
difficulty in discovering when it becomes available.

Unlike most red wines, Beaujolais
tastes best when served chilled, just the
way it comes out of the casks in the
cellars among the rolling hills where it
is produced. The wine will not suffer
greatly from not being chilled, but purists will prefer it below room temperature.

Bordeaux Tastings (Red)

Many connoisseurs are convinced that
the greatest red wines in the world come
from the Bordeaux District of France,
and few would argue that these are not
at least among the world's greatest. For
this reason they can be very expensive—in fact, far beyond the reach of
the average wine drinker. But prices
will vary sharply, depending on each
wine's ranking, breeding, and reputation. For this reason it can be rewarding
to compare some of the lesser châteaux
with some of the great classified growths
to determine whether fame and high
price necessarily mean superior quality.

At least one of the red Bordeaux you
serve should be a premier cru, or first
growth. There are five: Château Lafite-
Rothschild, Château Latour, Château
Margaux, Château Haut-Brion, and
Château Mouton Rothschild. (For a fuller
explanation of the Bordeaux Classification, see Bordeaux and Médoc in Part
II.) All of these wines are expensive, so
you may wish to join with another host
or two to share the cost. If possible,
you should also compare wines from
the same vintage. A young, acidic wine
that has not had the opportunity to
develop properly will compare poorly
with a wine that has spent a decade or
more in its bottle. Traditionally, red
Bordeaux require at least ten years to
become properly mellow, although some

of the more recent vintages, starting
with the 1969, have been early bloom-
ers.

Also include one or more of the other
classified growths, perhaps Château
Giscours, or a Château Lynch-Bages, or
a Château Palmer, or a Château Grand-
Puy-Lacoste. Then cross over into Saint-
Emilion and Pomerol as well as Graves,
where you may wish to choose a Château Bouscaut. (A complete listing is
available in the entry Médoc in Part II.)
Next pick a petit château, one of those
that exist outside the formal classifications. Most wine shops will carry several of these.

Arrange your Bordeaux in the order
of classification, proceeding from the
wines of least renowned heritage to the
ones of greatest fame. Remember to
keep the labels concealed and identify
each bottle only by number. Set out
morsels of bread in baskets on or near
your tasting table, so that your guests
will be able to clear their palates between wines. Also remember to open
the bottles at least one hour in advance
of the tasting (unless you are serving
very old wines), so that they will have
ample opportunity to breathe.

Some hosts provide an added touch
by introducing a non-French wine
alongside the others—for example, a
good Chianti Classico or a Cabernet

Sauvignon from California (made with the same grape variety that produces red Bordeaux). Your guests will be surprised when you reveal the identity of the non-French wine, especially if they have given it high marks on their tasting sheets. To be fair, though, be sure that it too is properly mature so that it can show itself to best advantage.

Burgundy Tastings (Red)

Because the Burgundy District of France has no formal system of classification comparable to the Bordeaux system, it is much more difficult to educate oneself about these noble wines. Nevertheless there is no question that some of the world's finest and most elegant table wines are Burgundies. The trouble comes in trying to find good Burgundies at reasonable prices. A Burgundy tasting is ideally suited for this.

To be truly educational, your tasting should include one of the great *tête de cuvée* or *grand cru* wines, such as one of the six produced by the Domaine de la Romanée-Conti or a Chambertin or a Musigny. Like the *premiers crus* of Bordeaux, these can be extraordinarily costly, so you may wish to join with one or more other hosts to spread out the expense. Then go down the line of breeding and heritage to other named vineyards, such as the Chambolle-Musigny Les Amoureuses or the Charmes-Chambertin, to the *commune* wines like ordinary Chambolle-Musigny (which may not taste ordinary at all) or Gevrey-Chambertin or Beaune or Nuits-Saint-Georges. (*See* Burgundy in Part II.)

To a great extent the quality of each wine will depend on the ability of the vineyard owner and the shipper. It is a fairly reliable rule of thumb that if you find one excellent Burgundy from a shipper, his other Burgundies will also be good. Therefore your guests will want to note the name of the shipper on their tasting sheets. There are hundreds of Burgundy shippers and even more growers, so this kind of information can be very valuable. Also be certain to present wines of the same vintage, because Burgundies that are too young or too old may not compare well with those of proper maturity. Generally, red Burgundies mature earlier than red Bordeaux. Depending on the characteristics of the vintage, you may be able to serve Burgundies of close to the proper maturity that are no more than four or five years old, although most connoisseurs feel they need a few years' more bottle-age.

Because the principal grape of Burgundy is the Pinot Noir, you may wish to serve a Pinot Noir varietal from California for the sake of comparison. A properly mature Barolo from Italy's Piedmont District may also provide an interesting experience. Keep their identities concealed until your guests have tasted them all. They may be surprised to learn that a California or Italian wine has compared very well with a noble Burgundy of great breeding.

Chianti Tastings

Some of the world's great red wines are produced in Italy and, although some connoisseurs are inclined to look down their noses at all Italian wines, no enthusiast should disregard them as being inferior. Innumerable Chiantis are available on the American market. Some of them have great class and breeding, while others are produced in bulk to be sloshed down only in pizza parlors or wine bars. In general, the amount of money you pay for a Chianti will provide an indication of its quality.

The best Chiantis usually are those of the Classico designation. A special label bearing a black rooster is sometimes attached to the neck of each bottle, attesting to its authenticity. Chianti Classicos almost always come in straight-sided bottles identical to the ones used for Bordeaux. The rounded, wicker-covered bottle known as the *fiasco*, or flask, is used most often for Chiantis of lesser distinction. For your tasting party try to obtain several different Classicos and several of the other type. Remem-

ber that Chiantis are robust wines that require an interval of breathing to be at their best, so uncork the bottles at least an hour in advance. As an added attraction, serve a red Bordeaux or a Zinfandel from California for the sake of comparison. Remember to conceal the identity of each wine so that your guests will not be prejudiced by the information on the label. You may even wish to decant the Chiantis that come in *fiascos* so that they will not be immediately identifiable by the shape of their bottles.

White Wine Tastings (Dry)

The number of white wines placed on the market in recent years has escalated drastically. Consumers are understandably confused by all the different labels and names, and sometimes it seems almost impossible to find a truly good white wine at reasonable cost. Dry white wines come from Italy, Portugal, Spain, Australia, Argentina, Hungary, England, the United States, Canada, and, of course, France. To educate your guests, choose a particular price range for your white-wine tasting. Then try to obtain a bottle from each country within that range. The Puligny-Montrachets and Pouilly-Fuissés of France have become very expensive; you should remember that it is unfair to compare them with wines from elsewhere that cost somewhat less. A simple Mâcon Blanc or Muscadet at a more modest price would be appropriate to compare with an Italian Verdicchio or a Chenin Blanc from California.

Chilling each bottle in advance will be a vital aspect of your preparations. If you plan to serve a half dozen or more different wines, you should plan your refrigerator space accordingly. And if you want to keep your wines well chilled during the tasting, you will need the appropriate number of ice buckets and an adequate quantity of ice. Generally, white wines do not require an extended period of breathing to display their merits, so you can plan to uncork the bottles just before your guests arrive. Remember not to disclose the identity of each wine until your guests have tasted all of them. Also, keep the cost a secret as well. At the conclusion of your tasting, ask your guests to guess what all of the wines had in common. When you tell them that all cost about the same, they will be able to make their own decisions as to value.

White Wine Tastings (Sweet)

Some of the best values can be found in dessert wines, mainly because numerous oenophiles with otherwise impeccable taste simply refuse to cast aside their prejudices against sweet beverages. The rich white wines of Sauternes

in France and the Rhine and Mosel rivers in Germany are among the best made wines in the world. The same can be said of the Tokay of Hungary and some other, lesser known dessert wines of other countries. Prices have stayed down nicely because of their limited popularity. They are best served to accompany sweet desserts or fruits, so your tasting party should include slices of ripe apples or pears, or perhaps an array of sweet pastries. Some aficionados contend that certain cheeses—an English Stilton or an Italian Gorgonzola or a Danish blue—also complement dessert wines. It is a question of personal taste, so you should experiment to determine your own preferences.

Truly elegant dessert wines are still within the price range of most budget-conscious tasters. From Germany select a Mosel of the Spätlese or Auslese degree of sweetness. (These words connote superior natural sugar content and will always appear on German labels whenever merited.) Then choose a Rhine, also of Spätlese or Auslese quality. Then perhaps two Sauternes (*see* Sauternes in Part II), plus a Tokay or two of at least three or four *puttonyos,* connoting superior sweetness (*see* Tokay in Part II).

More care is required in arranging a tasting of sweet dessert wines than of any other kind of tasting, because it is vital to progress up the scale of sweetness rather than down. The least sweet of the wines will be either the German Mosel Spätlese or the Sauternes if it comes from an inferior vintage. Examine the vintage chart to make this distinction. Generally, though, a Sauternes from a good vintage will be somewhat richer than most German dessert wines. Assuming you are able to obtain bottles from good vintages, progress through the following arrangement:

Mosel Spätlese
Mosel Auslese
Rhine Spätlese
Rhine Auslese
Tokay Aszu
Sauternes

You can carry your dessert wine tasting a step further by introducing a German Beerenauslese or Trockenbeerenauslese from a superior vintage, along with a Tokay Aszu of five *puttonyos* from a great Hungarian vintage, and perhaps a Château d'Yquem from one of the classic Sauternes vintages. But your cost will escalate drastically, reflecting the rarity of these wines. Their quality is so great, in fact, that they are best reserved only for extraordinarily cultivated taste buds and not presented in tastings for novices. If you should decide to serve one or more of these classics, however, be certain that they come at the climax of the tasting after all the lesser wines have gone before. Also, be certain that all of your dessert wines are kept very cold throughout the tasting. The degree of appreciation expressed by your guests is likely to decline as the temperature of these wines rises.

For the sake of comparison, you may wish to include a bottle or two of American wine carrying the "Sauterne" or the "Tokay" label. Generally such concoctions bear no resemblance whatever to the real thing and are best left to the unfortunates who drink them because they happen to be the least costly alcoholic beverages obtainable. The suspicion is strong that the American antipathy to legitimate dessert wines derives from youthful experiences with some of the beverages that have borrowed the names but not the quality of the real European products. By demonstrating the extraordinary differences, your tasting party can provide a true service to your guests and perhaps enable them to temper their prejudices against legitimate dessert wines in general.

All-American Tastings

Such a vast array of styles and qualities of wines are produced in the United States that consumers often experience difficulty selecting the truly superior products. Numerous comparison tastings over the years have demonstrated the quality of American wines, however, and it is no exaggeration that the best of them are firmly competitive with the best of France or anywhere else. Generally, the finest American table wines come from California, mainly because of its favorable climate. Some decent wines are produced in New York State as well, but eastern growers will concede that the climate in California is better suited to the production of wines comparable in quality to the best of Europe.

For your American tasting start with red wines at the low-cost end of the scale with one or two jug types without vintage designation. Decant them into normal bottles so that they will not be identifiable by their containers. Then progress up the quality scale to vintage wines. Many experts agree that a properly mature vintage Cabernet Sauvignon produced in California's Napa Valley is close to the summit in American wines. The best California wines generally are named after the grape variety used to produce them, so a Cabernet Sauvignon will be made mostly of that grape and may be comparable to a red Bordeaux made from the same grape. The Pinot Noir produces some good American wines, along with the Zinfandel, which seems to have no strict European counterpart. Your tasting might progress in this order:

Inexpensive jug wine
Expensive jug wine
Nonvintage varietal Pinot Noir
Nonvintage varietal Zinfandel
Nonvintage varietal Cabernet
Sauvignon
Vintage Pinot Noir
Vintage Zinfandel
Vintage Cabernet Sauvignon

Many other varietals are produced and blended in the American wine industry, and you may wish to experiment even further afield than the above listing suggests. You may also wish to offer a French or Italian wine to enable your guests to compare, and you may or may not discover a preference for the American product. Tastings of this kind can be especially useful for those of your guests who are convinced that the best table wines come only from Europe.

American white wines also can be compared favorably with those from other countries, but unfortunately the majority are designed to service a market in which low price seems to be the most important factor. Some American whites reach great heights, however, and connoisseurs hold those produced from the Chardonnay grape in especially high esteem. This is the grape of white Burgundy, and the best Chardonnays from the United States have been proven to be the equal of the finest Montrachet or Meursault from France. The costs of producing such magnificent wines are great, of course, and the version from California may cost as much as its French counterpart.

For your tasting of American whites, start with a couple of inexpensive jug wines from California or New York State or one of the other handful of states that produce wine in commercial quantities. Jug wines made in the United States often seem to be named after French places, so you may discover that you must shop for Chablis or Rhine even though they have no connection with the Chablis District of France or Germany's Rhine River Valley. Progressing up the quality scale, you will come to varietals without vintage designations and those identified as coming from a particular year. Here is a possible order:

Inexpensive jug wine
Expensive jug wine
Nonvintage varietal Riesling, Chenin, or Sauvignon Blanc
Vintage Riesling, Sauvignon, or Chenin Blanc
Nonvintage Chardonnay
Vintage Chardonnay

Numerous companies produce these wines, and many brands are available, mostly from California. The best wines from New York State, with some exceptions, bear brand names or hybrid names copyrighted by the companies producing them or else carry European names. Gold Seal, for example, pro-duces a very fine New York State white called Chablis Natur. To round out your tasting of American whites you should include one or two such wines. Then choose some European whites to enable your guests to compare. Remember, though, that you cannot expect a five-dollar American wine to compare favorably with a ten-dollar French wine, so be fair in your evaluations.

It is a simple matter to create your own tasting sheets for a tasting party. The following is an example to be used with eight wines, but a tasting sheet can be drawn up for any number. Use a ruler or other straightedge to make the lines, type or write in the headings, then photocopy as many as you will need for your guests, plus a few extra in case any are misplaced.

Tasting Sheet for Eight Wines

Name of Wine

	COLOR & CLARITY	BOUQUET	TASTE	RATING
No. 1				
No. 2				
No. 3				
No. 4				
No. 5				
No. 6				
No. 7				
No. 8				

Additional comments: e.g., aftertaste, general impressions.

Aging Wine and
the New Vinification

The question of when to drink a wine has become extraordinarily complex in this era of experimentation with changing methods of vinification. Generations ago, before the transportation of wine became a relatively simple routine matter, wine was vinified to assure its survival on the voyage. In the case of Port, Sherry, Madeira, and Marsala this meant it was fortified with grape brandy, a practice continued to this day. In the case of the best red wines of France—those from Burgundy and Bordeaux—it meant lengthy contact of the new wines with the skins, stems, and seeds of the grapes to provide a strong tannin content and assure a robust quality. The drinkers of these wines were accustomed to buying substantial quantities and laying them down in cellars for years until they reached a soft and pleasant maturity. For those without substantial cellars the leading wine merchants laid down supplies in their commercial cellars.

These practices continued well into the modern era, reflecting the position of fine table wine consumed outside the country of origin as primarily the drink of the aristocracy. Gradually the aristocracy diminished in numbers as well as wealth, while new converts to the

drinking of fine wines were won from the middle class—first in the European countries and later in the United States. A transformation occurred in the public's perception of the treatment of wine. Not only did the diminishing wealth of the upper classes mean fewer bottles could be laid down, but the converts from the middle classes had no supplies of aged wine in hand to drink while they laid down the younger vintages to await their maturity. So a great quantity of immature wine was consumed until producers all over the world perceived the change in their markets and began changing their vinification procedures to accommodate the circumstances of a new generation of connoisseurs.

It is not clear where the change in production methods occurred first, but it occurred most obviously with the pragmatic French. They suddenly—in the 1960s—began producing very different wines, much to the dismay of some of their loyal and traditional devotees. In Burgundy it seemed to be the 1966 vintage that started out with great promise but suddenly faded. "Drink your '66s!" was the cry in 1975 among people who had laid down the Burgundies of that vintage for consumption in some distant year. The 1966s suddenly "went over the hill" and into decline. In Bordeaux it seemed to happen in '67. The 1966 Bordeaux were big wines of great character which still seemed years away from ripeness after a decade. But the '67s were another matter. They were drinking nicely by 1973, and many had seen their peaks by '76. The 1969s tasted as though they had been watered down from the start. In 1970 and '71 everyone acknowledged that the best wines since 1966 had been made. Yet they were initially "forward"—meaning that they were precocious. Surprisingly, both vintages seemed soft and ready as early as the age of four, inciting doubts that they would be still alive at ten, although they later surprised the doubters and seemed likely to age gracefully through the 1980s.

The new vinification has meant great confusion for consumers who are trying to gauge the proper age at which to drink a wine. The situation is still in flux, but a good rule of thumb is that Bordeaux older than the 1966 vintage should have no trouble lasting through their second decade (this means Bordeaux of the better years, of course), while the same is true to a lesser extent of Burgundies from 1964 and earlier (the '65 was an off vintage in both Bordeaux and Burgundy). The wines produced since then may last as long, but the evidence so far indicates that they will be best before they reach ten. A similar change has occurred with many Italian reds, which now are ready to drink when less than a decade old—compared with the two or three decades previously needed. The beneficial aspect of the change is that it has become quite possible to dash down to the local merchant and obtain a fairly mature wine for dinner the same night.

Naturally, most questions about the proper age at which to drink a wine relate to reds. Whites are meant to be drunk much younger, because the vast majority of them are naturally more delicate. They are meant to be consumed as aperitifs or with more subtle foods, so their vinification did not change as much. But it does seem to have changed somewhat. The big white Burgundies of France, for example, do not seem to be as robust as they once were—robust, that is, relative to other white wines, not to reds. The sweet Sauternes of France seem to be drying out a bit—and not in response to poor weather. Nor are the changes confined to France. Some of Italy's Barolos now achieve a velvety smoothness after six or eight years, and Riojas from northern Spain are soft and smooth at a fairly young age.

So perhaps the rules for the aging of table wines need not be so rigid in this time of changing styles. Perhaps it is best for consumers to experiment on their own, determine what pleases them and stock up on it. The need to rely on periodic samplings or the tasting reports that appear in magazines and newspapers to determine the drinkability of a certain good vintage at a specific point in time has diminished. The new rule is: try it now, and if you like it, drink it now; don't lay it away in a musty cellar. Or if you don't like it now, try it in six months; it may have changed substantially.

Styles of vinification will also vary according to the producer, and not every producer has changed. Moreover, many modern producers continuously experiment, turning out a wine of one style one year and of a different style the next. The different characteristics of each vintage also play a role. No matter how the 1968 vintage in France was vinified, it would not have turned into a very good wine. So the same rule still applies: sample it now and see if you like it now.

Assuming that the vintage is of good quality, some rules of thumb for aging can be loosely applied:

White wines generally reach their peak within three years of the vintage. Sweet dessert wines are more durable; they will stay in fairly good condition for ten to twenty years, and some will last even longer. But dry white wines should be drunk young.

The best red wines of France—from Bordeaux, Burgundy, the Rhône Valley, Cahors, etc.—usually benefit from at least six years of age, and many knowledgeable wine lovers would be horrified at the notion that a red Bordeaux from a good vintage might be ready in fewer than ten. But styles are changing, so these wines should be sampled periodically. Once at their peaks, they should stay there for several years. Even with the new vinification, a ten-year-old Bordeaux or Burgundy should not be too old. Twenty years used to be a good drinking age for these reds, and it may still be. Most Beaujolais should be drunk before three.

The robust reds of northern Italy once needed at least a decade before they began to soften, and 20 years was not too long for a typical Barolo. But vinification methods are changing here too. Starting in the mid-1970s, many Italian producers began making wines that matured earlier, while some clung to the more traditional methods. The situation in Italy is in flux, and consumers should buy a bottle of Barolo, Gattinara, Chianti, or Brunello di Montalcino and try it before buying case lots. Bardolino and Valpolicella, on the other hand, have for many years been vinified to be drunk young—within five years of the harvest—so a reevaluation of these reds now seems not vital.

The better California reds are very long-lived. Cabernet Sauvignon from a good producer needs at least ten years, Zinfandel slightly less. Vinification methods vary widely in California, however, so there can be no hard-and-fast rule for the reds of this state.

Red wines from other countries tend to vary widely in style, so generalizations should not be made.

Labels and Wine Laws

The label on a bottle of wine is your guide to what you can anticipate inside. It often contains much more information than you might expect. Therefore it is wise to get into the habit of reading labels carefully, even if it means detaining the wine steward for another moment or two in a restaurant or taking a little more time when browsing through a wine shop. Wines with similar names may vary greatly in quality and the reason for the variance often will be evident on the label.

The information on a label is, in a number of countries, strictly controlled by law to protect you, the consumer, as well as the growers of the grapes and the vintners. As a result, it is rare to encounter fraud in wine labeling. The few examples of fraud that have been publicized in recent years represent exceptions that are extremely uncommon. Wine is vitally important in most of the countries or states where it is produced, and tampering with the credibility of the product that supports the local economy not only brings stiff legal penalties but public scorn as well. Generally the wine inside the bottle will be precisely what the label says it is. But it is up to you to interpret what it says.

As a rule, the more information that is printed on the label, the higher the quality of the wine. The reverse is also true: labels that do not tell you very much about the wine imply that there is not much to tell. The quality of the information is equally important. Some labels will inform you when the producer planted his first grapes and how many generations of the same family have been in the business. Such labels may be interesting, but they do not say much about the wine—which is what you want to know about.

The important information is where the wine comes from and who produced it—the more specific the description the better. A label that tells you that a wine is Beaujolais, without telling you the name of the specific village or vineyard where the grapes were grown, indicates that the wine is fairly ordinary and may be a blend of wines entitled to the Beaujolais name. The wine may prove to be excellent value when you taste it, but you have no way of knowing this from the label. On the other hand, the Beaujolais label that tells you the wine was produced at Château de la Chaize in Brouilly in 1981 by the Marquise de Roussy de Sales and that it was bottled at the château tells you all you need to know.

Wines from different parts of the world and even from different sections within the same country may be labeled in different ways. For example, a rule applicable to the Bordeaux District of France is that the closer the wine is bottled to the vineyard where the grapes were grown, the better it is likely to be. Wine that is bottled in bulk after being blended at a big plant far from the vineyard may taste like bulk wine. It may be quite palatable, but individual traits may have been lost. The good wines in the blend will have been used to render the mediocre ones drinkable. If a wine truly excels, it will fetch a higher price and is less likely to be blended. So you should look for the notation *"Mis en bouteille[s] au château"* on Bordeaux labels, literally meaning "put in bottles at the château."

But it is no use looking for the same notation on labels from the Burgundy District, on the other side of France. The reason is that the Burgundy trade is structured differently, and very few Burgundy wines are bottled at the château. Rather, the majority are bottled by dealers with centralized facilities in such towns as Beaune or Nuits-Saint-Georges, because the ownership of most Burgundian vineyards is divided among many growers with small parcels. These growers customarily sell to such firms as Louis Latour, Joseph Drouhin, Joseph Faiveley, Louis Jadot, Bouchard, Charles Noëllat, Prosper Maufoux, Roland Thévènin, and others. The standards followed by such illustrious houses are just as high as those followed in the Bordeaux châteaux, but the commercial method is different. All are strictly regulated in France by a legal system administered by the Institut National des Appellations d'Origine, and the notation *"Appellation contrôlée"* or *"Appellation d'origine contrôlée"* on a label is a government guarantee of the place of origin and the standards of quality gen-

erally met by the wines produced in that area.

A typical Bordeaux label might state: Château Giscours, Margaux, Médoc. This means the name of the château or winery is Giscours, that it is located in and entitled to the name Margaux, which is a *commune,* or township, in the Médoc, which is a large subdivision of Bordeaux. The label also says *"Appellation Margaux contrôlée,"* indicating that the wine has been classified as a Margaux under the French control laws. The statement *"Mis en bouteille au château"* indicates it was bottled at the château. Nicolas Tari is shown as the man who owns the property and the business. The vintage year on the label, 1961, was one of the best in Bordeaux history. This information comes close to being as specific as you will find on a Bordeaux label.

A typical Burgundy label might state: Pouilly-Fuissé, *Appellation contrôlée, Mis en bouteille par* Joseph Drouhin. This means the wine is a Pouilly-Fuissé under the control laws and that it was bottled by the Joseph Drouhin firm, one of the top wine houses in Beaune. The Joseph Drouhin name atop the label is in even larger type than the name of the wine itself, attesting to the fame of the firm and its reputation for quality and reliability. What Drouhin is saying is: There are many Pouilly-Fuissés, but here is mine, and I think it is the best because I've put my name on it and staked my reputation on it. At the bottom of the label is another notation: Dreyfus, Ashby & Co., the American importer and agent for the wine in New York. This firm also is demonstrating that it is proud to have its name associated with the wine. Lovers of white Burgundy know that a wine called Pouilly-Fuissé, without a specific vineyard name attached, is a dry white from Burgundy. The Drouhin name means it should be a superior *commune* wine, but it probably will not be as magnificent as wines entitled to the names of specific vineyards within Burgundy.

The amount of information that can be gleaned from labels on wines produced elsewhere in the world varies according to local tradition and how closely the wine industry is regulated. Some American wine producers adopted the curious practice years ago of giving their wines European names, so it is not unusual to find "Burgundy" or "Chablis" from California or New York State, even though they may not closely resemble their French namesakes and often are not made from the same kind of grapes. The more progressive American producers have begun naming their best wines after the variety of grapes used to make them. These so-called "varietals" differ according to the style and methods of the producer, whose name is crucial in American wine labels. A California Cabernet Sauvignon is made

from the same grape that tends to predominate in red Bordeaux and may taste very much like a Bordeaux. But you may find you prefer the Cabernet Sauvignon of Heitz Cellar to that of Beaulieu Vineyard, so you must learn to remember the name of the producer as well as the varietals that you like best.

German wine labels were among the most incomprehensible of all until the German government revised its laws controlling production and labeling in 1971. Effective with the vintage of that year—which, coincidentally, turned out to be one of the best in German history—a new and more precise system was established. German labels still are not as simple for the layman to understand as some others are, but a few terms are well worth learning.

The new law divided German wines into three basic categories: *Tafelwein, Qualitätswein,* and *Qualitätswein mit Prädikat. Tafelwein,* meaning "table wine," is the simplest and does not flow into the export markets in great quantities. Often it is given a brand name by the bottler, but it must carry the *Tafelwein* notation to assure that it can be identified as the relatively modest wine that it is.

Qualitätswein, or "quality wine," must be produced from approved grape varieties, must attain at least 8.5 percent natural alcohol and must come from one of the approved German quality-wine regions. It may carry the name of the region, subregion, collective vineyard, or individual vineyard as long as 85 percent of the wine comes from the smallest named area. It also may mention the type of grape—for example, Riesling, if at least 85 percent of the wine comes from that variety. Each bottle carries a control number from the government.

Qualitätswein mit Prädikat, meaning "quality wine with special attributes," is the highest category in Germany and must be produced from approved grape varieties and attain at least 10 percent natural alcohol. Control numbers awarded by the government attest to their authenticity. The various *Prädikats,* or special attributes, apply basically to degrees of sweetness. Cabinet, or Kabinett, wines cannot have sugar added to raise their sweetness and therefore must be made from mature grapes. Spätlese, or late-harvested wines, are made from grapes picked after the end of the normal harvest. Auslese, or selected wines, are made from especially ripe grapes individually selected. Beerenauslese, made from individually harvested grapes that have turned virtually into raisins, is very sweet because of the heavy concentration of juice. Trockenbeerenauslese, the sweetest of all, is also made of shriveled individually picked grapes that have contracted *Edelfäule,* or the "noble rot" that creates even greater natural sugar concentration and a deep, honeylike flavor. Eiswein is made of grapes picked so late in the autumn, following the regular harvest, that they have frozen. It is also quite sweet.

German labels state very specifically what category of wine is inside the bottle, but the basic name of each wine usually comes from the place where the vineyard is located and sometimes from the vineyard itself. A typical German label might state: Niersteiner Hipping, Riesling Spätlese, *Qualitätswein mit Prädikat.* The wine would be a Niersteiner from the village of Nierstein on the Rhine River. It would come from a specific vineyard within Nierstein, known as Hipping, would have the Spätlese degree of sweetness and would be estate-bottled. The control number also would be evident beneath the broad category—in this case *Qualitätswein mit Prädikat*—into which the wine was placed. The producer would be Franz Karl Schmitt.

What German wine labels have in organization, Italian wine labels are lacking. A system of *denominazione controllata* modeled after the French *appellation contrôlée* exists, but it covers only a portion of Italian vineyards, albeit most of the best. Place names are important, as are the names of shippers and bottlers. The control laws, enacted in 1963, specify three basic categories.

Denominazione di origine semplice, or "simple" wines, are those with the least specific origins. No government guarantee of quality goes with the designation and few efforts are made to assure that the areas of production specified by the government are observed. The boundaries of each named zone can be decreed by the Minister of Agriculture and Forestry, but in many cases no ministerial decrees have been made. Generally these simple Italian wines do not get into the export market, but some can be excellent value if you are traveling through Italy.

Denominazione di origine controllata, or "controlled" wines, meet specific government standards of quality in terms of maximum output per unit of land, methods of production, even the planting of the grapes. But the law also provides for exceptions, permitting wines to be produced by other methods in recognition of the "requirements" of foreign markets. Despite the obvious loopholes in the law, controlled wines available in the United States, Britain, and elsewhere usually are of good quality.

Denominazione di origine controllata e garantita, or "controlled and guaranteed" wines, carry a government seal attesting to their status in the traditional hierarchy of Italian wines. One factor in achieving this status is the price that the wine achieves in the market—not always a reliable indicator of quality but often accurate with Italian wines. These wines tend to be somewhat more expensive than other Italian wines, but this does not mean they are always superior in quality. Brunello di Montalcino and Barolo were the first Italian wines to be accorded the *garantita* designation.

Another guide to quality in Italian wines comes from the *consorzi,* or local clubs of growers. These groups usually predate the wine law by many years and still impose their own standards in an effort to maintain the reputation and boost the price of their produce. Their standards sometimes are low and occasionally are high. The *consorzio* that exists in Tuscany for Chianti Classico, one of the best types of Italian wine,

has been especially effective in promoting standards of high quality. The group's seal, a black rooster, is usually affixed to the neck of a bottle of Chianti Classico and attests to the authenticity of the wine. Chianti Classico tends to be superior to just plain Chianti, but this is not necessarily due to the local *consorzio.* Rather, it probably stems from the favorable soil and exposure of the vineyards in the Classico area, although the *consorzio* helps to keep up production standards. But not all of the best producers belong to the Chianti Classico Consorzio, so good Chianti without the black rooster can be found.

Other countries have their own wine laws and standards for truth-in-packaging, but few consumers can expect to keep track of all the variations. The formalization of the European Economic Community has helped to harmonize the situation by setting up regulations for wine sold within the Common Market, but it will be a long time before a uniform worldwide system of classification and regulation exists. It is possible that such a universal system will never exist, due to the differences in climate and customs among countries.

Vintages

Another crucial item of information that can be gleaned from a label is whether or not the wine is from a vintage year, and which year it was. Many wines consist of blends of various vintages and do not carry a vintage designation. This is especially true of the less expensive varieties from the United States, but it is not *necessarily* an indication of quality. Although the trend even in California is toward the use of vintage designations, some very good wines still are blends. Even in France some excellent and expensive wines are nonvintage, es-

pecially in the Champagne country. Nonvintage Champagne, which is produced every year, is preferred by some connoisseurs to the vintage variety, which is produced only in certain years.

Vintage designations will appear either on the main label or on a special neck label or on both. The designation can mean different things in different parts of the world. It is supposed to mean that the wine is produced entirely or predominantly from grapes harvested in the year specified. In Champagne and also in Oporto, where the fortified Portuguese wine known as Port is made, vintage designations are applied only in exceptional years when weather conditions have been good enough for superior wines to be produced. In other parts of the world a vintage designation is possible every year, regardless of the quality of the harvest, so great variations can occur from one vintage year to the next. In localities like California, where the weather tends to be good most of the time, the differences among vintages may be small, although connoisseurs will tell you they are nevertheless significant.

In general the best table wines are vintage, reflecting the desire of the leading producers to provide their customers with as much information as possible. A vintage label in Germany means that 85 percent of the wine came from the indicated year. In California since 1972 it has been legal to add 5 percent from another year, reflecting the need to top up the casks due to evaporation during the aging process. French vintage wines are expected to be entirely from the indicated year, but growers have been known to "improve" a modest vintage with surreptitious blending in of better wines left over from a better year when production was especially generous. When this is done strictly to make better wine, it is to the benefit of the consumer.

As wine drinkers gain experience, they develop an ability to distinguish among various vintages and to remember which ones are not as good as others. Use a vintage chart to determine which years are held in high regard by the experts. And beware of the appearance of off vintages, or less distinguished years, on restaurant wine lists or on sale at wine shops. Some producers rise above adverse weather conditions and make superior wines in poor years, but these are rare, and a noble label with a poor vintage year on it may not be the bargain that it seems to be.

P·A·R·T II

THE WINES
OF THE WORLD

NOTE TO THE READER

All wines are listed alphabetically by their principal names. Because so many foreign words are used in wine names, it is sometimes difficult to determine what the principal name of a wine is. In Bordeaux, for example, most wines are called "Château" something or other. All of these wines are listed under their principal names—e.g., Château Ausone is listed under "A" and Château Beychevelle under "B," etc. Articles such as *le* or *la* are not considered part of the principal name—e.g., Château La Tour-Haut-Brion is listed under "T." Prepositions such as *de* or *d'* are likewise not part of the principal name in alphabetizing this book—e.g., Château d'Yquem is listed under "Y."

For the sake of consistency, all California wines or wineries that have adopted French names are listed alphabetically in the same way. For example, Château St. Jean is listed under "S" and Château Montelena is under "M."

SYMBOLS FOR AGING POTENTIAL (☆) AND PRICE RANGE ($)

The aging potential for each wine, or the time it will take to reach its peak of drinkability, is indicated by one to five stars, as follows:

☆	=	Fewer than three years
☆☆	=	Three to six years
☆☆☆	=	Six to ten years
☆☆☆☆	=	Ten to twenty years
☆☆☆☆☆	=	More than twenty years

Multiple aging symbols may appear for some wines, wineries, or categories of wine, for example ☆/☆☆☆. This means the whites of that winery or producer are best drunk within three years and the reds should be best at six to ten years. It may also indicate a range of aging potential that is likely to vary according to vintage.

The retail price range of each wine or category of wines is indicated by one to four dollar signs, as follows:

$	=	Inexpensive, usually under $5 a bottle
$$	=	Moderately expensive, $5 to $15
$$$	=	Expensive, $15 to $50
$$$$	=	Very expensive, more than $50

Multiple pricing symbols appear for some wines or categories to indicate a price range that may vary according to the vintage or producer. Prices can fluctuate sharply, of course, due to currency exchange rates, local taxes, economic conditions, and competitive pressures, so the ranges are intentionally broad. Yet they are structured to provide a fairly clear indication of retail relationships.

·A·

Abboccato.

The Italian term for slightly sweet is *abboccato,* which indicates that the wine contains 1 to 2½ percent residual sugar. This is less sweet than *amabile* (2½ to 3 percent sugar) and *dolce* (at least 3 percent sugar).

Abruzzo.

Abruzzo is a region of Italy on the eastern side of the boot, where the two best known wines are Montepulciano d'Abruzzo and Trebbiano d'Abruzzo, with D.O.C. ratings. It is a rustic, mountainous area whose wines were little known outside of Italy until the 1970s, but its production is substantial and the quality level has finally been recognized. Montepulciano d'Abruzzo should not be confused with Vino Nobile di Montepulciano, a Tuscan wine of very high quality, although it is considered probable that the Montepulciano vines originated in Tuscany and were carried across the country to Abruzzo by traders. The principal grape of Tuscany is the Sangiovese, and although Montepulciano is the name of an old Tuscan town, the Montepulciano grape is no longer cultivated there.

☆/☆☆

$

Acacia Winery.

Many California oenophiles are convinced that the most Burgundian Pinot Noirs and Chardonnays can be extracted from the sparse soil of the Carneros district at the southern end of the Napa Valley, where the climate tends to be cooler (and therefore more Burgundian). Acacia Winery was established in 1979 and used leased premises for its first harvests while building a new winery on a 50-acre site in Carneros. The proprietors, Jerry Goldstein and Mike Richmond, were quite successful with their first offerings of Chardonnay, made largely from purchased grapes in the vintage of 1979. The wines, which included the names of the specific vineyards or areas where the grapes were grown, were creamy and rich and showed great character for such a new effort. Production of Pinot Noir also was under way, and early tastings indicated that considerable success had been achieved through minimal oakaging. As with the Chardonnays, the Pinot Noir labels carry the name of the individual vineyard where the grapes were produced, and nuances of difference are readily detectable among them. Production remains small, but the pro-

prietors are building toward an annual output of about 15,000 cases.
☆☆
$$

Adelsheim Vineyards.

David Adelsheim, a former sommelier in Portland, and his wife Ginny purchased 20 acres in 1972 and established a winery in the Chehalem Hills in northwestern Oregon. They grow some of their own grapes and also purchase grapes from other growers in Oregon and Washington. Adelsheim Vineyards is one of the few Oregon winemaking operations that produce wines from the Merlot grape, the primary varietal of Pomerol in the French Bordeaux district. The Adelsheim white Merlot, made by removing the dark skins from the juice immediately after the crush, is a very rare wine, one of the few white Merlots made anywhere. Adelsheim also produces the normal red Merlot as well as Sémillon, Riesling, Chardonnay, and Pinot Noir. In common with other Oregon Pinot Noirs, the Adelsheim version is peppery and spicy and slightly tannic. The winery is located near Newberg.
☆/☆☆
$/$$

Adler Fels Winery.

Adler Fels stands for "eagle rock" in German, and an eagle appears on the label of this small winery in the hills above the Sonoma Valley. Its first crush was in 1981, and the winery uses appellations from Sonoma Valley, Sonoma County, the Alexander Valley of the Sonoma region, and Mendocino County. The line of varietals includes Chardonnay, Cabernet Sauvignon, Johannisberg Riesling, and Gewürztraminer.
☆/☆☆☆
$/$$

Aglianichello.

This is an Italian red wine from the island of Procida in the Bay of Naples. The basic grapes are Aglianico and Barbera, and the wine is meant to be drunk young. Sometimes it is vinified slightly sweet and is best served at cellar temperature rather than room temperature.
☆☆
$

Aglianico del Vulture.

Basilicata is a sunny region stretching between the ankle and instep of the Italian boot, and its only D.O.C. wine is Aglianico del Vulture, which comes from grapes grown on the volcanic soil of Monte Vulture. Garnet in color, with an intensity of flavor typical of southern Italian reds, it is not often seen abroad and can be excellent value. It is vinified both dry and sweet and there is a *spumante* version.
☆☆/☆☆☆☆
$

Ahlgren Vineyard.

Although Ahlgren Vineyard, owned and operated by Val and Dexter Ahlgren, came into existence only in 1976, it has already built a reputation for excellent Cabernet Sauvignons and Zinfandels of deep color and intense flavor, wines that often place high in tasting competitions because of their strong character. The winery is near Boulder Creek, at an elevation of 1160 feet in Santa Cruz County, California. Production so far has amounted to only about 1000 cases per vintage, and the proprietors say their goal is only 2500. Their plantable land consists of 12 acres, but so far the Ahlgren wines have been made mostly from grapes purchased in the Napa Valley, Livermore Valley, Monterey County, and the Santa Cruz Mountains. The Ahlgren

Chardonnay is fermented in French oak barrels, the Sémillon in American oak. The intensity of the reds is derived from fermentation in contact with the skins and other grape solids, with the caps, or floating materials in the must, being punched down into the juice several times a day to achieve maximum extraction of color and flavor.

☆☆/☆☆☆☆

$$

Albana di Romagna.

Among the white wines of Italy is Albana di Romagna, often called simply Albana. It is vinified both dry, *secco,* or semisweet, *amabile,* and is produced in the region of Emilia-Romagna in the north-central part of the country. It is vinified 100 percent from the Albana grape.

☆

$

Alcamo, Bianco Alcamo.

This is a Sicilian white wine of fairly high quality that is recognized under the Italian D.O.C. law. It comes from the village of Alcamo, not far from Palermo, and is made mostly from Catarratto grapes, with small quantities of Trebbiano and a few others blended in. The wines are light, fresh, and soft and are produced by large cooperatives as well as private concerns.

☆

$

Aleatico.

The Aleatico is a red grape of the muscat family that is widely cultivated in Italy and often vinified fairly sweet. The wines are sometimes lacking in elegance and sometimes are fortified with brandy to bring their alcohol levels close to 20 percent. Often the varietal name will be followed with the name of the area of production, as in Aleatico di Bertinoro, Aleatico di Gradoli, Aleatico di Portoferraio, Aleatico di Puglia, or Aleatico di Terracina.

☆/☆☆

$

Aleatico di Puglia.

This is a sweet red wine made mostly from Aleatico grapes in the Puglia region of southern Italy. The production is modest and the wine is not well known outside the region.

☆☆

$

Alexander Valley Vineyards.

Alexander Valley Vineyards produces good premium varietals near Healdsburg in California's Sonoma County under the tutelage of Harry H. "Hank" Wetzel, the winemaker. His father bought 120 acres of property in 1963 in the Alexander Valley, consisting of part of the original homestead of Cyrus Alexander, who moved there in 1842 after a career as a fur trapper throughout the West. The winery was not established until 1975, when the first commercial harvest took place under the Alexander Valley Vineyards name. All of the grapes are purchased from the senior Wetzel's vineyards. Production is pushing toward 20,000 cases a year of such premium varietals as oak-aged Cabernet Sauvignon, Pinot Noir, Zinfandel, oak-aged Chardonnay and Chenin Blanc, plus slightly sweet Johannisberg Riesling and Gewürztraminer. The wines have developed a reputation for quality, especially the whites, and the Chardonnay can be rich and complex.

☆☆

$$

Algeria.

Hundreds of millions of gallons of Algerian wine were shipped to France each year during the French control of this part of North Africa, and its use was for blending to create the *vin ordinaire* drunk by millions of peasants so that the best wines of France could be exported. It is likely that Algerian wines also were used to "stretch" some of the better French wines, even though Frenchmen would not admit to such a deceptive practice. In any event, Algerian wines were sorely needed late in the 19th century, after the vine blight known as Phylloxera devastated the French vineyards. The Algerian Civil War that resulted in independence from France in 1962 crippled the country's export trade, and new markets had to be found for huge quantities of very ordinary wine. Virtually none is consumed at home, for the Moslem religion forbids drinking alcoholic beverages. Some of the vineyards of the flat plains areas have been permitted to lie fallow, although viniculture is still practiced with great enthusiasm in certain parts of the country. In fact, some very good premium wines, developed in the French style from French grapes, are made there. But Algeria will have difficulty overcoming her reputation for *vin très ordinaire*.

Almadén.

Almadén is a leading premium wine producer in California with a volume of 12 million cases per year. Frenchmen Etienne Thée and Charles LeFranc founded Almadén in 1852 at Los Gatos in Santa Clara County, making it the oldest of existing California wineries. As Thée's son-in-law, LeFranc inherited Almadén after Thée's death and in time acquired the help of another young Frenchman, Paul Masson, who had come over from Burgundy. Almadén continued to grow and prosper, and Masson became LeFranc's son-in-law, but eventually left to start his own winery.

Dormant during Prohibition, Almadén was acquired after repeal by San Francisco businessman Louis Benoist, a sophisticated gourmet and oenophile. Benoist knew what he was doing when he asked for advice from his friend Frank Schoonmaker, later acknowledged as one of America's foremost wine experts. Schoonmaker found him a winemaker (Oliver Goulet, formerly with Martin Ray) and served as adviser to Almadén for many years. The story is told that as Benoist toured the vineyards one day he noticed a basket of Grenache grapes that were to be used for making Port. Why not make a rosé, he suggested, as they do in the district of Tavel where France's best rosé is made? The result, some months later, was Grenache Rosé, now made by more wineries than any other type of rosé and still one of Almadén's most popular wines. By 1967, when Benoist sold the winery to National Distillers, he had expanded the vineyards to extensive holdings in San Benito County around Paicines and Hollister. Since then Almadén has moved into Monterey County and National Distillers has poured a great deal of money into production and promotion. The company now has 6400 acres in vines, among the largest vineyard holdings in the U.S.

Almadén makes over 50 different wines, including aperitifs, and sparkling and dessert wines of good quality. Varietal wines, particularly the whites, are rarely great, but consistently above average and reasonably priced. The grape surplus which reduced production costs somewhat was passed along to the consumer in 1976 when Almadén trimmed some of its retail prices. Few other producers could afford to do so. Almadén is perhaps best known for its jugs of Mountain Red and Mountain White. These wines still represent good value and have been so successful that many other premium producers have followed suit and brought out quality generics in half gallons and gallons.

Besides its jug wines in their graceful

teardrop-shaped bottles, Almadén produces two different lines of premium varietals, one under the Almadén label and one under the Charles LeFranc label. The latter was introduced in late 1978 and is said to represent the best winemaking that Almadén can accomplish. The grapes for the LeFranc line are chosen from selected vineyard sites that normally produce superior fruit, and the wines are aged for longer periods in Limousin, Nevers, and Hungarian oak casks. Some of the late-harvested Rieslings, Sauvignon Blancs, and Gewürztraminers are among the best from California. But the need to supply a large national market has prevented the quality of these wines from consistently reaching high levels, and they are often disappointing when compared with bottlings from producers specializing in only a few varietals.

☆/☆☆

$/$$

Aloxe-Corton.

The *commune* of Aloxe-Corton in the French Burgundy country is one of the few that produces both red and white wines of superb quality. Le Corton is the only red *grand cru* and the best red of the Burgundian Côte de Beaune. It often has great balance and elegance, with a seductive bouquet. The white wine of the *commune,* Corton-Charlemagne, has an exquisite earthy or nutty taste that is unique among white table wines. It shows some similarity to a good Meursault, but has more richness and fullness. Prior to a decade or so ago, it was not well known and could be obtained at modest prices. The author recalls seeing it used to make Kir, the Burgundian aperitif, at a fine French restaurant in suburban New York in the late 1960s. But now it has achieved full recognition, and Corton-Charlemagne is an expensive white wine. As its name implies, Charlemagne

once owned the vineyard area.

White *commune* wines simply called Aloxe-Corton are sometimes seen, and these tend to be inferior to the *commune* wines of nearby Meursault and Puligny-Montrachet. The red *premiers crus* of Aloxe-Corton are widely distributed and often are as charming as Le Corton itself. Among the better ones are Corton-Clos du Roi, Corton-Renardes, Corton-Languettes, Corton-Bressandes, Corton-Pougets and Corton-Maréchaudes. Le Corton has *grand cru* status, along with Corton-Charlemagne and a wine called simply Charlemagne, which is rarely seen. Louis Latour, who has substantial holdings in Aloxe-Corton, bottles a very good proprietary brand named Corton Château Grancey after his eighteenth-century château there. The lesser known *premiers crus* are the following:

Chaillots
Chaumes
Fournières
Guérets
Meix
Pauland
Valozières
Vercots
☆☆/☆☆☆☆
$$/$$$

Alsace.

Along the eastern edges of the Vosges Mountains of France and just west across the Rhine River from Germany lies Alsace, whose wines often are more German in character than French. The area, with its 60-mile-long stretch of vineyards, has been French for most of its history—at least for the last 300 years—except when it was under German control between 1870 and 1918 and during World War II. But the wines owe their character to the land, not to any German influence, and are produced with some of the same grapes that produce German wines because they grow well on Alsatian soil. Even the bottles for these French wines are very similar to German bottles, with their long, sloping sides.

Alsatian wines are almost always white and bear names that are based on an unusual system for France. They are generally named after the grape varieties used to make them, whereas virtually all of the other good French wines bear geographical names. Alsace has a different system mainly because the French appellation contrôlée laws were not applied there until 1962. When they came into force in Alsace, they reflected local custom, as they have elsewhere in the country, but the Alsatian custom was different. In fact, it is only the lesser wines of the district that bear place names, usually because they are not made with the more noble grapes that fetch higher prices in the market.

As in most parts of Germany, the Riesling is the most highly regarded grape variety in Alsace and produces wines with the most style and depth, drier than most German Rieslings, clean-tasting and fresh, with a flowery bouquet and strong character. But most experts believe that the Gewürztraminer is the most typically Alsatian grape, because the wine produced from it is unique in France. Gewürz means "spice," so Gewürztraminer means "spicy Traminer" and spicy it is, displaying a very unusual scent and taste which go well with the spicy Alsatian food. A chilled bottle of Gewürztraminer is perfect with one of the pâtés made in the region and with fresh, whole foie gras, one of the renowned Alsatian delicacies. Until recently, one could obtain both Gewürztraminer and Traminer from Alsace, but there has been an effort to produce only wines labeled Gewürztraminer if they are made from the Traminer grape. This means some are quite spicy and some are not, and it is questionable whether the consumer is being served by a system that does not make it simple for him to identify the product he wants. Although these wines display great fruit, they are relatively crisp and dry on the palate. Some connoisseurs prefer them to German wines for accompanying the main course of a meal.

The Riesling and the Gewürztraminer are by far the two most popular Alsatian wine varieties marketed abroad, but several others can also be found, including the Muscat, the Pinot Blanc and the Pinot Gris, which is used to produce Tokay d'Alsace, an inexpensive and often quite pleasant white table wine that bears no resemblance to Hungarian Tokay. The Alsatian Muscat tends to be somewhat drier than Muscat wines produced elsewhere in the world and certainly is worth trying. A quantity of Alsatian Sylvaner is also made. If the term grand cru or grand vin is applied in conjunction with the name of the grape, the wine must attain at least 11 percent alcohol. Blends of the better grape varieties, known as Edelzwicker, are also available. Some of the wines used for blending are the Chasselas and the Knipperlé. They are consumed mostly from carafes in Alsatian restaurants.

Blends of the lesser varieties are simply called Zwicker.

The vineyards of Alsace are broken up among thousands of small owners who often sell their grapes to large companies that vinify them and market them under their own names. This is similar to the structure of the champagne business. Sometimes the shipping company's name may even appear on labels in larger print than the name of the wine itself, reflecting pride in the product. Some of them are F. F. Hugel, F. E. Trimbach, and Dopff & Irion. Strasbourg, the best-known Alsatian town, is just north of the wine-growing area. Most of the leading firms are based in such picturesque villages as Riquewihr, Ribeauvillé, and Kaysersberg, or at Colmar, the Alsatian wine capital.

Alsace also is famous for its fruit brandies, or *eaux-de-vie,* which are distilled from fruit produced in orchards and fields interspersed among the vineyards. Framboise, perhaps the most famous of these spirited brandies, is made from raspberries. Fraise is made from strawberries, Mirabelle is made from plums, and Kirsch comes from cherries. They are best taken as *digestifs* after a meal and seem to be preferred to Cognacs and other grape brandies by ladies.
☆/☆☆
$/$$

Alsheimer.

German white wine produced around the village of Alsheim, which is south of Oppenheim on the west bank of the Rhine River in the Rheinhessen, one of the best German wine regions. Alsheimers are less distinguished than the Niersteiners and Oppenheimers that have made the Rheinhessen famous and not many of them flow into the export markets. Nevertheless, substantial quantities of wine are produced around Alsheim and are entitled to that name.

Among the best vineyards are the following:

Alsheimer Fischerpfad*
Alsheimer Fruhmesse*
Alsheimer Goldberg
Alsheimer Rheinblick
Alsheimer Sonnenberg*

The vineyards marked with an asterisk (*) are among those that retained their identities, if not their shapes, in the revision of the German wine law in 1971.
☆/☆☆
$/$$

Alto Adige.

This is a region that abuts the Austrian border in northern Italy and produces an array of D.O.C. wines that sometimes carry the name Sudtiroler in recognition of the bilingual personality of the populace. The better wines of the region include a variety of Rieslings, Pinot Grigio that is also called Rulander, and Traminer Aromatico that shares the name Gewürztraminer.
☆/☆☆
$

Amabile.

The Italian term indicating a fairly sweet wine is *amabile,* which suggests a residual sugar content of $2^1/_2$ to 3 percent. This is not quite as sweet as *dolce* (at least 3 percent sugar) and a little sweeter than *abboccato* (1 to $2^1/_2$ percent sugar).

Amador County.

Amador County lies roughly 45 miles east of Sacramento in the rugged foothills of the Sierra Nevada Mountain Range of California. It is not a populous area, and its chief claim to fame in recent years has been its Zinfandel wines, which are among the most robust, intensely flavored and characterful reds produced anywhere in the United States. They often display a deep purple hue, an intense bouquet of fruit, high alcohol levels, high tannin and great texture. At the same time, the richness and intensity of the fruit are so strong that it is nearly always evident, enabling the Amador Zins to exhibit great charm even in their youth. Some connoisseurs suggest that the Amador wines are unbalanced on the side of robustness, even coarseness, but there are others with a fanatical devotion to the Zinfandels from this region, and the rising production in response to sharply rising demand in the late 1970s and early 1980s attests to their quality.

An unusual microclimate is largely responsible for the singular nature of these wines. The bud break on the vines often is retarded in the spring by cool weather due to the fairly high elevation, and the growing season often is shorter than in such coastal regions as Napa, Sonoma, and Mendocino. Yet the daytime temperatures in the summer can be extremely high, enabling the Amador grapes to achieve great ripeness. Levels of 25° and 26° Brix (percentage of sugar in the juice) are common at harvest time, and Brix levels well over 30° occasionally are recorded. Zinfandels in the better known Napa and Sonoma districts generally achieve lower levels. The high sugar levels characteristic of Amador grapes lead to high alcohol levels, and 14 or 15 percent is not unusual for an Amador Zin. Some have been recorded at above 17 percent, and these are better used as Port after a meal than as table wines with food. While the sugar levels in the grapes rise under the hot Amador sun, the grapes are likely to undergo dehydration, which results in extremely concentrated juice and accounts for the intensity of the Amador flavor. High sugar levels elsewhere in California often are accompanied by low acid levels, resulting in flabby wines of little character. In Amador the nearby Sierra Nevada Mountains send cool breezes into the vineyards at night, keeping the average temperatures much lower than the daytime highs would indicate and enabling the acid levels to remain sufficiently high to produce wines of good character.

The Harbor Winery in Sacramento, owned by Charles Myers, a Sacramento teacher, is often credited with the modern discovery of Amador Zinfandel as a separate and different kind of wine. Myers made small amounts of Amador Zinfandel in his cellar in the early days, and they were noticed by Darrell Corti, a Sacramento wine merchant and Zinfandel enthusiast. Sutter Home, with its winery in St. Helena in the Napa Valley, began trucking Amador grapes northward in 1968 for crushing and bottling on the home premises, and several other well known producers began using Amador grapes. These included Ridge Vineyards, Carneros Creek, Mount Veeder and San Martín, all of which vinify their grapes outside Amador County. More recently, there has been a trend toward establishing wineries in Amador and neighboring El Dorado County to the north, partly because of the soaring costs of vineyard land in the more celebrated regions of California.

Any roster of producers of Amador Zinfandels is likely to be out of date as soon as it appears, for new wineries are cropping up rapidly and some of the older vinifiers of Amador grapes occasionally turn to other sources. But any list would have to include Monteviña Wines, Sutter Home, Ridge, Mount Veeder, San Martín, Carneros Creek, Story Vineyards, Harbor Winery, Amador Winery, Argonaut Winery, Baldinelli Shenandoah Valley Vineyards, D'Agostini Winery, Kenworthy Vineyards, Santino Wines, Shenandoah Vineyards, Stoneridge Winery, Bargetto Winery, Gemello Winery, Monterey

Peninsula Winery, ZD Wines, and Concannon Vineyard. Several Amador vineyards that do not make wines have established good reputations for their grapes, which are purchased by other producers. The best known of this group are the Deaver Ranch, Eschen Vineyard, and Esola Vineyard.

Historically, cultivation of Zinfandel grapes in Amador dates back to the 1880s and perhaps earlier. Following repeal of Prohibition, most Amador producers sold their grapes to the big Central Valley wineries that valued them highly because they provided the intensity and texture needed to offset the blandness of Central Valley grapes. The Amador producers should have received premium prices for their grapes, but they did not—at least not until the late 1960s and early 70s, when premium wine producers from the northern coastal counties began to compete for them. Now the quality of Amador Zinfandels is nationally recognized, and deservedly so.

Amalfi Bianco.

Amalfi Bianco is the pleasant white wine that many tourists have consumed in the seaside restaurants and taverns of Amalfi, in the Campania region of Italy near Naples. Unfortunately little of this wine travels abroad, and it is unlikely to taste as good anywhere else.

☆

$

Amarone.

Consistently the most magnificent red wines of Italy are made by the unusual Amarone process that is not unlike the method used to make Sauternes in France and the better sweet white wines of Germany. Unlike Sauternes and the German wines, however, Amarone is red and it is usually not sweet. The grapes are permitted to remain on the vines until quite late in the autumn after they have achieved great ripeness and in many cases have begun to dry up and shrivel into raisins. The grapes that have not begun to shrivel when harvested are laid out on indoor racks, so that all of the grapes used to make an Amarone have a minimal water content and an intense concentration of flavor. The sugar content of the grapes also is highly concentrated, but the sugar is turned into alcohol during the vinification, so there is usually no residual sweetness in Amarone wines. Because of this process, the alcohol level of a good Amarone sometimes will rise above 15 percent. These wines are rich yet dry, with a texture that is so thick that it can almost be chewed.

In Veronese dialect, the word *amarone* means "bone dry." The wines are made in the Veneto region of northeastern Italy, not far from Verona, from several grape varieties, including Corvina, Corvinone, Negrara, and Molinare. Only the grapes from the *recia,* or ears, of the grape bunches, meaning those on the top and outside and thus best exposed to the sun, are used for making Amarone. By harvest time they have begun to dry out, and further drying is encouraged when they are laid out on the racks. Because the volume of juice in the grapes diminishes with the drying, Amarones are expensive to make and are uncommon wines.

An Amarone will be similar to a Barolo, but usually will display a greater intensity of flavor. Like Barolo, Amarone benefits from considerable bottle age. Some examples of the 1964 vintage had achieved a velvety roundness by 1976, but the 1966 vintage had not yet reached the same level of perfection after a decade of aging. Some bottlings from the early 1960s were still not mature by the early 1980s.

☆☆☆/☆☆☆☆

$$/$$$

America. (See United States.)

Château l'Angelus.

One of the largest producers of Saint-Emilion wines is Château l'Angelus, which lies just to the west of the ancient village that sits atop a picturesque hill overlooking the Dordogne River as it winds toward the city of Bordeaux 20 miles westward. L'Angelus is one of the *côtes,* or hillside vineyards of Saint-Emilion, as opposed to the Graves, or flatland estates of this important Bordeaux District. L'Angelus, whose name dates back to the same period of Roman occupation as Château Ausone, was ranked among the sixty or more estates with *grand cru classé* status in the Saint-Emilion classification of 1955. Because the production is large and this wine has flowed readily into the export markets, it is widely available in the United States.
☆☆☆☆
$$

Anjou.

Many are the amateurs of wine whose first experience with an exciting bottle dates to their discovery of Rosé d'Anjou, the delightful pink and semidry wine from the Loire Valley of France. Its sweetness is fairly well balanced and innocent. It has no pretensions. Some connoisseurs of rosé prefer Tavel, but nobody would suggest that Anjou rosé is not a pleasant drink for a soft summer afternoon. It is one of the best-known Loire Valley wines, but not necessarily the highest in quality. Some is made from the Groslot grape, the best from the Cabernet.

The province of Anjou is west of Tours and its wines and those of the Touraine are very similar in many ways. More than half of the wines are white, with most of the balance rosé. Along the Layon tributary of the Loire south of Angers are wines entitled to the *appellation* Coteaux du Layon. These are white and can be fairly sweet. They are made with the Chenin Blanc grape. Subdivisions also entitled to their own *appellations* are Quarts de Chaume and Bonnezeaux, where some of the sweetest and most balanced wines of the region are produced. Specific vineyard names are often attached to them. These wines challenge sweet Vouvray in terms of quality and can be unusually alcoholic in good years when the grapes have achieved superior ripeness. The nearby Coteaux de l'Aubance, from another valley just north of the Layon, produces similar whites and rosés that do not quite reach the Layon level of fruity richness.

Savennières is on the Loire below Angers and above the Layon. Again, the Chenin Blanc is the principal grape, but here it produces drier wines. This area is adjacent to the eastern fringes of Muscadet and technically is within the Coteaux de la Loire. The best wines from this part of the Loire are: La Roche aux Moines and La Coulée de Serrant. Some others include Château de Savennières, Château de la Bizolière, Château d'Epire, and Clos du Papillon.

Farther east along the Loire on one of its southeasterly bends is Saumur, where both still and sparkling white wines are produced, as well as some reds. Labels from this area may carry the designation Saumur or Coteaux de Saumur, along with specific geographical subdivisions, such as Dampièrre or Souzay-Champigny. Wines labeled Saumur-Champigny are likely to be red and quite pleasant, although not up to the quality levels of some other French reds. The Anjou District, sometimes called Anjou-Saumur, ends here, and the Touraine and Coteaux de Touraine begins. (*See* Muscadet, Touraine.)
☆☆
$

Antinori, Villa Antinori.

Some of the best wines of Tuscany are produced by the House of Antinori, representing one of the oldest noble families in Italy, with a history in Florence, the capital of Tuscany, dating back nearly 800 years. The Antinoris originally were bankers and silk merchants, arriving in Florence in 1202. They soon began buying land and planting vines in the verdant hills between Florence and Siena and had gained admission to the Wine Guild of Florence by 1385. The family moved into its historic Palazzo Antinori in the heart of Florence in 1506, and the structure is considered an architectural jewel of the Renaissance.

Today the family is presided over by the Marchesi Piero and Lodovico Antinori, who also maintain the family estate, Santa Cristina, in the Chianti Classico portion of the Tuscan hills. Half of its 600 acres are devoted to grape vines and olive trees. The Antinoris also own and operate Belvedere, a 2000-acre estate in Bolgheri, where they produce Rosé de Bolgheri, which sells in large volume. More recently they have expanded their holdings to include the 800-acre La Sala estate in Umbria, near Orvieto, which gives them further coverage of the wine market. The Villa Antinori Castello della Sala Orvieto is the largest-selling Orvieto.

The most extraordinary wine of Antinori is Tignanello, a complex Tuscan red made partly from Cabernet Sauvignon grapes. There is also the very fine Villa Antinori Chianti Classico Riserva, a Chianti Classico, and a clean, simple white called Villa Antinori Bianco. The Antinoris also market Sassicaia, a wine produced by their uncle. (*See* Taurasi, Sassicaia, Chianti.)

Appellation Contrôlée.

This term, which appears on nearly every French wine label destined for the export market, is the shortened form of *appellation d'origine contrôlée,* which literally means "controlled" or "registered authentic name" and is sometimes more loosely translated as "controlled place-name." It is a guarantee that the name of the wine has been officially recognized and the geographical designation strictly established by the French Institut National des Appellations d'Origine des Vins et Eaux-de-Vie. The guarantee also covers the grape varieties used to make the wine, the process of vinification and a certain minimum alcohol level. The controls are occasionally violated, as in the Bordeaux scandal of 1973–74 when certain regional wines were upgraded to Bordeaux Supérieur, but in general they are observed and work very effectively to maintain high-quality standards in French wines. (*See also* Labels and Wine Laws in Part I, Vins Délimités de Qualité Supérieure.)

Aquileia.

This is a village in northeastern Italy, in the region known as Friuli-Venezia Giulia, with the city of Trieste in its southeastern corner. The wines of Aquileia are mostly varietal, meaning that they are named after grape varieties, and several have merited D.O.C. status under the Italian wine law. The Cabernet, made from both Cabernet Sauvignon and Cabernet Franc, and the Merlot are the best Aquileian reds, and there is also a good Pinot Grigio among the whites.
☆/☆☆
$/$$

Arbois.

One of the few *appellations* in the Jura Mountain area in eastern France is Arbois, where rosé, red, white, and yellow wines are made. Arbois rosé is fairly dark for a pink wine and is distinctive, with somewhat more character than the red or white produced there. A spar-

kling wine, or *vin mousseux,* also is produced and bottled under Arbois labels.
The yellow wine, or *vin jaune,* is made
with an unusual process, involving aging
for at least six years in partly filled casks
to produce an extraordinary, Sherrylike
taste and a deep yellow color. It is among
the longest-lived white wines of France,
if indeed it can be classified as a white.
(*See* Château-Chalon.)

Another unusual type of wine produced in the Jura under the Arbois and
other labels is *vin de paille,* or straw wine,
which also is very rich and holds up for
many years in the bottle. Traditionally
it was made by laying the grapes on
beds of straw after the harvest, to enable them to start drying almost into
raisins. The more modern method is to
hang the grapes for two months in drying rooms before the pressing to achieve
the same results as laying them on straw.
In either process, only small quantities
of wine can be made from the dried
grapes, and it can be rather expensive.
It should be considered a curiosity to
be served to wine-lovers who are interested in the unusual.
☆/☆☆☆
$/$$

Argentina.

Argentina produces more wine than all
but three other countries—Italy, France,
and Spain—and much of it is very good
indeed. The best growing regions are in
and near the foothills of the Andes
Mountains in the western part of the
country, where a unique combination
of circumstances makes wine production especially favorable. The area is
washed with sunlight at least 300 days
per year and, in some sections, the sun
shines 350 days. Thus, the grapes are
able to achieve great ripeness—assuming there is an adequate supply of water.
With so much sunshine, obviously there
can't be very much rain, and here is
what makes Argentine grape cultivation

unique: water is available in plentiful
amounts from the mineral-rich runoff
of melting mountain snow from the
Andes.

Argentina has six wine-growing
provinces, but the vast majority of the
wines come from Mendoza, which lies
some 500 miles due west of Buenos
Aires. European grape varieties have been
cultivated here with considerable success, and a Mendozan Cabernet Sauvignon, Malbec, or Merlot—all originally
from grapes native to the Bordeaux region of France—can be an exciting experience at modest cost. Argentine
Riesling and Pinot Blanc produce pleasant white wines, and small quantities of
sparkling wine are also made, using one
of the Champagne processes. The natural ripeness of the grapes means that
the addition of sugar to help fermentation is not necessary, so Argentine
wines tend to have a freshness that is
very charming.

The vinicultural history of the country is remarkably similar to that of the
United States. As in California, the first
vines were cultivated by the Spanish
missionaries, who produced wines in
the sixteenth and seventeenth centuries
mainly for the sacrament. Don Tiburcio
Benegas is credited with developing the
early vineyards of Mendoza Province.
He imported root stocks from Europe,
helped establish the banking structure
needed to finance wine production and
even played a role in bringing the railroad to Mendoza from Buenos Aires,
thus opening up the markets to the east.
So successful was Benegas that Argentina became a wine-drinking country,
and not until recently did she produce
adequate quantities for export. More
and more wines are flowing to the United
States and other countries nowadays,
however, and they can be among the
best bargains on the shelf of any wine
shop. The reds seem to be the most
successful and, of these, the Cabernet

Sauvignon has been the most consistent. The Rieslings tend to be the best whites.

Arkansas.

Arkansas wineries are scattered through the backwoods of the Ozark Mountains in the northern half of the state. The most important is Wiederkehr Wine Cellars in Altus, about 120 miles north-west of Little Rock. With a storage capacity of two million gallons, Wied-erkehr produces about one million gal-lons annually and is the largest winery in the South. On the last plateau of the Ozarks overlooking the Arkansas River Valley to the south, Wiederkehr's 600 acres of vineyards on St. Mary's Moun-tain enjoy a unique climatic situation. Shielded on the north by the Boston Mountains, the Ozarks' highest range, and by Mount Magazine of the Ouachita range south of the Arkansas River, the vines benefit from a thermal inversion that protects them from the cold Ca-nadian fronts bringing blankets of snow and subzero temperatures down the midwestern corridor. Natural rainfall and an abundant underground water table insure plenty of moisture for the vines year round. The altitude provides good drainage and a cool growing sea-son comparable to that of Germany. The southerly slopes offer excellent ex-posure for the ripening grapes.

Owner and cellarmaster Alcuin Wiederkehr is of the third generation to grow grapes here. He quit law school to transfer to the University of Cali-fornia at Davis where he studied oen-ology and viticulture. As an exchange student he spent a year in Bordeaux, traveling on weekends to Geisenheim, Germany, where he supplemented his study of French techniques with the best available in Germany. Returning with French hybrids such as Verdelet, Chancellor, and Baco Noir, he subse-quently planted Chardonnay and Jo-hannisberg Riesling. He now grows 135 acres of Vinifera varieties, including Gewürztraminer, Pinot Noir, Zinfandel, and Cabernet Sauvignon, in addition to Chardonnay and Riesling. One of Wiederkehr's most popular wines is Cynthiana, a dry red dinner wine from the native Cynthiana grape. Wieder-kehr continues to make quantities of sweet wines from native varieties and bulk champagne, and the winery also produces a bottle-fermented cham-pagne called Hans Wiederkehr, named for Alcuin's grandfather who started it all back in 1880.

There are other wineries in Arkansas. Post Winery, also in Altus, boasts nearly half a million gallons yearly. French hy-brids have been introduced here also. Other wineries operate in or near the towns of Paris, Harrisburg, Center Ridge, and Morrilton.

Arroyo Sonoma.

Arroyo Sonoma is the premium brand name for wines produced by a new con-cern called the California Wine Com-pany, established in 1980, with an operating winery at Cloverdale, Sonoma County. (The other brands marketed by the company include Potter Valley and Bandiera). Under the Arroyo Sonoma label there were plans for Special Re-serve bottlings of Cabernet Sauvignon, Chardonnay, and Sauvignon Blanc. A less expensive line of Arroyo Sonoma bottlings was to include Cabernet Sau-vignon, Zinfandel, and Pinot Noir. Pro-duction in 1981 was estimated at 28,000 cases in all for the Arroyo Sonoma label. One of the prime movers behind the venture was Adolph "Bud" Mueller, who played an important role in the Sou-verain operation.
☆☆
$$

Assmannshauser.

Nearly all of Germany's wine is white, produced from the Riesling, Sylvaner,

Müller-Thurgau, and other traditional white grapes. But a few vineyards produce red wines, and the best-known red is the Assmannshauser. It is mostly owned by the German State Domain and comes from the town of Assmannshausen just around the bend in the Rhine River from Rüdesheim, one of the great Rheingau wine villages. The basic red grape is the Spätburgunder and, as the name implies, it is virtually the same as the principal red grape of France's Burgundy country, the Pinot Noir. Because of the different soil and climate of the Rheingau, however, the wines produced by the Pinot Noir here bear little resemblance—except in color—to Burgundian reds. Eight hundred years of cultivation in Germany following their transplantation from France by the Cistercian monks has failed to improve the vines. Assmannshausers are pleasant enough, but they lack the depth and rich character of Burgundies and do not compare favorably with them. Very few ever get into the export markets and, when they are found, they can be enjoyable to taste as curiosities but not as superior red wines.

☆☆☆

$/$$

Asti Spumante.

Known as the "Champagne of Italy," Asti Spumante is a sparkling white wine produced in the provinces of Asti, Alessandria, and Cuneo in northern Italy's Piedmont region, which is better known for its great red wines. Asti Spumante is vinified mostly from the Moscato grape and is somewhat sweeter than true Champagne from France. It exudes a heady aroma and luscious soft taste that makes a superb accompaniment to a dessert of ripe pears or peaches. Although it is often served as an aperitif in the same way that Champagne is served, this is a mistake; it is best after a meal. A very small quantity of Asti Spumante is made by the traditional French process, the *méthode champenoise,* involving fermentation in bottles, but most of it is produced by the bulk, or *charmat* process, involving vinification under pressure in large vats and then bottling under pressure to retain the bubbles. Asti Spumante must attain a minimum alcohol level of 12 percent. Sometimes this wine can be found with "brut" added to its name, indicating that it has been vinified completely dry, but it still retains the taste of the Moscato grape. (*See* Champagne.)

☆

$/$$

Auslese.

This is one of the categories of wine with special attributes produced in Germany as *Qualitätswein mit Prädikat.* It tends to be quite sweet. Less sweet are Spätlese and Kabinett wines and higher on the sweetness scale are Beerenauslese and Trockenbeerenauslese. Auslese is produced from the ripest bunches of grapes individually selected late in the harvest and sometimes is made with the help of *Edelfäule,* or the "noble rot," a fungus or mold that penetrates the skins of the grapes and helps the water in the juice evaporate, leaving sweet, concentrated juice behind. Because it is a category or style of wine, it may come from virtually any good vineyard in Germany, assuming the correct weather conditions have prevailed. It should be consumed with a sweet dessert or very ripe fruit, or can be taken as an aperitif. An Auslese differs drastically from the cheap sweet wines produced in big quantities in some countries. It has an elegance and character which place it close to the top in the German wine hierarchy.

Château Ausone.

Along with Château Cheval Blanc, Château Ausone was ranked above all of the other Saint-Emilion wines in the

CHATEAU AUSONE

SAINT·EMILION

APPELLATION SAINT-EMILION CONTRÔLÉE

1962

Vᵛᵉ C. VAUTHIER & J. DUBOIS-CHALLON
PROPRIÉTAIRES A SAINT-ÉMILION (GIRONDE)

MIS EN BOUTEILLES AU CHATEAU

classification of this important district 20 miles east the city of Bordeaux in 1955. Both are *premiers grands crus classés,* reflecting a centuries-old tradition of good winemaking. According to legend, Ausone almost became the only Saint-Emilion estate to be included in the Bordeaux classification of 1855, so great were its wines in the early part of the 19th century, but apparently its production was too small and its location too distant from the Médoc.

Château Ausone lies along the *côtes,* or hillside, area of Saint-Emilion, as opposed to the *graves,* or gravelly plateau where Cheval Blanc, Figeac, and some other good vineyards are located. The wines of the *côtes* generally are more highly regarded, although certainly no one would challenge the quality of Cheval Blanc. The *caves* and other buildings of Ausone sit on one of the hilltops overlooking the Saint-Emilion vineyard area, adjacent to Château Belair, which is under the same ownership. Both wines are vinified and stored in the Ausone cellars. It has been suggested that they are very similar in taste and style, but Ausone definitely shows greater finesse. A sampling of the 1972 vintage of the

two wines from casks at Ausone in 1973 clearly showed the superiority of Ausone. 1972 was not a great vintage—just the type of year when the better estates demonstrate their superiority. Ausone also made a very pleasant 1956—a year when many vineyards were devastated by extremely cold weather in February.

Following World War II Château Ausone appeared to sink into decline, developing a reputation for not living up to its exalted status. The wines of Ausone lacked their traditional finesse and concentration, reflecting lackadaisical management of the property. Between 1959 and 1974, especially, Ausone simply did not measure up. But a metamorphosis has occurred since then, largely brought about by a new winemaker, Pascal Delbeck, who arrived at the chateau in 1975. He reverted to the old vinification methods, and the Ausone wines since then have returned to form. The 1978 was excellent, and Ausone once more is one of the leading chateaux of the region.

Château Ausone's name is derived from the fourth-century Roman poet, Ausonius, who, according to local legend, became a vineyard owner on or near the site of the present estate. Such was his influence that he no doubt would have chosen the best available location for cultivating grapes, and the Ausone estate is just that—facing south toward the Dordogne River a few miles distant and lying on sloping terrain that catches the sun during much of the day in the growing season.

☆☆☆☆

$$$

Australia.

The wine industry in Australia is booming, and the quality levels reached there are good, but, unfortunately, by the time an Australian bottle reaches the United States it has become fairly costly due to the lengthy journey it has undergone. As a result, little Australian wine is available in the U.S. and it is regarded more as a curiosity than something to take seriously. Because of the traditional ties of the Empire, considerable quantities go to Britain and Canada, but they are not really competitive on a price basis in these countries either. This doesn't mean Australian wines are terribly expensive when they reach the northern hemisphere, but why should consumers pay $4 for a bottle of "claret" from down under when very respectable red Bordeaux from *petits châteaux* are available at the same price?

Winemaking in Australia dates back to the late 1700s, when settlers from England brought vine cuttings with them aboard their ships. Great quantities of dessert wines and fortified wines were produced for many years, especially for the Canadian and British markets, although table wines have come into their own in the last couple of decades. The leading areas of production are South Australia, in the area around Adelaide, the Hunter Valley in New South Wales north of Sydney, and Victoria, the southernmost part of the country. Australian producers have borrowed the names Port, Sherry, Madeira and Tokay for their sweet fortified wines from the countries that rightfully own them— Portugal, Spain, Portugal and Hungary, respectively. They also market large amounts of "claret" and "Burgundy," although some of the more enlightened producers have begun using grape names, e.g., Cabernet Sauvignon, for their better table wines. But even this practice can become confusing when you learn that the French Semillon grape is called "Riesling" in some parts of Australia.

During the 1970s, as in the United States, a revolution occurred in the Australian wine business. Dry table wines replaced the sweet fortified wines that had dominated Australian production. By 1980 white wines were outselling reds by a margin of four to one in Australia, and per capita consumption of wine in the country had doubled. A measure of world renown was achieved in 1979 when the Pinot Noir 1976 of Tyrell, an Australian producer, took first prize in the Wine Olympiad in Paris organized by the Gault-Millau gourmet magazine. (A Clos de Vougeot 1969 from the heart of the French Burgundy country placed second.)

The Australian vineyard areas generally are about as far south of the equator as the major European growing areas are north. Across the bottom third of Australia, the vineyards exist roughly between south latitude 32° and 43°. The major European growing areas lie between 40° and 50° north latitude. But the Australian vineyards are far more spread out. For example, the distance from the Eastern State vineyards of the Hunter Valley to the west coast vineyards of the Swan Valley near Perth is some 2000 miles. Thus generalizations about Australian vintages are rarely valid.

While the Phylloxera wine blight was devastating the European vineyards in the latter half of the nineteenth century, it invaded only the area around Victoria in Australia, so many of the Australian vineyards still grow on their original rootstocks, in contrast to the European vineyards, which were grafted almost entirely onto disease-resistant American rootstocks. (*See* Phylloxera.) The most popular grape in Australia is the Shiraz, better known in France as the Syrah, where it is widely cultivated in the Rhône Valley. The Grenache, Cabernet Sauvignon, Sultana, Muscat, Doradillo, and Sémillon also are popular.

Austria.

Excellent white table wines are produced in surprisingly large quantities in

Austria, and in many cases they resemble the wines of Austria's neighbor, Germany. Until the 1970s Austria was basically a wine-importing country rather than a wine exporter, so her wines were little known in foreign markets. Only about 150,000 acres are planted in vines in Austria, and 84 percent of their output is white. A big national harvest amounts to fewer than 100 million American gallons. Yet Austrians drink an average of 36 liters per person each year, or about five times the volume that Americans consume. Wine has been made in Austria since about 700 B.C., so the tradition there is ancient. Now for the first time an export market has been established, and occasionally a Gumpoldskirchner or Neusiedler Riesling will be found abroad. These and the other wines of Austria come from vineyards surrounding Vienna and the Neusiedler See in the eastern part of the country. Ruster, the best-known wine from the Neusiedler, comes from the town of Rust near the lake. Other wines named after villages close to Vienna are Grinzinger, Neustifter, Nussdorfer, and Kahlenberger, whereas the well known Gumpoldskirchner comes from a few miles to the south. All of these wines are white, made from the Veltliner, Riesling, Sylvaner, Traminer, or Gewürztraminer grapes. Often they are crisp and dry, but sometimes an Auslese or Beerenauslese, with a honeylike sweetness, will be found.

Under the rigid Austrian wine law, the standards for producing sweet wines are high. To bear the Kabinett designation, the unfermented grape juice must be at least 20° Brix or 84 on the Oechsle scale. A Spätlese must be 23 Brix or 96 Oechsle, an Auslese must be 25 Brix or 106 Oechsle, a Beerenauslese must be 29 Brix or 124 Oechsle, and a Trockenbeerenauslese must be 34 Brix or 149 Oechsle. These standards are carefully enforced, yet the lack of knowledge of Austrian wines abroad means that these excellent wines usually cost less than German wines of comparable quality. (*See* Oechsle, Brix.)

The districts around Vienna are known as Burgenland, Weinviertel, and Südbahn. Farther to the west is Wachau, whose best-known wine is Schluck, made from the Sylvaner grape grown on the slopes above the Danube. Also from Wachau but less well known are Dürnsteiner, Kremser, and Loibner. Occasionally a red Austrian wine made from the Spätburgunder grape will turn up, but it will be in the same category as the German Spätburgunders—rather dull and lacking in character. The Spätburgunder is the same grape as the Pinot Noir of France's Burgundy District, but the wines it makes outside Burgundy are undistinguished. The best way to drink Austrian whites is from carafes in Viennese taverns, rather than from bottles sent abroad.

Auxey-Duresses.

In the hills above Meursault and adjacent to Monthélie in the heart of the Côte de Beaune of the French Burgundy country lies the small village of Auxey-Duresses, where good but rarely great red wines are produced as well as a very small quantity of whites. These wines lack the elegance and finesse of other Burgundies, but they tend to be low-priced and sometimes will represent good value. There are no *grands crus* in Auxey-Duresses, but the area has several recognized *premiers crus,* including:

Bas des Duresses
Bretterins
Climat-du-Val (or Clos du Val)
La Chapelle
Duresses
Ecusseaux

Grands Champs
Reugne
☆☆☆
$$

Avelsbacher.

The wines of Avelsbach are well known mainly because they are produced near Trier, the most important town for the wine trade in the Mosel-Saar-Ruwer region of Germany. Some wines are produced within the municipality of Trier itself, but most of those identified with Trier come from the surrounding hillsides, including the one at Avelsbach. The Tiergartener is the most important vineyard within Trier. Because Trier lies on the Mosel River, just north of the junction with the Saar, its wines are technically Mosels. But the nearby Avelsbachers and most of the other Trier wines more closely resemble those of the Saar and Ruwer. In the best vintages, when the weather has been kind and the sun has shone long and fully, these wines can rise to extraordinary quality heights, displaying an elegance and character that rank with the best of Germany. But fine vintages are less common in this part of the country due to the uncertain weather conditions, and in a mediocre year the Avelsbachers and other Trier wines will fall below the quality levels achieved by the wines of the central Mosel farther downstream to the north. The most identifiable trait of the Avelsbachers is a steely, or *stahlig,* quality which becomes more pronounced, even to the point of tartness, in lesser vintages. Many of these wines are produced by the Cathedral of Trier, which can be recognized by the prefix "Dom" added to the name of the wine on the label. Several other charities own vineyards in the area. Another of the big owners is the Staatsweingut, or State Domain, which has vineyard properties all over Germany.

Among the better known vineyards at Avelsbach near Trier are the following:

Avelsbacher Altenberg
Avelsbacher Hammerstein*
Avelsbacher Herrenberg
Avelsbacher Rotlei*
Avelsbacher Thielslei
Avelsbacher Vogelsang
Avelsbacher Wolfsgraben

The asterisk (*) indicates vineyard names that survived or were created by the German wine law of 1971. Other Trier wines are now bottled as Eitelsbachers or Mehringers, sometimes with specific vineyard names, to simplify their identification.
☆☆
$/$$

Ayler.

One of the better wine towns of the Saar River Valley at the southern end of the Mosel-Saar-Ruwer region of Germany is Ayl, whose Ayler Kupp vineyard produces some of the best German wines in good years. Like other Saar wines, however, Aylers can be hard and unyielding in poor years and do not measure up to the better wines of the central Mosel River Valley to the north. Ayler Herrenberg, Ayler Neuberg, and Ayler Scheidterberg also produce decent wines when the weather permits. In addition to the Kupp, the Scheidterberg and the Herrenberg vineyards survived the revision of the German wine law of 1971, although their boundaries may not be strictly the same.
☆☆
$/$$

· B ·

Baldinelli Shenandoah Valley Vineyards.

One of the newer winemaking operations in Amador County, California, is Baldinelli Shenandoah Valley Vineyards, which was established in 1979 and is concentrating on Zinfandel wines, which have made Amador County famous among oenophiles. Baldinelli is also producing some Cabernet Sauvignon there, but the winery has yet to prove itself. The Zinfandel vines are 57 years of age and are expected to produce extremely concentrated, tannic, and robust wines that will require extensive bottle-aging. The winery is located in Plymouth, the address of several other Amador wineries, and it turns out white Zinfandel, rosé Zinfandel, along with full-blooded red Zinfandel aged in small oak barrels plus Cabernet Sauvignon that receives the same treatment. Proprietors Ed, Kay, and Mike Baldinelli plan to raise production to about 6000 cases a year initially, but may expand more if the demand warrants.

☆☆

$$

Banfi, Villa Banfi.

Villa Banfi is one of the great American success stories, founded in the early years of the century as an importing company by John Mariani, Sr., and now run by his sons, John, Jr., and Harry. Its modern success is owed to Riunite, a Lambrusco from Italy that became the largest-selling imported brand in the U.S. in the 1970s, with volume in excess of ten million cases a year. The Marianis took a chunk of their profits from Riunite and built one of Italy's most modern wineries in San Angelo Scalo, near Montalcino, in the early 1980s. There they are making excellent premium wines, including Brunello di Montalcino, under the tutelage of their head oenologist, Ezio Rivella. Banfi is now one of the largest wine companies in the U.S.

☆/☆☆☆☆

$/$$$

Barbacarlo.

Lombardy, an important wine region in northern Italy, produces a number of very good red wines, and Barbacarlo is one of them. It has D.O.C. status under the Italian wine law and is made from Barbera, Uva Rara, and Ughetta grapes. The wine is dry and textured and gen-

erally should be drunk before age ten. Very little is seen in the export markets.
☆☆/☆☆☆
$

Barbaresco.

Sometimes called the younger brother of Barolo, which is the most celebrated wine of Italy's Piedmont region, Barbaresco is sturdy but not quite as robust as Barolo and tends to mature at a younger age. Like the other great red wines of the Piedmont, it is vinified from the Nebbiolo grape and displays a vigorous intensity, flowery bouquet, and great body. At maturity—usually after eight to ten years—a Barbaresco will be soft and velvety, but will retain the fruity taste of the Nebbiolo grape. It will usually be somewhat less costly than a Barolo and will not achieve the fullness of body displayed by Barolos from the best vintages. But there are exceptions, and among these would be the Barbarescos of Angelo Gaja, who makes wines of extraordinary depth and longevity that challenge the best Barolos. His single-vineyard bottlings are very expensive and are sought by connoisseurs of the best Italian reds.
☆☆/☆☆☆☆
$/$$$

Barbera.

Unlike the names of the other noble wines of the Piedmont region of northern Italy, Barbera is the name of a grape variety. It produces excellent red wines of supple body and an earthy flavor that are not unlike the best of the Rhône Valley of France. Barberas will vary widely in quality, depending on the style of each producer, but generally they will be somewhat fruitier and lighter than the Barolos, Barbarescos, and Gattinaras produced in the Piedmont from the Nebbiolo grape. The best Barberas have the name of the district of production attached, e.g., Barbera d'Asti, Barbera di Cuneo, Barbera d'Alba, Barbera del Monferrato, etc. The best examples are called *superiore* and must attain at least 13 percent alcohol.

Barbera d'Alba.

Made mostly from Barbera grapes but with some Nebbiolo blended in, this dry red comes from vineyards near Alba in Italy's Piedmont region. The D.O.C. law requires it to have two years of age, including one in wood, before it can be sold.
☆☆
$

Barbera d'Asti.

The Barbera grape is widely cultivated in Italy and yields wines of D.O.C. status in several areas, including the area around the city of Asti in the Piedmont region. It is full-bodied and dry and must be aged for two years, including one in wood, before it can be marketed.
☆☆
$/$$

Barbera del Monferrato.

This is another Piedmont version of Barbera, made near Monferrato in several different styles, including a *frizzante,* or sparkling, version. It tends to be less robust than some other Piedmontese Barberas and is entitled to a *superiore* designation if aged for two years before being sold.

☆☆

$/$$

Barbi, Fattoria dei Barbi.

One of the leading producers of Brunello di Montalcino, perhaps Italy's most consistently great red wine, is the Fattoria dei Barbi, presided over by Francesca Colombini-Cinelli. Her Brunellos are big, deep, and highly structured, needing 15 to 20 years to reach maturity in good vintages. Barbi also makes a nice second wine, Brusco dei Barbi, that matures earlier.

☆☆/☆☆☆☆

$$/$$$$

Bardolino.

The sunny vineyards on the eastern shores of Lake Garda in the Veneto region of northeastern Italy produce Bardolino, a pleasant light red wine that is well known in many countries. It is not a wine meant for laying down in cellars; it should be drunk when it is fresh and young, and many of its devotees insist that it is best when slightly chilled. It is made from the Corvina and Negrara grapes, with some Rondinella and Molinara blended in. Bardolino displays a very slight sweetness that is not unpleasant. It is the natural sweetness of the grape, and it seems appropriate as an accompaniment to a northern Italian meal.

☆/☆☆

$

Barengo Vineyards.

Barengo is a major producer of mostly jug wines in the Central Valley of California, with facilities at Acampo, just north of Lodi in San Joaquin County.

It is corporately owned by Verdugo Vineyards Inc., which is headed by Herbert R. Benham, Jr. The general manager is Albert Luongo. Benham is also chairman of Berrenda Mesa Farms, with 40,000 acres planted mostly in almonds and pistachios.

About half the Barengo wines are produced under the Barengo label, and the rest come under the Lost Hills label. (Lost Hills is a sleepy town in the San Joaquin Valley.) The winery was established in 1934. Besides red, white, and rosé jug table wines, Barengo produces a line of varietals, including Cabernet Sauvignon, Chardonnay, Johannisberg Riesling, Gewürztraminer, Zinfandel, Petite Sirah, etc. The winery also has been experimenting with an American Lambrusco. Barengo owns about 1000 acres of vineyards, which provide most of its grapes, but it still needs to buy about 20 percent of its total needs from outside producers. Barengo was originally known as Acampo Winery.

☆/☆☆

$/$$

Bargetto's Santa Cruz Winery.

Bargetto was established after the repeal of Prohibition and now has facilities in Soquel, in Santa Cruz County south of San Francisco. It is solely owned by Lawrence Bargetto, president and general manager, who grew up in the wine business. Production totals upwards of 40,000 cases a year, including magnum bottles of red and white generic table wines. But most of the output is now in premium varietals, including a pleasant Chardonnay aged in Limousin oak barrels. Bargetto also makes a bone-dry Gewürztraminer and a sweet, botrytised Gewürztraminer, Johannisberg Riesling, Chenin Blanc, plus Cabernet Sauvignon aged in American oak, Merlot aged in French oak, and Zinfandel aged in American oak. Most of the varietal labels carry designations of origin—either vineyard names or the name of a county or town—to let the consumer know where the grapes originated. Bargetto buys all of its grapes from other producers in Napa, Sonoma, San Luis Obispo, and Santa Barbara Counties. A line of fruit wines made from strawberries, apricots, raspberries, etc., is also produced.

☆/☆☆

$/$$

Barolo.

Italy's Piedmont region, in the northern part of the "boot," is where her greatest red wines are produced—wines that rival the best from France's Rhône Valley and that sometimes can be similar to a robust Burgundy from the Côte de Nuits. Among the best of Piedmont are the big and rich Barolos that sometimes require decades of bottle-aging to reach perfection. Barolo is a full-bodied red with a very intense texture sometimes described as "dusty," because of the almost dustlike taste particles that one senses on the tongue. It is a mouth-filling wine made from the noble Nebbiolo grape that also produces Barbaresco, Gattinara, Ghemme, and Spanna, the other great reds from this part of Italy. Barolos from the best vintages seem to take forever to mature into the velvety softness they are capable of achieving partly because they must reach at least 13 percent alcohol to merit the Barolo name. Charles Plohn, Sr., a New York investment banker with a summer home in Italy, laid down hundreds of bottles of the 1947 vintage of the Marchesi di Barolo, and it seemed to be at its peak in the mid-1970s, displaying extraordinary elegance and finesse. The 1961 of Bruno Giacosa, tasted in 1983, was one of the finest reds the author has ever experienced. Unfortunately, too few Italian wines are aged sufficiently, so it is extremely unusual to find Barolos of the proper maturity. Wines from lighter vintages, such as the 1967, are ready at a younger age, but never achieve the quality level of the wines from the truly great years. In general, Barolos made the traditional way in superior vintages tend to reach their peaks between ages 20 and 25.

In the mid-1970s many Barolo producers apparently began to vinify their wines differently in an effort to make them more palatable to consumers at a younger age, as well as to get the wines on the market sooner at a time when high inflation rates began to make holding wines ever more costly. Whereas Barolos traditionally had been aged at least four years in wood, many producers adopted the minimum of two years in wood (plus a mandatory third year in bottles) prior to release for sale. Barolos meriting the *riserva* designation must be aged a total of four years and those called *riserva speciale,* quite rare, require at least five years of aging. Consumers seeking the traditional style should look for the *riserve* and *riserve speciali,* which are costly.

Among the leading Barolo producers are Aldo Conterno, Giacomo Conterno, Paolo Cordero di Montezemolo, Fontana Fredda, Bruno Giacosa, Pira, Prunotto, Francesco Rinaldi, Giuseppe Rinaldi, Barale, Valentino, Luigi Einaudi, Granduca, Contratto, Dosio, Pio Cesare, Mauro, Ceretto, Abbazia dell'Annunziata Borgogno and Marchesi di Barolo.

☆☆☆☆

$$/$$$

Barry Wine Company.

In New York State's Lake Erie District in the town of Conesus is the Barry Wine Company, which produces a line of branded generics such as Mellow

Burgundy, Rosé of Iona, Barry Reserve Select White, Cream Sherry, etc. Two cousins from a well known California wine family operate the winery. They are Albert B. Cribari II, known to his friends as "Skip," and Theodore S. Cribari, Jr., known as "Ted." Both screwtop, inexpensive wines and a line of cork-finished Barry Reserve wines are produced. The Reserve line includes a crisp yet fruity Riesling. Barry has more than 65 acres of grapes planted in Labrusca, French-American hybrids and some European varietals. Annual production is 12,000 to 15,000 cases.
☆/☆☆
$/$$

Barsac.

Lying adjacent to the Sauternes District of southern Bordeaux is Barsac, whose sweet white dessert wines are fully the equal of the better Sauternes. Barsacs are entitled to the Sauternes *appellation,* and it is difficult to tell the two types apart. (For a full description, *see also* Sauternes.)
☆☆☆
$$

Château Batailley, Haut-Batailley.

Château Haut-Batailley and Château Batailley, two of the estates that won recognition in the Bordeaux classification of 1855, were together under one ownership until 1942. Both are *cinquièmes crus,* or fifth growths, producing big wines that lack some of the elegance of other Pauillacs, but nevertheless have a strong following in the export markets. The production of Batailley is somewhat greater than that of Haut-Batailley, which should not be confused with Château Haut-Bailly of Graves.
☆☆☆☆
$$

Bâtard-Montrachet.

Like its neighbor Montrachet, the vineyard of Bâtard-Montrachet lies in both Chassagne and Puligny, the two greatest white-wine *communes* of the Golden Slope of Burgundy in France and is partly responsible for the worldwide reputation of this area for producing the greatest dry white table wines to be found anywhere. Bâtard-Montrachet is often fully the equal of the great Montrachet itself, but is not quite as famous. The presence of a circumflex over a vowel in the French language often signals the former presence of an adjacent 's' in an earlier phase of the word and Bâtard is no exception. The word translates literally as "bastard," yet in Chassagne and Puligny it is considered an asset rather than an epithet. Only Corton-Charlemagne from the nearby *commune* of Aloxe-Corton is capable of challenging the Grand Bâtard for the position on the right-hand side of Montrachet. Two other very good *grands crus* include the Bâtard name, indicating the presence at one time of a prolific sire. These are Bienvenues-Bâtard-Montrachet in Puligny and Criots-Bâtard-Montrachet in Chassagne. The only other *grand cru* in the two communes is Chevalier-Montrachet in Puligny, and it is uncertain whether the existence of this estate relates to the parentage of the neighboring *bâtards.* (*See also* Chassagne-Montrachet, Puligny-Montrachet, Côte de Beaune.)
☆☆☆
$$$

Bear Creek Winery.

Bear Creek is a member of the big California cooperative called Guild Wineries and Distilleries. All of its wines are vinified and distributed by Guild. (*See* Guild.)
☆
$

Beaujolais.

There is a saying in the southern portion of the Burgundy country of France that three rivers flow through Lyon—the Rhône, the Saône and the Beaujolais. The Beaujolais, of course, is a river of mainly red wine, amounting to some 15 million gallons annually, and it is perhaps the freshest, simplest, and most delightful red made anywhere in the world. So much is produced on the rolling hillsides in this 45- by 10-mile district south of Mâcon toward Lyon that it does almost flow like a river. In fact, a great deal more Beaujolais is consumed each year than the district could possibly produce, reflecting the habit of many makers of light red wines to name them Beaujolais even if they are legally something else. The *vin de carafe* served in Paris bistros and most London restaurants is usually described as Beaujolais. Sometimes the description is accurate; often it is not. But there is no mistaking a true Beaujolais with its youthful zest, fruity taste, and great charm. It is a wine to be drunk young and, if you wish, chilled, the way it comes out of the casks in the cool cellars near the picturesque little villages that have somehow remained relatively free of tourist invasions. This is one of the most delightful areas of France, with twisting narrow country roads, green forests, spectacular little restaurants

hidden far from the beaten track and a slow and gentle life-style that could hardly be more remote from urban bustle.

In recent years Beaujolais has become a heavily promoted wine, but its price has stayed low, reflecting the substantial quantities made, and it can be one of the best buys among good French wines. The annual Beaujolais race, usually starting on the fifteenth of November, is an event of great fun as the producers vie with each other to be the first to take their new Beaujolais to Paris, London, and New York. The wine is variously called Beaujolais Nouveau, Tirage Primeur, Beaujolais Primeur, and sometimes Beaujolais de l'Année. It comes from the first fermentation of the grapes harvested only weeks earlier and is the youngest and freshest of all the Beaujolais, if not the best. Its color is light and its taste is extraordinarily fruity. It should be just as thoroughly chilled as a white wine when drunk, and it is often consumed in great mouthfuls instead of sips, because Beaujolais is not a sipping wine. The new Beaujolais is fun to drink and somewhat a curiosity because of its youth, but no serious producer of this wine will try to persuade you that it has the depth and character of Beaujolais that has been properly aged in casks and then allowed to rest quietly in bottles for a few months before being drunk.

The principal grape of Beaujolais is the Gamay, which rises to great quality heights only in this part of the world. Wines are made from the same grape in California, but they bear little resemblance to the ones produced from the claylike granitic soil of the Beaujolais District. Only a few miles to the north, in the Burgundian Côte d'Or, the Gamay fails to produce wines of the same fresh quality. The great Burgundian red grape, the Pinot Noir, is, by the same token, unable to achieve its accustomed superiority when nurtured in Beaujolais vineyards. This is what makes Beaujolais a unique wine. Nowhere else in the world has a strictly comparable wine been made.

The best Beaujolais comes from the nine villages entitled to the *grand cru appellation*. These are, running from north to south, St-Amour, Juliénas, Chénas, Moulin-à-Vent, Fleurie, Chiroubles, Morgon, Brouilly, and Côte de Brouilly. Each has distinctive characteristics yet each is undeniably Beaujolais. It is said that the Moulin-à-Vent is the most similar to the big Burgundies from the area to the north, but Morgon can also be a fairly robust wine. Both of these benefit from at least several years of bottle-age, whereas the other Beaujolais should be drunk within two years of their birth. The most charming *grand cru* widely available in the American market is the Brouilly. The Fleurie and Chiroubles are clean and fresh, with classic Beaujolais style. All of the *grand crus* will cost a bit more than the others and generally they display a little more character.

Wines called only Beaujolais, without the name of a more specific subdivision within the district, can represent excellent value. They need have only 9 percent alcoholic content and are delightful for summer picnics. Beaujolais Supérieur, a slightly better grade, can also be produced from grapes grown anywhere in the district, but must attain 10 percent alcohol. In good vintages it runs 12 percent or more. Between Beaujolais Supérieur and the *grand cru* level are wines entitled to the *appellation* Beaujolais-Villages, which means that they come from grapes produced in any of about three dozen villages whose names are not customarily used on labels. Under the French *appellation contrôlée* laws, the production of each category is strictly controlled. The yield

per acre of vines is restricted to the smallest amount for *grand cru* wines to assure higher quality. The yield in the plain Beaujolais vineyards is allowed to be about 20 percent higher, and the yield throughout the district can be expanded by government decree in especially fine vintages, so long as quality levels are maintained.

The upsurge in the popularity of table wines all over the world has benefited Beaujolais as much as any wine district, and now some of the wines from the area are even château- or estate-bottled. The Château de la Chaize of Brouilly, the Château des Jacques of Moulin-à-Vent, and the Château de Pizay and Château de Bellevue of Morgon connected with the Piat interests are excellent examples. Individual shippers' names are important with Beaujolais, and when you encounter an especially good one it is wise to remember it. Excellent Beaujolais also appears under the Prosper Maufoux, Bouchard, Joseph Drouhin, Chanson, Patriarche, Louis Jadot, Louis Latour, Pasquier-Désvignes, and Mommessin labels, and good ones are shipped by many of the big firms more famous for their Burgundies from the Côte d'Or.

Travelers through the Beaujolais country can stop at a number of tasting stations at such villages as Beaujeu (which is responsible for the Beaujolais name, but which does not produce the best Beaujolais wines). Romanèche-Thorins, St. Lager and several other villages along the Route du Beaujolais, the vineyard road that runs through the area. The Compagnons de Beaujolais, a merry-making society similar to the Confrérie des Chevaliers du Tastevin, is headquartered at Villefranche, one of the most important wine towns of the district. An extraordinarily pleasant way to pass an afternoon is to quaff fresh, cool Beaujolais from a *pot* or *pichet,* the jug-shaped bottles native to the area, at any of the little restaurants along the route. The Guide Michelin, by the way, has given high rankings to several of the nearby eating places.

A certain amount of white Beaujolais also is produced from the noble Chardonnay grape. But Beaujolais Blanc is not classic Beaujolais, and some of the whites from the Mâconnais District just to the north, where the famous Pouilly-Fuissé and the new *appellation* Saint-Véran come from, are usually superior. Still, Beaujolais Blanc from a good producer or shipper will be a well made wine.

☆/☆☆☆

$/$$

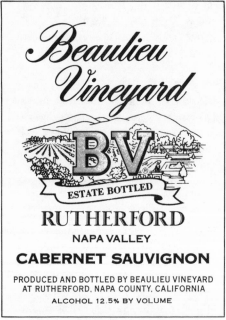

Beaulieu Vineyard.

Beaulieu Vineyard at Rutherford in the Napa Valley is one of California's most distinguished names in winemaking and is a major producer of premium varietal wines, including some of the best made in this country. For decades BV's Cabernet Sauvignon, especially, has set standards in quality and style, strongly French-influenced because Beaulieu, which means "beautiful place" in French, was founded in 1900 by a Frenchman from Périgord named Georges de Latour. He had greatness on his mind from the outset and traveled to France to collect vine cuttings of the finest varietals for his vineyards. He expanded rapidly and accumulated some of the best vineyard land on the floor of the Napa Valley. During Prohibition he made sacramental wines, thereby keeping his facilities operating so that they were ready to move back into high gear after repeal.

In 1937 Latour went to France in search of a new winemaker and returned with André Tchelistcheff, now regarded as the dean of American winemakers. He spent three and a half decades at BV and during that time enormously influenced California winemaking. His genius for evaluating grape quality and anticipating the special care demanded by each variety resulted in superbly balanced wines of depth and character. He was one of the earliest to use small oak barrels for aging and persuaded Latour to set aside portions of his Cabernet for maturation in French oak. This was the origin of the BV Georges de Latour Private Reserve Cabernet Sauvignon, whose first vintage was the 1936. Tchelistcheff also experimented with various yeast strains and fermentation techniques using colder temperatures. He sought special microclimates for vineyard sites and was an early advocate of the Carneros district in the southern Napa Valley for Pinot Noir and Chardonnay cultivation.

Perhaps his greatest contribution was the development of the Private Reserve Cabernet, consistently one of the best red table wines made in the United States. The grapes come from two vineyards—named BV No. 1 and BV No. 2, purchased in 1904 and 1907, respectively. Production of the Private Reserve fluctuates from vintage to vintage because of weather conditions, and not all of the 77 acres of Cabernet grapes in No. 1 or the 67 acres in No. 2 go into the Private Reserve bottlings, for only the best grapes are chosen. Production of the Private Reserve is believed to range between 7500 and 15,000 cases a year, although the figure is never disclosed and some analysts say it is somewhat more. The wine is nearly always one of the best Cabernet Sauvignons produced in California, competing on a par with the best red Bordeaux of France. It is also expensive.

Besides the Private Reserve, there is Beau Tour, BV's basic Cabernet Sauvignon, with production of about 30,000 cases a year, and Rutherford Cabernet Sauvignon, a cut above the Beau Tour, with output of 70,000 cases or more. Then there are such other varietals with proprietary names as Beaumont Pinot Noir, Beaufort Pinot Chardonnay, Beauclair Johannisberg Riesling, etc.

Heublein Inc., a food and beverage conglomerate, bought Beaulieu Vineyard in 1969 and expanded the production facilities. At the time of the Heublein purchase, BV was turning out 220,000 cases a year. Now it is producing about 300,000 cases of premium wines plus perhaps 150,000 cases more of 1.5-liter jug wines. The BV management bridles at the suggestion that any dilution of quality has occurred since the Heublein takeover. (In 1982 Heublein was in turn acquired by Reynolds Foods.) André Tchelistcheff retired from active winemaking at BV in 1973, to be succeeded by his assistant, Theo Rosenbrand, who later moved to Sterling Vineyards. Thomas B. Selfridge, with degrees in economics (from Berkeley and Wharton) and oenology (from the University of California at Davis), later took over as winemaker and has been maintaining the BV style and quality.

Amid the BV vines stands the Beaulieu mansion set in a small park with rose gardens, lawns, a swimming pool, tennis court, and 120-foot-long arbor of bent sycamore trees sheltering picnic tables. It has received many famous visitors and for years was the home of the Marquise Hélène de Pins, widow of the Marquis de Pins and daughter of the late Georges de Latour. Madame de Pins retained ownership of BV No. 1, which is called the "home vineyard," and she sold all of its production to the parent company, which means that the BV Private Reserve is a blend of wines from a private vineyard and from a corporately owned one (BV No. 2).

The BV line is broad, including most premium varietals: Chardonnay, Champagne, Sauvignon Blanc, Muscat, Gamay Beaujolais, Zinfandel, and so forth. But none of these has ever achieved the quality peaks of the Private Reserve Cabernet Sauvignon, which suggests that the BV vineyard sites are best suited for this red varietal. This possibility is tacitly acknowledged by the management, for 40 percent of BV's premium varietal production is in Cabernet Sauvignons of varying levels of quality. Interestingly, all of the cabernets are aged in American oak barrels, not French, yet still achieve extremely high levels of quality.

☆/☆☆☆☆
$$/$$$

Beaumes-de-Venise.

The place called Beaumes-de-Venise lies virtually in the shadow of Mont Ventoux in the Rhône Valley of France, and a number of good wines are made there, although most of them are simple country wines that do not attract attention among connoisseurs. But there is one local wine that stands above all the rest, a lightly sparkling wine of pinkish-orange hue made from the muscat grape and vinified slightly sweet. Its name is entirely geographical: Muscat de Beaumes-de-Venise. It is usually rich and full-bodied, a wine that warms the soul, for it is often fortified to contain 15 percent alcohol. Its flavor is of apricots and nectarines and cranberries, and it is intensely fruity, ideal for an aperitif or as a dessert wine. Its light sparkle, the quality known in French as *pétillance,* adds to its charm, although the bubbles are tiny and do not resemble those of a truly sparkling wine. At one time in the 1700s the Roman Catholic Church tried to ban consumption of the Muscat of Beaumes, for it was said to have mystical powers that triggered excessive consumption and unleased aberrant behavior among the citizenry of the Rhône region. Efforts were made to halt cultivation of the Muscat grape there, and not until the early part of the twentieth century did the vineyards recover. Most of the Muscat de Beaumes-de-Venise is produced by the Cave des Vignerons, a large winery cooperatively owned by some 300 growers who take their grapes there during the harvest each autumn. Individual *négociants* sometimes buy the finished wine from the cooperative and bottle it themselves, adding their own labels. Production runs 650,000 bottles in an average vintage, but only a modest portion is exported.

☆/☆☆☆

$/$$

Beaune.

The *commune* of Beaune is the namesake and center of the Côte de Beaune in the heart of the French Burgundy country, and its production of mostly red wines is among the largest of the Côte d'Or, or Golden Slope, of Burgundy. It lies between Pommard on the south and Savigny on the north, and its most important town is Beaune itself, the commercial center of the Burgundy wine trade. The medieval city, with its concentric rings of Roman walls built up during succeeding phases of growth, has narrow cobbled streets and numerous storage facilities bearing the most famous shippers' names of the region: Drouhin, Jadot, Bouchard, Patriarche, etc. Beneath the cobblestones are extensive cellars, some dating back hundreds of years, where millions of bottles of Burgundy wine are stored. The firm of Joseph Drouhin, now run by Robert Drouhin, has acquired much of the subterranean honeycomb in the old central part of the city, and hours can be spent exploring and tasting in the ancient vaulted passageways. Beaune is also the home of an excellent museum of wine artifacts that is open to the public. The annual wine auction at the Hôtel Dieu, or Hospices de Beaune, a charity hospital more than 500 years old, is the social and commercial event of the year in the Burgundy country.

Oenophiles in search of a silver *tastevin,* or wine-tasting cup, can acquire entire collections from the shops that ring the ancient square where fresh produce and meat, including freshly slaughtered rabbits with their heads and paws still attached, are marketed by hundreds of local farmers each Saturday morning. Beaune is a stopping-off place for members of the Chevaliers du Tastevin en route to a *chapitre* up the highway at Clos de Vougeot, and there is no better hostelry in the Burgundy country than the Hôtel de la Poste just on the outskirts of the old part of the city. Le Cep, appropriately named (the word means "vinestock"), is another good hotel in Beaune.

Beaune is just the way a wine capital ought to be and, if the streets and sidewalks are not exactly awash in the stuff, they sometimes seem that way. The vineyards entitled to the Beaune *appellation* slope upward from the city and produce mostly red Burgundies, with a sprinkling of whites. The reds are not the heaviest produced in the Côte de Beaune and have been widely imitated for many years. In fact, the word *beaune* was at one time interchangeable with red Burgundy. Other wines of the Côte de Beaune, especially Volnay and Pommard among the reds, tend to display more character when properly made. But this should not be taken to suggest that some excellent wines are not produced under the Beaune name. The Clos des Mouches produced by Drouhin is excellent in both red and white, and the Grèves called Vigne de l'Enfant Jésus made by Bouchard Père et Fils also has won an extensive following. The vineyard designations Bressandes, Marconnets and Fèves can be very good, depending on who produced them. Cent Vignes, one of the larger vineyards, can be classic, and Les Grèves, totaling 80 acres, produces the largest quantity of good red Beaune wines.

The French wine authorities have designated no *grand cru* parcels in the *commune* of Beaune, but there are several dozen *premiers crus,* the largest number in any of the *communes* of the Côte de Beaune. Among the better known are the following:

Avaux
Boucherottes
Bressandes
Cent Vignes
Clos des Mouches
Clos de la Mousse
Clos du Roi
Cras
Epenottes
Fèves
Grèves
Marconnets
Montée Rouge
Perrières
Teurons, or Theurons
Vignes Franches

Wines labeled Côte de Beaune or Côte de Beaune-Villages are blends from vineyards lying anywhere in the Côte de Beaune, and are not as high on the quality scale as those labeled simply Beaune, which must come from the *commune* of Beaune itself, rather than from any *commune* in the Côte de Beaune, a geographical area of which Beaune itself is only a part. (*See also* Côte de Beaune, Hospices de Beaune.)
☆☆/☆☆☆☆
$$/$$$

Château Beauséjour.

Among the *côtes,* or hillside, vineyards that were accorded *premier grand cru classé* status in the Saint-Emilion classification of 1955 is Château Beauséjour, which has been divided into two parts, each under different ownership, for more than 100 years. The Duffau-Lagarrosse family owns the original château and vineyards adjacent to it, while Dr. Jean Fagouet owns the rest, which has a slightly larger production of wine. The limestone cellars of Beauséjour extend for hundreds of yards under the hill of Saint-Emilion, providing an ideal storage area. They are said to meet the *caves* of Château Canon and Clos Fourtet at a point far underground.
☆☆☆☆
$$

Beerenauslese.

This is the very sweet German category of white wine produced from grapes that have been individually picked, often by hand, after they have been allowed to remain on the vines after the normal harvest in the autumn until they have begun to dry out and turn almost into berries. Beerenauslese is very rare and expensive. It is less sweet than Trockenbeerenauslese but somewhat sweeter than Auslese. The natural sugar in the juice is permitted to become extremely concentrated, often after the grapes have contracted *Edelfäule,* a fungus or mold that the French call the "noble rot" and which botanists call *Botrytis cinerea* in Latin. The fungus penetrates the skins of the grapes, permitting the water in the juice to evaporate into the air in the late autumn months until the grapes shrivel almost into raisins.

The term "Beerenauslese" refers to one of categories produced as *Qualitätswein mit Prädikat* and therefore may come from virtually any good vineyard in Germany when the autumn weather conditions permit. You are as likely to find a Beerenauslese from the Rheingau as the Rheinhessen or the Palatinate, but you probably will not find more than one in any wine shop if you are lucky enough to find any at all. Because only minute quantities of juice remain in the shriveled grapes when they are harvested for Beerenauslese and because the selection of the grapes must be done by hand, the production cost is extremely high and only small amounts are produced. A single bottle of a Beerenauslese is likely to cost as much as a case of a lesser wine from the same vineyard. Tasting one can be an extraordinary experience, and small groups of wine-lovers have been known to join together to buy a bottle and ceremoniously uncork it to the accompaniment of fresh *foie gras* or a dessert of overripe peaches or pears. A Beerenauslese should be treated with reverence and kept only for special occasions.

☆☆/☆☆☆
$$$/$$$$

Bel Arbres Vineyards.

Bel Arbres is the secondary label of Fetzer Vineyards of Redwood Valley, in California's Mendocino County. The wines are lower-priced than those bearing the Fetzer label and usually not of the same quality level. (*See* Fetzer Vineyards.)

☆
$

Château Belair.

Adjacent to Château Ausone on the *côtes,* or hillside, area of the important Saint-Emilion District east of Bordeaux is Château Belair, which was ranked a *premier grand cru classé* in the Saint-Emilion classification of 1955. Belair is under the ownership of the Dubois-Challon family that also owns Château Ausone. Its wines do not have the same elegance as Ausone, but they are good red Bordeaux. (*See* Château Ausone.)

☆☆☆☆
$$

Château Belgrave.

The *commune* of Saint-Laurent lies adjacent to Saint-Julien on the Médoc peninsula north of the city of Bordeaux, but its wines are entitled to carry only the Haut-Médoc designation under the French wine law, rather than the more specific name of the Saint-Laurent *commune* itself. Château Belgrave is the most widely distributed of the three classified growths there, and it has some of the characteristics of Saint-Julien due to its proximity to this better known township. Yet Belgrave sometimes lacks the breeding of the better growths of the Médoc because the soil is not quite as favorable there. The estate was ranked as a *cinquième cru,* or fifth growth, in the

Bordeaux classification of 1855. At one time it was under common ownership with Château La Tour-Carnet, a *quatrième cru* that lies just to the west in the same *commune* and that is not well known outside of France. The other classified growth of Saint-Laurent, Château de Camensac, a *cinquième cru,* has become better known in recent vintages through a marketing arrangement that also includes Château Larose-Trintaudon, an estate that has been revived after a long decline.

☆☆☆☆

$$

Belvedere Wine Company.

The Belvedere Wine Company has achieved considerable acclaim for its "Grapemaker" series, a group of wines made from vineyards owned by some of California's most respected growers. The wines tend to be very high in quality and can be fairly expensive. A 1980 Cabernet Sauvignon from Robert Young Vineyards was deeply concentrated and rich with Cabernet fruit. Pinot Noirs and Chardonnays from Bacigalupi Vineyards were equally stylish. Belvedere releases each wine with its own distinctive label. The company also makes low-priced wines from purchased grapes in its "Wine Discovery" series and has demonstrated considerable prowess with premium varietals.

☆/☆☆☆

$/$$$

Benmarl Vineyards.

Along the slopes of a prominent ridge above the Hudson River, about one hour and a half north of New York City, grow the vines of Benmarl Vineyards. They are mostly French-American hybrids such as Baco Noir, Chelois, Aurora, and Seyval Blanc, but also include such varieties of *Vitis vinifera* as Chardonnay, Riesling, and Pinot Noir. Here on this site in the Hudson River Valley,

vineyards were planted as early as 1827, and grapevines have continued to grow there. In 1959, Mark Miller, a magazine illustrator and sculptor, bought the A. J. Caywood property near the small town of Marlboro. He and his family named it Benmarl, the Gaelic term that means "slate hill." The slatey soil that nourishes the vines and the climate fostered by the Hudson River give the wines of Benmarl a *goût de terroir* that sets them apart from other New York wines.

The vineyards cover about 50 acres in all, with room to expand. Production is increasing rapidly. The goal is 30,000 gallons annually. On the ridge above the vines, with a spectacular view of the valley and river below, stand the handsome brick and wood buildings designed by Miller's wife Dene, an architectural draftsman. Miller tends the vines and makes the wines in this family operation. During the years that Mark illustrated for European publications, the family lived in Burgundy where their enjoyment of wines deepened and their knowledge of the techniques of winemaking and viticulture increased to the point where they felt ready to start a winery of their own. They have experimented with numerous varieties at Benmarl, with the advice and encouragement of such experts as Philip Wagner and Dr. Konstantin Frank. Experiments continue as they learn more from each vintage. In 1975 a small batch of Cabernet Sauvignon was made. Cabernet ripens late and the growing season here is not usually long enough for it to ripen fully. The same is true of Chardonnay, which Benmarl is also producing. The vines at Benmarl, however, enjoy a slightly longer season than elsewhere in the state. Often when frost hits the valley regions below in early autumn, it stops short of the slopes at Benmarl. Such fortuitous exposure has contributed to other successes, including Aurora, a soft, fruity white wine,

Seyval Blanc, a somewhat bigger white, and Baco Noir, a very agreeable dry red.

The Millers have formed an organization called the Société des Vignerons, a grape-growing association designed to encourage further development of vineyards in the Hudson River Valley. The society enables Miller to sell what he calls "vine rights," which give consumers the right to buy the production of his vineyard in case lots and also gives them a sense of participation in the fortunes of the winery. Annual dinners are held at the Culinary Institute of America in nearby Hyde Park for members of the society, and the income from the sale of vine rights gives Miller an inexpensive source of financing. The idea has been imitated in other parts of the country.

☆/☆☆☆

$/$$

Bereich.

Among the many subdivisions of the complex German wine universe is the Bereich, which can be roughly translated as a "district" within a major region. The word does not refer to a specific type of wine; rather, its use on a label implies that the wine in the bottle is a blend of wines from the district. A Bereich usually will involve several vineyards producing wines, of fairly similar style and taste. Its use is followed by the name of the area where the wine was produced. For example, Bereich Bernkastel means that the wine is a blend of the wines produced around the village of Bernkastel in the Mosel River Valley. The wine should display the characteristics of a Bernkasteler—full Riesling bouquet, rich and elegant taste. But it probably will not show as much depth and character as a Bernkasteler Doktor from the famous individual vineyard of that name. A Bereich wine should cost less than a wine from a specific vineyard in the same district and often will represent good value.

Bergerac.

East of Bordeaux by about 80 miles and straddling the meandering River Dordogne is the city of Bergerac, with its ancient castles and battlements dating back hundreds of years. The red wines produced in the area do not compare favorably with the great reds of Bordeaux, even though they are often made with the same grape varieties. One very good white is produced just south of the city in the area around Monbazillac. The Monbazillac is a sweet wine that sometimes challenges the better Sauternes and Barsac produced south of Bordeaux, but it suffers from the same lack of public demand as most other sweet wines. (*See* Monbazillac.)

The simplest *appellations* of the district are called Bergerac and Côtes de Bergerac. Most of this is white and rather undistinguished. There are three more specific place names within the district: Pécharmant, Rosette, and Montravel. Pécharmant, with a fairly small production, comes from northeast of the city and is fairly decent red wine. Rosette, which sounds as if it ought to be a red or rosé, actually is a name restricted to white Bergerac and is also produced in modest quantities. Montravel, including Côtes de Montravel and Haut-Montravel, also is mostly white and sometimes fairly sweet.

Beringer/Los Hermanos.

Beringer is one of the California Napa Valley's oldest wineries and one of the few in continuous operation through prohibition, when sacramental and medicinal wines could still be made. The Beringer brothers, Jacob and Frederick, came from a winemaking family on the Rhine in Germany and founded the Los Hermanos estate in St. Helena, California, in 1876. During its construction,

BARREL FERMENTED

Beringer

Chardonnay
Gamble Vineyard

PRODUCED AND BOTTLED BY
BERINGER VINEYARDS, ST. HELENA, NAPA VALLEY, CALIFORNIA
ALCOHOL 13.8% BY VOLUME

Jacob, having learned winemaking techniques in the French Médoc, spent the time working with Charles Krug, already well established just across the road, while Frederick oversaw the building of the Rhine House, as near a replica as possible to the old family castle on the Rhine River. Behind the house in the winery, over a thousand feet of storage tunnels were dug by Chinese laborers. These cellars, with their ideally constant temperature year-round, are still used for storing Beringer wines.

In 1970, the Nestlé company bought the winery and hired accomplished winemaker Myron Nightingale, formerly of Cresta Blanca, to upgrade and expand the line of wines. Two thousand acres of top varietals were planted in Napa and Sonoma Counties, others farther south around Santa Maria.

With increased acreage among the top varietals and a new fermentation facility, Beringer is producing limited bottlings from specific vineyards yielding wines of distinct characteristics.

Since 1977 Nightingale has been fermenting several lots of Chardonnay in small French oak barrels, an old Burgundian method intended to achieve greater complexity. Limited bottlings of these wines have been marketed and have won accolades from the experts. With nearly 2000 acres now planted in

premium varietal vines in the Napa and Sonoma Valleys, Beringer is able to market a diverse line of high-quality wines. Nightingale was one of the pioneers in late-harvested, botrytised wines, and his botrytised Semillon 1980, with 15.7 percent residual sugar, was a classic, superrich dessert wine with nuances of apricots and honeydew. His wife, Alice, plays an important role in making the sweet wines of Beringer.

Nightingale announced his retirement in December 1983, after 41 harvests, and assumed the title of Winemaster Emeritus. He continued as a consultant to Beringer, working with special lots of wine such as the 1980 botrytised Semillon, which was given the name "Nightingale" by Beringer when it was released commercially in 1984. Edward Sbragia, Nightingale's assistant for seven years, became the new Beringer winemaster.

A second line bottled in half gallons under the label Los Hermanos, has begun to garner a reputation for sound wines at reasonable prices. Beringer also produces two proprietary brands of table wine, the oldest being Barenblut, a robust blend of Zinfandel and Pinot Noir. To coincide with their centennial in 1976, Beringer launched Traubengold, a golden mellow wine that is sweet without being heavy. Beringer is a colorful place to visit, with limestone cellars and tasting rooms in the refurbished Rhine House. ☆/☆☆☆
$/$$

Bernkasteler.

Bernkastel is unquestionably the most renowned wine town of the Mosel River region of Germany. It is a fairy-tale village of gingerbread houses tilting over narrow alleyways, with geraniums hanging from window boxes and roofs made of the same native slate that lies in the vineyards. The village is perched on the side of the hillside and if you

enter it from above by car, you must wind down through extremely steep and sharp switchbacks comparable to those in the Alps. The village square is so tiny that a big American car would have difficulty turning around in it.

Bernkastel's fame derives from the Doktor vineyard, which produces some of the most elegant and expensive white wines in the world. The Bernkasteler Doktor has a richness and intensity that few German wines can match. The vineyard had three original owners: the Dr. Thanisch family, the Lauerburg family, and Deinhard & Company. Each makes superb wine and it is useless to rank one above another, although each owns a separate portion of the Doktor vineyard, which unfortunately was expanded by the new German wine law of 1971. The Lauerburg cellars are cut deep under the hillside and spread out some five stories beneath the vineyard. Built in the 17th century, they maintain a year-round temperature of 44° Fahrenheit and preserve old wines in superb condition. Herr Lauerburg keeps thousands of bottles of his own, many from the 1930s and 1940s, separate from those destined for the commercial market. His Bernkasteler Doktor Auslese 1949 was a masterpiece when tasted in 1973—deep tawny color, full bodied, with extremely rich intensity of Riesling flavor and extraordinary balance.

The Doktor bottlings of Dr. Thanisch

and Deinhard also rise to magnificent heights. Each of these growers owns interests in other vineyards in the area near the Doktor and one of their names on a label can be used as a guide to quality in the Mosel. Among the better known vineyards at Bernkastel are the following:

Bernkasteler Altenwald
Bernkasteler Amorpfad
Bernkasteler Badstube*
Bernkasteler Bratenhöfchen*
Bernkasteler Doktor*
Bernkasteler Graben*
Bernkasteler Held
Bernkasteler Lay*
Bernkasteler Pfaffenberg
Bernkasteler Pfalzgraben
Bernkasteler Rosenberg*
Bernkasteler Schlossberg
Bernkasteler Schwanen
Bernkasteler Steinkaul
Bernkasteler Theurenkauf
Bernkasteler Weissenstein*

The vineyard names given with an asterisk (*) survived the revision of the German wine law in 1971. The others have been merged and consolidated to simplify identification, but examples from pre-1971 vintages can still be found. Bernkasteler Badstube was turned virtually into a generic name for wines from the Bernkastel area. The name Bernkasteler Kurfürstlay has a similar connotation.
☆☆/☆☆☆☆
$$/$$$

Château Beychevelle.

This is one of the most celebrated estates of the Médoc peninsula that runs north of the city of Bordeaux, yet it was accorded only *quatrième cru,* or fourth growth, status in the Bordeaux classification of 1855. The wines are widely acknowledged to belong with the best of the second growths on a quality basis,

and sometimes a Château Beychevelle from an especially propitious vintage will challenge the first growths. Beychevelle is in Saint-Julien, the *commune* that is sometimes called Saint-Julien-Beychevelle. The name is believed to have come from the expression *baisse voile,* meaning "lower sail" in a reference to the demand of Admiral d'Epernon during feudal times, that all ships passing along the nearby River Gironde strike their sails in salute to the splendid vineyards. A stylized boat with lowered sails is depicted on the Beychevelle label. The château itself, owned by the Achille-Fould family that has been active in the French government and politics for many years, is one of the most beautiful of the Médoc, with terraced gardens overlooking the Gironde. Big and intense wines are made here, with a dark color and fullness of bouquet that can be overpowering in their youth. At maturity, a Beychevelle from a superior vintage will display great finesse and elegance, while retaining its celebrated intensity. The 1937, tasted nearly four decades later, remained a rich and fruity wine that required an hour's breathing to reach its mellow perfection. As in other Bordeaux estates, the vinification process apparently was changed late in the 1960s, so that earlier-maturing wines have been produced recently. The 1970 and '71 were surprisingly soft when sampled in 1975, although far away from their peaks.
☆☆☆☆
$$/$$$

Bianco.

Bianco is the Italian word for "white," and there are many Italian wines simply called Bianco with the name of the village or area of production attached, e.g., Bianco Capena from the Lazio region north of Rome, Bianco Colli Empolesi from the city of Empoli near Florence, Bianco dei Colli Maceratesi from the sloping vineyards of Macerata in the Marches region, etc.
☆
$

Bianco della Lega.

Bianco della Lega is a white wine recently introduced by members of the consortium of Chianti Classico producers in Tuscany. Its appearance is a direct result of the exclusive use of the Chianti name for red wines under the Italian wine law. It is vinified crisp and dry and is made from Trebbiano and Malvasia grapes. It is similar in style to Galestro, another recently developed white from Tuscany.
☆/☆☆
$

Binger.

German white wine produced in Bingen, which is one of the villages in the Rheinhessen. Bingen is the northern and westernmost outpost of Hessia, lying directly across the Rhine River from Rüdesheim near the opening of the Nahe River and within sight of Schloss Johannisberg. The wines are not as well known as some of the others of the Rheinhessen, for example Niersteiner and Oppenheimer, but some of them are strong rivals. The best-known Binger is the Scharlachberg, meaning the "scarlet hill" in a reference to the brick-red color of the soil that exists in some of Hessia's best vineyards. Bingers tend to be more robust than some others produced in the Rheinhessen, possibly reflecting their proximity to the Rheingau across the river. Some other communities, including Büdesheim and Kempten, are incorporated with Bingen and carry the Binger label on their wines. Among the best-known vineyards are the following:

Binger-Budesheimer Hausling
Binger-Budesheimer Scharlachberg*

Binger-Budesheimer Schnackenberg
Binger-Budesheimer Steinkautsweg
Binger Eiselberg
Binger-Kempter Kirchberg*
Binger-Kempter Pfarrgarten*
Binger-Kempter Rheinberg
Binger Mainzerweg
Binger Ohligberg
Binger Rochusberg
Binger Rosengarten*
Binger Schlossberg*
Binger Schwatzerchen*

The vineyards marked with an asterisk (*) are among those that retained their identities, if not their configurations, in the revision of the German wine law in 1971. In general, smaller vineyards were merged into large ones to simplify identification.
☆☆/☆☆☆
$$

Biondi-Santi.

The most traditional producer of Brunello di Montalcino, perhaps Italy's greatest red wine, is Biondi-Santi, whose labels are a symbol of quality. The property, called Il Greppo, is rum by Franco Biondi-Santi, a fiercely proud aristocrat who feels that most of his competitors are mere upstarts. His Brunellos are big, concentrated, complex wines that need decades to mature. The 1955, tasted at Il Greppo in 1983, was right at its peak.

It was still commercially available at the winery for $180 per bottle, which places Biondi-Santi in the same league as Romanée-Conti, the great Burgundy.
☆☆☆/☆☆☆☆☆
$$$/$$$$

blanc de blancs.

The term *blanc de blancs* literally means "white from whites," or white wine from white grapes. It is used by many Champagne producers in France to connote wines made entirely from the Pinot Chardonnay grape, as opposed to the Pinot Noir. Producers of sparkling wine outside the Champagne District in France sometimes call their wines *blanc de blancs* to indicate that they are similar to Champagne, at least in terms of their bubbles. The term is also used in California and elsewhere to connote a dry white wine, because the Champagnes vinified entirely from white grapes are supposed to be drier than those made from red grapes or from a combination of white and red. The process of making white wine from red grapes involves the removal of the red grape skins from the must, or fermenting grape juice, as soon as the grapes are crushed. It is the pigment in the skins that imparts color to the wine, if the skins are permitted to ferment with the juice. Sometimes a Champagne Blanc de Blancs will be more costly than a traditional one, but this does not necessarily mean it is better. Many Champagne lovers prefer the more robust and earthy taste of a wine made at least partly from red grapes.

blanc de noirs.

The term *blanc de noirs* means "white wine from dark grapes," and is used by some Champagne producers to indicate that their wines have been vinified entirely from the Pinot Noir grape, instead of the Pinot Chardonnay or a blend of the two. A Blanc de Noirs Champagne should be fuller-bodied and more earthy than a Blanc de Blancs. (*See blanc de blancs.*)

Blaye, Côtes de Blaye, Premières Côtes de Blaye.

Directly across the Gironde estuary from the celebrated Médoc near Bordeaux in southwestern France is a wine-producing area known as Blaye. The production of white wines here is enormous, although most of them lack character and finesse. A small portion of the output is red, and these are better, although rarely great. The best reds and whites are bottled under the *appellation* Premières Côtes de Blaye and sometimes Côtes de Blaye, while the lesser wines are marketed under the names Blaye, Blayais, or simply Bordeaux Blanc or Rouge. The area overlooks the merger of the Dordogne and Garonne Rivers at the Bec d'Ambès, forming the mighty Gironde that flows northward and westward into the Atlantic.

Blue Nun.

Blue Nun, produced by the Sichel firm in Mainz, West Germany, is the largest-selling Liebfraumilch and one of the world's largest-selling brands.
☆/☆☆
$$

Boca.

One of the better red wines from the Piedmont region of Northern Italy is Boca, produced near the town of the same name mostly from Nebbiolo grapes blended with portions of Vespolina and Bonarda. Boca is full-bodied and rich in flavor with a very dry finish. It can be quite tannic when young and is best not consumed before age eight.
☆☆☆/☆☆☆☆
$/$$

Bodegas Bilbainas.

One of the leading producers in the Rioja District of northern Spain is Bodegas Bilbainas, which produces large quantities of good table wines in a variety of price and quality categories. The Bilbainas reds and whites have become widely available in the United States in recent years, partly because they represent good value. (*See* Rioja.)
☆/☆☆☆
$/$$

Bodenheimer.

German white wine produced in Bodenheim, which is one of the villages in the Rheinhessen on the western bank of the Rhine River after it bends south at Mainz. Bodenheimers are less distinguished in general than the more elegant Niersteiners and Nackenheimers of the nearby Rheinhessen and many of them are bottled as Liebfraumilch. Some of the Bodenheimers are characterized by a taste of the earth that prevents them from achieving greatness. Exceptional wines are produced from the vineyards maintained by the Oberstleutenant Liebrecht'sche Weingutsverwaltung and the Staatsweingut, or state-owned property.

Among the better known vineyards are the following:

Bodenheimer Bock
Bodenheimer Braunloch
Bodenheimer Burgweg*
Bodenheimer Ebersberg*
Bodenheimer Hoch*
Bodenheimer Kahlenberg
Bodenheimer Kapelle*
Bodenheimer Leidhecke*
Bodenheimer Monchpfad*
Bodenheimer Rettberg
Bodenheimer St. Alban*
Bodenheimer Sandkaut
Bodenheimer Silberberg*
Bodenheimer Westrum*

The vineyards marked with an asterisk (*) are among those that retained their identities, if not their shapes, in the revision of the German wine law in 1971. St. Alban is now a *Grosslage,* or large vineyard area, encompassing wines from a major section of the Rheinhessen. In general, small vineyards were merged into large ones to simplify identification.

☆☆

$/$$

Boeger Winery.

Boeger is located in Placerville, in El Dorado County, California, just above Amador County, the home of robust Zinfandels. It was established in 1973 by Greg and Susan Boeger, both of whom have degrees from the University of California at Davis, Susan in philosophy and Greg in oenology. Greg is the grandson of Anton Nichelini, a Swiss-Italian who founded a winery and vineyards in California in 1883. This winery operates today under a different branch of the family as Nichelini Vineyard in St. Helena. The Boegers bought a pear ranch in Placerville in 1972 and decided to continue farming pears while clearing new ground for vineyards. In 1973 ten acres of Cabernet Sauvignon, Zinfandel, and Merlot were planted, followed by Chardonnay, Sauvignon Blanc, and Semillon the following year. They leased a small local winery with a seven-acre vineyard and thus were able to produce a 1972 vintage on the leased premises, called Gold Hill. The 1973 crush also took place there, while their own new winery was being finished. Production now totals about 10,000 cases a year of Cabernet Sauvignon, Zinfandel, Johannisberg Riesling, Chenin Blanc, Chardonnay, Sauvignon Blanc, and two brands called Hangtown Red and Sierra Blanc.

☆☆/☆☆☆☆

$$

Bonarda.

The Bonarda is a variety of red grape cultivated in the Novara Hills of Italy's Piedmont region and in Lombardy. It yields wines that lack the robustness and intensity of the Piedmont wines made from the Nebbiolo grape, such as Barolo and Gattinara, and is sometimes blended with the Nebbiolo for earlier maturation. When bottled as a varietal with its own name on the label, Bonarda is best drunk fairly young.

☆/☆☆☆

$

Bonnes-Mares

APPELLATION CONTROLÉE

Domaine G. Roumier et ses fils

PROPRIÉTAIRE A CHAMBOLLE-MUSIGNY (COTE D'OR) - FRANCE

Mise en bouteille au Domaine

Bonnes-Mares.

One of the most delicious red wines of the Burgundian Côte de Nuits in France is Bonnes-Mares, produced in a vineyard that lies partly in the *commune* of Chambolle-Musigny and partly in Morey-Saint-Denis. Bonnes-Mares is a charming *grand cru,* which means it has been officially recognized in French wine law as one of the 31 best Burgundy wines. It has a velvety texture, a highly perfumed bouquet evocative of the scent of lilacs or violets and a sensuous charm similar to Les Musigny, from a nearby vineyard. It is not as famous as Musigny, Chambertin, and some of the other *grand crus* of Burgundy, which means it can be excellent value. (*See also* Côte de Nuits, Morey-Saint-Denis, Chambolle-Musigny.)

☆☆☆☆

$$$

Bonny Doon Vineyard.

Just behind the Lost Weekend Saloon in the community of Bonny Doon, in the Santa Cruz Mountains of California, is the Bonny Doon Vineyard, established as a bonded winery in 1983, after existing at other locations earlier. A California Vin Rouge, 60 percent Cabernet Sauvignon, 37 percent Grenache, and 3 percent Merlot, was made in 1982 and won a gold medal at the Los Angeles County Fair in 1983.
☆/☆☆
$$

Boordy Vineyards.

If there is a single name that towers above others in the wine world of the eastern United States, it is undoubtedly that of Philip Wagner, former proprietor of Boordy Vineyards in Riderwood, Maryland. Wagner's story is well-known to American wine lovers. He was a journalist with the *Baltimore Evening Sun* in the 1930s who enjoyed the taste of good wine and attempted to make his own at home. Frustrated in his efforts with *Vinifera* varieties and finding the Labrusca flavor distasteful, he began to experiment with French hybrids imported from Bordeaux. Soon he was making enough wine to warrant a building of his own, so he and his wife Jocelyn built a winery that was first bonded in 1945. In 1964 Wagner retired as editor of the *Sun* to devote full time to making wine and act as consultant to other winemakers.

In 1980 Wagner announced the sale and relocation of Boordy to the family of Robert B. Deford, Jr., of Hydes, Maryland, a few miles north of Baltimore. The Defords had been suppliers of French hybrid grapes to Boordy for many years, but were primarily in the cattle-breeding business. The sale included all of the winemaking equipment and cooperage of Boordy as well as the existing inventory of wines. The 1980 vintage was the first under the Deford ownership, but the Boordy name continues at the new location, and the new relationships with outside growers should assure continuity. Production amounts to about 7000 cases a year, although the Defords are planting additional acreage.

Philip and Jocelyn Wagner held onto their nursery business and continue to send vines to growers all over the United States. They remain at their original location in Riderwood, Maryland.
☆/☆☆☆
$/$$

Bordeaux.

This is without question the most important viticultural area of France, and therefore of the world. It produces both red and white wines of extraordinary finesse and quality in huge volumes that are carried by every means of transportation to every corner of the earth. This has been the case for eight centuries—ever since King Henry II of England married Eleanor of Aquitaine in 1152 and received Gascony, or Guyenne, and Bordeaux as her dowry. With Britannia ruling the waves and carrying the wines from the Bordeaux seaport to all points in the British Empire, their fame spread far and wide, and deservedly so. The soil, the weather, and the general lay of the land in the Department of the Gironde spreading out mostly eastward from the seaport itself are ideal for cultivating vines. The soil is often coarse and rocky, laced with sand, gravel, and pebbles that are inhospitable to any other agricultural product. But they provide the perfect growing medium for the Cabernet, Merlot, Malbec, Sauvignon, and Sémillon grapes used to make the celebrated Bordeaux wines.

Actually, the term "Bordeaux" is extremely broad, covering just about any wine produced on nearly half a million vineyard acres in the region. But the area has many subdivisions, each with its own historic ties dating back to the Roman occupation that began in approximately 56 B.C. Many of the wine names that exist there now are versions of names the Romans used, and one can almost sense the taste of history in the red wines from the magnificent Bordeaux châteaux and estates that are now famous the world over. Some excellent white wines are made here too, but the reds are the ones most sought by connoisseurs. The production is so large— around 74 million gallons in 1970, a banner year—that the supply is usually adequate to fill the huge demand without pushing prices beyond the reach of the average wine-drinker. Although the prices for some of the more renowned Bordeaux can be extremely high, excellent wines from many less celebrated vineyards can usually be found at affordable levels. This situation is unique among the great wine-producing areas of the world. The total production of Burgundy, for example, is less than half that of Bordeaux, and it amounts to only about one-quarter if Beaujolais is subtracted. The best red Burgundies, in the view of a few wine-lovers, are superior to the best red Bordeaux, yet they are produced in only minute quantities, are very costly and are hard to find even if one can pay the price.

An understanding of the geography of Bordeaux is basic to the understanding of its great wines. The city of Bordeaux, with a population of about 270,000, lies in a crescent shape on the western bank of the Garonne River as it twists northward toward its union with the Dordogne River a few miles downstream to form the huge Gironde estuary that flows eventually into the Atlantic Ocean in southwestern France. Because of its shape, the city is known as *le port de la lune,* or the port of the moon. It provides worldwide access to the wines of the region—a fact which stimulated increasing production over the centuries. In common with nearly all of the other great viticultural areas of the world, the best vineyards of Bordeaux lie on or near the region's rivers, where alluvial deposits have been building up since the Ice Age.

The city of Bordeaux lies in the District of Graves, the oldest commercial wine area. The short distance from vineyards to piers made Graves important in the early days, before the growing areas farther afield came into their own. Graves lies along a 30-mile stretch of the Garonne River as it flows up from the southeast of France northwest toward the Atlantic. In a much smaller area surrounded by Graves, but also on the Garonne, lie Sauternes and Barsac, where the world's most luscious dessert wines are produced. The best Graves wines, both red and white, are produced south of Bordeaux, although the district extends a few miles north of the seaport to a river called the Jalle de Blanquefort, where the Médoc begins. (*See* Graves, Sauternes.)

The Médoc, consisting of the Haut-Médoc near the city and the Bas-Médoc farther north near the Atlantic estuary, lies mostly along the west bank of the Gironde in a band about 40 miles long and rarely more than ten miles wide. The Haut-Médoc portion has eclipsed Graves in both production and fame. It is here that most of the most famous Bordeaux vineyards lie today—Lafite, Margaux, Mouton Rothschild, and Latour—the most expensive wines in the world. The area was classified in 1855, and these classified growths, or *crus,* set the standards for elegant dry red wines everywhere. Besides the 62 classified growths, there are dozens of other vineyards here that produce excellent wines. Because they are not famous, their wines are much less costly. In the mid-1980s it was still possible to find excellent red Médocs for less than five dollars a bottle in the United States. (*See* Médoc.)

Directly across the Gironde from the Médoc are two lesser areas, Blayais and Bourgais, where large quantities of good, but not great, red and white wines are produced. Farther south, across the Garonne from Graves are Entre-Deux-Mers and its various subdivisions, where some good and many ordinary wines are made. (*See* Blaye, Bourg, Entre-Deux-Mers *and subdivisions*.)

About 20 miles due east of the city of Bordeaux is Libourne, another town very dependent on the wine trade. The Dordogne River passes under a bridge in Libourne and then winds circuitously northwest to its confluence with the Garonne at the spot known as the Bec d'Ambès. But the important vineyard areas are upstream, just beyond Libourne, in the hills and on the plateau above the river. Here are the great Saint-Emilion and Pomerol, whose wines are currently not as celebrated as those of the Médoc. But they are superb in their own right, with a slightly softer style and greater charm. The individual vineyard parcels are smaller here, and the people are closer to the land. They work the soil themselves, rarely leaving it to local managers as do some of the absentee landlords of the Médoc. Whereas the Cabernet Sauvignon is the dominant grape variety in the Médoc, the Merlot is much more important here, creating wines of richness and strength whose alcoholic content sometimes runs one or two points higher than elsewhere in Bordeaux. Yet these delicious reds (no whites are made here) tend to mature at an earlier age. Some are at their best in less than a decade, although the wines of the greatest châteaus of Saint-Emilion and Pomerol need at least 15 years and often 20 before they reach their summits of perfection. Several satellite areas around Saint-Emilion and Pomerol also produce decent wines, although generally they do not reach the same quality levels as those of the two major *communes*. (*See* Saint-Emilion, Pomerol.)

The methods of vinification in Bordeaux have evolved over the years in response to the public taste and the public pocketbook. Until the 1960s it was customary to make big and coarse wines that required many years of slow aging in cellars to reach proper maturity. It was unthinkable to drink a claret, as the British refer to red Bordeaux, that was less than 15 years old. Every good family laid in quantities of claret in their youth and waited patiently for them to mature, meanwhile drinking the wines that had been laid down decades earlier, perhaps by fathers or uncles. Gradually, however, the prices of Bordeaux wines began responding to demand from parts of the globe other than Britain. At the same time, heavy taxation and the socialist policies of the British Government wiped out much of the wealth that had enabled the British upper class to indulge in their taste for fine wines.

Meanwhile, the Americans had begun to develop a taste for wine and, true to their form, they rushed to make up for lost time, and suddenly the United States was competing to become the largest export market for Bordeaux. But the Americans did not have wine cellars in their houses and were impatient to drink good clarets, so they began consuming them within four or five years of the vintage. The Japanese, responding like the Americans to an unparalleled economic boom, also rushed into the Bordeaux market, buying whatever they could find. What they were able to get, often, were wines from off-vintages, and it is said in Bordeaux that more of the 1965 and 1968 went to Japan than any other country. Under this intense buying pressure, Bordeaux prices soared to unreasonable levels, prompting speculation by hoarders anticipating even higher prices. It was like the tulip craze that had swept Holland many years earlier.

Amid these extremely unsettled conditions, the Bordelais began making their wines differently, so that they were ready to drink at a much younger age. This, they hoped, would satisfy the great thirst for mature wines at the same time that it discouraged hoarding, for the wines that ripen in their youth are not likely to be as long-lived as those that take decades to become drinkable. In the vinification process, the pips and skins of the grapes are now often filtered out of the fermenting grape juice after a maximum of three weeks, instead of six weeks, and often the pips are no longer crushed. As a result, the tannin that gives a red wine its bigness, its harshness in youth, is less evident, and the wines tend to be softer and more supple at a young age.

Debate exists over whether the "new vinification" has resulted in inferior wines. Certainly the wines are now much more charming and enjoyable within a decade of production, and therefore the need to wait many years for them to mature has, in most cases, been eliminated. A few châteaus, for example Pétrus in Pomerol, still practice the old vinification for those who prefer such wines, but most seem to have shifted to the new. It seems likely that the new method will result in wines that lack the staying power of their forebears, but only time will tell if this is the case.

The first vintage in Bordeaux bearing the characteristics of the new vinification was the 1967, which was fairly light and reached its peak in most cases within six or eight years. The 1968 was a disaster, regardless of vinification, but the 1969, better but not great, again was light, thin and early-maturing. The 1970 and '71, widely accepted as excellent vintages, were soft and mellow even before they left the casks. A tasting of the first-growth '70s in London in 1975 provided ample evidence of early maturity and great charm after only five years. The 1972, closer in style to the 1969, was equally soft after only three years, and the '73 showed similar characteristics. Meanwhile, the 1966 Bordeaux reds seemed far away from adulthood after a decade of aging, and the 1961s displayed the high tannin content and heavy thickness of a young wine after 20 years. So 1967 seemed to be the turning-point vintage, but perhaps another decade will be needed to discover how gracefully these wines will age. It would be a pity indeed if the great 1970 clarets were consumed in the charming first decade of their lives— and then were found to have ripened into even finer wines in their second and third decades. In any event, buying clarets in their youth and waiting whatever time is appropriate for them to mature tends to be less costly than acquiring them in their adulthood. And storing red Bordeaux wines is the *raison d'être* of most of the world's wine cellars.

Château Boswell.

Richard Thornton Boswell established Château Boswell in 1979 and retained wine consultant André Tchelistcheff to oversee his initial production of Chardonnay and Cabernet Sauvignon. The property is in St. Helena, in the heart of California's Napa Valley, and the winery is a French-style château with slate roof and rock walls. Production of 8000 cases a year was planned.
☆☆/☆☆☆
$$

Botrytis cinerea.

The beneficial mold that afflicts very ripe grapes and imparts special qualities to them in German vineyards, in Sauternes and other parts of France, and sometimes in other countries, is known by the Latin term *Botrytis cinerea*. In France it is called *pourriture noble*, or the noble rot, and in Germany it is *Edelfäule*. (*See also* noble rot, Sauternes, Germany, Château d'Yquem.)

Botticino.

Botticino is a tannic, sometimes coarse red from the vineyards near the town of Botticino east of Milan in northern Italy. It is made mostly from Barbera and Schiava grapes and has a D.O.C. rating under the Italian wine law. After eight to ten years of aging, its harshness subsides and the wine becomes almost mellow.

☆☆☆☆

$/$$

Bottle Sizes.

The standard French wine bottle is the so-called American "fifth"—one-fifth of a gallon or four-fifths of a quart. It now contains 750 milliliters, and larger bottles usually contain multiples of this size.

The traditional terms for many French bottles and those from a few other countries patterned after the French are colorful and difficult to remember, because they come from Biblical kings. Nebuchadnezzar, for example, was not only the name of a king of Babylonia, but today stands for an enormous wine bottle with 20 times the capacity of a standard bottle. Here are the standard terms for Bordeaux bottles:

single bottle		25.4 ounces or 750 milliliters
magnum	two single bottles	50.7 ounces or 1.5 liters
Marie-Jeanne (rare)	about three single bottles	84.5 ounces or 2.5 liters
double magnum	four single bottles	101.4 ounces or 3 liters
Jeroboam	six single bottles	152.4 ounces or 4.5 liters
imperial	eight single bottles	203 ounces or 6 liters

Here are the standard terms for Champagne bottles:

single bottle		25.4 ounces or 750 milliliters
magnum	two single bottles	50.7 ounces or 1.5 liters
Jeroboam	four single bottles	101.4 ounces or 3 liters
Rehoboam	six single bottles	152.4 ounces or 4.5 liters
Methuselah	eight single bottles	203 ounces or 6 liters
Salmanazar	12 single bottles	305 ounces or 9 liters
Balthazar	16 single bottles	406 ounces or 12 liters
Nebuchadnezzar	20 single bottles	508 ounces or 15 liters

Château Bouchaine.

Château Bouchaine was established in Napa, California, in 1980 by David Pollak, Jr., who took over an existing winery that had been owned by Beringer Bros. since the 1950s. Prior to Pollak's takeover, the winery had been used to produce for other labels, but Pollak made known his intention to compete with his own label in the premium wine sweepstakes when he hired Jerry Luper away from Château Montelena in March of 1982 to become a partner and general manager of Bouchaine. Luper had achieved acclaim for making excellent Cabernet Sauvignons and Chardonnays at Montelena and at Freemark Abbey previously. Luper planned to focus on Pinot Noirs and Chardonnays at Bouchaine, which is located in the Carneros District of the Napa Valley, where the climate is considered most conducive to making Burgundy-style wines. Bouchaine Vineyards, the parent company for the Chateau Bouchaine label, planned to produce 20,000 to 25,000 cases by the 1984 crush and did not plan to release any wines at all prior to 1984. The winery is surrounded by 30 acres of Chardonnay, and the proprietors own additional acreage in Sonoma County. Wines of great character and finesse were expected from Bouchaine because of Luper's involvement.

Bourg, Bourgeais, Côtes de Bourg.

Just northwest of the city of Libourne and not far from Pomerol and Saint-Emilion in the Bordeaux country in southwestern France is a wine-growing area that takes its name from its principal town, Bourg-sur-Gironde. Actually, it is no longer on the Gironde estuary, but overlooks the Dordogne River, which has extended itself over the centuries through deposits of soil washed down from upstream. Some white wines are produced here, but the best are the reds, made from the Cabernet, Merlot, and Malbec grapes that produce the great wines of the Médoc a few miles to the west. The reds are full-bodied and fairly robust, but they sometimes taste sweetish and rarely aspire to greatness. They are entitled to the *appellations* Bourg,

Bourgeais, and Côtes de Bourg, but often are bottled simply as Bordeaux Rouge.

☆/☆☆☆

$/$$

Bourgogne Aligoté.

Some wines entitled to the generic name Burgundy in France have no geographic requirements on their origins, other than that they must be made from grapes grown somewhere in the Burgundy country. These are equivalent to the *vins ordinaires* of this part of France, and one of them is Bourgogne Aligoté, a white wine made from the Aligoté grape. It need be only 9.5 percent alcohol. Aligoté is always a modest wine without great character.

☆

$

Bourgogne Passe-Tous-Grains.

In the category of *vin ordinaire* in the French Burgundy country is Bourgogne Passe-Tous-Grains, which is a red-wine mixture made at least one-third from the Pinot Noir grape and the rest from the Gamay. It need reach an alcoholic level of only 9.5 percent, and is rarely seen in the export markets because it does not travel well. It can be fresh and pleasant on a summer afternoon in the Burgundy country, but it is not a wine to be taken seriously.

☆

$

Bourgueil.

The Loire Valley of France is noted mostly for its white wines, but a few good reds are produced there and Bourgueil is one of them. It is made from the Cabernet Franc grape in the Touraine portion of the Loire, around the village of Bourgueil. These wines have great charm rather than depth and should be drunk within three or four years of the vintage. Like Beaujolais, they are best served slightly chilled. Some of the better Bourgueils are called Saint-Nicolas-de-Bourgueil. (*See* Loire Valley, Touraine.)

☆☆/☆☆☆

$/$$

Château Bouscaut.

One of the loveliest mansions in all of Bordeaux is Château Bouscaut, where some of the best red and white wines of the Graves District are produced. The wines were classified in the Graves rankings of 1959 and are now among the superior wines of the Bordeaux District. Between 1968 and 1979, the château and surrounding 100 acres of vineyards were American-owned, and a great deal of American money was expended in upgrading the vineyards and restoring the château. The syndicate that purchased Bouscaut was headed by Charles Wohlstetter, a Wall Streeter who also is chairman of Continental Telephone Co. in Chicago, and Howard Sloan, an insurance man. They and another owner, Allan Meltzer, a public relations man now semiretired in Florida, promoted Bouscaut wines heavily, and bottles can be found on many of the best lists and in the better retail establishments around the United States.

Their efforts to improve the Château Bouscaut wines, especially the reds, involved additional plantings of Cabernet Sauvignon grapes and a higher concentration of these grapes in the end product. Thus, in recent vintages, Bouscaut red has become a bigger wine, with greater intensity and depth of character. Yet it retains the traditional dryness and full body of a classic Graves red, reflecting the gravelly soil that is the namesake of this area directly south of the city of Bordeaux. The Bouscaut whites are also well made wines and are equally characteristic of Graves.

At the end of 1979 the American group sold out to Lucien Lurton, also the proprietor of Château Brane-Cantenac and Château Durfort-Vivens in Margaux, thereby returning the property to French ownership. Lurton is a leading Bordeaux winemaker who can be expected to continue Bouscaut's upgrading.

The château itself, in Cadaujac just off one of the main roads leading south from Bordeaux, was constructed initially in 1710 and was then named Château Haut-Truchon. It became Château Bouscaut in 1847, when its round tower soared skyward. Much of the interior has been rebuilt since 1962, when a fire did substantial damage. There are six master bedroom suites, with high ceilings and sculpted plasterwork, a wood-paneled library and a ballroom whose dimensions are 32 by 65 feet where entertaining on a grand scale has occurred over the years.

When the American group acquired the vineyards and château for $1.35 million, they paid another $400,000 for an inventory of some 350,000 old bottles dating back as far as 1918, with substantial quantities of the 1949, 1953, and 1959. These show up on wine lists and in stores occasionally nowadays and are interesting curiosities, but it should be remembered that they were produced by former owners whose methods were different. To what extent any of these bottles suffered in the fire of 1962 is not known, but the fact is that not until the excellent 1970 vintage was the Wohlstetter-Sloan group fully in control of production. Subsequent vintages have been better and better, as the new Cabernet Sauvignon grapes have come to maturity and replaced some of the Merlot and Cabernet Franc that once dominated the mix.

☆/☆☆☆☆

$$

Château Boyd-Cantenac.

The production of this château, which is entitled to the Margaux *appellation,* is modest and not widely distributed. The estate was classified a *troisième cru,* or third growth, in the Bordeaux classification of 1855, but it has been undistinguished for a number of years. Boyd-Cantenac should not be confused with Château Brane-Cantenac, a Margaux of surpassing quality.
☆☆☆☆
$$

Brachetto d'Acqui.

Brachetto is the grape variety, and the town is Acqui, in Italy's Piedmont region. When Brachetto grapes are cultivated in the vineyards of Acqui, they produce red wines of fairly high quality that merit D.O.C. status under the Italian wine law. Brachetto is vinified both dry and sweet and in a spumante version.
☆/☆☆
$

Bramaterra.

Not well known outside Italy but an excellent red wine, Bramaterra is produced in the hilly vineyards near Novara in the Piedmont region that is also responsible for many other extraordinary red wines. Bramaterra is made mostly from Nebbiolo grapes, with portions of Bonarda, Croatina, and Vespolina blended in. The wine is robust and tannic in its youth but achieves suppleness with age.
☆☆☆/☆☆☆☆
$/$$

Château Branaire-Ducru.

Ranked a *quatrième cru,* or fourth growth, in the Bordeaux classification of 1855. Château Branaire-Ducru passed through the Du Luc and Ducru families in the nineteenth century. Until fairly recently, the labels carried both the Du Luc and Ducru names in one form or another, although neither family has been involved with the estate for many years. The name seems to be evolving toward, simply, Château Branaire, as it is generally known. The vineyards lie in the *commune* of Saint-Julien, but Château Branaire-Ducru seems to produce softer wines more characteristic of Margaux in some vintages. After passing through a mediocre phase in the post–World War II era, the estate has been improving.
☆☆☆☆
$$/$$$

Brander Vineyard.

Founded in 1975 by Fred Brander, Brander Vineyard has built a reputation for producing good Sauvignon Blancs at its property near Los Olivos in Santa Barbara County, California. Production so far has amounted to only about 3000 cases a year, including a small amount of Cabernet Sauvignon. Fred Brander is also the winemaker at the Santa Ynez Valley Winery.
☆☆/☆☆☆☆
$$

Château Brane-Cantenac.

The Baron de Brane, a renowned figure in Bordeaux wines in the early 1820s, gave his name to this château and made it the greatest in the *commune* of Cantenac at that time. The good baron also owned Château Mouton Rothschild, which then was named Brane-Mouton, but he sold Mouton to devote all of his energies to the estate then regarded as the better of the two. The property is now owned by Lucien Lurton, also the owner of Château Bouscaut and of Château Durfort-Vivens, but it is no longer in the same exalted category as Mouton. Brane-Cantenac was ranked a *second cru,* or second growth, in the Bordeaux classification of 1855, but Mouton has since moved up from second- to first-growth status (in 1973). The wines of Brane-Cantenac display great elegance and finesse, but they are less full-bodied than some other Margaux and sometimes do not live up to their reputation. Although the property technically is in the village of Cantenac, the wines are entitled to the Margaux *appellation*.

☆☆☆☆
$$/$$$

Brandy.

Distilled wine is brandy, although the meaning of the term has expanded over the years to include virtually all distillates of fermented fruit. Thus there is pear brandy, apple brandy, etc. The king of all brandies is Cognac, from the vineyards near the village of the same name in the Charente River District of western France north of Bordeaux. The grapes cultivated there make mediocre wine, but when the wine is distilled it produces an exquisite alcohol that retains the bouquet and aftertaste of the fruit, along with the strength of a typical distilled spirit—usually at least 80 proof, or 40 percent alcohol.

Challenging Cognac on the quality scale is Armagnac, from the part of France directly south of Bordeaux. Armagnac is neither better nor worse; it simply has a different style that many connoisseurs prefer. The other great brandy of France is in a class of its own: Calvados, which technically is not a brandy because it is not made from fermented grape juice but from fermented apple juice. It comes from Normandy, where wine production is minimal. Calvados can be an extraordinarily fine *digestif* after a meal, and it has its followers who suggest that it is far superior to Cognac or Armagnac.

Brandies are produced in almost every country that produces wine, for there is always a use for a local alcohol. In some countries, notably Spain, brandy production is big business, involving many foreign markets and enormous production. The Fundador brandy of Pedro Domecq, for example, could well be the largest-selling distillate in Europe, even if its designation as *coñac* is somewhat misleading. It is not a Cognac; it is a very good Spanish brandy that need not try to pass itself off as something else. The Carlos Primero brandy of Domecq, moreover, ranks among the better brandies of the world.

There are many other brandies that are not widely known but that have developed followings among people who have been fortunate enough to taste them. Among these are the *marcs* of France. The one produced in greatest volume is Marc de Bourgogne, which many Burgundy producers make. Sometimes it is given the designation of a specific vineyard, although just plain Marc de Bourgogne, consumed late at night by the Chevaliers du Tastevin at Clos de Vougeot, can be a memorable experience. It tends to be rather coarse and harsh when first tasted, but it is likely to improve with the hour.

Marc de Champagne is made in Epernay and Reims, and this is a more elegant alcohol. It displays a bouquet reminiscent of Champagne and a slightly fruity taste that is soon dissipated by the alcoholic aftertaste. It is made from the same leftovers as Marc de Bourgogne: the residue composed of split seeds, stems, and skins of the grapes that remains long after the last of the fresh juice has been squeezed out. It is a curiosity that, but for its rarity, could never compete with a good Cognac or Armagnac. The Italian and South American versions of the same product are known as *grappa*—and this, too, is a fiery brandy that is capable of putting the human system on alert following a siege at the dining table.

There are many designations that attempt to imply quality in brandies, e.g., the V.S.O.P. so often applied to Cognacs. It means Very Special or Superior Old Pale—which implies very little about the quality of the product. In foreign markets, brand names have become far more important than initials like V.S.O.P. or "Three-Star" or whatever. The best guide to Cognacs is through brands: e.g., Hennessy, Courvoisier, Martell, Remy Martin, Hine, Bisquit, Otard, Delamain. Some excellent California brandies are also produced, and the X.O. of Christian Brothers has begun to develop a national reputation.

Brauneberger.

One of the fullest, most assertive German white wines is from the wine town of Brauneberg, meaning "brown hill," in the better part of the Mosel River region near the famous Bernkastel. Braunebergers are big and rich, sometimes—in the best vintages—resembling the full-bodied wines of the Rhine. Braunebergers are overshadowed in popularity these days by the Bernkastelers, Wehleners, and Piesporters of the Mosel Valley, partly because the production is relatively small, but their quality is easily on a par with the others. Of all the Mosels, the Braunebergers of Auslese and sweeter categories serve best for laying down, although many connoisseurs prefer to drink them when they are young, fresh and flowery. The picturesque village is across the river from its vineyards, so that none of the southern-exposed hillside need be used for any purpose other than growing grapes.

Among the better-known vineyards at Brauneberg are the following:

Brauneberger Burgerslay
Brauneberger Falkenberg
Brauneberger Hasenläufer*
Brauneberger Juffer*
Brauneberger Kammer*
Brauneberger Lay

Brauneberger Nonnenlay
Brauneberger Sonnenuhr

An asterisk indicates a vineyard name that survived the revision of the German wine law in 1971. The law also made provisions for these other Brauneberg vineyard names: Juffer-Sonnenuhr, Klostergarten, and Mandelgraben.

☆☆☆

$/$$

Breganze.

An array of varietal wines that are recognized under the Italian D.O.C. law are produced in the vineyards around Breganze in the Veneto region in the northeastern part of the country. The reds, including Cabernet, Pinot Nero, and a Rosso that is mostly Merlot, generally mature fairly early. The Pinot Bianco, made from roughly equal amounts of Pinot Bianco and Pinot Grigio grapes, is the best white of the Breganze denomination.

☆/☆☆

$

Bridgehampton Winery.

The second winery constructed on Long Island, east of New York City, was Bridgehampton, built in 1983 in the town of the same name (Hargrave was the first). A 1982 Chardonnay and a 1982 Riesling were made under the Bridgehampton label by Hermann Wiemer, a noted Finger Lakes grower. The early efforts were promising.

☆

$$

Brindisi.

Brindisi is a seacoast city in the southern Italian region of Puglia and it is also the name of the wines produced there. A Rosato and a Rosso have merited recognition under the D.O.C. law, but the wines are not well known outside the region of production.

☆/☆☆

$

Brix.

Brix is the measurement of the sugar level in grape juice by weight. Growers measure the Brix in their grapes daily as the moment of harvest approaches, trying to achieve the maximum ripeness as indicated by a high natural level of sugar. These levels vary in different parts of the world because of different growing conditions, but generally Chardonnays harvested at 23° Brix are considered optimum, whereas dry Rieslings may be harvested as low as 17 Brix and sweet Rieslings may come in at more than 40 Brix in certain rare vintages. The German measurement of sugar by weight is known as Oechsle. Brix can be translated into Oechsle by multiplying the Brix level by four and adding four. Thus 23° Brix would be equal to 96° on the Oechsle scale. The Brix level at harvest normally is convertible into alcohol at a rate of 55 percent. This means grapes picked at 23° Brix theoretically should yield roughly 12.6 percent alcohol.

Brolio Chianti.

Much of the history of Tuscany, the home of Chianti wines in Italy, is wrapped up with Castle Brolio, which was acquired by the Ricasoli family in 1141. Baron Bettino Ricasoli pioneered in Chianti viticulture in the mid-1800s and is credited with having tried to establish the first Chianti Classico Consorzio, or consortium, in 1835. In 20 years of research at Castle Brolio, he demonstrated that the best wines from the area were made up of 70 percent Sangiovese, 15 percent Canaiolo and 15 percent Malvasia grapes—a ratio that is roughly maintained to this day under the Italian wine law governing Chianti

Classico. According to legend, the Baron decided to spend much of his life at Brolio after his bride of only a few months was courted by a suitor at a ball in Florence, prompting Ricasoli to have her taken immediately by coach to the castle in the Tuscan hills. Ricasoli was also a prominent statesman and served as Prime Minister of Italy after Cavour. Ironically, his heirs decided to drop out of the Chianti Classico Consorzio that most other Classico producers support, so Brolio bottles do not have the red seal with the black rooster on their necks. Nevertheless, this is one of the very best Chiantis, displaying great charm and character. The Brolio Riserva is one of the top Classicos that is widely distributed in foreign markets. It requires about a decade of aging to reach its peak. (*See also* Chianti.)

☆☆☆/☆☆☆☆

$$

Bronco Winery.

The Bronco Wine Company, with wineries in Ceres near Modesto and in Fresno, is a major California Central Valley producer that bottles under the JFJ and CC Vineyards labels—close to two million cases in all. These are basically jug wines made from purchased grapes and purchased wines. Bronco owns no vineyards of its own and relies entirely on outside growers. Total plant capacity is enormous—37 million gallons, and the excess beyond what is bottled under the Bronco brand names is sold off to other major producers. The operation was established in 1973 by Fred T. Franzia and Joseph S. Franzia, who are brothers, and their cousin John G. Franzia, Jr. These are the sons of the Franzia brothers who sold out their own Franzia Brothers business to the Coca-Cola Bottling Company of New York (not corporately related to the Coca-Cola Company of Atlanta). The sons wanted to stay in the wine busi-

ness, and that was the genesis of Bronco. The wines are in the inexpensive generic category—chablis, pink chablis, ruby rosé, burgundy, and rhine. Some wines are also produced under private labels for sale through chain stores in California. JFJ is the major brand under the Bronco aegis, and CC Vineyards is the secondary brand. Approximately three times as much wine is produced that never sees a Bronco label, which makes the enterprise one of the larger suppliers to other wineries in California.
☆
$

Brookside Cellars.

Brookside Cellars, based in San Bernardino County, produces fairly ordinary, low-priced wines under the Brookside, Vache, and Assumption Abbey labels in fairly large quantities, although distribution is limited mainly to California and nearby states. The operation is owned by the Brookside Vineyard Company in Guasti, with cellars in Etiwanda, Ontario, and Sacramento. The product line is broad, including generic table wines, Champagnes, and brandies.
☆
$

Brotherhood Winery.

Brotherhood Winery of Washingtonville, New York, in the Hudson River Valley, was started in 1839 and characterizes itself as the oldest active winery in America. Jean Jaques, a Frenchman, planted the first grapes and made sacramental wines for the Presbyterian church, of which he was an elder. He also made wines for friends and relatives, many of whom used them medicinally. The present owners of Brotherhood produce about 40,000 cases of 20 different wines annually, including fortified and sparkling wines. Brotherhood owns no vineyards of its own, but buys grapes from various vineyards in other parts of the state. The wines are blended from both hybrids and native Labrusca varieties and bear names such as Sauterne, Rosario, Rubicon, chablis, burgundy, and Rhineling. Aurora, a French-American hybrid, is the only varietal wine. Brotherhood welcomes visitors, and summer weekends bring crowds of them. Free tastings are offered to those who take the winery tour.
☆
$

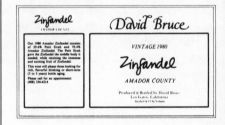

David Bruce.

This small vineyard, perched on a hilltop above Los Gatos in Santa Clara County, California, produces a very small quantity of fine varietal wines, including Chardonnay, Gewürztraminer, Zinfandel, Cabernet Sauvignon, Pinot Noir, and Petite Sirah. Wine buffs who favor big, intense wines seek them out knowing that owner and winemaker David Bruce, a physician from nearby San Jose, is dedicated to making wines of potent style and character. The Chardonnay in particular is noted for depth and complexity, always heavily oaked, and perhaps overly so for some palates. With proper balance of fruit and acidity, however, it is a magnificent wine, as luscious as the best Meursault. Zinfandel is another of Bruce's special pets and exhibits the loving care he gives it. One year, with a surplus of Zinfandel grapes on hand, he pressed them separately from the skins, resulting in an attractive, almost white wine. He also makes a Zinfandel Rosé. All the wines from David Bruce are powerful and full-bodied, some quite forcefully so, such as the Petite Sirah.

In more recent vintages, Dr. Bruce appears to have tried to produce more supple wines ready for drinking at a younger age. The tannin levels in some bottlings have appeared lower, and the robustness that was always a hallmark of the Bruce wines is not always the dominant characteristic. This moderating trend is in line with the philosophy of many California producers.
☆/☆☆☆☆
$$

Brunello di Montalcino.

One of the greatest red wines produced anywhere is the Brunello di Montalcino that comes from the Tuscan province of Siena in the Chianti region of north-central Italy. It is unusual among Italian wines in that it is not a blend, but is made entirely from the Brunello grape, which is a variety of the Sangiovese that dominates Chianti wines. Brunello is always aged at least four years in wooden casks and usually spends five to six years in wood before bottling. When aged more than five years in wood, it can be called *riserva*. This is an extraordinarily robust and tannic wine that exudes a bouquet of black currants and violets when it approaches maturity after a minimum of twenty years. Most Brunello requires far more aging than any well-known French wine and at maturity displays great depth and intensity.

In more recent vintages, some Brunello producers have been making softer wines, but the best Brunellos usually are very tannic and robust in their youth. Brunello achieved the distinction in 1981 of becoming the first Italian wine to win the *garantita* designation, meaning that its quality was guaranteed by the producers and the government. This was an outgrowth of the so-called D.O.C.

laws, or *denominazione di origine controllata e garantita* system of regulations enacted in 1963. Barolo and other reds followed Brunello, but the fact that Brunello was first with the designation attested to its preeminence among Italian reds. The leading Brunello producers include Biondi-Santi, whose vineyards yielded the original Brunellos more than a century ago, as well as Fattoria dei Barbi and Emilio Costanti, who also follow traditional production methods. Their wines are expensive and not easy to find, but they are worth looking for.
☆☆☆/☆☆☆☆☆
$$/$$$

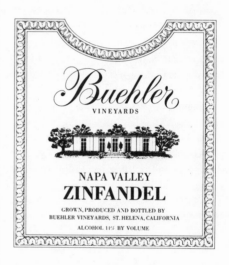

Buehler
VINEYARDS

NAPA VALLEY
ZINFANDEL
GROWN, PRODUCED AND BOTTLED BY
BUEHLER VINEYARDS, ST. HELENA, CALIFORNIA
ALCOHOL 11% BY VOLUME

Buehler Vineyards.

Deeply colored, richly flavored Cabernet Sauvignons and Zinfandels bearing the label of Buehler Vineyards began attracting national attention in the late 1970s and early 1980s, when they first reached the market. They were the products of John P. Buehler, Sr., the winemaker at Buehler, near the Napa Valley village of St. Helena in California, and head of a family corporation that owns the winery and vineyards nearby. The winery actually is six miles up into the hills east of St. Helena, and its first commercial harvest was in 1978. The land had been purchased in 1972 and planted in 1973. Now 60 acres in all are in vines and all Buehler wines are estate-bottled. Production grew to 8000 cases by 1981 and was headed toward 12,000 within a few years, a very small quantity in view of the rapidly growing reputation of the Buehler wines.

The financing for the Buehler operation came largely from the father of John Buehler, Sr., who had been with the Bechtel Corporation in San Francisco, one of the world's largest independent construction companies. There are now four shareholders: John P. Buehler, Sr., his wife Lisa, and his father and mother. Besides Cabernet Sauvignon and Zinfandel, there is a Muscat Blanc with about 1.5 percent residual sugar, or slightly sweet, and a Pinot Blanc that is vinified bone dry. Initially Buehler sold its excess production of Cabernet and Zinfandel to Burgess Cellars and its excess Muscat to Château St. Jean, two other outstanding wineries with fine national reputations. Their use of Buehler as an outside source of grapes was recognition of its accomplishments at an early stage.

☆/☆☆☆☆

$$

Buena Vista Winery.

Buena Vista Winery, an important producer in California's Sonoma Valley, claims a direct link with the origins of the California wine industry in the mid-nineteenth century. It was established, apparently, by Count Agoston Haraszthy of Hungary, who named it Buena Vista, Spanish for "beautiful view." He is said to have bottled his first vintage there in 1857. Later it was Count Haraszthy who traveled through Europe collecting vine cuttings, some 100,000 in all of the choicest varieties, including Cabernet Sauvignon, Pinot Noir, Chardonnay, and Gewürztraminer, and brought them back to California, not just for his operation at Buena Vista but for all of the winegrowers in the state. This was the beginning of California's development as one of the world's most important sources of premium wines, although more than a century was required before the state's wines began to measure up to their European counterparts on a quality basis.

Count Haraszthy's original stone winery buildings still stand at Buena Vista, although the operation has been vastly expanded and modernized. In 1979 A. Racke, a German company, acquired Buena Vista from Young's Market Company. Racke is a major European producer, exporter and importer of wine and spirits, with headquarters in Bingen, West Germany. Buena Vista maintains more than 650 acres of vineyards in Sonoma County and produces a broad line of premium varietals, including Chardonnay, Sauvignon Blanc, Cabernet Sauvignon, Zinfandel, Pinot Noir, Gamay Beaujolais, Cabernet Rosé, Sherry, and Port. Its best reds are bottled under the so-called "Cask" label, with the number of the individual aging cask appearing on the label. Its best whites are bottled under the "Cabinet" label, the term derived from the ancient German practice of reserving the best wines of each vintage in a cabinet for the proprietor.

The total Buena Vista line is broad, with more than 20 different bottlings available at any one time, reflecting the different cask and cabinet designations as well as different vintages and different sources of grapes. In a newly constructed facility in the southeastern part of the Sonoma Valley, total output of Buena Vista wines has been moving toward 200,000 cases a year, the new winery's capacity. The Buena Vista wines sometimes lack the complexity and flavor intensity of some of their competitors, although the Cask and Cabinet selections are a cut above the norm.

☆/☆☆☆

$$

Bulgaria.

Because of the political turmoil in Eastern Europe following World War II, the Bulgarian wine industry fell into disrepair and production dropped sharply. Since the early 1950s, however, the industry has been rebuilt almost from scratch, and the viniculture of Bulgaria is perhaps the most modern behind the Iron Curtain. The bulk of her wines are exported to other Communist countries and to Germany, Bulgaria's whites include Reatzitelli, Karlovo, Sangoularé, Dimiat, and Levskigrad. Some of the wines are named after geographical areas of production, others after grape varieties. The reds include Mavrud, Melnik, Pamid, and Gamza.

Most of Bulgaria's vineyards are owned by the government or by cooperatives, and all production and marketing are supervised by the government institute known as Vinprom. Many American consumers became acquainted with Bulgarian wines in the 1970s and '80s through Trakia, a brand imported by Monsieur Henri Wines Ltd. The Trakia Cabernet Sauvignon, Merlot, and Chardonnay were excellent values at around $3 per bottle. Another Trakia bottling, called Blanc de Blancs, is made from the Misket grape. The word Trakia means "Thracian," for Thrace was the ancient name for that area of eastern Europe.

Bully Hill Vineyards.

Bully Hill Vineyards is situated at Hammondsport, New York, about 1000 feet above Lake Keuka in the Finger Lakes region. In 1970 Walter Taylor, Jr., grandson of the founder of Taylor Wine Company, departed from Taylor and began making his own wine at Bully Hill, a vineyard he and his father had bought some years earlier for experimentation with French-American hybrids. Taylor is a controversial figure among winemakers in the East and has alienated himself from other producers through his outspoken criticism of their production methods—such as the use of wine from California to blend with their own and the use of water and various chemicals to make it more palatable. Nevertheless his vociferous position has brought him, and New York State wines, a good deal of publicity and attention. Perhaps he comes by his flair for showmanship naturally; an ancestor was first cousin to Phineas Taylor Barnum. More important are the wines produced at Bully Hill, which many experts have agreed are sound, well made and bear watching.

All of Bully Hill's vintage-dated wines are from French-American hybrids and include Chancellor Noir, Baco Noir, Chelois Noir (all reds) and Seyval Blanc and Aurora Blanc. The blended wines, Bully Hill Red, White, and Rosé, also carry vintage dates, a fairly unusual practice in New York State. Bully Hill Red, a blend of six red grape hybrids, is the most popular. Bully Hill White is slightly sweet, light-bodied, and pleasant. The vineyard now makes a dry sparkling wine out of Seyval Blanc using the traditional Champagne method.

In 1977 a Federal Court in upstate New York enjoined Walter Taylor from using the Taylor name in marketing or promoting the wines of Bully Hill. Two years later the same court found him guilty of contempt for using the injunction itself to promote Bully Hill wines in a manner that the court found derisive. The issue in the original case was whether Walter Taylor was improperly using the family name, which had been sold to the Coca-Cola Company with the Taylor Wine Company. Claiming that he had been robbed of his heritage, he blacked out the Taylor name on more than 100,000 Bully Hill labels and referred to himself as Walter Who? All the publicity did not hurt, however, and Bully Hill sales have boomed. The operation is one of the state's largest.
☆/☆☆☆
$/$$

Burgess Cellars.

Tom Burgess, a former corporate pilot for I.B.M., and his wife Linda purchased their winemaking operation in St. Helena in the heart of California's Napa Valley in 1972. They put the Burgess name on the business and held their first harvest that year. Since then the Burgess wines have established a reputation for high quality, complexity, and consistency.

The original vineyards and winery were established in 1880 by homesteaders, and there were numerous ownerships until 1943, when entrepreneurs associated with the Souverain name bought it. Another ownership change occurred in 1970, but the Souverain name stuck until 1972, when Tom Burgess bought it. Meanwhile Souverain moved to other locations and is no longer identified in any way with the Burgess operation.

Initially Burgess produced seven premium varietals, but, in common with a number of other California producers, Tom Burgess decided to reduce the number to three primary ones—Chardonnay (60 percent of production), Cabernet Sauvignon (20 percent), and Zinfandel (20 percent). All are aged in French oak barrels, and the Cabernet spends three and a half years at the winery before being released. The vineyard consists of 70 acres, much of it replanted in the mid-1970s, which required extensive purchasing of grapes from reliable outside sources. But the acreage in vines is sufficient to provide two-thirds of the grapes needed for the 30,000-case annual production of Burgess wines.
☆/☆☆☆☆
$$

Burgundy.

The picturesque and rustic hillsides of the Burgundy country of France produce some of the greatest wines on earth. The people live a calm and peaceful lifestyle that has remained steadfastly aloof from many of the pressures of modern civilization. It is a countryside of small hamlets populated mostly by vineyard workers, and the cultivation of vines and grapes dominates the daily existence here more than anywhere else. Most of the vineyards are owned by small farmers, rather than by large syndicates or consortiums as in Bordeaux, and some of the Burgundian landholdings amount to only fractions of an acre. In the Côte d'Or, where the greatest of all Burgundies are produced, some holdings consist of only a few rows of vines. Many vineyards have the appearance of patchwork quilts, reflecting the different styles of pruning the vines, weeding the soil and turning it that are practiced by the various owners.

The Burgundian wines that are produced from this soil run an extraordinary gamut of styles and quality. The wines of Beaujolais, the Mâconnais, and the Chalonnais in the southern portion of the district are fresh and fruity, made for drinking when young and not to be taken too seriously by either neophytes or connoisseurs. It is said in this part of France that three rivers flow there: the Rhône, the Saône and the Beaujolais, so vast is the quantity of charming wine produced from the Gamay grape. The large supply has kept prices down, and many wine-drinkers all over the world have begun their experience with the wines of France with Beaujolais. The most famous white wine of southern Burgundy is the Pouilly-Fuissé of the Mâconnais, which is very fine and elegant and ranks among the best dry white table wines produced anywhere.

Farther north, there are a number of minor producing areas before the Côte d'Or, the celebrated Golden Slope, where some of the very best wines of the world are made. In the southern part of the Golden Slope lies the Côte de Beaune, named after the ancient town that is the capital of the Burgundy wine trade. Here is where the famous Montrachet is produced—a white wine of great elegance and finesse that is extremely rare and expensive. Farther north on the Golden Slope is the Côte de Nuits, where the great reds that have carried the Burgundy name into every corner of the world are produced. The villages of Chambolle, Gevrey, and Vosne are tiny and rustic, belying the renown of the wines produced on the nearby hillsides. Here are the vineyards of Chambertin, Musigny, and the magnificent Romanée-Conti that has achieved almost deity status among connoisseurs who can afford to pay the high prices it automatically brings. A trip along the narrow vineyard road known as the Routes des Grands Crus is an experience that no wine-lover should miss. Stopoffs at the little restaurants and hostelries along

the way can be charming experiences, and the food of Burgundy is acknowledged to be among the best cuisines of France.

Still farther north, about halfway to Paris, is the last Burgundian outpost, the vineyards of Chablis, where the famous dry white wine with its steely, flinty taste is produced. In the best vintages, when weather conditions are ideal, the *grands crus* of Chablis can rival the big whites of the Côte de Beaune. Chablis is one of the northernmost table-wine producing areas in the world, and it can suffer from frost and lack of sun when the other Burgundy areas farther south are experiencing much better conditions. Still, these are great wines, widely imitated in name if rarely in quality in many other countries.

Wine has been a part of Burgundian life for more than 2000 years. The Romans found vines already growing there when they invaded this part of Gaul, and some of the Burgundian vineyards have origins clearly dating back more than 2000 years. Construction of the monastery at Clos de Vougeot was begun by the Cistercians in the twelfth century. They also built Kloster Eberbach in the German Rheingau near Hattenheim, signifying the importance of the church in the early years of viticulture all over Europe. Following the French Revolution, however, the vineyards in Burgundy were expropriated by the State and ultimately were sold to the French people. This explains the extremely fragmented pattern of ownership. Another explanation is that concentrated vineyard holdings in one area exposed the owner to greater risks from bad weather, whereas geographically dispersed holdings reduced the risk of total loss of a crop due to a local storm or frost.

Because of the system of fragmented ownership that prevails, there is virtually no château-bottling in Burgundy as it is known in Bordeaux. About the closest the Burgundians come to this is what they call estate-bottling, indicated by the phrase *mis en bouteilles au domaine* or *mis en bouteilles par le propriétaire* or shortened forms and variations thereof. This means, simply, that the grower himself has also vinified the grape juice and bottled it, although the bottling is unlikely to occur on the estate, or vineyard property itself, because most of the Burgundy vineyards have no buildings on them. Production facilities are centered in the towns and villages of the countryside, and it is common for *négociants,* or dealer-shippers, to buy the production from several growers and bottle it. These wines can be just as good as estate-bottled wines when handled properly.

Most of the *appellations contrôllées* regulations of Burgundy were established during the Depression, between 1936 and 1938. Under these controls, a maximum yield in gallons per vineyard acre was imposed, to assure that quality would not be sacrificed for quantity, and minimum alcohol levels were established for the various grades of wine. This was based on the premise that the best wines come from the ripest grapes, and the ripest grapes have the highest natural sugar content, and the higher the sugar content, the greater the level of alcohol resulting from fermentation. The great reds of the Côte d'Or must be made only with the Pinot Noir grape, whereas the Chardonnay is specified by law for the best whites. The Gamay was officially banned from the Côte d'Or by the Duke of Burgundy who reigned in 1395, because it produced inferior wines, yet it is the required grape of Beaujolais, where it produces wines of great charm and freshness.

Minimum alcohol level for the most ordinary Burgundies, no matter where produced, is 9 percent. The *grands crus* reds of the Côte d'Or must reach 11.5 percent, the whites 12 percent. The *premiers crus* must be 11 percent for reds, 11.5 percent for whites, and the *commune* wines need reach levels one-half percent lower. The alcohol requirements are not quite so high for Chablis because of its location somewhat farther north: 11 percent for *grands crus*, 10.5 percent for *premiers crus,* 10 percent for the *commune* wines of Chablis, and only 9 percent for Petit Chablis. These are minimums, of course, and the actual alcohol level may be much higher in great vintages. The author has a Romanée-Saint-Vivant 1959 whose label proclaims a reading of 14.6 percent. Even a Beaujolais *grand cru,* which must by law reach only 10 percent to merit its name, can rise to 15 percent when the weather conditions are ideal. Failure to reach the required alcohol means a demotion in grade, e.g., from *premier cru* to *commune* wine.

The greatness of Burgundy naturally lies in its individual wines, which are discussed under their own headings. The broadest categories are:

> Beaujolais
> Chablis
> Chalonnais
> Côte d'Or
> Mâconnais

The Côte d'Or is broken down into separate headings for the Côte de Beaune and the Côte de Nuits. Most of the *grand cru* estates of the Côte d'Or also have their own separate entries.

No general discussion of Burgundy can omit reference to the practice of labeling wines from other parts of the world as "burgundy." It is perhaps the most misused name in all of winedom, and its indiscriminate application in parts of the world far removed from the Burgundy country of France creates confusion for the consumer. The use of

French or other European names for wines produced elsewhere is sometimes justified with the statement that they connote a certain style with which the consumer is familiar, based on experience with the real products. This rationale might be acceptable if all the wines called "burgundy" closely resembled Burgundy. But they do not. An Argentine wine with "burgundy" on its label was recently marketed in the United States in Bordeaux-shaped bottles; it tasted not like a Burgundy, nor even a Bordeaux, but more like the thick reds produced in Southern Italy. The term "burgundy" has come to mean almost anything vaguely red and alcoholic, and this is a shame in that the practice detracts from the glory of the only true Burgundies—the ones from that extraordinary area in eastern France. Neophytes should remember that name from anywhere else in the world are rarely comparable to the real thing—a fact that becomes obvious in any comparison tasting.

Buttafuoco.

This is a decent dry red wine produced in the Oltrepo' Pavese part of Italy's Lombardy region and vinified from Uva Rara, Barbera, and Bonarda grapes. The word "Buttafuoco" is translated as "fire-sparking," implying that the wine has a fiery quality in the mouth. With the proper age, perhaps a decade, however, it becomes soft and silky and is sometimes compared with the better Piedmont reds. The leading producer is Casa Alberici, whose proprietor is Bianchina Alberici, a leading figure in the area. Buttafuoco is recognized under the Italian D.O.C. law.
☆☆☆☆
$$

Davis Bynum Winery.

L. Davis Bynum, a former home winemaker, opened his first commercial winery in 1965 in Albany, California, adjacent to Berkeley. He purchased wines in bulk, bottled them and sold them entirely at the winery. So the Davis Bynum name, although it still is ranked among California's small boutique wineries, has existed for somewhat longer than many of the others. Bynum spent 15 years with the *San Francisco Chronicle* as a newsman and feature writer, then got into public relations and advertising and briefly ran a group of weekly newspapers in southern California before turning his attention entirely to wine.

After more than seven years of selling his wines only from the tasting room in Albany, he established a corporation, with himself as president. There are now 19 other friends and associates who are shareholders, but he holds 63 percent of the equity. With the corporate structure came more financing in 1973, when he acquired his present property in the Russian River Valley near Healdsburg in Sonoma County.

Wide distribution of the Davis Bynum wines began in 1974 and production now runs 22,000 cases a year of such premium varietals as Cabernet Sauvignon, Pinot Noir, Zinfandel, Fumé Blanc, and Chardonnay. Seven and a half acres of the Russian River property belong to the corporation and the rest belong to him and his wife. Most of the grapes, however, are purchased from outside sources—60 percent from shareholders in the corporation who have growing operations and the rest from growers who are unaffiliated. Oak-aging gives the Davis Bynum wines a degree of complexity. All of them tend to be pleasant and charming, less intensely flavored than those of some other boutiques but nevertheless well made.

· C ·

Cabernet di Pramaggiore.

The Cabernet Sauvignon and Cabernet Franc grapes have been widely cultivated in Italy, and one of the better versions is made from Cabernet Franc, grown in the vineyards near Pramaggiore in the Veneto region, north of Venice itself. This one has achieved D.O.C. recognition under the Italian wine law.

☆☆☆

$

Cabernet Sauvignon.

Among the noble red grape varieties cultivated in the vineyards of France, the Cabernet Sauvignon of the Bordeaux region is perhaps the noblest of all. Usually, although not always, it is the dominant variety used in making wines at the greatest estates. The celebrated Châteaux Latour and Mouton-Rothschild, for example, are made almost entirely from Cabernet Sauvignon grapes, with small amounts of Merlot and Cabernet Franc or Malbec blended in. Cabernet Sauvignon is also extensively cultivated in California, where it produces unquestionably the best American red wines. The grape is also planted extensively in South America, Australia and elsewhere, reflecting the efforts of winemakers the world over to produce wines of a style and quality similar to that of the great Bordeaux. The Cabernet does not yield copious quantities, so it is more expensive to produce than other grape varieties. But what it lacks in volume it more than compensates for in quality.

When the soil and growing conditions are proper, the great reds vinified from the Cabernet Sauvignon display extraordinary complexity, with an intense bouquet of fresh cedarwood or lead pencils, or freshly melted road tar. The scent of violets and lilacs can also be detected in the wines from certain vineyards. The best reds of Bordeaux and the best California Cabernets have an intense, almost chewy texture that softens in maturity, creating great balance, and that special characteristic known as finesse. Cabernet Sauvignons tend to live for many years, requiring at least a decade or perhaps two before they reach their peak of perfection. Unfortunately, the vast majority are consumed in their youth, before being given the chance to fulfill their poential.

Cabinet, Kabinett.

One of the categories of wine under the German designation *Qualitätswein mit Prädikat,* literally "quality wine with special attributes." Cabinet or Kabinett is the lowest of the quality wines on the sweetness scale—less sweet than Spätlese, Auslese, Beerenauslese, or Trockenbeerenauslese. Cabinet wines cannot have sugar added to increase their sweetness and therefore must be produced from fully mature grapes. This is important, because full maturity may not be achieved in vintages hampered by poor weather.

The term comes from the ancient practice of reserving the best wines from a vineyard in the owner's cabinet and had no legal standing prior to the restructuring of the German wine laws in 1971. But generally a Cabinet wine was understood to be of superior quality and sometimes was not offered for sale but was retained by the grower for his guests. Prior to 1971 it was up to the grower to decide whether to add the term to his label, but "Cabinet" took an official standing as indicative of a certain minimum quality level in that year. As with Auslese and Spätlese and the other *Qualitätsweins,* Cabinet wines must attain 10 percent natural alcohol and must be produced from approved grape varieties. Before receiving the designation, they are tasted and analyzed by a German government agency, which then awards a control number to assure consistent quality.

Cahors.

Certainly one of the finest regional red wines of France is produced around the ancient city of Cahors, which nestles in a horseshoe bend of the River Lot in the rustic and rolling countryside about 110 miles east and slightly south of Bordeaux. It is known as *vin noir,* or black wine, because of the extremely dark color derived from a heavy tannin content imparted from the local grapes as well as from the old-fashioned methods of vinification that prevail in this sleepy section of southern France. It requires a good decade in the bottle before it is ready to drink and can go on developing for several decades until it reaches a full peak that is comparable to a young Saint-Emilion or Pomerol from Bordeaux.

A Cahors Clos de Gamot 1947, tasted at La Taverne, the best restaurant in town, in the summer of 1974, was superb, with plenty of fruit left and an extraordinary, velvety finish. The wine was produced by Jouffreau & Fils, a prominent local firm. A Cahors Clos des Batuts 1970, sampled at the same time and produced by Tesseydre, another good local grower, showed great promise. Most common are the wines bottled by Les Caves d'Olt, a big local cooperative. Because Cahors did not receive its *appellation contrôlée* designation until fairly recently, it lived for many years in obscurity and is still not one of the better known French wines. But its quality can be quite high and it deserves a place in any serious wine cellar.

☆☆☆/☆☆☆☆

$/$$

Cakebread Cellars.

Cakebread Cellars was established in 1973 by Jack and Dolores Cakebread on a 22-acre vineyard near Rutherford, 13 miles north of Napa in one of California's best growing areas. Their wines developed a reputation for quality almost immediately, especially their Chardonnay, which is fermented partly in small oak barrels and partly in temperature-controlled steel tanks, after which it is placed in small oak barrels for aging—20 percent in new oak, 40 percent in one-year-old oak and 40 percent in two-year-old oak. This type of careful treatment, the Cakebreads believe, provides the balance and complexity sought by discerning consumers.

A Sauvignon Blanc, a Cabernet Sauvignon, and a Zinfandel are also produced, but total production amounts to little more than 15000 cases a year, supervised by Jack and Dolores Cakebread's son Bruce, a graduate in oenology from the University of California at Davis, who is the winemaker. The Cakebread vineyard now has a deepwater retrieval system as well as irrigation and frost-protection systems. They still must buy up to 50 percent of their grapes, depending on the vintage, but they buy only from growers who share their philosophy about grape quality.

Cakebread Cellars is truly a family operation. Bruce's wife Rosemary, also a graduate in oenology from Davis, supervises the Cakebread laboratory that plays an important role in assuring the quality of the Cakebread wines. Besides the winery, Jack Cakebread runs an automotive garage, restores classic cars, and teaches photography.

☆☆/☆☆☆
$$

Caldaro.

Sometimes called Lago di Caldaro, this red wine is made in the Trentino-Alto Adige region of northern Italy. It consists mostly of Schiava grapes, with some Pinot Nero blended in, and tends to be soft and dry. It should be drunk young and slightly chilled.

☆
$

Calera Wine Company.

Calera's winemaking operations are in the Cienega District in San Benito County, California, southeast of San Francisco. The winery is best known for its Zinfandels, which it calls "Zin" on its labels, often followed by the name of a locality or vineyard where the grapes were produced. The winery itself is at Hollister, but there are Calera bottlings

bearing designations from Cienega, Central Coast, Templeton, and Doe Mill, as well as the broad appellation California, suggesting a blend from geographically separated sources. Calera also bottles a Zinfandel that it calls Essence, a late-harvest wine that generally is high in sugar and alcohol. In fact, most Calera Zinfandels are high in alcohol.

Calera's first vintage was in 1975, vinified in rented facilities. By 1977 construction had begun on a new winery, which was completed in 1981 and is believed to be one of the few wineries in the world that operates completely by gravity flow. It was built into the side of a mountain on the site of an old lime kiln. (The word *calera* is Spanish for "lime kiln.") Calera's wines have great style and personality and therefore are controversial. The sweet late-harvest Zinfandel Cienega District 1978, for example, was 13.9 percent alcohol and contained 12 percent residual sugar—possibly a dessert wine, but nevertheless a wine that many consumers might find difficult to match with any food. (Production totaled only 350 cases.) Calera's regular Zin Cienega District 1979 was 15.6 percent alcohol, quite high and possibly out of the table wine category. Production totaled 1780 cases. Calera also produces stylish Pinot Noir on a 24-acre site at an elevation of 2200 feet in the Gavilan Mountain Range.

☆☆☆☆
$$

California.

The American wine boom has its roots in California, where dramatic changes during the 1970s vastly upgraded wine quality and led to expanded production of the best varieties. Partly in response to persistent consumer demand for better products and partly because of increased winemaking sophistication, California's wine industry suddenly shifted its focus from fairly ordinary, often sweet or fortified products to wines capable of competing with the best available anywhere in the world. California Cabernet Sauvignons began defeating the top-ranked Bordeaux reds in blind comparison-tastings, and California Chardonnays vanquished the best white Burgundies. Whereas many California producers had grown accustomed to denying the validity of comparing their wines with the best wines of Europe, now such comparisons became not only valid but often rewarding. Consumers eagerly tracked down every available bottle from the wineries that began capturing the headlines not only in the home wine country but also in New York, Paris, and London.

The proven ability to produce superior wines attracted many newcomers. At the end of 1975 there were 67 operating wineries in the state's best known growing region, the Napa Valley. By 1979 there were 82 and by 1980 there were more than a hundred. The growth in the adjacent Sonoma Valley was equally dramatic—from 46 wineries in 1975 to 64 in 1979 and roughly 80 in 1980. The number of wineries in Amador, Monterey, El Dorado, and Mendocino Counties approximately doubled in five years as the prime Napa and Sonoma vineyard sites were grabbed up, prices for acreage soared and new locations were sought. The number of acres bearing wine grapes in the Napa region rose 35 percent, from 16,161 in 1975 to 21,888 in 1980. Mature vineyard acreage in Sonoma climbed 50 percent in the half-decade, from 15,773 to 23,903. Significantly, the gains occurred in plantings of premium European varieties—Chardonnay, Sauvignon Blanc, Gewürztraminer, Cabernet Sauvignon, Zinfandel, and the like. Toward the end of the 1970s it became evident that American consumers preferred white wines, so some producers began grafting over some of their red varieties to white. But the emphasis remained on premium varieties planted in the best locations so that wines of the highest quality could be produced.

Meanwhile California continued to account for roughly seven out of every ten bottles of wine consumed in the United States, including imports. In 1980 other states combined held less than 10 percent of the market, and imports accounted for about 21 percent. California producers made nine out of ten bottles made in this country, and California growers had even a larger share of the grape market, reflecting the practice of many non-California wine producers of buying California grapes for vinification in their own states. Great Western Champagne, possibly the best known American-made sparkling wine, was made partly from California grapes, even though it was produced in a New York State winery.

Not only did the wine boom reflect population growth and rising affluence among consumers, it also reflected higher per capita consumption. Between 1976 and 1980 the number of gallons consumed by each American rose to 2.12 per year from 1.73, while adult per capita consumption climbed from 2.71 gallons to 3.01. With the French and Italians drinking more than 20 gallons a year each, moreover, the growth potential among Americans appeared enormous. In spite of this potential, economists began forecasting a shakeout among wineries and a leveling off of consumption. The market was becoming saturated, they suggested, but as the decade of the '80s opened, the trend remained strongly upward.

Good wines have existed in California for more than a century, of course, and California's 70 percent share of the market for all wines sold in the U.S. has remained steady for many years.

Within the market, however, an upgrading in quality occurred and continued into the 1980s. Once the 70 percent represented mostly cheap jug wines with generic names borrowed from Europe, such as chablis, burgundy, Rhine, Sauternes, Sherry, and Port. The misleading names aroused confusion and gave rise to the conception that California was incapable of producing premium wines. Many were inferior, of course—some still are—but the breakdown of that 70 percent has changed radically, reflecting the steady improvement of California wines that began after World War II. Some Californians still feel that the comparison with European wines is unfair in principle because the grapes are grown on different soils under different climatic conditions. But since the same grape varieties are used, it is difficult to resist comparing the results, particularly for those who have experienced and enjoyed good European wines.

The attitude that presumed the inferiority of California wines was reinforced by the fact that distribution of California's finer wines was limited, some of the best never leaving the state. Relatively few people outside California had tasted the better wines, so that most judged the California product by the sweetish substance, high in alcohol, that was widely available for the first 30 years following the repeal of Prohibition in 1933. Gradually, however, persistent reports by experts of the excellence of California's varietal wines (those containing 51 percent or more of the grape variety stated on the label, such as Cabernet Sauvignon, Chardonnay, Pinot Noir) began to filter through to the wine-drinking public. (In 1983 the percentage required for a named varietal rose to 75 from 51.) As the state moves into its third century of viticulture, the wines are indeed getting better every year.

California's hospitality for the grapevine was discovered almost immediately by European immigrants who were accustomed to tables graced by wine. The arable plains and broad valleys and the accommodating climate prompted early settlers to begin planting vines as soon as they could stake out vineyards. The history of California winemaking has been thoroughly explored in the recent proliferation of wine books and is familiar to many wine lovers. The first grapes planted in 1769 were a variety of the European *Vitis vinifera* family brought from Mexico by the Franciscan Father Junipero Serra, who founded the earliest of California's missions at San Diego de Alcalá. As he moved up the coast, establishing a chain of missions as far north as Sonoma, vineyards sprouted in his wake, providing wines mostly for medicine and the celebration of the Eucharist, but also for table use among the friars.

The Mission grape, as it became known, is still widely grown in central and southern California, yielding prodigious quantities of rather poor quality wine. In the 1830s, the first premium varietals were planted by a Frenchman from Bordeaux, Jean Louis Vignes (whose surname, interestingly enough, means "vines" in French), who received cuttings from relatives in his homeland. A number of colorful figures contributed to the development of California wine, but probably the most colorful of all was Hungarian-born Agoston Haraszthy. A self-made man in the most literal sense of that term, the dynamic Count Haraszthy was the first to import large quantities of European varietals, which he successfully established in vineyards north of San Diego. By 1858 he had acquired extensive acreage in Sonoma, a vast estate known as Buena Vista where he built a palatial villa. During the next ten years or so Haraszthy became the most potent force in the burgeoning wine industry. In 1861 the governor of California commissioned him to go to Europe and seek out the choicest vines he could find. Setting out with his son Arpad he spent three years doing so and returned with 100,000 cuttings of some 300 varieties. When the state government refused to reimburse him due to his sympathies toward the Confederacy before the Civil War, he was keenly disappointed but, undaunted, he distributed the vines personally up and down the state. One of them apparently was the famous Zinfandel, whose mysterious origins are as yet in doubt (a great deal of searching seems to indicate at the moment that it may be related to certain Italian varieties). Despite continued efforts in behalf of California winemaking, Haraszthy was plagued by a series of misfortunes and in 1868 he left California for new ventures in Nicaragua. In 1869 he disappeared, allegedly devoured by alligators as he attempted to cross a stream on his property. A tragic end indeed, but somehow in keeping with the heroic aura surrounding this flamboyant man who with good reason is called "the father of California viticulture."

Vineyards and winemaking flourished in California in the late nineteenth century, spurred initially by the gold rush of 1849 that brought an influx of people and increased demand for wine. This was the first in a cycle of boom-and-bust periods that marked the second half of that century. In the 1870s Phylloxera, the vine louse that caused destruction also in European vineyards, worked its evil in California, raging unchecked until 1894. As in Europe, new cuttings were grafted on resistant American rootstocks and good wines were made once more. By 1900 some of the finest were winning prizes at the annual Paris Exposition, and California was well on its way to becoming a top contender in the world market. The

wine industry continued to grow until its destiny collided with another cruel working of fate—Prohibition.

During the 14 years following 1919, the industry, with the exception of a few wineries that continued to make sacramental and medicinal wines, was almost totally wiped out. Vineyards lay fallow or were replanted with coarser varieties for table use. Machinery rusted. Winemakers turned to other trades. It was disastrous, and after repeal in 1933 recovery was slow. Most of the wine made then was in bulk and of decidedly poor quality. Not until the 1940s did California winemakers evince much interest in upgrading their wines and it took new impetus from an outsider to awaken their interest. The late Frank Schoonmaker, in California to select wines for eastern distribution, discovered some that interested him. He encouraged the winemakers at Wente Brothers, Almadén, and Louis M. Martini to use varietal names for them rather than the generic holdovers from before Prohibition. (For years California law required that 51 percent of the grape variety named on the label be used in the wine, but the regulation was changed to 75 percent as of January 1, 1983. In any event, many top-quality producers customarily use much more, often 100 percent.) Prior to the wine revolution of the 1970s, wines labeled Grey Riesling, Chardonnay, Gamay, Grenache Rosé, and Sémillon had a strange and exotic sound, for in Europe the wines from these vines had geographical or vineyard names. But, sold in fifths, they were better than the jug wines Americans were accustomed to from California, and Schoonmaker's excellent selections commanded higher prices, a fact soon noticed by other American winemakers. Thus the trend toward varietal labeling was begun. Now firmly established, the practice is so successful in California that it has become common with certain wines made in France, such as Pinot Chardonnay, Gamay, Pinot Noir, even Cabernet Sauvignon, when produced outside the most renowned vineyard areas.

The quality of California wines steadily improved after World War II. Per capita consumption for table wines increased dramatically and by the mid-60s an upsurge of interest in the quality wine market was attracting investors from big business. Large national companies such as Pillsbury, Nestlé, Heublein, Seagram's, and others purchased premium wineries, investing huge sums of money with the hope of good returns. Small new wineries sprang up that specialized in three or four top varietals, and names like Chappellet, Heitz, Mayacamas, Ridge, Freemark Abbey, David Bruce, and Chalone became synonymous with quality (as well as high prices).

By the early 1970s a genuine wine boom had erupted on the world wine market. Small harvests in Bordeaux and Burgundy in the late 1960s produced limited quantities of premium wines that sent prices skyrocketing. Speculators added to the pressure by purchasing for storage, not drinking. With the demand for Europe's finest exceeding supply, prices for all grades of wines increased out of all proportion to value. New attention focused on California and American wines in general. For a couple of years it was a grape grower's paradise—in 1972 a single ton of Cabernet grapes sometimes commanded over a thousand dollars. A feverish flurry of excitement swept the state; land was bought for new vineyards and thousands of acres were planted in premium wine grapes, some in areas never before used for vines. But the grower's glory was short-lived. By 1974, as recent plantings came into bearing, a grape glut reversed the situation. Also, the energy crisis and resultant world reces-

sion inhibited consumption. In 1975 the supply of grapes far exceeded demand. The wineries had more wine than they knew what to do with. Quantity had increased, but markets and distribution had not expanded rapidly enough to absorb it. Nor in fact had the wineries themselves the production capabilities and storage facilities to handle such quantities. Some of the newer vineyards not yet up to production capacity made and stored wines for wineries that could not handle their own overflow. It was a typical example of boom economics that brings disaster to speculators—the price for Cabernet grapes sank as low as $175 a ton in 1975. Growers who could not find buyers were forced to rip out vineyards and plant other crops in order to survive.

But the situation proved temporary, and the wine boom resumed with gusto in the late 1970s. Profits began rising again and the notable thing about California winemakers, or at least the most dedicated among them, is that profits are plowed right back into the business of growing grapes and making wines. Now at last there is more time and more incentive than ever before to pay attention to detail—the development of microclimates, further experiments with yeast strains in fermentation, clarifying the wines without overfiltering (which can take the guts out of a wine and happens too often in California), aging in various types of cooperage. Today 600,000 acres of grapevines are growing in California, far more than at any other time in its history. Plantings of premium varietals make up roughly half, about 300,000, some of which are just now coming into bearing.

California wine districts can be roughly divided into coastal valleys and inland valleys. The cooler climates of the coastal valleys, tempered by breezes from the Pacific, best accommodate superior grape varieties such as Chardonnay, Pinot Noir,

Cabernet Sauvignon and Riesling, to name a few. The famous North Coast counties of Napa, Sonoma, and Mendocino lie above San Francisco Bay, stretching as far north as the town of Ukiah. East and south of the bay are the Central Coast counties of Alameda (the Livermore Valley), Amador, Santa Clara, San Benito, Santa Cruz, and Monterey. Farther down the coast in San Luis Obispo and Santa Barbara counties are other newly developed vineyards around the towns of Santa Maria and Paso Robles.

Inland, the Great Central and San Joaquin Valleys spread in broad, flat, sun-baked plains from Sacramento to just above Bakersfield. Farther south around Los Angeles are the districts of Cucamonga and San Bernardino, which extend down to the Mexican border. Here grow the prodigious bearers such as Berger, Mission, Thompson Seedless, and other varieties that yield enormous quantities of wine that is rather ordinary and without great character. Dessert wine grapes, however, such as those used for sherry and port-type wines, do quite well here and some quite creditable sweet wines are made.

One of the most useful projects undertaken by the University of California at Davis was the division of California's wine districts into five growing regions according to climate, based on a method known as heat summation. Collecting data over a period of years, researchers monitored the average number of degree days (those in which the temperature went over 50°, the minimum necessary for grapes to grow) for each area during the growing season from April 1 to October 31. The difference between 50° and the mean temperature over a five-day period was multiplied by five (65 − 50 = 15 × 5 = 75 degree days). The sum totals for the season were plotted into five growing regions:

Region I—2500 degree days or fewer
Region II—2501 to 3000
Region III—3001 to 3500
Region IV—3501 to 4000
Region V—4,000 or more

Climatic conditions in Region I, the coolest, approximate those of northern Europe—the vineyards along the Rhine and Mosel Rivers in Germany, northern Burgundy and the Champagne District in France. Region I, therefore, is most favorable to varieties such as Chardonnay, Pinot Noir, and Riesling that ripen early and develop better balance of sugar content and fruit acid in cooler climates.

Region II is similar to Bordeaux and is best suited for late-ripening Cabernet and other grapes from the Bordeaux region, such as Merlot, Malbec, and Sauvignon Blanc. Chenin Blanc grows best in Region II, but is also suited to Region I. Regions I and II comprise most of Napa and Sonoma, parts of Mendocino, all of the Central Coast counties, including Monterey, San Luis Obispo, and Santa Barbara.

The warmer zone of Region III resembles the Rhône Valley in southern France, and Gamay varieties, Zinfandel, Barbera, and Sémillon thrive here.

Regions IV and V are the warmest and most suitable for dessert wine grapes found in Spain and Portugal, such as Palomino, Tinta Madeira, Souzao, Mission, and Thompson Seedless, varieties that are used also for table grapes and raisins. The inland valleys and the vineyards of southern California are all Regions IV and V, with some percentage of Region III in the Central Valley. Within all of the regions microclimates exist that have conditions like those of other regions because of drainage, exposure to the sun or wind. As these become better known they are taken advantage of and replanted in varieties most suited to them.

The most important wine regions of California are discussed further under their own alphabetical listings, including Napa, Sonoma, Mendocino, Livermore, Amador, Santa Clara, and Monterey. The leading wineries with national distribution also have their own listings.

Calistoga Vineyards.

Calistoga Vineyards is the second label of Cuvaison, and the Calistoga wines represent good value. They are made by Cuvaison's winemaker. (*See* Cuvaison.)

☆☆/☆☆☆

$

Callaway Vineyard.

Until Callaway Vineyard and Winery of Temecula, California, introduced its varietal wines in the fall of 1975, no one believed that outstanding wines could be made in the southern part of the state. There were too many days of too much warm sun drenching the earth to yield anything more than ordinary wine that was pleasant enough in many cases but rarely distinguished. In 1969, however, Ely Callaway, retired president of Burlington Industries, purchased a uniquely situated stretch of land in the Rancho California District east of San Diego. The vineyard, 23 miles inland from the Pacific Ocean and 70 miles west of Palm Springs, lies on a 1400-foot plateau below the peaks of the Palomar range in a microclimate of ideal conditions for wine grapes. Morning mist hovers over the vines until the sun is high around ten o'clock, and by one o'clock in the afternoon Pacific breezes flow in to cool the vine leaves and grape-skins during the hottest part of the day. The Palomar range blocks the hot air of the desert to the east which draws the cooling marine air from the coast. Virtually no rain falls during the growing season, so the 135 acres of granitic

soil are irrigated. The growing season is long, the harvest in some years continuing until December.

The first wines released were three whites from the 1974 vintage and a late-harvested Chenin Blanc from 1973. Connoisseurs were enthusiastic about the 1973 Chenin Blanc, known also as Sweet Nancy. *Botrytis cinerea,* the grape mold that concentrates grape sugar and flavor, developed in 1973. Cabernet Sauvignon was available in late 1976. The Zinfandel and Petite Sirah are robust and interesting reds. But the emphasis at Callaway shifted almost entirely to white wines in the late 1970s.

In 1981 an agreement was reached to sell Callaway to Hiram Walker & Sons, the American subsidiary of the Canadian distilling company, Hiram Walker Resources Ltd. Ely Callaway and his management team were expected to continue to run the Callaway operation under the new ownership, which should provide additional capital for expansion. Ely Callaway issued a statement at the time, asserting that the same standards of high quality would be maintained under the new ownership. He also announced plans for a new, 150-acre vineyard for the Callaway winery.

☆/☆☆☆☆

$/$$

Château Calon-Ségur.

Château Calon-Ségur is a completely typical Saint-Estèphe, with vineyards lying in the northernmost of the great wine-producing *communes* of the Haut-Médoc peninsula above Bordeaux. It is a big and hard wine that is best drunk after two decades or more of aging. At its maturity, it is rich and supple, displaying great finesse. Calon-Ségur was classified a *troisième cru,* or third growth, in the Bordeaux classification of 1855, but it is clearly one of the best of the thirds and, with Château Palmer in Margaux, ought to be raised to second-growth status. The origins of Calon-Ségur date back to the Roman occupation of France. In the seventeenth century, Alexandre de Ségur owned Châteaux Lafite and Latour, as well as Calon-Ségur, in one of the most extraordinary unions of ownership in Bordeaux history. But Calon-Ségur was his favorite, a fact reflected in his motto: "I make wine at Lafite and Latour, but my heart is at Calon." A heart is an integral part of the design of Calon-Ségur's label. The production from these vineyards is high, surpassing 20,000 cases in a copious vintage, so prices have stayed attractively low.

☆☆☆☆
$$/$$$

Cambiaso Winery & Vineyards.

Here is an example of a California winery that has been acquired by overseas interests because of the high potential they see in the Golden State's viticulture. Cambiaso was purchased in 1973 by Somchai Likitprakong of Thailand and other members of his family, who also have a whisky-distilling business in their native country. The ownership of Cambiaso is under the name of the Four Seas Corporation, a family company. Likitprakong attended the New York Institute of Technology in Old Westbury, New York, and is the winery's general manager.

Immediately after the purchase, the winery near Healdsburg in the Sonoma Valley was rebuilt and its capacity was quadrupled. The first commercial harvest was in 1973 and production has grown to more than 100,000 cases a year, of which 60 percent are such jug wines as burgundy, chablis, and rosé and the remaining 40 percent are premium varietals, including Cabernet Sauvignon, Petite Sirah, Zinfandel, Barbera, Fumé Blanc, Chenin Blanc, and Chardonnay. Cambiaso owns 52 acres of property, but still buys 95 percent of its grapes from growers in the Napa, Sonoma, Mendocino, and Amador County areas. Barrel-aging in American, Yugoslavian, and French oak is practiced, but the Cambiaso wines generally are not complex and lack strong character.

☆/☆☆☆
$/$$

Château de Camensac.

The production of Château de Camensac, which lies in Saint-Laurent on the Médoc peninsula north of Bordeaux, is quite small and the wine is not widely distributed. The estate was ranked among the *cinquièmes crus,* or fifth growths, of the Bordeaux classification of 1855. Despite the modest volume of output, Château de Camensac is available in the export markets, partly because it is under common ownership with Château Larose-Trintaudon, a *cru bourgeois supérieur,* whose production is becoming fairly large and has recently been distributed in the United States by the giant House of Seagram. Château de Camensac produced an excellent 1970 that was supple and pleasing at a fairly young age. Under the French wine law, the production of the *commune* of Saint-Laurent is entitled to the Haut-Médoc *appellation,* rather than the more specific *commune* designation, which means that Château de Camensac and the other Saint-Laurents are identified as Hauts-Médocs in the classification of 1855.

☆☆☆/☆☆☆☆☆
$$

Cammellino.

The Cammellino is the gimmicky, long-necked Chianti bottle that seems to be used mostly for display purposes in Italian restaurants. The base of the bottle is encased in straw, and the neck extends about four feet, enabling the bottle to hold more than three liters of wine. The Chianti that comes in a Cammellino is not likely to be the best that Italy can produce.

Campania.

Campania is a wine-producing region in southwestern Italy surrounding the coastal city of Naples. It is the region of Mt. Vesuvius, Pompeii, and the Isle of Capri in the Bay of Naples. The principal wines are Lacrima Christi, Greco di Tufo, and Taurasi. Most of the wine is still consumed locally, but exports have increased in recent years in response to the rising demand for Italian wines in foreign markets.

Campidano di Terralba.

Terralba is one of the superior red wines of Sardinia, the productive island lying in the Mediterranean off the west coast of Italy. It is made mostly from the Bovale grape and has won D.O.C. recognition under the Italian wine law. It is a dry red that lacks robustness and should be consumed when fairly young.
☆☆
$

Canada.

If it is true that Leif Ericson discovered North America before Columbus with an expedition that landed somewhere in Canada, then his decision to name the New World Vinland must be accepted as proof that grapevines grew there naturally long before man tried to make wine from their bounty. Apparently the first Canadian viniculture was undertaken by settlers in the early 1600s, although the first commercial winemaking did not occur until perhaps 200 years later. Most of Canada's vineyards lie in the Niagara Peninsula bounded by Lake Erie and Lake Ontario. These two huge lakes exert a moderating influence on the winter temperatures, although experimentation with the more sensitive European grape varieties has not produced great wines. The most durable grape varieties of the region are the same that are cultivated in New York State just to the east. These include the Niagara, Delaware, Concord, Catawba, etc., which produce wines with the "foxy," or musty, taste that almost any wine drinker can identify blindfolded. Some hybrids with European vines have been successful, but their taste is not exactly European. Wines are also produced in British Columbia on the west coast of Canada, where the winter temperatures are fairly moderate, but these, too, are undistinguished. The fact is that Canadian winters in general are simply too cold to permit the production of great wines in substantial quantities.

Canaiolo Nero.

Canaiolo is one of the grapes used to produce Chianti in the Tuscan region of Italy. All Chianti consists of at least 50 percent Sangiovese, but as much as 30 percent of the blend may be Canaiolo, with the balance Trebbiano or Malvasia and Colorino.

Cannonau di Sardegna.

Cannonau di Sardegna is one of the better red wines produced on the island of Sardinia off the west coast of Italy. It is made 90 percent from Cannonau grapes and tends to be robust in flavor and high in alcohol, sometimes reaching 15 percent. It is vinified in dry as well as sweet versions and in a fortified version. The wine has won recognition under the Italian D.O.C. law.
☆☆☆
$

Château Canon.

This estate in Saint-Emilion, east of Bordeaux, was named a *premier grand cru classé* in the Saint-Emilion classification of 1955. It has a lovely iron-fenced courtyard and lies on the flatlands not far from the celebrated Château Ausone. Rich and robust wines are produced here. They are very grapey and tannic in their youth, before maturing gracefully into very well-balanced, full-bodied wines. The estate is planted mostly in Merlot, one of the predominant grapes of the district.

☆☆☆/☆☆☆☆
$$/$$$

Château Canon-la-Gaffelière.

In one of the more confusing mixtures of estate names in Saint-Emilion, Château Canon-la-Gaffelière is a separate vineyard from both Château Canon and Château la Gaffelière, which were ranked as *premiers grands crus classés,* or first great growths, in the Saint-Emilion classification of 1955. Yet Canon-la-Gaffelière, which bears both names of the other two estates, was ranked beneath them on the quality scale as a *grand cru classé.* The estate lies less than half a mile due south of Château la Gaffelière and is adjacent to Château L'Arossée. The production of Château Canon-la-Gaffelière is fairly large for a Saint-Emilion, and the wines have been distributed in the United States for some years. In a good vintage, they can be rich and full-bodied, although perhaps not quite as elegant as some of the *premiers grands crus* of the district.

☆☆☆/☆☆☆☆
$$/$$$

Château Cantemerle.

Château Cantemerle is one of the more consistent Bordeaux estates, producing good wines when other estates are experiencing difficulty and always making superior wines that compete with the best of the Médoc in the better vintages. Yet it was ranked as only a *cinquième cru,* or fifth growth, in the Bordeaux classification of 1855. Cantemerle lies in the *commune* of Macau, one of the southernmost wine-growing areas of the Médoc, and is entitled to use the Haut-Médoc *appellation,* rather than the *commune* name. For many years the estate has been in the Dubos family, and the late Pierre Dubos kept perhaps the best viticultural records in the entire Bordeaux region. The supple reds of Cantemerle have won acclaim in England and Holland, especially, and are becoming better known in the United States. Château Cantemerle should not be confused with another estate also named Cantemerle that lies outside the Médoc across the Dordogne River in Saint-Gervais.

☆☆☆☆
$$/$$$

Château Cantenac-Brown.

The wines produced at this stately château in Bordeaux were rated among the third great growths in the Médoc classification of 1855. Cantenac-Brown is one of the more robust wines of Margaux, a *commune* better known for its delicate, or "feminine," wines. The château's fame dates back to the 16th century, when its vineyards covered not only parts of Margaux and Cantenac, but also nearby Arsac and Avensan. In those days it was known simply as Château de Cantenac. Its ownership passed through Dutch hands to John Lewis Brown, a Bordeaux wine merchant of British nationality, in 1826 and his name was attached shortly afterwards. The vineyards went through a succession of owners after Mr. Brown went bankrupt in 1840. More recently, in 1968, the Bordeaux shipping firm of A. de Luze & Fils purchased Cantenac-Brown from Jean Lawton, a member of a prominent Bordeaux wine family. Reflecting their early ownership, the wines of Cantenac-Brown are especially popular in Holland and England. In the United States they have achieved less renown than Château Brane-Cantenac, whose wines are more typically Margaux, although not necessarily superior. Under the de Luze proprietorship, Cantenac-Brown has been made from 60 percent Cabernet Sauvignon and Cabernet Franc grapes, 30 percent Merlot, and 10 percent Petit Verdot.

☆☆☆☆
$$/$$$

Capri.

Tourists know that Capri is the sparkling island of romance and song that lies in the Bay of Naples, and those who have visited the island and sipped wine in the local restaurants and bars know that Capri also stands for the local red and white wines that come in carafes. There is a Bianco and a Rosso, both with D.O.C. status under the Italian wine law, even though little wine bearing the Capri name is either vinified on the island or made from grapes grown there. This is one of the areas where the D.O.C. law appears not to have been true to its purpose.

☆/☆☆
$

Caramino.

One of the better wines of the Piedmont region of northern Italy is Caramino, which in good vintages can be intensely rich, filled with the fruit of the Nebbiolo grape yet dry and elegantly balanced. The wine attracted attention among connoisseurs of Italian reds when it began appearing on the American market in the mid-1970s, but quantities were small. The quality level of Caramino is generally quite high and less variable than Barolo or Gattinara, which seem to be produced in much greater amounts. One of the better Caramino producers is Dessilani.

☆☆☆/☆☆☆☆☆
$/$$

Château Carbonnieux.

Six of the thirteen red-wine estates that received *grand cru* recognition in the Graves classification of 1959 lie in the *commune* of Léognan about six miles south of the Bordeaux city limits. Château Carbonnieux is one of these, and the wine has been widely distributed in the United States and England, reflecting a fairly large production. The Carbonnieux reds are not on a par with the top-ranked Graves such as Château Haut-Brion, Château La Mission-Haut-Brion, or Domaine de Chevalier. They seem to lack that extra quality known as finesse. The dry whites of Carbonnieux are somewhat better known and also are widely available. They, too, won *grand cru* status in the Graves classification.

☆☆☆/☆☆☆☆☆
$$/$$$

Château La Cardonne.

This 156-acre property in Blaignan, in the lower Médoc of Bordeaux, has achieved prominence since being acquired by the Groupe Lafite-Rothschild in 1973. The wines are entitled to the *cru grand bourgeois* appellation and are

well made, reflecting the Rothschild influence.
☆☆☆
$$

Carema.

Devotees of the intensely flavored reds of Italy's Piedmont region have discovered Carema, from the town of the same name, as a viable and less costly alternative to Barolo and Gattinara. Carema is made from the same Nebbiolo grape responsible for the other great reds of the Piedmont, and it is a richly flavored, dry, robust wine that is best not drunk before age eight. The production is not large, but the wine has begun to establish a reputation in overseas markets.
☆☆☆/☆☆☆☆
$/$$

J. Carey Cellars.

This is another of the many small wineries that sprang up in California during the 1970s. The original vineyard was planted in 1973 with Cabernet Sauvignon and Merlot, and additional plantings of Chardonnay, Sauvignon Blanc, and Cabernet Franc came later. The winery was built in 1978 in Solvang, in Santa Barbara County, and Carey estate-bottles its Santa Ynez Valley wines. It also buys grapes from the Edna Valley and the Santa Maria Valley. The Carey Sauvignon Blanc is considered its best wine.
☆/☆☆☆
$$

Carmignano.

Carmignano is an excellent red wine produced in the Italian region of Tuscany, west of Florence. It is similar in style to the Chianti produced from nearby vineyards because it is made from the same grapes: about half Sangiovese, with the balance in Canaiolo, Trebbiano, and a few others, plus as much as 10 percent

Cabernet Sauvignon, which gives it an extra dimension. The wine tends to be full-bodied and robust and should not be drunk before about age eight.
☆☆☆/☆☆☆☆
$/$$

Carneros Creek Winery.

For years the conviction has been growing among California wine producers that some of the state's best Pinot Noirs and Chardonnays ultimately will come from the Carneros District at the southern end of the Napa Valley, where the temperatures are cooler because the area is closer to San Francisco Bay and experiences its cool breezes. The phenomenon is called the "marine influence." In the early afternoon each day during the growing season, a wind begins blowing from the south, moderating the hot temperatures, and it keeps blowing until around five o'clock in the evening.

Carneros Creek Winery, owned and operated by Balfour Gibson and Francis Mahoney and their wives, was one of the early wine-making operations in Carneros. The winery was built in 1974, although Carneros Creek had been using

borrowed premises and purchased grapes for two years before that. Now there are ten acres of Pinot Noir vines planted adjacent to the winery, with the Carneros Creek itself meandering through a nearby valley. There are also 27 acres of Chardonnay planted about one mile south. The winery also purchases some Pinot Noir that carries a Napa Valley—rather than a Carneros District—label, and some Chardonnay also is purchased. The Carneros Creek Zinfandel 1974, made from grapes from the Isola Vineyard in Amador County, was famous, but now the winery buys its Zinfandel from Yolo County, northeast of Napa County, and plans to phase out Zinfandel production. Sauvignon Blanc also is now being made from purchased grapes in response to the white-wine boom. Total production at Carneros Creek has passed 15,000 cases a year and is approaching the winery's capacity of 20,000. The wines are clean and well made, but the Pinot Noirs still do not match their Burgundian counterparts.
☆☆/☆☆☆
$$

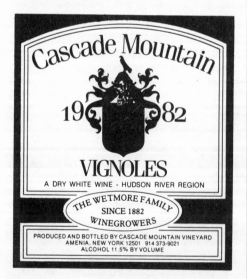

Cascade Mountain Vineyards.

In Amenia, New York, not far from the Connecticut border, William Wetmore operates Cascade Mountain Vineyards, which produces a line of inexpensive generics and branded wines, some with such prosaic names as Le Hamburger Red and A Little White Wine. A New Harvest Red is usually bottled each autumn in Cascade's version of Beaujolais Nouveau. Wetmore encourages visits to the winery and offers so-called subscription futures to customers, whereby they "subscribe" to cases of wine in one year for delivery two years later at current prices. The wine is aged in the Cascade Mountain cellars at no cost to the customer, who has the right to exchange it for the new vintage two years later if he finds the older one fails to meet expectations. This arrangement also provides the proprietor with a very inexpensive method of financing his inventory, which can be extremely costly during periods of high interest rates. It also gives customers a sense of participation in the winery itself.
☆/☆☆
$/$$

Cassayre-Forni Cellars.

The partners in charge of Cassayre-Forni are Paul and Jim Cassayre and Mike Forni, the winemaker, and they are producing good premium varietals at their winery in Rutherford, in California's Napa Valley. The winery was established in 1977 in a barn, then moved to a new building in 1981. The first wine marketed under the Cassayre-Forni label was produced on borrowed premises in 1976, a Cabernet Sauvignon that was released in 1978. The three partners in the venture all were in the engineering business, mainly in northern California, and they designed wineries, among other projects. They produce close

to 10,000 cases a year of Cabernet Sauvignon, Zinfandel, Chardonnay, and Chenin Blanc entirely from purchased grapes that come mostly from Napa growers, although some of the Zinfandel comes from the Dry Creek area of the Sonoma Valley. The reds tend to be fairly intense and high in alcohol, although they appear to become mellow with no more than three to four years of bottle-aging.
☆☆/☆☆☆
$$

Cassis.

Cassis is the French word for "black currant," and liqueur or crème de Cassis is the basis for the most popular aperitif of France, the Kir, named after the late Canon Félix Kir, a famed Resistance fighter during World War II and once a mayor of Dijon. Liqueur de Cassis or crème de Cassis is fortified, usually to at least 16 percent alcohol and most often to at least 20 percent, or 40 proof. The alcohol used to bring the strength up from the normal 10 or 12 percent that the cassis might achieve through natural fermentation is usually grape brandy, the result of distilling wine. Cassis is sometimes drunk by itself, but its most popular use is to make Kir, which is about one part Cassis to four parts white wine. (*See* Kir.)

Castel Chiuro.

Castel Chiuro is the premium brand of both red and white wines made by Nino Negri in the Valtellina district of the Lombardy region of northern Italy. The red, lacking the intensity of the Piedmont reds produced to the south, still benefits from at least a decade of age before drinking.
☆/☆☆☆☆
$$

Catalonia.

Like most other major wine-producing countries, Spain has an area that makes sparkling wines. This is Catalonia, a region that runs north and south of Barcelona on the Mediterranean coast. Actually, Catalonia produces far greater amounts of cheap, bulk wine used mainly for blending. But among its best are the *espumosos,* or bubbling wines, produced in the area known as Panadés, some 30 miles south of Barcelona. These wines do not measure up to Champagne on the quality scale, but they are as good as any of the other Champagne imitations. The sparkling wine from the cellars of Codorniu is fairly widely distributed abroad.

Panadés produces table wines as well. They are linked in style to the wines of Alella, just to the north of Barcelona. These are fresh and fruity, and one of the better known Alellas is Marfil Blanco. Like Alella, Priorato, farther south, produces relatively modest quantities of palatable wines. It is best known for its very dark reds made from the Garnacha Negro and Cariñena grapes, but some sweet Priorato dessert wines are also produced. Tarragona is yet another subdivision of Catalonia entitled to produce wines under its own place name, but most of these are used for blending. The most important producer of premium table wines in the entire region is Miguel Torres, whose reds, especially, have attracted a big following in the U.S., where the Torres line is now the largest-selling table-wine brand. Big export houses like the Vinícola Ibérica buy production from all over Catalonia and create such items as Sangría, Spanish Burgundy, and Spanish Port, nearly always for foreign markets. These wines tend to be well sugared to cover up their natural coarseness.

Caymus Vineyards.

Charles Wagner and his son and winemaker Chuck operate Caymus Vineyards on the Napa Valley floor in Rutherford. Their wines bearing the

Caymus label come from grapes grown on the 70-acre estate adjoining the winery, while those produced under the Liberty School label are made mostly from purchased grapes. Their prices are reasonable, and the Liberty School Cabernet Sauvignon Lot 6 was one of the bargains of the late 1970s. The Liberty School wines are intended to reach a lower-priced market, but they are usually very well made. The Caymus Chardonnays can be big, creamy, and rich, with citric overtones, while the Fumé Blanc tends to be fruity yet dry and medium-bodied. The Pinot Noir is the least successful of the Caymus varietals, often displaying a lack of fruit and stemmy overtones. The Caymus Cabernet Sauvignons are the best that the Wagners produce, and they tend to approach maturity after only a few years, which will be welcome news to consumers without storage facilities. The 1977 was already pleasing in 1981, and the 1978 was medium-bodied, subtle and quite palatable at age three. Caymus also has begun bottling limited amounts of Special Selection Cabernet Sauvignon, which tends to be spicier and richer and more textured than the standard cabernet. Total production of Caymus Vineyards is upwards of 20,000 cases a year, including about one-third under the Liberty School label.
☆☆/☆☆☆☆
$$

Cellatica.

The Lombardy region of northern Italy produces some excellent red wines, and Cellatica is one of them. The grapes come from vineyards near the town of Cellatica, near Lake Garda, and the wine is a blend of Schiava, Barbera, Marzemino, and a few others. It is relatively light and dry, but should not be drunk before age five.
☆☆
$

Cerasuolo di Vittoria.

The word means "cherry-red in color," and the wine comes from vineyards near the city of Vittoria on the island of Sicily, off the toe of the Italian boot. The grapes of Cerasuolo di Vittoria are roughly 60 percent Calabrese and 40 percent Frappata, sometimes with a few others blended in. They achieve great ripeness in the heat of the Sicilian sun, and the wines commonly reach 14 and 15 percent alcohol. They need considerable aging.
☆☆☆/☆☆☆☆☆
$

Château Certan-de-May.

At one time Château Certan and Vieux-Château-Certan were united in one estate, and the two estates lying in Pomerol east of Bordeaux now produce wines of similar style, although Vieux-Certan has achieved greater standing among connoisseurs. The production of Château Certan, now called Château Certan-de-May, is relatively modest even for Pomerol, which is heavily populated by small estates. Two other vineyards of similarly modest production and with similar names, Château Certan-Marzelle and Certan-Giraud, lie nearby and make less distinguished wines. Certan-de-May brings prices comparable to the second and third growths of the Médoc.
☆☆☆☆
$$/$$$

Cerveteri.

Cerveteri is a village near the seaport of Rome, and the Bianco and Rosso produced from the vineyards there have won D.O.C. recognition under the Italian wine law. The Rosso, made with 25 to 30 percent Sangiovese grapes, sometimes resembles Chianti.
☆☆/☆☆☆☆
$

Cesanese.

Cesanese is the name of a red grape cultivated fairly extensively in Lazio, the region adjacent to Rome. Several versions with the names of towns attached have won recognition under the Italian D.O.C. law, e.g., Cesanese del Piglio, Cesanese di Affile, Cesanese di Olevano, Cesanese di Romano.

☆/☆☆

$

Chablis.

In an outpost some 100 miles north of the main portion of the Burgundy country of France lies the village of Chablis, whose fame has spread throughout the world for the fine white wine it produces. In fact, Chablis is regarded as the quintessential dry white table wine, and it is widely copied in name if not in character. But only the wine from the town in France that bears the name has the logical right to call itself Chablis. Wine of the same name produced in California or New York State may be quite decent, but it is only a copy that really ought to have a name of its own. A great quantity of carafe wine sold by the glass in restaurants also is loosely called Chablis, but it rarely is the real thing, for the production of true Chablis is fairly small and the taste is unique.

The traditional terms for describing the taste of Chablis are "flinty" and "steely," but these do not mean that the wine actually has metallic qualities. Rather, they refer to the wine's dryness—a fresh, crisp, almost tart but clean dryness imparted to it by the bituminous clay soil that prevails in the area. This dryness acts almost as an overlay, or surface coating, through which the underlying fruit of the Chardonnay grape can easily be perceived in good vintages. At the same time, the best Chablis has a bigness and richness that makes it a king among the world's foremost white wines. The bouquet is of freshly mown hay, with less power and depth than the scent of a big Meursault or Puligny from the Côte de Beaune. The color is light gold, with glints of green, and as the years pass it deepens to a burnished gloss.

More than any other white Burgundy, Chablis benefits from bottle-age, for in its youth it can be a bit hard and unyielding. Perhaps three years in bottle is a minimum for the best Chablis and a good one will hold up well for a decade. In 1973, the author tasted a rare bottle from the 1928 vintage and was astonished to discover that it still had plenty of fruit and ripeness. Even more surprising, the bottle's cork had been sucked inward when it was transferred from a cellar several days before the wine was drunk, so that its only protection from the atmosphere was the lead capsule covering the neck. Yet the wine showed virtually no trace of maderization, the process of deterioration which old white wines tend to undergo. This does not suggest that Chablis should be laid down for long periods of time before drinking. But a few years of bottle-age are advisable.

One of the classic marriages of food and wine is shellfish, especially raw oysters, with Chablis. They were made for each other. But Chablis also goes well with nearly all other seafoods and even with poultry, although many gastronomes prefer a big white from the Côte de Beaune or perhaps a red Burgundy when poultry is served with any but the lightest of sauces. Chablis also tends to be better whenever seafood or poultry are served cold. The wine itself, of course, should always be drunk well chilled.

There are four different categories of Chablis: Grand Cru, Premier Cru, just plain Chablis and Petit Chablis. Even Petit Chablis can be excellent in good vintages, so long as it genuinely comes from the Chablis District of France. The Grands Crus are usually the best, and their cost shows it, although they tend not to be as expensive as wines of comparable quality from the Côte de Beaune. There are seven *grand cru,* or great growth, vineyards: Blanchots, Bougros, Les Clos, Grenouilles, Les Preuses, Valmur and Vaudésir. Experts differ on which of these should be considered the best, but some opt for Les Clos and some for Vaudésir. They are all superior. Another vineyard, La Moutonne, lying between Vaudésir and Les Preuses, supposedly merited *grand cru* recognition at one point in its history, but it is not regarded with quite the same esteem as the others.

The *premier cru,* or first growth, vineyards are more numerous and come from a much larger area that produces approximately ten times as much wine. They must have an alcoholic content of at least 10.5 percent, compared with 11 percent for the *grands crus.* The ones most often seen in the export markets are Fourchaume, Mont de Milieu, Montée de Tonnerre, Vaucoupin, Côte de Lechet, Les Forêts, Montmain, and Vaillon. Some of the first-growth wines also are simply labeled "Premier Cru." Wines called only Chablis or Petit Chablis need attain only 10 percent and 9.5 percent alcohol respectively and usually come from outside the *grand cru* or *premier cru* vineyards, although excess production from these vineyards in abundant

vintages may fall into the simple Chablis category. This is one more reason to try a simple Chablis or Petit Chablis. If they are genuine, they can represent excellent value.

☆☆/☆☆☆☆
$$/$$$

Chadwick Bay Wine Company.

In western New York State, south of Buffalo in Fredonia, the Chadwick Bay Wine Company opened its doors for business with the 1980 vintage, one of the best in the state in many years. The winery is owned by George Borzilleri, Jr., and his partner Rick Mazza. It lies in the broadly defined Lake Erie District, where the lake has a moderating impact on winter temperatures. Much of the vineyard land is in New York's Chautauqua County. Chadwick Bay opened with an ambitious roster of wines made from purchased grapes, including Seyval Blanc, Vidal Blanc, Chambourcin, and Chardonnay, as well as such brands as "Classic New Yorker," "White Cat," and "Pink Cat" made from the Catawba grape, among other offerings.

☆/☆☆☆
$/$$

Château de la Chaize.

Very few Beaujolais are château-bottled, but here is one that is: Château de la Chaize, from the hills of Brouilly. Owned by the Marquise de Roussy de Sales, the château is a magnificent structure surrounded by lilacs, formal gardens—and vineyards bursting with Gamay grapes. The luscious wine of Château de la Chaize is often one of the best Beaujolais, displaying all of the lively freshness and charm that any Beaujolais could hope to achieve. Because it is slightly fuller-bodied than some other Beaujolais, it seems to taste best about one year after the vintage and remains very pleasant well into its third year, after most other Brouillys have begun to fade. Château de la Chaize is widely distributed in the United States and is usually a good bargain. (*See* Beaujolais.)

☆/☆☆

$$

Château-Chalon.

In the Jura Mountains east of the Burgundy District of France and far from Chalon-sur-Saône is Château-Chalon, which is the name of a village and of the *vin jaune,* or yellow wine, that is produced there in an unusual process. The grapes are harvested late in an effort to achieve extra ripeness. The fermenting wine is placed in relatively small casks, only partly filled, and allowed to age for six to ten years while turning a deep yellow color. A yeasty film forms on the surface of the wine in each cask in a process similar to the making of Sherry in Spain, and the *vin jaune* that results has some Sherry-like characteristics. It is perhaps the longest-lived white wine of France, lasting a half century or more, all the while turning a deeper and darker color. If maderization, a process of deterioration, sets in, the wine is considered all the more unusual. It is bottled in squarish containers unique to that type of wine. *Vin jaune* is also produced at Arbois and L'Etoile nearby, but the Château-Chalon is the best known.

☆☆☆/☆☆☆☆

$$/$$$

Chalone.

Tiny Chalone Vineyard may be one of the smallest vineyards in Monterey County, but it is also one of the most prestigious. Nestled on a mountaintop in the Gavilan range, 2000 feet above Soledad, California, Chalone produces some of the best Chardonnay and Pinot Noir made in the U.S. Richard Graff provides a fine example of the single-minded dedication that can be found among California winemakers. Nothing is too much trouble when you are doing

what you love to do—especially if you do it particularly well. Chalone wines were among the earliest to prove that superb wines could be made in Monterey, once the problem of no rainfall was solved. For Graff this means bringing the water up from the valley floor, so periodically a truck from Soledad hauls it up to the vineyard, where it is fed through ground-level pipes to thirsty vines. The wines are made by hand and aged in small oak. Everything is on a small scale except the quality of the wines and their considerable, ever-widening influence.

In 1970 Dick Graff got together with Phil Woodward, a former certified public accountant, and Phil's brother-in-law, John McQuown, who became partners and brought in some 150 other shareholders to bolster finances. Peter Watson-Graff, Dick's brother, is now the winemaker. Two reservoirs have been built to supplement the water supply that arrives by truck, and production now totals about 12,000 cases a year, about half Chardonnay. Further expansion is occurring through a 50 percent interest in Edna Valley Vineyards, which Phil Woodward calls a "clone of Chalone." This operation, producing 20,000 cases a year of mostly Chardonnay, is in San Luis Obispo. At Chalone itself a "reserve" bottling was established with the 1978 vintage for wines produced from the older vines on the Chalone estate. The winery still has no electricity except for its own butane-powered generators, and it has no telephone. There is only a radiophone for contact with the outside world.

☆/☆☆☆☆

$$/$$$

Chalonnais.

Bordering the Côte de Beaune on the south is the Chalonnais, named after the town of Chalon-sur-Saône, and its wines sometimes attain quality levels that rival the good Burgundian growths, both red and white, from farther north. Chalonnais wines were "discovered" in the late 1960s and early 1970s when the more famous Burgundies achieved so much popularity that their prices climbed out of the reach of the average wine lover. They still represent good value, although occasional bottles will be rather ordinary.

The better red wines are the Mercurey, sometimes quite similar to a Pommard or Volnay from the Côte de Beaune, the Rully, and the Givry. The latter two are less elegant than Mercurey but display the same dark color and robust personality. Mercurey has a number of *premiers crus,* including Barraults, Byots, Champmartins, Crets, Clos l'Evêque, Nogues, Tonnerre, Vignes Blanches, Petits Voyens, and Grands Voyens. These must attain 11 percent in alcoholic strength. Sometimes they are called simply Mercurey Premier Cru. Givry has some specific vineyards of its own, including Barande, Bois Chevaux, Cellier-aux-Moines, Champ Nallot, Clos St-Paul, Clos St-Pierre, Clos Salomon, Marolles, and Survoisine. Rully produces a good deal of sparkling Burgundy but also quantities of still red, sometimes with a *premier cru* designation and sometimes with a specific vineyard name. The reds are made almost entirely from the Pinot Noir grape and must attain at least 10.5 percent alcohol.

Some whites are produced in Mercurey, some better ones in Rully, and some in Givry, but the best whites of the Chalonnais come from Montagny, whose reputation has been enhanced by the Louis Latour firm of Beaune, one of the most prestigious Burgundy houses. Montagny has several dozen vineyards entitled to the *premier cru,* or first growth, designation, but few attain the quality levels of any *premier cru* from the Côte d'Or, farther north. Made mostly from the Chardonnay grape, they are earthy,

with a *goût de terroir* that has been known to overwhelm the basic fruit, which seems to come to the fore more readily when the Chardonnay is cultivated at Meursault or Puligny in the Côte de Beaune. Still, some excellent Montagny is produced, and the wine has found increasing popularity among connoisseurs. Lesser wines from the area are ideal for making Kir, the Burgundian aperitif named after Canon Félix Kir, who was mayor of Dijon. It is a mixture of white Burgundy and Cassis, the liqueur made of black currant juice.

Chambertin.

At the very top of the great wine aristocracy of Burgundy is Chambertin and the wine from the adjacent vineyard, Chambertin-Clos de Bèze. Napoleon is said to have taken comfort in being able to have a regular supply of this magnificent red wine during the long and arduous battle on the Russian front, and the fame of Chambertin dates from that era. It is the biggest and most robust of the red wines of the Burgundian Côte d'Or, or Golden Slope, yet it displays a velvety texture and great balance at maturity, which may be after a decade or more of aging. The vineyard area is only 32 acres, compared to the 36 acres of Clos de Bèze, but more wine is marketed as Chambertin, because Clos de Bèze is legally entitled to use the Chambertin name, which is better known. Both vineyards lie on the Route des Grands Crus as it winds south through the *commune* of Gevrey-Chambertin toward Morey-Saint-Denis. (*See also* Côte de Nuits, Gevrey-Chambertin.)
☆☆☆☆
$$$/$$$$

Chambolle-Musigny.

One of the greatest red wines produced anywhere comes from the vineyard known as Le Musigny, sometimes called

Les Musigny, lying in the *commune* of Chambolle-Musigny in the best part of the Burgundian Côte d'Or. Musigny is big and robust at the same time that it is delicate and feminine. Its bouquet evokes the scent of violets and raspberries, and it develops in the bottle for many years. The name of this single magnificent vineyard has been added onto the name of the picturesque village of Chambolle, creating confusion for nonexpert Burgundy lovers.

Commune wines blended from vineyards anywhere within Chambolle-Musigny and called simply Chambolle-Musigny rank with Vosne-Romanée as the most reliable of the Côte de Nuits. But they should not be confused with the noble Musigny itself. The *commune* shares two other *grands crus* with the neighboring *commune* of Morey-Saint-Denis. These are Bonnes-Mares, an exquisite, more feminine wine than Musigny, and Clos de Tart, which also displays great elegance.

Chambolle-Musigny also has a number of *premiers crus,* ranking in between the *grands crus* and the *commune* wines. The best of these are Les Amoureuses and Les Charmes, which are among the best *premiers* to be found in Burgundy. The best producer in the area is Comte Georges de Vogüé, whose name on a label is a guarantee of quality and is comparable in stature to the Domaine de la Romanée-Conti. He is related to the de Vogüés of the Moët et Chandon Champagne firm. (*See also* Côte de Nuits, Musigny.)

☆☆☆/☆☆☆☆☆
$$/$$$

Chamisal Vineyard.

Chamisal Vineyard was a pioneer in the Edna Valley of San Luis Obispo County, California, planting its first vines in 1973. A winery was built in 1980, and production has risen to about 3000 cases a year, mostly Chardonnay, with a small amount of Cabernet Sauvignon. A secondary label is Corral de Piedra. In common with some other Edna Valley Chardonnays, those of Chamisal are full-bodied, rich, and sometimes heavy.

☆/☆☆☆☆
$/$$

Champagne.

> De ce vin frais l'écume
>   pétillante
> De nos Français est l'image
>   brillante.
>
> (This wine where foaming
>   bubbles dance
> Reflects the brilliant soul
>   of France.)
>   Voltaire

"Champagne" is without question the most evocative word in the entire vocabulary of wine. Strictly speaking, it refers to the district in France named Champagne and to the unique process invented there for producing sparkling white wine, as well as to the wine itself. But the word means so much more. It stands for gaiety, celebration, and festivity, for wealth and splendor, for love. It means New Year's Eve, the launching of ships, toasts to kings and presidents. Its reputation has spread farther than that of any other wine. In fact, so unique is Champagne that many people do not even refer to it as wine but rather as some sort of magical potion with an identity all its own. How often have you heard someone say, "I prefer Champagne to wine"?

Yet wine it is, made from the fermented and refermented juice of the Chardonnay and the Pinot Noir grapes produced on a select group of hillsides and slopes near Reims and Epernay, in northeastern France, about 90 miles from Paris. Sparkling wines erroneously called Champagne are produced in other parts of the world, including some good ones in California and New York State, but these have borrowed the name from a geographical region of France. Some of them are distinctive enough to merit their own identities, yet they are called Champagne, as if the term were generic for a particular type of wine. The use of the name is strictly legal of course, because the French *appellation contrôlée* laws cannot be applied outside the Common Market. But somehow the need to copy a name downgrades the product, and it is interesting to note that Moët et Chandon, the biggest Champagne producer and also a major producer of sparkling wines in California under the name Domaine Chandon, does not call its California product Champagne. Rather, it is simply Napa Valley Brut or Cuvée de Pinot Noir, and the only reference to Champagne on the label is the notation that the wine is made by the *méthode champenoise,* or "traditional" Champagne process.

The sparkle is what sets Champagne apart from other wines. It consists of bubbles of carbon dioxide gas, one of the by-products of fermentation. Quantities of carbon dioxide are thrown off by all fermenting wines, but in the *méthode champenoise* the bubbles are retained in the bottle, where they wait to be released, and rise steadily to the surface after uncorking and pouring. For some elusive reason the presence of the bubbles transforms the relatively modest white wine produced in the Champagne District into an exciting and extraordinary beverage capable of thrilling and exhilarating the drinker. Some good still wines are produced in Champagne, but they do not have the same almost magical powers as when the bubbles are present. Still Champagnes are rare outside France because the French government discourages their export.

Several theories exist about the discovery of Champagne, and one of them involves Dom Pérignon, a Benedictine monk who was cellar-master at the abbey of Hautvillers, not far from Epernay, in the late seventeenth and early eighteenth centuries. The growers around Champagne had already noticed that their wines went through an upheaval during the spring following the harvest. They worked and bubbled, and sometimes the bubbles were captured in the bottles in small quantities. This was not terribly unusual, because *vin pétillant,* or slightly sparkling wine, could be found occasionally in most wine-producing areas. Whenever too many of the bubbles were captured, the bottles exploded, so the bubbles were not an altogether desirable development.

But Dom Pérignon is said to have perceived the possibility of intentionally capturing the bubbles and producing sparkling wine on a commercial scale. The task took him twenty years, but eventually he came up with cork stoppers (wood or cotton had been used previously), the practice of tying down the stoppers with string, and the use of stronger bottles capable of containing the gas without exploding. He also is credited with starting the practice of blending wines from various parts of the Champagne District to produce the most pleasing result. This practice continues today, and Champagne remains one of the few noble wines of France that is almost always a blend of wines from various vineyards.

According to another theory, it was the English who created commercial sparkling Champagne—and by accident. For centuries the English imported much of their French wine in bulk—that is, in casks or barrels—and then bottled it in their own country. If the bulk importation of Champagne was timed just right, the wine would be undergoing its second fermentation in the spring following the harvest, just as it was being bottled in England. The result was sparkling wine, which English wine lovers found to be a delightful and unique experience. But regardless of who it was who made the discovery, it was the basis for a new and different kind of wine. The key factor was to make sure that the second fermentation, the one that began after the first fermentation had been halted by the cold of the winter, took place in bottles rather than in casks or vats that would permit the carbon dioxide to escape into the open air, as it does when all still wines are produced.

The production of Champagne is different even before the grape juice is fermented. The wine is made from grapes produced by some 15,000 vineyard owners with holdings, mostly very small, in the carefully defined Champagne District. The soil is almost pure chalk and is responsible for the wine's distinctive taste. The main growing area is on the mountain of Reims, which runs roughly between Reims and Epernay, in the Marne Valley and in the Côte des Blancs. The grapes are either Pinot Noir or Chardonnay, which are also used for red and white Burgundy, respectively. In Champagne the Pinot Noir is vinified in such a way that it produces white wine, the dark skins having been removed very early in the process. There has been a trend in recent years to produce *blanc de blancs*— white wine strictly from the white, or Chardonnay, grapes—and these Champagnes seem to be lighter and drier. But they also lack the distinctive character of traditional Champagne, with its fuller body and greater depth. Generally, Champagne is made from a blend of both red and white grapes, and the blend, or *cuvée,* will change with each producer.

The growers sell their grapes to the producers at prices that vary according to where they were grown. The price for the best growths, or *crus,* is worked out in advance of the harvest each autumn. This is the standard by which all the others are priced—each as a percentage of the price of the best. The quality of the growths depends on geography and tradition: the vineyards that have always produced superior wines are usually the ones with better soil, drainage, and exposure to the sun. The district is divided into cantons, each with its own specific *crus.* In the canton of Ay, for example, the Bouzy *cru* receives 100 percent of the negotiated price, whereas the Romery *cru* receives 83 percent. An excellent Champagne may, however, contain portions of both, reflecting the desire of the producer to achieve what he considers an ideal *cuvée,* or blend. Obviously, under this system there is no such thing as wine made from the grapes of only one vineyard— the prevailing system for making the best Bordeaux and Burgundies.

Once the big Champagne houses have bought their grapes, they are taken to one of the *vendangeoirs,* or press houses, strategically positioned around the district so that the grapes do not have to be transported long distances and risk premature fermentation en route. There are generally three or four pressings, but only the juice of the first two or three is retained by the better houses. The result of the final pressing is usually sold off to smaller houses making lesser Champagnes or for the production of *vin ordinaire* for the workers. Some 10 million gallons or more of Champagne are made each year, as well as smaller quantities of still white wine often called Champagne Nature, and even smaller amounts of the local red wine, Bouzy Rouge, which does not seem to reach the same quality levels as good Burgundies. Pink Champagne is also produced by leaving the purple skins of the Pinot Noir grapes in the fermenting juice a little longer, but only very small amounts are produced. About 100,000 men, women, and children work in the

Champagne harvest, including 60,000 to 70,000 from elsewhere in France. Many come from the northern coal mines and use their two weeks in the vineyards as a semiholiday for clearing out their lungs in the local fresh air. Of course all the vineyard workers receive their daily ration of wine, which is sometimes trucked in from southern Beaujolais and other points south. As in the other major wine-producing areas of the country, it is a time of merriment and revelry, especially if the weather has been good through the autumn and it seems likely that a vintage will be declared.

Vintage Champagne is made only in the best years, when large amounts of grapes have reached just the proper ripeness. This happens perhaps once every three years, although sometimes several vintage years in a row may occur. Vintage Champagnes will vary substantially in style and character, each having the traits peculiar to the wines produced in that particular year. The 1969s were soft and rounded, for example, while the 1966s were more robust, with a higher level of acidity and more backbone. Most Champagne, however, is nonvintage, meaning that it is a blend of wines produced in two or more years. Each Champagne house tries to blend its nonvintage wines to have similar characteristics year after year, so that customers will keep coming back in the knowledge that they can obtain a consistent product. Vintage Champagne is not necessarily any better than nonvintage, although it costs more. It is likely to be more distinctive, but some very sophisticated connoisseurs prefer the nonvintage variety. It is a question of personal taste and, of course, economics. But no host need fear that he is serving something second-rate when he offers a nonvintage Champagne, for it will be one of the best made wines in the world.

From the presses in the *vendangeoirs* the wine is placed in vats and then barrels to be taken to the cellars of the producing houses, which are mainly in Reims, Epernay, and Ay. Sugar may be added in the process known as chaptalization to make sure that enough fermentation occurs to bring the wine up to at least 10 percent in alcoholic content. The purpose of the sugar is not to sweeten the wine, for eventually it is all fermented out, and other methods are used to make sweeter Champagne. The wine stays in the barrels, fermenting for perhaps three weeks, and in this, the first fermentation, the carbon dioxide gas is allowed to escape into the atmosphere. Toward the end of the year, after the bits of grapes and the exhausted yeasts, which are the agents of fermentation, have settled to the bottom, the wine goes through its first racking. This involves drawing the wine off the residue, or lees. Then the blending occurs, as each house tries to produce its own distinctive wine. At least two more rackings take place before the crucial second fermentation.

During the cold winter months the young wine lies relatively dormant. Bottling takes place in the spring and early summer, and it is at this point that the unique *méthode champenoise,* which separates Champagne from all other wines, is invoked. It involves the addition of the *liqueur de tirage*—a bit of liquid cane or beet sugar mixed with wine—for each bottle produced. After it is bottled, the *liqueur de tirage* begins to react with the yeasts in the wine, producing slightly more alcohol (about 1 percent) and the vital carbon dioxide gas which this time is kept in the bottle. This second fermentation must occur inside each bottle for the *méthode champenoise* to be fulfilled. (Sparkling wine can also be made by a bulk method, in which the second fermentation takes place in large, sealed tanks, but not legally in Champagne.)

The second fermentation occurs deep in the cellars carved out of the chalky subsoil of the Champagne District, with the bottles lying on their sides. The fermentation switches on and off, depending on the activity of the yeasts, and more sediment is produced. To prevent it from sticking to the sides of the bottles, they must be moved at least every six or eight months, even if only from one huge stack to another. When they are moved, bottles from the middle of the stack, where the heat of fermentation is most concentrated, are shifted to the outside, so that all will undergo the same maturation and development. Each bottle has a temporary cork or cap at this point. The fermentation takes about three months, but the bottles are left in the cellars for two years or more in all to develop additional character.

Toward the end of their aging period the bottles are removed from their stacks and placed in *pupitres,* so that the newly formed sediment inside can be induced to slide toward the corks. *Pupitres* are wooden boards with holes in them for the necks of the Champagne bottles. In each *pupitre* two boards about five feet tall and three feet wide are hinged together and stand upright in an inverted "V," whose angle can be changed in order to change the tilt of the bottles stuck in the holes. Each bottle's butt receives a white mark so that its position in the *pupitre* can be altered and closely monitored in the process known as *rémuage.* Working deep underground along row after row of *pupitres* bristling with bottles, expert *rémueurs* deftly twist and rotate each bottle individually with a motion that takes five years of training to perfect. Each man has his own technique and decides whether to give each bottle a quarter turn or an eighth turn. A good *rémueur* can turn 70,000 bottles in an eight-hour day, all the while keeping close track of the white marks and the angle at which each bottle is tilted. Gradually, over a period of weeks, the bottles are worked almost into a vertical upside-down position, and the sediment, which has been induced to move downward by the *rémuage,* finally nestles against the cork in a compact ball.

Next comes the *dégorgement,* or the disgorging of the sediment, so that each bottle contains only crystal-clear sparkling wine. In preparation, the bottles are taken from the long subterranean rows of *pupitres* and are stacked again, but this time upside down, with the neck of one bottle inserted in the indentation in the butt of the one below it. Sometimes the bottles are stored like this for years before the *dégorgement,* and at least one firm, Bollinger, markets a premium "R-D" Champagne, one that has been *récemment dégorgée*—recently disgorged—after spending a decade upside down with the sediment stored in the neck. The Bollinger R-D 1961, for example, was disgorged on February 23, 1973, and tasted fresh, fruity, and full-bodied when sampled at the firm's tasting room in Ay in May of the same year. Ordinarily, however, the *dégorgement* takes place shortly after the *rémuage*.

This process involves just as much skill as the *rémuage,* although it has been automated successfully by the big Champagne houses. Still upside down, the necks of the bottles are placed for a few minutes in a brine solution that is well below the freezing point of water (the brine prevents the solution from freezing). The result is that the sediment and a bit of wine are frozen against the cork. The bottles are then stood upright, and the corks—or metal caps, if true corks have not been used—are removed. The pressure inside the bottle forces out the frozen sediment with surprisingly little loss of wine when the *dégorgement* is accomplished with the proper skill. Then a bit of sugary wine, the *dosage,* is added, and the bottles receive their final corks.

The *dosage* is necessary with even the driest Champagnes, because the fermentation eliminates virtually all of the natural sugar in the wine. The amount of *dosage* will vary according to how sweet a Champagne is desired, and it will contain a tiny bit of brandy to act as a stabilizing agent. Most people prefer their Champagne bone dry, so the majority receives only a minute *dosage* and is then topped up with some of the same wine from another bottle. Each producer follows his own practice, which is usually kept secret, but typical *dosages* are as follows:

Brut	0.5 percent *dosage*
Extra Dry	1 to 2 percent
Sec or Dry	2 to 4 percent
Demi-Sec	4 to 6 percent
Doux	8 to 10 percent

Bottles to be made into *doux,* the sweetest Champagne, usually reserved for drinking with dessert, often need to have some of their contents syphoned off to make room for the *dosage,* or *liqueur d'expédition.* The *dosage* does not mean that these wines are 8 to 10 percent sugar, because only a portion of the *liqueur d'expédition* is sugar. *Brut,* the driest Champagne, must have a tiny *dosage* to add to its character. For American and British palates anything sweeter than *brut* or extra dry (sometimes called extra-sec) seems almost cloying, and examples of the sweeter varieties are difficult to find in these countries. Yet they go very well with sweet desserts and with ripe fruits—so well, in fact, that some gourmets contend that a Champagne demi-sec is a better accompaniment with a very ripe pear than a German Mosel of the Auslese degree of sweetness.

Brut Champagnes tend to be the best of all, because the quality of the wine used to make them must be the highest. They are so dry that any flaws are readily detectable. The additional sweetness of the other types tends to mask any shortcomings in the wine. It also impedes the ability to taste superior wine, so the best tends to be reserved for making the driest. In recent years there has been a trend toward the production of premium brands of the highest quality. Moët et Chandon's Dom Pérignon, for example, now has many competitors, including Louis Roederer's Cristal, Charles Heidsieck's Royal Cuvée, Mumm's René Lalou, and Laurent Perrier's Grand Siècle, as well as a range of *blanc de blancs* from such houses as Taittinger and Mercier which sell at premium prices. The basic nonvintage product from all of the big Champagne houses, however, is always excellent wine, and the consumer must decide for himself whether the premium bottlings are worth the extra cost, which can be substantial.

After the *dégorgement,* the *dosage,* and the insertion of their permanent corks the bottles are closely inspected to assure that they are in perfect condition. Then they are returned to the cellars of the Champagne houses for more bottle-age so that the alcohol in the wine can soften the natural acidity and create the balance of lightness and body that consumers have come to expect over generations. These storage cellars, by the way, are often open to public inspection, and some of the leading firms run tours in the hope of creating converts to their products. The *caves* of the largest house, Moët et Chandon in Epernay, stretch for 18 miles beneath the town and contain some 40 million bottles. Even a smaller house, such as Bollinger, keeps an inventory of six million bottles in its cellars at Ay, and it is estimated that the subterranean Champagne vaults in Reims extend for 200 miles. They are cold the year round, helping the wine stored there to mature in the slow and balanced way that results in the best Champagne.

There are 25 major Champagne houses that account for more than 90 percent of the production, plus a host of smaller firms and cooperatives that market their wine either under their own names or as private brands. Some two-thirds of the output is accomplished by only three firms: Moët et Chandon, Mumm, and Piper-Heidsieck. To say that one is better than another is merely to state a preference for the style and character of the Champagne it produces and markets, for all follow the high standards established by a governing organization, the Comité Interprofessionel du Vin de Champagne, known throughout the trade as the C.I.V.C. The group was organized in 1941 and, among other things, lays down regulations for the production and distribution of all Champagne wine. It levies a tax of 1 to 1.5 percent on each harvest and raises additional funds with a tax on the sale of bottles. All growers and producers must adhere to its rules, and, as a result, the standards for Champagne are among the highest anywhere in the world. People who want to lay in a stock can choose among these top houses:

Ayala
Bollinger
Castellane
Charbaut
Deutz
Gosset
Charles Heidsieck
Heidsieck Monopole
Henriot
Krug
Lanson
Laurent Perrier
Louis Roederer
Mercier
Moët et Chandon
G. H. Mumm
Perrier-Jouët
Philipponnat
Piper-Heidsieck
Pol Roger
Pommery et Greno
Ruinart
Taittinger
Venoge
Veuve Clicquot-Ponsardin

Mercier and Ruinart are now controlled by Moët et Chandon, which makes it the giant of the industry. It also controls Hennessy Cognac. In another consolidation, Mumm, Perrier-Jouët, and Heidsieck Monopole have been brought under the Seagram's umbrella. Yet each of these Champagnes has maintained its own individuality. Some of the smaller houses have won renown for producing especially distinctive Champagnes, usually with the greater body and fuller flavor that come from the use of the Pinot Noir grape heavily in their *cuvées,* rather than the Chardonnay white grape. In this category would be Bollinger, presided over for many years by Madame Lily Bollinger, Krug, Louis Roederer, and Veuve Clicquot.

CHAMPAGNE AND FOOD.

Because it has traditionally been the wine of celebrations, Champagne is generally not consumed during a meal. It is best as an aperitif or during and after the dessert course. A few years ago 50 members of the New York Chapter of the International Wine and Food Society undertook an unusual experiment. They prevailed upon André Soltner, the chef and part owner of the New York restaurant Lutèce, to produce a five-course meal for them, each course designed to be accompanied by Cham-

pagne with a different degree of sweetness. The sweeter varieties had to be
specially imported for the event, which
was planned by George J. Nelson, one
of the leading gastronomes of the United
States. The black-tie dinner was a marvelous success as a social event and as
an experiment, but at its conclusion Mr.
Nelson stated with unimpeachable cer-
tainty, "I don't think we will try it
again." In other words, the operation
was a success but the patient died. The
meal was splendid and the wines were
splendid, but Champagne simply was
not appropriate during the main courses.
At Château de Saran, the country house
maintained outside Epernay by Moët et
Chandon for fortunate guests, vintage
dry Moët is served as an aperitif. The
firm's still Champagne Nature is served
with the fish course, a red Bordeaux
comes with the meat course, and
Champagne is served again with dessert.
Not even the biggest and presumably
the most knowledgeable of all the
Champagne houses would serve its excellent sparkling wine throughout a meal.

It is worth noting that Champagne
at Château de Saran is served in fairly
tall tulip-shaped glasses—not in the
shallow saucerlike glasses that seem to
be so popular at American restaurants.
Shallow glasses cause the bubbles in the
wine to dissipate too rapidly and they
tend to spill easily. The best Champagne
glasses are tall tulips or flutes that enable the bubbles to rise from a single
point at the very bottom. They also
capture the wine's bouquet more efficiently and are easier to handle. (*See*
Glassware in Part I.)

☆☆/☆☆☆

$$/$$$$

Chappellet Vineyard.

This is another of Napa Valley's small
wineries, which has established a rep-
utation for fine varietals such as Chenin
Blanc and Cabernet Sauvignon. Donn

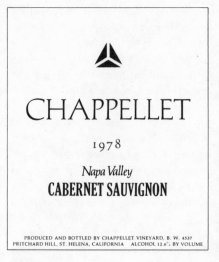

CHAPPELLET

1978

Napa Valley

CABERNET SAUVIGNON

PRODUCED AND BOTTLED BY CHAPPELLET VINEYARD, B. W. 4537
PRITCHARD HILL, ST. HELENA, CALIFORNIA   ALCOHOL 12.6% BY VOLUME

Chappellet has created an exquisite and
functional facility to try to realize his
dream of making some of the finest
wines California can produce. The set-
ting itself and its view of the valley are
something to behold. Winding up into
the hills east of the Silverado Trail, which
courses north on the eastern side of the
valley, a visitor wonders at certain points
if the trail has been lost, when suddenly
a dark and unusual shape takes form
amid the trees. A triangular pyramid,
12 feet on each side at the base, its
russet roof burnished by afternoon sun,
seems to rise right out of the earth.
Inside, the sloping, three-sided roof soars
to 50 feet in the center of its cathe-
drallike structure, which is filled with
new equipment and cooperage.

The Chappellet Vineyard is really a
family operation. In 1967 Donn Chap-
pellet quit the high life in Beverly Hills
which a successful vending-machine
business, the Interstate United Corpo-
ration, had fostered and sank his for-
tune into 100 acres on top of Pritchard
Hill. Total production at Chappellet
amounts to 25,000 cases a year. The
best are the Cabernet Sauvignon, con-
sistently elegant and complex, and the
Chardonnay, also made in an elegant

style. Would-be visitors should not drop by without calling first, because these people are involved and busy; but if they say "Come ahead," go—the view from the top is spectacular.

☆/☆☆☆☆

$$/$$$

Chaptalization.

The practice of adding sugar to the must, or fermenting grape juice, to increase the alcoholic content of the wine is known as chaptalization. Because sugar is a natural product of mature grapes and is responsible for the alcoholic content of wine, its addition can be helpful in mediocre vintages when there has been too little sun and an imbalance of rain, resulting in low natural sugar development. Too often, however, more sugar is added than is necessary, reflecting the efforts of winemakers to produce more alcoholic wines that qualify for higher ratings under national wine laws. Chaptalization is especially prevalent in the Burgundy District of France and is practiced to a lesser extent in Bordeaux. The process derives its name from Chaptal, Minister of Agriculture under Napoleon, who is credited with promoting its use. When abused, chaptalization can be employed to create additional quantities of wine and therefore to increase the profits of the producer, because the addition of sugar to the must, along with water, adds to the bulk while maintaining the alcoholic level. Widespread suspicions exist that the process is abused, but most winemakers agree that it is often appropriate to chaptalize under strict controls.

Chardonnay.

The best grape of white Burgundy is the Chardonnay, which also produces the finest white table wines of California and some other states. It makes wines of great depth and finesse, with an al-

most creamy or buttery richness in the best vintages. All of the best white Burgundies come from this grape—Le Montrachet, Corton-Charlemagne, Chablis, and Pouilly-Fuissé, for example. Some California Chardonnays have proved in recent years that they are the equal of the great whites of Burgundy. The same grape is used to produce Champagne in France, usually blended with the Pinot Noir.

Chassagne-Montrachet.

Good red wines are made in Chassagne-Montrachet, one of the excellent *communes* of the Côte de Beaune in the heart of the French Burgundy country, but the *commune* is best known for its magnificent whites. Chassagne-Montrachet shares the *grands crus* vineyards of Le Montrachet and Bâtard-Montrachet with the neighboring *commune* of Puligny-Montrachet. These are two of the greatest white wines produced in the world. Chassagne also has a *grand cru* of its own in Criots-Bâtard-Montrachet, which is another truly superb white. These are big and rich whites, with a touch of earthiness and a flavor subtly evocative of herbs and spices. Sometimes their texture is so full that it can best be described as creamy. Only the superb Corton-Charlemagne ever challenges them, and many experts say the challenge usually falls short. The production is limited and these wines are always extremely expensive. Sometimes they are attacked by the *pourriture noble,* or beneficial noble rot, which is important in the production of Sauternes and the best German whites.

La Domaine de la Romanée-Conti owns a slice of Le Montrachet, as does the Marquis de Laguiche, who often produces the best wine. Other important owners include Baron Thénard, Bouchard Père et Fils, Jacques Prieur and Mme Boillereault de Chauvigné. The total annual production of genuine Le

Montrachet available for commercial sale is believed to be less than 1000 cases. These wines should not be confused with the *commune* wines Chassagne-Montrachet or Puligny-Montrachet. Among the *premiers crus* of Chassagne are the following:

Abbaye de Morgeot
Boudriotte
Brussolles
Caillerets
Champs Gain
Chenevottes
Clos St-Jean
Grands Ruchottes
Macherelles
Maltroie
Morgeot
Romanée
Vergers

(*See also* Puligny-Montrachet.)
☆☆/☆☆☆☆
$$/$$$

Château.

Many vineyards and wineries in France include the word "château" in their names. It means "castle" or "mansion" and implies wines of character and renown, although the implication is not always accurate. Virtually all Bordeaux wines available in export markets are called "Château" something or other, even if in many cases they are not château-bottled. The names of all of the most famous Bordeaux wines start with "Château," e.g., Château Latour, Château Margaux, Château Haut-Brion, Château Lafite-Rothschild, and Château Mouton Rothschild. Some Beaujolais wines also use the word, e.g., Château de Pizay and Château de la Chaize. A few Burgundies use the word, and its use has spread to some other countries as well. In general, "Château" can be regarded as part of a brand name but implies little about the quality of

the wine. (In this book all wines whose names start with "Château" are listed alphabetically under the specific name of the vineyard or winery—e.g., Château Ausone is listed under "A" and Château Beychevelle under "B," etc.)

Châteauneuf-du-Pape.

The best known wine from the Rhône River District of France is Châteauneuf-du-Pape, a big and robust red produced under strict quality controls in the area north of Avignon and south of Orange. Some white Châteauneuf is made, but the name has achieved world renown because of the durable red that is highly unusual among French noble wines in that it is produced with as many as 13 grape varieties blended to achieve balance, depth, and longevity. These include Grenache, Syrah, Clairette, Picpoul, Mourvèdre, Terret Noir, Counoise, Muscardin, Vaccarèse, Picardan, Cinsault, Roussanne, and Bourboulenc. Châteauneuf-du-Pape is a very full-bodied, earthy wine that occasionally will challenge the big red Burgundies of the Côte d'Or in character if not elegance. It is best after ten years of bottle-age and can remain in excellent condition for two decades or more. It is a traditional accompaniment to wild boar, venison, and other game, but also goes well with almost any red meat.

The wine takes its name from the "new castle of the pope" built in the fourteenth century when Avignon, rather than Rome, was the base of the papacy. Pope Clément V, once the Bishop of Bordeaux, started the construction, and it was completed by Clément VI. Its purpose was to function as a summer home in the picturesque hills above the Rhône River. Today the castle is in ruins, but its name lives on in the form of the wine produced in the sunny vineyards nearby. Round stones, perhaps deposited there thousands of years ago by a glacier, lie everywhere among the vines, reflecting the heat of the sun and enabling the grapes to achieve great maturity and a natural sugar content capable of producing unusually high alcoholic strength. The legal alcohol level must be at least 12.5 percent, the highest minimum in France, and wines of somewhat greater strength are made in good years. This adds to their longevity.

It was in the Châteauneuf area that the French *appellation contrôlée* laws were born 13 years before they were applied in 1936 to other parts of the country. The leader in this movement was the late Baron Le Roy de Boiseaumarié, whose name still appears on Châteauneuf labels in connection with Château Fortia, where some of the best wine is produced. The rules specify the areas where the grapes can be grown, the type of grapes, the yield per acre, and the specific name to which the wine is entitled. As a result, quality standards are high, and consumers as well as legitimate growers are protected from misnamed wines. In Châteauneuf the blend of grape varieties may vary according to the style of the producer, so that individual wines display differing personalities while maintaining the essential robust and earthy character of the area.

Besides Château Fortia, the wine appears under a number of other specific vineyard or estate names, including Château des Fines Roches, Château Maucoil, Château Rayas, Château de Vaudieu, Clos de l'Oratoire, Clos des Papes, Clos St-Jean, Domaine de Beaucastel, Domaine de Beaurénard, Domaine de Mont-Rédon, Domaine de Nalys, Domaine de la Nerthe, Domaine de Saint-Préfert, Domaine de Sénéchaux, Domaine du Vieux Télégraphe, la Gardine, and Père Cabache. In addition, there are many bottlings simply labeled Châteauneuf-du-Pape, with no vineyard name.

A small quantity of white Châteauneuf-du-Pape is also produced, but it is rarely seen in export markets. It is worth trying when encountered, because it tends to be fairly robust and earthy for a white wine and lasts longer than most. Red Châteauneuf bears a certain similarity to Hermitage, another great wine from the Rhône District, but does not have quite the same longevity, reflecting a tendency in recent years to produce less robust wines which are ready to be consumed at a younger age, although still not as early as a Beaujolais or simple Côtes-du-Rhône.
☆☆☆/☆☆☆☆
$$/$$$

Chenin Blanc.

The wine grape of the Loire Valley in France, Chenin Blanc is responsible for such delightful wines as Vouvray, Saumur, and *vins du pays* of Anjou and La Touraine. Also known as Pineau de la Loire, the variety is widely planted in California, where it produces fresh, fruity wines, best enjoyed quite young. It is often used in blended California wines bearing the generic label Chablis, but as a varietal it often achieves considerable grace on its own, whether vinified completely dry or slightly sweet.

Château Cheval Blanc.

If it is possible for a wine to display all of the best traits of both Saint-Emilion and Pomerol, Château Cheval Blanc does so. The vineyard reigns supreme among the great red wines produced in Saint-Emilion in the Bordeaux region of southwestern France, and consistently brings prices equal to the first growths of the Médoc. Yet it lies on the northeast edge of Saint-Emilion, and only a ten-foot border separates Cheval Blanc from Château La Conseillante, one of the leading growths of Pomerol. This is the *graves,* or gravelly and flat portion of Saint-Emilion, as opposed to the *côtes,* or slopes, immediately surrounding the village of Saint-Emilion itself. The better wines generally are produced on the *côtes,* but Cheval Blanc and the neighboring Château Figeac are exceptions. They and Châteaux l'Evangile, Vieux-Certan, and Pétrus in Pomerol lie along a slightly elevated ridge running northward through the two great Bordeaux *communes.* The soil on this rise tends to be less sandy and more calciferous than in the lower vineyards and is believed responsible for producing better wines.

In the Saint-Emilion classification of 1955 Cheval Blanc and Château Ausone were ranked atop the other *premiers grands crus classés* in a separate category all their own. In recent years Cheval Blanc has been regarded as superior in quality to Ausone, and the prices it consistently brings show it. It is a big and rich wine, with extraordinary fullness and depth. Yet at maturity it displays great elegance and finesse. It clearly deserves to be ranked in the "Big Eight" reds of Bordeaux, which also include Château Ausone, Château Pétrus in Pomerol, Château Haut-Brion in Graves, and Châteaux Lafite-Rothschild, Margaux, Latour, and Mouton Rothschild in the Médoc. Cheval Blanc's annual production of about 10,000 cases is smaller than all of the Médoc first growths but several times the volume produced by Ausone and Pétrus.

☆☆☆☆
$$$/$$$$

Château Chevalier.

Château Chevalier is one of the older wine estates in California's Napa Valley, with origins dating back to the 1870s, when Jacob Beringer bought land 1000 feet above sea level on Spring Mountain and planted a vineyard. He sold a piece of the estate to a Frenchman named Fortune Chevalier in 1884, and Chevalier, a San Francisco wholesaler of wine and spirits, decided to get into wine production. He expanded by acquiring nearby vineyards, and built a Victorian stone château in 1891 that still stands. This became Château Chevalier. Greg and Kathy Bissonette bought the château and 280-acre estate in 1969, but only 40 acres were plantable at the time, so they began clearing the land, and expanded the vineyard to 60 acres. The winery was opened in 1973, and the operation was sold in 1978. The buyers were Gil Nickel, owner of the Far Niente Winery in Oakville, and his brother, John Nickel. All of the Château Chevalier wines are estate-bottled, meaning that they are made only from grapes grown on the nearby estate. Wines made from purchased grapes are marketed under the Mountainside label.

Château Chevalier attracted attention with a Cabernet Sauvignon 1975 Private Reserve made from grapes harvested from the best section of vineyard, which often yields wines of greater intensity and flavor. Most of the Château Chevalier wines are aged in French oak barrels, and production now totals about 10,000 cases a year of Cabernet Sauvignon, Chardonnay, and Pinot Noir under the principal label, and Chardonnay, Pinot Noir, Merlot, Zinfandel, and Cabernet Sauvignon under the Mountainside label.

☆☆/☆☆☆☆
$$

Chevaliers du Tastevin.

The most famous wine society in the world is, under its full name, La Confrérie des Chevaliers du Tastevin, which translates as the Brotherhood of Knights of the Wine-Tasting Cup. It was conceived in 1933, which was to be the fourth mediocre vintage in succession following the great 1929, and was formally established in 1934—a good vintage year. The world was deep in the throes of the Depression, and the goal of the Chevaliers was to promote the sale of Burgundy wines. Among the founders were the late Camille Rodier and Charles Faiveley, and it is probable that they did not foresee how successful their society would become. The initial meetings were held in a wine cellar in Nuits-St-Georges, the principal town of the Côte de Nuits subdivision of the French Burgundy country, where the working headquarters of the Confrérie still exists.

The true home of the society, however, is the Château du Clos de Vougeot, which stands in the middle of the famous Clos de Vougeot vineyard, a few miles north of Nuits. The immense stone château was built by the Cistercian monks starting in the twelfth century, and was restored in 1891 before falling into disrepair again. Since the Chevaliers acquired it, shortly after their formation, it has been continuously renovated, largely with donations from wealthy members from all over the world, including many from the United States. The gravel-floored banquet hall can seat upward of 500 people for the spectacular feasts held there each Saturday night in the spring and fall. Ancient stone arches support the high ceilings, and the tables are arranged in formation around a stage next to the tapestried south wall.

The central table, where the aristocrats of Burgundy sit with their guests, is set up in a long horseshoe shape and is named Clos Vougeot. All of the other long tables, each with places for 30 to 40 diners, are named after a famous Burgundian *cru*—for example, Romanée, Richebourg, Corton, Chambertin, etc. Participants receive tickets that identify their tables by these names. Induction ceremonies are held in a room off to the side in advance of the dinner, which usually begins with the blaring of elongated trumpets at 8 P.M. The celebrants are serenaded with Burgundian folk songs by the Cadets de Bourgogne, a group of surprisingly talented local *vignerons,* who loll about the stage extolling in song the virtues of Burgundy wines, all the while consuming bottle after bottle of their subject matter. Arrayed above the Cadets is a banner proclaiming the motto of the Confrérie: *Jamais en vain, Toujours en vin.* Around the tables toasts are drunk to their *"bon maître"* François Rabelais, and an array of Burgundian wines are served by waiters who are somehow able to clutch the necks of four bottles in one hand while pouring with the other. The men traditionally wear tuxedos and their bejeweled ladies are in long gowns. The symbol of membership, the silver *tastevin,* is hung on a scarlet and gold ribbon around the neck.

The banquet involves six courses, all of which miraculously arrive properly hot or cold, depending on what is appropriate, and the feast goes on until after one o'clock in the morning. The first course is often cold roast suckling pig Dijonnaise—with the famous mustard of Dijon from the northern end of the Burgundy country. The author was present for the fortieth-anniversary feast of the Confrérie, held November 16, 1974, as part of *Les Trois Glorieuses,* or Three Days of Celebration, surrounding the annual wine auction at the Hospices de Beaune. Following is the menu for that occasion, reproduced in French. An English translation could not do jus- | tice to the subtle humor of the French wording, so none will be attempted.

Première Assiette
Le Jambon Persillé Dijonnaise
relevé de bonne Moutarde forte de Dijon
escorté d'un Bourgogne Aligoté frais et gouleyant
des Hautes Côtes de Nuits

Deuxième Assiette
Le Loup Farci en Croûte Brillat-Savarin
humidifié d'un Pouilly-Fuissé 1971 subtil et bouqueté

Entremets
Les Oeufs en Meurette
arrosés d'un Côte de Nuits-Villages 1971 soyeux et prenant

Dorure
Le Poulet Gaston-Gérard
accompagné d'un Beaune Montée Rouge 1971 suave et caressant

Issue de Table
Les Bons Fromages de Bourgogne et d'Ailleurs
rehaussés d'un Clos de la Roche 1964 de mémorable lignée

Boutehors
L'Escargot en Glace et les Poires Clos de Vougeot
Le Tastevin Anniversaire en Nougatine et les Petits Fours

Le Café Noir, Le Vieux Marc et la Prunelle de Bourgogne
fort idoines à stimuler vapeurs subtiles du cerveau

The membership of the Chevaliers du Tastevin is theoretically made up of people with a prodigious knowledge of wine, especially Burgundy wine, but in practice the inductees are those whose membership can help fulfill the principal goal of the society: to promote the consumption and prestige of Burgundy. Thus the worldwide membership roster includes many prominent citizens whose oenology is limited. Their participation, however, is considered valuable for promotional reasons. Inductions are held not only at Clos de Vougeot but at various local chapters around the world. The Sous-Commanderie de New York, headed by Edward Hartley Benenson, one of the great American Burgundy lovers, inducts candidates each January, but the waiting list is so long that joining at Clos de Vougeot itself has been more easily accomplished for some years. Through the inspiration of the late Clifford Weihmann, long the Grand Pilier Général of the Confrérie in the United States, many other chapters have been established in such cities as San Francisco, Toledo, Washington, D.C., New Orleans, St. Louis, Palm Beach, and Los Angeles.

Many *sous-commanderies* around the world, including the one in New York, do not admit women members, although many have been inducted at Clos de Vougeot. The French, it seems, have been more sexually egalitarian than the Americans. In his book *The Wines of Burgundy* (Stein & Day, 1970), H. W. Yoxall gave this superb explanation of the role of women: "Women are admitted to the order, and woman guests welcomed. In my recollection half at least of these were chic, which is a high proportion anywhere; and here and there one sees a type—not chic, indeed, but something much more interesting—who seems a pure Toulouse-Lautrec character coming from the Parisian music halls of the 1890's. These are undoubtedly the ones who best understand Burgundy."

Wherever they occur, inductions into the Confrérie are highly ceremonial events. The leaders wear robes of gold and scarlet, and each inductee takes an oath to drink nothing but Burgundy wines before being tapped solemnly on each shoulder with a Burgundian vine root. From time to time the oath is compromised of course, and it is interesting to note that H. Gregory Thomas, who heads the Commanderie de Bordeaux in the United States, is also a member of the hierarchy of the Chevaliers du Tastevin. Cries of *"scandale"* were heard when Mr. Thomas once inadvertently substituted the words "Chevalier du Tastevin" for "Commandeur de Bordeaux" during an induction ceremony for the Commanderie in New York. The *faux pas* was quickly corrected, but the startled inductee thought for a moment that he had come to the wrong party.

Château Chevre.

Château Chevre was one of the few California wineries established in the 1970s that devoted its initial production to Merlot, the principal red grape of the Pomerol subregion of Bordeaux. The property is in Yountville, in the Napa Valley. Annual production has risen to about 2000 cases, and Pinot Noir and Chardonnay were to be added to the product line.

☆☆/☆☆☆

$$

Chianti.

The Italian city of Florence may be best known for its art treasures, but in the Tuscan hills around Florence there is a different kind of treasure: Chianti. Some very great wines are made in the vineyards of Tuscany, but unfortunately the foreign image of Chianti is quite different. Generations of Americans have grown up identifying Chianti as the wine in the straw-covered basket, or *fiasco,* which is consumed in pizza parlors rather than in serious restaurants. Then, when the *fiasco* is empty, it becomes a candle holder that stands on the red-and-white-checkered tablecloths of the same pizza parlors. A huge amount of the Chianti exported from the Tuscan hills above Florence is consumed in just this way, and much of it is fairly ordinary wine, but it is not representative of the quality levels that Chianti can achieve.

The best Chiantis come in straight-sided bottles of the classic Bordeaux shape, and they display a rich elegance and charm that places them in the top rank of Italian wines and in the forefront of the red wines of the world. These are not frivolous wines; they require considerable bottle-age, should sometimes be decanted before serving, and complement fine food. Some of them keep on improving for a decade or more, and it can be interesting to compare a properly mature Chianti from one of the better Tuscan producers with a French Bordeaux of similar maturity. The better Chiantis are aged in oak casks for at least two years; this entitles them to add the designation *vecchio*—"old"—to their names. After three years in cask a Chianti can be called *riserva.*

The Chianti name dates back to the fourteenth century during the period when civil wars ravaged northern Italy, but the credit for developing the Chianti style is generally given to Baron Bettino

Ricasoli of Castle Brolio in the mid-1800s. According to legend, Ricasoli resented the advances of a young man toward his bride of only a few months at a ball in Florence, so he took her to Brolio and kept her there, out of the mainstream of Tuscan life, for the rest of their existence. At Brolio he experimented with viniculture and developed a blend of Sangiovese and Malvasia grapes which he vinified in two separate fermentations, the second starting about a year after the harvest with the addition of a quantity of rich dried grape must. Ricasoli was also a leading academic and political figure of his era, and, according to another legend, he spent many years at Castle Brolio because he found it convenient to experiment with grapes and vines during the periods when he was in political disfavor. He founded a Tuscan wine consortium in 1835, and, although it was short-lived, it was the predecessor of the *consorzio* of Chianti Classico established in 1924. Today Chianti is 50 to 80 percent Sangiovese, 10 to 30 percent Canaiolo, and 10 to 30 percent Trebbiano, Toscano, and Malvasia del Chianti grapes. The addition of dried must is known as the *governo,* and it gives the wine its freshness. The *governo* system is not used with the best Chiantis intended for lengthy bottle-aging.

The Chianti Classico Consorzio was used as an example when the Italian government established its *denominazione di origine controllata* in 1963. Ironically, the heirs of Baron Ricasoli have decided to drop out of the Classico Consorzio because they felt their financial support was doing more for their competitors than for themselves. The symbol of Chianti Classico is a roundish red neck label with a black rooster on it, and each bottle will carry one (except for the Ricasoli wines, even though they are made in the Classico zone, and the wines of a few other producers who also have dropped out). All of these labels must be registered and approved by the council of the *consorzio,* which has an agency in each community. The seals are issued to the growers by the branches of local banks, and the records go back to 1924, which means the authenticity of a bottle dating back that far can be verified. The growers pay for each seal, and this finances the activities of the *consorzio.*

Other *consorzi* have been formed in the Chianti areas surrounding Classico, and they have comparable rules and procedures to assure high quality. These groups include Chianti Colli Aretini, Chianti Colli Fiorentini, Chianti Colli Senesi, Chianti Colline Pisane, Chianti Montalbano, and Chianti Rufina. The latter group should not be confused with Ruffino, a family and brand-name Chianti widely available in the export markets. Each group has its own type of seal, or neck label, attesting to the authenticity of the wines, but this is not necessarily a guarantee of quality. After Classico the best wines are produced in Rufina, Montalbano, Fiorentini, and Senesi, although the production from Senesi is substantially larger than any other, including Classico, and includes some mediocre wines.

Brunello di Montalcino, perhaps the most magnificent and costly Italian wine, is produced in the Senesi area, but it is not a Chianti. It is one of the world's great red wines. Some other very good Chiantis play down their Chianti heritage and emphasize brand names. Among these are Ricasoli's Brolio Riserva, the Riserva Ducale of Ruffino, the Stravecchio of the Melini firm, the Villa Antinori of the House of Antinori, and the Nipozzano of Frescobaldi. Some of the smaller producers also make very good wines, and one of these is Olivieri, which is produced at La Romola, a thirteenth-century hilltop villa filled with antique

furniture and colorful muraled walls. Marcello Olivieri, who heads the firm, is one of the leading citizens of the district, and, as his name implies, he is also in the olive oil business. In fact, olive trees grow throughout many of the Chianti vineyards in a reminder of the fast-disappearing system of *mezzadria,* or share-cropping, which involves the cultivation of several crops on each parcel of land tilled by peasant farmers for their landlords. Visitors to estates such as La Romola may not only enjoy a wine tasting but an olive oil tasting as well. Another fine but lesser known producer is Poggio al Sole, whose Classicos are superbly balanced and textured. Experimentation with the wines of small Chianti producers that lack the reputations of the big companies can be rewarding. (*See also* Brunello di Montalcino, Brolio Chianti, Ruffino Chianti.)
☆☆☆/☆☆☆☆
$/$$$

Chicama Vineyards.

Chicama Vineyards, the property of George and Cathy Mathiesen, is making the island of Martha's Vineyard, beyond Buzzards Bay in the Atlantic Ocean off Massachusetts, live up to its name. The Mathiesens' first modest harvest of a half barrel of Chardonnay was in 1973, but production has grown in recent years to more than 5000 cases annually. They have plantings of such European varieties as Cabernet Sauvignon, Zinfandel, Pinot Noir, Chardonnay, and Gewürztraminer on a 30-acre tract. Some of the Chicama wines are made partly from grapes purchased from growers in California. The Zinfandel and Pinot Noir are especially successful.
☆/☆☆
$/$$

Chile.

In the middle of the last century Chile imported a group of French viniculturists and French vines in a serious effort at building up the wine industry, which had already existed for 200 years or more, since the early days of the Spanish missionaries. The new vines, along with others imported later from Europe, were planted in the area known as the Central Valley, which formed the nucleus of what was to become South America's leading producer of quality wines. Although Argentina now produces substantially more wine than Chile, and the Argentine reds have won a reputation for high quality, Chile is still regarded as the premium-wine country of South America. Unlike virtually all of the world's other major wine-producing countries, Chile has never been confronted with the vine blight known as Phylloxera, which wiped out most of the European vineyards in the second half of the last century. Whereas nearly all European vines are now grafted onto disease-resistant American roots, Chile's European vines grow on their own roots. Probably because of the Andes Mountains on the east and the Pacific Ocean on the west, Chile has been protected from an invasion of Phylloxera and thus can make the boast made by only a handful of European vineyards: that her vines are pre-Phylloxera.

Although lots of ordinary Chilean wine is produced, the better wines tend to be exported. Chilean Cabernet Sauvignon is the best of the reds and is not unlike claret from one of the *petits châteaux* of Bordeaux. Some Pinot Noir is also produced, along with Malbec, Merlot, and Cabernet Franc, among the other reds, but the Cabernet Sauvignon is usually the best. The best white of Chile is usually the Riesling, although some Sémillon and Sauvignon are also made. More robust, sweeter wines of less elegance are produced in the hot northern zone, closer to the equator.

Production is closely controlled by the Chilean government, partly in an effort to curb alcoholism, which has been regarded as a national problem. But, as in France and elsewhere, holding the yield per acre of vines to a specific maximum tends to result in higher quality wines. For the export markets Chilean whites must be at least 12 percent alcohol and the reds at least 11.5 percent. Wines bearing the *reservado* designation must be at least four years old, and those called *gran vino* must be at least six.

Chinon.

The production of Chinon, one of the best red wines of the Loire Valley of France, is limited, and the wine is not easily found in foreign markets. But it can be very fresh and charming when encountered. Chinon is best consumed within three or four years of the vintage and should be slightly chilled, like Beaujolais. It is made from the Cabernet Franc grape, which also produces Bourgueil in the Loire Valley and which is cultivated extensively in Saint-Emilion as well. The village of Chinon is in the Touraine portion of the Loire and is the birthplace of Rabelais, who wrote about the good local wines. (*See* Loire Valley, Touraine.)

☆☆/☆☆☆

$/$$

Chorey-les-Beaune.

Among the smaller *communes* of the Burgundian Côte de Beaune in France is Chorey-les-Beaune, whose 350 acres lie just north of Beaune, the capital of the Burgundy wine trade. This wine is rarely seen under its own name and is usually bottled as Côte de Beaune-Villages after blending with one or more wines from the other designated *communes* of the area. It has no *grands crus* or *premiers crus*.

☆☆☆

$$

Christian Brothers.

The Redwood Road to Mont La Salle winds sharply up into the foothills of the Mayacamas range of California's Napa Valley. In a clearing on a plateau, surrounded by vines that cover the curving hills, stands the monastery and novitiate of the Christian Brothers, a teaching order founded in Reims by Saint Jean Baptiste de la Salle in 1680. Today the worldwide order has schools and colleges in 80 countries. To support this endeavor the brothers at Mont La Salle make wine, here on the mountain and also down in the valley at St. Helena.

It is quite an operation. Christian Brothers has the largest holding of premium vineyards in the Napa Valley. With a storage and aging capacity of eight million gallons, they have the largest stock of aged premium wines in all of Napa County. Historically, in many famous wine regions of the world, vineyards were owned and tended by the church, the wines made by monks and priests. It is interesting that today Christian Brothers is the largest church-owned operation of its kind in the world.

The best known face at Christian Brothers is that of Brother Timothy, a tall, gracious man with warm blue eyes and a gift for conversing on many subjects. As cellar-master he supervises all of the winemaking activities at Christian Brothers. He has figured large in the development of California wines and the constant effort to improve them.

Christian Brothers wines, widely distributed in the United States and to over 40 countries abroad, include both generics and excellent varietals. Until 1979 all wines marketed by Christian Brothers were blends. The winery was one of the last major holdouts against vintage dating, on the theory that blending for consistency from year to year created customer loyalty. Since the vagaries of the weather could be virtually eliminated by not having to rely on a single harvest to produce a wine, it was felt that over the long term the Christian Brothers' reputation would benefit.

But this philosophy ignored the modern evolution of the market for California wines. Christian Brothers had devoted great effort and energy to the blending process, so it was understandable that a decision to change was difficult. But virtually all of the new California wineries were marketing vintage wines exclusively, and Christian Brothers seemed to be losing its share of the market. It was time for a change.

So the first Christian Brothers vintage wines were introduced in 1979 in a move that had long been predicted in the wine world despite frequent denials from Brother Timothy and others. This was an acknowledgment of the new face of the American consumer, who was curious about the differences between vintages and wanted to know precisely what year a wine had been made. A Cabernet Sauvignon 1974 and a Pinot Saint George 1975 were among the first Christian Brothers vintage wines, and they were superior products.

The Christian Brothers array of products is among the largest in the American wine industry. The generics include burgundy, claret, chablis, rhine, sauterne, La Salle Rosé, Napa Rosé and *vin rosé*. All are blended from several grape varieties. The burgundy, for example, is made from Pinot Noir, Napa Gamay, Petite Sirah, and Zinfandel.

Among varietals Christian Brothers not only makes vintage wines but also continues to produce nonvintage blends, which cost less. All of the major varietals are covered. There are also estate-bottled Napa Fumé Blanc, vintage Pinot Saint George, and vintage Pineau de la Loire made from grapes produced

entirely on the Christian Brothers' own estates. Brandies, Sherries, and Ports round out the line, and there are vermouth and several sparkling wines.

Christian Brothers' Greystone Cellars in St. Helena is one of the handsomest tasting facilities in Napa County, and visitors throng to its portals during the tourist season, which is now virtually year-round.

☆/☆☆☆
$/$$

Chusclan.

In the southern Rhône Valley of France, many wines of distinction are made. Most of the best are full-bodied reds, such as Hermitage and Châteauneuf-du-Pape, but the southern Rhône is also the home of some excellent rosés. The most famous is Tavel, from the village of the same name, but good rosé is also produced at Chusclan, just a few miles north. These rosés tend to be drier than others, and, if you close your eyes, you might mistake them for light-bodied red wines. Some red is also produced in Chusclan, and it can be good value, like the rosé. In general the wines of Chusclan are not meant for laying down in cellars. A bottle more than five years old should be viewed with suspicion. (*See* Rhône Valley, Tavel.)

☆☆/☆☆☆
$/$$

Cilurzo Vineyard & Winery.

Cilurzo was one of the early producers of grapes in Temecula, in Riverside County in southern California, not far from San Diego, with its first plantings there in 1968. A second vineyard and a winery were started in 1978, and production has risen to about 8000 cases a year of Chenin Blanc, Fumé Blanc, Petite Sirah, Cabernet Sauvignon, and Gamay Beaujolais. The wines have been distributed so far almost exclusively on the West Coast.

☆/☆☆☆

$/$$

Cinqueterre.

Cinqueterre is the white wine made mostly from Bosco and Albarola grapes in the Liguria region of northern Italy, which encompasses the Italian Riviera just below the Piedmont. Much of it is served in Riviera restaurants, and the wine has won D.O.C. recognition under Italian law. Sciacchetrà is a sweet, high-alcohol version of the same wine which is made from *passito* grapes that have been allowed to dry into raisins before pressing.

☆/☆☆☆

$/$$

Cinzano.

Cinzano is a major producer of ver-mouth, with extensive operations in Torino, Italy, and in the Italian Pied-mont District, where it produces good Asti Spumante. Cinzano also controls the Spalletti Chianti firm, which pro-duces excellent wines in the Rufina Chianti zone.

Ciró.

Ciró is the most famous wine of Cal-abria, the Italian region that comprises the toe of the boot, and its producers say it is the oldest wine region in the world. A Bianco, a Rosato, and a Rosso are made under the Italian D.O.C. law, and the one taken most seriously is the Rosso, made 95 percent from the Gag-lioppo grape. It is a big, strong wine that sometimes achieves 15 percent al-cohol.

☆/☆☆☆☆

$/$$

Claret.

The British term for red Bordeaux wine is "claret," and the word has a fairly strict meaning in that country, where it refers only to Bordeaux red. But claret has no legal standing in France, much less Bordeaux, and the term is widely used in other countries to refer to red wines in general. Because the word is English, not French, the "t" on the end is pronounced. One of the most ridic-ulous affectations in the discussion of wines is to pronounce claret as "clair-ay," as if the word were French.

Château Clarke.

This property in the central Haut-Médoc community of Listrac rose from obscu-rity when it was purchased in 1973 by Baron Edmond de Rothschild, who built a new winery and a new château. The estate got its name from the Clarke family, which bought the land from the Seigneur de Blanquefort in 1806, who had owned it since 1750. The wines of Clarke, about two-thirds Cabernet Sau-vignon and one-third Merlot, are firm and full. They are also expensive for a *cru bourgeois* whose chief distinction is Rothschild proprietorship.

☆☆☆☆

$$

Château Clinet.

Among the better estates of the Pom-erol District east of the city of Bordeaux is Château Clinet, which produces ro-bust wines with an elegant bouquet in good vintages. The estate is adjacent to Clos L'Eglise in the heart of Pomerol. If the district were to be included in a broad classification of Bordeaux estates, Château Clinet might rank with the fifth growths of the Médoc, but so far there has been no formal classification of the Pomerol wines. Clinet made a very ac-ceptable 1969, when many Bordeaux estates produced quite mediocre re-sults.

☆☆☆/☆☆☆☆☆

$$/$$$

Clinton Vineyards.

Clinton Vineyards in Clinton Corners, in New York's Hudson Valley, is one of those eastern wineries that is demonstrating that excellent wines can be made consistently from European-American hybrid grapes. Clinton produces a crisp, dry Seyval Blanc that is reminiscent of the better Muscadets of the French Loire Valley and of some of the Chablis that have been produced in France for hundreds of years. Clinton's Seyval Blanc displays good fruit balance with its crisp finish and has developed a strong following among eastern consumers.

The property, in Dutchess County, was operated as a dairy farm for 70 years before Ben Feder bought it in 1969. Feder was a graphic designer in New York, specializing in book publishing, and he later moved into the real estate business. Now he and Kathie, his wife, devote much of their attention to their 98-acre farm. In 1974 they planted 2000 Seyval vines, and later planted 2000 more, for a total initial planting of only four acres. Contrary to most northern hemisphere wineries, Clinton's primary vineyard faces north, but the air drainage is excellent. Feder's success has astonished the experts from Cornell University's agricultural school, and now growers from all over the state visit Clinton to try to determine its secret for success. But Feder says the answer simply lies in the soil. There have been additional plantings, all in Seyval Blanc, but some experimentation with Riesling may take place soon. Total production is only about 3000 cases, of which about 2000 are sold right there at the winery, which is in a converted cow barn. There is a tasting room, and visitors are welcomed during certain hours on weekends.

☆/☆☆
$$

Clos.

Clos is the French word for "enclosure" or "field," and it is sometimes used in vineyard names to connote that the vineyard is, or once was, enclosed to keep its vines strictly separated from neighboring vines and theoretically to maintain high quality standards by preventing the production of one vineyard from being used under another's name. In Bordeaux some estates use the term "clos" in place of "château," and in Burgundy the term is also used in connection with named vineyards, as in Clos de la Roche or Clos de Vougeot.

Clos du Bois Vineyards.

Clos du Bois produces a fairly broad and varied line of premium varietals at a winery built in 1974 in Healdsburg, in California's Sonoma Valley. The winery is owned by Frank M. Woods and is supplied by grapes from 200 to 300 acres of vineyards owned by Woods, his associates, and his family. The 1974 was the first vintage for Clos du Bois, although the vineyards had been planted in 1964. At one time the wines were bottled at Souverain, but the Clos du Bois winery has been expanded to ac-

commodate all phases of production. The wines are variable, sometimes rising to quality peaks and at other times falling into the modest category. The line includes Cabernet Sauvignon, Pinot Noir, Merlot, Chardonnay, Johannisberg Riesling, and Gewürztraminer. Beginning in 1978 Clos du Bois began to offer occasional bottlings of vineyard-designated wines, and it also occasionally produces wines bearing the unfined and unfiltered description on the labels. The Clos du Bois Marlstone, consisting of 54 percent Cabernet Sauvignon and 46 percent Merlot, is a superb wine.
☆/☆☆☆
$$

Clos L'Eglise.

One of the estates clustered around the church in the heart of the Pomerol District east of Bordeaux is Clos L'Eglise, which has developed a far-reaching reputation even though its production is less than 3000 cases in a bountiful vintage. Good wines are produced on this estate, equivalent to third or fourth growths of the Médoc. In the absence of a formal classification of Pomerol, prices for many of the wines of this district are lower than for wines of comparable or lower quality produced in the Médoc.
☆☆☆/☆☆☆☆☆
$$/$$$

Clos Fourtet.

Just west of the ancient village of Saint-Emilion near the wine-trading city of Libourne, lies Clos Fourtet, one of the few Saint-Emilion estates that does not use the word "château" in its name. Clos Fourtet was ranked a *premier grand cru classé*—a first great growth—in the Saint-Emilion classification of 1955. The wines are less full-bodied and robust than some of the other *premiers* of this important district in the Bordeaux region, but they have long been held in high regard all over the world. The estate was once owned by the Ginestet family that also once owned Château Margaux in the Médoc. The cellars of Clos Fourtet are cut deep in the limestone that makes up the hill of Saint-Emilion, extending hundreds of yards underground and touching the *caves* of two other *premiers,* Châteaux Canon and Beauséjour. Clos Fourtet is best drunk ten to twenty years after the vintage.
☆☆☆☆
$$/$$$

Clos René.

One of the few Bordeaux estates that does not use the word "château" in its name is Clos René, which lies between Château Mazèyres and Château l'Enclos in the western part of the Pomerol District east of Bordeaux. The wines of Clos René are sometimes a bit lighter than those of some other small estates of Pomerol, but they are available in the United States and can provide a worthwhile introduction to the district. Clos René can be drunk eight to ten years after the vintage and remains good for 15 to 20 years before declining.
☆☆☆/☆☆☆☆☆
$$/$$$

Clos de la Roche.

Clos de la Roche is a ten-acre vineyard in the *commune* of Morey-Saint-Denis lying in the Golden Slope of the French Burgundy country. It was awarded *grand cru* status under the French wine laws, which means it is one of the greatest Burgundies. Only 23 other red-wine vineyards have *grand cru* designations, including three others from Morey-Saint-Denis: Bonnes-Mares, Clos de Tart, and Clos Saint-Denis. Although Clos de la Roche merits its *grand cru* ranking, it is one of the lesser known of this category, and even the *premier cru* Morey-Saint-Denis Clos des Lambrays is more famous. But Clos de la Roche is a very good wine. Although it tastes best at about age ten, a bottle of the 1928 vintage tasted in 1976 was full-bodied and fruity, with a delicate but fine bouquet. (*See also* Morey-Saint-Denis, Côte de Nuits.)

☆☆☆☆

$$/$$$

Clos de Tart.

One of the few *monopoles,* or vineyards under a single ownership, in the Golden Slope of Burgundy is Clos de Tart, whose origins date back at least eight centuries. The vineyard, consisting of barely 18 acres, is the property of the Mommessin shipping firm of Mâcon. It con-

sistently produces firm but fairly light wines, whose principal characteristic is their delicacy. Clos de Tart is a *grand cru* of Morey-Saint-Denis, one of the important *communes* of the Côte de Nuits, yet the wines of Clos de Tart often seem more akin to the elegant reds of Aloxe-Corton of the Côte de Beaune farther south. Their delicacy is an unusual attribute in the Côte de Nuits, where fleshiness is a more prevalent characteristic among the leading vineyards. (*See also* Morey-Saint-Denis, Côte de Nuits.)

☆☆☆☆

$$$

Clos du Val.

Bernard Portet, general manager and winemaker at Clos du Val, has a background steeped in wine. He grew up at Château Lafite-Rothschild in Bordeaux, where his father was the *régisseur,* which translates roughly as "technical director." Young Bernard helped in the harvests at Lafite and then took degrees in oenology and viticulture at the French Institutes of Agronomy at Toulouse and Montpellier. He taught agriculture briefly in Morocco and was a consultant in agricultural investment in France before moving to California to launch Clos du Val. The winery is on the Silverado Trail on the eastern side of the Napa Valley near the city of Napa.

Clos du Val is owned by a corporation whose shareholders, all said to be Americans, have not been publicly identified. Bernard Portet does not have an ownership interest. The Clos du Val plantings were begun in 1972, and now more than 150 acres are in vines, including some Chardonnay and Pinot Noir in the Carneros District at the southern end of the Napa Valley. The first wines to appear under the Clos du Val label were made from purchased grapes in 1972, but now some 90 percent of the winery's production is from its own vines.

Production now totals some 25,000 cases a year of mainly Cabernet Sauvignon, plus smaller amounts of Merlot, Pinot Noir, Zinfandel, and Chardonnay. Chardonnay production will increase drastically as the Carneros vines mature, and Pinot Noir from Carneros will be added to the Clos du Val roster. The winery also bottles a Cabernet under a second label, Grand Val, which is reserved for wines that do not reach the higher quality standards of Clos du Val itself. Grand Val is 100 percent Cabernet, and Clos du Val Cabernet is usually 8 to 20 percent Merlot, depending on the vintage. All of the wines are aged in French oak barrels.

☆☆/☆☆☆

$$

Clos de Vougeot, Vougeot.

So famous is Le Clos de Vougeot, one of the *grands crus* of the Burgundian Côte d'Or, or Golden Slope, of France, that it surprises some wine lovers to learn that Vougeot is actually a *commune* or township, where the celebrated *clos* happens to exist. But it is also probable that Vougeot would not even be on the map were it not for the *clos,* which is the largest single vineyard in the Côte d'Or. It covers slightly less than 125 acres, which stretch from within a few yards of Route 74 above Nuits-Saint-Georges up onto the fabled hillside that catches the sun throughout the day.

Acreage of this quantity is substantial in the Burgundy country, and the assumption is sometimes made that a copious flow of magnificent wines emanates from the Clos de Vougeot. The fact is that the flow is copious, but the wine is extremely variable in quality, reflecting the fragmented ownership of the vineyard. The 125 acres are broken up into at least 60 syndicates of owners, and it is said that more than 100 individuals can claim a share. Some of the plots involve only a few rows of vines; obviously the quality of the production must vary with so many individuals involved. At its best Clos de Vougeot (sometimes simply Clos-Vougeot) is a superb wine, deserving of its status as a *grand cru* of Burgundy. At its worst it can be rather ordinary and undistinguished, although the name on the label often persuades drinkers that it is better than it really is. A portion of the vineyard is devoted to white-wine production. These wines are called Clos Blanc de Vougeot or Vignes Blanches de Vougeot; they are crisp and dry, displaying a certain elegance, but they are not up to the great white wines of the Côte de Beaune produced in Chassagne, Puligny, and Meursault to the south.

Much of the latter-day fame of Clos de Vougeot may be attributed to the Chevaliers du Tastevin, that great international fraternity of Burgundy lovers that owns the magnificent stone château standing in the middle of the vineyard. Every Saturday night in the spring and fall and at least once a month during the other seasons the Chevaliers hold their feasts at the château, whose floodlit walls are visible from many a neighboring vineyard. The huge banquet hall, with its arched ceilings and gravel floor, can and often does seat more than 500 Chevaliers and their guests. The revelry goes on into the small hours of the morning, and each visitor carries away with him the unforgettable memory of an evening at the celebrated Château du Clos de Vougeot. His inclination to drink the wines of Clos de Vougeot is increased, and he is more likely to order them, no matter where in the world he may be. At the same time, it has become traditional for Clos de Vougeot to be served at dinners of the Chevaliers du Tastevin wherever they are held. This constant demand on the resources of the vineyard pushes prices ever higher and should make the Chevaliers thankful that the vineyard surrounding their château is the largest in the Côte d'Or. Clos de Vougeot wines are best seven to 15 years after the vintage.

Besides Clos de Vougeot itself, several other vineyards exist in the *commune* of Vougeot. Among these are Cras, Clos de la Perrière, and Petits Vougeots. Sometimes a *commune* wine simply labeled Vougeot will also be found, but very rarely. (*See also* Chevaliers du Tastevin, Côte de Nuits, Côte de Beaune, Hospices de Beaune, Beaune.)

☆☆☆☆

$$$

Codorniu.

Good sparkling wines are made in huge quantities under the Codorniu label in San Sadurni de Noya, on the outskirts of Barcelona. Codorniu was the first in Spain to use the *méthode champenoise* on a large commercial basis, and the company is believed to be one of the world's largest sparkling-wine producers. The wines are high in quality and moderate in price. The Codorniu Brut Classico English Cuvée bottling became a runaway best-seller after it won a blind tasting conducted by the author and publicized in *The New York Times* in 1982. There are several other bottlings of Codorniu.

☆/☆☆

$/$$

Cold Duck.

Cold Duck is supposed to be a mixture of Champagne and sparkling Burgundy, but why anybody would want to ruin either of these wines by mixing them remains a mystery. Its discovery in the United States is alleged to have occurred in or near Detroit, Michigan. No doubt the wines involved were cheaper American versions of true Champagne and sparkling Burgundy, or perhaps they weren't even sparkling. It is also said that the first version of Cold Duck was Kalte Ente, a German wine punch created when the latest vintage had failed to produce anything with a sufficiently low acid content to be palatable. There were enough additives, however, so that the punch more closely resembled a Spanish Sangría. Yet another theory is that Cold Duck was the mixture of wines that servants in bygone days were able to collect by gathering the leftover dregs from glasses after their masters had stopped partying. In any case, the Food and Drug Administration has never suggested that Cold Duck may be injurious to the health and well-being of the populace.

☆

$

Colli Albani.

White wines in great quantities have been produced for many years in the hillside vineyards near Lake Albano, just a few miles south of Rome in the region called Lazio, or Latium. At one time the bottles that traveled abroad often contained dull, uninteresting wines with a penchant for premature oxidation. They were not competitive with the crisp, dry whites from France or California. But vinification procedures in the area have changed, and now the whites of Colli Albani are fresh and clean for the most part. They should be drunk within a few years of the harvest and should be regarded as quaffing wines. The dominant grape variety is the Malvasia, but usually there are portions of Trebbiano as well as some Bonvino or Cacchione blended in.

☆/☆☆
$

Colli Altotiberini.

The hills of Umbria and the Tiber River Valley of central Italy produce great quantities of wine, and one of them that has won D.O.C. recognition under the Italian wine law is Colli Altotiberini, of which there are Bianco, Rosato, and Rosso versions. The Rosso is 50 to 70 percent Sangiovese, 10 to 20 percent Merlot, with the balance a blend of other grapes.

☆/☆☆
$

Colli Berici.

The Colli Berici are the hills running south from Vicenza into Italy's Po Valley, and the vineyards that grow on the slopes there produce good varietal wines. Labels usually will carry the name Colli Berici to connote the region of production, plus the name of the grape variety. The best reds are called Cabernet, and they are made from the Cabernet Franc rather than the Cabernet Sauvignon grape. They are inclined to lack the flavor intensity of the great reds of the Bordeaux Médoc in France, made mostly from the Cabernet Sauvignon grape, but they tend to be elegant, balanced, and representative of some of the best reds that Italy has to offer. Another Bordeaux red grape, the Merlot, also is produced here, as well as the Sauvignon, Pinot Bianco, Garganega, and Tocai Bianco, and Tocai Rosso.

☆/☆☆☆
$/$$

Colli Bolognesi di Monte San Pietro.

This wine, also sometimes called Colli Bolognesi dei Castelli Medioevali, is produced in the hills southwest of Bologna in Italy's Emilia-Romagna region, which stretches across the north-central part of the country. Besides the geographical name, the D.O.C. wines of the area carry such varietal names as Barbera, Merlot, Pinot Bianco, Riesling Italico, and Sauvignon, as well as Bianco. The Merlot, a soft red, can be good value.

☆/☆☆☆
$

Collio Goriziano.

Northwest of Trieste in Italy and not far from the Yugoslavian border, within the larger region of Friuli-Venezia Giulia, is the province of Gorizia. Often labels will carry only the name Collio to indicate the province, and the most popular wine there bears the same name. The white wine called Collio is blended from Ribolla, Malvasia, and Tocai grapes, but varietal wines are also produced here, including Pinot Grigio, Pinot Bianco, Pinot Nero, Malvasia, Merlot, Riesling, Sauvignon, Tocai, and Traminer. In general, quality levels are high.

☆/☆☆☆
$/$$

Colli Orientali del Friuli.

The eastern hills of Friuli above Venice and Trieste yield varietal wines of high quality that are increasingly seen in the export markets as part of the boom in popularity of Italian wines. Among connoisseurs the best known wine of the region is Picolit, which is made from *passito,* or grapes that have been allowed to dry virtually into raisins, so that a sweet wine of intense flavor and fairly high alcohol results. But many other wines come from the same region and have devoted followings. These include Verduzzo, a golden-yellow wine often vinified slightly sweet, and very good Pinot Grigio, which is more often made crisp, dry, and full-bodied. The Colli Orientali of Friuli also produce Cabernet, Merlot, Pinot Nero, and Refosco among the reds, as well as such whites as Pinot Bianco, Ribolla, Riesling Renano, Sauvignon, and Tocai. Labels always carry the regional designation under the Italian wine law, followed by the grape variety.

☆/☆☆☆☆

$/$$$

Colli di Parma.

The hills of Parma in the Emilia-Romagna region of north-central Italy are perhaps more famous for their spicy hams than their wines, but they also yield some good bottlings that occasionally reach the export markets. One of them, Lambrusco, is not taken seriously by connoisseurs but is produced in substantial quantities.

☆/☆☆

$

Colli del Trasimeno.

The hills of Trasimeno lie in the Italian region of Umbria and yield decent Bianco and Rosso wines that have won D.O.C. recognition under the Italian wine law. The Rosso runs 60 to 80 percent Sangiovese grapes and is best after at least eight years of age, although most of it is probably consumed much younger.

☆/☆☆☆☆

$/$$

Commanderie du Bontemps du Médoc et des Graves.

This is a society made up largely of Bordeaux wine producers and their friends whose goal is to promote the grandeur of Bordeaux wines and commemorate the historic past of the region. It meets periodically for feasts at which wines and foods native to Bordeaux are served in copious quantities. The society takes its name from the bontemps, a small wooden utensil in the shape of a scoop or pail, commonly used by Bordeaux cellar-masters for a variety of purposes. The Commanderie's headquarters are at the Maison du Vin in Pauillac, on the docks, facing the Gironde. Visitors are welcome.

An independent American affiliate, the Commanderie de Bordeaux, has chapters in a number of American cities and a headquarters in New York. Led for many years by H. Gregory Thomas, a retired chairman of Chanel Inc., who is known as "Le Grand Gregoire" because of his imposing stature and elegant speaking manner, the Commanderie in the United States also holds periodic feasts at which great Bordeaux wines and haute cuisine française are featured. The underlying purpose, both in the United States and France, is good fellowship in advancing the causes of fine wine and good food. During the Commanderie's repasts it is customary to drink toasts to the president of France and the president of the United States. Extensive discussion of Bordeaux wines also is encouraged, and the Commanderie is one of the nation's most prestigious gastronomic societies.

Commonwealth Winery.

Commonwealth Winery in Plymouth, Massachusetts, is part of the wine revival in New England. It was established in 1978 by David Tower, and its initial production came entirely from purchased grapes, mostly from New York State. The winery has been turning out Seyval Blanc, Aurora, Cayuga, and Vidal Blanc, which resemble the same varieties from New York. Tower spent two years as an apprentice winemaker in

Germany and has a bachelor's degree from Williams College as well as master's degrees from Columbia University and from the University of California at Davis, whose oenology school is the most renowned in the nation.

☆/☆☆

$/$$

Commune.

Reflecting the national orientation toward the church throughout France, most villages or communities grew up around a place of worship. A *commune* is a parish or township, after which the wines of the area are likely to be named. In the Médoc peninsula north of Bordeaux, for example, the *communes* of Margaux, Pauillac, Saint-Estèphe, and Saint-Julien are the principal wine-producing townships. The area involved in a *commune* varies widely, but generally it is no more than that needed to draw worshipers in support of the local church.

Compagnons de Beaujolais.

The Compagnons de Beaujolais is a largely social organization, established in 1947 and devoted to glorifying the wines of the Beaujolais District of France. The group's headquarters is a vaulted cellar in Lacenas, not far from Villefranche. Induction ceremonies take place here four times annually, and they are marked by a great deal of merrymaking and vast consumption of the charming wines of the region. Inductions also are carried out in foreign countries by emissaries sent out from the Beaujolais vineyards. In all cases the ceremony is the same. After sipping from a silver *tastevin,* inductees are tapped on each shoulder with a vine, are handed a diploma, and receive their own Beaujolais *tastevin,* which hangs around their necks on a green braid. The officials of the *confrèrie* are always decked out in their folkloric costumes of black jackets, green vig-

neron aprons, and broad-brimmed black hats with green ribbons. Beaujolais lovers in foreign countries often partake of the ceremonial dinners at Lacenas, where the enthusiasm for Beaujolais wines is exceeded only by the volume of Beaujolais consumed.

Concannon Vineyard.

Southeast of San Francisco and the Bay area in northern California is the Livermore Valley, best known for the white wines that come from its gravelly soil. But as one of the valley's leading vineyards, Concannon, has proved, it is quite capable of producing red wines of complexity. Brothers Joe and Jim Concannon were third-generation Irish winemakers who put their heads together in the early 1960s to determine what new varietals the vineyard should try to develop. With advice from the University of California at Davis and other experts, they settled on Petite Sirah. They already knew that this variety did well in Livermore, as they had for some time blended it into their Concannon Burgundy to add depth, body, and color. In 1964 California's first varietal Petite Sirah was introduced and was successful enough to encourage further vintages and refinements. A number of other vineyards have since followed suit, but Concannon's Petite Sirah is still considered one of the best.

In 1980 the Concannons sold out to Agustin Huneeus, a Chilean, who had at one time worked for Seagram's. A major expansion and upgrading of the winery was undertaken with the infusion of new capital. Yet another change in ownership occurred in 1983, when Concannon was acquired by Distillers Company Ltd. of Edinburgh, Scotland. Most of the Concannon whites and all of the reds now undergo barrel-aging for added complexity, and the wines already are showing improvement. Jim Concannon remains active in managing

the winery along with the new owner and several other new officers. Sergio Traverso was hired away from Sterling Vineyards in 1981 to be the new Concannon winemaker. (Joe Concannon died in 1978.) Production totals about 35,000 cases a year.
☆/☆☆☆☆
$/$$

Condrieu.

The Rhône Valley in eastern France is renowned for its full-bodied red wines such as Hermitage and Châteauneuf-du-Pape, but some good whites are produced there too, and one of them is Condrieu, from the area of the same name adjacent to the Côte Rôtie in the northern part of the district. They are big and earthy, with a flowery bouquet, and do not flow into the export markets in great quantities. They are made with the Viognier grape, which gives wine with spicy overtones detectable above the basic earthiness imparted by the soil. Château Grillet, with only four acres in vines, is the best Condrieu, but very little of it ever goes abroad. (*See* Château Grillet.)
☆☆/☆☆☆☆
$/$$$

Confrérie Saint-Etienne.

The Confrérie Saint-Etienne is a largely social organization whose purpose is to bring together people who have a taste for the wines and gastronomy of the French province of Alsace. The Confrérie was established in the small Alsatian town of Ammerschwihr in the fifteenth century. Originally its function was to supervise the wines leaving the Alsatian cellars to ensure their quality. Under the rules of procedure, *confrères* and *consoeurs* gathering at official functions (mainly wine tastings and dinners) are barred from engaging in any discussions of political or religious matters or of subjects of an acrid nature of any

kind. Smoking is not permitted during gatherings, and fines amounting to forfeiture of three bottles of wine must be levied against anybody who calls a *confrère* bad names, such as "liar" or "thief," and against anyone who behaves in an unseemly or indecent fashion. The same fine is to be imposed against *confrères* who make unseemly gestures to, take base liberties with, or speak unbecomingly of *consoeurs*. Various chapters of the Confrérie have been established around the world, but the only one in the U.S. with a record of continuous operation is in Fort Worth, Texas. This chapter celebrated its tenth anniversary in 1980.

Congress Springs Vineyards.

The vineyards of Congress Springs were planted in 1892 and were reestablished under the current management in 1976. They lie in the Santa Cruz Mountains of California, in Santa Clara County, not far from Saratoga, and yield excellent Zinfandels that have won a strong following among Zinfandel devotees all over the nation. The winery, with production of some 5000 cases a year, also turns out Chardonnay, Pinot Blanc, Fumé Blanc, Chenin Blanc, Sémillon, Cabernet Sauvignon, and Pinot Noir.
☆/☆☆☆
$/$$

Conn Creek Winery.

Conn Creek was founded in 1974, one of California's great vintage years, by William and Kathleen Collins on the Silverado Trail in St. Helena in the Napa Valley. Their wines were of high quality from the outset, especially their Cabernet Sauvignon 1974, which was a prizewinner. William Collins had been a Napa grape grower since 1967. Conn Creek also produces good Chardonnays and Zinfandels. Production totals about 20,000 cases a year, much of it aged in small oak barrels. In 1980 the Collinses sold a minority interest in Conn Creek to Mr. and Mrs. Francis Dewavrin-Woltner, coproprietors of Château La Mission Haut-Brion in the Graves subregion of Bordeaux. La Mission Haut-Brion is one of the finest producers of red and white wines in Graves. No major changes were planned initially at Conn Creek as a result of the new ownership structure, but plans were being made to export Conn Creek wines to the European continent.

☆/☆☆☆

$$

Connecticut.

Wines have been produced for many years in neighboring New York State just to the west, so why not in Connecticut? With that point of view in mind, several new vineyards and wineries have been established in Connecticut in recent years, and they produce mostly European-American hybrids, with a smattering of pure European varietals that do not yet quite challenge wines made from the same grapes in California. The Farm Winery Act of 1978, a new state law, opened the way for small wineries. The three pioneers in modern Connecticut viticulture are Haight Vineyards in Litchfield, St. Hilary's Vineyard in North Grosvenor Dale, and Stonecrop Vineyards in Stonington.

Sherman Haight started planting Haight in 1975 with Riesling and Chardonnay vines in small amounts, then added Maréchal Foch, De Chaunac, Van Buren, and Rougeon, among others. St. Hilary's got its first plantings in the early 1960s, but they were strictly the hobby of the owner, Peter Kerensky. More recently, however, he has gone commercial with Concord, Captivator, Van Buren, Aurora, and Golden Muscat. At Stonecrop, Tom and Charlotte Young have planted such hybrids as Rayon d'Or, Seyval Blanc, Vidal, Aurora, Maréchal Foch, and Cascade, among others. Several other Connecticut growers also are producing in small quantities and are experimenting with various varieties to determine which will stand up under the sometimes arduous winters in the state.

Château La Conseillante.

Just inside the Pomerol boundary line and adjacent to the great Château Cheval Blanc of Saint-Emilion lies Château La Conseillante, one of the best estates of Pomerol. Like Cheval Blanc, Vieux-Château-Certan, Château l'Evangile, and Château Pétrus, La Conseillante lies on a slightly elevated ridge running in a northwesterly direction across the flatlands of this district 20 miles east of Bordeaux. In any classification of Pomerol, La Conseillante would rank near the top because of its consistent and proved ability to produce full-bodied, rich, and velvety wines that are classically Pomerols. It brings prices comparable to the second growths of the Médoc. The property has been owned for many years by the Nicolas family.

☆☆☆☆

$$$

R. & J. Cook.

Roger and Joanne Cook established their winery near Clarksburg in Yolo County, California, in 1979 after producing grapes used for years by other wineries. Their property consists of 130 acres, and it is best known for its Chenin Blanc, which is vinified in three styles ranging from bone-dry to slightly sweet. They also make Fumé Blanc, Cabernet Sauvignon, Petite Sirah, and a Merlot Blanc, a rarity in California or anywhere else. Production grew rapidly to 50,000 cases a year, and the Cooks continue to sell portions of their grapes to other wine producers.

☆/☆☆☆

$/$$

Cordtz Brothers Cellars.

The original winery at Cordtz Brothers, in the northern end of the Alexander Valley in Sonoma County, California, was built in 1905 and mainly produced bulk wines for sale to other producers, who bottled them under their own labels. Dr. William Cordtz and his son David bought the winery in 1979 after it had been out of production and empty for 15 years. They immediately began renovating it, and were able to produce their first vintage under the Cordtz Brothers label in 1980, some of it in the refurbished winery and some of it in borrowed premises nearby. William and David Cordtz head a family corporation that owns the winery and 50 acres of grapes that had been planted in 1972 and are now bearing Cabernet Sauvignon, Sauvignon Blanc, and Sémillon, although Cordtz still buys most of its grapes from outside growers. Production now exceeds 12,000 cases a year of such premium varietals as Cabernet Sauvignon, Zinfandel, Sauvignon Blanc, Chardonnay, Gewürztraminer, and a small amount of Muscat Blanc vinified sweet and marketed in half bottles. (The goal is 20,000 cases a year in all.) The Cordtz Sauvignon Blanc, crisp and clean, has won a big following.
☆/☆☆☆
$$

Corks.

The purpose of the cork is to keep the wine in the bottle and keep the air out. As a rule, the longer the cork, the better. Short corks are more likely to admit air that would cause a wine to age prematurely or deteriorate. The better producers in France always use corks at least two inches long. Producers who try to save money by reducing the length of the corks they use are not doing their best for their customers. Of course wines that are meant to be drunk young need not have corks as long as those requiring decades of bottle-age. And in recent years there has been a trend toward using screw caps and plastic stoppers for the common or ordinary wines of many countries. These wines do not improve in the bottle, so the use of corks is not necessary. But the minute amounts of air that a proper cork permits to pass are probably beneficial for the development of good wines.

Corks come from Spain, Portugal, and a few other countries and are made of tree bark that is cut off in great sheets. The discovery of this type of stopper for wine bottles in the eighteenth century was one of the most significant developments in the history of viniculture, for it meant that wine could be stored in bottles. Previously, bottles were used mainly for transporting small quantities, and wine was stored in casks or barrels. It didn't last much longer than the year until the next vintage. The use of corks meant that wine could be stored in bottles, and suddenly a whole new range of possibilities opened up. Vintage comparisons became possible, and wines could be made in such a way as to mature over a period of years. All because of corks.

Cornas.

Cornas is one of the good red wines of the Rhône Valley of France which has begun to achieve recognition in recent years. It is made from the Syrah grape, which also produces Hermitage, but Cornas rarely measures up to Hermitage on a quality basis. It often displays a pronounced earthiness. Cornas is best drunk between four and seven years after the harvest. (*See* Rhône Valley.)
☆☆/☆☆☆
$$

Cortese.

Cortese is one of the few good white wines of the Piedmont District of

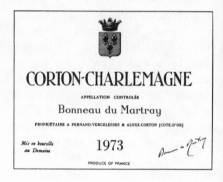

northern Italy, and it is also cultivated in the Lombardy region and in Sicily. It is pale in color and light, running as little as 10 percent alcohol. Clearly the best is the Cortese di Gavi, sometimes called simply Gavi, that comes from the southeastern part of the Piedmont. It is usually full-bodied and textured and is one of the better Italian whites available in the export markets.

☆☆

$/$$

Corton.

The only red *grand cru* in the Côte de Beaune of the French Burgundy country is Corton, which produces an elegant if delicate wine of great finesse. Like most other red Burgundies of the Côte de Beaune, it is not as big and robust as the *grands crus* of the Côte de Nuits farther north on the Burgundian Golden Slope. It is important to distinguish Le Corton from Aloxe-Corton, the name of the *commune* where the Corton vineyard lies. *Commune* wines called simply Aloxe-Corton can be good value, but they will rarely measure up to Le Corton itself. Besides this fine vineyard, several others have been given *premier cru* status. The best of these are Corton-Clos du Roi, Corton-Maréchaudes, Corton-Languettes, Corton Clos des Cortons, Corton-Pougets, and Corton-Renardes. But only Le Corton stands

by itself, without another vineyard name added. The most famous wine of Aloxe-Corton is the white *grand cru* Corton-Charlemagne, which rivals the best whites of Puligny- and Chassagne-Montrachet for charm and finesse. (*See also* Aloxe-Corton, Côte de Beaune.)

☆☆☆☆

$$/$$$

Corton-Charlemagne.

The Emperor Charlemagne once held substantial vineyard properties in the French Burgundy country, and his name has been attached to the greatest estate of the *commune* of Aloxe-Corton, the white-wine vineyard known as Corton-Charlemagne. This is a *grand cru* of Aloxe-Corton and one of only seven active vineyards in the entire Burgundy country that have been awarded *grand cru* status specifically for their white wines. Corton-Charlemagne has an earthy taste that suggests fresh walnuts or roasted hazelnuts laced with an exquisite suggestion of fruit that only the Chardonnay grape could impart. It is not as widely renowned as Le Montrachet or even Bâtard-Montrachet from nearby Puligny and Chassagne, but its followers know that it can surpass all of the other great white Burgundies under the right conditions. (*See also* Aloxe-Corton, Corton, Côte de Beaune.)

☆☆☆

$$$/$$$$

Corvo.

One of the best wines of Sicily, the Italian island whose wines are increasingly flowing into the export markets, is Corvo di Casteldaccia, which comes in both red and white varieties. The red reaches an alcohol level of close to 15 percent as the grapes achieve a fleshy ripeness under the hot Sicilian sun. This is one of the better red wines of Italy and deserves greater recognition than it has received. Corvo Bianco can also be quite pleasant, displaying an earthy quality that is common in many Italian white wines, especially those from the southern part of the "boot."
☆/☆☆
$

Château Cos d'Estournel.

Louis Gaspard d'Estournel planted the vineyards of Château Cos d'Estournel in 1810 and began building the château itself in 1830. The structure is one of the most spectacular in all of the Médoc, with its Chinese-Gothic combination of accents. Monsieur D'Estournel wanted it to reflect the distant markets for his great wine, so he created a castle in what is now regarded as a Laotian style, with a pagoda roof indicating Chinese influence. The word "Cos" is said to have entered the Bordelais lexicon when it was brought by crusaders returned from the island of that name near Rhodes just off the Turkish coast. This explains why the final "s" is pronounced rather than being silent as with most other French words ending in "s." The vineyard lies just across a stream from Château Lafite-Rothschild, marking the boundary between Pauillac and Saint-Estèphe. Cos d'Estournel was ranked a *second cru,* or second growth, in the Bordeaux classification of 1855, and it is consistently the best wine of Saint-Estèphe. It is big and robust, with great depth and character, contrasting with the refined elegance of Lafite, whose vines grow only a short distance to the south. A Cos d'Estournel from a good vintage has no trouble living for fifty years. The estate is owned by the Prats family, which acquired it along with Château de Marbuzet, another Saint-Estèphe, from the Ginestet family. Prats Frères also owns the Châteaux Petit-Village and Certan-de-May in Pomerol and the Châteaux Petit-Figeac and La Fleur-Pourret in Saint-Emilion.
☆☆☆☆
$$/$$$

Château Cos-Labory.

With vineyards bordering on those of Château Lafite-Rothschild and Château Cos d'Estournel, Château Cos-Labory is in an ideal location on the northern side of the boundary between Pauillac and Saint-Estèphe in the Médoc peninsula running north of Bordeaux. It was accorded *cinquième cru,* or fifth-growth, status in the Bordeaux classification of 1855. Although it is on the border of two great wine-producing *communes,* it is more typically a Saint-Estèphe, reflecting the actual designation of the estate. The wines of Cos-Labory are hard in their youth and long-lived, although not as big as those of neighboring Cos d'Estournel, which was once under the same ownership. The prices at which Cos-Labory usually sells reflect the estate's fifth-growth classification rather than its quality and proximity to the other great estates of the area.
☆☆☆☆
$$/$$$

Côte de Beaune.

The renowned Burgundy District of France is separated into several subdivisions, including the Côte de Beaune and the Côte de Nuits, which together comprise the Côte d'Or, or Golden Slope. This is the heart of Burgundy, where some of the best wines in the world are produced—big, robust, and assertive wines that display great balance and charm along with their bigness. The Côte de Beaune is the southern part of the Côte d'Or, stretching from Pernand-Vergelesses on the north to just south of Santenay. The area is named after its principal town, Beaune, where much of the Burgundian wine trade is centered. The red wines of the Côte de Beaune are not quite as assertive and robust as those of the Côte de Nuits, but they can be extremely fine and elegant, combining a flowery bouquet with great depth of flavor. The most famous wines of the Côte de Beaune, however, are the whites, which are produced in relatively minute quantities around the villages of Puligny-Montrachet, Meursault, and Aloxe-Corton.

Here is where the great Montrachet, perhaps the best dry white wine produced in the world, is made, along with several other very good wines that share its name. The splendid earthy whites of Meursault often rival the best of Montrachet, but have never been quite as popular, perhaps because the name is not quite as catchy on the foreign tongue. The least expensive whites—those simply named Puligny-Montrachet or Meursault, after the townships where the grapes are grown—can display great character when produced by one of the better growers. It is here that the Chardonnay grape reaches its peak, although in recent years it has also done nearly as well in California's Napa and Sonoma valleys. Besides the California Chardonnays, the only true rivals of the Montrachets and Meursaults are the *grands crus* of Chablis, somewhat farther north in the Burgundy country. But even they cannot quite match the best whites of the Côte de Beaune.

Whereas Le Montrachet has attained almost deity status among white Burgundies, some very well known reds are produced here as well, including Pommard, which may be the best known red Burgundy of all. It is a velvety red wine of great character when properly made, but unfortunately it has many imitators. The other good reds of the area are Volnay—which can be excellent value because of its lack of fame —Santenay, Chassagne-Montrachet, Beaune, Savigny-les-Beaune, Chorey-les-Beaune, Pernand-Vergelesses, and Aloxe-Corton, where the great red Corton is made, as well as Corton-Charlemagne, an extraordinary white wine. Some good wines are also made at Auxey-Duresses, Monthélie, and Saint-Romain, although they are not quite as well known.

Among the lesser *appellations* of the area is Côte de Beaune-Villages, which refers to a blend of red wines from any two or more designated villages of the Côte de Beaune. The wines must be at least 10.5 percent alcohol, the same as for the *communal* wines entitled to the individual *commune* names, which are also used in blends for Côte de Beaune-Villages. This contrasts with the 11.5 percent alcoholic level required for the *grands crus,* or great growths, which bear only the names of specific vineyards, and the 11 percent required for *premiers crus,* which are specific vineyard names attached to the *commune* name. When a good and reliable shipper is doing the blending, Côte de Beaune-Villages can be a very decent wine. This is especially true in copious vintages when the actual production of individual vineyard areas exceeds the limits set by the French wine laws. The only legal commercial alternative in such cases is to sell off the excess production under a lesser *appellation.* Thus a Santenay might become part of a Côte de Beaune-Villages in a large vintage.

Most striking to visitors is the smallness of the vineyard holdings and the shortness of the distance between individual *communes.* For instance, a single three-mile stretch of the highway running south of Beaune passes through Pommard, Volnay, part of Meursault, and part of Beaune itself. At one point on the hillside above Pommard it would be possible for a man with a strong arm to throw a rock that would land in Beaune on his left or in Volnay on his right. Yet the wines from each area have their own traits, which experts can readily identify.

Besides the harvest itself the most important annual event in the Côte de Beaune is the wine auction on behalf of the Hospices de Beaune, a charity hospital within the walls of the ancient city of Beaune. The hospital was established in 1443 as the Hôtel-Dieu by Nicolas Rolin, who was tax collector for the Duke of Burgundy. It is said that he was trying to make amends for his extortions when he built the hospital and that the indigent Burgundians who have benefited from its care have merely been recovering some of what had been wrongfully taken from them or from their forebears. In any event, Monsieur Rolin and his wife, Guigone de Salins, endowed the hospital with their own vineyards on the surrounding hillsides, and the production is sold at the auction each November to benefit the charity. Over the years other Burgundian producers have also bequeathed vineyard parcels to the Hospices, and these are among the best wine-producing areas in the Côte de Beaune. The auction sets the prices for each vintage and establishes relative values among the various *communes*. Special labels are printed for wines sold at the auction, and these bottles tend to be more expensive than others of comparable or even superior quality.

The sale is usually held on the third Sunday in November during the three-day celebration known as *Les Trois Glorieuses*. The revelry begins on Saturday night with a banquet for La Confrérie des Chevaliers du Tastevin at the Château du Clos de Vougeot, which this international group of Burgundy-drinkers owns. Upward of 500 people are seated in the great gravel-floored banquet hall of the château, and they do not leave their tables until after one o'clock in the morning. Following the auction itself on Sunday, another banquet is held in an ancient hall in Beaune. Then on Monday is the *Paulée* at Meursault, yet another banquet, at which the wine is furnished by the growers themselves. Survival is difficult for the neophyte wine lover who does not restrict his intake, and even if the annual event is entirely commercial in its goal to promote Burgundy wines, it is something that visitors never forget. (Individual *communes* and their vineyards are discussed under their own headings, and there is more about the Chevaliers du Tastevin under a separate entry.) (*See* Hospices de Beaune.)

Côte des Colombes Vineyards.

This small winery is in Banks, in northwestern Oregon, where it produces a balanced Cabernet Sauvignon plus small amounts of Chardonnay, Pinot Noir, Chenin Blanc, and Riesling. Grapes are purchased from both Oregon and Washington. The winery was established in 1977, and initial vintages of Chardonnay and Cabernet Sauvignon appeared well made, but production is quite small. The goal, not yet achieved, is 10,000 cases a year.
☆/☆☆
$/$$

Côte de Nuits.

The heartland of the French Burgundy country is the Côte d'Or, or Golden Slope, which is divided into two subdivisions: the Côte de Beaune on the south and the Côte de Nuits on the north. The red wines with the greatest depth, fullest bodies, and most balanced character come from the northern part, the Côte de Nuits. These are among the most celebrated red wines produced in the world, and the tiny vineyard parcels where the vines grow are among the most valuable pieces of agricultural land anywhere. The vineyard of Romanée-Conti, certainly the most famous in the world among the cognoscenti of wine, consists of only four and a half acres. The annual production is a meager 600 to 700 cases, but it sells for a minimum of $100 per bottle wholesale. What other legitimate agricultural crop fetches a price of nearly $200,000 per acre of production?

Romanée-Conti is, of course, not typical of the vineyards of the magnificent Côte d'Or in terms of its size and value, but it is the archetypical red wine of Burgundy: robust without being harsh, intense but not obvious, wonderfully balanced and highly seductive. Several other great wines from the Côte de Nuits share these traits, and even if their production is somewhat greater, it cannot be considered large by any standards of viniculture. The entire Côte d'Or is only about 30 miles long and an average of less than one mile wide. The Côte de Nuits comprises less than half of this, and visitors are continually astonished at how small are the vineyards that produce such famous wines as Le Chambertin, Clos de Bèze, Le Musigny, and Bonnes-Mares, to name only a few. Even more surprising is the fragmentation of individual vineyards. Some owners have only two or three rows of vines and will make a style of wine slightly different from their neighbors who cultivate the next few rows.

Besides the great wines, some of lesser quality are cultivated in the Côte de Nuits. For instance, there are *commune* wines such as Vosne-Romanée that can be produced from vineyards anywhere within the geographical boundaries of the *commune* of Vosne-Romanée. Ro-

manée-Conti comes from the same *commune* but from a very specific part of it. Wines of even less specific origin, called Côte de Nuits-Villages, which can come from any of the *communes* of the Côte de Nuits, are also widely available. They lack the character of the *grands crus* produced in single vineyards, but they can be very good Burgundies indeed. A host of wines, some very good and some mediocre, are labeled Nuits-Saint-Georges, which means they come either from that fairly large *commune* or from the neighboring Prémeaux, whose wines are also entitled to use the Nuits-Saint-Georges *appellation* under French wine law.

It is well for the neophyte to remember that the broader the geographical area included in a wine name, the less distinguished the wines will be. Thus wines called Côtes de Nuits-Villages have the broadest and least specific origins of the Côtes de Nuits and are comparable to the wines named Côte de Beaune-Villages from the area just to the south. Some of them can be quite good, but little should be expected of a wine carrying such a general designation. Next higher on the quality list come the *commune* wines, named after the individual community or single township where the grapes are grown. In the Côte de Nuits, these are the following:

Fixin
Gevrey-Chambertin
Morey-Saint-Denis
Chambolle-Musigny
Vougeot
Flagey-Echézeaux
Vosne-Romanée
Nuits-Saint-Georges
Prémeaux

Within most of the *communes,* or townships, there are individual vineyards that have a right to use their own

names. Some of these are *grands crus* and
some are *premiers crus*. The *grands crus* of
the Côte de Nuits are the best red Burgundies made and arguably are the best
red wines made, although lovers of the
great châteaux of Bordeaux might quib-
ble with this contention. The *premiers
crus* vineyards stand between the *commune* wines and the *grands crus* on the
quality scale. Following is a list of the
premiers crus. Each vineyard is preceded
by the name of its *commune* just as it
would appear on a label.

Fixin-Arvelets
Fixin-Cheusots
Fixin-Clos du Chapitre
Fixin-Hervelets
Fixin-Meix-Bas
Fixin-Perrière

Gevrey-Chambertin-Bel Air
Gevrey-Chambertin-Champeaux
Gevrey-Chambertin-Champonnets
Gevrey-Chambertin-Champitonnois
Gevrey-Chambertin-Cherbaudes
Gevrey-Chambertin-Closeau
Gevrey-Chambertin-Clos du Chapitre
Gevrey-Chambertin-Clos Saint-
    Jacques
Gevrey-Chambertin-Clos Prieur
Gevrey-Chambertin-Combe-aux-
    Moines
Gevrey-Chambertin-Combettes
Gevrey-Chambertin-Corbeaux
Gevrey-Chambertin-Craipillot
Gevrey-Chambertin-Ergots
Gevrey-Chambertin-Estournelles
Gevrey-Chambertin-Fontenys
Gevrey-Chambertin-Gémeaux
Gevrey-Chambertin-Goulots
Gevrey-Chambertin-Issarts
Gevrey-Chambertin-Lavaut
Gevrey-Chambertin-Perrière
Gevrey-Chambertin-Petite Chapelle
Gevrey-Chambertin-Poissenot
Gevrey-Chambertin-Veroilles

Morey-Saint-Denis-Bouchots

Morey-Saint-Denis-Calouères
Morey-Saint-Denis-Chabiots
Morey-Saint-Denis-Chaffots
Morey-Saint-Denis-Charmes
Morey-Saint-Denis-Charnières
Morey-Saint-Denis-Chénevery
Morey-Saint-Denis-Clos Baulet
Morey-Saint-Denis-Clos Bussière
Morey-Saint-Denis-Clos des Lambrays
Morey-Saint-Denis-Clos des Ormes
Morey-Saint-Denis-Clos Sorbés
Morey-Saint-Denis-Côte Rôtie
Morey-Saint-Denis-Faconnières
Morey-Saint-Denis-Fremières
Morey-Saint-Denis-Froichots
Morey-Saint-Denis-Genevrières
Morey-Saint-Denis-Gruenchers
Morey-Saint-Denis-Maison-Brûlée
Morey-Saint-Denis-Mauchamps
Morey-Saint-Denis-Meix-Rentiers
Morey-Saint-Denis-Millandes
Morey-Saint-Denis-Monts-Luisants
Morey-Saint-Denis-Riotte
Morey-Saint-Denis-Ruchots
Morey-Saint-Denis-Sorbés

Chambolle-Musigny-Amoureuses
Chambolle-Musigny-Baudes
Chambolle-Musigny-Beaux-Bruns
Chambolle-Musigny-Borniques
Chambolle-Musigny-Charmes
Chambolle-Musigny-Chatelots
Chambolle-Musigny-Combottes
Chambolle-Musigny-Cras
Chambolle-Musigny-Derrière la
    Grange
Chambolle-Musigny-Fousselottes
Chambolle-Musigny-Fuées
Chambolle-Musigny-Groseilles
Chambolle-Musigny-Gruenchers
Chambolle-Musigny-Hauts-Doix
Chambolle-Musigny-Lavrottes
Chambolle-Musigny-Noirots
Chambolle-Musigny-Plantes
Chambolle-Musigny-Sentiers

Vougeot-Vigne Blanche (Clos Blanc
    de Vougeot)
Vougeot-Cras

Vougeot-Clos de la Perrière
Vougeot-Petits Vougeots

Vosne-Romanée-Beaux Monts
(Beaumonts)
Vosne-Romanée-Brûlées
Vosne-Romanée-Chaumes
Vosne-Romanée-Clos des Réas
Vosne-Romanée-Gaudichots
Vosne-Romanée-Grande Rue
Vosne-Romanée-Malconsorts
Vosne-Romanée-Petits Monts
Vosne-Romanée-Reignots
Vosne-Romanée-Suchots

Nuits-Saint-Georges-Aux Argillats
Nuits-Saint-Georges-Les Argillats
Nuits-Saint-Georges-Boudots
Nuits-Saint-Georges-Bousselots
Nuits-Saint-Georges-Cailles
Nuits-Saint-Georges-Chaboeufs
Nuits-Saint-Georges-Chaignots
Nuits-Saint-Georges-Châine-Carteau
Nuits-Saint-Georges-Champs-Perdrix
Nuits-Saint-Georges-Clos des
Argillières
Nuits-Saint-Georges-Clos Arlots
Nuits-Saint-Georges-Clos des Corvées
Nuits-Saint-Georges-Clos des Forêts
Nuits-Saint-Georges-Clos des Grandes
Vignes
Nuits-Saint-Georges-Clos de la
Maréchale
Nuits-Saint-Georges-Clos Saint-Marc
Nuits-Saint-Georges-Corvées-Paget
Nuits-Saint-Georges-Cras
Nuits-Saint-Georges-Crots
Nuits-Saint-Georges-Damodes
Nuits-Saint-Georges-Didiers
Nuits-Saint-Georges-Hauts Pruliers
Nuits-Saint-Georges-Aux Perdrix
Nuits-Saint-Georges-Perrière
Nuits-Saint-Georges-Perrière-Noblet
Nuits-Saint-Georges-Porets
Nuits-Saint-Georges-Poulettes
Nuits-Saint-Georges-Sur Premeaux
Nuits-Saint-Georges-Procès
Nuits-Saint-Georges-Pruliers
Nuits-Saint-Georges-Richemone

Nuits-Saint-Georges-Roncière
Nuits-Saint-Georges-Rousselots
Nuits-Saint-Georges-Rue de Chaux
Nuits-Saint-Georges-Les Saint-
Georges
Nuits-Saint-Georges-Sur Nuits
Nuits-Saint-Georges-Thorey
Nuits-Saint-Georges-Vallerots
Nuits-Saint-Georges-Vaucrains
Nuits-Saint-Georges-Vignes-Rondes

The above listing is fairly comprehensive, although the articles have been left out of the vineyard names for the sake of brevity—a practice which many vineyard owners also follow. But it is easy to find a Nuits-Saint-Georges-Les Vaucrains as well as one without the *Les,* and Vosne-Romanée-La Grande Rue is just as likely to appear as Vosne-Romanée-Grande Rue. The best vineyards of Flagey-Echézeaux are included in Vosne-Romanée by tradition, so there is no separate listing for them. The *premiers crus* of the Côte de Nuits in general are good wines and are rarely inexpensive, although they should always be less costly than any of the *grand crus* from the same *communes.*

The greatest wines of Burgundy are the *grands crus,* and they are recognized the world over as being among the best red wines that money can buy. Opinions vary as to which ones are the best of all. Certainly La Romanée-Conti is the most expensive, but to some connoisseurs this does not mean that it is superior in quality to the magnificent Musigny produced by the Comte de Vogüé. Chambertin and Chambertin Clos de Bèze are known as the *grands seigneurs* of Burgundy and are at the very top of many lists. Bonnes-Mares also reaches great heights, as does Clos de Vougeot, although the latter vineyard has so many owners that finding the better made wines can be exceedingly difficult. A list of the *grands crus* of the Côte de Nuits follows. These wines appear under the vineyard names alone, without the *commune* names:

Gevrey-Chambertin:
Chambertin
Chambertin Clos de Bèze
Chapelle-Chambertin
Charmes-Chambertin
Griotte-Chambertin
Mazis-Chambertin
Mazoyères-Chambertin
Ruchottes-Chambertin

Morey-Saint-Denis:
Bonnes-Mares
Clos de la Roche
Clos Saint-Denis
Clos de Tart

Chambolle-Musigny:
Bonnes-Mares
Clos de Tart
Le Musigny

Vougeot:
Clos de Vougeot

Vosne-Romanée:
Echézeaux
Grands Echézeaux
Richebourg
La Romanée
Romanée-Conti
Romanée-Saint-Vivant
La Tâche

Because of civic pride the names of the most famous vineyards have been attached to the *commune* names, creating confusion for the neophyte in Gevrey-Chambertin, Chambolle-Musigny, and Vosne-Romanée. All of these are *commune* names, and wines bearing these names rank below the *grands crus* and *premiers crus*. It would be much simpler if the Burgundians would swallow their pride and revert to the simpler names of yore: Gevrey, Chambolle, and Vosne. Then the layman would have no trouble

differentiating between the *commune* wine Gevrey (now called Gevrey-Chambertin) and Le Chambertin itself, one of the greatest wines produced anywhere. In the absence of such a decision the supposition must be made that the Burgundians benefit from the confusion— that perhaps significant quantities of Gevrey-Chambertin are sold because buyers cannot readily differentiate between it and Le Chambertin or any of the other *grands crus* of Gevrey that carry the Chambertin name. The same obviously goes for Chambolle and its Le Musigny and for Vosne and its La Romanée and Romanée-Conti. (Discussions of individual *communes* and their wines appear under their own headings.)

Côte d'Or.

Some of the greatest red and white wines of the world are produced on the Côte d'Or, the fabled Golden Slope in the heart of the Burgundy region of France. The Slope consists of a hillside roughly 30 miles long and rarely more than one mile wide, extending south of Dijon to Santenay about ten miles above Chalon on the Saône River, in eastern France. Although the wines of the Beaujolais, Chalonnais, and Mâconnais subdivisions of Burgundy are far more plentiful, they do not reach the same pinnacles of quality and finesse achieved in the Côte d'Or, where the vineyards are tilted toward the southeast, enabling them to catch the intense morning sun and hold its heat throughout the day. At the same time the hillside itself protects the vineyards from the adverse weather that might otherwise blow in from the west.

The soil is alluvial, having been deposited there thousands of years ago by glaciers and subsequently washed by the flow of the Saône as it receded into its present banks. It consists of clay and limestone, as do many of the other great vineyard areas of the world, and to the eye or the touch it does not seem especially fertile. Yet it provides the perfect medium for cultivating vines, because it makes them reach deeply into the subsoil and work hard to produce the superb Pinot Noir and Chardonnay grapes used for the best red and white Burgundy wines. More fertile soil, the type prevalent in the valleys below the hillsides of the Côte d'Or, produces soft wines of little character and distinction. Because of erosion and the steep pitch of the Slope in certain parts of the Côte d'Or the soil sometimes washes away from the vineyards and must be carted back up in a process similar to that carried out in the Mosel Valley of Germany.

The Côte d'Or is divided into two sections: the Côte de Beaune on the south and the Côte de Nuits on the north. They are named after the two principal towns of the area, Beaune and Nuits-Saint-Georges. Some Burgundy enthusiasts feel the wines of the Côte de Nuits have more character and depth, and it is certainly true that the more expensive reds—indeed, some of the costliest reds in the world—come from the Côte de Nuits. But some very fine reds also are produced in the Côte de Beaune to the south, as well as the greatest dry white wines found anywhere. The differences among the reds often come down to a question of style: the wines of the Côte de Beaune are not as big and robust as those of the Côte de Nuits, but they sometimes display more charm and certainly tend to be more pleasant in their youth. The best wines of the Côte de Nuits are quintessential Burgundies, full-bodied and robust, with great depth and intensity. The wines from both sections produce overpowering bouquets evocative of the scent of violets, truffles, and other romantic essences.

The production of wine in the Côte d'Or is very small when compared with that of Bordeaux. In a typically generous vintage the 150 Burgundian *grands crus* and *premiers crus* altogether might yield 120,000 cases of red wine. In contrast, the five *premiers crus,* or first growths, of the Médoc would yield well over 100,000 cases, while the other 57 classified growths of the Bordeaux Médoc, mostly comparable to the great growths and first growths of the Côte d'Or on a quality basis, would yield at least 500,000 cases more. Obviously, good Burgundy wines are not plentiful.

The estates of the Côte d'Or are ranked in four categories according to quality: *grands crus* or *têtes de cuvées* at the top, followed by *premiers crus* in the second category, *communal* wines in the third, and simply Bourgognes, or Burgundies with no other names attached, in fourth. Among the *grands crus* are the wines named only after the vineyards from which they were produced—for example Le Musigny, which is produced in the village of Chambolle-Musigny. Among the *premiers crus* would be Chambolle-Musigny Les Charmes—a specific vineyard name following the name of the township, or *commune*. Les Charmes is a fine wine produced in Chambolle-Musigny but not quite as fine as Le Musigny. Sometimes the *premiers crus* from two or more vineyards in the same town are blended—for example, Les Charmes and Les Combettes in Chambolle-Musigny. In this instance the wine would be called Chambolle-Musigny Premier Cru. In the third category would be wines simply labeled Chambolle-Musigny—produced anywhere in the *commune* and not entitled to any kind of vineyard identification. Finally, in fourth place, there are the wines of inferior alcoholic content and those not produced from specified grape varieties in designated areas, which are entitled only to the geographical designation Bourgogne, or Burgundy.

The blending of two *premiers crus* of

a Burgundy *commune* is done frequently because of the highly fragmented ownership of the vineyards in this part of France. A specific Burgundian vineyard may have dozens of individual owners, each one of them cultivating only a few rows of grapes. These individuals usually sell their production to one of the shippers located in the principal villages of the Côte d'Or, and the shipper will decide whether to bottle them as blends or as individual vineyard wines. Often the shipper may have too little wine from a single vineyard to bottle by itself.

The prime example of fragmented ownership is the famous Clos de Vougeot, in Vougeot on the Côte de Nuits. With 124 acres in all, this is the largest estate in the Côte d'Or, with production totaling around 10,000 cases a year. Its ownership is divided up among anywhere from 60 to 100 individuals and syndicates, depending on whose estimate is used, and such is the prestige attached to owning a slice of this celebrated estate that many of the owners try to have their wines bottled under their own names. The production from each small piece of the estate obviously will vary in quality according to the age of the vines, the care with which they are cultivated, the date of the harvest, and the lay of the land. So the knowledge provided by a label that proclaims that the wine is Clos de Vougeot (sometimes Clos-Vougeot) may be insufficient to make a judgment as to quality. Anyone who has tasted several different Clos de Vougeots from the same vintage knows how variable they can be.

For this reason it has become common practice to buy Burgundy wines according to the shipper or bottler rather than the vineyard owner. In some cases, of course, the vineyard owner is also the shipper and bottler (e.g., La Domaine de la Romanée-Conti), but this is unusual in this part of France. The need to know the names of the better shippers makes identifying the better Burgundies more difficult. But the situation is not hopeless for the neophyte, because a relatively small number of shippers dominate the business. It should be noted, of course, that small shippers without substantial reputations can be responsible for excellent wines, and an obscure shipper may accomplish an especially fine blend in a specific vintage. But it is easier to rely on the big or well known houses that have proven themselves year after year.

No listing of the leading Burgundy firms can hope to be all-inclusive, but there are certain names that always come to the fore in any discussion of the wines from this great section of France:

Bouchard Aîné et Fils
Bouchard Père et Fils
Calvet
Caves de la Reine Pédauque
Chanson Père et Fils
F. Chauvenet
Doudet-Naudin
Joseph Drouhin
Joseph Faiveley
Grivelet
Jabóulet-Verchèrre
Lémé Frères
Liger-Belair
Prosper Maufoux
J. Mommesin
Morin Père et Fils
Charles Noëllat
Pasquier-Desvignes
Patriarche Père et Fils
Piat Père et Fils
Pierre Ponnelle
Poulet Père et Fils
Louis Jadot
Jaffelin
Louis Latour
Lebègue-Bichot
Georges Roumier
Ropiteau Frères
Sichel

Roland Thévenin
Charles Vienot
Comte de Vogüé

Often the name of the shipper will not appear on the bottle, but in these cases the name of the producer will be prominently displayed. Sometimes the producer also ships his own wine but not the wines of other producers. The listing of shippers above includes mostly firms and individuals that have built up substantial reputations for bottling or shipping the production of others, although many also have important vineyard holdings as well. The Domaine de la Romanée-Conti is not listed above because it is primarily an owner and producer rather than a major shipper of other producers' wines. It is worth repeating that the list above is not intended to be comprehensive; it merely reflects a cross-section of the leading shippers familiar to the author.

Neophytes are constantly admonished in wine literature to look for the designation mis en bouteilles au domaine or mis en bouteilles par le propriétaire, which provides an indication that the wine was bottled at the estate or vineyard where it was produced rather than at the centralized facilities of a shipper. But the fact is that many highly reputable shippers bottle wines for other producers, and the lack of the notation mis en bouteilles au domaine on their labels is not a sign of inferiority. At the same time, an estate owner who bottles on his own property may not have standards as high as those of a good shipper, yet he would be entitled to the above designation.

Some notations that resemble the ones with official standing are used by less scrupulous shippers in an effort to mislead the buyer. For example, mis en bouteilles dans mes caves translates literally as "bottled in my cellars," but it does not restrict where those cellars might be. Thus the designation could be used by a Bordeaux firm that purchased Burgundy wines shipped in bulk from, say, Nuits-Saint-Georges and bottled them in its own caves in Bordeaux. The notation mis en bouteilles au château also is virtually meaningless in the Burgundy region because few châteaux exist there, whereas it is a guarantee of quality in Bordeaux, where nearly all the good wines are château-bottled. The best rule to follow is to experiment with the wines of a reputable dealer until several good Burgundy shippers' or producers' names have been identified. Then rely on those names as the sources of good Burgundy wines. The alternative would be to make a list of all the grand cru Burgundy domains and buy only these wines—regardless of cost. Obviously a little self-education will save money. (A listing of individual Burgundy vineyards appears under the entries for the Côte de Beaune and the Côte de Nuits. In addition, the more prominent estates are discussed under their own headings.)

Côte Rôtie.

Some very good red wines are produced in the Rhône River District of France and one of them is Côte Rôtie, which comes from the northernmost part of the district, near Vienne. The name means "roasted hillside" and refers to the slope overlooking the Rhône on its west bank and facing generally south and southeast so that the vineyards can absorb the warm rays of the sun and produce very ripe grapes. The wines are dark-colored, like the full-bodied Hermitages produced about 25 miles south, and tend to be hard and tannic when young. They have an almost sharp quality, which can be detected even in mature vintages, and it is not altogether pleasing to some connoisseurs. But they are also earthy and rich and do not require as much bottle-age as a big Hermitage.

Côte Rôtie is made with the Syrah

grape, although Viognier white grapes may be added to provide a softening effect. The vineyard area is divided into two subdivisions: the Côte Brune and the Côte Blonde. According to local folklore, they were named after the daughters of an early landowner; one had blond hair and one brown. The Côte Brune soil is darker and is said to produce superior wine, but the wines from the two are generally blended. Devotees of Côte Rôtie wines say they are the best of the Rhône District in the vintages when fruit and tannin are balanced, but good wines from Châteauneuf-du-Pape and Hermitage seem to be more highly esteemed among Rhône connoisseurs.

☆☆☆☆

$$/$$$

Côtes de Canon-Fronsac.

This *appellation* is applied to the better red wines produced on the slopes of Saint-Michael-Fronsac above the Dordogne River near Libourne in the fringe areas of Bordeaux, in southwestern France. The knoll of Fronsac goes back a thousand years in French history because of its strategic importance overlooking the Dordogne Valley. Several fortresses existed on the site, including one built by Charlemagne. Other wines from the area are entitled to the *appellations* Côtes de Fronsac and Fronsadais, the latter referring to lesser vineyards. The same grapes that are used in the Médoc. Saint-Emilion, and Pomerol are used here, but they produce wines of less character and breeding.

☆☆☆

$/$$

H. Coturri & Sons.

The family of Harry Coturri established H. Coturri & Sons in Glen Ellen, in California's Sonoma Valley, in 1979 and began making Chardonnay, Johannisberg Riesling, Sémillon, Gewürztrami-

ner, Pinot Noir, Zinfandel, and Cabernet Sauvignon, mostly from purchased grapes. Production has amounted to less than 2000 cases a year, and the wines have been distributed exclusively in California.

☆/☆☆☆

$/$$

Château Couhins.

Excellent dry white wines are produced at Château Couhins, an estate lying in the *commune* of Villenave d'Ornon in the Graves District south of Bordeaux. The estate was accorded *grand cru* status in the Graves white-wine classification of 1959. Château Couhins is owned by relatives of the late Edouard Gasqueton, who also was proprietor of the great Château Calon-Ségur in Saint-Estèphe. Couhins lies not far from Château Bouscaut and Château Carbonnieux, two other well-known Graves estates. A separate property, Château Couhins-Lurton, has been split off from the original estate and is operated by André Lurton, a prominent local grower who also owns Clos Fourtet in Saint-Emilion and who is the brother of Lucien Lurton, proprietor of Château Brane-Cantenac and of Château Bouscaut.

☆☆

$$

Crémant de Bourgogne.

Sparkling wines are being produced in rising quantities all over the world in efforts to capitalize on the almost magical reputation of the most famous of them all, Champagne. One of the newer entries from France is Crémant de Bourgogne, which is not quite as bubbly as Champagne. It is produced in the Burgundy country from Pinot Noir, Pinot Chardonnay, and Aligoté grapes and differs from Sparkling Burgundy in that it is white. One of the best examples, produced in Nuits-Saint-Georges by the Countess Michel de Loisy, consists of a mixture of one-third Pinot Noir and two-thirds Aligoté. Other producers use the Chardonnay instead of the Pinot Noir grape. These wines generally are full-bodied yet dry, with slightly less character than Champagne. Yet they also are less costly. They tend to be superior to most American champagnes and to the sparkling wines produced elsewhere in Europe. (*See also* Champagne.)

☆☆

$$/$$$

Crépy.

Among the lesser known white wines of France is Crépy, produced just across the border from Switzerland, near Geneva, in the area known as the Haute-Savoie. It is made from the Chasselas grape, which also is grown in Alsace and, more extensively, in Switzerland. It is light and dry, with an interesting tang that is similar to the taste of Swiss white wines.

☆

$

Cresta Blanca.

The old Cresta Blanca winery, founded by Charles Wetmore in the Livermore Valley of California in 1882, produced award-winning wines, some from cuttings that he had brought over from the great Château d'Yquem in Sauternes. Wetmore was an active promoter of California wines, constant in his effort to improve the wines and make people aware of them, abroad as well as at home. Many of his wines won prizes at Paris expositions before the turn of the century. In 1941 the winery was bought by Schenley, which sponsored the famous singing commercial that spelled out the name Cresta Blanca in an unforgettably singsong refrain.

Cresta Blanca is now a member of the big cooperative called Guild Wineries and Distilleries, based in San Francisco, although Cresta Blanca is the only member of Guild that still makes wine on its own premises, in this case Ukiah, in Mendocino County. The Cresta Blanca wines are among the better bottlings marketed by Guild, but they generally lack character and rarely achieve quality peaks.

☆/☆☆☆

$$

B. Cribari and Sons Winery.

Cribari and Sons is a member of the big cooperative called Guild Wineries and Distilleries. All of its wines are vinified and distributed by Guild. (*See* Guild Wineries and Distilleries.)

☆

$

Château La Croix de Gay.

Among the small but high-quality Pomerol estates is Château La Croix de Gay, located in the heart of the Pomerol District east of Bordeaux. Production is only about 2000 cases per year, but the wine is available in the United States and other export markets. La Croix de Gay would probably rank as a fourth or fifth growth if Pomerol were classified in the same way as the Médoc.

☆☆☆☆

$$/$$$

Château Croizet-Bages.

Surrounding the tiny hamlet of Bages in the *commune* of Pauillac, on the Médoc peninsula north of Bordeaux, are several estates with Bages attached to their name. The most famous is Château Lynch-Bages, but Château Croizet-Bages is almost as well known, although its wines are less supple and elegant. A Croizet-Bages in a robust vintage will be a very coarse wine in its youth and may retain the same roughness into maturity. The estate consists mostly of Cabernet Franc and Merlot, with only a minority of Cabernet Sauvignon grapes going into the blend. Plans to increase the percentage of Cabernet Sauvignon have been disclosed and should improve the wine. Croizet-Bages was ranked a *cinquieme cru,* or fifth growth, in the Bordeaux classification of 1855.

☆☆☆☆
$$/$$$

Cru, cru classé.

In Bordeaux the word *cru* has a very specific meaning, referring to a private estate or specifically delineated vineyard area. It is also roughly equivalent to *château,* to the extent that virtually all Bordeaux vineyards are named after a château—for example, Château Palmer or Château Giscours or Château Lynch-Bages. Literally the word is commonly translated as "growth," because in French it is the past participle of the verb *croître,* "to grow." Thus a *cru* of Bordeaux is a growth of Bordeaux. But this translation obviously leaves much to be desired, and the looser usage, as in château or estate or even vineyard area, is preferable. A *cru classé,* or *grand cru classé,* in the Médoc portion of Bordeaux is a vineyard that was recognized in the Médoc classification of 1855 as being of superior quality. Sixty-one existing châteaux were accorded *cru classé* designations in the 1855 Médoc classification, plus one château not in the Médoc, Château Haut-Brion in Pessac, Graves, which was included because of its renown. The ranking is broken down into five numerical categories: *premier grand cru, deuxième,* or *second, grand cru,* etc.

Graves, the district directly south and west of Bordeaux, was not officially classified until 1953. This classification was revised in 1959, and the designations *grand cru, grand cru classé,* etc., can be found on Graves labels. Because they came more than a century after the Médoc classification, the Graves ratings are taken less seriously than those of the Médoc. Saint-Emilion was classified in 1955, using four basic categories: Saint-Emilion Premier Grand Cru Classé, Saint-Emilion Grand Cru Classé, Saint-Emilion Grand Cru, and Saint-Emilion. Both the Graves and Saint-Emilion classifications were alphabetical within each level, although Château Ausone and Château Cheval Blanc were given special status atop the *premiers grands crus classés* in Saint-Emilion. The Médoc classification was not alphabetical. Attempting to evaluate the wines of the Médoc, Graves, and Saint-Emilion through comparing their classifications is futile. The terms *cru classé* and *grand cru classé* should be used only as a general guide to quality and should not be considered a guarantee in any way. (*See also* Médoc, Saint-Emilion, Graves, Sauternes, Pomerol, etc.)

Cuvaison Vineyard.

Cuvaison was established in 1970 and has consistently produced excellent Cabernet Sauvignons, Zinfandels, and Chardonnays at its whitewashed winery with red-tiled roofs, which was completed in 1974 on a site on the eastern slopes of the Napa Valley, not far from Calistoga. The proprietor is Dr. Stephan Schmidtheiny and the winemaker is John Thacher.

Cuvaison purchased 392 acres in the Carneros District of the southern Napa Valley in 1979 and was planting the former hayfield in vines during the early 1980s. Prior to this purchase Cuvaison owned no vineyards of its own and made wine entirely from purchased grapes. Production totaled 10,000 cases of Chardonnay, 7000 cases of Cabernet Sauvignon, and 3000 cases of Zinfandel per year before the new Carneros vineyard came into production.

Cuvaison also bottles wine under a secondary label, Calistoga Vineyards, which the winery describes as two-thirds the quality of Cuvaison at half the price. Production of Calistoga Vineyards runs about 3000 cases of white wine a year, plus up to 3000 cases of Cabernet.

The Cuvaison wines receive especially careful treatment prior to bottling. For example, they are fined, or filtered, using the ancient European method of dropping egg whites into the aging wine to cause the solids to precipitate out. The wines tend to be robust and intensely flavored, with relatively high alcohol content. The reds are matured in oak barrels imported from Bordeaux, and the Chardonnay also is oak-aged. Occasionally, when growing and harvesting conditions have been ideal, a Reserve wine is made, and these tend to be even more intense and textured than the regular Cuvaison bottlings. All of the Cuvaison wines benefit from years of bottle-aging.
☆☆/☆☆☆☆
$/$$

Cygnet Cellars.

Cygnet Cellars, in Hollister in San Benito County, California, has been most successful with a Paso Robles Carignane aged in oak barrels. The property, established in 1977, uses purchased grapes and also produces Chardonnay, Pinot St. George, and Zinfandel. The wines have been undistinguished.
☆/☆☆
$/$$

Cyprus.

The island of Cyprus in the eastern Mediterranean has been producing thick, sweet wines at least since the Crusades and probably even earlier. The island was the home of the goddess Aphrodite, according to Greek legend, and her name is found today on Cyprus wine labels. The most famous of the island's wines is Commanderia, so named by the Knights Templar after Richard I gave Cyprus to them in 1191 and the commanders monopolized its production and export. Commanderia is made from a blend of red and white grapes and is very sugary, with an almost molasseslike consistency. It is produced on the sloping vineyards of the Troodos Mountains, which stretch across the western part of the island. In the last decade or two Cyprus has developed a substantial "Sherry" business in competition with the producers of genuine Sherry in Spain. Cyprus Sherries are produced in big volume and are priced to undercut the Spanish Sherries, enabling them to carve out a major share of the market for this type of fortified wine. Only three important grape varieties are cultivated on the island: the red Mavron, which dominates most of the vineyards, the white Xynisteri, and a small amount of the Muscat of Alexandria. The table wines of Cyprus, produced high in the Troodos range, tend to be fairly coarse and alcoholic and are rarely seen abroad.

· D ·

Dāo.

The rich and velvety red table wine of northern Portugal is Dāo, and it has flowed increasingly into the export markets in response to growing public awareness of its qualities. It is a dry and full-bodied wine of great depth and intensity, and it is sometimes compared to the wines of Saint-Emilion and Pomerol in the eastern part of the Bordeaux region of France, although a Dāo from a good vintage will be earthier and less beguiling in its youth. A decade of aging is usually required for a Dāo to reach maturity, but the amount of time will vary according to the style of the producer. Some lighter-bodied Dāos that mature at a younger age are made by blending quantities of white grapes in with the red. A Dāo 1952 tasted in an Oporto shipper's home in 1975 displayed a classic Bordeaux bouquet, a deep color, and full body. It was produced by the Vinicola do Vale do Dāo, the same concern that makes Mateus Rosé. The bouquet was so similar to the aroma of a Bordeaux produced from Cabernet Sauvignon and Merlot grapes that the Dāo's taste was almost surprising, since it did not resemble a Bordeaux taste. Rather, it had an earthy personality of its own, with an intensity and richness that were extraordinary for a 23-year-old wine.

Dāo is produced in central Portugal, south of the Douro Valley where Port is made. The wine is named after the Dāo River, which runs through the area. The Dāo wine trade is centered in Viseu, an ancient town with an eleventh-century cathedral and the sixteenth-century Três Escalões Palace, which is now a museum. Viseu was the home of Grão Vasco, a painter of the primitive school, whose name is on one of the better Dāo wines. Viseu is also the home of the Federação dos Vinicultores do Dāo, the region's supervisory confederation.

The grape varieties approved by the Dāo confederation are the Tourigo, Tinta Pinhiera, Tinta Carvalha, Baga de Louro, Alvarelhão, and Bastardo for red wines, as well as the Arinto, Dona Branca, Barcelo, and Fernão Pires for the small amounts of white Dāo that are produced. Several of the red grapes are the same as those used to make Port, although the production methods are somewhat different. Whereas Port is a fortified wine with a fairly high sugar content, Dāo is completely fermented, so that very little residual sugar remains.

A Dão produced for export must be at least 13 percent alcohol—a standard table-wine percentage all over the world—whereas Port is always about 20 percent alcohol, due to the addition of grape brandy. A number of wine co-operatives have been formed in the Dão region, and the small vineyard owners bring their production to these cooperatively run facilities for vinification. The young wine remains here for no more than six or eight months and is then sold to shippers, who age it in wooden casks, usually for at least two years and often for three years, before bottling. Thus Dão, like Port, is nearly always a blend from numerous vineyards in the region, and the distinctions among the various Dãos available result from the handling by the shippers, whose facilities are more likely to be in or near Oporto on the Atlantic Coast than in the Dão area itself. The wines are usually vintage-dated and are likely to be rather pungent if drunk before they reach the age of eight.

☆☆☆/☆☆☆☆☆

$/$$

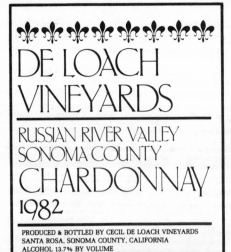

De Loach Vineyards.

This family operation headed by Cecil O. De Loach had originally grown grapes for other producers, but established its own winery in 1979 near Santa Rosa in California's Sonoma Valley. Using French and American oak cooperage as well as stainless steel tanks, De Loach began producing excellent red and white Zinfandels, a decent Chardonnay and Gewürztraminer, Fumé Blanc, and Pinot Noir. Production has climbed to 20,000 cases a year.

☆/☆☆☆

$$

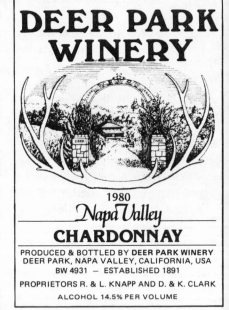

Deer Park Winery.

Deer Park Winery was established in 1979 on a historic site in Deer Park in California's Napa Valley. The winery owns six acres of vineyards and buys additional grapes from other Napa Valley producers. The initial product line consisted of Sauvignon Blanc, Chardonnay, and Zinfandel.

☆/☆☆

$$

Dehlinger Winery.

Tom Dehlinger worked at Beringer, Hanzell, and Dry Creek and did graduate work in oenology at the University of California at Davis before opening his own business in 1975, when he made the first Dehlinger wines from purchased grapes in a borrowed winery. He built the Dehlinger Winery in 1976 in Sebastopol in the Sonoma Valley and began planting his own grapes. He is still tearing out apple orchards to make way for vines and, in 1981, produced more than half of his own grape requirements for the first time. He buys the rest from other Sonoma growers. Production is now about 9000 cases a year of Chardonnay, Cabernet Sauvignon, and Pinot Noir, as well as Zinfandel, which he makes entirely from purchased grapes. All of his wines are aged in 130-gallon French oak barrels. A typical batch of Chardonnay, for example, will be aged for ten months, one-third in new oak and two-thirds in used oak. The size of the barrels (about double the standard size) and the moderate exposure to new oak give his wines a subtle complexity lacking in some of the more robust bottlings produced by some of his competitors. Production at Dehlinger is expected to double by the late 1980s as more of the winery's own vineyards are planted and come into bearing.

☆☆/☆☆☆☆
$$

Deidesheimer.

Deidesheim, one of the principal towns in the center of the Rheinpfalz, or Palatinate, is Germany's southernmost region for producing superior white table wines. Deidesheimers can reach quality peaks unmatched anywhere else in Germany and are revered by connoisseurs. They exude character with their full bodies, great depth and balance. The area is planted mostly in the noble Riesling grape, which produces the most elegant wines. The town is the home of the imposing fifteenth-century mansion of Dr. Ludwig Bassermann-Jordan, son of the late Dr. Friedrich Bassermann-Jordan, who wrote extensively on wine and established one of the world's most outstanding private wine museums beneath Deidesheim's streets. The town is the most important in the Pfalz in terms of fine wine trade, although Bad Durkheim probably does a bigger volume of business.

Most important to Deidesheim are its vineyards, whose names will appear on labels unless the wine is a blend or regional bottling entitled only to the Deidesheimer name. Among the most highly regarded vineyards are the following:

Deidesheimer Dopp
Deidesheimer Fleckinger
Deidesheimer Forster Strasse
Deidesheimer Geheu
Deidesheimer Grain
Deidesheimer Grainhübel*
Deidesheimer Hahnenböhl
Deidesheimer Herrgottsacker*
Deidesheimer Hofstück*
Deidesheimer Hohenmorgen*
Deidesheimer Kalkofen*
Deidesheimer Kieselberg*
Deidesheimer Kränzler
Deidesheimer Langenmorgen*
Deidesheimer Leinhöhle*
Deidesheimer Mäushöhle*
Deidesheimer Mühle
Diedesheimer Reiss
Deidesheimer Rennpfad
Deidesheimer Weinbach

The vineyards marked with an asterisk (*) are among those that retained their identities, if not their former configurations, in the revision of the German wine law in 1971. The new law also made provision for one other vine-

218   TERRY ROBARDS' NEW BOOK OF WINE

yard name, Paradiesgarten. Hofstück is now a *Grosslage,* or large vineyard area, roughly equivalent to a generic term for wine from the area.

☆☆/☆☆☆

$$

Dienheimer.

German white wine produced in Dienheim, one of the wine villages of the Rheinhessen, which lies mostly south of Mainz along the west bank of the Rhine River. Dienheim adjoins Oppenheim and shares two of its most important vineyards—Goldberg and Kröttenbrunnen. But most of its vineyards produce undistinguished wines that probably wind up as Liebfraumilch, a blend.

Among the better Dienheimer vineyards are the following:

Dienheimer Goldberg
Dienheimer Guldenmorgen
Dienheimer Kröttenbrunnen*
Dienheimer Rosswiese
Dienheimer Siliusbrunnen*
Dienheimer Tafelstein*

The vineyards marked with an asterisk (*) are among those that retained their identities, if not their shapes, in the revision of the German wine law of 1971. Kröttenbrunnen has evolved into a generic name for wines from a fairly large vineyard area.

☆☆

$/$$

Del Rio Winery.

Del Rio is a member of the big California cooperative called Guild Wineries and Distilleries. All of its wines are vinified and distributed by Guild. (*See* Guild Wineries and Distilleries.)

☆

$

Delicato Vineyards.

Delicato Vineyards was founded in California's San Joaquin Valley in 1924 by Gaspare Indelicato and Sebastiano Luppino and has been in the same family since the beginning. Frank, Anthony, and Vincent Indelicato are the present proprietors, and they produce wines mostly for other California bottlers. Their annual production is substantial, 14 million gallons, and they now bottle a full line of varietals and generics that are mostly in the low-priced category.

☆/☆☆

$/$$

Denominazione di Origine Controllata (D.O.C.).

This Italian term is nearly always abbreviated by its initials, D.O.C., and literally stands for "controlled appellation of origin," closely equivalent to the French *appellation d'origine contrôlée.* The words on an Italian wine label indicate that the wine was produced within a specific geographical territory, that only certain approved varieties of grapes were used and that they were vinified according to procedures mandated by law and custom. The D.O.C. law came into being in Italy in 1963 as part of a general effort to upgrade the quality and reputation of Italian wines, and it has been highly successful. Italian wines are taken far more seriously now than they used to be, partly because they are simply better, reflecting the standards imposed by the D.O.C. law. Consumers seeking an indication of quality on an unfamiliar Italian label should look for the words *denominazione di origine controllata.* Wines without a D.O.C. rating may be surprisingly good, but virtually all of the most consistently superior Italian wines are in the D.O.C. category.

Three types of D.O.C. wines exist. The first consists of the best-known wines with geographical names, e.g.,

Chianti, Barolo, Soave. The second consists of two-part names that indicate both the variety of grape and the geographical place of origin, e.g., Vernaccia di San Gimignano, Albana di Romagna, Aglianico del Vulture. The third consists of names that have much tradition or historical background but lack geographical origins, e.g., Est! Est! Est! There is no need for consumers to memorize which wines fall into a D.O.C. category, for the producers of such wines take pride in their ratings and always print the words on their labels.

An even rarer category suggesting the ultimate in quality is the D.O.C.G., for *denominazione di origine controllata e garantita*, for "controlled and guaranteed appellation of origin." The key word is *garantita*, for "guaranteed," implying an official guarantee of quality. Tasting panels judge each wine at different stages of production and vinification to assure that the highest standards are met, and wines that do not pass the tests must be decontrolled into simple table wine. All producers of a type of wine with D.O.C.G. ranking must submit to the judging and must meet the applicable standards in order to win the government seals that are placed on bottles to attest to their superiority. The first wines to win D.O.C.G. designations were Vino Nobile di Montepulciano, Barbaresco, Barolo, and Brunello di Montalcino, comprising a hierarchy of northern Italian reds. Others probably will qualify as time passes.

Diamond Creek Vineyards.

Very dark, tannic, robust, textured Cabernet Sauvignons are produced by Al Brounstein, the proprietor and winemaker at Diamond Creek Vineyards, from grapes grown at three adjacent tracts totaling 20 acres, on Diamond Mountain above Calistoga on the western slopes of California's Napa Valley. The production of each vineyard has its own personality and style and therefore is identified by name on the Diamond Creek labels. The three are Volcanic Hill, Red Rock Terrace, and Gravelly Meadow, and each has developed a following among Cabernet enthusiasts who prefer big, intense wines that require years of bottle-aging before they reach their peaks. A fourth vineyard, Lake, is usually blended with one of the others.

Brounstein sold his wholesale and proprietary drug business in 1969, opting for the wine business instead. He had bought his property on Diamond Mountain in 1967 and planted part of it in Cabernet vines in 1968 and part a few years later. An operating winery was established in 1972 and was upgraded and expanded to include modern storage facilities in 1981. Production runs no more than 3500 cases a year, but the Diamond Creek reputation for fine wines is large. The composition of the wines is similar to that of a typical vineyard in the Médoc subregion of Bordeaux: Merlot, Cabernet Franc, and Malbec grapes blended in small amounts with the dominant Cabernet Sauvignon. All of the Diamond Creek wines are aged in French oak barrels from Nevers. All are estate-bottled; no grapes are purchased from outside sources.
☆☆☆☆
$$$

Diamond Oaks Vineyard.

Diamond Oaks Vineyard, not to be confused with Diamond Creek Vineyards, was established in California's Sonoma Valley in 1980 and has its wines vinified at Souverain Cellars. Its grapes come from both the Napa and Sonoma regions. Production has risen to about 16,000 cases annually of Fumé Blanc, Chardonnay, Cabernet Sauvignon, and a blended red table wine.
☆/☆☆☆
$/$$

D.O.C.

D.O.C. stands for *denominazione di origine controllata,* the basis for the Italian wine law. (*See denominazione di origine controllata.*)

Dolan Vineyards.

Dolan Vineyards is one of numerous California wineries owned and operated by winemakers whose primary work is for other producers. The man behind Dolan Vineyards is Paul Dolan, who also happens to be the winemaker at Fetzer Vineyards. Dolan is in Redwood Valley in Mendocino County. The first harvest, in 1980, yielded 800 cases of Chardonnay and 250 cases of Cabernet Sauvignon. Because of Dolan's role at Fetzer, however, his wines have attracted attention from coast to coast.
☆☆/☆☆☆
$$

dolce.

The Italian term for "very sweet" is *dolce,* which indicates that a wine contains at least 3 percent and sometimes a somewhat higher percentage of residual sugar. *Dolce* is sweeter than *amabile* (2½ to 3 percent sugar) and *abboccato* (1 to 2½ percent sugar).

Dolcetto.

One of the commoner red wines of the Piedmont region of northern Italy is Dolcetto, produced from the Dolcetto grape. Although the name indicates that this is a sweet wine, it is often quite dry and can be very pleasant, if not truly great. Its name usually is followed by the name of the district where it is produced—e.g., Dolcetto d'Alba, which is considered the best of the Dolcettos.

Domaine de Chevalier.

One of the few Bordeaux estates that does not include a château in its name is Domaine de Chevalier, which lies in Léognan in the Graves District south of Bordeaux. The red wines of this estate rank just below the most celebrated Graves, Château Haut-Brion, and are on a par with La Mission-Haut-Brion in many vintages. They display an elegance and finesse comparable to the best reds of the Médoc to the north. A dry white wine is also made at Domaine de Chevalier, and it is one of the leading white Graves. Both the red and the white were accorded *grand cru* recognition in the Graves classification of 1959.
☆/☆☆☆
$$/$$$

Domaine Chandon.

Domaine Chandon opened in April 1977 in Yountville in California's Napa Valley as an American outpost of the Moët et Chandon Champagne house based in Epernay, France. Four years of development lay behind the opening of the modern winery and the rest of Chandon's extensive facilities. Success came almost immediately. Domaine Chandon's Napa Valley Brut sparkling wine was one of the best sparklers produced in California from the outset and its Blanc de Noirs, made from black grapes, also developed a wide following. By the late 1970s the wines had become so popular that they were put on allocation while production facilities were expanded from 100,000 cases a year to 350,000 cases. A restaurant serving excellent food has been opened on the premises, and tours are available to the public.

Domaine Chandon's success is attributable partly to the expertise of John Wright, a former management consultant who was based in Paris, and to the careful supervision of the parent French company through the guidance of Edmond Maudière, *chef de caves* of Moët et Chandon, who is largely responsible for the quality of the Chandon wines and who works closely with Chandon's on-premises winemaker, Dawnine Sample Dyer. The traditional *methode champenoise,* involving fermentation in bottles, is employed. (This is not unique in California; most of the other producers of superior sparkling wines use the same method.) The Napa Valley Brut is made from a blend of Pinot Noir and Chardonnay grapes, with some Pinot Blanc, as are the Moët et Chandon Champagnes made in France. The Blanc de Noirs is fuller-bodied because it is made entirely from Pinot Noir grapes.

Initially Chandon made its sparkling wines from purchased grapes, but extensive vineyards have been cultivated since. The concern owns 900 acres of vineyards in the Napa Valley, including a 600-acre plot in the Carneros district which spills over into the Sonoma Valley. It also owns a 200-acre vineyard on Mount Veeder, along with the 130-acre vineyard surrounding the winery just west of Yountville.

Besides its sparkling wines (which do not carry the Champagne name out of deference to the accurate geographical origin of that name in France), Domaine Chandon produces a modest amount of still wine under the name Fred's Friends, made from second pressings of the same grapes used for the sparkling wines. The concern also produces an aperitif wine

called Panache that is sweet, with about 10 percent residual sugar, and high in alcohol, about 18 percent. It is similar to the Ratafia produced by some Champagne houses in France.
☆
$$

Domaine Laurier.

Excellent Chardonnays in the French Chablis style have been produced by Domaine Laurier since its founding in 1978 in California's Sonoma County. The wines are full-bodied yet crisp and tart and require considerable breathing to reach their peaks, in contrast to many other California Chardonnays. Production has amounted to about 7000 cases a year of Sauvignon Blanc, Pinot Noir, and Cabernet Sauvignon as well as Chardonnay.
☆/☆☆☆
$$

Donna Maria Vineyards.

Fred and Donna Furth became interested in the Sonoma wine region of California in the early 1970s and established Donna Maria Vineyards in 1980. They own 180 acres in the Chalk Hill area of Sonoma County, where they produce mostly Chardonnay as well as Cabernet Sauvignon, Gewürztraminer, and Sauvignon Blanc. Production so far has amounted to only about 10,000 cases a year, but the total will expand substantially as the vineyards reach maturity. Fred Furth, a San Francisco lawyer, also has major additional landholdings in the area and could undertake further plantings.
☆/☆☆☆
$/$$

Dry Creek Vineyard.

Dry Creek Vineyard, near Healdsburg in the Sonoma Valley, was founded by David Stare, who built the winery in

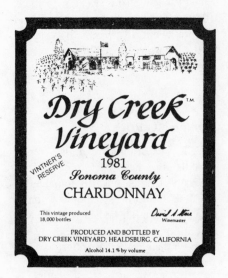

Dry Creek Vineyard T.M.

VINTNER'S RESERVE

1981

Sonoma County

CHARDONNAY

This vintage produced 18,000 bottles

David I. Stare Winemaster

PRODUCED AND BOTTLED BY
DRY CREEK VINEYARD, HEALDSBURG, CALIFORNIA

Alcohol 14.1 % by volume

1973 after spending two years as a special graduate student in oenology and viticulture at the University of California at Davis. Earlier he had received a bachelor's degree in civil engineering from the Massachusetts Institute of Technology, then won his master's in business administration from Northwestern University. His first job, with the Baltimore & Ohio Railroad in the corporate planning area, took him to Baltimore, where he encountered Philip Wagner of Boordy Vineyards and planted vines in his own backyard. He also worked in Germany briefly before moving to California.

Little of this background suggests that Stare would become one of the better winemakers of the Sonoma Valley, but the Dry Creek wines usually are very well made, with intense varietal character. They have developed a wide following over the years, and production has risen past 30,000 cases a year. The first Dry Creek wines were made in the Cuvaison cellars at Calistoga in 1972. These were all whites—Chenin Blanc, Fumé Blanc, and Chardonnay. Once his 3500-square-feet winery in Healdsburg was completed in 1973, he also began

to produce Cabernet Sauvignon, Zinfandel, and Petite Sirah. Dry Creek occasionally also turns out small amounts of Merlot and Gewürztraminer. The winery's size was tripled in 1977, mainly for barrel-aging and storage, plus creating a tasting room for visitors. About 40 percent of Dry Creek's production comes from its own vineyards, and the rest comes from grapes purchased from outside growers. Stare is one of the very few producers who is able to continue buying Chardonnay grapes from the Robert Young Vineyard, whose production now goes almost entirely to Château St. Jean.

☆☆/☆☆☆☆

$$

Duckhorn Vineyards.

Duckhorn is a relatively new winery established in St. Helena in the Napa Valley in 1976. Its first crush came in 1978, with vintage-dated bottlings of Napa Valley Cabernet Sauvignon and Napa Valley Merlot in very limited quantities. Proprietors Dan and Margaret Duckhorn have also planted 6.5 acres in Sauvignon Blanc and Sémillon and purchase grapes from a half-dozen other Napa Valley growers. Aging takes place in small oak barrels, and the Duckhorn wines tend to be rich in varietal intensity and character.

☆☆☆☆

$$

Château Ducru-Beaucaillou.

The name of this estate overlooking the Gironde and adjacent to Château Beychevelle in Saint-Julien means "beautiful pebble." The soil in this part of the Médoc is very gravelly, a characteristic that produces great wines wherever it is found in this part of France. Ducru-Beaucaillou was ranked a *second cru,* or second growth, in the Bordeaux classification of 1855, and it clearly merits this distinction today. The wines are full-bodied and elegant, with a flowery bouquet.

The property was known only as Beaucaillou until the early nineteenth century, when its owner, whose name was Ducru, added his name to that of the château. The property was sold to Nathaniel Johnston in 1863, to a Monsieur Desbarats de Burke in 1928 and finally to Francis Borie in 1941. He died in 1953, and since then his son, Jean-Eugène Borie, has been the proprietor. He has made substantial investments in the vineyards, and the wines seem to keep improving year after year. The property consists of 275 acres, of which 100 acres are planted in vines—65 percent Cabernet Sauvignon, 25 percent Merlot, and 10 percent Cabernet Franc and Petit Verdot.
☆☆☆☆
$$$

Château Duhart-Milon-Rothschild.

The barons Guy and Elie de Rothschild, of the Paris banking family, expanded their Bordeaux interests in 1962 with the purchase of Château Duhart-Milon, which lies adjacent to their celebrated Château Lafite-Rothschild in the *commune* of Pauillac on the Médoc peninsula north of the city of Bordeaux. They immediately changed the label of Duhart-Milon so that it closely resembles that of Lafite, and a few years later they added the Rothschild name. The 1959 and '61 vintages of Duhart-Milon, under the previous ownership, were quite decent wines, and the 1962, also the result of the previous owners, was good. But the Rothschilds have been upgrading the vineyard since then, and the wine is no longer quite as robust and full as it used to be, although it displays a touch more finesse. During this transition the price of Duhart-Milon has escalated sharply, perhaps because unsophisticated buyers have been responding to the addition of the Rothschild name on the label. Duhart-Milon was ranked as a *quatrième cru,* or fourth growth, in the Bordeaux classification of 1855, but it now consistently brings prices equivalent to the second growths. Although the wine has improved under the Rothschild influence, its character is more that of a secondary Lafite than of a wine that displays its own distinctive merits.
☆☆☆☆
$$/$$$

Château Durfort-Vivens.

Ranked a *second cru,* or second growth, in the Bordeaux classification of 1855, Durfort-Vivens is owned by Lucien Lurton, who also owns Château Brane-Cantenac, another *second cru* of great renown. Durfort-Vivens lies in the heart of the *commune* of Margaux on the Médoc peninsula, not far from Château Margaux itself. The wine is supple and elegant and has a reputation for longevity.
☆☆☆/☆☆☆☆☆
$$/$$$

Dürkheimer.

German white and red wine produced in Bad Dürkheim, one of the better wine towns in the Rheinpfalz, or Palatinate, the country's southernmost region for superior table wines. More wines are produced in this town than anywhere else in the Pfalz, and it ranks among the largest in Germany in terms of output. Yet the reds are no better than the cheapest California jug wines and are not responsible for the fame of Bad Dürkheim, which has mineral baths, a casino and most of the other trappings of a typical German resort. The best Dürkheimers are the rich and full-bodied whites made from the Riesling grape. They tend to lack the finesse of a Forster or Deidesheimer, but in good vintages some excellent wines are produced, worthy of the attention of connoisseurs.

Although quantities of Dürkheimer are sold in bulk for blending and bottling elsewhere in Germany, some specific Dürkheimer vineyards have won recognition abroad. Among the better known are the following:

Dürkheimer Feuerberg*
Dürkheimer Forst
Dürkheimer Fuchsmantel
Dürkheimer Halsberg
Dürkheimer Hochbenn*
Dürkheimer Hochmess*
Dürkheimer Klosterberg
Dürkheimer Michelsberg*
Dürkheimer Schenkenbohl
Dürkheimer Spielberg*

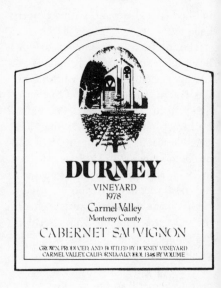

DURNEY
VINEYARD
1978
Carmel Valley
Monterey County
CABERNET SAUVIGNON
GROWN, PRODUCED, AND BOTTLED BY DURNEY VINEYARD
CARMEL VALLEY, CALIFORNIA/ALCOHOL 13.4% BY VOLUME

The vineyards marked with an asterisk (*) are among those that retained their identities, if not their shapes, in the revision of the German wine law in 1971. The others were merged and consolidated to simplify identification. Hochmess and Feuerberg were made *Grosslage,* or virtually generic names for wines from the Bad Dürkheim area.
☆☆/☆☆☆
$/$$

Durney Vineyard & Winery.

One of the more spectacular wineries in California is Durney Vineyard, which lies on a remote hillside in the Santa Lucia Range looking out across the Carmel Valley in Monterey County, south of San Francisco. The farm there is called Rancho del Sueño, with 1200 acres that produce cattle as well as wine. It is the first winemaking operation ever established in the Carmel Valley, and no expense has been spared by Bill Durney and his wife, Dorothy Kingsley, the writer, to create a jewel of an enterprise.

They built a Spanish mission-style house on the hill above the winery. It has a reddish tiled roof, arched door-

ways, high ceilings with open beams, and a huge stone fireplace with a sunken seating area nearby. The bar is called the Bacchus Room, after the god of wines, and the grape motif is everywhere—in the stained-glass windows, in the carvings on the furniture, in the paintings that hang on the walls, even in the kitchen tiles. Behind the main house is a wine cellar dug into the hillside, complete with tasting table, and across a courtyard from the house is a chapel, with pews salvaged from an old church that was being demolished and a big bronze bell from Portugal that swings high in a stucco belfry. The chapel also contains an apartment for visiting priests, who perform the marriages and christenings for the Durney family. The Durneys' daughter Chrissie was married there to David Armanasco, general manager of the vineyards.

The Durneys have one of the few winemaking operations that use no herbicides or spraying of any kind and that does not need irrigation, despite the 1200-feet elevation of the vineyards. The vines are irrigated naturally by underground springs that flow beneath the soil, apparently carrying nutrients and minerals down the hillside to the roots at a depth of three to four feet. The surface soil appears chalky and dry, but the subsoil is moist.

Production totals only about 12,000 cases a year, and 60 percent of this is Cabernet Sauvignon. The Durney Cabernet is a big, mouth-filling wine of tremendous character which needs at least eight to ten years to reach maturity. Chenin Blanc, Johannisberg Riesling, and Gamay Beaujolais have also been produced, and Chardonnay has been planted. Unlike many other Monterey County wines, the Durney wines lack a grassy, vegetal quality and more closely resemble those from the Napa or Sonoma valleys to the north.

☆☆/☆☆☆☆

$$/$$$

· E ·

Echézeaux, Grands Echézeaux.

Listed among the seven *grands crus* vineyards of Vosne-Romanée, one of the best wine-producing *communes* in the Burgundian Côte d'Or, or Golden Slope, of France are Echézeaux and Grands Echézeaux, which do not actually lie in Vosne-Romanée. Rather, they are in Flagey-Echézeaux, a nearby *commune,* but have been given the right under French wine law to the Vosne-Romanée *appellation.* There are only 24 red *grands crus* in all of the Burgundy country, so these two vineyards rank with the very best. They are full-bodied, velvety wines of great intensity that exude a bouquet of truffles and violets. Grands Echézeaux is usually held in higher regard, but André Noblet, the *régisseur* at the Domaine de la Romanée-Conti, ex-presses a preference for Echézeaux in many vintages. The Domaine is a principal owner of these two vineyards and produces wines of great finesse. Echézeaux tends to be the least expensive of the Domaine's wines, although it is by no means a cheap Burgundy. (*See also* Romanée-Conti, Vosne-Romanée, Côte de Nuits.)
☆☆☆☆
$$$

Edelfäule.

The German term for *Botrytis cinerea,* or the "noble rot," a fungus or mold that afflicts grapes very late in the autumn after the normal harvest if the weather conditions remain good. The parasite penetrates the skins of the grapes, helping the water to evaporate into the air, leaving behind a highly concentrated juice with natural sugar content. The *Edelfäule* will be evident in Auslese, Beerenauslese, and Trockenbeerenauslese—the sweeter wines in the German *Qualitätswein mit Prädikat* category. In France it is called *pourriture noble* and is sought after in the production of such French sweet wines as Sauternes, Barsac, and Monbazillac, as well as Tokay in Hungary. Grapes that have contracted the noble rot appear moldy and ugly, but they produce the best sweet wines. *Edel-fäule* is also seen in certain Austrian wines, especially the Ruster wines from the shores of the Neusiedler See in the province of Burgenland.

Edmeades Vineyards.

Dr. Donald Edmeades, a Pasadena physician, purchased a 108-acre apple ranch in 1964 near the Navarro River in Philo, in Mendocino County's Anderson Valley. The microclimate there is said to create the rainiest viticultural region in California, and one of the Edmeades products is a brand called Rain Wine, which is vinified from a blend of Johannisberg Riesling, French Colombard, and Chardonnay. Dr. Edmeades died in 1972 after planting Cabernet Sauvignon, Chardonnay, French Colombard, and Gewürztraminer on the property. The initial harvest, in 1968, and subsequent crops through 1974, were sold to Parducci, which won awards for its wines made from Edmeades grapes.

Deron Edmeades, Dr. Edmeades' son, took over upon his father's death and established a small winery in a converted apple dryer below the main house on the estate. Production grew gradually but steadily and recently was around 50,000 cases a year. The winery itself has been expanded and upgraded with new cooperage and equipment. Besides grapes from the estate's own vineyards, Edmeades purchases grapes from other Anderson Valley growers who were attracted there by the pioneering success of the physician who launched Edmeades.
☆/☆☆☆
$/$$

Edna Valley Vineyards.

Edna Valley Vineyards, in San Luis Obispo, California, is a joint venture of Chalone Vineyard of Soledad and Paragon Vineyard, a grape-growing concern that sells to other wineries. Chalone regards Edna Valley as its primary means of expansion, mainly because of the difficulty in expanding the low-yielding vineyards that Chalone maintains high in the Gavilan Range above Soledad. Production at Edna Valley rose quickly to 16,000 cases of Chardonnay and 5000 cases of Pinot Noir after the enterprise was established in 1980. The wines reflect the careful handling that has characterized the Chalone wines, although they lack the same finesse. The Chalone proprietors refer to Edna Valley as a "clone of Chalone."
☆☆
$$

Eiswein.

Rare German wine made from grapes that have been left on the vines so late in the autumn that they have frozen. The customary practice is to harvest the grapes for Eiswein early in the morning while they are still frozen and take them for pressing before they thaw out. In some years Eiswein is produced from grapes harvested as late as January. It usually is made as a curiosity from some of the better vineyards. It has great elegance and richness, although it tends to lack the intensity of a Beerenauslese or Trockenbeerenauslese.

Eltviller.

The wines of Eltville in the German Rheingau are not as famous or elegant as some of the other whites of the region, but the town is well known as a center of the Rheingau wine trade. It is one of the Rheingau's biggest vineyard towns as well, producing a major quantity of sound and reliable wines at prices that compare quite favorably with those of the more renowned vineyards in neighboring communities. The headquarters and administrative office of the Staatsweingut, or German State Domain, are here, along with its central storage and bottling facilities for the Rheingau. The Graf Eltz, whose Schloss

Eltz label is a symbol of quality, also has substantial cellars in Eltville, as does the Freiherr Langwerth von Simmern, another producer of excellent wines, whose seventeenth-century mansion is a local landmark.

Among the better vineyards at Eltville are the following:

Eltviller Albus
Eltviller Altebach
Eltviller Freienborn
Eltviller Grauer Stein
Eltviller Grimmen
Eltviller Hahn
Eltviller Kalbspflicht
Eltviller Mönchhanach
Eltviller Posten
Eltviller Rheinberg*
Eltviller Sandgrub
Eltviller Schlossberg
Eltviller Setzling
Eltviller Sonnenberg*
Eltviller Klümbchen
Eltviller Langenstück*
Eltviller Steinmacher
Eltviller Taubenberg*
Eltviller Weidenborn

An asterisk (*) indicates vineyard names that survived or that were created in the revision of the German wine law of 1971.
☆☆/☆☆☆
$/$$

Emilia-Romagna.

One of the largest wine regions of Italy is Emilia-Romagna, which roughly surrounds the city of Bologna and produces huge quantities of fairly ordinary wines. These include the most popular Italian wine in the United States, the frothy product known as Lambrusco that accounts for most of the Italian wine consumed by Americans, largely because it is cheap and slightly sweet. (*See* Lambrusco.) The dominance of Lambrusco in the export markets has over-shadowed the better wines of Emilia-Romagna, which do not enjoy great recognition abroad.
☆/☆☆☆
$

England.

A number of small wineries with relatively limited production have sprung up in England in recent years, partly because of the steadily rising costs of imported wines in the island nation and partly because of the weak British pound, which has been buying less overseas. But the British climate is capricious, and the result can be devastating in some vintages when the grapes simply do not ripen properly and acid levels remain high. The popular grape varieties are those that thrive in Germany, whose climate also can be difficult, although rarely as poor as the British climate. Most of the British vineyards are planted with Müller-Thurgau, Riesling, and Reichensteiner.

There are believed to be some 300 wineries in England now, but many of these can scarcely be called commercial, and only about 20 produce wine in significant quantities. Many producers of other fruits, such as apples and pears, were lured into wine-growing by the great 1976 vintage, when virtually all of the British growers fortunate enough to have grapes already growing experienced bumper crops and made fine wines. The Three Choirs vineyard near Cheltenham harvested enough grapes in 1976 to make 17,000 bottles of wine, but then made only 4000 bottles from twice as much acreage in vines in 1980. Penshurst and Lamberhurst Vineyards in the verdant Kent countryside south of London had similar experiences, as did many other English vineyards.

Grapes had been cultivated for wine in England five centuries ago, but the vineyards went to seed after French imports became readily available. The coup de grâce for the British planting was delivered in 1152, when Eleanor of Aquitaine married Henry Plantagenet, Count of Anjou and King of England, which brought Bordeaux under English control through Eleanor's dowry. The British vines continued to be cultivated for centuries after this event, but slowly they withered and went fallow as French wines flowed increasingly into the country. The replanting that has occurred in recent years has reversed this trend, although England still does not produce red wines in any way comparable to the better reds of France.

Some 27 English counties now have vineyards, including the Isle of Wight (where "Wight" wine, naturally, is produced at Adgestone). The most prolific growing areas seem to be in Kent, Essex, and Sussex, south and east of London and therefore with ready access to the metropolitan market. Such names as Boyton, Felstar, Fyfield Hall, New Hall, Biddenden, Lamberhurst Priory, Penshurst, Barnsgate, Chilsdown, and Westfield along with many others are now cropping up occasionally in shops and cellars. Usually the wines are white, and sometimes they lack the depth and body of wines from the Continent, but the fact that they are now being produced in commercial quantities is a testimonial to British determination.

Entre-Deux-Mers.

The large triangular area created by the confluence of the Dordogne and Garonne Rivers where they form the Gironde estuary at Bordeaux in southwestern France is called Entre-Deux-Mers, which literally means "between two seas," although it should be more loosely translated as "between two rivers." Some of the greatest wines of the world are produced all around Entre-Deux-Mers, but the ones actually made within this specific area are rather common. Sometimes they are sweetish,

sometimes fairly dry, but rarely very attractive. Within Entre-Deux-Mers are several Bordeaux subdivisions, including Premières Côtes de Bordeaux, Loupiac, Graves de Vagres, Sainte-Croix-du-Mont, and Sainte-Foy-Bordeaux.

In good vintages the wines from these areas can present exceptional values to price-conscious consumers, for some of the producers there have upgraded their vinification methods and are making fresher, cleaner-tasting white wines in substantial quantities. Some of the sweet wines made there also can be good value, at times competing with the luscious dessert wines of Sauternes and Barsac across the Garonne River, but at a fraction of the price.

Erbacher.

Most of the great Rheingau vineyards of Germany are situated on the hillsides overlooking the Rhine River, where they can catch the direct rays of the sun and produce fat, juicy Riesling grapes to make noble wines. A major exception is at Erbach, where the famous Marcobrunn (sometimes Markobrunn) vineyard lies down by the river on flat ground near the railroad tracks. The Marcobrunn actually rests partly in Hattenheim and is named after a fountain (*Brunnen* in German) which marks the boundary between the two villages. Marcobrunners are big wines, among the best of the Rheingau, demonstrating that not all the great wines come from hillside vineyards. One of the biggest landholders is Schloss Reinhartshausen, the domain of Prince Heinrich Friedrich of Prussia. The castle itself has been turned into a hotel. Other big producers include the Graf von Schonborn, the Staatsweingut (State Domain), and the Freiherr Langwerth von Simmern, whose house and cellars are in the middle of Eltville but whose vineyard holdings are in several of the better villages.

The Marcobrunner, which sometimes appears without the village name, tends to overshadow the other wines of Erbach, but most are big and full-bodied, with enough backbone to be among the longest-lived of the Rheingau. Sometimes they lack the elegance of the best Rheingau wines, including the Marcobrunner, but in good vintages they represent excellent value.

Among the better-known vineyards at Erbach are the following:

Erbacher Bachhell
Erbacher Bruhl
Erbacher Germark
Erbacher Herrenberg
Erbacher Hinterkirch
Erbacher Pellet
Erbacher Rheinhell
Erbacher Schlossberg*
Erbacher Seelgass
Erbacher Siegelsberg*
Erbacher Hohenrain*
Erbacher Honigberg*
Erbacher Kahlig
Erbacher Kränzchen
Erbacher Langenwingert
Erbacher Michelmark*
Erbacher Steinchen
Erbacher Steinmorgen*
Erbacher Wormlock
Marcobrunner (sometimes
    Markobrunner and sometimes
    Erbacher Marcobrunn)*

An asterisk (*) indicates vineyard names that survived or that were created in the revision of the German wine law of 1971.
☆/☆☆☆☆
$/$$$

Erdener.

German white wine is produced at Erden, one of the better wine towns of the Mosel River region. The town is one of the northernmost of the Mittelmosel, where the best wines come from, and its vineyards across the river can be reached, from the town whose name they bear, only by boat. Erdeners are not considered quite as elegant as the Bernkastelers and Wheleners produced to the south, although the Erdener Treppchen vineyard produces top-quality wines that rival the best in some vintages.

Among the better known vineyards at Erden are the following:

Erdener Busslay
Erdener Herrenberg*
Erdener Herzlay
Erdener Hodlay
Erdener Prälat*
Erdener Rotkirch
Erdener Treppchen*

The vineyard names marked with an asterisk (*) survived the revision of the German wine law in 1971. One goal of the law was to eliminate most vineyards of fewer than about 12 acres to reduce confusion over German names. As a result, many small vineyards were merged into larger ones.
☆/☆☆☆☆
$/$$

Château Esperanza.

On a steep hillside overlooking the north end of Keuka Lake in New York's Finger Lakes wine-growing district stands the run-down but majestic Château Esperanza. The house was built in 1823 and was being restored in the early 1980s to receive guests in the same grand style that they were received in during the nineteenth century.

The house was turned into a winemaking enterprise in 1979, when it was purchased by a group from Syracuse. Most of the early vintages were made from grapes purchased from other farmers—Seyval Blanc, Cayuga, Chancellor, some Cabernet Sauvignon, some Merlot. Meanwhile, plantings have been under way on parts of the 46-acre property, and crops of Gewürztraminer,

Riesling, and Chardonnay were expected, weather permitting. There were also experiments with Aurora, Maréchal Foch, and some Pinot Noir, as well as Léon Millot, a spicy red hybrid grade not produced by many wineries. Eventually, the focus will be narrowed to fewer varietals as the proprietors discover which grapes are best for their microclimate. The first vintage, 1979, totaled 3700 cases, and the total had risen to more than 10,000 cases in the early 1980s, much of it sold to winery visitors.

☆/☆☆
$/$$

Est! Est! Est!.

One of the more peculiar names in the world of wine is Est! Est! Est!, which must properly appear on labels complete with the exclamation points. It is an Italian white wine produced in and around the village of Montefiascone in Lazio, or Latium, which is the province of Rome. According to legend, the German Bishop Johann Fugger set out in the year 1110 on a trip from Augsburg to Rome to attend the coronation of Emperor Henry V. The good bishop was a man of Lucullan tastes and was determined to dine on the best foods and drink the best wines during his journey, so he sent a scout ahead to sample the fare at the inns along the way. The servant was ordered to write the word "Est," meaning "it is," on the door of each stopping place that served acceptable wines. When he came to Montefiascone, some 60 miles north of Rome, he found white wines that were so delicious that he scrawled the term on the door three times: Est! Est! Est! Bishop Fugger and his trusted servant never made it to the coronation, according to the legend, and spent the remainder of their lives ensconced in the inn at Montefiascone, consuming the local wine. The bishop's remains are entombed there to this day at the church of San Fla-

viano, and a barrel of the young wine is donated each year to the local seminary on behalf of the estate of the bishop, which endowed part of the production. The wine is made from the Trebbiano and Malvasia grapes and is vinified both dry and semisweet.

☆/☆☆
$/$$

Estrella River Winery.

On a hilltop above the Estrella River six miles east of Paso Robles, California, stands the Estrella River Winery, which was established when Clifford R. Giacobine traveled north from California in search of a rural life and began planting vines on a 710-acre tract in 1973. Zinfandel had been the primary viticultural crop in that area of San Luis Obispo County, but Giacobine decided to experiment with other varietals. His son Clifford, Jr., and younger brother Gary Eberle joined him, and now the winery is turning out substantial quantities of estated-bottled Cabernet Sauvignon, Zinfandel, Zinfandel Rosé, Barbera, Syrah, Chardonnay, Fumé Blanc, Chenin Blanc, Muscat Canelli, as well as Johannisberg Riesling purchased partly from a Santa Barbara County Vineyard.

The soil varies from a light sandy clay loam to gravelly clay loam. Deep wells tap into a large underground water table and supply five reservoirs built into natural depressions on the estate. A modern winemaking facility was constructed in time for the 1977 harvest, and a major expansion took place in 1979 and '80 with the addition of a large refrigerated warehouse. An aging room contains 1600 American and French oak barrels, and the winery's total storage capacity is substantial—about 550,000 gallons. *Estrella* (pronounced Es-tray-ya) is Spanish for "star."

☆/☆☆
$/$$

Etna.

Wines bearing the Etna label come from the volcanic mountain of the same name on the Island of Sicily off the southwestern coast of Italy. A Bianco, Bianco Superiore, Rosato, and Rosso are made, and the Etna Rosso sometimes shows considerable character, although it is often flaccid and dull. The Etna wines are produced in large quantities and can be good value.
☆/☆☆
$

Château L'Evangile.

If the Pomerol District east of Bordeaux were to be classified on the basis of quality, Château L'Evangile would be ranked near the top. The estate consistently makes full-bodied red wines of great character. They bring prices comparable to the second or third growths of the Médoc.
☆☆☆☆
$$/$$$

Evensen Vineyards.

Richard and Sharon Evensen established a winery in the basement of their home in California's Napa Valley in 1979 and have focused their efforts so far exclusively on Gewürztraminer, an unusual choice. They have planted 5.5 acres with this spicy white varietal and planned to plant 12 more acres shortly. So far their Gewürztraminers have been vinified bone dry. Production is less than 1000 cases a year, but the wines have received national distribution.
☆/☆☆
$/$$

Eyrie Vineyards.

The wines of the State of Oregon, specifically those made from the Pinot Noir grape, were spotlighted on the world vineyard map in 1979 and 1980 when the Pinot Noir 1975 of tiny Eyrie Vine-

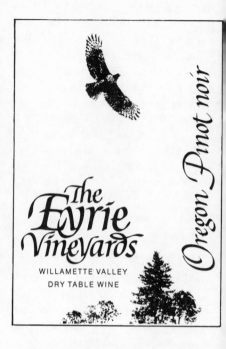

yards took high honors in blind tastings in Paris and Beaune against some of the best red Burgundies. Eyrie, with production of only about 5000 cases, has vineyards in Dundee, in northwestern Oregon, and a winery in a converted turkey-processing plant a few miles down the road at McMinnville. The proprietors are David and Diana Lett, and they produce excellent Chardonnay as well as Pinot Noir. David Lett is a graduate of the University of California at Davis. The Chardonnays are buttery and rich, but slightly more austere than those produced in California. The Eyrie Pinot Noirs do not all live up to the exquisite 1975, but they tend to be elegant, balanced wines similar to the lighter, less robust red Burgundies of the French Côte de Beaune. They display a peppery, spicy bouquet and require four to six years to approach maturity.
☆/☆☆☆
$$/$$$

· F ·

Far Niente Winery.

When Far Niente introduced a Chardonnay in the 1979 vintage, it represented the revival of a very old California winery. Far Niente was founded by John Benson, a San Francisco entrepreneur, in 1885 and operated until Prohibition. Then it was abandoned for more than six decades before a renovation was undertaken, starting in 1980. The old stone

building, just south of Oakville in the Napa Valley, has been placed on the National Register of Historic Places. Prior to completion of the renovation, the wines were made in temporary quarters in Sausalito. The grapes for the revival vintage were purchased from four Napa Valley vineyards—ABC Farms, Emil Hoffman Vineyard, Reese Ranch, and Rennick Harris Vineyard. Gilliland "Gil" Nickel is the new proprietor. The Far Niente Chardonnay is a big, rich, oaky wine filled with creamy complexity. Its stay of some six months in new French Limousin and Alliers oak barrels is evident in the bouquet and flavor. The wine is expensive and production is limited. Far Niente is translated "without a care."
☆☆
$$$

Fara.

One of the lesser known but very good Piedmont reds is Fara, from the region's Novara Hills. It is usually a blend of Nebbiolo, Vespolina, and Bonarda grapes. The wine has the same robust, full-bodied personality as Barolo and Gattinara, although its flavor intensity and texture are likely to be more modest. Fara needs at least six years of age to reach maturity and several more years are advisable. Fara should not be confused with Faro, another Italian wine made in Sicily.

☆☆☆

$/$$

Faro.

Some very good red wines are produced in Sicily, and one of these is Faro, although it is rarely seen outside Italy. It is blended from Nerello, Nocera, and several other grape varieties. It should not be confused with Fara, a Piedmontese red.

☆☆

$

Feine, Feinste.

Terms applied to German wines, literally meaning "fine" or "finest," but no longer having legal standing following the revision of the German wine laws in 1971. Prior to that year, if a grower took special pride in a particular vintage or portion of a vintage, he was free to add such terms to his labels. Thus, such names as Niersteiner Hipping Riesling Feinste Auslese existed, meaning "finest wine of the Auslese degree of sweetness made from Riesling grapes in the Hipping vineyard at Nierstein." The use of the terms—including hochfein, meaning "extra-fine"— was highly subjective and might change from vineyard to vineyard according to the whim of the owner. Generally it was a sign of higher quality, but not always, and the government finally decided the terms were so subjective that they defied the type of specific interpretation which was one of the principal goals of the new German laws.

Felton-Empire Vineyards.

Felton-Empire produces mostly white wines, often in a German style, and has begun to build a reputation for excellent white Riesling vinified both dry and sweet. Even the winery's presses come from Germany, and the Riesling, like some German Rieslings, usually is blended with small portions of Sylvaner and Scheurebe. Leo McCloskey established Felton-Empire in 1976, naming it after the road in Felton, in Santa Cruz County, California, where the winery is located. He and some partners purchased the former Hallcrest Winery, built in 1941. McCloskey, who is the president and winemaker, made a white Riesling in 1976 that was fully botrytised and honeylike in flavor, immediately attracting attention among devotees of this style of sweet wine.

After graduating with a degree in biological sciences from Oregon State, McCloskey went to work for Ridge Vineyards in 1971 and continued to maintain close ties with Ridge even after starting his own winery. Felton-Empire has about 60 acres of vineyards owned or under long-term lease and buys the majority of its grapes from outside growers. Production has risen to roughly 28,000 cases a year of Chenin Blanc, Gewürztraminer, and Chardonnay. The wines are aged mostly in 550-gallon American white oak ovals, similar to many German aging casks, although 55-gallon American oak barrels are used for the finest Rieslings.

McCloskey is a one-third owner of Felton-Empire and has two active partners who each own almost as much— John Pollard and Jim Beauregard. In addition, a Swiss group holds a 15 percent interest in the business.

☆/☆☆

$$

Fetzer Vineyards.

The late Bernard Fetzer established Fetzer Vineyards in Mendocino County, California's most northern coastal wine-producing region, in 1968 and main-

1980 Lake County
Zinfandel

fetzer

1980
Lake county
zinfandel

produced and bottled by fetzer vineyards
redwood valley, california, u.s.a. alcohol 12.9% by volume

Some of Lake County's finest vineyards are located just below Mount Konocti, near the town of Kelseyville. The Zinfandel grapes from these vineyards gain greater varietal character and distinction each year as Lake County grape growers continue to develop the viticultural practices which promote the production of high quality winemaking grapes.

In 1980, the Zinfandel grapes were harvested at 23.5° Brix. The wine was aged for 11 months in small American oak barrels. fined with fresh egg whites and bottled in January 1982. It is an excellent example of how Zinfandel from Lake County, when properly grown, can make a red wine of spicy fruit, without excessive tannin.

fetzer vineyards

tained two wineries there on a 750-acre estate—one for red wines (built in 1968) and one for whites (built in 1978). The property was originally settled by Anson Seward, who planted Mission and Zinfandel grapes there in 1855 and built the house that is now the Fetzer residence, which is depicted on Fetzer's secondary label, Bel Arbres Vineyards. Fetzer bought the property in 1956 and ran his wine business as a family affair, with most of his eleven children involved. The production has become substantial.

Red wines produced by Fetzer have proven far superior to the whites, and the Fetzer Zinfandels have developed a considerable following among devotees of this spicy varietal. Fetzer produces Zinfandels from several different vineyards, which usually are identified on the labels. For example, there are the Lolonais Zinfandel, the Ricetti Zinfandel and the Scharffenberger Zinfandel, all produced in Mendocino County. There are also a Lake County Zinfandel as well as a number of other varietals under the Fetzer name, including Cabernet Sauvignon, Petite Sirah, Gamay Beaujolais, and Pinot Noir among the reds, plus Chardonnay, Pinot Blanc, and Sauvignon Blanc among the whites. Some of the wines are estate-bottled, some are not, but the difference usually is prominently noted on the label and evident in the price. The wines bottled under the Bel Arbres label are lower-

priced and not quite as intensely flavored as those under the Fetzer label. Following Barnie Fetzer's death in 1981, management of the winery shifted to other family members.
☆/☆☆
$/$$

Fiano di Avellino.

The Fiano grape makes good red wines in the Campania region of southwestern Italy, and the Fiano di Avellino is one of the better examples. It comes from vineyards near the village of Avellino, east of Naples, and is often found in the city's restaurants. It tends to be smooth and sometimes approaches elegance.
☆/☆☆
$/$$

Ficklin Vineyards.

Ficklin Vineyards is one of the pioneers in the production of California Port, which is produced from authentic Portuguese grapes grown on the 50-acre Ficklin vineyards near Madera in Madera County. The grapes, produced from vines obtained through the University of California at Davis, are the Tinta Madeira, Tinta Cao, Touriga, and Souzao. These were planted in the 1940s after David Ficklin and his father established Ficklin Vineyards in 1946. The winery was completed in 1948 and the first Ficklin Ports were produced that year, although they were not released until 1952. Because Port is a fortified wine, the alcohol level in the Ficklin bottlings runs $18^{1}/_{2}$ to 19 percent, while the residual sugar is 10 to 12 percent. The wines are aged in American white oak barrels for about four years, using the Ficklin version of the solera system, whereby the wines are moved from barrel to barrel and blended. Thus, Ficklin does not produce a vintage Port. Alcohol is added to the fermenting grape juice after about half the sugar has fermented out. This leaves the wine sweet and achieves the relatively high alcohol level that is typical of Port-style wines. Production is a maximum of 3000 cases a year. Before establishing their own winery, the Ficklins had been in the fruit and grape business in Madera County for many years. Ficklin Vineyards is still a family enterprise, with at least seven members of the family involved.

☆☆☆☆

$$

Field Stone Winery.

Wally Johnson and his wife Marion, who had been in the grape business since the 1960s, built the Field Stone production facilities in 1977, when the first crush occurred under the Field Stone label. The winery is near Healdsburg in California's Sonoma Valley, and the Johnsons bought some very old vineyards and raised their acreage in vines to 150 in all. Before opening their own winery, they had sold grapes to Simi, Montelena, and Grgich Hills, among others. Wally Johnson died in 1979, and Marion Johnson had continued to operate the winery since then. The winemaker is Debby Cutter, a graduate in oenology of the University of California at Davis, who worked at Dry Creek Vineyards before joining Field Stone. Production has been pushing toward 20,000 cases a year of Johannisberg Riesling, Gewürztraminer, Chenin Blanc, Cabernet Sauvignon, and Petite Sirah, all grown on the Field Stone estate, plus a rosé of Petite Sirah and a rosé of Cabernet called Spring Cabernet.

☆/☆☆☆

$$

Château de Fieuzal.

This château was among those accorded grand cru recognition in the Graves classification of 1959. The Fieuzal estate lies in the commune of Léognan about nine miles south of the Bordeaux city limits. Both red and white wines are made here, but only the reds were classified. The production is rather small, and the wines of Château de Fieuzal are not frequently seen in the United States or Great Britain.

☆/☆☆☆

$$

Château Figeac.

Among the premiers grands crus classes, or first great growths, of Saint-Emilion, Château Figeac has achieved a reputation in recent years nearly equal to that of Château Cheval Blanc and Château Ausone, traditionally regarded as the two greatest estates of the district. In fact, some lovers of these excellent Bordeaux wines suggest that Figeac has eclipsed Ausone on a quality basis, although Ausone is one of the côtes, or hillside vineyards, generally given higher marks simply because of location, and Figeac is on the graves, or gravelly flatlands. Nevertheless, Figeac is adjacent to Cheval Blanc and the two lie on a gravelly ridge that also includes some of the best vineyards of nearby Pomerol. Figeac's production is among the largest of the great Saint-Emilion estates, and the new chais, or storage facilities, constructed by Thierry Manoncourt, the proprietor, are perhaps the most modern and efficient of any in the area. Manoncourt is a leading figure in Saint-Emilion, deeply involved in the affairs of the district and highly knowledgeable about the land and the good wines it yields. Figeac is a big and rich wine that needs more time to mature than some other Saint-Emilions. The 1947, tasted at the château in 1973, was an intense wine with an abundance of fruit remaining. The 1966 was ready for drinking in 1980.

☆☆☆☆

$$$

Joseph Filippi, Château Filippi.

Large quantities of inexpensive table and dessert wines are produced in Fontana, California, by the J. Filippi Vintage Company. Production runs in excess of 350,000 gallons a year, and the wines are sold almost entirely at the company's eight retail sales and tasting rooms in southern California. The Filippi family had been in the grape and wine business for many generations in northern Italy before Giovanni Filippi emigrated to the United States in 1922 and planted his first vines in California's Cucamonga Valley in 1923. The first portion of the present winery was built in 1934, and the vineyard holdings have been expanded to 300 acres. The brands include Pride of Cucamonga, Château Filippi, and Joseph Filippi. The company remains family-owned and -operated.
☆/☆☆
$/$$

Filsinger Vineyards.

The Filsinger family owned a winery in Germany that was seized by the Nazis prior to World War II, so they emigrated to the United States and dreamed of starting another winery in this country. Dr. William Filsinger, a physician, did so in 1980 in Temecula, an area of growing interest in southern California near San Diego. Production remains small, and the wines are distributed mostly in California. The product line includes Fumé Blanc, Chardonnay, a late-harvested Riesling, Petite Sirah, Zinfandel, and Cabernet Sauvignon.
☆/☆☆☆
$/$$

Firestone Vineyard.

The Firestone name has been well known to generations of Americans for its leading role in the tire industry, but members of the same family have gone into

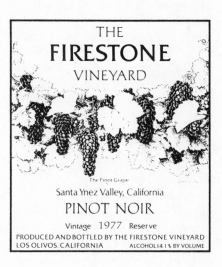

THE **FIRESTONE** VINEYARD

The Pinot Grape
Santa Ynez Valley, California
PINOT NOIR
Vintage 1977 Reserve
PRODUCED AND BOTTLED BY THE FIRESTONE VINEYARD
LOS OLIVOS, CALIFORNIA   ALCOHOL 14.1% BY VOLUME

the California wine business with a major commitment to quality that has begun to win recognition for the Firestone name in a new field. Leonard Firestone, then United States Ambassador to Belgium and a former top executive with the Firestone Tire & Rubber Company, found property in the Santa Ynez Valley not far from Santa Barbara in 1972 and joined with his son, Brooks Firestone, in the new venture. They bought 300 acres near Los Olivos and began planting vines in 1973 after consulting with André Tchelistcheff, an oenologist who has been involved in the establishment of many leading California wineries. Besides the two Firestones, there is a third partner in Firestone Vineyard—Suntory of Japan, which is a major factor in the Japanese wine and spirits trade. As a result of this relationship, a portion of the Firestone wine production each year is exported to Japan. Both Brooks and his wife Kate, a former ballerina, are active in the winery and also operate a nearby cattle ranch. The first Firestone wines were rosés, released in 1975, and now the product array includes well-made Pinot Noirs, Cabernet Sauvignons, Merlots, Chardonnays, Johannisberg Rieslings, Sauvignon Blancs, and Gewürztraminers. Production, at 65,000 cases a year, is rapidly rising past the point where Firestone can be called a boutique winery. All of the grapes come from the 300-acre estate, which means all Firestone wines are estate-bottled.

☆/☆☆☆

$$

Fisher Vineyards.

Fred and Juelle Fisher bought 84 acres on the Sonoma side of the Mayacamas Mountain Range in 1973, built a winery of rough-sawn redwood and Douglas fir in 1979, and began making excellent Chardonnays and Cabernet Sauvignons that immediately attracted the attention of connoisseurs of well-structured California wines. Fred Fisher, of the Fisher Body family of Michigan, also owns a 56-acre vineyard on the Silverado Trail in the Napa Valley, so the Fisher wines carry the Napa–Sonoma appellation. The wines are high in quality.

☆/☆☆☆☆

$$

Fixin.

The northernmost wine-growing *commune* of the Burgundian Côte d'Or in France is Fixin, where very robust wines of great intensity and longevity are produced. Because these wines are not as well known as most of the others of the Côte d'Or, they can be good value for Burgundy-lovers willing to lay down bottles and wait patiently for them to mature over a period of five years or more. Wines simply labeled Fixin are likely to be inexpensive and authentic as well, since the *appellation* is too little known to warrant imitating. The *commune* has six *premiers crus*, and the most consistently good of these are Clos de la Perrière and Clos du Chapitre. As with other wines of Burgundy, they will be identified on labels by the *commune* name first and then by vineyard name,

e.g., Fixin-Clos du Chapitre. They resemble the full-bodied reds of Gevrey-Chambertin, the next *commune* to the south, but lack the same depth and finesse. A small inn with a good restaurant, Chez Jeanette, is located there. (*See* Côte de Nuits.)

☆☆☆☆

$$

Flagey-Echézeaux.

Perhaps because the name is so difficult for the non-Gallic tongue to pronounce, very few wines produced in the *commune* of Flagey-Echézeaux are marketed as Flagey-Echézeaux. Rather, they are sold under the labels of the nearby Vosne-Romanée, where the greatest wines in the French Burgundy country are produced. Flagey-Echézeaux lies between Vougeot and Vosne-Romanée in the heart of the Burgundian Côte de Nuits. Its two most famous vineyards, both *grands crus* under French wine law, are Grands Echézeaux and Echézeaux. Important portions of these estates are owned by the Domaine de la Romanée-Conti. They are full-bodied, balanced, and elegant red Burgundies that can be very expensive. (*See also* Vosne-Romanée, Romanée-Conti, Côte de Nuits.)

☆☆☆/☆☆☆☆

$$/$$$$

Château La Fleur.

In the center of the Pomerol District east of Bordeaux and not far from the great Château Pétrus lies Château La Fleur, where some very good Pomerol wines are produced in quite modest quantities. Because this important vineyard area of Bordeaux has never been formally classified as to quality, tradition and reputation are the only guides to the relative merits of the various estates. La Fleur certainly would rank with the classified growths of the Médoc if all were classified together.

☆☆☆☆

$$/$$$

Château La Fleur-Pétrus.

Just across the vineyard road from the celebrated Château Pétrus in the Pomerol District 20 miles east of Bordeaux lies Château La Fleur-Pétrus, where some very pleasant, supple wines are made. The estate is owned by Jean Pierre Moueix, the Labourne shipper who has extensive vineyard holdings in Pomerol and Saint-Emilion. The production at La Fleur-Pétrus is not large and the wine lacks the reputation of some other Pomerol estates, but it is fairly consistent and of good value from this important part of France. If Pomerol were classified, La Fleur-Pétrus would rank among the upper third, equivalent to a classified growth of the Médoc.

☆☆☆☆

$$/$$$

Flora Springs Wines.

Stylish Chardonnays and a crisp, clean Sauvignon Blanc are produced by Flora Springs at its winery at the end of Zinfandel Lane near St. Helena in California's Napa Valley. The winery building, restored and reopened in early 1983, once housed the Sherry cellars of the late Louis M. Martini. Production was expected to rise rapidly past 10,000 cases annually as vineyard plantings matured. A Cabernet Sauvignon scheduled for release in 1983 was just as well made as the Flora Springs whites.

☆/☆☆☆

$$

Foppiano Vineyards.

Foppiano Vineyards is a family organization led by Louis J. Foppiano, whose son Louis M. Foppiano is in charge of production and sales while another son, Rod, is the winemaker. The two sons represent the fourth generation in the business. The winery was bought by John Foppiano, Louis Foppiano, Sr.'s, grandfather, in 1896. It was closed during Prohibition, then reopened after repeal and has been turning out wines under the Foppiano label from the winery in Healdsburg in California's Sonoma Valley ever since. Production totals more than 100,000 cases a year, of which 70 percent are in the jug category. The line of Foppiano premium varietals occasionally turns out some surprises— e.g., the rich and supple Cabernet Sauvignon 1974. Besides Cabernet this line includes Pinot Noir, Zinfandel, Petite Sirah, Chardonnay, Chenin Blanc, and Sonoma Fumé (Sauvignon Blanc). Foppiano owns some 200 acres of vineyards, which are responsible for 75 to 80 percent of the varietal line. Nearly all of the grapes for the jug wines are purchased from other growers.

☆/☆☆☆

$/$$

Forster.

German white wine produced in Forst, one of the most important towns in the center of the Rheinpfalz, or Palatinate, the country's southernmost region for producing superior wines. Forsters are always ranked among the finest German wines—indeed, among the best white wines of the world. They and the nearby Deidesheimers usually are regarded as equally outstanding, although some connoisseurs will argue that the Forster Jesuitengarten is superior to the Deidesheimer Hohenmorgen or any of the other top vineyards, or *Lagen,* in Deidesheim. It is a moot question, because both are extraordinarily full and rich when made with the predominant Riesling grape. In years when the weather has been favorable, with plenty of sunshine until late in the autumn, Forst produces as much Trockenbeerenauslese as any other town in Germany and perhaps more. The Forsters also are noted for their elegant bouquet, which is believed to come from the dark and rocky soil of the area. The town itself is much smaller than Deidesheim or Bad Dürkheim, the two principal centers for the wine trade of the Pfalz, but vines grow everywhere, even in the yards of the houses.

Forst has dozens of vineyards whose names have appeared on labels in the export market, but the best-known are the following:

Forster Alser
Forster Altenburg
Forster Bolander
Forster Elster*
Forster Fleckinger
Forster Freundstück*
Forster Gerling
Forster Hellholz
Forster Jesuitengarten*
Forster Kirchenstück*
Forster Kranich
Forster Langenacker
Forster Langenmorgen
Forster Langkammert
Forster Mühlweg
Forster Musenhang*
Forster Pechstein*
Forster Pfeiffer
Forster Sechsmorgen
Forster Trift
Forster Ungeheuer*
Forster Walshohle
Forster Ziegler

Vineyard names marked with an asterisk (*) are among those that retained their identities, if not their former configurations, in the revision of the German wine law in 1971. The others were consolidated and merged to simplify identification, although examples from pre-1971 vintages can still be found. The name Mariengarten now refers to a large vineyard area around Forst and

is roughly equivalent to a generic term for good local wines.

☆/☆☆☆☆

$$/$$$

Fortified wines.

Through the natural process of fermentation, the sugar that is a component of freshly squeezed grape juice undergoes a chemical reaction that converts it to alcohol and carbon dioxide gas. The agents of fermentation are yeasts, and these microorganisms are killed by the very alcohol they create, thus halting the fermentation process. This generally occurs when the alcohol level in the wine rises to around 12 to 14 percent. Unfortified wines thus are rarely more than 14 percent alcohol, although the percentage can rise several points higher when the weather conditions during the growing season are ideal and the sugar content of the grapes is extraordinarily high.

In some parts of the world, it was discovered that wine traveled better and lasted longer when brandy was added to it. The addition of the brandy raised the alcohol level of the wine beyond what the yeasts could produce, thus fortifying it. A fortified wine is one with additional alcohol—usually enough to bring the level to 20 percent. Any wine can be fortified, but the ones that benefit most from it—the ones for which fortification has become a vital part of the production process—are Port, Sherry, Madeira, and Marsala. All are roughly 20 percent alcohol and are best consumed before or after a meal—not during. They are usually fairly sweet, because the alcohol is intentionally added before all of the natural sugar has been fermented out. The addition of the alcohol kills the yeasts, leaving residual sugar that gives the wine part of its character. The point at which the alcohol is added determines how sweet the wine will be. For example, the fermentation process is allowed to continue longer with a dry Sherry than with a sweet Sherry.

A number of fortified wines are produced in the south of France as well as in the United States. Those made in this country usually bear the name of their European counterparts, but are rarely of the same quality, and the practice of giving them European names is questionable. True Port comes only from the region in northern Portugal just east of the ancient city of Oporto. True Sherry comes only from the region of Spain surrounding the city of Jerez, from which the name Sherry comes. True Madeira comes only from the island of that name lying off the coast of Africa in the Atlantic Ocean. And true Marsala is made only in Sicily, off the "toe" of Italy. (*See* Port, Sherry, Madeira, Marsala.)

Fortino Winery.

Ernest Fortino learned the art of winemaking in the family-owned winery in Calabria, in southern Italy, before emigrating to the United States in 1959 and settling in the Santa Clara Valley of California. He worked for several prominent northern California wineries before buying his own in 1970. Production totals about 15,000 cases a year of numerous varietals, generics, and branded wines. The best is the Fortino Zinfandel, made in a style reminiscent of some rich southern Italian reds.
☆/☆☆☆
$/$$

Château Fourcas-Hosten.

Château Fourcas-Hosten is a *cru bourgeois supérieur* under the Bordeaux classification of 1855, and it has been owned by a largely American syndicate since 1971. The group is headed by Arnaud de Trabuc and includes Phillip Powers, Peter M. F. Sichel, Bertrand de Rivoyré, and others. The property is located in the commune of Listrac on the so-called Hill of Fourcas, which it shares with Château Fourcas-Dupré. Fourcas-Hosten's vineyard consists of more than 100 acres planted with 35 to 40 percent Cabernet Sauvignon, about 35 percent Merlot, and the balance in Cabernet Franc. Production totals an average of 12,000 to 14,000 cases a year, of which 5000 are exported to the U.S. The wines generally have lacked the depth and concentration of the better Médocs, but the owners are committed to continuous upgrading, and improvements can be expected.
☆☆☆☆
$$

France.

The greatest wines in the world are produced in France. Producers and connoisseurs with other allegiances—perhaps to the wines of Italy, Germany, or California—must concede that French wines provide the benchmarks for the best wines from elsewhere, and on the basis of general quality no other wines have come close to the French. The soil, the climate, perhaps the natural character and disposition of the French people all play important roles. Italy, whose vinicultural heritage is older than that of France, now produces and consumes more wine, but most of it falls below French quality standards.*

Any general book that attempts to discuss the wines of many countries must devote more attention to France than to any other country. Thus, much of this book is about French wines, and

---

* Italy produces a number of magnificent wines that deserve to be taken far more seriously than they customarily are. Some of these have not yet developed export markets, while others are made in such small quantities that they are consumed entirely by the few connoisseurs who know them. Yet most objective evaluations of Italian vs. French wines demonstrate that the *average* quality level in France is somewhat higher.

the heritage, history and subjective data about them comes under the individual entries for the wines themselves and their regions, rather than under a general entry for France. The wines of France are also discussed generally under regional headings:

Alsace
Bordeaux
Burgundy
Champagne
Languedoc
Loire Valley
Provence
Rhône Valley

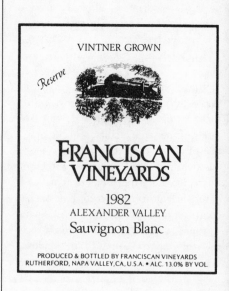

VINTNER GROWN

Reserve

FRANCISCAN VINEYARDS

1982
ALEXANDER VALLEY
Sauvignon Blanc

PRODUCED & BOTTLED BY FRANCISCAN VINEYARDS
RUTHERFORD, NAPA VALLEY, CA, U.S.A. • ALC. 13.0% BY VOL.

There are also many good wine-growing sections of France outside the main regions. These also have their own entries, e.g., Arbois, Cahors, Gaillac, Jurançon. Major regions such as Bordeaux and Burgundy have numerous subdivisions with their own separate entries, and some individual vineyards are so famous that they too merit separate treatment. Virtually any French wine that a reader is likely to encounter is listed either under one of the regions, regional subdivisions, or else under its own heading.

Franciacorta.

Franciacorta Pinot and Franciacorta Rosso are produced from vineyards near the town of Cortefranca in the Lombardy region of northern Italy. The Rosso, consisting of 40 to 50 percent Cabernet Franc, with quantities of Barbera, Nebbiolo, and Merlot blended in, can be a complex, interesting wine that is best aged at least eight years before drinking.
☆/☆☆☆
$

Franciscan Vineyards.

Franciscan Vineyards in Rutherford, California, is a Napa Valley winery that was founded in 1972, encountered financial distress in the early 1970s and was purchased out of bankruptcy in 1975 by Raymond Duncan of Denver and Justin Meyer, a former assistant cellarmaster at Christian Brothers. They acquired substantial vineyard acreage in Napa, Sonoma, and Lake Counties and sold grapes to other wineries besides making their own wines at Franciscan. Then, apparently dissatisfied with profitability themselves, Meyer and Duncan sold out in 1979 to the Peter Eckes Company of West Germany, a producer and distributor of spirits, liqueurs, and juices. Meyer remained as president and winemaker for a brief period, but then resigned to devote full time to another joint venture with Raymond Duncan, Silver Oak Cellars, just south of Rutherford. Tom Ferrell, formerly of Inglenook, succeeded Meyer as winemaker in 1982.

Franciscan Vineyards produces good Cabernet Sauvignon and Johannisberg Riesling and very good Chardonnay. With the 1979 vintage the winery began offering estate bottlings for the first time, made from grapes planted near Oakville by Meyer in the early 1970s. The new

line included a Johannisberg Riesling, a Pinot Noir Blanc, and a Zinfandel (from the 1978 vintage). To come later were estate-bottled Cabernet Sauvignon, Merlot, and Chardonnay. In 1981 came a Napa Valley Brut sparkling wine made from Chardonnay and Pinot Noir grapes by the traditional *méthode champenoise.*
☆/☆☆☆
$$

Franconia, Franken.

Along the Main River Valley eastward from Mainz toward Würzburg and beyond is a major wine-growing region that lacks the international reputation of the Mosel, the Rheingau, and some of the other important German areas. Franconia, or Franken, nevertheless produces a vast quantity of wines and many of them more closely resemble French white wines than the other wines of Germany, mainly because they are less sweet and have an earthy quality that permits them to be consumed all through a meal, instead of only with hors d'oeuvres or dessert. Many tasters liken them to the wines of Chablis because they have a flinty quality, but the comparison is probably optimistic. The Franken wines are not often great, but they are different and interesting.

They come in a jug-shaped bottle which is similar to the bottles for some Portuguese rosés and which is unique in Germany. It is called the *Bocksbeutel,* which has been in use in Franconia since 1728. The reason for the name is uncertain, but, according to one theory, it derives from the bottle's similarity to the scrotum of a billy goat—*der Beutel des Bocks* in German. Not many Franken wines flow into export markets, partly because most connoisseurs prefer French or California dry white wines and partly because their prices are fairly high. Most of the production is sold in Germany, where these wines are admired, and as long as Germans are willing to pay good prices for them there is little reason for the producers to attack the export trade.

Franconia is one of the most beautiful parts of Germany, with its rolling hillsides, numerous rivers, verdant forests, and many castles dating back hundreds of years, some to the Roman occupation. The area has traditionally been underdeveloped and poor, with relatively high unemployment. It was one of the first parts of Germany to go Nazi, reflecting the willingness of the people to grasp at a different philosophy which they hoped would lead them out of their poverty. In Würzburg, the principal city, many old buildings stand, including the enormous Prince-Bishop's castle towering over the Main River. Much of the wine trade is concentrated here and perhaps the best-known wine of the region is Würzburger Stein from the Stein vineyard, one of the largest in Germany. The town is also renowned for its beer, Würzburger Eldelbräu, which is probably better known than any of its wines.

The principal grape of Franconia is the Sylvaner, also known locally as the Franken, and a large quantity of Müller-Thurgau is grown here as well. The microclimate of the Main Valley is not as even as in other parts of Germany and early autumn frosts tend to cut short the growing season. The Sylvaner has a shorter maturing season than the Riesling, so it is better suited to the area, producing excellent wines in the best years. Another grape, a Riesling-Sylvaner crossbreed known as the Mainriesling, is also produced here, but it should not be confused with the true Rieslings grown elsewhere in Germany. In the effort to produce grapes that will withstand the climatic conditions most readily, some growers have experimented extensively and some unusual wines can be found. The owner of the vineyards surrounding the feudal hamlet of Castell, for example, has planted

20 different varieties and some are worth sampling if you are willing to travel there to taste them.

Franconia has four separate subdivisions for the purpose of wine production, reflecting the four major types of soil that exist: clay mixed with chalk, limestone, reddish sandstone, and primary rock stratum. Some red wines are produced in Franconia and are much loved by the local residents. But they tend to be quite mediocre when compared with the reds from the world's other wine-growing regions and taste something like the lesser wines from the Finger Lakes District of New York State. Vintage charts applicable to the rest of Germany do not always accurately reflect the vintages in Franconia because of the different climate there, but in warm, sunny years some big wines are produced. Examples of Auslese, Beerenauslese, and Trockenbeerenauslese are rare in this part of Germany but, when encountered, can be magnificent. An Iphofer Julius-Echter-Berg Sylvaner Beerenauslese 1971 from the magnificent Juliusspital Weinguter of Würzburg, tasted in London early in 1975, displayed great depth and character, with a richness and balance that turned its basic earthiness into a splendid asset. This was one of the greatest Sylvaners ever tasted by the author and demonstrated the heights to which some Franken wines can aspire.

Examples of Franken wines are uncommon outside Germany, but they deserve to be experimented with because of their basic contrast with other German wines. About half of them are sold through cooperatives involving groups of growers, another 25 percent are produced by public institutions such as churches, local municipalities, and the state, and the balance—often the best—come from individual private estates or growers. Any Franken wines that you are likely to encounter outside Germany will probably bear one of these names: Casteller, Escherndorfer, Frickenhauser, Homburger, Hoersteiner, Iphofer, Kitzinger, Klingenberger, Nordheimer, Randersacker, Röedelseer, Schloss Saalacker, Sommeracher, Sulzfelder, Thüngersheimer, Veitshöchheimer, Volkacher, or Würzburger. The names come from the towns where the wines are produced and the wines will display the characteristics of their geographical areas. Some are bottled with individual vineyard names from within each town, for example the Würzburger Stein from the outstanding Stein vineyard of Würzburg or the Casteller Trautberg from the much smaller but equally noble Trautberg vineyard of Castell.

☆/☆☆☆

$$/$$$

Franzia Brothers.

Franzia Brothers, one of California's larger winemaking enterprises, is the principal holding of a company called the Wine Group Inc., which was purchased by members of Franzia management from the Coca-Cola Bottling Company of New York (not related to the Coca-Cola Company of Atlanta) in 1981. The New York bottling concern had purchased Franzia in 1973. Earlier, a group of Wall Street investors had purchased Franzia from the Franzia family and sold it to public investors in a stock offering. Franzia had been established in Ripon, in San Joaquin County, California, in 1906. Franzia owns and cultivates between 3500 and 4000 acres of vineyards, yet still buys 75 to 80 percent of its grape and/or wine requirements from other growers and producers. The concern has a production capacity of eight million cases a year and has 30 million gallons of cooperage. Eighty to 85 percent of the Franzia production consists of generic wines in the jug category, with the rest in such varietals as Cabernet Sauvignon, Zinfandel, Chenin

Blanc, French Colombard, and Grenache Rosé. The Wine Group also owns the Tribuno vermouth operation and the Mogen David wine business, which produces mostly kosher wines.

☆/☆☆

$

Frascati.

In Roman cafes and even the more serious restaurants, the local white carafe wine is Frascati, produced in the vineyards of Lazio (Latium) not far from the city. Any visitor who spends a few days dining in Roman restaurants will soon discover that Frascati comes in a variety of colors, from very pale straw to brownish yellow, and that its taste can be equally variable, from very dry to semisweet, yet almost always quite fresh and pleasant. This is a good example of a wine that does not always travel well. Frascati is available in the export markets, but the exported product always seems to have lost that freshness and zest that is displayed in the carafes of Rome. It is one of the wines that is included in the category Castelli Romani, which covers an area of about 50 square miles southeast of Rome. It is made largely from the Malvasia and Trebbiano grapes. Sweeter versions are known as Cannellino and are produced with the assistance of the *muffa nobile*, the same noble rot so valued in French Sauternes and the better wines of the German Mosel and Rhine Valleys. A *superiore* version will have an alcohol level of 12 percent, compared to the 11.5 percent that is more common.

☆

$

Fred's Friends.

Fred's Friends is the prosaic name for still wines produced from the same grapes that produce the excellent sparkling wines of Domaine Chandon in Napa, California. Using Chardonnay and Pinot Noir from second and third pressings of the sparkling wine grapes, nonsparkling table wines are the result. Production is around 10,000 cases a year. (*See* Domaine Chandon.)

☆

$$

Freemark Abbey.

One of the fine small wineries of California's Napa Valley near St. Helena, Freemark Abbey makes about 25,000 cases of premium varietals, including Cabernet Sauvignon, Pinot Noir, Pinot Chardonnay, Johannisberg Riesling, and Petite Sirah. The winery is a native graystone building erected in 1895, today surrounded by a complex of newer buildings in similar architectural style that includes a candlemaking shop and a restaurant called The Abbey.

Revived and restored in 1965 by a new partnership, Freemark Abbey burst on the wine scene in 1970 with its 1969 Chardonnay, a rich wine of depth and complexity and strong evidence of oak aging. All of the wines at Freemark are aged in French oak barrels except for the Johannisberg Riesling, a soft, flowery wine of fine varietal character. Most of the vines are grown and tended by three of the owners, Charles (Chuck) Carpy, Frank Wood, and William P. Jaeger. Other owners are John Bryan and distinguished wine consultant R. Bradford Webb.

The owners are especially proud of a new wine called Edelwein. In 1973 some of the Johannisberg Riesling grapes developed *Botrytis cinerea*, a beneficent mold that attacks the ripened grapes and results in a high concentration of sugar. The luxuriantly sweet Edelwein has been likened to a fine German Beerenauslese. The 1978 vintage, for example, contained 15.5 percent residual sugar, but was high enough in acidity not to be cloying.

☆/☆☆☆☆

$$/$$$

Freisa.

The Freisa is one of the better red grapes of the Italian Piedmont region, and wines from this grape are produced in large quantities. Labels usually will indicate the name of the area where the grapes were grown, as in Freisa d'Asti, Freisa Delle Langhe, or Freisa di Chieri. Generally the Freisas should be drunk when younger than such robust Piedmont reds as Barolo and Gattinara, perhaps within six years of the harvest. Some Freisa Spumante, or sparkling wine, is also produced.
☆☆☆
$

Freixenet.

This is one of several huge producers of *méthode champenoise* sparkling wines based in San Sadurni de Noya, just outside Barcelona. The wines are high in quality and moderate in price, and have helped to establish a beachhead for Spanish sparkling wines in the American market. The Carta Nevada Brut and the Cordon Negro Brut are the two most popular Freixenet bottlings among American consumers.
☆/☆☆
$/$$$

Fresno Winery.

Fresno Winery is a member of the big California cooperative called Guild Wineries and Distilleries. All of its wines are vinified and distributed by Guild. (*See* Guild Wineries and Distilleries.)
☆
$

Frey Vineyards.

Frey Vineyards is a small, family-owned and -operated winery in California's Mendocino County, north of the more famous Napa Valley. Dr. and Mrs. Paul Frey and their eight sons and four daughters are responsible for every phase of the business, from grape to label. The family began planting vines in the late 1960s. The winery itself was built by the Frey sons and opened in 1980. The grape presses are hand-made. Production has grown to a total of about 2000 cases of Cabernet Sauvignon, Grey Riesling, Gewürztraminer, French Colombard, and Chardonnay. Some of the grapes are purchased.
☆/☆☆☆
$/$$

Frick Winery.

Bill and Judy Frick established their first winery in 1976 in an old, isolated gasoline station made mostly of corrugated steel in Bonny Doon, in California's Santa Cruz County. Their first two vintages were crushed there, before the operation was moved to new facilities in the city of Santa Cruz in time for the 1979 harvests. Production totals about 3000 cases annually of Pinot Noir, Petite Sirah, Chardonnay, and Zinfandel.
☆/☆☆☆
$$

Friuli-Venezia Giulia.

One of Italy's most important growing areas for fine wines is Friuli-Venezia Giulia, which lies in the northeastern part of the country north of the city of Trieste. It is on the frontier with Austria on the north, Yugoslavia on the east, and the Adriatic Sea on the south, and

the Austro-Yugoslavian influence that is apparent in the food of the region can be perceived also in the wines, especially the whites. The wines include Aquileia, Collio Goriziano, Colli Orientali del Friuli, Grave del Friuli, Isonzo, and Latisana. Numerous grape varieties are produced there, including the Pinot Grigio, Riesling, Traminer, Cabernet Sauvignon, Merlot, and Malvasia.
☆/☆☆☆☆
$/$$

Frog's Leap Winery.

Frog's Leap Winery attracted national attention in 1982 with its first release, a 1981 Napa Valley Sauvignon Blanc, largely because of the Frog's Leap name, which somehow captured the imagination of wine fanciers. The winemaker, John Williams, was unable to resist suggesting that the wine would make a big splash in California and that it exuded a grassy bouquet that fairly jumped out of the glass. He also suggested that it was ideal for picnics at creekside and that it had good legs as well as a nose, rather than a bouquet or aroma. Actually, the wine was extremely well made, and its name comes from the location of the winery, at a spot along Mill Creek in the Napa Valley known as the Frog Farm. Frogs were raised there around the turn of the century and according to an old ledger were sold for 33 cents

a dozen, apparently destined for San Francisco restaurants. John Williams, his wife Julie, and Larry and Jeannine Turley planted the Frog Farm vineyard with Sauvignon Blanc grapes in 1978, and an old stable was converted into a winery in time for the 1981 crush. Frog's Leap is a sideline for the proprietors. John Williams spends most of his time at Spring Mountain Vineyards, where he is the winemaker. Larry Turley is a physician. They made about 2000 cases of the 1981 vintage and increased production in succeeding vintages. A Chardonnay has been added.
☆/☆☆
$$

Fronsac, Fronsadais.

Overlooking the Dordogne River a mile or two north of Libourne outside the city of Bordeaux in southwestern France is the village of Fronsac, where some good, but rarely great, wines are produced. The *appellation* Côtes de Fronsac is accorded to the red wines produced on the land surrounding the hill of Fronsac, Saint-Michel-de-Fronsac, Saint-Germain-la-Rivière, Saint-Aignan-la-Rivière, Saillans, and a small portion of the nearby *commune* of Galgon. Cabernet Sauvignon, Merlot, Cabernet Franc, Malbec, and Bouchet grapes are used here, but they produce less elegant wines than are produced by the same grapes 20 miles west in the Bordeaux Médoc and a few miles east in Pomerol and Saint-Emilion. A lesser *appellation* is simply Fronsadais, referring to wines from parts of the district not entitled to the *appellations* Côtes de Fronsac or Côtes de Canon-Fronsac. The latter *appellation* is considered one of the best of the minor districts around Bordeaux. The red wines are spicy and interesting, but lack the vigor and finesse of the best of Bordeaux.
☆/☆☆☆
$/$$

· G ·

Château La Gaffelière.

Most of the châteaus of Saint-Emilion are fairly modest in comparison with the great castles of the Médoc peninsula north of Bordeaux, but Château La Gaffelière is a precious jewel lying in the *côtes*, or hillside, area of the Saint-Emilion District. It has a splendid courtyard with reflecting pool adjacent to the medieval château itself. The estate was ranked a *premier grand cru classé* in the Saint-Emilion classification of 1955. Bottles from older vintages bear labels that indicate the wine was called La Gaffelière-Naudes, but the name has been shortened. Wines of elegance and finesse are produced at this excellent estate. They are best when ten to 15 years old.
☆☆☆☆
$$/$$$

Gaillac.

Once renowned for its sweet white wines, Gaillac has suffered the fate of many of the sweet-wine-producing areas due to public rejection of any but the driest of table wines. The area is in the south of France, south of Cahors and north of Toulouse. Today it produces a broad array of reds, whites, rosés and *vins mousseux*, or sparkling wines—all of little distinction, even though Gaillac is a designated *appellation contrôlée*, which should imply greater quality. To qualify for the Premières Côtes de Gaillac name, the wines must attain 12 percent alcohol; for simple Gaillac, 10.5 percent. They are not often seen outside France, but visitors to this picturesque and rustic area where the River Tarn cuts gorges through the hillsides have found some interesting bottles.
☆/☆☆☆
$/$$

Galestro.

Because Italy's wine laws so far have not permitted white wines to be produced under the Chianti name, some of the Chianti producers in Tuscany have begun producing a white called Galestro, made mostly from the Trebbiano grape but also with portions of Pinot Bianco, Chardonnay, and Sauvignon permitted. It is vinified crisp and dry, and production has been rising rapidly in response to the growing demand for white wines, especially among American consumers. Several of the major Chianti producers have been

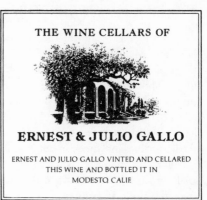

making Galestro, including Ricasoli, Antinori, Ruffino, and Frescobaldi. The wine is similar to Bianco della Lega, which also comes from Tuscany.
☆/☆☆
$

Gallo.

E. & J. Gallo Winery of Modesto, California, is the giant of the California wine industry, with 40 percent of the market. Gallo sells over 54 million cases of wine per year—one million per week—in a wide-ranging spectrum of products that includes table wines, sparkling wines, fortified dessert wines, and fruit-flavored "pop" wines. Gallo's enormous impact on the wine industry is readily acknowledged by California winemakers, for it has been Gallo's reasonably priced jug wines that have brought new wine drinkers into the fold.

Brothers Ernest and Julio Gallo, now in their seventies and still sole owner-managers of Gallo, started out modestly enough. As boys they helped their father, an immigrant from the Piedmont Dis-

trict of northern Italy, in a small vineyard at Modesto. After the repeal of Prohibition the brothers scrounged up $6,000, bought a $2,000 grape crusher and a couple of redwood tanks, rented a railway shed to house them and they were all set to go—with just one small problem. They knew a lot about growing grapes but nothing about making wine. Ernest read up on the subject, learning fermentation techniques from a two-page pamphlet in the local library, and as soon as a quantity of grapes was purchased they were in business. First-year profits of $34,000, mostly from distribution in the East, were plowed right back into the business. Growth and expansion steadily continued, largely helped by shrewd salesmanship and a sharp eye for what the public wanted. Catering to the mass market, Gallo concentrated on sweet dessert wines such as Thunderbird and muscatel and inexpensive table wines like Paisano. As their fortunes increased so did their diversification, and the quality of their wines.

Gallo was first to use stainless steel

fermenters and the fresher, cleaned-up taste of the wines prompted other wineries to follow suit. They were also the first to come out with flavored wines like Ripple and Spanada. Recently they have begun to improve their better quality table wines, buying grapes from the North Coast counties (Napa, Sonoma, and Mendocino) to upgrade bottlings of Hearty Burgundy and Chablis Blanc. Though wine connoisseurs tend to denigrate Gallo wines, some have taken notice of Gallo's better efforts and have been quick to point them out as the best values in American wines. Such encouragement must have pleased the Gallo brothers. Despite their aloofness from the press and the rest of the industry and their couldn't-care-less attitude toward critics, the Gallos seem interested in continued improvement of their wines. In 1974 Gallo brought out its first varietal wines, sold in fifths— Zinfandel, French Colombard, Sauvignon Blanc, and Ruby Cabernet, once again at reasonable prices for everyday drinking. The Sauvignon Blanc was perhaps the best among them, fresh and dry, with a pleasant bouquet.

Later in the 1970s Gallo expanded its commitment to the varietal market with the introduction of several other wines in the category, including Chenin Blanc, Riesling, and Barbera. All represented decent value and were well made, if lacking complexity. In 1981 the commitment was carried a step further when an oak-aged Chardonnay was introduced. This was by far the most interesting Gallo wine so far, although it was nonvintage, like all its other varietals, and still lacked complexity. Nevertheless, the subtly oaky nuances in the flavor and the clean finish represented another step up the quality ladder. A year later came a Cabernet Sauvignon that pleased many critics, and finally, in 1983, Gallo released its first vintage wine, a 1978 Cabernet Sauvig-non that was of very high quality, proving that Gallo is capable of producing some of the best wines in California.

The betting is that Gallo will be estate-bottling an entire line from its Dry Creek satellite facility in Sonoma County. Meanwhile the family company continues to grow and prosper. It is estimated that Gallo crushes perhaps 30 percent of all wine grapes crushed in California, including one-fourth of the crop even in the Napa Valley, and the Gallo brothers' business is probably the largest winemaking enterprise in the world. Speculation abounds as to what will happen when Ernest and Julio give up control, but it is probable that no drastic or rapid changes will occur. After all, Gallo has become an institution, and institutions do not change quickly.
☆/☆☆
$/$$

Gattinara.

Italy's Piedmont region produces the country's best red wines, and among the best of these is Gattinara, which comes from the vineyards around the village of the same name. Like the other great Piedmont reds, Gattinara is made from the noble Nebbiolo grape that imparts great depth and intensity and an unusual texture that can almost be chewed. If Barolo is the King of Italy's red wines, then Gattinara is the Queen, displaying a softer, more elegant style and perhaps somewhat more finesse. The finest of all the Gattinaras are called Spanna Gattinara, possibly to underscore that they have been made entirely from the Spanna, or Nebbiolo, grape. The production is quite small and these wines are difficult to find outside Italy, but they are worth seeking out because of their high quality. Gattinara must be aged for four years, including two years in cask, before it can be marketed, and it must attain an alcohol level of at

least 12 percent. (*See also* Barolo, Spanna.)
☆☆☆☆
$$/$$$

PRODUCT   OF ITALY

GAVI
DENOMINAZIONE DI ORIGINE CONTROLLATA
DRY WHITE WINE

Contratto

IMBOTTIGLIATO DA GIUSEPPE CONTRATTO · CANELLI (ITALIA)

750 ml.   AT/130   Alc. 11,5% by vol.

Sole U.S.A. Agents: Lake Success N.Y.
MEDITERRANEAN   IMPORTING CO.

Gavi.

The Piedmont region of northern Italy is best known for its Barolo, Gattinara, and other robust red wines, but some white table wine is made there, and perhaps the best is Gavi, produced in the southeastern sector of the region. Gavi is made from the Cortese grape and sometimes is called Cortese di Gavi. It is fresh and light but displays ample character when vinified with the modern techniques that have become prevalent in the area in recent years. At one time Gavi was a wine prone to premature oxidation and heaviness, like many other Italian whites, but nowadays it is not allowed to sit around in casks and is bottled with a fresh crispness that marries well with fish dishes. Gavi also has increasingly become available in foreign markets as its popularity has expanded, and versions from a number of different producers are exported. Some sparkling (*spumante* or *frizzante*) Gavi is also made. (*See* Cortese.)
☆/☆☆
$/$$

Château Le Gay.

The gravelly soil in the heart of the Pomerol District 20 miles east of the city of Bordeaux produces excellent red wines of robust character and hearty texture. Château Le Gay, which lies adjacent to Château La Croix de Gay and not far from Château Pétrus, is one of these. The estate's production is small, but the wines can be found in the export markets. If Pomerol had been included in the Médoc classification of 1855, Château Le Gay would probably have ranked among the fourth or fifth growths.
☆☆☆/☆☆☆☆
$$/$$$

Château Gazin.

One of the larger producers in the Pomerol District east of Bordeaux and adjacent to Saint-Emilion is Château Gazin, whose wines are fairly widely distributed abroad. They are good, robust reds that occasionally lack finesse, but can be stylish and intense in the best vintages. If the Pomerol District were classified according to the quality of the vineyards, Gazin probably would rank in the middle third, comparable to a fourth or fifth growth of the Médoc.
☆☆☆☆
$$/$$$

Geisenheimer.

Germany's Rheingau region produces some of the finest white wines of the world and many have achieved great fame. But the Geisenheimers from the village of Geisenheim adjacent to Johannisberg are not well known outside Germany. This means they can represent excellent value, for they are superior wines produced in fairly large quantities. No Geisenheim vineyard has the panache of a Marcobrunner or a Schloss Vollrads or a Schloss Johannisberger, but many Geisenheimers are nevertheless sound in vintages when more renowned vineyards have trouble producing wines that measure up to expectations. The village is probably more famous for its excellent School and Research Institute for Viticulture, where much German wine technology has been developed. The school is also a substantial vineyard owner under its German name, the Lehr- und Forschungsanstalt für Wein.

Among the better vineyards at Geisenheim are the following.

Geisenheimer Altbaum
Geisenheimer Decker
Geisenheimer Fuchsberg*
Geisenheimer Hinkelstein
Geisenheimer Hoher Decker
Geisenheimer Katzenloch
Geisenheimer Kilsberg*
Geisenheimer Kirchgrube
Geisenheimer Klaus*
Geisenheimer Kläuserweg*
Geisenheimer Kosankenburg
Geisenheimer Kreuzweg
Geisenheimer Lickerstein
Geisenheimer Marienberg
Geisenheimer Mäuerchen*
Geisenheimer Mönchspfad*
Geisenheimer Morschberg
Geisenheimer Rosengarten
Geisenheimer Rothenberg*
Geisenheimer Schlossgarten*

*An asterisk (*) indicates vineyard names that survived or that were created in the revision of the German wine law of 1971.
☆/☆☆☆
$/$$

Gemello Winery.

John Gemello, Sr., emigrated from Italy in 1898 after learning the winemaking trade in the Piedmont District, home of Barolo and Gattinara, among other great red wines. He established the Gemello Winery in Mountain View, Santa Clara County, California, in 1934. More recently his son Mario Gemello has been the dominant owner and winemaker. The winery was sold to the Felice family, which had owned San Martin, in 1974 but returned to Gemello ownership in 1976. The premium varietals are produced under the Gemello name, while jug wines are made under the Mountain View name. Case production runs about 6000 a year of red wines, including Zinfandel, Cabernet Sauvignon, Pinot Noir, Petite Sirah, and Barbera, although a return to white-wine production was planned. All of the grapes for Gemello wines are purchased from other growers.
☆☆
$$

Generic Wines.

Generic wines are those made in America ostensibly in the style of certain European wines such as Sherry and Port, or are blended wines that are given European place names even though they may bear no resemblance whatever to their namesakes. In themselves, however, these wines—for example, "Chablis," "Burgundy," "Rhine," and "Chianti"—can be attractive and reasonably priced for everyday drinking. Unlike varietal wines, which in California must contain at least 75 percent of the grape name that appears on the label, generics can be blended from any number of varieties, and unfortunately a great many of the generic jug blends have been made from inferior grapes that produce insipid wines. Many premium producers in California make generic wines, however, and when the blending is carefully done using better varieties the result can be extremely good value. The surplus of premium grapes in the early 1970s promoted a general upgrading of many California generics as surplus Cabernet, Pinot Noir, Zinfandel, and Chenin Blanc found their way into domestic burgundy and chablis. Producers such as Gallo, Italian Swiss Colony, Guild, and Franzia Brothers achieved their fortunes largely with generic wines, but huge quantities of generics have also been produced by such well-known companies as Almadén, Paul Masson, Christian Brothers, Louis Martini, and others. The system of generic labeling is so entrenched in California and the Americas in general that it will probably always be in use, despite objections from Germany's Rhineland and France's districts of Chablis and Burgundy. Generic wines from California and other states, as well as from South America, represent an excellent introduction to the world of wine for the neophyte. But his palate will soon demand greater depth and complexity than the generics can provide, and he is likely to step upward to premium varietals and imports as his knowledge and appreciation expand.

Germany.

Without question Germany is the greatest white-wine producing country in the world. Its vineyards are among the northernmost of all and the weather is perhaps the most adverse of any major wine-growing area, but somehow the cultivation of the grape here is superior in terms of quality if not quantity. France produces ten times as much wine as Germany, but it does not produce as much first-class white wine. The achievements of German viniculture are extraordinary, not only because of the weather but because Germany is the only major wine-producing country in which wine is not the national drink. Most Germans drink beer, whereas wine is the national beverage in Italy, France, Spain, Portugal, and other countries where the grape is extensively cultivated and most babies are born with wine already coursing through their veins. What the Germans lack in natural

advantages, however, they make up for in skill, craftsmanship, and perseverance. It is hard to imagine how anything can be cultivated on the extraordinarily steep vineyard slopes of the Mosel River Valley, for example, where the vineyard workers often have to be secured by ropes to keep from falling hundreds of feet to the river below. Yet they manage to produce wines of incredible bouquet, great natural sweetness, and delicate finesse, even it if means carting the soil back up the gorges by hand after it washes away in winter rainstorms. In many parts of Germany quantity is sacrificed for quality. The noble Riesling grape, which produces by far the best German wines, is stingy in its yield, yet it is grown wherever possible, even when much more wine could be made by growing Sylvaners, Müller-Thurgaus, or other higher-yielding grapes instead.

The bouquet of the best German wines is incomparable—flowery and full, redolent of peaches, honey, hyacinths, and spring daffodils. The taste is rich and full, displaying great fruit, fullness, depth and an almost magical finesse. Good German wines are clean on the palate, light in body and often relatively low in alcoholic content. Depending on their degree of sweetness, they are ideal as aperitifs to be sipped well chilled on warm summer afternoons, or as an accompaniment to a first dinner course of shellfish or smoked salmon or pâté. They harmonize well with most full-flavored seafood, but they tend to be at their most formidable as dessert wines, especially when nature has been generous and permitted the growers to harvest the grapes late in the autumn after the juice inside has become highly concentrated and intensely sweet.

The main difficulty with German wines is that they *are* sweet and, as a result, many otherwise open-minded people reject them out of hand, almost as if there were something objectionable about the natural sweetness that the producers strive so diligently to achieve. This rejection is bred of a prejudice that is difficult to understand, but which probably stems from the fact that so many low-quality alcoholic drinks produced in the United States and some other countries have a cloying artificial sweetness. The suspicion is strong that these drinks, sometimes made from wine and sometimes from almost any other fermented liquid, have created prejudices against even the best dessert wines. Moreover, the cheapest American-made wines, the ones often identified with hoboes and derelicts, are sometimes called "Tokay" or "Sauterne" or "Rhine" even though the only characteristics they have in common with their namesakes is that they are wet and contain alcohol.

The sweetness of a great Rhine or Mosel is entirely natural, as it must be under German law. It is the same sweetness that exists in a ripe peach or pear or strawberry, not a sweetness of processed sugar. It is achieved with the help of plenty of warm sunshine and the proper amount of moisture. If the weather conditions remain ideal, the growers leave the grapes on the vines late in the autumn until they begin to shrivel into raisinlike berries. The water in the juice evaporates through the grape skins, leaving behind concentrated nectar. Under ideal circumstances, the grapes will contract a mold or fungus called *Botrytis cinerea* and known as *Edelfäule* in German and *pourriture noble* in French, meaning "noble rot." The mold digs into the skins but does not break them, facilitating the evaporation of the water until an extremely small amount of highly concentrated juice is left. Obviously, conditions must be perfect to produce such wine and the result is very expensive, reflecting the much larger volume of grapes required to make very small quantities of wine.

Some of the most tongue-twisting words in German wine terminology are used to describe the varying degrees of sweetness achieved through late harvesting. "Spätlese" refers to late-picked grapes. "Auslese" means selected late-picked bunches of grapes. "Beerenauslese" means that each grape is harvested individually after it has begun turning into a dried berry. "Trockenbeerenauslese" refers to wine made after the berries have shriveled and produced the most concentrated juice of all, often with the help of the *Edelfäule*. The majority of German wines, however, are not nearly as sweet and need not be regarded only as dessert beverages.

The two major types of German wines are Rhines and Mosels. They are easily recognized and identified in their tall, narrow bottles—the Rhines in brown bottles and the Mosels in green bottles. But there are numerous subdivisions in each area, as well as other areas that also produce good wines. As in other countries, the more specifically identified a wine is, the better it is likely to be. A wine simply called Mosel or Moselle, using the French spelling, will probably be rather modest, as will a wine called nothing more than Rhine. Such ordinary types tend to reach the export markets through generic names like Moselblümchen and Liebfraumilch, which are discussed under their alphabetical listings.

The major German wine regions are strictly controlled as to nomenclature. The six most important are the Mosel-Saar-Ruwer, the Rheingau, the Rheinhessen, or Hessia, the Pfalz, or Palatinate, the Nahe, and Franconia, or Franken. All are involved with the mighty Rhine River, which snakes its way from Switzerland in the south to Holland and the North Sea. The Rheingau, Rheinhessen, and Pfalz are directly on the Rhine, while the Mosel flows into the Rhine at Koblenz and the Saar and Ruwer are Mosel tributaries. Franconia is on the Main River, which reaches the Rhine from the east at Mainz. The Nahe River flows into the Rhine at Bingen east of the junction with the Mosel. Each area is discussed separately under its alphabetical entry.

Germany has a number of other big wine-producing districts, but examples from these areas are uncommon in the export markets. Occasionally a Markgräfler, Ihringer, Neuweierer, or Steinbacher will show up from the Baden region. From the Mittelrhein northwest of the Rheingau come Bacharachers, Caubers, and Steegers of minor distinction, and red wines are produced in the Ahr south of Bonn. But none of these regions or their wines are serious challengers to the noble produce of the six leaders and they are rarely seen abroad.

Because the weather conditions for growing grapes can be so adverse in Germany, vintages are extremely important. Wide variations in style and quality exist from year to year. For instance, the 1964 vintage in many parts of Germany produced wines of unusually high alcoholic content, which imparted a heavier taste to them. But they are long-lived. The 1971 vintage was so magnificent that it virtually defies description—astonishing fruit, great depth, perfect balance. The 1972 at first vintage was considered almost worthless (after all, it couldn't match the superb '71), but some quite decent wines were made. The 1973 was excellent, rich and fruity. Use the vintage chart on the inside cover of the book for indications of quality.

Grape varieties are also important with German wines and are likely to be mentioned on most of the best bottles exported. The Riesling is the noblest of all and hardly anybody would suggest that it does not consistently produce the best German wines. But the Sylvaner and Müller-Thurgau account for a major share of Germany's whites. The Traminer and Gewürztraminer make spicier wines. Examples of the Hüxelrebe, Scheurebe, Ruländer, and Gutedel may also be found. The Spätburgunder, originally the Pinot Noir of France's Burgundy District, accounts for the most important share of Germany's red-wine production, which amounts to only 27 percent of total output. Blends of various grapes are not uncommon, sometimes involving five or more varieties in a single wine.

In 1971 a new German wine law was passed in an effort to simplify identification and establish more rigid quality controls. The information that appears on each label is strictly regulated and standardized now and the discretion which a grower could use in naming his wine has been virtually eliminated. The most important result of the legislation, however, was a drastic reduction in the number of vineyard names. More than 22,000 names were wiped out, leaving about 2500 for the consumer to contend with. Previously, some vineyards were not much larger than somebody's backyard. Now they all must be at least 12.5 acres to merit an entry on the official lists. The remaining names, of course, cover much more territory and in some cases do not connote the same level of quality as before. The tiny Doktor vineyard at Bernkastel in the Mosel Valley was expanded substantially, for example, to cover much more acreage. Now, unless you know where the grapes were picked and who produced the wine, you will be unable to determine whether a Bernkasteler Doktor bottled since 1971 came from that famous and special plot of fertile ground. (Additional information on the new German regulations is presented under the section on Labels and Wine Laws in Part I. All of the German wines that you are likely to encounter outside Germany are discussed under their individual alphabetical entries.)

Gevrey-Chambertin.

It is said that the very best red wines of the world are made in the Burgundian *commune* of Gevrey-Chambertin, and few connoisseurs would argue with this statement. Gevrey is the northernmost of the great *communes* of the Côte d'Or, or Golden Slope, that produces an abundance of exquisite wines. Its two most celebrated vineyards are Le Chambertin and Chambertin-Clos de Bèze, which lie just above the vineyard road known as the Route des Grands Crus running south of Gevrey toward Morey-Saint-Denis. Clos de Bèze has slightly more than half of the 68-acre vineyard, although more wines called Chambertin are produced. This is because the wines of Clos de Bèze have the legal right to the Chambertin name and sometimes use it because of its greater fame. Yet Burgundy experts suggest that if either vineyard produces superior wines, it is Clos de Bèze. These are the firmest, sturdiest wines of the Côte d'Or, and they benefit from considerable bottle-age. A decade is required for a Chambertin to approach the mellow, velvety, almost thick but elegantly balanced and rich perfection that it is capable of achieving. If Le

Musigny can be regarded as the greatest of the feminine red wines of Burgundy, then Chambertin and Clos de Bèze are the most masculine, although their masculinity is neither chauvinistic nor crude, but instead is highly refined. According to legend, Chambertin was the favorite of Napoleon, and it is not difficult to appreciate why.

The name of the *commune*'s most famous vineyard was tacked onto the name of the *commune* itself, a practice common in the Burgundy country but confusing to nonexperts. If the blended wines of the *commune* were called, simply, Gevrey, there would be little difficulty in differentiating them from the eight *grands crus*, all of which have Chambertin in their names. It is significant that nine of the 24 red *grands crus* in all of Burgundy are in Gevrey. Besides Chambertin and Chambertin-Clos de Bèze, these are Chapelle-Chambertin, Charmes-Chambertin, Griotte-Chambertin, Latricières-Chambertin, Mazis-Chambertin, Mazoyères-Chambertin, and Ruchottes-Chambertin. None of these should be confused with the *commune* wine, Gevrey-Chambertin, which is good but less distinguished and less costly. In addition, there are more than two dozen *premiers crus*, which rank between the *grands crus* and the Gevrey-Chambertins. Most of these are excellent wines.

The name Chambertin, according to legend, is derived from a long-departed peasant named Bertin, who established a vineyard or field (*champ*) adjacent to Clos de Bèze, which had been planted by the monks of the Abbey of Bèze near Dijon in the seventh century. The *champ de Bertin* evolved into Chambertin. The Route des Grandes Crus passes through the heart of Gevrey, a typical Burgundian wine town, where most of the wine-producing facilities are centered. An excellent subterranean restaurant with vineyard museum, La Ròtisserie du

Chambertin, is located here. The owner has his own vineyard parcels and serves his own wines in the restaurant, the distance from vine to table being only a few hundred yards, so there need be no concern about its traveling poorly. The Rôtisserie has a rosette in the *Guide Michelin*. (*See also* Chambertin, Côte de Nuits.)

☆☆☆/☆☆☆☆

$$/$$$$

Gewürztraminer.

The Gewürztraminer grape was introduced to many American consumers through the wines of Alsace, an important viticultural region in the eastern part of the country, where the grape has been widely cultivated for many years. *Gewürztraminer* means "spicy traminer" and refers to the pleasantly spicy quality of the varietal wines made from the grape. Many German wines are produced from the Gewürztraminer grape, and its popularity has spread to California, where a number of producers are making Gewürztraminer in both dry and sweet versions. The sweet versions, with a high level of residual sugar, can be superb aperitifs or dessert wines. The grape is a member of the same European *Vitis vinifera* family that produces most of the other premium table wines of the world. It is sometimes likened to the Riesling because it thrives in similar climates, but its flavor is much spicier and it is considered less elegant. The California versions often are fully the equal of the Alsatian and German versions.

☆/☆☆

$/$$$

Geyser Peak.

Geyser Peak Winery at Geyserville in Sonoma County, California, is an old winery that for years made wines and brandy in bulk for other producers. In 1972, the Joseph Schlitz Brewing Company decided to go into the wine business and purchased Geyser Peak. They immediately began expansion of the physical plant and vineyards. Schlitz put Geyser Peak back into the bottled table wine business on a full-scale basis, not only with the Geyser Peak label but also with a second label, Summit, mostly for jug wines. The Geyser Peak line consists of vintage-dated varietals such as Chardonnay, Chenin Blanc, Fumé Blanc, Johannisberg Riesling, Gewürztraminer, Pinot Noir Blanc, Rosé of Cabernet Sauvignon, Pinot Noir, Zinfandel, and Cabernet Sauvignon. A sparkling wine also is made. Of the two and a half million cases produced each year, about 200,000 are premium varietals. Geyser Peak has 1,100 acres, but purchases grapes for its Summit line. Henry F. Trione and his family bought Geyser Peak in 1982. A year later they hired John R. Mc-Clelland, formerly president of Almadén, to be chairman of Geyser Peak in an effort to increase their share of the market.

☆/☆☆☆

$/$$

Ghemme.

Perhaps not as well known as Barolo or Gattinara, two of the best red wines of Italy, is Ghemme, which also comes from the Piedmont region in the northern part of the country bordered by the French, Swiss, and Italian Alps. Ghemme is vinified about two-thirds from the noble Nebbiolo grape, with portions of Vespolina and Bonarda blended in. It is aged three years in wooden casks and another year in bottles before it can be marketed. Ghemme is not quite as robust as Barolo and not quite as elegant as Gattinara, but it is an excellent red wine that deserves much greater recognition. It is produced in the province of Novara in the communities of Ghemme and part of Romagnano.

☆☆☆/☆☆☆☆

$/$$

Girard Winery.

Girard Winery was established in Oakville, in California's Napa Valley, in 1979 and includes 44 acres of prime Napa vineyards producing Chardonnay, Cabernet Sauvignon, Chenin Blanc, and Sauvignon Blanc grapes. A secondary label, Stephens, is used for wines made from grapes grown in the Alexander Valley of Sonoma County. Production has risen to about 12,000 cases a year.

☆/☆☆☆

$$

Château Giscours.

Château Giscours is one of the most popular wines of the *commune* of Margaux in the Médoc peninsula north of the city of Bordeaux. The château was classified a *troisième cru*, or third growth, in the Bordeaux classification of 1855. Giscours produces rich yet supple wines with a flowery bouquet. They tend to mature slightly earlier than some other reds of the Médoc, but still should not be consumed before the sixth or seventh year following a favorable vintage. The château is owned by the Tari family, which bought it in 1952 and undertook an improvement program that has resulted in a series of excellent vintages. The owners contend that the Giscours vineyards benefit from an unusually mild climate that allows the grapes to ripen up to six days earlier than average in the Médoc, permitting an earlier harvest and the possible avoidance of adverse weather.

The average age of the Giscours vines is about 30 years, and the vineyard consists of 65 percent Cabernet Sauvignon, 15 percent Merlot, and the balance Cabernet Franc, Petit Verdot, and Malbec.

Even in mediocre vintages, Giscours excels, reflecting the care and attention of the Tari family.

☆☆☆☆

$$/$$$

Giumarra Vineyards.

Giumarra is one of the largest owners of vineyards in the United States and perhaps in the world. The family organization, headed by brothers Giuseppe, George, and John Giumarra and their brother-in-law, Dominic Corsaro, all of whom emigrated from Sicily in the early part of the century, owns 3000 acres of the wine grape vineyards and 5000 acres of table grape vineyards in California. Giuseppe came to the U.S. in 1912 and moved to California in 1922. The others followed later, settling near Los Angeles initially with a fruit business before moving to the San Joaquin Valley in the 1940s. They built their first winery in 1946, making wines from table grapes and selling them in bulk to other producers, ranging from such giants as Gallo and Almadén to Mondavi.

Giumarra remained in the bulk wine business from 1946 until 1974, when the first wines under the Giumarra label appeared following a revamping and upgrading of the winery in Edison, not far from Bakersfield. At least 50 percent of the Giumarra production is still sold in bulk, but the winery turns out some 500,000 cases a year under the Giumarra label plus perhaps 400,000 cases more under private labels and a secondary label, Breckenridge Cellars, which is sold largely to the restaurant trade. Despite their substantial acreage in vines, Giumarra still buys about 25 percent of its grape requirements from other growers, and the enterprise remains one of the largest providers of table grapes in the world. Three generations of Giumarras now work in the operation. The product array covers virtually all premium varietals and generic wines as well as sherries and sweet dessert wines. In general, the level of quality reflects Giumarra's relatively recent entry into the wine business under its own name, but quality is improving and prices are attractive.

☆☆

$$

Glen Ellen Winery.

The original vineyards of the Glen Ellen Winery in California's Sonoma Valley were planted in 1868, and the property as well as some of the buildings have landmark status. The property consists of a glen on the west side of Mount Sonoma below the Mayacamas Range that separates the Napa and Sonoma Valleys, and the growing conditions there are next to ideal for Cabernet Sauvignon and Sauvignon Blanc grapes. The vineyards had fallen into disuse until discovered by Bruno and Helen Benziger and their family in 1980. Bruno sold his interest in a family wine- and spirits-importing business in New York and moved with five of his seven children and some grandchildren to Glen Ellen in 1982 to begin making wine.

Terracing from the old vineyards of the last century was evident as trees and brush were ripped out to make way for the new vineyard. Several patches of marijuana also were torn out in the process, and some 55 acres were planted in vines by early 1983, with a few more acres still to be replanted. Besides Cabernet Sauvignon and Sauvignon Blanc there are Merlot and Cabernet Franc for blending. In addition, 100 acres have been leased in the Carneros District of the Napa Valley for growing Chardonnay. Bruno's son Mike Benziger is winemaker and another son, Joe, is assistant winemaker. A new, 5000-square-foot winery was built with family labor in 1981, and oak barrels have been purchased from suppliers in the Burgundy district of France.

The early efforts of the Benziger family have been successful. A 1981 Chardonnay made from grapes purchased from a nearby vineyard called Les Pierres was fruity yet crisp and dry, with toasty nuances. A line of secondary wines, called Proprietor's Reserve, represented excellent value at under $5 a bottle. The quality was very high, and the only question was whether that quality can be maintained as production climbs. In 1982 Glen Ellen turned out about 7000 cases in all, and the goal is 20,000 cases a year of estate-bottled wines.

☆/☆☆☆

$/$$

Glenora Wine Cellars.

In Dundee, N.Y., on the shore of Seneca Lake is Glenora Wine Cellars, one of the more successful winemaking operations in the Finger Lakes district. The winery was built in 1977 and has been used to process up to ten varieties of wine per vintage, including such European varietals as Riesling and Chardonnay. The operation basically runs on purchased grapes—grapes grown by the four principal owners of Glenora: Eastman Beers, Ed Dalrymple, Howard Kimball, and Gene Pierce. All are grape growers who sell parts of their annual production to Glenora for bottling under the Glenora label. Output surpassed 12,000 cases in 1980 and was moving higher, amid efforts to shift production more heavily into white wines to better reflect consumer preferences. Initially only about one-third of production was white.

The four partners who own Glenora had been selling grapes to such big producers as Taylor, but decided that they also could produce premium wines on their own. Seneca Lake, about 40 miles long, provides a moderating influence on the winter temperatures, the kind of microclimate conducive to grape cultivation. Experiments have taken place at Glenora with very sweet wines equivalent to the German Trockenbeerenauslese and to eiswein. Oak-aged Chardonnay has also been produced, along with such European-American hybrids as Ravat and Maréchal Foch. The wines are clean and well made and are available for sale and tasting at the winery's handsome tasting room.

☆/☆☆

$/$$

Château Gloria.

One of the best-known estates of the Médoc peninsula north of the city of Bordeaux is Château Gloria, although it was not accorded *cru classé* status in the Bordeaux classification of 1855. Its prominence is due partly to the popularity of its owner, Henri Martin, mayor of Saint-Julien, former manager of Château Latour, and one of the leading personages in the Bordeaux region. Château Gloria, a *cru bourgeois* of Saint-Julien, consists of vineyard tracts acquired from Châteaux Beychevelle, Talbot, Duhart-Milon, Saint-Pierre, Léoville-Barton, Léoville-Poyferré, and Gruaud-Larose. The first parcel was acquired in 1942, and the Gloria vineyard now consists of 110 acres in all. The production facilities came from Château Saint-Pierre. Château Gloria produces rich and mellow wines that mature at a fairly young age. They can be consumed as early as five years after the vintage while the bigger wines of the Médoc are just passing through their adolescence. The property is now managed by Jean-Louis Triaud, son-in-law of Henri Martin.

☆☆☆☆

$$/$$$

Gold Seal.

Gold Seal Vineyards of Hammondsport, New York, is one of the largest and

best-known American wine companies. The winery is located on the western bank of Lake Keuka in the Finger Lakes District and is one of the oldest and most picturesque in the East. Gold Seal was started in 1865 by a group of men from Hammondsport and Urbana who wanted to make Champagne. It was then known as the Urbana Wine Company and later the name was changed to Gold Seal. The company continued to operate during Prohibition, making sacramental and medicinal wines. In 1979 it was purchased by Seagram's, the big Canadian distilling and wine-importing company.

Most of the winemakers at Gold Seal have been Frenchmen from the Champagne District of France. After Prohibition, wishing to raise production standards to their pre-Prohibition position, the firm hired Charles Fournier of the distinguished house of Veuve Clicquot de Ponsardin in Rheims. He introduced plantings of French hybrids and began making the Charles Fournier New York State Champagne that received acclaim everywhere. In 1953, hearing Dr. Konstantin Frank express the conviction that European wine grapes could grow in the Finger Lakes Region, despite their past failures, Fournier hired Dr. Frank as viticultural consultant for plantings of Chardonnay and Riesling in an experimental vineyard at Gold Seal. The first vintage in 1959 was so successful that Dr. Frank later went off to begin his own vineyard and winery nearby. (*See* Vinifera Wine Cellars.)

Although Fournier died in 1983, Gold Seal has continued to produce its Charles Fournier line of special wines: Chablis Nature, from a blend of Chardonnay and French hybrids, and Blanc de Blancs, a Champagne initially made from the first pressings of Chardonnay and French hybrids, but now made entirely from Chardonnay grapes. It is one of the best sparkling wines produced in New York State. The winemaker now is a Frenchman named Guy Devaux.

Besides the Blanc de Blancs produced under the Fournier signature, there are Gold Seal Brut, Extra Dry and Pink Champagnes, a sparkling Burgundy, Cold Duck, Spumante, and such Gold Seal table wines as chablis, Rhine, dry Sauterne, *vin rosé,* chablis rosé, and burgundy among the generics. There is also a line of Gold Seal "native" wines made from local grapes, including Catawba red, white, and pink, Concord red, and Labrusca. The concern also produces a line of Sherries and Ports mainly from local grapes and hybrids.

☆/☆☆☆
$/$$

Governo.

Governo is the process used in the vinification of certain Italian red wines by which a quantity of *passito*, or raisined grapes, is added to the juice after fermentation, thereby inducing a refermentation. The *governo* enhances the depth of color, raises the alcohol and glycerol levels and creates a rounder, richer, more complex wine. The process has been in decline, largely because it is troublesome to set out the grapes to dry or to reserve a portion of the pressed grape solids for the same purpose. There has also been speculation that use of the *governo* decreases the longevity of the wines, but this may simply be rationalization related to the

extra effort required. The Chianti La Querce made by Attilio Pieri using the *governo* is consistently very high in quality. So is the Chianti Poggio al Sole made by Aldo Torrini, another charming and complex wine that benefits from the *governo.*

Graacher.

German white wine produced in Graach, one of the foremost wine towns in the best part of the Mosel River region, north or downstream from Wehlen and Bernkastel as the river twists toward the Rhine. Graachers have not won the renown of the Wehleners or Bernkastelers, but they are excellent wines with great fullness and balance and are regarded by connoisseurs as the equals of the more famous growths of the Middle Mosel. One vineyard at Graach is simply called Josephshöfer because its owners feel it need not be identified with the name of the town. Some of the best growers of the Mosel own slices of the Graacher vineyards, including members of the Prüm family that dominates the Wehleners, as well as the estate of Dr. Thanisch, one of the three owners of the celebrated Bernkasteler Doktor vineyard.

Among the better known vineyards at Graach are the following:

Graacher Abtsberg*
Graacher Domprobst*
Graacher Goldwingert
Graacher Heiligenhaus
Graacher Himmelreich*
Graacher Homberg
Graacher Kirchlay
Graacher Lilenpfad
Graacher Monch
Graacher Münzlay*
Graacher Nikolauslay
Graacher Stablay

An asterisk (*) indicates a vineyard name that survived the revision of the

German wine law in 1971. The new law also made provision for the Josephshöfer name in connection with Graach. The Münzlay is now a *Grosslage,* or large vineyard area, similar to a generic wine from Graach.

☆/☆☆

$/$$

Grand Cru Vineyards.

Grand Cru, established in 1970 by Robert Magnani and Allen Ferrera, has developed a reputation for producing excellent Gewürztraminers at its Sonoma Valley winery in Glen Ellen. Using a technique involving the spraying of *Botrytis cinerea* spores over the grapes, Grand Cru incubates the Botrytis to assure that the grapes shrivel and become dehydrated so that a super-sweet, concentrated wine with honeylike qualities similar to the German Trockenbeerenauslese results. In 1977 the finished wine contained an extraordinary 32 percent residual sugar and was only 7.1 percent alcohol. Production was extremely limited, but national distribution took place.

Grand Cru also produces good dry Chenin Blanc and Sauvignon Blanc as well as Cabernet Sauvignon and Zinfandel. Production has risen to around 30,000 cases a year. In 1981 Walter and Bettina Dreyer, who already held an interest in Grand Cru, acquired the ownership interests formerly held by several other stockholders and partners, although Ferrera and Magnani agreed to remain manager and winemaker, respectively. A major expansion of the winery was undertaken.

☆/☆☆☆

$$

Château Grand-Puy-Ducasse.

The house and cellars of Château Grand-Puy-Ducasse are directly on the waterfront in Pauillac, one of the most important wine-growing *communes* on the Médoc peninsula north of Bordeaux, and the house itself has been turned into the local *Maison du Vin,* headquarters for the Commanderie du Bontemps du Médoc et des Graves. The vineyards of Château Grand-Puy-Ducasse are separated from the production facilities and lie in three parcels outside the village. The estate was ranked as a *cinquième cru,* or fifth growth, in the Bordeaux classification of 1855. Its wines tend to be less polished than some other Pauillacs and sometimes display a certain coarseness. In the excellent 1971 vintage, however, the estate made a supple and generous wine aspiring to greatness. Grand-Puy-Ducasse needs at least eight years of aging before it should be drunk. (*See* Commanderie du Bontemps, etc.)

☆☆☆☆

$$/$$$

Château Grand-Puy-Lacoste.

Château Grand-Puy was broken up in the early part of the 1700s, and the Lacoste that was added to the name indicates the ownership of the Lacoste family at that time. Although the estate is almost universally known as Grand-Puy-Lacoste, its name also includes Saint Guirons, for yet another former proprietor. The estate lies in Pauillac, one of the most important Bordeaux *communes* on the Médoc peninsula running north of Bordeaux. The production of Grand-Puy-Lacoste runs about twice that of Grand-Puy-Ducasse, and the wine of Lacoste has developed a better reputation over the years. It is typical of Pauillac, fairly big but elegant, and displays considerable longevity in some vintages. It needs about 10 years of aging before reaching its peak. In the Bordeaux classification of 1855, it was ranked a *cinquième cru,* or fifth growth. It would probably be upgraded in any reclassification of the Bordeaux wines.

Since 1978 the property has been owned by Jean-Eugène Borie, also the proprietor of Châteaux Ducru-Beau-caillou and Haut-Batailley. The vineyard is one of the largest among the classified growths of Bordeaux, with 225 acres in vines—75 percent Cabernet Sauvignon and 25 percent Merlot. The wines of Grand-Puy-Lacoste are better than ever under the Borie ownership.

☆☆☆☆

$$/$$$

Granite Springs Winery.

El Dorado County, California, is capable of producing excellent Zinfandels of deep color and high fruit, and the new Granite Springs Winery, completed in time for the crush of 1981, is vying to turn some of them out. Twenty-three acres have been planted by proprietors Lester and Lynne Russell, and they made about 2500 cases of wine in 1982. The product line includes three different Zinfandel bottlings—an El Dorado red, an El Dorado white and a Sierra Foothills red—as well as a Cabernet Sauvignon and a Chenin Blanc.

☆/☆☆☆

$/$$

Grave del Friuli.

Several important subregions producing good wines exist within the broad geographical area in northeastern Italy known as Friuli-Venezia Giulia, and one of these is Grave del Friuli. The word *grave* refers to the gravelly soil of the area. Much of the wine is made from the Merlot grape, but Grave del Friuli also produces such other varietals as Cabernet, Pinot Bianco, Pinot Grigio, Refosco, Tocai, and Verduzzo.

☆/☆☆☆

$/$$

Graves.

One of the best producing areas in the Bordeaux region of southwestern France is Graves, which lies immediately south and west of Bordeaux between the Médoc and Sauternes. It encompasses the southernmost of the noble vineyard districts of Bordeaux. The word *graves* means "gravel" and pertains to the type of soil that is prevalent in the Graves District. Although it is virtually useless for any other kind of agriculture, it is ideal for viniculture, and gravelly portions of other vineyard areas around Bordeaux also use the word *graves*. But under the French *appellation d'origine* laws, only the specific district encompassing roughly 100 square miles mainly south and west of the city is entitled to the Graves place name for its wines.

Because the city of Bordeaux actually lies within Graves, the wines of this district have long been famous all over the world, especially in England and the outposts of the former British Empire, reflecting the English involvement in the Bordeaux wine trade exemplified in the marriage of King Henry II to Eleanor d'Aquitaine in 1152. Her dowry was Bordeaux and its environs, known as Aquitania. Following the Middle Ages, the Dukes of Aquitania began rebuilding the Bordeaux vineyards, and it was natural to begin with those that were closest to the seaport—the Graves. Over the years, however, the fame of Graves diminished as the renown of the Médoc a few miles to the north grew. By the year 1855, when the famous Bordeaux vineyard classification was made in connection with a Paris exposition, the wine trade was focused almost entirely on the Médoc. Only one Graves estate, the magnificent Château Haut-Brion, was mentioned in the 1855 classification, although it was fitting that Haut-Brion was named one of only four *premiers grand crus*, along with the celebrated Châteaux Lafite, Margaux and Latour of the Médoc.

Starting around the turn of the century, the reputation of Graves began to grow again, and now the wines of the district are acknowledged to be on a par with those of the Médoc, Saint-Emilion, and Pomerol once more. Unlike the other important Bordeaux Districts, however, Graves produces a large quantity of white wines, and many wine lovers automatically assume all Graves must be whites, even though reds account for fully one-fourth of the district's production. Moreover, the greatest wines of Graves are the reds, whereas the whites, with their dry, almost steely taste, will never challenge the great whites of the Côte de Beaune in Burgundy. Some of the white Graves, in fact, taste like dry Sauternes, and this is appropriate in light of the fact that the Sauternes District is an island entirely surrounded by the southern parts of Graves.

With the sole exception of Château Haut-Brion, Graves missed out on the 1855 Bordeaux classification, and it was not until 1953 that a formal Graves classification, albeit an unsatisfactory one, was instituted. This was revised in 1959, and its major fault is that it lists so few châteaux, implying that all the rest must be of decidedly inferior quality, when this is hardly the case. Only 13 châteaux are mentioned in the red-wine category, while eight are in the white, but of these eight, six are also cited in the red, so that only 15 châteaux in all are accorded *cru classé* status in Graves.

The whites are the following:

Château Laville-Haut-Brion in Talence
Château Bouscaut in Cadaujac
Château Couhins in Villeneuve-d'Ornon
Château Carbonnieux in Léognan
Domaine de Chevalier in Léognan
Château Malartic-Lagravière in Léognan
Château Olivier in Léognan
Château La Tour-Martillac in Martillac

These are the classified red wines of Graves:

Château La Mission-Haut-Brion in Talence
Château La Tour-Haut-Brion in Talence
Château Haut-Brion in Pessac
Château Pape Clément in Pessac
Château Bouscaut in Cadaujac
Château Carbonnieux in Léognan
Domaine de Chevalier in Léognan
Château de Fieuzal in Léognan
Château Haut-Bailly in Léognan
Château Malartic-Lagravière in Léognan
Château Olivier in Léognan
Château La Tour-Martillac in Martillac
Château Smith-Haut-Lafitte in Martillac

The celebrated Haut-Brion remains the costliest and most renowned wine of Graves, although La Mission Haut-Brion has also become one of the most expensive red Bordeaux in recent vintages, surpassing the prices brought by most of the second growths of the Médoc. Price is, of course, a reflection of the demand for a particular wine. Domaine de Chevalier is another excellent red Bordeaux capable of challenging the best of the Médoc, while Château Bouscaut clearly is the most improved wine of Graves, reflecting substantial investments by its American owners. Haut-Brion also is American-owned, giving Americans an important stake in the wines of this excellent Bordeaux District. Haut-Brion Blanc, undisputedly one of the superior whites of Graves, was omitted from the white classifications of both 1953 and 1959, but finally was included in 1960 when its absence raised questions about the entire classification's validity. All of the classified Graves merit the same *cru classé* designation on their labels, but in practice most call themselves *grands crus classés*.

The reds of Graves differ in style from the big wines of the Médoc, Saint-Emilion and Pomerol. They tend to be less robust, with a more elegant fullness and great finesse at an early age, which means they do not last as long in the bottle as some of the others. They reach their maturity after about a decade, although an Haut-Brion or La Mission Haut-Brion from a good vintage may take twice as long, and the reds of Château Bouscaut, increasingly dominated by the Cabernet Sauvignon grape, are requiring more and more bottle-age. As in the Médoc, the Cabernet Sauvignon and Cabernet Franc are widely used in Graves reds, along with the Merlot, the Malbec and the Petit Verdot. The Sauvignon Blanc and Semillon grapes dominate the white Graves, and small amounts of Muscadelle are vinified. Some sweet whites are also produced in Graves, but they generally fall short of the luscious wines of nearby Sauternes and Barsac.

The vineyards in and near Pessac along with Haut-Brion itself have progressively become surrounded by the suburbs of Bordeaux and stand as green oases amid urban sprawl, while lesser Graves vineyards also in the northern portion of the district closest to the city have been wiped out.

If yet another official classification of Graves is undertaken (and it ought to be), a number of the smaller, less renowned estates should be included, as they have been, for example, in Saint-Emilion. A number of relatively unknown Graves *crus* produce excellent wines that deserve recognition in the export markets.

Graves de Vayres.

This vinicultural area in Entre-Deux-Mers east of Bordeaux in southwestern France should not be confused with the Graves District of Bordeaux, where some of the world's greatest red wines are produced. Graves de Vayres produces both red and white wines, but few of great character. The area's name, like that of the celebrated Graves District itself, comes from the small pebbles, or gravel, that are prevalent in the soil.
☆/☆☆☆
$

Great Western.

Great Western is a brand name for the New York State wines produced by the Pleasant Valley Wine Co., which was acquired by the Taylor Wine Co. in 1962. Because of its name, a widespread impression exists that Great Western Champagne is from California. It has always been a New York wine, although some California wines shipped in bulk may find their way into the Great Western blend. After Taylor was acquired by the Coca-Cola Company in 1977, an upgrading program was begun for Great Western (as well as Taylor) wines. By 1981 a line of "Special Selection" Great Western table wines made from European hybrid grapes had been introduced, and the level of quality was high. All were vintage-dated, initially 1980, and a Vidal Ice Wine was of special interest to oenophiles who admire naturally sweet, late-harvested bottlings. Ten other varietals were marketed under the Great Western name in the remarkable 1980 vintage, and the company also upgraded its generic chablis, Rhine, rosé, and burgundy. In 1983 Taylor and the other Coca-Cola wine properties were acquired by Seagram's, and further changes were likely under the new ownership. (*See* Taylor Wine Co.)
☆/☆☆
$/$$

Greco.

The Greco is a variety of grape widely cultivated in Italy. On labels it normally appears with the name of the town or region of production. Among the better known are Greco di Bianco, Greco di Gerace, Greco di Todi, and Greco di Tufo. Perhaps the best of these is Greco di Tufo, which is a rich and full-bodied white produced in Campania, east of Naples. The grape here yields a dark yellow, highly concentrated juice that is almost immediately separated from the skins and is fined, or filtered, with gelatin or egg whites, to assure that the resulting wine is not overly heavy and oxidized. The wine tends to be yellowish in color and slightly musty in bouquet. In other parts of Italy the Greco is sometimes vinified light and dry but often slightly sweet. The Greco di Gerace of the Calabria region is made partly from *passito*, or grapes that have been allowed to turn into raisins. The result is a sweet wine that is often fortified up to 19 or 20 percent alcohol. As it ages it turns slightly tawny in color and displays a fairly pungent bouquet. Greco di Todi comes from the Umbria region and usually is vinified slightly sweet.

☆/☆☆☆

$/$$

Greece.

Thousands of years ago in ancient Greece there arose the cult of Dionysus, the God of Wine, who won followers all over the world and made wine an important item in trade. Homer's *Iliad* and *Odyssey* are sprinkled with references to wine and wine-dark seas, and wine played a major role in Greek tragedy. Such was its prominence in ancient Greek life that it must have been a wonderful potion indeed—far superior to the coarse and resiny products of the grape that seem to dominate the Greek wine trade nowadays. In Greek restaurants the word *retsina*, for resin, is synonymous with wine, and it appears that the majority of Greek table wines have been laced with the stuff, which imparts a turpentine-like taste that is not altogether unpleasant, especially when the wines are served well chilled. These wines seem especially pleasant when drunk with oily Greek food, but they are somewhat overpowering when consumed with more delicate cuisines.

The Peloponnesan Peninsula produces the largest volume of Greek wines, and the best of them are rather sweet. One of these is Mavrodaphne, a surprisingly flavorful red. Others from the area include Demestica, Santa Helena, and Antika. From Attica come Hymettus, Marco, and Pallini. Macedonia, along the Yugoslavian and Bulgarian frontier, produces both reds and whites, and superior wines are made on the Islands of Rhodes, Crete, Thíra, and Samos. Monemvasia is a type of wine from anywhere in Greece, rather than from a particular district, and it is usually fairly sweet. The name Monemvasia is believed to be the derivation of several other types of grapes and wines from other parts of the world: the Malmsey of Madeira, Malvasia of Italy, Malvoisie of France, and Malvagia of Spain, although it is not clear whether they are actually related in anything more than name.

Greenstone Winery.

Stan and Karen Van Spanje and Durward and Jane Fowler founded Greenstone early in 1980 in the historic Jackson Valley of Amador County, California, the land of the Gold Rush of the last century. Twenty-three acres have been planted in vines, including ten in French Colombard, six in Zinfandel, and smaller amounts in Palomino and Chenin Blanc. Amador County is famous for its robust and textured Zinfandels, and Greenstone's first crush, in 1981, consisted of 40 tons of Zinfandel grapes purchased from Bowman Vineyards of the nearby Shenandoah Valley. A white, rosé, and red Zinfandel were vinified. An Amador Cream Sherry also was cellared, and French Colombard was added to the roster in 1982. Production has grown to about 5000 cases a year.

☆/☆☆☆

$/$$

Grey Riesling.

Grey Riesling is not a true Riesling, but is the anglicized name of the Chauché Gris grape variety used in minor and undistinguished wines in parts of France. In California the grape produces a fresh white wine not unlike Sylvaner. It was first popularized by Wente Brothers and it is still one of their best-selling wines. Many other domestic producers now offer this varietal and, when properly made, it can represent good value among domestic white wines. It is vaguely similar to German Rieslings, but the better American types are usually somewhat drier.

Grgich Hills Cellars.

Miljenko "Mike" Grgich is one of men who helped put California wines on the world wine map. While working at Château Montelena, another Napa Valley winery, as the winemaker in 1973, he made a Chardonnay that took first place in a widely publicized blind tasting

competition in Paris in 1976, defeating many of the finest white Burgundies from France and signaling the presence of California wines among the world's best. Born in Croatia-Yugoslavia, he grew up as the son of a vineyard owner and recalls stomping the grapes when he was three years old. He still speaks with the rolling accent of his native land.

With backing from Austin Hills, formerly of Hills Brothers Coffee, he went into business for himself at Grgich Hills Cellars in Rutherford in the Napa Valley in 1977. His first Chardonnays made that year won prizes, and he has been winning prizes ever since. Most of the grapes for the Grgich Hills operation are grown on the 20 acres adjacent to the winery or on the 140 acres planted elsewhere by Austin Hills. Mike Grgich (pronounced Gur-gich) would prefer to produce only Chardonnay, at which he has proven himself a master, but he recognizes the need for diversity, even though total production is not much over 10,000 cases a year. There are also a Grgich dry Fumé Blanc, Johannisberg Riesling, Cabernet Sauvignon, and Zinfandel of excellent quality.

☆☆/☆☆☆

$$/$$$

Grignolino.

Grignolino is the light red and rosé wine made in huge quantities in the Piedmont region of northern Italy and in small quantities in California and a few other places. It should be drunk young and slightly chilled. Some versions, e.g., the Grignolino d'Asti and the Grignolino del Monferrato Casalese, have won D.O.C. recognition under the Italian wine law.

☆

$

Château Grillet.

One of the rarest white wines of France comes from the tiny vineyard of Château Grillet on the west bank of the Rhône River about a half mile from the water. Since 1936 Grillet has had its own *appellation contrôlée,* one of the smallest parcels in France to merit such a distinction. The vineyard is less than five acres in size and runs up a steep, terraced hillside from the village of Vérin in the broader geographical area known as Condrieu. Because of the steep slope, each vine of Grillet is tied to stakes to prevent it from leaning downhill, and all of the harvesting is accomplished by hand, with a work force totaling 25, picking over two days. An average harvest is 10,000 bottles, although a bumper crop of 14,000 was brought in during the 1980 vintage.

The wines of Grillet, made from the Viognier grape that also produces Condrieu, spend 18 months in wooden casks, much of this time in contact with the lees, or grape sediment. The wine is bone dry, with a slightly citric flavor melded with nuances of wood and the subtly earthy quality that is common to many of the whites of the northern Rhône Valley. The vineyard has been owned for many years by the Neyret-Gachet family, and their "château" is an old stone mansion built on many levels at the end of a steep dirveway adjacent to the vineyard. The cellar is 20 feet wide by 60 feet deep and contains 34 barrels in all, capable of holding two vintages at a time. The walls are three feet thick, built that way to repel invaders hundreds of years ago. Part of the house was standing at the time that the Mayflower landed at Plymouth Rock. Contrary to a popular impression, the majority of the production of Château Grillet is not sold at La Pyramide, the celebrated restaurant founded by Fernand Point in Vienne. Grillet is available in the U.S.

☆☆☆

$$$

Château Gruaud-Larose.

This is one of two well-known Bordeaux estates operated by the Cordier family, the other being Château Talbot, also in Saint-Julien. Gruaud-Larose was rated a *second cru,* or second growth, in the Bordeaux classification of 1855, and it deserves this high ranking. Its wines are full-bodied and fairly intense, with a rich bouquet. On wine lists all over the world, the château's name is frequently misspelled to read "Grand" Larose; the wine may be *grand,* but the name is Gruaud, pronounced Grew-oh, accenting the second syllable.

☆☆☆☆

$$/$$$

Guenoc Winery.

Guenoc Winery was established in 1981 in Guenoc Valley, Lake County, California, on property once owned and cultivated by Lillie Langtry, the British actress who was the toast of London society in the late 1880s and was said to have engaged in a liaison with the Prince of Wales. The present owners, Bob and Orville Magoon, have replanted the original vineyard as well as 250 additional acres and have plans to use the recently renovated Langtry house to promote their wines. About 7500 cases of Guenoc were produced in 1980, followed by 20,000 cases in 1981, with a projected goal of 100,000 cases a year of Cabernet Sauvignon, Zinfandel, Petite Sirah, Chardonnay, Sauvignon Blanc, and Chenin Blanc. The initial vintages were made partly from purchased grapes. The vineyard has been managed for the Magoons by Roy Raymond, Jr., of Raymond Vineyards in the Napa Valley, and the wines have been made by his brother, Walter.

☆/☆☆☆

$$

Grumello.

Some very good red wines are produced from the Nebbiolo grape in the Valtellina subdivision of Lombardy in northern Italy east of the Piedmont region. Grumello is one of these, lying just to the east of the Inferno. Grumello is not quite as intense and robust as Inferno or the nearby Valgella and reaches maturity at a younger age, after perhaps four years.

☆☆/☆☆☆

$/$$

Grüner Veltliner.

The Grüner Veltliner is a white grape that is widely cultivated in Austria, where it may account for as much as one-third of total vineyard plantings. Very good dry table wines are made from the Grüner Veltliner, but it is often vinified sweet as well, and these wines—best used with *foie gras* or sweet desserts—can be very special. The grape is also cultivated in Hungary and Yugoslavia.

☆/☆☆

$/$$

Emilio Guglielmo Winery.

Emilio Guglielmo is a third-generation winery founded in 1925 by Emilio Guglielmo and presently operated by his grandsons, George and Eugene Guglielmo, at Morgan Hill in California's Santa Clara County. A line of low-priced varietals is produced, along with a line of jug wines. Production totals some 65,000 cases a year.

☆/☆☆

$/$$

Guild Wineries and Distilleries.

Guild is an integrated cooperative owned by the California wineries that make up its membership. The members deliver their grapes to Guild, mostly at the Central Cellars in Lodi, and then are paid according to the quantities they deliver and how much the cooperative can earn from them in the marketplace. Guild crushes grapes in six different quality categories and turns out 5.5 million cases annually. Much of the total, more than 3.2 million cases, is accounted for by B. Cribari and Sons in Fresno, one of the cooperative's members. The other members are Bear Creek Winery in Lodi, Del Rio Winery in Lodi, Fresno Winery in Fresno, L.K. Marshall Winery in Delano, and McCall Winery in Sanger, as well as Cresta Blanca Winery in Ukiah, which is the only member that bottles on its own premises rather than in the Central Cellars.

As an "integrated" cooperative, Guild handles all marketing, production, and distribution for its members. Most of the wines are in the so-called "popular-priced" category, which means basically jug wines, although about $10^1/_2$ percent of the production is in single bottles. The product lineup runs through varietal, generic, sparkling wines, brandy, and vermouth. Guild, whose president for some years has been Robert M. Ivie, also vinifies considerable quantities of grapes that are sold as bulk wine to other producers that do not belong to the cooperative. Finished wines, Sherries, brandies, and concentrates are among the products sold anonymously to other producers whose names Guild does not disclose. But Gallo, Almadén, and Paul Masson are believed to be among the Guild customers. Guild's headquarters are in San Francisco.

☆/☆☆

$

Gundlach-Bundschu Winery.

This winery traces its origins back to 1858 and is now a family business run by Jim Bundschu, who represents the fifth generation with the winery, and by his brother-in-law, John Merritt, Jr. The winery and vineyards have existed in the same place in Vineburg in California's Sonoma County since the beginning, but Jim Bundschu's grandmother was a prohibitionist who saw to it that the winery did not operate during Prohibition. It was revived in 1970 by Jim and his late father Towle Bundschu, and the winery was rebuilt and modernized by 1973. Gundlach-Bundschu owns some 375 acres of vineyards on three different ranches in Sonoma County. Substantial quantities of grapes are sold to Sebastiani under a long-standing contract, so Gundlach-Bundschu must buy about 20 percent of its grape requirements from outside growers despite its acreage in vines. Case production will total about 30,000 per year until the Sebastiani contract expires, at which point those grapes probably will be used for the Gundlach-Bundschu line of varietals, which includes Cabernet Sauvignon, Zinfandel, Pinot Noir, Merlot, Johan-

nisberg Riesling, Sonoma Riesling (made mostly from Sylvaner grapes), Gewürztraminer, Chardonnay, and Kleinberger (a German variety rare in the United States). The Cabernet Sauvignon made from grapes grown on the Batto Ranch is one of the better Cabernets produced in California.
☆/☆☆☆
$$

Gutturnio dei Colli Piacentini.

Gutturnio is a deeply colored red of good quality made from 60 percent Barbera and 40 percent Bonarda grapes in the Emilia-Romagna region of Italy. It is vinified dry as well as sweet, and there is also a spumante version. It has been accorded D.O.C. recognition under the Italian wine law.
☆☆☆
$

· H ·

Hacienda Wine Cellars.

On part of the estate originally established by Count Agoston Haraszthy in the 1850s near Sonoma, California, lies Hacienda Wine Cellars, a producer of high-quality premium varietal wines. Haraszthy was the Hungarian who traveled to Europe and brought back thousands of European vine cuttings that provided the basis for the premium wine industry in California. His original estate was Buena Vista Vineyards, purchased in 1943 by Frank H. Bartholomew, a San Francisco newspaperman, who revived Buena Vista and later sold it to the Young's Market Company, which sold it to a German concern in 1979. But Bartholomew retained the property that is now Hacienda Wine Cellars, which was established in 1973 in an existing building constructed in 1926, which once served as the Sonoma Valley Hospital. In 1976 control of Hacienda was purchased by Crawford Cooley, an investment banker whose family held vineyards in Sonoma County since 1860. Steve MacRostie, who has a degree in oenology from the University of California at Davis, has been the winemaker since 1974.

Some of the grapes for Hacienda's wines are produced on the 50-acre vineyard adjacent to the winery that Bartholomew kept separate from Buena Vista, and some are purchased from other growers. Hacienda's oak-aged Chardonnay is a rich, complex wine. The other whites include Chenin Blanc, Johannisberg Riesling, and Gewürztraminer, and the reds are Cabernet Sauvignon, Zinfandel, and Pinot Noir. Hacienda also makes an interesting California Port. Production now totals more than 20,000 cases a year.
☆/☆☆☆
$$

Hallgartener.

This is not one of the better-known wines of Germany's formidable Rheingau region, but its quality is high. The village of Hallgarten lies up in the hills above the Rhine River, some 1000 feet above sea level, near Hattenheim, and the famous Steinberg vineyard, which is technically in Hattenheim but is really closer to the village of Hallgarten. Because of the proximity of the Steinberg, some of the Hallgarteners, especially those from the Deutelsberg, Jungfer and Schönhell vineyards, are well known to connoisseurs of good values. They are big and robust wines that achieve high levels of quality after long, hot summers, but they have a reputation for being sub-par when the weather conditions are not ideal. Hallgarteners should not be confused with the German wine shipping firm of the same name, whose wines are widely marketed in the United States.

Among the better vineyards of Hallgarten are the following:

Hallgartener Deez
Hallgartener Deutelsberg
Hallgartener Frühenberg
Hallgartener Hendelberg*
Hallgartener Jungfer*

Hallgartener Kirchgrube
Hallgartener Kirschenacker
Hallgartener Mehrhölzchen*
Hallgartener Rosengarten
Hallgartener Schönhell*
Hallgartener Würzgarten*

An asterisk (*) indicates vineyard names that survived or that were created in the revision of the German wine law of 1971. The Mehrhölzchen is now a *Grosslage,* or large vineyard area, similar to a generic term for Hallgarten wines.
☆/☆☆
$/$$

Hamlet Hill Vineyards.

Hamlet Hill is a new winery in Pomfret, Connecticut, owned by A. W. Loos, whose modernistic nearby residence is called Elsinore. Vines under cultivation there include both European and European–American hybrids. A red blend called Brunonian Reserve has been bottled for the exclusive use of Brown University in nearby Providence, Rhode Island.
☆/☆☆
$/$$

Hanzell.

In the late 1940s, James D. Zellerbach, U.S. Ambassador to Italy, bought 16 acres in Sonoma. He had become such a fan of the wines of Burgundy that he was determined to produce similar wines on his own estate in California. He built a winery modeled after the great château at Clos de Vougeot, hired winemaker Bradford Webb, a fine oenologist trained at the University of California at Davis, and began to make Chardonnay and Pinot Noir as close to the style of Burgundy wines as possible. He ordered the same oak barrels he had seen in the cellars of Romanée-Conti and Montrachet. It was generally agreed when the first wines appeared in 1956 that they did indeed possess the inimitable Burgundy character and style that had so far eluded the California winemakers who sought it. The answer was partly in the wood used for aging. New oak from Limousin, Nevers, or Yugoslavia imparts unmistakable flavor and bouquet, quite different from that of American white oak.

Zellerbach died in 1963 and the winery was closed down for a while until Douglas and Mary Day bought it in 1965. They sold out in 1975 to Barbara deBrye, an English woman who resides in her native country but pays frequent visits to Hanzell. Bob Sessions has been the general manager since 1973 and is responsible for the continued high quality of the Hanzell wines, which come from 32 acres of Sonoma vineyards. Production remains very modest at about 2000 cases a year, but the Hanzell reputation is big. Besides the Chardonnay and Pinot Noir, there are plantings of Cabernet Sauvignon, Malbec, Merlot, Cabernet Franc, and Petit Verdot that will be used to produce a Bordeaux-style red.
☆/☆☆☆☆
$$/$$$

J. J. Haraszthy & Son.

This wine business, established in 1977, represents a revival of sorts of a famous California wine name. It was Count Agoston Haraszthy who brought thousands of European vine cuttings from Europe to California in the last century and was responsible for a big share of the success of the Golden State's wine industry with superior European varietal wines. Count Haraszthy's own property was Buena Vista, which still operates. The people behind the relatively new J. J. Haraszthy operation are Jan James Haraszthy and his son Vallejo Haraszthy, direct descendants of the count. Jan Haraszthy worked at Buena Vista before opening his own winery with his son. They neither crush nor ferment grapes at their facility, but buy grapes from other Sonoma County producers and have them crushed elsewhere. The wines are finished in the Haraszthy cellars. This complicated arrangement is a result of zoning laws, whereby the Haraszthy operation has a "blender's" license rather than a grower's license. Haraszthy has been selling 5000 to 8000 cases of premium varietals a year and is under contract to a national distributor to raise its output to 15,000 cases a year. The bulk of the production is in Zinfandel, but the enterprise also turns out Pinot Noir, Pinot Noir Blanc, Chardonnay, Gewürztraminer, and Johannisberg Riesling.
☆/☆☆☆
$$

Harbor Winery.

Charles Myers, an English teacher at Sacramento City College, is one of the pioneers of California Zinfandels produced in Amador County, which is increasingly being recognized as the prime Zinfandel-growing area of the state. Myers first made Amador Zinfandel in 1964, long before it was fashionable, and introduced Bob Trinchero of Sutter Home Winery to the Amador phenomenon, an introduction that led to a major commitment to the region by Sutter Home. The Harbor Winery is located in West Sacramento and produces Cabernet Sauvignon, Chardonnay, and Mission del Sol as well as Zinfandel. The winery was not commercial until 1972 and production remains small at fewer than 2000 cases a year.
☆/☆☆☆
$$

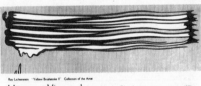

Hargrave Vineyard Long Island Chardonnay "Collection Series" 1981
Estate Grown. Produced & Bottled By Hargrave Vineyard, Cutchogue, N.Y. 13.0% Alcohol By Volume
The bottling consists of 575 cases, 250 magnums and 21 double magnums, offered for sale in New York only.

Hargrave Vineyard.

On Long Island's North Fork near the village of Cutchogue is the Hargrave Vineyard, owned and operated by Alex and Louisa Hargrave, who are demonstrating that the warming influence of the Atlantic Gulf Stream as it flows past the easternmost tip of New York State can help in the cultivation of Eu-

Deaver Vineyard Unfined Unfiltered

HARBOR WINERY
1976
Amador County
CABERNET SAUVIGNON

Produced and bottled by Harbor Winery
West Sacramento, California
Alcohol 13.5 % by Volume

ropean grapes. Alex Hargrave, with a Master's degree in Chinese from Harvard, and Louisa, with a Master's in education from Simmons College, established their operation in 1973 with their first plantings and converted an old potato barn to a winery in 1975, the year of their first commerical crop. Since then production has risen past 10,000 cases a year of such varietals as Cabernet Sauvignon, Pinot Noir, Merlot, Chardonnay, Sauvignon Blanc, Riesling, and Gewürztraminer. About 55 acres have been planted and more plantings are taking place. The Hargraves have some 400 barrels made of French, Yugoslavian, and American oak for aging their wines. The Cabernet Sauvignon, for example, spends about two and a half years in wood before bottling. The Hargrave wines in general sometimes lack the complexity and balance of comparably priced wines made from the same grape varieties in California, but they seem to keep improving with each vintage, and the Hargrave Chardonnays are often equal to the better California Chardonnays. The vineyard has become the most successful in New York State producing European varietals, largely because of the special microclimate on the North Fork.

☆/☆☆☆
$$

Hattenheimer.

Of the great vineyards of Germany, those surrounding Hattenheim in the Rheingau are among the best of all. The wines are big and have great character, displaying all of the better qualities that the Riesling grape is capable of producing. The most famous Hattenheimer, indeed one of the most renowned wines made in Germany, comes from the Steinberg vineyard on the hillside well back of the Rhine River. So famous is this vineyard that it is one of the few German wines whose labels do not bear the name of the town. They say simply "Steinberger" along with the other information required under Germany's wine law. The vineyard itself, consisting of more than 60 acres, is owned by the German state and is perhaps the country's most prized wine possession. Steinbergers are the biggest, most assertive of Germany's white wines, sometimes overwhelming in their power and body, but they also have great elegance and finesse, while sometimes lacking in delicacy. The vineyard is surrounded by a wall, just as the Clos de Vougeot in Burgundy is walled, and was established by monks of the same Cistercian order that created the Burgundian vineyard hundreds of years ago.

Nearby is Kloster Eberbach, the magnificent Gothic monastery which the Cistercians took over in the early twelfth century. It was secularized under Napoleon after becoming one of the best-known outposts of the German wine trade. Today it is owned by the state, which bottles and stores its Steinbergers there along with many of the other wines produced in German State Domains. The walls of the Kloster's tasting room are lined with bottles from famous vintages, including some from the vintages of the 1930s that bear the Nazi swastika on their labels. The cellar, with arched ceilings 30 feet tall, contains big casks with vineyard names stenciled in white on their butts. The cellar once served as a hospital under the Cistercians, but it is hard to imagine a hospital that remains so chilly for most of the year. The temperature is obviously more conducive to the good health of wines than humans.

Although the Steinberg vineyard and Kloster Eberbach tend to overshadow the town itself, Hattenheim is a delightful little place with narrow streets and quaint old houses. More than 400 acres of vineyards outside the walls of the

Steinberg are entitled to the Hattenheim name, and some of the wines produced in them rank among the best of the Rheingau, which means the best in Germany. The Graf von Schönborn has his cellars in Hattenheim, where he bottles and ages not only his Hattenheimers but also the wines from his extensive other holdings in the Rheingau.

Among the better known vineyards at Hattenheim are the following:

Hattenheimer Aliment
Hattenheimer Bergweg
Hattenheimer Bitz
Hattenheimer Boden
Hattenheimer Boxberg
Hattenheimer Deutelsberg*
Hattenheimer Dillmetz
Hattenheimer Engelmannsberg*
Hattenheimer Gasserweg
Hattenheimer Geiersberg
Hattenheimer Hassel*
Hattenheimer Heiligenberg*
Hattenheimer Hinterhausen
Hattenheimer Kilb
Hattenheimer Klosterberg
Hattenheimer Mannberg*
Hattenheimer Nussbrunnen*
Hattenheimer Pfaffenberg*
Hattenheimer Pflanzer
Hattenheimer Rothenberg
Hattenheimer Schützenhäuschen*
Hattenheimer Stabel
Hattenheimer Weiher
Hattenheimer Willborn
Steinberg*
Hattenheimer Wisselbrunnen*

An asterisk (*) indicates vineyard names that were created or that survived in the revision of the German wine law of 1971. The survival of the name does not always indicate that the same vineyard boundaries are being observed, because many smaller vineyards were merged into larger ones. The Steinberg vineyard became a suburb of Hattenheim so that it could retain its traditional name. The only difference now is that Steinberg is, in effect, a place where a vineyard that is also called Steinberg happens to exist. Thus the Steinberger wine is no longer technically a Hattenheimer. The Deutelsberg is now a *Grosslage,* or large vineyard area, similar to a generic wine from Hattenheim.

☆/☆☆☆☆
$/$$$

Château Haut-Bailly.

Château Haut-Bailly, often confused with Château Haut-Batailley of Pauillac in the Médoc, is a very good estate lying in the *commune* of Léognan in the district of Graves, south of Bordeaux. Haut-Bailly makes soft, rich and full-bodied wines that lack the hardness characteristic of some other red Graves, probably because the vineyard is less than 50 percent Cabernet Sauvignon and contains a nearly equal amount of Merlot, a somewhat softer grape. The 1964 vintage Haut-Bailly was a luscious wine that established a strong reputation for the estate in the United States and England, although it reached its peak by the early 1970s. The estate was classified a *grand cru* in the Graves classification of 1959. Production is relatively small; the vineyard is less than 40 acres.
☆☆☆☆
$$/$$$

Château Haut-Batailley.

Château Haut-Batailley has achieved substantial improvement in recent years as a result of the devoted efforts of Jean-Eugène Borie, who also is the proprietor of Château Ducru-Beaucaillou and Château Grand-Puy-Lacoste. Haut-Batailley, which lies in the Bordeaux *commune* of Pauillac, actually is owned by Borie's sister, Madame des Brest-Borie. The château was accorded fifth growth, or *cinquième cru*, status in the Bordeaux

classification of 1855. Its wines have been rich and elegant in recent vintages.
☆☆☆☆
$$/$$$

Château Haut-Beychevelle-Gloria.

The vineyard of Château Haut-Bey-chevelle-Gloria is a very small parcel within the estate of Château Gloria, lying roughly between Gloria and Château Beychevelle on a small hill in the plain of Saint Julien in the Bordeaux Médoc. It is owned by Henri Martin, mayor of Saint Julien, proprietor of Château Gloria and Château Saint-Pierre, who is the former manager of Château Latour. It was managed by Martin's father before him. Production is very limited, but the wine is sometimes as good as that of Château Gloria itself, although it usually is less expensive and therefore can be good value in superior vintages. (*See* Château Gloria.)
☆☆☆/☆☆☆☆
$$

Château Haut-Brion.

In 1855, when the red wines of the Médoc District just north of Bordeaux were classified according to quality, the wines of one château outside the Médoc were included. Château Haut-Brion, in the *commune* of Pessac in the district of Graves directly south of Bordeaux, was designated a first growth, or *premier cru classé*, along with three great Médocs: Châteaux Lafite, Latour, and Margaux. (Château Mouton Rothschild, classified a second growth in 1855, was elevated to first-growth status in 1973, so there are now five first growths.) Haut-Brion was drawn into the 1855 classification because of the consistent superiority of its red wines over a period of years and because of the relatively high prices brought by them in the open market. So great was the renown of Haut-Brion that it would have been unthinkable to leave it out, although all of the other châteaux of Graves were omitted.

Haut-Brion's reds are classic Graves—full-bodied, rich, and elegant, although perhaps not as big and fleshy as some of the Médocs produced farther north. Yet Haut-Brion remains an excellent red wine, with a balance and dryness that are hard to match. It ages gracefully and tends to reach proper maturity only after 20 years, although the superb 1970 and '71 vintages were just as precocious at Haut-Brion as elsewhere in Bordeaux and should reach their peaks somewhat sooner than normal. Haut-Brion Blanc, an excellent white Graves, is also produced in small quantities and tends to be quite costly. It is flinty and dry, ranking as one of the best white Bordeaux, and is a superb accompaniment to shellfish and lobster. The white vines at Haut-Brion were transplanted from the exquisite Château d'Yquem vineyard in Sauternes in the hope that a sweet wine of equal or similar quality could be made in Pessac. But the *vignerons* at Haut-Brion discovered that these same vines that produced such a luscious sweet wine at the illustrious Yquem made a very good dry wine at Haut-Brion—a rare demonstration of how important the soil is in wine production.

The estate is one of several in Bordeaux that are American-owned. The heirs of the late Clarence Dillon, including his son Douglas Dillon, the former U.S. Secretary of the Treasury, are the proprietors, although the management is under Jean Delmas. The name Haut-Brion, contrary to one popular theory in Great Britain, is not a "Franglais" version of O'Brien, although the pronunciation is quite similar. In the early 1500s a Manor of Brion existed in the area, and its name passed through various versions, including d'Obrion and Hault-Brion. The estate went through the hands of various officials of Bordeaux and Libourne, where the Saint-Emilion trade is based, and a portion was taken over by the government during the French Revolution. Talleyrand owned it from 1801 to 1804.

The soil at Haut-Brion epitomizes Graves, which got its name from the gravelly terrain. The stones and pebbles through which the vines grow not only reflect the heat of the sun back onto the grapes in daytime, but also retain the heat of the day well into the evening, enabling the grapes to ripen more readily than at vineyards less favorably situated. Urban sprawl has virtually enveloped Haut-Brion, and it is now an oasis of roughly 100 acres amid the encroachments of Bordeaux on the road to Arcachon on the Atlantic Coast to the west. Directly across the road lies Château La Mission-Haut-Brion, another excellent red Graves vineyard that was acquired by Domaines Clarence Dillon in 1983, bringing the two most illustrious estates of Graves under one ownership.
☆☆☆☆
$$$/$$$$

Haywood Winery.

Haywood undertook its first plantings in 1975 and made its first wines in 1980 in Sonoma, California, on a 100-acre tract called Los Chamigal Vineyards. All of the wines are estate-bottled, and production has risen to about 6000 cases annually of Cabernet Sauvignon, Zinfandel, Chardonnay, White Riesling, and a blended white wine.
☆/☆☆☆
$/$$

Hectare.

In Europe, vineyards are measured not in terms of acres but in hectares, the metric measure of surface area. One hectare equals 2.471 acres, or 10,000 square meters. Rounding off to 2½ acres per hectare is a common practice among Americans not accustomed to metric measurements.

Hectoliter.

A hectoliter is a measure of liquid volume amounting to 100 liters, or 26.42 American gallons. The hectoliter is the standard measurement for French wines sold in bulk.

Heitz Cellar.

In a picturesque stone winery off the Silverado Trail in California's Napa Valley, Joe Heitz pursues with vigor his ideal of superior wines. He is acknowledged inside California and out as one of the prime forces in bringing worldwide attention to wines from the Napa Valley. Many of his wines are excellent; some are merely good, but generally, in such cases, that was his intention—to make honest, agreeable wines reasonably priced for daily drinking. Lots of people wonder why, with his gift for making extraordinary wines, he insists on making such a wide range of them, including eight varietals as well as fortified wines and Champagne. But Heitz is a man of tireless energy and wide-ranging curiosities. He makes certain wines because they intrigue him. He was one of the first to make special lots of wine from designated vineyards and at various times may have three different lots of Cabernet Sauvignon available. Like many of the better winemakers in Napa he holds back some batches of superior wine for further maturing and development in bottle, releasing them in stages. Naturally they are more expensive but well worth trying when you can find one. 1968 was a fine year for Cabernet in Napa Valley and one of the best wines from that vintage is the Heitz Cabernet from "Martha's Vineyard," a hugely round wine with many years of life remaining in it. It has now become very rare and expensive.

The Martha's Vineyard Cabernets often display a minty flavor that is highly unusual. But at the same time the fullness of the Martha's Vineyard is so great and the depth of fruit so enormous that it is usually among the best Cabernets made in California in each vintage. In more recent years Heitz has introduced other individually named Cabernets, including "Bella Oaks" and "Fay Vineyard," neither of which quite measures up to the Martha's Vineyard. The 1974 Martha's, some of which was bottled with a special anniversary label, has become a collector's item and may well be one of the best Cabernets ever produced in California.

Heitz inherited a vineyard planted with Grignolino grapes, a variety used for making some of the great Piedmont wines of northern Italy. In California the wine is not quite so hearty but nevertheless very agreeable. A blend of vintages, it will keep well but does not improve in bottle. Another special pet of Joe's is Angelica, a rich and mellow dessert wine which he tends with loving care. Heitz also makes a sound and balanced Pinot Noir and a Chardonnay of depth and complexity.

☆/☆☆☆☆

$/$$$$

Hermitage.

One of the great wines of France is produced at Tain-l'Hermitage north of Valence in the Rhône River District. It is Hermitage, from the hill by the same name overlooking the river from the east bank, where wine has been produced since the days of the Roman occupation. Both red and white are made there, but the reds are the better. They are robust and full-bodied, with a dark color and a strong, flowery bouquet. In their youth they tend to have a certain harshness which takes years of bottle-age to soften into the smooth and elegant wine that a great Hermitage can be. Twenty years is not too long to wait for it to develop, because Hermitage is one of the longest-lived wines of France. It has also been described as the most "manly" of all wines because of its robust character. It is made mostly from the Syrah grape, the principal red grape of the Rhône District, and is similar in personality to the Châteauneuf-du-Pape that comes from farther south in the Rhône, although connoisseurs are convinced that no Châteauneuf could ever achieve the depth and fullness of a good Hermitage.

The wine takes its name from a hermit who planted vines and meditated on the hillside above Tain after one of the crusades of the early thirteenth century. He was the knight Gaspard de Stérimberg who, according to folklore, gave wine to his many visitors, who praised it so much that Hermitage at one time was listed among the most famous reds of France. The production is relatively small, however, and the wine is the most expensive of the Rhône, so it is not as well known as it used to be. The hillside is divided into relatively small, terraced parcels called *mas*, whose names are sometimes applied to the wines produced there. Hermitage *blanc* is a dry, earthy, and full-bodied white. The most widely available one seems to be the Chante-Alouette produced by Chapoutier. It is long-lived for a white and bears a resemblance to white Châteauneuf-du-Pape.

Red Hermitage is the classic accompaniment to smoked meats and full-flavored game, such as wild boar, venison, and wild goose. It also goes well with most red meats and strong cheeses. After five years or so of bottle-age, the wine begins to throw sediment, and properly mature vintages should be decanted. Just to the north of Tain is Crozes-Hermitage, which produces a larger quantity of often good wines, although rarely of the quality achieved by Hermitage itself. A Crozes-Hermitage will be ready for consumption at a much younger age and can represent excellent value in good vintages, when it displays more depth and character than, for example, a simple Côtes-du-Rhône. (*See* Rhone Valley.)
☆☆☆☆
$$/$$$

Heron Hill Vineyards.

A valiant struggle against the weather is being waged by Peter Johnstone of Heron Hill Vineyards in Hammondsport, New York, focal point of the state's Finger Lakes wine region. At Heron Hill, on a sloping vineyard, Johnstone has plantings of Chardonnay and Riesling, two of the most popular European grape varieties, and the winter weather in New York does not treat them kindly. In some vintages, such as 1980, the Heron Hill Chardonnay and Riesling are superb examples of what the European *Vitis vinifera* vine can accomplish in the state. In other years, such as 1981, winter freeze can kill the vines right back to the ground, wiping out the crop. To make up for such eventualities, Johnstone also produces European-American hybrids, which are more durable. These include Aurora, Seyval Blanc, Cayuga, and Ravat, most of which are grown by his partner, John Ingle, Jr., in a separate vineyard. In a good year Heron Hill grows 80 percent of its own grapes and buys 20 percent. In a poor year the reverse can be the case. The Chardonnay is oak-aged, and the Riesling is crisp and clean.
☆/☆☆
$/$$

High Tor Vineyard.

High Tor is one of the most charming vineyard sites in America, its 78 acres nestled into the top of a craggy mountain on the western bank of the Hudson River only 28 miles from New York City. High Tor was founded in 1949 by playwright Everett Crosby, a Californian who had long yearned to have his own vineyard and make his own wines. He named the vineyard, appropriately enough, after the mountain that Maxwell Anderson immortalized in his Pulitzer Prize-winning play, *High Tor*.

Crosby retired to the Caribbean in 1971 and sold the estate, but since then production has been halted and High Tor's future is uncertain.

William Hill Winery.

William Hill started making wines in 1976 after becoming convinced that the best grapes came from mountain vineyards. He began accumulating land along the western peaks of the Napa Valley, joining with a group of investors who remain with him, and later acquired property on the eastern hills above the valley, including a large parcel on Atlas Mountain above the Silverado Country Club. A winery was planned for this site, but meanwhile he has been crushing his grapes at a leased facility in the town of Napa after using facilities provided by other wineries, including Stonegate and Cuvaison. Plans call for a 20,000-case capacity at the new winery initially. His 1976 vintage totaled only 5000 cases and by 1980 his volume had crept up to 6400 cases.

Because of the mountainous locations of his vineyards, William Hill must settle for lower yields from his acreage. But the wines bearing the William Hill label—Cabernet Sauvignons and Chardonnays—are intensely flavored, with great varietal concentration. They are big and rich, wines of longevity that are hard to find because production is so small. Hill plans eventually to raise his production to 100,000 cases a year, once the new winery is completed and then expanded in a later phase of development. The wines are fairly expensive, but they are among the better selections from that rapidly expanding group of California wineries with small production but fierce devotion to quality.
☆/☆☆☆☆
$$/$$$

Hochheimer.

The only wines that truly have the right to be called "Hocks" are the ones from the village of Hochheim above the Main River a few miles upstream from its junction with the Rhine. The fame of Hochheimers spread far and wide during the reign of Queen Victoria of England because of her avowed partiality to hock and nowadays the word is used by the English to refer to any wine produced along the Rhine River in Germany. The wine lists in many English restaurants refer to hock when they really mean Rhine, and it seems too bad that

the identity of the wines of Hochheim has been obscured by such linguistic shortcuts. Nevertheless, Hochheimers are excellent wines and are classified as coming from the Rheingau, even though Hochheim is somewhat to the east. Their taste and character are comparable to the best of the Rheingau and certainly Hochheimers deserve to be ranked among the superior white wines of the world. They have great texture and bouquet even in vintages when other German wines fall short. The two best vineyards are generally agreed to be the Domdechaney and the Kirchenstück, although the Königen-Viktoria-Berg has achieved a certain celebrity because of its identification with the English monarch.

Among the better known vineyards at Hochheim are the following:

Hochheimer Beine
Hochheimer Berg*
Hochheimer Daubhaus
Hochheimer Domdechaney*
Hochheimer Falkenberg
Hochheimer Gehitz
Hochheimer Hofmeister*
Hochheimer Hölle*
Hochheimer Kirchenstück*
Hochheimer Königen-Viktoria-Berg*
Hochheimer Neuberg
Hochheimer Raaber
Hochheimer Rauchloch
Hochheimer Reichesthal*
Hochheimer Sommerheil*
Hochheimer Stein*
Hochheimer Steinern Kreuz
Hochheimer Stielweg*
Hochheimer Wiener

An asterisk (*) indicates vineyard names that survived or that were created in the revision of the German wine law of 1971.
☆/☆☆☆
$/$$

Hoffman Mountain Ranch (HMR).

Dr. Stanley Hoffman, a cardiologist who moved his practice from southern California to Paso Robles, established Hoffman Mountain Ranch there in 1972. Within three years the San Luis Obispo County winery expanded into new facilities and later its Pinot Noir 1975 began finishing high in blind tastings in Paris and elsewhere, establishing an international reputation for the HMR wines. Dr. Hoffman had owned the ranch for 15 years and planted his first vines there in 1964 and '65. By the early 1980s, about 60 acres were bearing, but HMR still was buying most of its grapes from outside growers. The property, consisting of 1000 acres in all, had been planted in walnuts and almonds. The first fairly large vintage for HMR was the 1975, and now the annual production totals some 50,000 cases of Cabernet Sauvignon, Pinot Noir, Chardonnay, and Sylvaner produced mostly from HMR's own vines, plus White Riesling, Chenin Blanc, Cabernet Sauvignon, and Zinfandel, as well as some additional Chardonnay bought from other growers.

In 1980 HMR filed under Chapter XI of the Federal Bankruptcy Act and was being reorganized under protection from its creditors. (Chapter XI is the so-called voluntary bankruptcy law.) Under the reorganization plan, some 400 acres of the original 1000 were being sold off to raise cash, and new investment money was being sought. The bankruptcy filing occurred when a note came due and cash was not available to pay it off. Substantial quantities of wine were in the HMR inventory, and the use of the bankruptcy law was employed partly to enable these wines to reach maturity before being sold off to satisfy debts.
☆/☆☆☆
$$

Louis Honig, HNW Vineyards.

Excellent Sauvignon Blanc is produced under the Louis Honig label by HNW Vineyards in Rutherford, in California's Napa Valley The general partners include Bill Honig, Superintendent of Public Instruction for the State of California, and his brother-in-law, Superior Court Judge Daniel Weinstein. The winemaker is Rick Tracy, who also manages vineyards for Austin Hills. The Louis Honig label replaced the original HNW label in the 1982 vintage. The late Louis Honig, Bill Honig's father, bought the property in 1966, and the grapes were sold to other wineries until the family decided to produce some of their own wines, starting in 1980. The 1981 Sauvignon Blanc won a gold medal at the Orange County Fair in 1982.
☆/☆☆
$$

Hop Kiln Winery.

The Hop Kiln Winery building is one of the most picturesque in the California wine country and has landmark status. It was built in 1905 and was used for drying hops, an element in making beer and ale. The facility is located in the Sonoma Valley's Russian River region near Healdsburg and was converted to a winery in 1975 by Dr. Martin Griffin, Jr., a public health physician, who is the sole owner. Hop Kiln has about 75 acres in vines and also buys grapes from outside growers. Annual production amounts to some 10,000 cases of Zinfandel, Petite Sirah, Napa Gamay, Chardonnay, Gewürztraminer, French Colombard, and Riesling, both dry and late-harvested. Most of the cooperage for aging is American oak. The Zinfandel has developed a following among fanciers of this spicy varietal. The other Hop Kiln wines are less successful.
☆/☆☆☆
$/$$

NET CONTENT 1 PINT 8 FL. OZ.   PRODUCE OF FRANCE   ALC. STR. 13° BY VOLUME

GRANDS VINS
DES
Hospices de Beaune
Volnay-Santenots
APPELLATION CONTROLÉE
Cuvée Jehan de Massol
Adjudicataires
Roland Thévenin & Fils
Négociants-Eleveurs à Saint-Romain (Côte-d'Or)

Imported by : **Monsieur Henri Wines Ltd New-York-N.Y.**

Hospices de Beaune.

In the medieval city of Beaune, where the Burgundy wine trade has been centered for many years, stands a charity hospital built in 1443 by Nicolas Rolin, who was the tax collector for the Duke of Burgundy. It is known as the Hôtel Dieu, and is part of the Hospices de Beaune, which, as the plural form of the noun implies, is a charity house that includes other worthwhile interests besides the magnificent Hôtel Dieu itself. An orphanage is sponsored in Beaune, as well as the hospital, and local legend has it that Rolin started the project in expiation for the tax-collecting zeal that enabled him to amass a fortune. Like most other members of the Burgundian aristocracy of his day, he owned vineyards, and he and his wife Guigone de Salins left their vineyard holdings to the Hospices as an endowment. Over the years other Burgundians have done the same, and now many excellent vineyard parcels are cultivated for the benefit of the charity.

The most important social event of the year—and perhaps the most significant commerical event as well—is the annual wine auction in Beaune for the benefit of the Hospices. At one time it was held in the Hôtel Dieu itself, but the event has become so crowded that it is now held in the arcade that normally houses the agricultural market just off the central square of the town. Buyers come from all over the world, ostensibly to bid at the auction but more probably to partake of the revelry that attends the occasion. The auction is always scheduled for the third Sunday in November, and it involves three days of celebration that have come to be known as *Les Trois Glorieuses*. The festivities officially get under way with a feast in the splendid banquet hall of the Chevaliers du Tastevin at the Château du Clos de Vougeot on Saturday night, followed by the auction in Beaune after lunch on Sunday.

Then on Monday comes the *Paulée* in Meursault, to which the growers bring their own bottles for passing around the tables. A formidable constitution is required to survive the three days in good fettle, and it is said that only the men of Burgundy remain to sing the songs of their region by Monday evening when all of the outsiders have long since collapsed into bed for a day or two of respite and repose. The *Trois Glorieuses* represent the highlight of the year for the Chevaliers du Tastevin, who travel from all over the world to attend, but the central event of the three days, the auction, has more than social importance.

The Hospices de Beaune's endowment of vineyards involves more than 100 acres in the Côte de Beaune, and the wines from this acreage must be sold to generate the revenues that support the charity. Thus buyers can rationalize overbidding with the thought that it is all going for charity anyway. More important, however, the prices set at this auction serve as benchmarks for the price level of that particular vintage throughout Burgundy, and the system is not as far-fetched as it may seem. If economic conditions around the globe are such that a multitude of buyers gravitate to Beaune for the auction and bid up the prices for the wines of the Hospices, it is logical to suppose that comparable prices will be obtained for the other wines of the region.

Perhaps a thousand people jam the long hall where the bidding occurs, and many of them have generated considerable enthusiasm at the hearty pre-sale luncheons given at such splendid local restaurants as the Hôtel de la Poste and the Relais de Saulx. Tickets to gain entry are difficult to obtain for the individual who is not in the wine trade, and it is best to make arrangements far in advance with a shipper or hotel proprietor if you want to attend merely as an observer.

For the sake of tradition, the auction takes place *à la chandelle,* or according to the candle. Three candles are permitted to burn while each batch is being auctioned, and supposedly the last bid before the last candle burns out wins the wine. This system poses obvious difficulties, and it has become largely ceremonial in recent years, especially as the prices for good Burgundy wines have escalated and the dying of a candle flame could not be allowed to forestall a still higher bid.

The end result of all the hoopla is the sale of some very good Burgundy wines that will be bottled under the special label of the Hospices de Beaune. The labels vary in style, but generally they feature a drawing of the Hôtel Dieu. In contrast with other Burgundy labels, the name of the wine itself is usually in smaller print than the words Hospices de Beaune, which dominate the label. But some famous vineyard names appear on those labels and, if they are not the best wines of Burgundy, surely they are the most celebrated.

Here is where Burgundy nomenclature reaches its most difficult level, because not only does the buyer need to recognize the name of the *commune* as well as the vineyard, but he also needs to know the name of the particular owner of the slice of vineyard that has been donated to the Hospices—that is, if he wants to know precisely what he is buying. But if he is content to know that the label of the Hospices de Beaune provides marketability in itself, then perhaps the individual vineyard names are not so important. The wines with a special cachet are as follows:

Aloxe-Corton Bressandes-Docteur
    Peste
Aloxe-Corton-Clos du Roi-Docteur
    Peste
Beaune-Bressandes-Guigone de Salins
Beaune-Champimonts-Guigone de
    Salins
Beaune-Bressandes-Dames
    Hospitalières
Beaune-Mignotte-Dames Hospitalières
Beaune-Cent Vignes-Nicolas Rolin
Beaune-Grèves-Nicolas Rolin
Aloxe-Corton-Renardes-Charlotte
    Dumay
Aloxe-Corton-Bressandes-Charlotte
    Dumay
Pommard-Epenots-Dames de la
    Charité
Pommard-Rugiens-Dames de la
    Charité
Volnay-Santenots-Jéhan de Massol
Beaune-Avaux-Clos des Avaux

All of the above are red wines of the Côte de Beaune, but white wines are auctioned as well, although their quantity is small. All of the whites are Meursaults, except for the Corton-Charlemagne of François de Salins. Because of their modest supply, they are rarely seen in the export markets. More than a dozen other named vineyard parcels are involved in the auction, but most of them do not benefit from wide foreign distribution. Moreover, the consumer need know little more than that the Hospices de Beaune label stands for quality in the Côte de Beaune. The quality is not often the highest in this part of the Côte d'Or, or Golden Slope of Burgundy, but it is certainly above average. And there is always the comforting thought that these wines came from vineyards owned by a charity. (*See* Côte de Beaune.)

☆☆/☆☆☆☆

$$$/$$$$

Hudson Valley Wine Company.

Hudson Valley Wine Company of Highland, New York, sits on a bluff overlooking the Hudson River a two-hour drive north of New York City. The winery was founded 70 years ago by a wealthy Italian family, the Bolognesis, who became bankers in New York City and winemakers here in the Hudson Valley. The winery was bought by wine importer Herbert Feinberg in 1970. The 325-acre estate, with 160 acres in French and American hybrid grapes, produces sweet and dry table wines and Champagne. Winemaker Sam Johnson grew up on the estate, succeeding his father in the post. Hudson Valley encourages visits to the winery, and the well-organized tours through the stone buildings and elegant Manor House end in the tasting room, where the company's products can be sampled. Visitors can also picnic on the grounds if they like (throngs of them do)—all for the price of parking their car.

☆

$

Hultgren & Samperton Winery.

Ed Samperton and Len Hultgren established their winery in 1978 in Healdsburg, in California's Sonoma Valley, and have been making Cabernet Sauvignon, Chardonnay, Gamay Beaujolais, and Petite Sirah from purchased grapes. Production had climbed to 22,000 cases

annually by the early 1980s. The wines are clean and well made.

☆/☆☆☆

$$

CABERNET SAUVIGNON
SONOMA COUNTY
1980

PRODUCED AND BOTTLED BY

HULTGREN & SAMPERTON

HEALDSBURG, CALIFORNIA, B.W. 4919 ALCOHOL 13% BY VOLUME

Hungary.

Vast quantities of wine, both red and white, are produced in Hungary, but only a few have achieved any fame outside of Eastern Europe. The best known of these is Tokay, produced in the northeastern part of the country not far from the Russian border. The Tokaji Aszu (using the Hungarian spelling that appears on labels) is a wonderfully rich and sweet wine comparable to French Sauternes or German Beerenauslese. It displays the bouquet and taste of *Botrytis cinerea*, the noble rot that happily afflicts the other great white dessert wines of the world, although a good Tokaji Aszu will lack the intense sweetness of the best Sauternes or German sweet wines.

One other wine, a red, has developed a following abroad, probably because of its unusual name. It is called Egri Bikavér, or "bull's blood" and is made in the town of Eger a few miles northeast of Budapest. Egri Bikavér is an intense, full-bodied and robust red that requires more bottle-aging than it generally gets. It is made mostly from the Kadarka grape and is not unlike some of the better reds of the French Rhône Valley, such as Châteauneuf-du-Pape or Hermitage. It comes in Bordeaux-shaped bottles with a bull's head on the label and is exported by Monimpex, the Hungarian state monopoly. Good wines also come from vineyards on the shores of Lake Balaton, Europe's biggest lake, but they are infrequently encountered abroad. (*See also* Tokay.)

Husch Vineyards.

Hugo A. Oswald, Jr., and six other members of his family are the driving forces behind Husch Vineyards, which produces excellent premium varietals, mostly from its 23-acre vineyard near Philo in the Anderson Valley of Mendocino County, California. The Oswalds had been grape growers selling to other wineries prior to purchasing Husch in 1979. The business had been established by Tony and Gretchen Husch, who built the winery there in 1971. The vineyards had been planted in 1967 and '68. Husch's own vineyards plus some grapes from Oswald family vineyards nearby yield some 6000 cases a year of estate-bottled Sauvignon Blanc, Gewürztraminer, Chardonnay, Pinot Noir, and Cabernet Sauvignon. The winery has ceased producing Johannisberg Riesling and Pinot Noir Rosé.
☆/☆☆☆
$$

· I ·

Indiana.

The first vines in Indiana were planted at Vevay, a small town on the Ohio River whose Swiss founders named it after their hometown of Vevey on Switzerland's Lake Geneva. Winemaking flourished in Indiana before it was killed off by Prohibition. But it is starting to revive. Since 1971 the number of wineries has grown. In that year, Indiana law was changed to make it economically feasible to grow grapes and make wine for the first time in nearly a century. The new wineries are small but growing. A small operation called Swiss Valley Vineyards has revived winemaking in Vevay, and others are sprouting up around the state. Two of the most interesting are Banholzer Vineyards and Oliver Wine Company. Carl and Janet Banholzer left Chicago in the early 70s to devote full time to their 72 acres in the northern part of the state near Lake Michigan, cultivating mostly hybrid grapes and some Vinifera varieties. The vines exist in a microclimate behind the dunes of Lake Michigan where warm lake air moderates the harsh climate. The first crush of Cabernet Sauvignon was in 1975. Oliver Wine Company near Blooming-

ton is operated by Professor William Oliver of the University of Indiana Law School, and his wife Mary. They also grow hybrids and are expanding the vineyards and production yearly. Ben Sparks, first president of Indiana's newly formed Winegrowers' Guild, owns another winery quaintly named Possum Trot Farms. Golden Rain Tree Winery in Wadesville and Villa Medeo Vineyards in Madison, both established in the mid–1970s, have won devoted, but mostly local, followings.

Inferno.

In Lombardy, the region immediately east of the Piedmont in northern Italy, lies a small subregion known as Valtellina, where the vineyards are cut into the mountainsides and produce the noble Nebbiolo grape. One of the best wines of the Valtellina is Inferno, which is robust and intense, with a deep red color, earthy taste, and rich bouquet. It is made mostly from the Nebbiolo grape, with some Brugnola blended in, and can be similar to a Ghemme from the Piedmont when made by one of the better Valtellina producers, such as Negri or Polatti.

☆☆/☆☆☆

$/$$

Ingelheimer.

German wine produced around the village of Ingelheim on the south bank of
the Rhine River west of Mainz in the
northern section of the Rheinhessen,
one of the principal wine regions of the
country. Ingelheim is one of the few
German towns that produces red wine
in recognizable quantities, although the
quality is not great relative to French
or Italian reds. Nevertheless, Ingelheim-
er reds are better known than Ingel-
heimer whites, which is ample comment
c the whites. Very few get into the
export markets.

☆/☆☆

$

Inglenook.

Gustave Niebaum, a Finnish sea captain,
made his first fortune in sealskins at the
age of 26. At the urging of his wife he
left the sea and began to search for a
place to settle down and pursue his new
goal, making fine wines that could rival
those of Europe. In 1879 he finally found
the spot that suited him in the tiny
town of Rutherford in California's Napa
Valley. Inglenook, a Scottish term for
"a cosy, fireside nook," was the name
bestowed by the vineyard's former

owner, Scotsman G. B. Watson, and
Niebaum liked it well enough to retain
the name. Setting to work with prodigious energy, Niebaum planted new
vineyards with vines imported from Europe, dug storage tunnels for his German casks, started construction of the
imposing three-story winery still used
today and fashioned its distinctive oak-
paneled tasting room, windowed with
stained glass. A perfectionist, he inspected the winery daily wearing white
gloves and never permitted the name
Inglenook to appear on any wines except the best. These were fine enough
to win prizes and fame at Paris expo-
sitions. Niebaum died in 1908, but his
wife continued the winery operation until
Prohibition, when it closed down. After
repeal, responsibility passed into the
hands of Niebaum descendent John
Daniel, Jr., and under his care and guid-
ance Inglenook regained its former em-
inence and became widely known for
soft, highly perfumed wines of elegance
and breed.

Daniel sold the vineyard in 1964 to
United Vintners, Inc., a cooperative of
grape growers owned by Heublein. For
a time devotees of Inglenook registered
dismay at the quality of wines turned
out under the new management. But in
more recent vintages the wines have
begun to show renewed evidence of the
finesse that made Inglenook famous. In
1971 the company hired as winemaker
Thomas Ferrell, a graduate of the University of California at Davis. Inglenook
was formerly known mostly for its red
wines, but under Ferrell's guiding hand,
the whites came into their own. Superb
vineyards acquired long ago still produce notable Cabernet Sauvignon and
Pinot Noir. In 1982 John Richburg, formerly assistant winemaker, succeeded
Ferrell as Inglenook's top oenologist.
Ferrell moved to Franciscan Vineyards.

Three lines of wines are produced at
Inglenook. The premium varietals are

always vintage-dated and come exclusively from Napa Valley vineyards, labeled estate-bottled. Superior lots of wine from a single vineyard are available as Cask Selections. Inglenook's vintage line consists of blends of varietal and generic grapes from a single vintage. The Navalle line, named for the stream that runs down from the Mayacamas Range above the estate, consists of generic wines and varietals such as French Colombard and Ruby Cabernet. These are the least expensive wines produced, available in both fifths and half-gallons. Inglenook made about seven million gallons of wine in 1982.

☆/☆☆☆☆

$/$$$

Iron Horse Vineyards.

Iron Horse was planted in 1970 and '71, but the winery itself was not constructed until 1979, with previous vintages made in borrowed premises. The operation was purchased in 1976 by Barry and Audrey Sterling and Forrest Tancer, the winemaker. All of the grapes for the Iron Horse premium varietals come from the winery's own 126-acre vineyard at Sebastopol in Sonoma County and from Tancer's 40-acre vineyard at his T-Bar-T Ranch in the nearby Alexander Valley. Iron Horse owns 250 acres in all, and the T-Bar-T consists of 450 acres in all, so new plantings could expand production considerably from the present 15,000 to 20,000 cases a year. It is Iron Horse's stated policy to prune back all vines to produce only two and a half tons of grapes per acre, a relatively small volume for most California vineyards. Four varietals are produced: Chardonnay, Pinot Noir, Sauvignon Blanc, and Cabernet Sauvignon. The Chardonnay, which is extremely well made with a rich texture and long finish, comes from the vineyard adjacent to the winery, along with the Pinot

Noir. The T-Bar-T Ranch produces Cabernet Sauvignon and Sauvignon Blanc. All harvesting is by hand, and the wines have a devoted following.

☆☆/☆☆☆☆

$$

Ischia.

Ischia is a small island that lies off Naples and is technically within the Italian region of Campania. The wines from Ischia usually are labeled simply Bianco, Bianco Superiore or Rosso and are blended from local grape varieties. Generally they are light and pleasant and are not meant for keeping.

☆/☆☆

$

Isonzo.

The wines of Isonzo, virtually all named after grape varieties, have for many years been among the most consistently high in quality in Italy. They are named after a river that flows south from the Alps toward the Gulf of Trieste in the superior Italian wine region known as Friuli-Venezia Giulia. The best red is the Isonzo Cabernet, and the best whites are the Pinot Grigio and the Pinot Bianco. Ten Isonzo varietals merit D.O.C. recognition under the Italian wine law.

☆/☆☆☆

$/$$

Israel.

The Rothschilds of France are well known among wine connoisseurs for their ownership of two of the greatest estates of Bordeaux: Château Lafite-Rothschild and Château Mouton Rothschild. Not so well known is the fact that an ancestor, Baron Edmond de Rothschild, was largely responsible for today's burgeoning wine industry in Israel. It was Edmond who brought vines from France and established Israel's first winery at Richon Le Zion southeast of Tel Aviv in 1886, after the country's vineyards had lain fallow for centuries. The Baron and his wife are buried in a tomb atop a vineyard-covered hill near Haifa, a vantage point from which his contribution to Israel's viniculture is quite apparent. Contrary to a widespread impression, the majority of Israel's wines are not sweet and are not produced for religious purposes. Most of them are dry table wines produced in a French style, and they can be charming and pleasant, although the climate is too hot to produce truly great vintages. The largest commercial winemaking operation is conducted by the Carmel Wine Co., whose products include Avdat, one of the better reds. Cabernet Sauvignon, Carignan, Grenache, Sauvignon Blanc, and Semillon grapes are among the French varieties cultivated in Israel.

Italian Swiss Colony.

Italian Swiss Colony, long one of California's largest producers of bulk and jug wines, was founded in 1881 by Anthony Sbarboro, a native of the Piedmont area of Italy. In altruistic spirit, he set up the winery and vineyards to employ other Italian and Swiss immigrants who were homesick and struggling in an unfamiliar land. Buying 1500 acres in northern Sonoma County along the Russian River, he named the settlement Asti to make them feel even more at home. Sbarboro's plan was to deduct a small amount from wages which would purchase shares in the winery, making all of them owners eventually. The workers were suspicious of the plan, however, preferring dollars in hand over shares in the business. At first the only customers of Italian Swiss were other Italians—and most of them in New York, at that. Gradually the firm prospered and expanded. After repeal it was bought by National Distillers, and later Louis Petri, another bulk producer, bought it.

Yet another owner was Heublein, the food and liquor conglomerate, which sold Colony and six other brands to Allied Grape Growers in 1983. Allied is a cooperative, representing some 1300 growers.

A great many types of wine are produced by Italian Swiss Colony under various labels other than its own. Under the Lejon label the company makes vermouth, Champagne, and brandy. Fruit-flavored pop wines, such as Annie Green Springs and Bali Hai, are made in the Central Valley at Madera, as are various other flavored wines. Generic wines, such as Tipo Red, Pink and Gold Chablis, are sold under the Italian Swiss Colony label, as are some quite decent and very reasonably priced varietals made at Asti, mainly the nonvintage Zinfandel and Cabernet Sauvignon.

In 1981 Colony announced a new thrust into the varietal field with the introduction of four wines with a drier taste, new labels, and corks instead of screw caps. The four were Cabernet Sauvignon, Chenin Blanc, Zinfandel, and French Colombard. Colony had used corks selectively before, but the new varietals represented the first time since Prohibition that Colony had used corks for all four varietals. The wines were priced very low and were packaged in standard bottles and 1.4-liter magnums. ☆/☆☆
$/$$

Italy.

More wine is produced and consumed in Italy than in any other country, including France. In fact, France is an importer of Italian wines across her southern borders for blending in the production of *vins ordinaires* for peasant consumption. The heritage of Italian wines dates back to earlier civilizations than any known to have existed in France. The country is, indeed, the land of the grapevine. It grows everywhere, and rare is the farmer who does not have his own vines producing for his own consumption if not for commercial gain. Often the Italian vineyards are planted in combination with other crops, especially olives, and in some parts of the country the olive trees are used to help support the vines. Wine is the national drink, and few Italian babies are born without a strong *vino rosso* already coursing through their veins.

Partly because the production is so vast and has flowed fairly indiscriminately into the export markets, Italian wines tend not to be taken seriously by wine-drinkers and are relegated to a second tier below those of France, Germany, and the United States (California) on the quality scale. This is a mistake. Some Italian wines compete on a quality basis with the best of France and merit the consideration of the most exacting connoisseurs. In fact, the man with a cellar full of mature Brunello di Montalcino from Tuscany owns a supply of wine as precious as the man with a cellar full of the first growths of the Bordeaux Médoc. It is true that Italy does not produce white wines of the same high quality as France and Germany, but her reds can be magnificent, displaying an intensity and body that no other wines can achieve.

The best Italian reds come from the Piedmont region in the northwestern corner of the country, hard by the French, Swiss and Italian Alps. Here is where the Nebbiolo grape reaches perfection, producing dark-colored wines of great character and finesse that sometimes require decades of bottle-age to reach their properly soft and velvety maturity. The king of the Italian wines is Barolo, big and robust, with a haunting bouquet and an almost chewy texture. The queen is Gattinara, softer and more elegant, but with similar intensity.

Barbaresco, Barbera, and Ghemme have characters of their own that few wines outside Italy ever match. Asti Spumante, the famous sweet Italian sparkling wine, also comes from the Piedmont, or Piemonte.

Lombardy, the region adjacent to the Piedmont in northern Italy, also produces excellent wines from the Nebbiolo grape, including the Valtellina varieties such as Sassella, Grumello, Valgella, and Inferno. Excellent reds come from Tuscany, the home of Chianti. Bardolino, Valpolicella, and Soave all come from the Veneto region, and no meal at a Venetian restaurant is complete without one of these lighthearted wines. Orvieto, a pleasant and charming white, comes from Umbria, and Frascati, the carafe wine of Rome, is found on the outskirts of the capital city in Lazio, or Latium, which also produces Est! Est! Est!, a wine with one of the most peculiar names in all winedom. Verdicchio in its fish-shaped bottle comes from the Marches, and there is Marsala from Sicily. All are regulated under a system similar to the French *appellation contrôlée*, known as *denominazione di origine controllata*.

During the 1970s Italian wines emerged as the favorites of American consumers among all the imports, partly because of rising prices for French wines and partly because of overdue recognition for the quality of the Italian imports. In addition, Italian producers began changing the vinification of their white wines, so that they were fresher and cleaner-tasting and thus more competitive with American and French whites. There was also the phenomenon of Lambrusco, which gained immense popularity among younger people in the U.S. In 1982 the three biggest-selling imported brands all were Lambruscos: Riunite, Cella, and Giacobazzi. Their popularity and the rising popularity of

Italian wines in general enabled Italy to capture about 60 percent of the imported-wine market in the U.S., while French wines were declining in popularity. The growth of Italian imports will continue as long as prices remain competitive, for the majority of American consumers are now aware of the quality available from Italy. (*See also* Labels and Wine Laws, as well as entries under various geographical and regional designations.)

· J ·

Jekel Vineyard.

William and August Jekel were born five minutes apart and resemble each other so closely that even some of their closest friends sometimes mistake one for the other. In 1972 they planted 140 acres of vines on the Salinas Valley floor in Greenfield in Monterey County. The biggest section, 40 acres, was Johannisberg Riesling, and there is nearly as much Chardonnay. The growing season there is long, with budbreak sometimes occurring as early as February and harvesting continuing into December in some vintages. Fog enshrouds the vineyards nearly every morning, which makes for slow growing. But rainfall is sparse, so the slow growth is not viewed as a major liability by the bearded Jekel twins.

Besides the Riesling, which is crisp and dry with a citric bouquet, and the equally dry Chardonnay, there are plantings of Pinot Blanc, Pinot Noir, and Cabernet Sauvignon. In addition, the Jekels also buy some of their grapes from other producers. Production runs 35,000 cases in a favorable vintage. Both the Pinot Blanc and the Chardonnay are austere and dry, in the style of French Chablis or Mâconnais wines. The Pinot Noir tends to be slightly vegetal, as does the Cabernet Sauvignon, a characteristic common to other Monterey County wines. The Jekels have a modern winemaking and storage facility at Greenfield built in 1978 and expanded in 1981.

Reflecting their other business interests, the Jekel brothers' business office is at Studio City, Hollywood, where they operate Film Fare, a company that makes television commercials and feature films. Bill Jekel was a fine arts major at U.C.L.A. and later took a law degree at Southern Cal. Gus was an animator for Walt Disney Productions.

☆/☆☆☆
$$/$$$

Johannisberger.

No doubt the most famous of all the Rhine vineyards of Germany are those surrounding the village of Johannisberg in the heart of the Rheingau on that 20-mile stretch of the river that runs roughly east to west. Johannisbergers have won such renown the world over that the name has been copied in Switzerland, the United States, and South Africa, where Johannisberg or Johannisberger on a label is used to mean Riesling or simply white wine. But these imitations cannot compare with the great whites produced from the steep slopes below Schloss Johannisberg, the castle whose Schlossberg vineyard is the most renowned of all.

According to some accounts, Charlemagne established the first vineyards near the Schloss and it is known that wines were being produced on Johannisberg's steep hillsides as early as the twelfth century. It was presented to Prince Metternich in 1816 after Napoleon's defeat, with the provision that an annual tithe consisting of 10 percent of the production be paid to the Imperial Court at Vienna. The payment is still being made, although not in wine. The magnificent castle with its commanding view over the Rhine gives the impression of having stood there for centuries, but actually it is a new

structure. In a regrettable error during World War II, bombers of the Royal Air Force wiped out the previous Schloss, although the cellars buried deep in the hillside were not destroyed. Inside are fantastic hand-carved wine casks that provide an inspiring background for tasting sessions. The subterranean vaults contain all the good vintages dating back to 1818, as well as some bottles as old as 1748. These mold-covered specimens of bygone times lie quietly behind iron gates and are said to taste fresh and young on those rare occasions when they are sampled.

Schloss Johannisbergers are the most balanced wines of the Rheingau. They have what experts call finesse, with their fruity Riesling depth, their elegant sweetness, and even character. They are not as robust as the Steinbergers, but display a refined subtlety that is unique among Rhine wines. They have traditionally been bottled with capsules (the lead or plastic coverings over the neck and cork) of varying colors indicating quality levels. Gold capsules are reserved for Beerenauslese and Trockenbeerenauslese, while the lesser wines have red, orange, green, or white capsules. This system of identification is confusing even to the experts. The more important information has been on the labels themselves since the revision of the German wine laws in 1971. With the new law Schloss Johannisberg in effect became a suburb of Johannisberg so that it could retain its traditional name.

So great is the fame of Schloss Johannisberg that it is easy to forget the other fine wines produced around the village of Johannisberg. The Schloss itself controls only 66 acres, and some 200 acres more are entitled to the Johannisberger name. In exceptional vintages they may even surpass the wines of the Schloss, reflecting their fortunate location in the Rheingau. They tend to be somewhat less costly than the wines of the Schloss and therefore often represent better value.

Among the better known vineyards at Johannisberg are the following:

Johannisberger Erntebringer*
Johannisberger Goldatzel*
Johannisberger Hansenberg*
Johannisberger Hölle*
Johannisberger Kahlenberg
Johannisberger Kerzenstück
Johannisberger Klaus
Johannisberger Kläuserberg
Johannisberger Kläuserpfad
Johannisberger Kochsberg
Johannisberger Mittelhölle
Johannisberger Nonnhölle
Johannisberger Schwartzenstein*
Johannisberger Steinhölle
Johannisberger Sterzelpfad
Johannisberger Unterhölle
Johannisberger Vogelsang*
Johannisberger Weiher
Schloss Johannisberg*
    (Johannisberger Schlossberg)

An asterisk (*) indicates vineyard names that survived or that were created in the revision of the German wine law of 1971. The survival of the name does not always indicate that the same vineyard boundaries are being maintained, because many small vineyards were merged into larger ones. Johannisberger Erntebringer, for example, is now a *Grosslage*, or large vineyard area, and the name is virtually a generic term for some of the better—but not the best—Johannisbergers.
☆/☆☆☆☆
$$/$$$

Johnson's Alexander Valley Wines.

The Johnsons founded this family-operated winery in 1975 near Healdsburg in California's Sonoma region and have planted 70 acres in vines. The wine building is said to be the oldest in the Alexander Valley, with a pipe organ dating back to 1924 in the tasting room. James Johnson, a Chicago attorney, purchased part of the old Whitten Ranch near Healdsburg in 1952 and tore out the vines that had been planted in the last century because prunes and pears were more valuable crops at the time. One of his sons, Tom Johnson, began home winemaking after returning from military service in 1961, took some courses in oenology and went to work at a local winery. He got his brothers, Jay and Will, interested in making wines, and ultimately they turned their father's orchard back into a vineyard. Production has risen to 12,000 cases a year of Chenin Blanc, Johannisberg Riesling, Gewürztraminer, Chardonnay, Zinfandel, Pinot Noir, Cabernet Sauvignon, and pear wine. Open-house organ concerts are conducted monthly at the winery, with organists from far and wide journeying to Healdsburg for the opportunity to play the old organ.
☆/☆☆☆
$/$$

Jordan Vineyard and Winery.

One of the more spectacular new wineries in California is Jordan, overlooking the Alexander Valley outside of Healdsburg in the Sonoma Valley. It is the project of Tom Jordan, a Denver oil man who made millions exploring for petroleum in Indonesia. His goal was to reproduce a French Bordeaux-style château in California, and that is what he has done. The yellow stucco château has an orange tiled roof and has a full dining room and kitchen plus bedroom suites overlooking the fermenting and aging rooms of the winery. There are huge redwood beams everywhere, looking down on Oriental carpets, Louis XV reproduction furniture, plus some genuine antiques, extravagant bathrooms with marble sinks and goldplated fixtures, wet bars in each suite, and French magazines lying about.

With so much attention to form, the devotion to substance—the making of fine wines—came as a surprise to some observers. Jordan hired Mike Rowan, trained at the University of California at Davis, as his general manager, and Rob Davis as his winemaker. The vineyards were planted in 1972, initially all in Cabernet Sauvignon with just a few vines of Merlot—typical of a Bordeaux Médoc vineyard. But with white wine beginning to boom, Tom Jordan lost his nerve and pulled out 92 acres of two-year-old Cabernet and Merlot and planted them in Chardonnay. Production of Cabernet Sauvignon totaled 34,000 cases with the 1976 vintage, which was not released until 1980, then rose to 35,000 cases in 1977, 45,000 cases in 1978 and sank to 40,000 cases in 1979. The 1976 vintage was only 35 percent vinified from Jordan's own grapes, while the 1977 was 85 percent Jordan and the 1978 and subsequent vintages were 100 percent Jordan and therefore estate-bottled. The Jordan Cabernets are about 8 percent Merlot. Chardonnay production totaled 1200 cases in 1979.

No expense has been spared to assure that the Jordan wines receive the best available handling. A total of 2800 barrels, half French oak and half American, were purchased for aging the wines, and at least 400 new barrels are being purchased every year to assure that the wines of each vintage will see new oak. Jordan also bought 600 used barrels from Château Lafite-Rothschild's 1964 vintage. "We decided that whatever problems Lafite had with the cooperage, we were willing to live with," said Mike Rowan.

The Jordan wines are very well made, although some critics argue that they lack the bigness and intensity of some other California wines in the same rel-atively high price category. However, it was Jordan's intention to produce wines that would not require many years of bottle aging to reach their peaks, wines that restaurants would be happy to order and put on their lists immediately. The best word to describe the early Jordan Cabernets would be "elegant" or perhaps "balanced" in the French style. The 1976 was very good, the 1977 fair, the 1978 excellent, the 1979 and 1980 more intense. Mike Rowan left in 1983, but Tom Jordan remains committed not to produce any so-called "monster" wines similar to those from some other vineyards, the wines that are high in alcohol and so heavy in tannin that many years of aging must pass before they are drinkable. So far, they are living up to that commitment. The Jordan Chardonnay, on the other hand, is creamy and rich, not a small wine that will finish poorly in blind tastings.
☆☆/☆☆☆
$$$

Jug Wines.

This slang term for American wines sold in gallon and half-gallon jugs is a little less pejorative in connotation than it used to be, due to the general upgrading of many such wines over the last decade. Wines of poor quality are still to be found among them and always will be, but such California producers as Gallo, Guild, Italian Swiss Colony, Almadén, Paul Masson, CK Mondavi, and others can generally be counted on for relatively good jug wines at fair prices. Their success has prompted a number of premium producers from Napa and Sonoma to produce generic and varietal jug wines, including Inglenook (the Navalle line), Beringer/Los Hermanos, Robert Mondavi, and Sebastiani.

Jurançon.

Among the many rather obscure wines produced in the south of France are some fairly good sweet ones, and Jurançon is one of these. It comes from the area around Pau about 125 miles almost due south of Bordeaux in the foothills of the Pyrenees that separate France from Spain. The grapes, basically local varieties, are left on the vines until late in the autumn in the hope of attracting *pourriture noble*, or the noble rot, a mold that is desirous in the production of most sweet white wines in Germany as well as France. The best Jurançons have a deep golden hue and a perfumy bouquet. Unfortunately, the extra effort required to produce concentrated sweetness in this part of France has not been rewarded by higher prices, so much of the Jurançon produced today is rather dry and lacking in character. ☆/☆☆

$/$$

· K ·

Kalin Cellars.

Terrance and Frances Leighton founded Kalin Cellars in Emeryville, California, in 1977 and established their winery in Novato, in Marin County just across the Golden Gate Bridge from San Francisco in 1979. Their grapes come from Mendocino, Sonoma, the Livermore Valley, and the Santa Maria Valley, and their most successful wines seem to be Zinfandels and Cabernet Sauvignons. Production was about 5000 cases in the 1982 harvest.
☆☆/☆☆☆
$$

Kallstadter.

German white and red wine produced in Kallstadt, one of the better wine towns in the Rheinpfalz, or Palatinate, the country's southernmost region for superior table wines. The reds are mediocre but the whites are big, full-bodied, and assertive, lacking only the finesse of the more famous Forsters and Deidesheimers produced a few miles to the south. Kallstadters, when they can be found, often represent excellent value and sometimes challenge the greatest German wines when the weather conditions are just right.

Among the better known vineyards are the following:

Kallstadter Annaberg*
Kallstadter Horn
Kallstadter Kirchenstück
Kallstadter Kobnert*
Kallstadter Kreuz
Kallstadter Kronenberg*
Kallstadter Nill
Kallstadter Saumagen
Kallstadter Steinacker*

The vineyards marked with an asterisk (*) are among those that retained their identities, if not their shapes, in the revision of the German wine law in 1971. Kobnert became a *Grosslage* and wines identified with this name come from a fairly large area around Kallstadt. Smaller vineyards were merged into large ones to simplify identification.
☆/☆☆
$/$$

Robert Keenan Winery.

High on Spring Mountain above St. Helena on the western side of California's Napa Valley, some 1500 feet above sea level, stands the Robert Keenan Winery, built by Robert Keenan in 1977 on the premises of another winemaking facility that had been constructed in 1904. Keenan, a retired San Francisco insurance man, made his first commercial harvest with the 1977 vintage, and production rose to about 7000 cases a year of Chardonnay and Cabernet Sauvignon. The Chardonnay has proven to be especially fine and has established a national reputation, despite the relatively small production, which cannot be expanded without an expansion of production facilities. (Keenan now has some 45 acres in vines.) The winery plans to be 90 percent self-sufficient in grapes when new plantings come of age. Both the Chardonnay and the Cabernet are aged in 60-gallon oak barrels and are complex, well-made wines.

☆/☆☆☆

$$

Kendall-Jackson Vineyards.

The winery boom in California has expanded north from the Napa Valley to Lake County, and Kendall-Jackson is one of the newer, more elaborate facilities. Vineyards now totaling 100 acres were acquired by San Francisco attorney Jess Jackson and his wife Jane Kendall Jackson in 1974, and the winery at Lakeport was completed in 1982. The harvest of '82 yielded 38,000 cases, a sizable quantity, and the winery's capacity is 60,000 cases. Chardonnay, Sauvignon Blanc, and Cabernet Sauvignon are the principal varieties. From time to time, small lots will be bottled under the Château du Lac label.

☆/☆☆☆

$$

Kenwood Vineyards.

Kenwood Vineyards derives its name from the town in California's Sonoma Valley where the winery is located. The operation is the property of a family corporation headed by Martin Lee, Sr., a retired chief of inspectors of the San Francisco Police Department. The busi-

ness was established in 1970 when the Lees bought out the old Papani Brothers Winery, which had been built in 1906 and was mainly in the bulk wine business. The old redwood tanks have been largely replaced with stainless steel fermenters, and 1000 American oak barrels and 300 made of French oak have been added for aging the wines. The first Kenwood vintage was in 1970, when 2000 cases of wine were made. Now production has reached the 60,000-case level, and the total is about equally divided between red and white.

Kenwood has 38 acres of its own in vines and long-term leases on four other vineyards. Most of its grapes come from outside growers. The products include Chardonnay, Sauvignon Blanc, Chenin Blanc, Johannisberg Riesling, some Gewürztraminer, Cabernet Sauvignon, Pinot Noir, and Zinfandel. The Zinfandel and Cabernet are the most consistently superior. Besides Martin Lee, Sr., the members of the ownership group are his son Mike Lee, Mike's brother-in-law John Sheela, Neil Knott, and Bob Kozlowski, who is the winemaker.

☆/☆☆☆

$$

Kiedricher.

Although some of Germany's Rheingau vineyards have won worldwide reputations, others are best known strictly to connoisseurs. The wines of Kiedrich, a picturesque village up in the hills behind Eltville north of the Rhine River, rise to extraordinary heights of quality in the best vintages, but they suffer from a lack of fame. As in the other Rheingau villages, the Riesling grape produces full-bodied but elegant whites here, and Kiedrichers can represent good values.

Among the better vineyards at Kiedrich are the following:

Kiedricher Berg
Kiedricher Dippenerd

K 299

Kiedricher Gräfenberg*
Kiedricher Heiligenstock*
Kiedricher Klosterberg*
Kiedricher Sandgrub*
Kiedricher Turmberg
Kiedricher Wasserrose*
Kiedricher Weihersberg

An asterisk (*) indicates vineyard names that survived or that were created in the revision of the German wine law of 1971. Kiedricher Heiligenstock has become a *Grosslage*, or large vineyard area, and can be regarded as a generic wine of Kiedrich.

☆/☆☆
$

Kir.

The standard aperitif in the Burgundy country of France and, often, in Paris restaurants is *un kir*, which is a mixture of white Burgundy and Cassis, the liqueur made from black currant juice. It is pronounced "keer" and is named after Canon Félix Kir, a late mayor of Dijon, who became renowned as a resistance fighter during the German occupation in World War II. The drink is known as *vin blanc cassis* in other parts of France, but in the classic fashion it should be made of four parts Bourgogne Aligoté and one part Cassis. The ratio can be changed to suit individual tastes: a smaller quantity of Cassis makes for a drier, lighter drink. Actually, any white Burgundy can be used, but the American restaurant that once made Kir with Corton-Charlemagne was committing a crime against that noble white wine. Some prebottled Kir has been marketed in the United States in recent years, and it has the advantage that it can be kept chilled in a refrigerator so that the drinker need not take the trouble to mix it himself. Ice cubes can be added if prechilled wine is not available, and a dash of soda water is also permissible. A slightly different drink can be made by mixing Cassis with red Beaujolais. This is called a Cardinal, and Cassis mixed with Champagne is a Kir Royal. The leading producers of Cassis, whose bottlings are available on foreign markets are Gabriel Boudier, Cartron, Heritier-Guyot, Trenel Fils, and Marie Brizard.

Kirigan Cellars.

With extensive experience in winemaking in his native Yugoslavia and a degree in oenology from the University of Zagreb in 1941, Nick Kirigan-Chargin came to the United States in 1959 and took over the Bonesio family winery near Gilroy in the Uvas Valley of southwestern Santa Clara County in 1976, changing the name to Kirigan Cellars. The winery and adjacent 50-acre vineyard stand on the site of the Solis Rancho homestead, and the Kirigan family residence is in one of the original buildings dating back to the early part of the nineteenth century. Kirigan is a family operation, with Nick Kirigan-Chargin, Jr., active in the business. Besides grapes from their own estate, the Kirigans also make wines from purchased grapes, with production totaling more than 10,000 cases a year of Chardonnay, White Riesling, Gewürztraminer, Chenin Blanc, Cabernet Sauvignon, Pinot Noir, and some Malvasia Bianca, a slightly sweet wine from the Muscat family of grapes. Initial vintages of the Chardonnay, which was austere in the style of some of the Mâconnais wines of France, were made mostly from grapes grown in Temecula vineyards, not far from San Diego.

☆/☆☆
$/$$

Kistler Vineyards.

Kistler Vineyards, near Glen Ellen in California's Sonoma Valley, produces wines from grapes grown in the Mayacamas Range separating the Napa and

Sonoma regions. The business was launched in 1978, and the Chardonnays from the 1979 vintage were excellent, achieving national acclaim. The 1980 Chardonnays from the same winery, however, were far less successful. Because the 1979 versions had been so superior, far more attention than probably was deserved was focused on the shortcomings of the 1980s. Kistler rebounded in 1981, and Cabernet Sauvignons and Pinot Noirs were added to the product roster. Production totaled about 5000 cases in 1982, and the goal of about 8000 was to be reached shortly.
☆☆/☆☆☆
$$/$$$

Knudsen-Erath Winery.

One of the pioneers in modern winemaking in northwestern Oregon is Dick Erath of the Knudsen-Erath Winery near the town of Dundee in Yamhill County. He purchased 50 acres in 1969 in the lower reaches of the Chehalem Mountains and later bonded the Erath Vineyards Winery. After meeting Cal Knudsen Erath joined forces with him to establish Knudsen-Erath, with 86 acres of vineyards. They built a new winery in 1976 and produce mainly Chardonnay, Pinot Noir, and White Riesling.
☆/☆☆☆
$$

Königsbacher.

German white wine produced in Königsbach, one of the better wine towns in the Rheinpfalz, or Palatinate, the country's southernmost region for superior table wines. This is one of the smaller towns of the Pfalz in terms of wine production, but it grows a strong percentage of Riesling grapes which make rich and full-bodied wines of great character in good years. Königsbachers are not so well known as some of the other big wines of the Pfalz, but they can represent good value and certainly rank

among the better wines produced in Germany.

Among the better known vineyards are the following:

Königsbacher Bender
Königsbacher Falbert
Königsbacher Harle
Königsbacher Idig*
Königsbacher Jesuitengarten*
Königsbacher Muckenhaus
Königsbacher Mühlweg
Königsbacher Oelberg*
Königsbacher Reiterpfad*
Königsbacher Rolandsberg
Königsbacher Satz
Königsbacher Weissmauer

The vineyards marked with an asterisk (*) are among those that retained their identities, if not their former shapes, in the revision of the German wine law in 1971. Most small vineyards were merged into larger ones to simplify identification.
☆/☆☆
$/$$

Konocti Cellars Winery.

Konocti Cellars, founded in 1974, is a California cooperative named after Mt. Konocti, a 4200-foot inactive volcano near the winery in Lake County. The operation is owned by Lake County Vintners, with 27 members, and is based in Kelseyville. The members have an average of ten to 20 acres of vines each, which yield grapes for vinification at the Konocti facility. Production is upward of 20,000 cases a year of such varietals as Cabernet Sauvignon, Zinfandel, Sauvignon Blanc, Johannisberg Riesling, Cabernet Blanc, and Gamay Blanc. The first Konocti Cellars wines were released in 1976 and new facilities were built in 1979 at Kelseyville. In 1983 John and George Parducci purchased a 50 percent interest in Konocti, and plans for expansion were announced. The

Parduccis invested in Konocti as individuals, and the operation was to be kept separate from Parducci Wine Cellars of Ukiah, in Mendocino County.
☆/☆☆☆
$$

Korbel.

To many people the name Korbel means California Champagne. Located at Guerneville in Sonoma County, F. Korbel & Bros. was founded by three brothers about a century ago. The Korbel brothers emigrated from Czechoslovakia and were involved in several enterprises—lumber, tobacco, the manufacture of cigar boxes—before the University of California advised them that the best use of their land overlooking the Russian River was to plant it in grapevines. The price of grapes was so low when they harvested their first vintage that they decided to make their own wine rather than sell the grapes to other producers. During the 1890s, when San Francisco society was at its glittering height and celebrations were held in a constant stream, Korbel began to make Champagne in the traditional French manner. Its popularity soon outstripped the sales of Korbel's other wines.

In 1954 Tony Korbel sold the winery to another trio of brothers. Adolf, Paul, and Ben Heck, whose father had made sparkling wine in Alsace. The Hecks expanded the vineyards and instituted a number of innovations while continuing to make good Champagne in the proper way, fermenting it in the original bottle as the label conspicuously states. One innovation was an automatic riddling machine invented by Adolf. Riddling is the California term for *rémuage,* the process of turning each bottle by hand daily, giving it a shake and pointing the neck ever more downward until all the sediment has collected on a temporary cork. This is a laborious and time-consuming process, still performed by hand in France and at such California Champagne cellars as Schramsberg and Hanns Kornell. The automatic riddler is set to vibrate the bottles at regular intervals, accomplishing the process with more uniformity and saving man-hours for other winery work. Korbel Brut and Extra Dry Champagnes are extremely popular, but the brisk and bone-dry Natural has a strong following too.

Korbel continues to use the *méthode champenoise,* the traditional Champagne process whereby the second fermentation takes place inside the bottles, enabling the bubbles to be captured. Both Chardonnay and Pinot Blanc are used in blending Korbel sparkling wines, along with some other grape varieties. The Korbel Natural is 0.5 percent residual sugar, and so is the Blanc de Noirs, made from black grapes. The Brut is 1 percent residual sugar, the Extra Dry and Rosé 1.25 percent, the Sec 1.5 percent, and the Rouge 2 percent, or fairly sweet. The quality of the Korbel Champagnes has risen since the mid-1970s, and now its best bottlings are fully competitive with Domaine Chandon, Schramsberg, and Piper Sonoma.

Branching out, Korbel introduced a full line of varietal and generic table wines in 1974, including burgundy, chablis, Gamay Rosé, and Zinfandel. The Cabernet, Pinot Noir, and Chardonnay are aged in small oak. The winery also makes brandy. Gary Heck succeeded his father, Adolph Heck, as president of Korbel in 1982 and remains committed to producing sparkling wines of the highest quality.
☆/☆☆☆
$$

Hanns Kornell.

It must make Hanns Kornell very proud to stand in his winery and survey the results of all his years of hard work and determination. Nearly one and a half million bottles of Champagne lie neatly stacked at one stage or another in their development, here at one of California's leading wineries in the celebrated Napa Valley—a situation far different from that in 1940 when Hanns arrived in New York at Ellis Island, a virtually penniless refugee from Germany. Hanns, now a stocky, energetic man with a great mane of white hair, was practically weaned on Champagne; his father and grandfather had produced it in Germany and he himself learned to make sparkling wines at his uncle's winery in Mainz. Hanns disagreed with German policies under the Nazis and left. Eventually he went to California and found a job at Fountain-Grove winery in Sonoma. Subsequently he made sparkling wines in Ohio and was production manager for the American Wine Company in St. Louis (makers of Cook's Imperial Champagne). Finally, in 1952, he started his own winery in Sonoma; he made the wines at night and delivered them to customers during the day.

At his present site in the Napa Valley, Hanns Kornell makes only sparkling wines, and all of them are made in the true French method. Each label carries the phrase "naturally fermented in this bottle," and each step, from the time the wines are blended until the final bottling, is undertaken with care, a process that takes a minimum of four years and sometimes more if need be. Though he does not grow his own grapes, he selects with great care the Johannisberg Riesling, Chardonnay, Pinot Blanc, and Sémillon grapes that are used for his wines. The driest of the sparkling wines is Sehr Trocken, from 100 percent Johannisberg Riesling. The *brut* is almost as dry, with a marvelous froth the color of straw. The extra dry is pleasant, fruity rather than sweet. Pink champagne and demi-sec dessert Champagne are also made, as well as a sparkling Burgundy.

Production totals more than one million cases a year.

☆☆

$$

Kosher Wines.

To be certified as kosher, wine must be made in strict accordance with regulations established by ancient Jewish law. The regulations set standards for purity and naturalness of ingredients and demand that the end result be sound, clean, and properly made, with every step of the winemaking process, from grape picking to bottling, supervised by an Orthodox rabbi. Kosher wines are officially made for use in Jewish ceremonies, but the wines became popular with the wine-drinking public, and by far the greatest amount is now sold to non-Jewish wine drinkers. American kosher wines are made mostly from the Concord grape grown in upstate New York, where, pressed into juice and frozen in bulk, it is delivered to kosher wineries when needed. Doses of grape concentrate are added during fermentation to counteract the Concord's high acidity and to achieve the desired degree of sweetness.

The largest producers of kosher wines in America are Manischewitz of Brooklyn and Mogen David of Chicago. A number of kosher wines are now shipped to the United States from Israel.

Kröver (Cröver) Nacktarsch.

One of the better known German wine labels, especially in the export markets, bears a picture of a child with his pants pulled down being spanked. He is the Kröver Nacktarsch, or "naked bottom," whose fame has spread far and wide because he is depicted on most of the labels from the ancient wine town of Kröv, or Cröv, which is downstream on the Mosel River as it twists and turns toward its junction with the Rhine. Kröver Nacktarsch certainly is well known, but not for its wines, which are not among Germany's best. They lack the elegance and depth of the better wines from the central portion of the Mosel-Saar-Ruwer region, which probably explains why a slightly naughty label has been employed to sell them. This is not to say that good value cannot be found in the wines of Kröv. In good vintages some excellent wines are made there. Some of them are bottled as Nacktarsch and some under the other vineyard names of the area: Kröver Letterlay, Kröver Kirchlay, Kröver Paradies, Kröver Burglay, Kröver Herrenberg, and Kröver Stephansberg.

☆/☆☆

$/$$

Charles Krug.

A true landmark in California's Napa Valley, this winery is one of the largest still owned and run by a single family, the Mondavis. Charles Krug emigrated from Prussia at age twenty-two and came to northern California, where, encouraged by the legendary Agoston Haraszthy, at Buena Vista in Sonoma, he learned the art of winemaking. In 1860 he founded the winery in St. Helena that still bears his name. Krug was a key figure in the history of California winemaking and the development of Napa Valley as perhaps the most illustrious, certainly the most famous wine region of California. He spared neither effort nor expense to foster excellence in California winemaking and set standards that others strived to emulate. His wines were well received in the eastern United States as well as abroad in Mexico, Germany, and England. The Krug family operated the winery until Prohibition.

In 1943 the winery and cellars were bought by Cesare Mondavi, who started life in this country as an Italian immigrant working in the Minnesota iron mines. When his Italian friends sent him to California on a grape-buying expedition, he fell in love with the place and moved his family (by this time he had returned to Italy, married his childhood sweetheart and brought her back to the Midwest) to Lodi, where he began a successful wholesale fruit business. The Mondavi family restored and expanded the Charles Krug Winery, emphasizing varietal wines, and were one of the earliest families in the Valley to do so. When Cesare died in 1959 his wife Rosa became president of the company, with sons Peter and Robert in charge of operations. Robert left in 1966 to begin his own winery down the road at Oakville; Peter remained to continue making wines in the tradition of his father and the man who began it all, Charles Krug.

This winery pioneered in cold fermentation techniques which enhance the varietal character that Krug is noted for. The varietal wines contain 100 percent of the grape for which they are named. Many are aged in oak barrels—some Cabernet Sauvignon spends as much as 26 months in oak and 25 more in bottle before it is released. The Chardonnay may spend only three months in oak. The Mondavis prefer the dominance of varietal flavor for this and other white wines such as Johannisberg Riesling, Blanc Fumé, Gewürztraminer, and Sémillon. Charles Krug produces a wide range of wines, generics as well as varietals, that include Zinfandel and a Pinot Noir of considerable character. The Gamay Beaujolais is often a spirited wine with a large and pleasing bouquet. Unlike most premium wineries, Krug bottles a full line of half bottles, a good way to get acquainted with the range of varietals. Under a separate label, CK Mondavi, inexpensive gallon and half-gallon generic wines are produced, such as chablis, burgundy, and claret.

Charles Krug is owned corporately by C. Mondavi and Sons, the family company now of Peter Mondavi, Robert's brother. Peter's sons Marc and Peter, Jr., and their mother Mary Westbrook Mondavi are active in management. The parting with Robert Mondavi and his branch of the family in 1966 was not amicable, and lawsuits followed. The two family companies are totally unrelated, and Peter and Robert rarely speak any more. Among premium varietals, the wines of Robert Mondavi are usually superior to those of Charles Krug.

Peter's company, C. Mondavi and Sons, owns some 800 acres of vineyards, a substantial holding, while 400 acres more are owned by the family itself. Production totals 1.5 million cases a year of mostly jug wines under the CK Mondavi name, although the Krug wines remain popular among premium varietals.

☆/☆☆☆☆

$/$$

· L ·

Lacrima Christi.

The name of this wine means "tears of Christ," and it is produced in many parts of Italy, although, strictly speaking, it should come only from the Campania region in the south-central part of the country, around Mount Vesuvius. It can be red, rosé, or white, dry or sweet, and is usually quite fruity, with a pleasant bouquet. Were it not for its catchy name, Lacrima Christi would not be nearly as popular as it is.
☆/☆☆
$/$$

Château Lafite-Rothschild.

Among the renowned châteaux of Bordeaux, none enjoys a reputation as great as Lafite, classified first growth, or *premier grand cru,* in the Médoc classification of 1855 in Paris. The wines of this splendid château in the *commune* of Pauillac are held in near reverence by connoisseurs, and they are always among the most expensive on any restaurant list or in any retail establishment. Lafite is the quintessential claret, big but not overwhelming, delicate but not light, displaying extraordinary balance and elegance. Almonds and violets are evident in its bouquet, and richness and breeding are in its body. Some wine lovers prefer the more robust clarets of Château Mouton-Rothschild or Château Latour, also Pauillacs, or the elegance of a Château Margaux or a Château Haut-Brion, which round out the list of Bordeaux first growths. But no one would challenge Lafite's nobility and prestige.

In the Middle Ages the owners of the Lafite vineyards were always among the most influential families in French politics and justice. In the reign of Louis XV, Lafite was served at the royal table, and Madame Pompadour also favored it. It passed through the Alexandre de Ségur family, which also owned Château Latour and Château Calon-Ségur. Its owner during the French Revolution was a Monsieur de Pichard, a leading political figure of his time and a delegate to the Third Estate in Paris. He was guillotined in 1794, and the property was nationalized. Then it passed into Dutch ownership before being acquired by Samuel Scott, an English banker. Baron James de Rothschild of the Paris banking family purchased Lafite in 1868, and it has been in the family ever since, although in a different branch of the Rothschilds from that of Philippe de Rothschild, owner of Château Mouton-Rothschild. A certain amount of rivalry has existed between these two magnificent estates, partly because of Mouton's classification as a second growth prior to its elevation to first-growth status in 1973. Now that Mouton has achieved its proper rank, the rivalry seems to have diminished.

The Lafite vineyards are situated in the most elevated part of Pauillac, and the name itself is said to be derived from an old French word, *lahite,* for "the height." The château, with its conical towers, which appear on the Lafite label, is not far from the banks of the Gironde. The elevated hillside exposure of the vineyards to the sun and their proximity to the great river that flows past the Médoc en route to the Atlantic Ocean are important factors in the ripening of the Cabernet Sauvignon, Cabernet Franc, Merlot, and Petit Verdot grapes that make up the Lafite blend. Less Cabernet Sauvignon is used in Lafite than in the more robust Latour and Mouton-Rothschild, whose vineyards abut Lafite's, and this is the principal explanation for Lafite's softer and more delicate character. With ample quantities of the supple Merlot, Lafite tends to mature earlier than the wines dominated by Cabernet, but it still does not reach its peak for at least a decade after the harvest, even with today's modern vinification procedures.

The 1970 Lafite should not be drunk

before 1985, although it was an early-maturing wine, and the 1961 was far from ready in 1984, due to its deep concentration and intensity. The 1960, an off vintage, represented excellent value in the latter years of its first decade. But the 1968, another poor vintage all over France, probably will never display noble breeding, and the 1969, although better than the '68, will never be great. For drinking in the early 1980s, Lafite's '71 vintage is best, while the excellent '66 will take longer to mature. Lafite also was one of those châteaux whose 1979 appeared capable of surpassing the '78, and the 1981 also showed great promise.

The Lafite cellars in Pauillac are cool and so damp that water constantly oozes from the walls and ceilings. As in other Bordeaux cellars, most of the bottles bear no labels, for they would disintegrate in the moisture. Individual bins and sections of the Lafite cellars are identified by vintage dates, and not until the bottles are ready for shipping do they receive their labels. In one section is the Lafite "library"—with vintages dating as far back as 1797 and with many from the nineteenth century, including the renowned 1846, which brought $5,000 for a single bottle, then a record price, at the Heublein Wine Auction in San Francisco in 1971. Record prices for wine are customarily set by Lafites. The 1806 brought $28,000 at an auction in Chicago in 1979, and the 1822 brought $31,000 at the Heublein auction in San Francisco in 1980. (Both were uncorked by the author, and neither was worth the sum paid for it, except as publicity value.) Because the old bottles in the Lafite cellars are moved only to be recorked every quarter century and because the temperature there is so cool and consistent, these wines tend to remain in good condition. As soon as they leave the cellar, however, they are subject to sudden temperature changes and to the jostling and shaking that inevitably occur in transportation, so the old Lafites that seem to turn up at auctions so frequently are of doubtful quality for drinking and might best be set aside for show.

A secondary wine, Carruades de Château Lafite-Rothschild, is also produced, ostensibly from the grapes that do not attain sufficient quality each year to be bottled as Lafite itself, although this does not explain why the Barons Guy and Elie de Rothschild bothered to bottle any of the Lafite '68, which was a mediocre wine. In 1962 they purchased Château Duhart-Milon, a fourth-growth Pauillac that also abuts the La-fite vineyards, and soon changed its name to Château Duhart-Milon-Rothschild. Duhart-Milon is a good Pauillac but not good enough to warrant the price increases imposed on it since the Rothschilds acquired it. The Lafite vineyard totals about 150 acres, and about 60 more are cultivated at Duhart-Milon, but the production will probably never be adequate to fill the demand for these celebrated Rothschild wines.
☆☆☆☆
$$$/$$$$

Château Lafon-Rochet.

Château Lafon-Rochet is a *quatrième cru,* or fourth growth, in the Bordeaux classification of 1855. For some years it did not merit such a high rank, but now, under the capable management of its proprietor, Guy Tesseron, it has regained much of its former eminence. It tends to be one of the more supple wines of Saint-Estèphe, the northern-most of the great wine-producing *communes* of the Médoc above Bordeaux, although some majestically big wines have been made by Monsieur Tesseron. High tannin content and a nearly as-tringent hardness in youth are typical of Saint-Estèphe. A handsome château has been constructed by M. Tesseron.
☆☆☆☆
$$/$$$

Château Lagrange.

Château Lagrange was ranked a *troisième cru,* or third growth, in the Bordeaux classification of 1855. The estate lies in Saint-Julien, but the wines tend to lack the finesse of some of the others produced in this *commune* in the Médoc north of Bordeaux. They are said to benefit especially from greater bottle-age than some other Saint-Juliens, but older vintages of Lagrange are rarely seen in the United States or Great Britain. In 1983, Suntory Limited of Japan, one of the largest producers of beverages, announced the purchase of La-grange. Suntory also said it would double the production of 20,000 cases annually by planting additional portions of the 300-acre estate.
☆☆☆☆
$$/$$$

Château La Lagune.

Château La Lagune is one of the few estates ranked in the Bordeaux classification of 1855 that does not lie in one of the four great wine-producing *com-munes* of the Médoc: Margaux, Pauillac, Saint-Estèphe, or Saint-Julien. Rather, La Lagune lies in Ludon, just north of Blanquefort, the closest superior vineyard area to the city of Bordeaux. But Ludon is not entitled to an *appellation contrôlée,* so Château La Lagune is designated as an Haut-Médoc. It was ranked a *troisième cru* in 1855. Much vineyard replanting and refurbishing of the production facilities have been accomplished in recent years, resulting in wines that are somewhat more robust and longer-lived than those of Margaux, a few miles to the north.
☆☆☆☆
$$/$$$

Lalande-de-Pomerol.

Just to the north of the *commune* of Pomerol in southwest France are two smaller *communes,* Lalande-de-Pomerol and Néac, which are entitled to the name Lalande-de-Pomerol on their wines. These are fairly rare in the export markets, but they can represent excellent values when found, for they display many of the characteristics of the better Bordeaux. (*See also* Pomerol.)

☆☆☆/☆☆☆☆

$$

Lambert Bridge.

Excellent Chardonnays of texture and complexity are produced by Lambert Bridge in the Dry Creek area of Sonoma County, California. The winery, established in 1975, is owned and operated by Gerald and Margaret Lambert. Gerry Lambert, an heir to the Warner Lambert pharmaceutical empire, is committed to quality, and his wines show it. The first commercial harvest was in 1976, and Lambert Bridge immediately established a strong reputation for its Chardonnay. The winery, near Healdsburg, also produces Cabernet Sauvignon, but it rarely measures up to the Chardonnay. About 80 acres have been planted in vines, and Lambert Bridge buys no grapes from outside growers. Production runs about 10,000 cases a year.

☆☆

$$

Lambrusco.

Lambrusco is a red grape grown in enormous quantities in Italy, especially in the regions of Emilia-Romagna, Trentino-Alto Adige, and Lombardy. The wine it yields, sold under such brand names as Riunite, Giacobazzi, and Cella, is light and frothy and usually semisweet, and it has grown extremely popular with young people in the United States. In fact, were it not for Lambrusco, the Italian wine boom in the U.S. would be virtually nonexistent, for Italy's 60 percent share of the imported-wine market in America is due almost entirely to Lambrusco. In no small sense, Lambrusco has been responsible for introducing a generation of American consumers to wine, so it is taken seriously even by connoisseurs who never drink it. Sales in the U.S. now run into the hundreds of millions of bottles annually. The wine is totally lacking in complexity and firmness, but it is not meant to be a serious wine in any case. There are many labeled with the name of a town or region, e.g., Lambrusco di Parma, Lambrusco di Sorbara, Lambrusco Grasparossa di Castelvetro, Lambrusco Reggiano, etc.

☆

$

M. La Mont Winery.

A broad array of mostly mediocre wines are produced in huge quantities by M. La Mont, based in DiGiorgio, California, using Central Valley grapes that betray the unsuitably hot climate there for premium table wines. La Mont at one time was a cooperative jointly owned by a group of local grape growers, but it was sold to a Canadian company, John Labatt Ltd., in the late 1970s. The wines are bottled under the La Mont, Mountain Gold, and Mountain Peak labels. Production totals a massive 10 million cases a year, which makes La Mont one of the larger California winemaking enterprises.

☆

$

Lancers.

One of the world's most popular wines is Lancers rosé, a pink wine that is produced in great quantities in Portugal for the export markets. It is pleasant and charming, but, like all rosés, is lacking in character. It is one of the largest-selling wines in the United States, and much of its appeal derives from its bottle, a reddish-brown jug that can be turned into an attractive vase or candleholder after the wine has been consumed. It should be drunk well chilled as an aperitif, although many people drink it during meals. At one time Lancers was a so-called "crackling," or lightly sparkling wine, but the bubbles, which placed Lancers in the same import-duty category as Champagne, have long since been removed. A white Lancers is also produced and it is equally pleasant and innocuous. (*See also* Rosé, Mateus.)

☆

$$

Landmark Vineyards.

Landmark is a small winery producing premium California varietals near Windsor in California's Sonoma Valley. The name comes from the two rows of hundred-year-old cypress trees that border the driveway and have been a local landmark for many years. The winery is a family operation headed by William R. Mabry, whose wife, Maxine, and daughter, Katherine, are active in management and whose son, William R. Mabry III, is the winemaker. Landmark's first vintage was in 1974, and production has grown to 15,000 cases, with a goal of 25,000. There are 91 acres of vineyards, with 60 more due for planting. Grapes are also purchased from several outside growers. The winery initially turned out Chardonnay, Chenin Blanc, Johannisberg Riesling, Gewürztraminer, Pinot Noir, and Cabernet Sauvignon, but has concentrated on Chardonnay and Cabernet in recent vintages.

☆/☆☆☆

$$

Château Langoa-Barton.

This excellent estate lies adjacent to Château Léoville-Barton in the *commune* of Saint-Julien, one of the great wine-producing townships of the Médoc peninsula north of Bordeaux. Both are owned by Ronald Barton, great-great-grandson of Hugh Barton, the Irishman who bought the two vineyards in the 1820s and who was part of the Barton & Guestier shipping firm. Although Ronald Barton is a well-known Bordeaux personage today, he has maintained Irish citizenship, which enabled him to keep his châteaux ostensibly neutral during World War II. Barton & Guestier, still one of the major Bordeaux wine houses, is now part of the Seagram empire. Both Léoville-Barton and Langoa-Barton are vinified and bottled at Langoa, where huge wooden fermenting casks containing wine from the two vineyards stand side by side. The wines of Langoa tend to be less costly than those of Léoville-Barton, possibly reflecting the greater fame of the Léoville vineyards among connoisseurs. (Léoville-Las-Cases, Léoville-Poyferré, and Léoville-Barton once were united in one vineyard.) But Langoa consistently makes very fine wines, with great intensity and fullness. The Langoas of the 1940s are famous and are still in extraordinary condition. Most vintages of Langoa reach maturity after ten to 12 years.

☆☆☆☆

$$/$$$

Languedoc.

In southern France, west of the mouth of the Rhône River toward the Spanish border, is the hot and relatively flat plain known as Languedoc, where *vin très ordinaire* is produced in vast quantities. So mediocre is most of this regional wine that it is often "helped" with stronger imported wines from Algeria, Spain, or Italy, to be sold to farmers and workingmen of the area. Very little is ever seen outside southern France, except for Minervois, from the area just east of the ancient walled city of Carcassonne, and St-Chinian, adjacent to Minervois. From slightly farther south comes Corbières, which was sucked into the export markets in surprising quantities during the great price escalation of French wines in the late 1960s and early 1970s but which will probably recede into obscurity just as quickly as prices come down. From even closer to the Spanish border comes Roussillon, another sturdy and inexpensive red. The Corbières-Roussillon area also produces some sweet white wines which do not compare favorably with Sauternes or Barsac and are rarely exported.

Two interesting dry whites, Clairette de Bellegarde and Clairette du Languedoc, have been given *appellation contrôlée* recognition. Both are named after the Clairette grape variety, which is not held in the same esteem as the noble white grapes of Burgundy and Bordeaux. The Bellegarde variety is slightly fresher and lighter than the Clairette du Languedoc, but the latter tends to have a higher alcoholic content. Besides the two Clairettes, Languedoc has very few *ap-pellation contrôlée* designations. Much more common is the V.D.Q.S. rating, meaning *vins délimités de qualité supérieure,* or "delimited wines of superior quality." The V.D.Q.S. designation is mainly for decent local wines but has been seen increasingly in the export markets in recent years. Whenever they appear on a restaurant wine list, they should be far less expensive than other French wines.

☆/☆☆

$

Laubenheimer.

German white wine produced around the town of Laubenheim at the northern end of the Rheinhessen. The wine is generally undistinguished and ranks below the better wines of the region.

☆

$

Château Lascombes.

This excellent estate, ranked a *second cru,* or second growth, in the Bordeaux classification of 1855, achieved widespread popularity under the ownership of a group headed by Alexis Lichine (the author of wine books and a wine exporter) which took control in 1952. Under Lichine, the château was heavily promoted, and the name Lascombes became familiar to many Americans. Its renown was aided by an annual art show sponsored there by the Lichine group. The vineyard lies on a knoll in Margaux and had been subdivided by several owners until it consisted of only about 40 acres, when the Ginestets, who once owned Château Margaux, bought it in the early 1920s and began putting it all back together. The Lichine group then took over and continued reaccumulating parcels that had been sold off, and now it consists of 125 acres, although the ownership has changed hands once again. The wines are typical of Margaux—full-bodied yet elegant and not

as robust as the better wines of Pauillac and Saint-Estèphe farther north in the Médoc. A Lascombes from a good vintage is best consumed at between ten and 20 years of age.
☆☆☆☆
$$/$$$

Château Latour.

For some connoisseurs a properly mature Château Latour provides all that can be demanded of a red wine. It was one of four Bordeaux châteaux classified first growths, or *premiers grands crus,* in the Médoc classification of 1855 in Paris, and over the years it has proven that it merited the distinction. Latour lies in the *commune* of Pauillac, not far from such other great vineyards as Châteaux Lafite-Rothschild and Mouton Rothschild, in the Médoc region north of Bordeaux. Its wines are famous the world over for their fullness and depth. In their youth they are dark and tannic, with a powerful bouquet of cedarwood. As they age, the bouquet grows, but the tannin ebbs, and great balance is achieved. A Château Latour from a good vintage should last three decades without fading, assuming it is stored properly. In poor vintages, Latour often makes excellent wines, and it is perhaps the most reliable red Bordeaux in those off years

when no other château seems capable of surmounting adverse weather conditions. Latour is almost entirely made from Cabernet Sauvignon grapes, which account for its bigness.

The ancient tower depicted on Latour's label was constructed as part of a wall in defense against marauding pirates that sailed up the Gironde looking for plunder in the Middle Ages. At one point in the seventeenth century the châteaux Latour, Lafite, and Calon-Ségur all belonged to Alexandre de Ségur in a union of great vineyards that was spectacular indeed. More recently Lord Cowdray of Lazard Brothers, the London merchant banking house, has been in control, which makes Latour one of a number of excellent Bordeaux properties in foreign hands. Yet the owners have continued to use the time-honored production methods that, together with the rocky soil, have made the château's wines great. A secondary wine, Les Forts de Latour, is also produced, but it does not measure up to the great Château Latour itself.
☆☆☆☆☆
$$$/$$$$

Château Latour à Pomerol.

Many French vineyards and estates have names that include the French word for tower, *"la tour,"* but considerable confusion exists in the Bordeaux region because one of the half dozen most famous estates is Château Latour in Pauillac of the Haut-Médoc, which many other châteaux would like to imitate. There is also a Château Latour in Pomerol, and, to assure that it will not be confused with the great Latour of the Médoc, the name includes "à Pomerol," meaning "in Pomerol." Château Latour à Pomerol is one of the better estates of this important vinicultural district east of Bordeaux near Saint-Emilion. Pomerol estates have never been formally classified according to quality, but Latour à Pomerol would rank with the second or third growths of the Médoc in any broad classification of Bordeaux. It requires eight to ten years to reach maturity. Bottles 20 and 30 years old have shown remarkable character.

☆☆☆☆

$$$

Château Laville-Haut-Brion.

Château Laville-Haut-Brion is one of the white-wine estates of Graves in the *commune* of Talence, south of Bordeaux. It was ranked a *premier cru* in the Graves white-wine classification of 1959 and is one of the better producers of the district.

☆/☆☆

$$

Lawrence Winery.

Lawrence Winery was established in 1978 by Jim Lawrence and two partners in San Luis Obispo, California, and relies on grapes grown in the county of that name for a full line of premium varietal wines. Production grew rapidly to more than 700,000 gallons a year of Chardonnay, Johannisberg Riesling, Gewürztraminer, Sauvignon Blanc, Chenin Blanc, French Colombard, Cabernet Sauvignon, Zinfandel, Pinot Noir, Gamay Beaujolais, and Napa Gamay, along with a line of blended red, white, and rosé table wines. Initial marketing

efforts involved packaging the Lawrence wines in handsome wooden cases that could be turned into wine racks. The wines share the herbaceous quality of many other central-coast wines, yet they have won numerous awards at wine festivals.

Jim Lawrence is the winemaker. He has a Bachelor of Science degree in oenology from Fresno State College and a Master's in Business Administration from the same institution. He worked at Bear Mountain Winery and Giumarra Vineyards before starting his own operation in partnership with Don Burns and Herman Dreyer. In 1982 the business was purchased by Glenmore Distilleries, a major producer and distributor of wines and spirits.

☆/☆☆☆

$$

LeBay Cellars.

This Sonoma County winery was founded as Rege Winery in 1939. It was purchased by Helen Dauphiney and Doug Shaffer in 1980 and was undergoing extensive upgrading. The vineyard was being shifted to such premium varietals as Sauvignon Blanc, Zinfandel, and Petite Sirah. A Chardonnay made from purchased grapes was stylish. Production of 10,000 cases of various varieties was projected. Besides LeBay Cellars, the winery also uses the Château Rege name on certain bottlings.

☆/☆☆☆

$/$$

Charles Lefranc Cellars.

This is the name for the premium line of Almadén wines, including Château Lefranc, a late-harvested Sauvignon Blanc of superb quality. (*See* Almadén.)

Jean Léon.

Excellent Cabernet Sauvignons are made in Spain by Jean Léon, proprietor of La Scala, the Los Angeles restaurant, and they have wide distribution in the U.S. A small amount of Chardonnay is also produced. The *bodega* is in Penedés.

☆☆/☆☆☆☆
$$

Château Léoville-Barton.

Classified a *second cru,* or second growth, in the Bordeaux classification of 1855, Château Léoville-Barton is the property of the Barton family, whose Bordeaux firm, Barton & Guestier (now owned by Seagram's), is one of the best known. The vineyard once was joined with Léoville-Las-Cases and Léoville-Poyferré. Léoville-Barton produces big, rich wines that are consistently among the best of Saint-Julien. They have greater intensity and less elegance than the wines of Léoville-Las-Cases but tend to age more gracefully and develop more character, if less finesse. Léoville-Barton generally makes bigger and more charming wines than Léoville-Poyferré as well. The Barton wines are bottled at nearby Château Langoa-Barton. (*See* Château Langoa-Barton.)

☆☆☆☆
$$/$$$

Château Léoville-Las-Cases.

This is perhaps the most renowned of the three Léovilles of Saint-Julien in Bordeaux, and, like the others, was classified a second growth in the rankings of 1855. It is the largest producer among the three châteaux and tends to be especially appealing to oenophiles who prefer their reds to have greater delicacy and elegance than bigness. The château takes its name from the Marquis de Las-Cases, who owned it until the turn of the century. The arched stone gateway that appears on the Léoville-Las-Cases label is a landmark of Saint-Julien.

☆☆☆☆
$$$

Château Léoville-Poyferré.

Among the three great Léovilles that once were combined in one vineyard, Léoville-Poyferré is the least renowned today, although it produces very good wines that have many devoted followers all over the world. Like Léoville-Barton and Léoville-Las-Cases, it was accorded *second cru,* or second growth, status in the Bordeaux classification of 1855. Its wines lack the depth and intensity of the other Léovilles.

☆☆☆☆
$$$

Château de Leu.

Château de Leu, a French Tudor building overlooking 80 acres of vineyards, is operated by Ben Volkhardt, Jr., and Ben Volkhardt III, who are also proprietors of Volkhardt Vineyards, which has cultivated grapes for other California wineries since the 1950s. The Volkhardts decided to begin making their own wines in 1982, when they established the Château de Leu label and a secondary brand called Green Valley Vineyards. Their property lies in Suisun in Solano County, near the Napa County border, and was originally planted with vines in the 1880s. The first wines, 1500 cases in all, were released in 1982, and 8000 cases were to be released in 1983. Volkhardt Vineyards, which supplies the grapes for Château de Leu, owns 20 acres of Chardonnay, 14 acres of French Colombard, ten acres of Napa Gamay, and smaller plantings of Fumé Blanc, Chenin Blanc, and Petite Sirah. The French Colombard is barrel-fermented and is aged in French oak.

☆/☆☆☆
$/$$

Liebfrauenstift.

Name for wines grown exclusively in the vineyards surrounding the Liebfrauenkirche, or church, in Worms in the Rheinhessen. Not synonymous with Liebfraumilch, the listing of which follows.

☆

$

Liebfraumilch, Liebfrauenmilch.

German white wine which is no longer identified with a particular vineyard and usually represents a blend of wines from a number of Rhine vineyards. The word literally means "maiden's milk" or "Holy Lady's milk" when used in connection with the Liebfrauenstift vineyard near the Liebfrauenkirche, or church, in Worms just south of Nierstein in the Rheinhessen. Publications mentioned the Liebfrauenmilch of Worms several centuries ago, implying that it was one of the renowned wines of time past. Shortly after the turn of the century the Chamber of Commerce of Worms, where very few noble wines are produced, formally recognized that the wine trade had been making free and unrestricted use of the Liebfraumilch name for some time and suggested that it should be applied to any Rhine wines of good quality.

Today not all Liebfraumilch is of good quality, however, and the suspicion is widespread that virtually anything that is white and semisweet is used to produce it. That is why it has become widely available in shops all over the world as a bin wine of very low cost. This is not to suggest that all Liebfraumilch is mediocre. Some is delightful and can serve as an excellent introduction to German wines in general. The most successfully marketed Liebfraumilch in foreign countries in recent years has been the Blue Nun of the Sichel firm based in Mainz. Hundreds of thousands of gallons of Blue Nun are blended at one time, and exhaustive precautions are taken to preserve the Blue Nun taste, which is semisweet like many Liebfraumilchs but not so sweet that it can-

not be served throughout a meal. Anyone who has witnessed a Blue Nun blending session at the Sichel facilities in Mainz will take the wine seriously thereafter. A few other big and solid firms with high standards also produce excellent Liebfraumilch, and generally these cost more. Among them are Deinhard's Hanns Christof and Julius Kayser's Glockenspiel. Sadly, though, most Liebfraumilch that you will encounter in wine shops is cheap stuff that would have disappointed the town fathers of Worms if they had tasted it at the start of the century when they decided Liebfraumilch should be good-quality wine.

☆

$/$$

Liguria.

Liguria is the crescent-shaped region of northwestern Italy that encompasses the Italian Riviera, with Genoa at its center. Many different wines are produced there, but perhaps the most famous are Cinqueterre and Dolceacqua. Production is not large, because the region itself is small and is focused almost exclusively on tourism.

Livermore.

The Livermore Valley of Alameda County, east of San Francisco Bay, is an important wine region of California and is the home of famous wineries such as Wente Brothers and Concannon. During the 1960s a number of Livermore vineyards were engulfed by suburban expansion and covered over with housing divisions and shopping centers. This was unfortunate, as the gravelly soil and climate of Livermore are excellent for the wine grape. It has been mostly famous for its white wines, but as in the Graves District of Bordeaux, where the climate and soil are similar, excellent reds are made also, particularly Gamay Beaujolais and Petite Sirah. One of California's most famous vineyards, Cresta Blanca, originated here. Owner Charles Wetmore was a reporter for San Francisco newspapers who became so interested in wine that he finally established a winery of his own. Through a friend he made contact with the Marquis de Lur-Saluces in France, owner of the top château in Sauternes, Château d'Yquem. He was able to obtain cuttings from the Marquis of Sauvignon Blanc, Sémillon, and Muscadelle Bordelais, the three varieties that make up the glorious Yquem—and he was in business. During the 1960s, however, the winery closed down. It has since reopened in Mendocino County, and the Cresta Blanca label is seen once again.

Llords & Elwood Winery.

Llords & Elwood is a small family-owned winery based in Fremont in Alameda County, California. Production and aging of its wines take place in three separate facilities in the Santa Clara Valley—one in Fremont and two in San Jose. All of the grapes are purchased from outside growers. The business was established by the late Mike Elwood, a former wine and spirits retailer in the Beverly Hills area. After opening one store there, he bought another called Llords, and the Llords & Elwood name was born. The retailing business eventually grew into five stores, all in the Beverly Hills-West Los Angeles vicinity.

The Llords & Elwood winemaking business was founded by Mike Elwood in 1955 and is operated now by his son Dick. In 1961 the Elwoods retired from their retailing business and went into the winemaking business full time. They claim to have been pioneers with the first rosé of Cabernet Sauvignon in 1966 and with the first Spätlese style of Johannisberg Riesling in California. Using the solera system of outdoor storage and blending from cask to cask by gravity feed, Llords & Elwood produces a line of very good Sherries as well as Port. The operation also produces Chardonnay, Johannisberg Riesling, rosé of Cabernet, Pinot Noir, Cabernet Sauvignon, and sparkling wine.

☆/☆☆☆

$$

J. Lohr (Turgeon & Lohr Winery).

The J. Lohr label adorns the production of the Turgeon & Lohr Winery in San Jose, in Santa Clara County, California. The partners in the venture, formerly in the construction business, are Jerry Lohr and Bernie Turgeon, and they produce an array of Monterey reds and whites from 280 acres of vineyards near Greenfield, in Monterey County. The vineyards were planted in 1972, the winery was built in 1974, and the first J. Lohr wines reached the market in 1976. Production now exceeds 100,000 cases a year of such varietals as Chenin Blanc, Chardonnay, Pinot Blanc, Johannisberg Riesling, Cabernet Sauvignon, Napa Gamay, Zinfandel, and Petite Sirah, as well as a branded wine called Jade, which is *pétillant,* or slightly effervescent. The winery, on part of the premises of the old Freidricksburg Brewery in San Jose, has more than 1500 small oak barrels for aging. The J. Lohr wines often display the herbaceous quality common to many Monterey County wines.

☆/☆☆

$/$$

Loire Valley.

Some of the pleasantest, most unassuming and inexpensive wines of France come from the Loire River Valley, which extends from the Atlantic Ocean near Nantes on the west some 550 miles east through Angers, Tours, the famous château country, Orléans, and on southward, where its headwaters rise in the rugged hills near St-Etienne. Most of the good Loire wines come from the 260-mile stretch between Nantes and Pouilly-sur-Loire southeast of Orléans. They are mainly white, produced from either the Chenin Blanc grape or the Sauvignon Blanc. Rarely do they attain the quality heights of the better white Burgundies produced from the Chardonnay grape, but rarely do they cost as much, either. Lots of sparkling Loire wines are also produced, and they are usually available at bargain prices compared to Champagne. Loire wines have charm and a pleasant personality. Some are rather heavy and earthy, others are clean and light. Sometimes they are known as "country wines," reflecting their honest and unassuming character.

Among the driest and most refreshing are the Muscadets that come from the area around Nantes, just before the Loire empties into the Atlantic. Unlike most other French wines, this one is named after the grape variety, the Muscadet, originally the Mélon de Bourgogne, and it has an almost musky flavor that makes it good company with shellfish. Heading east and upriver is the Anjou District which includes Saumur, Savennières, and the Coteaux du Layon. As a group, the wines from this area are not usually as crisp and dry as Muscadet; the most famous wine is the Rosé d'Anjou, one of the world's best known rosés. Farther east is the Touraine, where lots of ordinary still and sparkling whites are produced, as well as some better ones, including Vouvray. The best reds of the Loire also come from Touraine; they are Chinon and Bourgueil. At the easternmost reaches of the important Loire wine-growing area are Sancerre and Pouilly-sur-Loire, with its renowned Pouilly Fumé. After this point the valley winds almost due south and eventually reaches headwaters in the rugged Massif Central, where noble wines are not produced.

On the Loire tributary known as the Cher, about 50 miles due south of Orléans, are Reuilly and nearby Quincy, whose whites made from the Sauvignon Blanc are favored by some connoisseurs. But they are not often seen in export markets. Equally rare is the Jasnières, produced not far from Vouvray in the central Loire Valley's Touraine District. Its wines are similar to Vouvray and are most distinctive when they are sweet. The Loire has numerous subdivisions and outposts where decent wine is made, and most of these are worth sampling, if only to satisfy curiosity.

Few wines are actually called "Loire." Most of them are entitled to more specific geographical designations and some are produced in specific vineyards whose superiority qualifies them to use the vineyard names on their labels. For example, Clos de la Coulée de Serrant has its own *appellation contrôlée* within Savennières, one of the Anjou subdivisions. This implies that it is one of the very superior wines of the area, which it is. The bulk of Loire wines are consumed by local citizens and by tourists making their way through the château country. They are rarely great but are often good, and they nearly always represent excellent value. (*See also* Anjou, Touraine, Muscadet, Pouilly Fumé, Sancerre, Vouvray.)

☆/☆☆☆

$/$$

Lombardy.

One of the better wine-producing regions of northern Italy is Lombardy, lying just to the east of the more famous Piedmont. The best part of Lombardy is the mountainous Valtellina, which produces Grumello, Inferno, Sassella, and Valgella on steeply terraced hillsides. These are earthy, full-bodied red wines vinified from the Nebbiolo grape which produces the best wines of the Piedmont region as well. The best producers are Bettini, Negri, Polatti, and

Rainoldi. The vineyards look down upon the River Adda that flows into Lake Como. Perla Villa and Fracia are lesser known, producing lighter wines. Elsewhere in Lombardy good red wines are also produced, but generally not up to the standards of Valtellina. Among these are Bellagio, vinified from French grapes grown on the shores of Lake Como, Chiaretto del Garda, from the shores of Lake Garda, and Montelio. The wines of Frecciarossa in the Oltrepo Pavese are produced entirely by one owner, Giorgio Odero, who has a reputation for maintaining very high standards.
☆☆/☆☆☆☆
$/$$

Long Vineyards.

Long Vineyards, with 15 acres equally divided between Chardonnay and Johannisberg Riesling, lies in the hills of the Napa Valley facing north across Lake Hennessey toward Mount St. Helena. Originally the property was mostly Riesling, but half has been grafted over to Chardonnay. The enterprise was founded with the 1977 vintage and is owned by Zelma Long, who also is the winemaker at Simi in the Sonoma region, and by her former husband, Bob, who operates the Long winery and vineyards while Zelma makes the wines. Production is fewer than 2000 cases a year, but the wines are well made, displaying good varietal intensity. At the first annual Napa Valley Wine Auction in 1981 the Long Vineyards Chardonnay 1977 sold for $50 a bottle and the 1978 version sold for $100 a bottle, far above the retail prices for either vintage.
☆/☆☆
$$/$$$

Château Loudenne.

Among the better Bordeaux vineyards not given an official classification in 1855 is Château Loudenne, a *cru bourgeois* whose red wines are the equal of many

of the classified growths. In 1975 the château celebrated a century of ownership by W. & A. Gilbey Ltd., the producer of Gilbey's gin in Britain and an important part of International Distillers & Vintners of London. The château is situated near St. Yzans in the northern part of the Médoc peninsula beyond the boundary of Saint-Estèphe, and its wines carry the Médoc *appellation*. The involvement of Gilbey's over the years has meant that Château Loudenne's wines have enjoyed great popularity in foreign markets and are widely available, usually at moderate prices. The château, a low-slung country house surrounded by terraces, has for many years been the scene of elegant house parties attended by guests from many countries, including prime ministers and other heads of state. It also serves as the home base for Gilbey Société Anonyme Bordeaux, a major Bordeaux shipping house that exports many fine wines from other châteaux to markets all over the world. Château Loudenne is a reliable name in both red and white Bordeaux. The reds are made in the traditional way, with maturation in new oak casks and bottling by hand. The whites are vinified in temperature-controlled stainless steel tanks to preserve the freshness, the taste of fruit, that sometimes is lacking in other Bordeaux whites. The reds of Loudenne are not as hard and tannic as many of the nearby Saint-Estèphes and tend to mature at a younger age. They are soft and elegant and in recent vintages have been ready for drinking within seven years of the harvest, although older vintages have displayed remarkable staying power.
☆☆/☆☆☆☆
$$

Loupiac.

Directly across the Garonne River from Barsac, south of Bordeaux in southwestern France, is the town of Loupiac, where pleasant sweet white wines are made. Despite the area's proximity to Barsac and Sauternes, however, the whites of Loupiac rarely reach the same luscious and elegant quality levels. They seem heavier and ordinary, and the relatively low prices at which they sell are appropriate.

☆/☆☆

$/$$

Lower Lake Winery.

The Lower Lake Winery is said to be the first winery established in Lake County, California, since the repeal of Prohibition in 1934. Founded in 1977 by members of the Stuermer and Scavene families, it has specialized in Cabernet Sauvignon, producing both red and white versions, as well as a Fumé Blanc. Production amounted to about 4500 cases in the 1982 vintage. (Lake County, just north of Napa County, is the scene of increasing vineyard activity as Napa property becomes ever more scarce and expensive.)

☆/☆☆☆

$/$$

Château Lynch-Bages.

In blind tastings, Château Lynch-Bages consistently ranks well above its fifth-growth status in the Bordeaux classification of 1855. It displays great intensity, with the classic bouquet of freshly cut cedarwood or black currants that

is characteristic of the better Bordeaux reds. The estate lies in Pauillac, one of the important *communes* of the Médoc peninsula that runs north of Bordeaux, and its production is among the largest in the Médoc. Partly because it is produced with 75 percent Cabernet Sauvignon grapes, Lynch-Bages tends to be a big and robust wine that some of its admirers compare with Château Mouton Rothschild, also of Pauillac. Lynch-Bages does not show quite the same finesse as Mouton, but it is a fully flavored and rich wine. Its name comes from a one-time proprietor of Irish origins who was mayor of Bordeaux in the early 1800s. Monsieur Lynch also owned Château Lynch-Moussas, another Pauillac estate. Lynch-Bages lies near the little village of Bages, which has also lent its name to the Châteaux Haut-Bages-Libéral, Croizet-Bages, and Haut-Bages-Averous. Lynch-Bages begins to mellow about eight years after the vintage and is best at 12 to 15 years of age.

☆☆☆☆

$$$

Lytton Springs Winery.

Superb Zinfandels are produced by Lytton Springs at its winery near Healdsburg in the Sonoma Valley, and the focus will remain on this spicy varietal, although small amounts of Cabernet Sauvignon are produced in some vintages. The first commercial harvest for Lytton Springs was the 1975, when Zinfandel was made in borrowed premises. Another batch followed in 1976, also made in borrowed facilities, before the winery was finished in 1977. The winery is leased by a small corporation headed by Bura W. "Walt" Walters, the Lytton Springs proprietor, and it buys 100 percent of its grapes, mostly from an adjacent vineyard. Walters retired from the navy in 1970 after 23 years in naval food service, and in 1971 he went to work for Richard Sherwin, a vineyardist who now is a primary source of the grapes vinified by Lytton Springs. The same vineyard once supplied Ridge Vineyards. Production stands at about 10,000 cases a year and is expected to remain at that level for the foreseeable future. The wines are aged in small barrels made of American, French, and Yugoslavian oak. The Zinfandels are rich, textured, and spicy.

☆☆☆

$$

· M ·

Mâcon-Clessé, Mâcon-Fuissé, Mâcon-Lugny, Mâcon-Viré.

Several vineyard areas in the Mâconnais subregion of the French Burgundy country have been entitled to add the name of the local village to the name Mâcon for purposes of identification. Technically, these wines come under the Mâcon-Villages *appellation,* and their full names are long—for example, Mâcon-Villages Commune de Clessé. But they are shortened on labels, to be read Mâcon-Clessé, Mâcon-Fuissé, Mâcon-Lugny, or Mâcon-Viré. All are made with the Chardonnay grape and all are the products of vineyards not far from Pouilly-Fuissé, the most famous wine of the region. They rarely achieve the depth, fullness and balance of a good Pouilly-Fuissé, although they tend to be much better value at a fraction of the cost of Pouilly-Fuissé. Mâcon-Fuissé is produced from vineyards in the *commune* of Fuissé which were planted later than the awarding of the official *appellation contrôlée* of Pouilly-Fuissé in 1936 and therefore could not be included in the more celebrated *appellation.* In fact, not until the 1977 vintage did Mâcon-Fuissé appear commercially. In com-

mon with all Mâcon-Villages whites, the hyphenated *commune* wines of Mâcon-Fuissé and the others must achieve 11 percent alcohol in order to merit their *appellation.*
☆/☆☆☆
$/$$$

Mâconnais.

Just north of the Beaujolais country in eastern France is another area that produces good wines. It is named after Mâcon, the principal town of the area, and its most famous wine is Pouilly-Fuissé, an excellent white that has become so popular in the United States in recent years that its price has shot up to fairly high levels. Because of Pouilly-Fuissé's renown, some other Mâconnais whites with similar names—Pouilly-Vinzelles and Pouilly-Loché—have also become popular. They tend to lack the depth and finesse of the better Pouilly-Fuissés, but occasionally they rise to extraordinary heights. One of the newest *appellations,* Saint-Véran, also comes from the area. It tends to be not quite as rich as a Pouilly-Fuissé, but has a character all its own, showing a touch more earthiness. It is usually a good value. Another inexpensive white wine from the Mâconnais is the Mâcon-Viré, named after the village of Viré, north of Mâcon. Other Mâcon village names also sometimes appear on labels. All of the best whites of the Mâconnais are made from the Chardonnay grape, also called the Pinot Chardonnay, the same variety that produces the big and noble whites of the Côte de Beaune section of the Côte d'Or in Burgundy. Generally, though, the Mâconnais whites do not match those from the Côte de Beaune in quality or finesse and ought to cost somewhat less. (*See* Pouilly-Fuissé.)

A certain quantity of Mâcon Rouge is also produced, but none of it rises to the quality levels of the district's whites, except the small amounts that come from the area around Romanèche-Thorins at the northern end of the Beaujolais country. Because of the great popularity of Beaujolais, it is said that good red Mâcons somehow find their way into Beaujolais bottles, while only the less noble Mâcon Rouge is actually sold under its own name. Higher standards apply to the ones that merit the names Mâcon Supérieur or Mâcon-Villages. Some of the *rouge* comes from the Pinot Noir grape of the Côte d'Or; the best is made with the Gamay Noir à Jus Blanc, but this grape does better in Beaujolais soil than in the Mâconnais. A Mâcon Rouge should cost less than a Beaujolais or any red from the Côte d'Or. It must attain 9 percent in alcoholic strength, whereas a simple Pinot-Chardonnay-Mâcon, the comparable white wine of the simplest level, must reach 10 percent. The Mâcon Supérieur or Mâcon-Villages must reach 10 percent if red, 11 percent if white. The Pinot-Chardonnay-Mâcon and the Mâcon Blanc are roughly equivalent. All Mâconnais wines are best drunk within five years of the vintage.

☆/☆☆

$/$$

Madeira.

One of the world's best known fortified wines is Madeira, whose reputed powers as an aphrodisiac have long been regaled in song and verse. No scientific evidence has been produced to indicate that Madeira is any more capable of arousing human emotions than other fortified wines, but its reputation no doubt will linger. The wine is produced on the island of Madeira, lying off the west coast of Africa in the Atlantic Ocean. Like such other great fortified dessert wines as Port, Sherry and Marsala, Madeira is largely the result of British enterprise, although the island is part of Portugal. It was the British who developed the Madeira trade in the eighteenth century and discovered that the addition of grape brandy to the wine prior to its voyage to English and American markets helped it to survive the journey in good condition. The journey, moreover, was found actually to improve the wine, once the brandy had been added. The theory was that the pitching and rolling of the sailing vessels of the British merchant fleet assured that the brandy would be thoroughly mixed with the wine. The constant movement also probably aged the wine prematurely, giving it the velvety softness which is still one of its important characteristics.

The island was claimed for Portugal in 1418 by Captain João Gonsalves Zarco and Tristão Vaz Teixera, representing Prince Henry the Navigator, who named it Madeira, the "Isle of Trees," because of its extremely dense forests. Due to the warm and accommodating climate, the vegetation was so dense that it was virtually impenetrable, so the Portuguese sailors set it afire to enable them to explore it. Legend has it that the island burned for seven years, and layer upon layer of ashes built up on top of the already rich humus deposited by the forest over the centuries, creating ideal soil for growing vines. A less credible legend has it that the burning of the island is responsible for the burnt taste that is Madeira's most recognizable characteristic even now. In any event, substantial vineyard acreage is cultivated there, and Madeira has become a pleasant and beautiful vacation area, its rugged mountains and lush greenery attracting many thousands of visitors each year.

Several varieties or styles of Madeira are produced, and they are usually named after the type of grape used to make the wine.

Sercial: the driest of the Madeiras, sometimes compared with *fino* Sherry, although a Sercial will tend to be slightly sweeter. Scholars of wine have linked the Sercial grape to the great Riesling of Germany, but the wine produced on the island of Madeira bears no resemblance to Riesling from Germany or anywhere else.

Rainwater: another name for dry Madeira, although it does not refer to a variety of grape. An American from Savannah, Georgia, named Habisham imported his own Madeira in casks in the early nineteenth century and, according to legend, used a secret method of filtering the wines so that they were especially light and clear—like rainwater. These became Rainwater Madeiras, and the name stuck, although now it is much more widely used.

According to another story, Rainwater obtained its name from a shipment of casks that were drenched with rain while lying at dockside in Oporto en route to Boston. Somehow the rain worked its way into the casks, diluting the Madeira. The New Englanders found the light, diluted wine pleasant and asked for more. Still another theory is that Rainwater Madeira comes from grapes grown so high on the hillsides of the island that irrigation is impossible, so the wine is produced only in years of sufficient natural rainfall. In any event, Rainwater is a pleasant, light Madeira.

Verdelho: sweeter than Sercial or Rainwater, but remains light and refreshing. It is sometimes likened to an Amontillado Sherry.

Malmsey: the Madeira most adored by connoisseurs and probably the one that produced the stories of aphrodisiacal powers. It is a rich, velvety dessert wine made from the Malvoisie grape. It is comparable to a cream Sherry, although it has somewhat more character.

Bual: similar to Malmsey, but not quite so sweet. It is often drunk while cheese is being served at the end of a meal and is similar to a well-made tawny Port.

The sweeter Madeiras are vinified in a manner similar to that for Port. Grape brandy is added to the fermenting wine before all of the natural grape sugar has been converted to alcohol. The addition of the brandy halts the fermentation process by killing the yeasts that cause the fermentation, leaving residual sugar in the wine. Sufficient brandy is added to raise the alcohol level to around 20 percent, compared to the 12 to 13 percent that wine achieves through normal fermentation. Then the Madeira is blended, using a *solera* process similar to the method for blending Sherry in Spain. Young wines are mixed with old ones, so that a consistent quality is maintained. The "vintage" dates on Madeira labels actually refer to the year when the *solera* was started—when the very first wine was put into the casks. A Malmsey from the 1876 *solera* might have an iota or two of the 1876 vintage in it, but it will really be a blend of vintages since then. The better Malmseys will sometimes display a *solera* year on their labels, but this should not be construed to mean the same thing as a

vintage designation, which should mean entirely wine from a single year.
☆/☆☆☆☆
$/$$$

Maderization.

The process by which white and rosé wines deteriorate, turning a brownish color and taking on a slightly rotten odor, is known as maderization. The term is derived from "Madeira," the fortified sweet wine produced on the Island of Madeira, in the Atlantic Ocean off the coast of Morocco, and it is true that maderized wines resemble Madeira. The breakdown of white wines involves oxidation, implying improper storage, permitting the corks to dry out or rapid temperature fluctuations, causing an air exchange through the corks. Maderization also occurs from aging in cask for long periods prior to bottling and is sought in the production of Madeira, sherry, and Marsala, as well as a few other dessert or aperitif wines. The French terms are *maderisation* and *maderisé*.

Madroña Vineyards.

Madroña, with vineyards planted in the early 1970s, built its own winery in time for the 1980 harvest in El Dorado County, California, an area noted for full-bodied Zinfandels and Cabernet Sauvignons. Thirty-five acres are now in vines, and production reached about 4000 cases in the 1981 vintage. Besides Cabernets and Zinfandel, Madroña produces Merlot, Chardonnay, White Riesling, Gewürztraminer, and a white Zinfandel.
☆/☆☆☆
$/$$

Château Magdelaine.

This excellent estate was ranked as a *premier grand cru classé* in the Saint-Emilion classification of 1955. It is one of the *côtes,* or hillside vineyards, surrounding the ancient village of Saint-Emilion itself, about 20 miles east of Bordeaux. Château Magdelaine is owned by the Libourne shipping firm of Jean Pierre Moueix, which has extensive interests in the Pomerol District, including part ownership of Château Pétrus. The wines of Magdelaine are supple and pleasant, coincidentally not unlike some of the better wines of Pomerol. The estate lies not far from Châteaux Belair and Ausone on one of the best slopes of the district. Magdelaine begins to reach maturity at about age eight.
☆☆☆☆
$$$

Château Malartic-Lagravière.

Among the better estates of Graves, south of the city of Bordeaux, is Château Malartic-Lagravière, whose red and white wines were given *grand cru* status in the Graves classification of 1959. Malartic lies in Léognan, which is also the *commune* of Domaine de Chevalier and several other good estates. Malartic is not one of the better red Graves in light vintages, but it makes big and robust wines in good years when the grapes achieve full ripeness. It is best after about eight years of age and remains pleasant and full well into its second decade.
☆☆☆/☆☆☆☆
$$/$$$

Malbec.

Among the principal grape varieties cultivated in the Bordeaux region of France, the Malbec has a long tradition. It has never been dominant or comparable in use to the Cabernet Sauvignon or the Merlot, but it exists in many château-bottled wines of the region. It has also been cultivated to some extent in California, although its use has diminished recently. The Malbec has a reputation for sparse yields and lack of fruit on the tongue, although it provides texture—that mouth-filling characteristic that makes a good wine almost chewy. For this reason, principally, it continues to survive, although vintners from the Napa Valley to the Médoc keep hoping that the weather conditions in their respective microclimates will create such robust and full-bodied Cabernets and Merlots that the need for a bit of Malbec in the blend will be eliminated.

Château Malescot-Saint-Exupéry.

In 1697 this estate in Margaux on the Médoc peninsula north of the city of Bordeaux was acquired by Simon Malescot, a court official in Bordeaux. Count Jean-Baptiste de Saint-Exupéry bought it 130 years later and added his own name to that of Malescot. Château Malescot-Saint-Exupéry was ranked a *troisième cru,* or third growth, in the Bordeaux classification of 1855. It has been under the same ownership as Château Marquis-d'Alesme-Becker. Château Malescot produces fairly robust wines that are not always typical of Margaux, generally needing five to ten years more bottle-age than most other wines produced in this excellent *commune.* A Malescot from a good vintage should not be drunk before its tenth birthday.
☆☆☆☆
$$$

Malvasia.

The Malvasia is a white grape that belongs to the Muscat family and is widely cultivated in Italy and other countries. It is most often fairly deep yellow or golden in color and is usually vinified sweet for use as a dessert wine or, perhaps, as an aperitif. Many versions are made in Italy, sometimes with the name of a town or district attached, e.g., Malvasia delle Lipari, Malvasia di Bosa, Malvasia di Cagliari, Malvasia di Castelnuovo Don Bosco, etc. Sometimes they are fortified for added punch and longer

life, but they are best drunk when fairly young.
☆/☆☆
$

La Mancha.

The most bountiful wine-producing region of Spain is the elevated plateau known as La Mancha, southeast of Madrid. Light and dry reds and whites are produced here, but the reds predominate and can be found at modest cost in the export markets under the general name Valdepeñas, which also happens to be the name of the bustling, principal wine town of the region. Valdepeñas is not great wine, but it can be very pleasant. It can be described as a Spanish version of Beaujolais and, like Beaujolais, should be drunk slightly chilled. Most Valdepeñas is sold as carafe wine in the bars and restaurants of Spain, and its name tends to change according to the part of the country where it is served.
☆/☆☆
$/$$

Manischewitz.

The millions of gallons of kosher wines that are labeled Manischewitz each year actually are made by Monarch Wine Company, housed in the vast Bush Terminal in Brooklyn, New York. After repeal, when Monarch got started, the owners realized that it would be a great advantage if their wines could be marketed under the Manischewitz label, the most famous name in kosher foods. Under an agreement that still stands, Monarch pays Manischewitz for use of the name. The wines are made from the Concord grape harvested in vineyards upstate, where the grapes are pressed and the juice frozen in bulk. It is stored in Monarch's processing plants near Buffalo until the winery in Brooklyn is ready to use it. Monarch makes wine year-round in the Brooklyn plant and carefully observes the regulations for kosher wine. A rabbi supervises each step in the process and even the Champagnes that Monarch produces for house labels are kosher. Red and white wines are made from the Concord and in both versions range from medium dry to quite sweet. Monarch also makes fruit wines and vermouth. The firm imports European wines which it sells under the Tytell label.

☆

$/$$

Margaux.

Among the four *communes,* or townships, that comprise the Haut-Médoc north of Bordeaux, Margaux is the most famous, possibly because it is the only *commune* that has a *premier cru classé* estate named after it. Château Margaux is one of the world's great red-wine producers, but there are a number of other excellent estates within the *commune.* The wines of Margaux are invariably described as the most "feminine" of the Médoc, because they are soft, supple, and charming, with great sensuality. Within this definition, however, individual styles assert themselves, and a Château Palmer from a good vintage may display greater finesse than a Château Giscours of the same year, while a Château Lascombes may be more robust. Besides Château Margaux, twenty other vineyards within the *commune* achieved *cru classé* status in the Bordeaux classification of 1855. They are the following:

Premier Cru (First Growth)
Château Margaux

Seconds Crus (Second Growths)
Château Rausan-Ségla
Château Rauzan-Gassies
Château Lascombes
Château Durfort-Vivens
Château Brane-Cantenac

Troisièmes Crus (Third Growths)
Château Kirwan
Château d'Issan
Château Giscours
Château Malescot-Saint-Exupéry
Château Boyd-Cantenac
Château Cantenac-Brown
Château Palmer
Château Desmirail
Château Ferrière
Château Marquis d'Alesme

Quatrièmes Crus (Fourth Growths)
Château Prieuré-Lichine
Château Pouget
Château Marquis-de-Termes

Cinquièmes Crus (Fifth Growths)
Château Dauzac
Château du Tertre

The most widely distributed of the Margaux in the United States are the Châteaux Palmer, Giscours, Brane-Cantenac, Prieuré-Lichine, Lascombes, and Rausan-Ségla, in addition to Château Margaux. All of these are fine wines, competing to be among the best red Bordeaux. Besides the classified growths, however, there are a number of other very good estates within the *commune.* Among these are Château d'Angludet, ranked as a *cru exceptionnel* and owned by the Sichel family, Château Labégorce, a *cru bourgeois supérieur,* Château Paveil-de-Luze, another *bourgeois supérieur,* and Château La Tour-de-Mons, in the same category. These wines of lesser renown sometimes offer excellent value, although they are not as consistent as most of the classified growths. (*See also* Médoc, Bordeaux.)

☆☆☆☆

$$/$$$$

Château Margaux.

In 1855 the wines of four Bordeaux châteaux were classified as first great growths, or *premiers grands crus,* in connection with an exposition in Paris. These were Châteaux Margaux, Lafite, Latour, and Haut-Brion, and they have remained among the greatest producers of red wines in the world ever since. Château Margaux, whose 150 acres of superb vineyards are situated in the *commune* of Margaux, is the most delicate of the top-ranked Bordeaux. Softer than Latour and Mouton Rothschild (which joined the other four as a *premier cru* in 1973), Château Margaux displays great balance and elegance, with a perfumy bouquet evocative of violets or freshly hewn cedarwood. Like other wines from the *commune* of Margaux, Château Margaux is considered more "feminine" than the robust Saint-Estèphes and Pauillacs from elsewhere in the Médoc.

The château itself is a magnificent edifice constructed in 1802 by the Marquis Douat de La Colonilla after he tore down the former Gothic mansion. King Edward III of England, who was made Duke of Aquitaine in 1325 and who assumed the title of King of France in 1340, lived there during part of his reign, when the château was one of the most imposing fortified castles in the region. In 1977 the property was purchased by André Mentzelopoulos, a native of Greece who owned the Felix Potin supermarket chain, with some 1800 stores, in France. The purchase price was 62 million francs, then equal to about $13.5 million, and Monsieur Mentzelopoulos and his charming wife, Laura, spent another 40 million francs refurbishing the mansion and upgrading the vineyard. The wine of Château Margaux, which disappointed some connoisseurs when the Ginestet shipping family owned it prior to the sale to Mentzelopoulos, has improved under the new ownership. André Mentzelopoulos died in December 1980, but his wife has continued to manage Château Margaux, as she did even before the death of her husband.

A white wine (unusual in the Médoc) is also produced there under the name Pavillon Blanc du Château Margaux; it tends to be crisp and dry, but it is never on the same quality level as Château Margaux itself, which needs a good decade of age to reach maturity. Because it is delicate, however, most vintages of Château Margaux should be drunk before their twentieth birthday. (*See* Margaux.)

☆☆☆☆

$$$/$$$$

Mark West Vineyards.

In the Russian River Valley of Sonoma County in one of California's prime growing areas lies the Mark West Vineyards, owned and operated by Bob and Joan Ellis. Bob is an airline pilot, and Joan is a former accountant who is now one of the few female owner-winemakers in the country. Their first plantings took place in 1972 and their first wines were bottled from the harvest of 1976. As of 1981 some 62 acres had been planted in vines: about one-quarter Chardonnay, one-quarter Gewürztraminer, one-quarter Johannisberg Riesling, and one-quarter Pinot Noir. Twenty acres more were to be planted entirely in Chardonnay. All of the wines have been estate-bottled since 1977, and all are initially slightly high in acidity, which gives them greater longevity than some others from the Golden State. Joan Ellis says her Chardonnays and Pinot Noir Blancs (whites made from the black Pinot grape) need at least two full years from the date of the harvest to achieve their full fruit and complexity. When consumed younger, they tend to seem slightly green and tart. Half of the Chardonnay of Mark West is barrel-fermented in new French oak casks and then is aged a year in old French oak for added complexity.

☆/☆☆

$$

Markham Winery.

H. Bruce Markham is another of those individuals who was lured away from the business world to enter California winemaking. He had been president of a fifty-year-old family-owned advertising agency, the Markham Advertising Company, when he began acquiring vineyard property in the Napa Valley in 1975. The family business was sold, and Markham began buying additional Napa property in preparation for a full commitment to wine. The Markham holdings now include some 300 acres in three separate sections of the Napa Valley—the Calistoga, Yountville, and Oak Knoll areas.

A century-old stone winery building was acquired in St. Helena, and one-third of Markham's vineyard properties were set aside for the Markham wines. The grapes from the other two-thirds are sold to other premium wineries. The first Markham vintage was 1978, when 17,000 cases were made under the Markham and Vin Mark labels. The product lineup includes Chardonnay, Chenin Blanc, Johannisberg Riesling, Muscat de Frontignan, Gamay Beaujolais Blanc, Cabernet Sauvignon, Merlot, and such types as red and white table wine.

☆/☆☆☆

$$

Marqués de Cáceres.

One of the better red wines of the Rioja District of northern Spain is the Marqués de Cáceres, a soft, elegant wine that has attracted a wide following in the United States because of its early drinkability. It is vinified in such a way that it does not require years of bottle-aging in order to achieve the mellowness of maturity; normally it is ready within five years of the harvest. The wine is made by Henri and Elysée Forner, who have a background in Bordeaux. They have major ownership interests in Château Larose Trintaudon and Château de Camensac, and the Cáceres label bears a resemblance to the Larose Trintaudon label. Henri Forner supervises the Bordeaux part of the business and Elysée Forner runs the Rioja operation. The first vintage of Cáceres shipped to the United States was the 1970, which was vinified at a large co-operative winery in Rioja. Two years later, separate facilities at the cooperative were constructed for the Cáceres wines. Members of the cooperative are still the major source of the wines for the Cáceres blend, although Elysée Forner oversees the vinification. Production runs some 200,000 cases a year, of which 10 to 20 percent have been coming into the American market. In certain vintages a *reserva,* with more aging, is produced, and it tends to be a more complex wine than the regular bottling. The only fault with the regular Cáceres is that it lacks complexity, but possibly for this reason (and because of attractive pricing) it has attracted a significant following in the United States.

☆☆/☆☆☆☆

$/$$

Marqués de Murrieta.

One of the very finest Rioja wines from Spain is produced by the Marqués de Murrieta at Ygay near the town of Logroño on the River Ebro. Reds, whites and rosés are made at this *bodega,* but the reds are taken most seriously abroad. The Rioja Valley stretches across the northern part of the country and for many years has produced Spain's best red table wines. The *reservas* of the Marqués de Murrieta spend at least a decade in oaken casks before bottling and can provide intriguing taste experiences. (*See also* Rioja, Marqués de Riscal.)

☆☆/☆☆☆☆

$$

Marqués de Riscal.

Very few winemaking establishments in Spain have achieved international reputations comparable to any of the major châteaux of Bordeaux, but there are some. The Marqués de Riscal is one of them. This *bodega* was established in 1860, predating the invasion of the French viniculturists from the north who were fleeing the Phylloxera vine blight that had devastated their vineyards. Making red wines in the Bordeaux style was the credo of Riscal's founders, and these wines resemble good Bordeaux to this day. They need eight to ten years to reach maturity. Riscal is at Elciego, in the heart of Spain's Rioja Valley, where the best red wines of the country have traditionally been produced. The facilities of the Marqués de Riscal include a fairly comprehensive library of old bottles. Recent vintages of Riscal are more widely available on the American and British markets than any other good Riojas, and the prices are attractive. These wines merit consideration for inclusion in any thoughtfully planned cellar. (*See also* Rioja, Marqués de Murrieta.)

☆☆/☆☆☆☆

$$

Château Marquis-de-Terme.

This vineyard took its name from one of its proprietors in the latter half of the eighteenth century, the Lord of Pe-

guilhan, who was also the Marquis de Terme and whose wife was a member of the Rausan family that had widespread vineyard interests in Bordeaux in the seventeenth, eighteenth, and nineteenth centuries, e.g., Châteaux Rausan-Ségla and Rauzan-Gassies. Marquis-de-Terme lies in Margaux on the Médoc peninsula north of the city of Bordeaux and was ranked a *quatrième cru,* or fourth growth, in the Bordeaux classification of 1855. The proportion of Cabernet Sauvignon grapes, at 25 percent, is relatively small for one of the good reds of Bordeaux, and the blend has fairly large percentages of Cabernet Franc, Merlot, and Petit Verdot. The wine is sometimes less supple and balanced than others from Margaux. It needs a decade to reach maturity.

☆☆☆☆

$$/$$$

Marsala.

The Island of Sicily, lying in the Mediterranean Sea off the "toe" of Italy, is the second-largest Italian wine-producing region, partly because of the substantial quantities of Marsala that come out of it. Marsala is a fortified wine in the same category as Madeira, Port, and Sherry; its alcohol level is usually 18 to 20 percent, and it is fairly sweet. In common with Port, Sherry, and Madeira, Marsala achieved international recognition largely through the efforts of British merchants. John Woodhouse of Liverpool has been credited with recognizing Marsala as a generic competitor to the other fortified wines in 1760. Marsala is made from the Catarratto and Grillo grapes, with a modest blending of Inzolia. To reach its high alcohol level, a mixture consisting of 25 percent wine brandy and 75 percent *passito,* or dried grape must, is added to the wine, along with another additive consisting of fresh unfermented grape juice that has been boiled down to a thick texture. The combination results in additional fermentation and the dark brownish-red tinge that is a Marsala characteristic. Some Marsala is produced under the same *solera* system used in Jerez for Sherry. This involves the continual blending of older wines with young wines, so that every bottle contains at least a minute quantity of old wine.

Marsala is vinified and blended in four different grades: Marsala Fini, Marsala Superiori, Marsala Vergini, Marsala Speciali. The Fini have an alcohol level of 17 percent, and the others are all at least 18 percent. The Superiori must be aged at least two years. The Vergini are usually made by the *solera* system and lack some of the additives of the others. The Speciali usually have a special flavor added, e.g., eggs or strawberries, and are very thick and sweet. Marsala is an interesting fortified wine that has a certain following around the world, but it lacks the finesse of the other fortified wines.

☆/☆☆☆☆

$/$$

Marsannay-la-Côte.

About two miles above the last vineyards of the Burgundian Côte d'Or and just south of the city of Dijon is Marsannay-la-Côte, which at one time was part of the old Côte de Dijon before it virtually disappeared as a serious winemaking area. There are two reasons for mentioning Marsannay. The first is that one of the better rosé wines of the Burgundy country is produced here from the Pinot Noir grape in substantial quantities. The Rosé de Marsannay is drier than some other rosés and makes a pleasant aperitif when served well chilled. The second is that one of the best Burgundian restaurants, appropriately named Les Gourmets, is operated here by M. and Mme. Daniel Gauthier.

The wine cellar is good, as it should be.

☆/☆☆☆☆

$$

L. K. Marshall Winery.

L. K. Marshall is a member of the big California cooperative called Guild Wineries and Distilleries. All of its wines are vinified and distributed by Guild. (*See* entry for Guild.)

Louis M. Martini.

One of the best-known and most esteemed names in California wine is that of Louis M. Martini, an Italian who went to the American West Coast in 1900. Involved in winemaking very early in life, he established the present winery in St. Helena in 1934. Soon he began acquiring vineyards, including 300 acres atop the Mayacamas Range between the Napa and Sonoma Valleys that he named Monte Rosso after the red volcanic soil. Other acquisitions followed, with acreage in the cool Carneros Region at the lower end of Napa, up around Healdsburg near the Russian River in Sonoma and, later, the Chiles Valley east of St. Helena. Martini's son, Louis Peter Martini, joined the family venture after World War II, first as viniculturist, then as winemaker. With his father's retirement in 1968 he became president and general manager. In true patriarchal fashion, however, the elder Martini remained actively involved until his death in 1974.

It is said that Louis P. knows his grapes well and both grows and buys some of the best in the valley. He has substantial vineyard holdings, mostly in upland regions where the vines must struggle, producing low yields but high quality. He fills 70 percent of his grape requirements from his own vineyards. The word "Mountain" that appears on all Martini labels is not there to arouse romantic notions but is used because most of the grapes are grown on mountainsides. "A vine has to be stressed to produce good grapes," says Martini. Most of his attention is concentrated on the reds, and the Cabernet Sauvignon, Pinot Noir, and Zinfandel consistently are full-bodied, complex wines of long life. Louis Martini sometimes makes small batches of special wines, although he prefers to use his premium varietals for maintaining the high quality of his main blends.

An exception, however, is Cabernet Sauvignon, the variety that intrigues him most, and the 1968 vintage was high enough in quantity and quality to permit some experimentation. Five lots of Special Selection wines were made with variations in blending and aging. Lots 2 and 3 contain percentages of Merlot and Malbec, grape varieties used in Bordeaux to add complexity and soften the almost astringent impact exerted by Cabernet in its early years. Lots 4 and 5 were 100 percent Sonoma Cabernet, the first aged in 50-gallon oak barrels, the second in 1300-gallon oak casks. Martini watched the wines carefully, tasting them as they developed, and felt that after four years in bottle they were ready for release in 1975. Lot No. 1, a blend of 50 percent Napa Cabernet and 50 percent Sonoma, was quickly sold out, as was Lot No. 4, the one aged in small oak. Generally the flavor of oak is somewhat in the background with Martini wines, allowing the varietal fruit to predominate. Pinot Noir is also aged in 1300-gallon oak casks, Zinfandel in redwood tanks.

Martini whites are always vinified completely dry, even the least expensive half-gallon wines, in the belief that they taste better this way with meals. The white varietals are fresh and appealing, particularly the spicy Gewürztraminer and soft, fragrant Johannisberg Riesling. Generic wines, among the best values in California, are available both in fifth sizes and half-gallons. Mountain Burgundy, a sturdy blend of Petite Sirah, Gamay, and Pinot Noir, is aged two years or more before bottling. The Mountain Claret, intentionally lighter, is made from Zinfandel, Gamay, and Grenache and aged only six months. Mountain Chablis is mostly French Colombard but contains Chenin Blanc. Chardonnay, and Folle Blanche whenever surplus is available.

A man of great warmth and generous nature, Louis Martini is vigorously involved in every phase of the winemaking process; during harvest he is on the scene by 5 A.M. each morning to check the temperature of the fermenting wines and leave instructions for what is to be done that day. It makes him very happy that his children are carrying on the family tradition.

☆/☆☆☆☆

$/$$

Martini & Rossi.

Martini & Rossi is a leading producer of vermouth and Asti Spumante, with extensive facilities in Torino, Italy, and a winemaking history that dates back two centuries. Its vermouth and sparkling wine from Asti are major sellers in the American market, and in recent years the company has begun marketing a line of dry table wines in the United States in an effort to capitalize further on its widely recognized name. Early entries from Emilia-Romagna and the Veneto were well-made wines.

Maryland.

The most famous wines in Maryland are those from Philip Wagner's Boordy Vineyards at Riderwood. (The winery has its own listing alphabetically.) Another vineyard of interest at present is Montbray Wine Cellars in Westminster, a small operation owned by G. Hamilton Mowbray. His wines include Seyval Blanc and Maréchal Foch from French hybrids, as well as Chardonnay. Other Vinifera varieties planted are Johannisberg Riesling, Cabernet

Sauvignon, and Gamay. Production will eventually reach 22,000 gallons a year. All Mowbray's wines are vinified dry and receive varying periods of aging in American white oak.

Paul Masson.

Paul Masson came to Santa Clara County in California at the age of 19, burning with the ambition to make fine wine. The family vineyards in Burgundy, where he was born and grew up, were devastated by Phylloxera in the 1870s so he set out for America. Once here, he had the good fortune to go to work for Charles LeFranc, and the company became known as LeFranc and Masson, later evolving into Almadén. Masson married Louise LeFranc. It was a most beneficial association for both Frenchmen and profitable as well. They constantly worked on ways to improve the wines. Masson was keen on making Champagne, and by the time the first Champagne was available LeFranc had made him a full partner. Eventually, however, Masson purchased a piece of land all his own and began to make Pinot Noir, Cabernet, Pinot Blanc, Gamay, and other varietals. High above Saratoga, La Cresta Vineyard, the "vineyard in the sky," became such a celebrated site, visited by traveling dignitaries and famous people, such as actress Anna Held and Charlie Chaplin, all of whom were wined and dined by the ebullient Masson. He was a potent force in the California wine industry and remained active until his death in 1940 at age 81.

The Paul Masson winery today is a subsidiary of Seagram. The original winery with its twelfth-century portal, the Champagne cellars and the "vineyard in the sky" have all been retained and expanded. Volume is nearly 20 million gallons per year, second only to Almadén among premium producers. When Masson heard University of Cal-

ifornia Professor E. W. Hilgard say that "judicious blending is the height of the art of winemaking," he took it very much to heart. As a Champagne-master he had refined the blending art to a high degree, and he applied his knowledge to table wines of quality and consistency, ready for drinking the moment they are opened. This tradition of winemaking continues at Paul Masson and while at times one might wish for a greater depth or complexity in the Cabernet Sauvignon or Chardonnay, they are always pleasant drinking and reasonably priced. Not until 1976 did Masson introduce vintage-dated wines, and now all of the Masson varietal table wines carry a vintage year on their labels. But Paul Masson himself would not have done it this way. A number of proprietary wines were developed at Paul Masson and they are among the best values from the winery—for example, Emerald Dry, a white from the Emerald Riesling grape. Masson Light, a low-alcohol wine, was introduced in 1981, and the company's "California Carafe"—literally a winery-sealed carafe container—remains one of the most successful packaging innovations in the American wine business. The Masson carafes are used over and over again by consumers, and now they are even turning up as collectibles at flea markets, even though they date back only to 1972.

A very respectable line of Sherries, Port, and other dessert wines are also produced as well as Champagne, aperitifs, and brandy.

☆/☆☆☆

$/$$

Matanzas Creek Winery.

The Matanzas Creek Winery in Santa Rosa, Sonoma County, California, produces mostly Chardonnay of good quality, but also makes Pinot Blanc, Gewürztraminer, Pinot Noir, Cabernet

Sauvignon, and Merlot. Occasionally small amounts of Sémillon, Sauvignon Blanc, or Muscat Canelli are also turned out, depending on what grapes are available in the California market and whether Sandra MacIver, the owner, or Merry Edwards, the winemaker, are in an experimental mood. Merry Edwards, a graduate in oenology from the University of California at Davis, worked for three years at Mount Eden Vineyards in Saratoga and is one of the few female winemakers in the country, although their number is growing rapidly. The winery was built in 1977 and the first Matanzas Creek wines were produced in 1978. Production is approaching a modest 5000 cases a year, but the wines are well made and have attracted a following. Matanzas Creek has about 25 acres planted in Cabernet Sauvignon, plus additional acreage in Merlot and Chardonnay. It buys about half of its grapes from outside growers. Its Chardonnay is about 75 percent barrel-fermented. Small Limousin oak barrels are used for aging both the Chardonnay and the Pinot Noir, while small Nevers oak barrels are used for Cabernet Sauvignon and Merlot.
☆/☆☆☆
$$

Mateus.

The old and ornate palace called Mateus stands next to the road running north of the Douro River in northern Portugal to the city of Vila Real. The proprietor, a Portuguese nobleman, charges admission to the grounds, which have become a popular stopping place for tourists familiar with Mateus rosé wines. Behind the palace lies a beautiful garden filled with passageways between extraordinary sculpted boxwood hedges. Mateus Rosé, one of the largest-selling imported wines in the United States, does not really come from vineyards associated with the palace. The wine is produced from grapes grown all over northern Portugal and is blended to create the particular Mateus style in a big plant outside the city of Oporto on the Atlantic coast.

Mateus achieved its enormous popularity mainly because it is a pleasant and charming wine that has been successfully marketed by Schenley, the big American beverage company. It is medium dry, light in color, innocuous and undistinguished. It is a wine for people who do not ordinarily drink wine, as are most rosés, although it must be said that Mateus lacks the coarseness of some of the cheaper ones. It is best consumed well chilled as an aperitif, although many people drink it with their meals. The Portuguese pronounce the name "Ma-TAY-us," but Americans are more inclined to call it "Ma-TOOS." (*See* rosé.)
☆
$$

Maximin Grünhäuser.

This is the best-known of the Ruwer River wines in the Mosel-Saar-Ruwer region of Germany. Its picturesque label, showing the manor house framed in rich green leaves, is striking and no doubt is responsible for at least a small share of the wine's reputation. The vineyard name has eclipsed the name of the nearby village, Mertesdorf, and comes from the name of one of the ancient owners, the St. Maximin Abbey of Trier. The owner now is the Von Schubert family, whose name appears on the label, usually accompanied by the name of a specific plot of ground, such as Herrenberg, Abtsberg, or Brüderberg. The Maximin Grünhäuser can be a rich and elegant wine in the best vintages, displaying a delicate bouquet and fresh character that place it among the best in Germany. It is made with the noble Riesling grape, like nearly all of the other top wines of the Mosel-Saar-Ruwer region, and its remarkable fruity character is accompanied by a slight *stahlig,* or steely, taste. In the mediocre vintages, which unfortunately occur more often in this part of Germany due to the cooler weather, the steely taste tends to be much more pronounced and overwhelms the taste of the grape. Still, whenever good wines are made in the Ruwer, the Maximin Grünhauser will be among the best. To retain its identity under the new German wine law of 1971, the Maximin Grünhäus became a suburb of Mertesdorf. The Abtsberg, Herrenberg and Brüderberg vineyards retained their names also.

☆/☆☆☆

$$

May Wine.

May Wine (Maiwein, in German) traditionally is a light German wine punch flavored with Waldmeister, or sweet-scented woodruff, a woodland herb, along with strawberries and perhaps other fruit. It also may have sugar added and is generally somewhat sweet. Bottlings of May Wine have increasingly become available in the United States, and they do not appear to contain fruit flavors. Rather, they are simple, sweet German wines promoted in the spring months at low prices to attract consumer interest. The sweetness is usually sufficient to mask any flaws in the wine itself. An American version of May Wine punch calls for mixing simple white wine of almost any origin with Champagne, brandy, Benedictine, and sugar, plus a quantity of Waldmeister, creating a far more potent concoction than the traditional German Maiwein.

☆

$

Mayacamas.

Mayacamas is one of the smallest of the California Napa Valley's premium wineries but widely acknowledged as one of the best. Winemaker Robert Travers is a relative newcomer to the wine business. Formerly a stockbroker in San Francisco, Travers' love of fine wine and interest in making it grew serious, and eventually he quit his business to go to work for Joe Heitz of Heitz Cellars and learn firsthand some of the techniques in oenology he had studied at the University of California at Davis. In 1968, in a limited partnership with six others, he bought the winery and its 40 acres of vines, terraced on hillsides over 2000 feet above the valley floor. By the early 1980s, about 60 acres were in vines, supplying about half the winery's requirements.

The first buildings on the property had been constructed by a pickle merchant from San Francisco in 1889. John Henry Fisher, an immigrant from Stuttgart, Germany, planted Zinfandel and Mission grapes for red and white table wines and also built a small distillery out of native gray stone (where Bob and Nonie Travers now live). Fisher sold the winery around the turn of the century, and it lay dormant through Prohibition. In 1941 it was bought and revived by Jack and Mary Taylor, who renamed it Mayacamas, an Indian term meaning "howl of the mountain lion." The Taylors planted Chardonnay, Cabernet, and other top varietals and for some 20 years made small amounts of highly regarded wines.

Mayacamas is still a small and compact operation: only five or six thousand cases are produced each year. Since Travers bought the winery he has gradually narrowed his range of production and at present concentrates his abilities on three varietals: Chardonnay, Cabernet Sauvignon, and Zinfandel. Most are 100 percent varietal and aged in French and American oak. Pinot Noir and Sauvignon Blanc are also produced in some vintages. The Late Harvest Zinfandel is a deep and powerful wine that Travers likes to serve only with cheese or just by itself. It is really too big to accompany a meal. A number of California growers market a Late Harvest Zinfandel nowadays, but in 1968 it happened at Mayacamas by accident. Unable to pick the Zinfandel until late September, Travers found the grapes so ripe they produced a wine of 17 percent alcohol instead of the usual 12 or 12.5 percent. This fortuitous occurrence was repeated in 1972 and in 1978, each time resulting in a wine of intense aroma and flavor—an extraordinary experience well worth seeking.

☆/☆☆☆☆

$$/$$$

McCall Winery.

McCall is a member of the big California cooperative called Guild Wineries and Distilleries. All of its wines are vinified and distributed by Guild. (*See* entry for Guild.)

☆

$

McDowell Valley Vineyards (McDowell Cellars).

McDowell Valley Vineyards, owned and operated by Richard and Karen Keehn, is a small winemaking and growing enterprise located in the McDowell Valley about four miles east of Hopland in the southern end of California's Mendocino County. It was settled by Paxton McDowell in 1852 after he failed to strike pay dirt in the California gold rush. Much of the valley had been planted by the turn of the century, and now 360 acres are owned by the Keehns, who bought the estate in 1970 and began selling grapes to other producers. They built their own winery in 1979, and it is believed to be one of the first to use solar heat, a measure decided upon because of the proprietors' environmental concerns.

The vineyards lie between 750 and 1000 feet above sea level. The microclimate there is affected by moist air from the Pacific Ocean which moves into the valley about midday. The Keehns have records showing that their peak temperatures are five to seven degrees cooler in summer than in surrounding areas, while in winter and spring they experience less frost because of the moderating influence of the Pacific. Their grapes are picked partly by a mechanical harvester, and the harvest is accomplished entirely at night to preserve grape freshness. Their cellars are about 15 feet below ground level, enabling them to maintain temperatures at 55° Fahrenheit the year round.

McDowell Valley Vineyards is a family operation. Both Richard and Karen Keehn are native northern Californians, and they have eight children. Besides McDowell Valley Vineyards, they also bottle under the Mendocino Cellars brand. Production totals about 60,000 cases a year of Chardonnay, Chenin Blanc, Sauvignon Blanc, French Colombard, Grenache, Cabernet Sauvignon, Petite Sirah, and Zinfandel.

☆/☆☆☆

$$

Mead.

Mead is an alcoholic beverage made by diluting honey with water and allowing the mixture to ferment. It may have been the first alcoholic beverage, for it is known that the Greeks and Romans made mead 2000 to 5000 years ago. Normally two or three parts water must be mixed with the fresh honey of bees in order for a fermentation to begin, for pure honey is too dense to ferment on its own. Often fruit juices and other nutrients are also added to the honey in order to assure a complete fermentation through the action of yeasts and to enhance the flavor of the ultimate product. Mead is often defined as honey wine, which is an accurate general definition, although, technically, wine is the product of fermented grape juice and not of other fermented substances.

Médoc.

The Médoc is a large triangular peninsula running north from the city of Bordeaux, bounded on the west by the Atlantic Ocean and on the east by the Gironde estuary. It is an area where some of the greatest red wines of France, and therefore of the world, are produced. The western two-thirds of the peninsula is dominated by sandy hills and pine woods. The great vineyards lie along the banks of the Gironde in the eastern portion, and a local maxim is that the vines growing in sight of the river are superior, while those that cannot see the water produce lesser wines. The vinicultural area is divided into two sections, the Haut-Médoc and the Bas-Médoc, although the Bas-Médoc has come to be known simply as the Médoc, in common with the entire general area of the peninsula. Wines from the area also are sometimes called simply Médoc, to differentiate them in a generic sense from Saint-Emilion, Pomerol, Graves, and Sauternes, which are the best-known of the other Bordeaux vineyard areas. Château Lafite-Rothschild, for example, is an Haut-Médoc, informally a Médoc, as well as being a Pauillac and Lafite itself.

The Médoc starts at the Jalle de Blanquefort, a small river just north of the Bordeaux city limits, and extends farther northward some 50 miles in a band rarely more than seven miles wide. The hills are modest, and most of the vineyards are on flatlands. It is the soil that makes the area virtually worthless for growing anything except grapevines, but magnificent for cultivating the Cabernet Sauvignon, Cabernet Franc, Carmenère, Merlot, Malbec, and Petit Verdot grapes that are used to make red Bordeaux wines. In what geologists call the Tertiary Epoch, thick layers of gravel and yellowish pebbles were deposited there on foundations of clay, limestone, and sand. The best wines come from the coarsest, rockiest soil, which tends to lie in more elevated areas, while lesser wines are produced in the lower, alluvial soil that actually is more fertile but less capable of cultivating grapes properly.

The French *appellation contrôlée* designations tend to reflect the differences in soil quality. The broadest categories of wines produced in the Médoc, and therefore those with the least specific names, are simply called Haut-Médoc, Bas-Médoc, or Médoc. Although Bas-Médoc means "Lower Médoc," the term refers to the downstream part of the peninsula on the Gironde, while Haut-Médoc refers to the upstream portion. To make matters more confusing, the Gironde flows from south to northwest, so the Haut-Médoc is below the Bas-Médoc on any map of the area. The best wines are produced in the Haut-Médoc, although many excellent wines also come from the Bas-Médoc.

The Haut-Médoc is only about 30 miles long, extending from Blanquefort on the south to Saint Seurin-de-Cadourne on the north. Here is where some of the most famous vineyards in the world lie. Twenty-six *communes*, or townships, exist in this extraordinary band of vineyards, but only six are entitled to *appellations communales*. These are Margaux, which includes the *communes* of Cantenac, Arsac, and Soussans; Moulis, including parts of Listrac; Saint-Julien, which includes parts of Pauillac, Cussac, and Saint-Laurent; Pauillac, the greatest *commune* of all, which contains parts of Saint-Julien, Saint-Estèphe, and Saint-Sauveur; and Saint-Estèphe, which is self-contained.

About 500 individual vineyards exist here, averaging fewer than 25 acres in size, although the most celebrated estates are somewhat larger. For the most part, the greatest vineyards are those that were ranked in the Médoc classification of 1855 by the Bordeaux Chamber of Commerce in connection with the Paris Exposition held in that year. Only 62 crus, or estates, also known as châteaux or "growths," were designated as Great Classified Growths of the Médoc, while all the rest had to be content with cru bourgeois, cru grand bourgeois, or similar designations. Many of these are fine wines, but they lack the automatic access to fame accorded by a numerical classement.

The basis for the rankings in 1855 was the quality of the wines produced at each château. This was determined not only by actual tasting, but also by reputation and price achieved in the marketplace. Thus, Château Haut-Brion, which is in Graves, far to the south of the Médoc, was classified as a premier grand cru, or first great growth, in the 1855 classification because of its fame and the high prices it fetched, even though it should have been excluded from the rankings on a geographical basis. There is little doubt today that the 1855 classification remains the single most important determinant of prices for Bordeaux wines, even though the ownership and the quality of many of the vineyards obviously have fluctuated in the years since then. To some extent, moreover, the classification is self-fulfilling, because its tendency to create greater demand and therefore to foster higher prices for specific châteaux enables those châteaux to invest more in their vineyards.

Within the classification are five nu-merical subdivisions. The first growths, or premiers grands crus, are supposed to be the best, while cinquième cru, or fifth growth, is the lowest category. This would imply that being a fifth growth was of dubious distinction, but the opposite is true, considering that hundreds of other Bordeaux vineyards did not achieve a cru classé designation at all. Among the 62 that did merit cru classé status were four first growths (plus Château Mouton Rothschild, which was raised from second to first in 1973), 15 second growths, 14 third growths, 11 fourth growths, and 18 fifth growths. On a quality basis, some of the fifth growths now merit recognition at least as second growths if not first growths, while others perhaps should be demoted. Outside the first growths, the particular numerical classification of a château is no longer given great weight by many knowledgeable wine-lovers. It is enough to know that a château received cru classé recognition in 1855.

It has been well over a century since the classification was adopted. Some of the vineyards have been merged in the intervening decades, others have been subdivided, and the spelling of names has changed, sometimes drastically. Here is a list of the châteaux in the 1855 classification, using their present names:

Premiers Crus (First Growths)
château
Château Lafite-Rothschild
    Pauillac
Château Margaux
    Margaux
Château Latour
    Pauillac
Château Haut-Brion
    Pessac, Graves[1]

---

[1]Château Haut-Brion, in Pessac, Graves, was included in the 1855 classification because of its renown and high price, although it is not a Médoc.

Château Mouton Rothschild[2]
Pauillac

Seconds Crus (Second Growths)
Château Rausan-Ségla
Margaux
Château Rauzan-Gassies
Margaux
Château Léoville-Las-Cases
Saint-Julien
Château Léoville-Poyferré
Saint-Julien
Château Léoville-Barton
Saint-Julien
Château Durfort-Vivens
Margaux
Château Gruaud-Larose
Saint-Julien
Château Lascombes
Margaux
Château Brane-Cantenac
Cantenac-Margaux
Château Pichon-Longueville
Pauillac
Château Pichon-Longueville
(Comtesse de Lalande)
Pauillac
Château Ducru-Beaucaillou
Saint-Julien
Château Cos-d'Estournel
Saint-Estèphe
Château Montrose
Saint-Estèphe

Troisièmes Crus (Third Growths)
Château Kirwan
Cantenac-Margaux
Château d'Issan
Cantenac-Margaux
Château Lagrange
Saint-Julien
Château Langoa-Barton
Saint-Julien
Château Giscours
Labarde-Margaux

Château Malescot-Saint-Exupéry
Margaux
Château Boyd-Cantenac
Cantenac-Margaux
Château Cantenac-Brown
Cantenac-Margaux
Château Palmer
Cantenac-Margaux
Château La Lagune
Ludon
Château Desmirail
Margaux
Château Calon-Ségur
Saint-Estèphe
Château Ferrière
Margaux
Château Marquis-d'Alesme-Becker
Margaux

Quatrièmes Crus (Fourth Growths)
Château Saint-Pierre
Saint-Julien
Château Talbot
Saint-Julien
Château Branaire-Ducru
Saint-Julien
Château Duhart-Milon-Rothschild
Pauillac
Château Pouget
Cantenac-Margaux
Château La Tour-Carnet
Saint-Laurent
Château Lafon-Rochet
Saint-Estèphe
Château Beychevelle
Saint-Julien
Château Prieuré-Lichine
Cantenac-Margaux
Château Marquis-de-Termes
Margaux

Cinquièmes Crus (Fifth Growths)
Château Pontet-Canet
Pauillac
Château Batailley
Pauillac

[2]Château Mouton Rothschild was classified a second growth in 1855, but was elevated to first growth in 1973 in the only change in the original classification until that time.

Château Haut-Batailley
Pauillac
Château Grand-Puy-Lacoste
Pauillac
Château Grand-Puy-Ducasse
Pauillac
Château Lynch-Bages
Pauillac
Château Lynch-Moussas
Pauillac
Château Dauzac
Labarde
Château Mouton-Baron-Philippe
Pauillac
Château du Tertre
Arsac-Margaux
Château Haut-Bages-Libéral
Pauillac
Château Pédesclaux
Pauillac
Château Belgrave
Saint-Laurent
Château Camensac
Saint-Laurent
Château Cos-Labory
Saint-Estèphe
Château Clerc-Milon-Mondon
Pauillac
Château Croizet-Bages
Pauillac
Château Cantemerle
Macau

Many critics have suggested that the Médoc Classification of 1855 be given a thorough revision to reflect the changes that have occurred not only among the classified châteaux but also among some of the better unclassified estates. For example, Château Lynch-Bages, a fifth growth, is held in such high regard that it is sold at prices above some second growths, and the same is true of Château Talbot and Château Beychevelle, both well-made fourth growths. Now that Mouton Rothschild has been raised from second- to first-growth status, say some critics, ample precedent exists for making other changes. But the situation

is fraught with politics, mainly because the same grounds for elevating some châteaux would call for the demotion of others. In recognition of Mouton Rothschild's proven ability to sell at the same or higher prices than some first-growth Médocs over the years, virtually no dissension was heard when it was upgraded. But considerable controversy could erupt over other changes that might not be so universally accepted. It will take an abundance of fortitude for any body of Bordeaux judges to undertake any substantial reclassification. (*See also* individual château and *commune* entries.)

☆☆/☆☆☆☆☆
$/$$$$

Mendocino.

Mendocino County is the northernmost wine district of California in the United States and is the third of the important North Coast counties (Napa, Sonoma, and Mendocino). A much smaller number of wineries and vineyards operates here than in the other two because until fairly recently it was mostly a lumbering region, dotted with pear orchards. Excellent red wines, principally Cabernet, Pinot Noir, and Zinfandel, have been made here over the past few years, however, by producers such as Parducci, Weibel, Cresta Blanca, Fetzer, and Husch Vineyards.

Mercurey.

The Côte Chalonnaise immediately to the south of the Burgundian Côte d'Or in France yields some good wines that resemble those from farther north. Mercurey is one of these and, in good vintages, it will display some of the characteristics of wines from the Côte de Beaune only a few miles away. The most important producer here is the firm of Antonin Rodet, which also acts as a négociant with wines from the Côte d'Or. The Mercureys of Rodet represent excellent value—they are skillfully made and usually are priced competitively. Most Mercurey is red and it is produced from the same Pinot Noir grape that is responsible for the best Burgundies. Mercurey is not as long-lived as the better reds from the Côte d'Or, however, and it tends to lack the elegance of the best Burgundies. In good vintages, Mercurey can represent excellent value. It is best drunk from five to eight years after the harvest, although some more robust examples have been known to last considerably longer. (*See* Chalonnais.)

☆/☆☆☆
$/$$

Meredyth Vineyards.

Meredyth Vineyards began producing estate-bottled wines in the State of Virginia in 1975 and was the first winery to be licensed under Virginia's Farm Winery Law of 1980. The winery is in Middleburg, in the Bull Run Mountains, 55 miles west of Washington, D.C. Its production consists mainly of European-American hybrid wines such as Seyval Blanc, Rougeon, Villard, Maréchal Foch, and De Chaunac. Meredyth also produces an occasional European varietal, and successful efforts in this category have included a Gewürztraminer. The winery is owned and operated by Archie M. Smith, Jr., and his family.

☆/☆☆
$/$$

Merlot.

This French grape has a reputation for producing soft wines of limited character and, in fact, it is true that the addition of some Merlot to the noble Cabernet Sauvignon in the fermenting vats of the Médoc will help to reduce the youthful astringency of the great red wines of Bordeaux. The Merlot's reputation as merely a secondary grape

variety falls by the wayside, however, at one of the greatest vineyard estates in the world: Château Pétrus, the King of the Pomerols. Pétrus is vinified at least 95 percent from the Merlot. The few Cabernet Sauvignon vines that sprout in the Pétrus vineyard might, indeed, make good wines on their own. But Pétrus is essentially Merlot, and it is no secondary wine. The consistent ability of the Pétrus vineyard to produce extraordinary wines from the Merlot grape provides one of the best examples available in support of the thesis that the climate and the soil play dominant roles in the creation of great wines.

In California the Merlot came into its own as a premium varietal in the late 1970s, and now more than 50 are on the American market. Largely because most of them are produced by wineries experienced with making Cabernet Sauvignon, the California Merlots often resemble Cabernets, although they tend to be slightly softer and earlier-maturing. They are also usually less expensive because Merlot has not yet achieved quite the panache of Cabernet. Some of the better producers of Merlot in California are Sterling Vineyards, Clos du Val, Duckhorn Vineyards, Keenan Winery, Rutherford Hill, and ZD Wines. The Merlot is also widely cultivated now in northern Italy.

Meursault.

The *commune* of Meursault lies adjacent to Puligny Montrachet in the heart of the Côte de Beaune of Burgundy and shares with Puligny a reputation for producing some of the most magnificent white wines in France and therefore in the world. Some reds are produced in Meursault, but they are marketed as Volnays, and all but a tiny portion of the output is white. The production of Meursault is the second largest in the Côte de Beaune, behind Pommard, and the wines are widely available. This, and the fact that they are not quite so fashionable as the wines of Puligny-Montrachet, has kept their prices within reach of most wine drinkers. A *commune* wine named simply Meursault, without a specific vineyard name attached, can be the best value obtainable in white Burgundies.

Meursault is a big and earthy white, with a hint of spices and herbs and a depth of flavor that is similar to a Puligny-Montrachet. Yet a good Meursault is slightly drier, often displaying a woody or nutty taste comparable to a Corton-Charlemagne. Unlike the neighboring Puligny, the *commune* of Meursault has no *grands crus,* but some of its *premiers crus,* especially the Genevrières, Perrières, and Charmes, are superb wines. Among the *premiers crus* are the following:

Bouchères
Caillerets
Charmes
Cras
Genevrières
Goutte d'Or
Perrières
Pectures
Poruzots
Santenots Blancs
Santenots du Milieu

Lying roughly between Meursault and Puligny-Montrachet is the tiny hamlet of Blagny, which produces small quantities of both red and white wines. Some of the white is marketed as Puligny-Montrachet and some as Meursault-Blagny. It tends to be an earthier wine than Meursault itself. The reds of Blagny are similar to Volnays.
☆☆/☆☆☆☆
$$/$$$

Château Meyney.

As one of the vineyards operated by the Cordier family of Bordeaux, Château Meyney consistently produces robust but supple wines. The estate was not ranked among the *grands crus classés* in the Bordeaux classification of 1855, but the quality of its wines has been good for many years. Meyney is a Saint-Estèphe, which means its wines tend to age gracefully and should not be drunk prior to ten years following the vintage.
☆☆☆
$$

Michigan.

Michigan is the fourth-largest wine producer in America—and has produced wines since the middle of the nineteenth century. Records for 1880 show that over 62,000 gallons were made that year. Today the figure is several million. Three of the largest wineries, St. Julian, Bronte, and Warner, are in Paw Paw. All produce wines from French-American hybrids, though the majority of their production consists of sweet dessert and sparkling wines. St. Julian was founded by Mariano Meconi, an Italian immigrant who started his first winery in Ontario, Canada. Bronte Champagne and Wines Company was founded after repeal by a Detroit dentist, Dr. Theodore Wozniak. Bronte planted the first Baco Noir grapevines in Michigan in 1954 and has expanded its acreage and production of French hybrids consistently since. Bronte also claims to have introduced Cold Duck in America, and it is true that this concoction apparently came from Michigan. Warner Vineyards, formerly Michigan Wineries established in 1938, produces French hybrid wines such as Aurora and Chelois, Champagne, and *solera*-aged Port and Sherry. Warner has become by far the largest wine producer in the state.

Another sizable operation is at Harbert and is called the Lakeside Winery, which bought out and continues to make Molly Pitcher wines, named for one of the Revolution's heroines. The most promising new winery to come on the scene is Tabor Hill on top of Mount Tabor in Berrien County. It is small and produces eight varietal wines from French hybrids and *Vinifera* varieties, the first in Michigan to carry vintage dates. (*See also* Cold Duck.)

Mill Creek Vineyards.

Charles Kreck has been in the grape-growing business for years, selling his production to such other wine producers as Simi, Sonoma Vineyards, and Widmer's Wine Cellars of Naples, New York. In 1974 he established Mill Creek as a label, but the grapes for his wines were crushed and finished at Korbel. Sonoma Vineyards did the same service in 1975, before the new Mill Creek winery was completed in 1976. Before his own winery was built he continued to sell to other producers, and some of Kreck's wine made at Korbel in 1974 went to Caymus Vineyards, which used it for its second brand, Liberty School Lot 1, which attracted national attention as a very sound wine at a modest price. Mill Creek is a family business involving Charles Kreck's son James, who is the winemaker, as well as other family members. The senior Kreck was in the cattle and sheep business in Sonoma County (besides the grape business) before opening Mill Creek, which owns 60 acres of vineyards that provide more than enough grapes for the 12,000 cases or so of Merlot, Cabernet Sauvignon, Pinot Noir, and Chardonnay that are produced each year. Gewürztraminer and Gamay Beaujolais are made from grapes purchased from another grower, and Kreck continues to sell grapes from his own vineyard.
☆/☆☆
$$

Mirassou.

Mirassou Vineyards, just outside San Jose in California's Santa Clara Valley, has been in continuous operation since it was begun in 1854. Pierre Mirassou came to the region from France and married the daughter of vineyard owner Pierre Pellier, sire of a five-generation dynasty of winemakers. In the mid-60s the energetic members of the fifth generation—Daniel, Steve, Peter, Jim, and Don—approached the men in charge, their fathers Norbert and Edmund, and informed them that it was time to let more people know about the good wines of Mirassou. Given a free hand, they set about expansion, buying 650 acres in Monterey County near Soledad and new equipment for the winery.

It is interesting to try the wines from Mirassou year after year because, as the fifth generation gains experience and learns to extract more from their Monterey varietals, the wines show it. Most are big wines of spirit and gusto, with the marked varietal character that bespeaks their origin in Monterey County. Superior batches of the best varietals are designated as Harvest Selections; there is a stronger expression of wood in these wines, and some of the reds are not released until they are five years old.

The grapes from the Monterey County vineyards are machine-harvested and crushed in the field. The juice is pumped into tankers and is taken immediately to the winery in San Jose, where the processing varies according to the variety of grape. Mirassou's wines cover a broad range of styles. The whites range from bone-dry to slightly sweet, while the reds may be mellow and early-maturing or big and robust. The typically vegetal or herbaceous flavor of Monterey-County can be detected in many of the Mirassou offerings.

Besides table wines Mirassou also makes sparkling wines, using the French *méthode champenoise,* in which the grapes undergo a second fermentation inside the bottles to capture the bubbles. Four types of "Champagne" are made: Brut, Au Naturel, Sparkling Gamay Beaujolais, and L.D. (for Late-Disgorged). The Mirassou line of table wines includes a dozen varietals.

☆/☆☆☆

$/$$

Château La Mission-Haut-Brion.

Across the road from the famed Château Haut-Brion in the Graves District south of Bordeaux lies Château La Mission-Haut-Brion, which sometimes challenges Haut-Brion itself. Although Haut-Brion is in the *commune* of Pessac, La Mission-Haut-Brion is in Talence, because the highway is the dividing line at that point. As of 1983, Haut-Brion and La Mission-Haut-Brion were unified under the ownership of the Dillon family of the U.S., and devotees of both wines wondered whether any change in style or substance would occur. La Mission can be especially good in off vintages, displaying excellent fruit and depth when other châteaux are producing thinnish wines. In general, it is a fruitier wine than Haut-Brion—fruitier in the sense of grapiness rather than sweetness. The vineyard is planted about two-thirds in Cabernet Sauvignon, with most of the balance in Merlot. La Mission needs a decade to mature and retains plenty of fruitiness and body after two decades.

☆☆☆☆

$$$

Missouri.

Missouri was once the second-largest producer of wines in America and was the home state for one of the country's finest Champagnes, Cook's Imperial, which was made and bottled in St. Louis. Cook's was sold after World War II and eventually was moved to California. Its Champagne-maker, Adolph Heck, is now one of the owners of Korbel, a leading Champagne producer in Sonoma County, California. Small wineries are once again thriving in Missouri, mostly in the eastern central part of the state in the Missouri River valleys.

Missouri is responsible for a crucial contribution to European viniculture. George Husmann, professor of horticulture at the University of Missouri, and Hermann Jaeger, a grape breeder from Neosho, discovered nearly a hundred years ago that Ozark grape stock was resistant to Phylloxera, the vine parasite. They advised French horticulturists, who were in despair over the many vineyards devastated by the pest, to graft their vines onto the Missouri rootstocks. Soon carloads of roots were on their way to France, allowing some of the world's greatest vineyards to begin anew. Jaeger was awarded the French Legion of Honor for his contributions to the wines of France.

Mogen David Wines.

Mogen David is a producer of sweet kosher wines, mostly from Concord grapes grown in New York State. The production is substantial, and the wines are mediocre. The operation is owned by the Wine Group Inc. of San Francisco, which bought it from Coca-Cola Bottling of New York in 1981. The Wine Group also owns Franzia Brothers and Tribuno vermouth. (*See* Franzia Brothers.)

Monbazillac.

This is a fairly sweet dessert wine produced just south of Bergerac in the Périgord area east of Bordeaux which is more famous for its cuisine than for its wines. Monbazillac can occasionally challenge a good Sauternes or Barsac in richness and depth, although it usually lacks the same intensity, except in very good vintages. Château Monbazillac, now cooperatively owned, is the best-known example. These wines, usually very well made and capable of displaying a certain elegance, will never be exported in great quantities unless the public distaste for sweet wines is eliminated. Since this antipathy is based mainly on a lack of knowledge and not on objective evaluation, it is possible that Monbazillac some day will take its rightful place among the world's more highly regarded wines.

☆☆/☆☆☆

$/$$

Château Monbousquet.

One of the more prolific vineyards of Saint-Emilion in the eastern part of the French Bordeaux region is Château Monbousquet, owned by Daniel Querre, an activist in the promotion of Saint-Emilion wines. Monbousquet is widely available because of its large production, and tends to be a supple and mellow wine at a fairly young age—perhaps six years after the vintage. It is usually available at attractive prices and in good vintages often is excellent value.

☆☆☆

$$

CK Mondavi.

The wines under the CK Mondavi label are produced and bottled by C. Mondavi and Sons, the family company headed by Peter Mondavi, which also produces the Charles Krug line of varietals. (*See* Charles Krug.)

☆

$

Robert Mondavi.

Robert Mondavi, a leading figure in modern California viniculture, has great respect for tradition but too much energy and innovative spirit to be content with making a great many wines of the same type in the same way year after year, however excellent they may be.

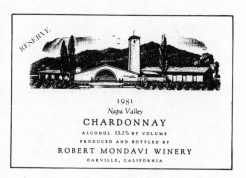

1981
Napa Valley
CHARDONNAY
ALCOHOL 13.2% BY VOLUME
PRODUCED AND BOTTLED BY
ROBERT MONDAVI WINERY
OAKVILLE, CALIFORNIA

So in 1966 he left the family business, Charles Krug, in St. Helena, and started his own winery from scratch under his own name, down the road in Oakville, in the Napa Valley. He felt then as he feels now that there are new levels of excellence to achieve and much yet to be discovered about the making of wine. "One has to be totally involved to achieve the maximum from a wine," he says. For Bob Mondavi this means concentrating on a relatively narrow range of top varietals and devoting the utmost care and attention to them at every stage of development. By the early seventies he and his sons Michael and Timothy were establishing new bench marks for excellence in classic California varietals such as Sauvignon Blanc, Cabernet Sauvignon, Zinfandel, Chardonnay, and others. Tireless in his effort to discover every nuance of flavor and bouquet that a wine is capable of reflecting, Mondavi has stocked his handsome winery with the finest equipment advanced technology has to offer and an impressive variety of oak cooperage, which enable him to test out his theories.

Robert Mondavi wines must be tasted often in order to keep up with what is going on, for judicious experimentation is the very essence of his philosophy of winemaking. A number of winemaking practices he has developed have been incorporated at other wineries. Mondavi's open-mindedness has led to many discoveries during visits to the vineyards of Germany and France. He found in Germany, for example, that the soft elegance and delicacy of Rhine wines resulted in part from centrifuging, a method of cleaning the grape remnants and sediment from the wine before (or after) fermentation which is less harsh than the traditional clarification methods. After importing the best centrifuge available, he eventually began to wonder about its effect on reds, and found that when not overdone, they retained more flavor and fullness of body when treated in this way.

Mondavi is credited with popularizing the Fumé Blanc name for Sauvignon Blanc. His Cabernet Sauvignons have achieved great heights, and experts are always eager to try new offerings of this great red varietal as well as older vintages to see how they are developing. Oak influence is very evident in most of Mondavi's wines, though perhaps a little less so than formerly. Aware of the differences imparted by various oaks, he owns quantities of each. American white oak from the Ozarks produces heavier wines with more aggressive bouquet; Limousin from France is also strong, a little coarser than that from Nevers; Yugoslavian oak is similar to that of Nevers but more subtle, more plentiful, less costly.

The Mondavi operation has grown rapidly since its inception in 1966. Now some 375,000 cases a year of premium varietals are turned out by the Oakville winery, and, despite the volume, the quality remains high. Another winery, the Woodbridge operation in Lodi, 80 miles away, was acquired in 1979 and produces more than one million cases a year of low-priced wines under the R. Mondavi Vintage Red, White, and Rosé brand names. This line replaces the line of Mondavi "Table Wines" pro-

duced at the same facility until 1982. The new line is made from better grape varieties, is exposed to some barrel-aging, and consists of vintage wines, unlike the other line.

In 1980 Bob Mondavi joined forces with Baron Philippe de Rothschild of Château Mouton Rothschild in Bordeaux to produce a wine through a joint effort of winemaking technology in the Napa Valley. Initially referred to informally as Napamédoc, a new name, Opus One, was decided upon in time for the release of the 1979 vintage in early 1984. Two thousand cases of the joint-venture wine were made in the 1979 vintage and 5000 cases in subsequent vintages. Plans were under way to establish a separate vineyard and winery for the joint effort, but the initial vintages all were made at Mondavi from Mondavi grapes.

A great air of excitement is evident at the Mondavi winery, most of it generated by Bob Mondavi himself. His enthusiasm is contagious. The Robert Mondavi label stands for quality in California wines, and the reds, especially, are held in high regard by connoisseurs. (*See also* Charles Krug.)

☆/☆☆☆☆

$/$$$

Monopole.

Monopole is the French term for "monopoly," and it appears on labels, especially Burgundy labels, when a vineyard is exclusively owned by one proprietor. The distinction is important in Burgundy, because most of the major Burgundian vineyards have multiple ownership, which makes for confusion in assessing the potential quality of a particular wine prior to tasting it. For example, there are several owner/producers of Richebourg, each making wines of a slightly different style, but the Domaine de la Romanée-Conti owns the adjacent La Tâche vineyard as a *monopole,* or exclusively. In another example, Clos de Tart in Morey-Saint-Denis is a *monopole* of the Mommessin shipping firm of Mâcon.

Mont La Salle Vineyards.

Mont La Salle Vineyards is the corporation that owns and operates Christian Brothers, one of the largest American wine brands. The headquarters has been at Mont La Salle, high in the hills above the Napa Valley of California, since 1930. It is named after Saint Jean Baptiste de La Salle, who founded the Christian Brothers Catholic teaching order in France in the seventeenth century. Christian Brothers celebrated its centennial of winemaking in California in 1982. (*See* Christian Brothers.)

Montagne-Saint-Emilion.

To the north and northeast of Saint-Emilion itself in southwestern France are several satellite areas entitled to attach their names to that of Saint-Emilion in marketing their wines. Among the more widely recognized of these is Montagne-Saint-Emilion, where some good red wines are produced. (*See* Saint-Emilion.)
☆☆☆
$/$$

Monte Antico.

Monte Antico is one of several very good red wines made in the Tuscany region of northern Italy but not entitled to the name of Tuscany's most famous wine, Chianti. It is made of roughly the same grapes as Chianti: 80 percent Sangiovese and 20 percent Canaiolo and a few others. It lacks the longevity of the better Chiantis, but it can be good value.
☆☆☆
$

CHATEAU MONTELENA
ESTABLISHED 1882

SONOMA
Cabernet Sauvignon
1977
PRODUCED AND BOTTLED BY CHATEAU MONTELENA
WINERY • CALISTOGA, NAPA VALLEY, CALIFORNIA
ALCOHOL 13.4% BY VOLUME

Château Montelena.

Château Montelena is one of California's leading producers of Chardonnay and Cabernet Sauvignon, among other varietals. The winery is located on Tubbs Lane in Calistoga at the foot of Mount St. Helena in the northern Napa Valley and was built in 1882 by Alfred E. Tubbs, who tried to imitate a French château. The Montelena vineyards were established from cuttings brought over from France. The operation fell into disuse during Prohibition, went through a period of ownership by a Chinese family that installed ponds and gardens reminiscent of their native country, then finally was revived in 1972 by a group of new owners, James Barrett, Lee Paschich, and Ernest Hahn. Château Montelena established a world reputation in 1976 when its Chardonnay from the 1973 vintage took first place in a widely publicized blind tasting in Paris. That wine was made by Mike Grgich, who has since left to form Grgich Hills Cellars. When the new owners took over in 1972, new equipment was installed along with new Limousin and Nevers oak barrels from France as well as barrels from elsewhere in Europe and the United States. Besides its Chardonnay and its elegant, balanced Cabernet Sauvignon, Montelena produces a spicy Zinfandel and at one time made a Johannisberg Riesling.

☆/☆☆☆

$$/$$$

Monterey.

Enormous interest is focused on Monterey County, California's largest premium wine district and potentially one of the best in the United States. Here on the flat plain of the Salinas Valley, just inland from the Monterey peninsula, more than 40,000 acres of grapevines have been planted, some of them only recently coming into bearing. The whites in particular—Chardonnay, Chenin Blanc, Johannisberg Riesling, and Pinot Blanc among others—possess exquisite fruit and aroma, far bigger in many cases than we find elsewhere in California.

Salinas Valley used to be known as the nation's "salad bowl" because of the abundant lettuce and celery plantings here. Due to a lack of rainfall, it was assumed that grapes could not be grown, despite the long cool growing season that made it seem ideal. Researchers at the University of California at Davis determined that growing conditions were similar to those of Burgundy and Bordeaux. During the hottest months, morning mists shield the vines from too much sun and gentle breezes from the Pacific sweep through in the afternoons. Today, sophisticated irrigation systems tap the water table, fed by the underground flow of the Salinas River, to provide the perfect amount of "rainfall" from overhead sprinklers.

Although it was in the 1930s that Professors A. J. Winkler and Maynard Amerine predicted great possibilities for Monterey County, it was not until 1962 that the Paul Masson and Mirassou wineries, pressed with the need for new vineyards, planted the first premium wine grapes between Soledad and Greenfield. Wente Brothers of Livermore followed soon after, establishing 300 acres at Arroyo Seco. The notable success of these three vintners attracted attention from others. More than a dozen other growers have established vineyards in Monterey, scattered up and down the 80-mile valley.

There is much still to be learned about this new area. Microclimates exist here as everywhere and it takes time to discover them and determine how best to take advantage of them. Some plots may turn out to be unsuited to the grape, or at least to the variety planted there now. But if the promise of the first years holds, it has been predicted that by the end of the century 100,000 acres or more will be planted in vines, more than all other coastal counties (including Napa, Sonoma, and Mendocino) combined.

Monterey Peninsula Winery.

Monterey Peninsula has adopted a maverick approach to winemaking and marketing since it was established in an old stone house called Rancho Sausito in Monterey, California, in 1973. The enterprise decided to issue numerous bottlings of the same varietals in an effort to preserve the integrity of the origins of all of the grapes that it purchases from different regions or growers. At one point, for example, there were as many as 30 different bottlings of Zinfandel for sale under the Monterey Peninsula name, including a Zinfandel Champagne, a white Zinfandel, late-harvested Zinfandel and Zinfandels from various vintages in various parts of California, including Amador County, the Salinas Valley, Alameda County, and Monterey County. By meticulously not-

ing the origins on the labels, the winery certainly has preserved the identity of each batch of grapes, but consumers often are confused by the proliferation of sources and find it difficult to keep track of the diversity. Monterey Peninsula neither filters nor centrifuges its wines and likes to call itself old-fashioned. Production totals about 18,000 cases a year in prolific vintages. Besides Zinfandel, the winery produces Cabernet Sauvignon, Chardonnay, Pinot Blanc, late-harvested Johannisberg Riesling, and late-harvested Chenin Blanc. Since the first vintage under the Monterey Peninsula label in 1974, all of the grapes have been purchased from outside growers. The enterprise is owned by Dr. Roy Thomas, a dentist, and Dick Nuckton, a retired orthodontist.
☆/☆☆☆
$$

Monterey Vineyard.

Monterey Vineyard, which produces well-made premium varietal table wines from grapes purchased mostly in Monterey County, California, had its origins in 1973, when a group of investors approached Dick Peterson, then the winemaker at Beaulieu Vineyard in the Napa Valley, and offered him 5 percent of Monterey Vineyard and carte blanche to design and build a winery. The investor group, known as McFarlands, had developed a number of land-purchase ventures as tax shelters. One of these ventures had involved the purchase of 9600 acres in Monterey County. They planted 7000 acres and then needed a winery and a winemaker. That was when they approached Peterson. The company set up for him was separate from the vineyards, and to this day Monterey Vineyard is a purchaser of grapes from other producers.

The new winery was built in 1974, and in that year a marketing agreement was signed with Foremost-McKesson, the big wine and spirits wholesaling company. Still another company was formed for marketing purposes, and finally the entire Monterey Vineyard concept went awry because of financial reverses and was threatened with collapse. One more company was formed, Gonzales & Company, 80 percent owned by Peterson and 20 percent by Daniel Lucas, and they bought all of the remaining assets of Monterey Vineyard—wines, name, label, employee contracts. They could not afford the winery, which by now was owned by the John Hancock Insurance Company, but Hancock became a partner in Gonzales and rented the winery to it for a dollar a day on a two-year contract. Wines began appearing under the Monterey Vineyard label, and the company finally was on track. In 1977 it was sold to the Coca-Cola Company through its Wine Spectrum subsidiary, assuring Monterey Vineyard of the kind of long-term financial support it needed. Dick Peterson has remained president and winemaker, and Dan Lucas is now vice-president in charge of finance and administration. The deal with Coca-Cola enabled Monterey Vineyard to resolve its problems and concentrate on producing wines, and now sales total more than 100,000 cases a year of premium varietals, as well as a line of branded wines called Classic California Red, White, and Rosé. The most interesting varietals appear under the "Special Selection" designation and only in certain vintages. Among these have been a Thanksgiving Harvest Johannisberg Riesling, a Botrytis Sauvignon Blanc, and a December Harvest Zinfandel. In 1983, Seagram's bought Monterey Vineyard from Coca-Cola through the purchase of the Wine Spectrum, assuring Monterey of a continuing source of capital.
☆/☆☆☆
$/$$

Montescudaio.

Montescudaio is a rugged area southeast of Livorno on the Tyrrhenian Sea yielding a Bianco, a Rosso, and a Vin Santo that have been accorded D.O.C. status under the Italian wine law. The wines are Tuscan but not Chiantis. The Bianco is made mostly from Trebbiano grapes and is light and dry. The Rosso is made mostly from Sangiovese grapes, like most Chiantis. The Vin Santo is produced from Trebbiano and Malvasia grapes; it is strong, sweet, and best served with dessert.
☆/☆☆☆
$

Monteviña Vineyards.

Monteviña's location in Plymouth, in the heart of California's Shenandoah Valley in Amador County, has been crucial to its success as a leading producer of Zinfandels. Amador County is hot during the day and cool at night, and it has proven to be a source of robust, intensely flavored, spicy, and complex Zinfandel wines. Monteviña was established by Cary Gott and his father-in-law, Walter H. Field, a banker, in the basement of a house. The surrounding vineyards had supplied Christian Brothers with Zinfandel grapes, but Cary Gott and his wife, Vickie, undertook a major effort to establish Monteviña as a force in California Zinfandel. Besides the existing Zinfandel vines planted some years earlier, new plantings of Sauvignon Blanc, Cabernet Sauvignon, Merlot, Barbera, and Ruby Cabernet were undertaken on the 450-acre estate, which is now about 50 percent planted. A new winery, involving three new buildings around a central courtyard, was built in 1980 and '81, and production has climbed rapidly, now totaling about 50,000 cases a year. A White Zinfandel is produced, plus a fresh and fruity Zinfandel Nuevo which is released in the fall shortly after the harvest, and there are the standard Monteviña Zinfandel, Cabernet Sauvignon, Barbera, Ruby Cabernet, Chardonnay, Sauvignon Blanc, and white Cabernet Sauvignon. Cary Gott resigned as winemaker in 1982, and his role was taken over by existing personnel.
☆/☆☆☆
$$

Monthélie.

The production of this hillside area above Volnay in the Côte de Beaune in the heart of the French Burgundy country is rather modest and the wines are not well known. A Monthélie will taste something like a Volnay or a Pommard, but usually will be less charming and sometimes will display a coarseness uncharacteristic of the Côte de Beaune. Its lack of fame, however, means its price will usually be lower than for most other wines produced in this part of Burgundy. Monthélie can be good value in superior vintages, especially when Burgundy production is bountiful. At one time, Monthélie was bottled as Volnay and Pommard, before the French wine laws were strengthened. Monthélie has a number of *premiers crus,* but they do not seem to be widely distributed.
☆☆/☆☆☆
$$

Montilla-Moriles.

Many lovers of true Spanish Sherry have probably tasted the wines of Montilla-Moriles, produced not far from the Sherry country, and never knew it. Much of the production was sold under the far more famous name of Sherry until the wines of this part of Andalusia began to develop a reputation of their own. They are very similar to Sherry and achieve something that Sherry cannot achieve—a natural alcoholic content of 16 to 17 percent. Sherries are always fortified with grape brandy; there is no need to fortify a Montilla. It is probable that substantial quantities of Montilla are still sold as Sherry in England, where many wine merchants still import in bulk and do their own bottling under private labels.

The chalky vineyards that produce Montilla cover about half the territory of the Sherry vineyards and lie in the area east of Jerez and south of Córdoba. The terrain is more hilly and the temperatures are hotter, enabling the grapes to ripen further and develop the higher sugar content that is responsible for the high natural alcohol level of the wines. Montilla wines are Finos—pale gold in color, subtle and charmingly dry in taste, with a delicate, earthy bouquet. They are produced with the help of the same *flor,* or film of yeasts, required to make Sherry Finos. The yeasts feed on the developing wine, extracting color and harshness and creating the unique Fino character. Most Montilla is consumed in Spain from casks before it is two years old, and it tastes best this way. Bottled Montilla for the export markets seems to lack the same native freshness and charm, although it can be very pleasant and inexpensive. The name Montilla-Moriles comes from the town of Montilla about 75 miles due east of Seville and from the village of Moriles, but the wine is generally called simply Montilla.
☆/☆☆☆
$/$$

Montrachet.

The greatest dry white table wines of France and probably of the world are produced in the *communes* of Puligny-Montrachet and Chassagne-Montrachet in the Côte de Beaune of the French Burgundy country. Both *communes* attached the name of the greatest vineyard, Montrachet, to their names, creating confusion among nonexpert Burgundy-lovers. Le Montrachet straddles both Puligny and Chassagne and produces big whites of an almost creamy texture with a perfumy bouquet and great elegance. Wines of nearly equal caliber are produced in the neighboring Bâtard-Montrachet, Chevalier-Montrachet, and Bienvenues-Bâtard-Montrachet. But the most regal are from Montrachet itself. None of these should be confused with the *commune* wines called Puligny-Montrachet, which come from areas outside the named vineyards. (*See also* Chassagne-Montrachet, Puligny-Montrachet, Côte de Beaune.)
☆☆/☆☆☆
$$$/$$$$

Château Montrose.

Château Montrose was ranked a *second cru,* or second growth, in the Bordeaux classification of 1855, and today it is one of the very best wines of Saint-Estèphe, the northernmost of the great wine-producing *communes* of the Haut-Médoc above Bordeaux. Montrose makes big, hard wines that age gracefully for decades, and it is probable that most of them are consumed before they reach their peaks. Partly for this reason, Château Cos d'Estournel is usually held in higher regard among the Saint-Estèphes. But a properly mature Montrose from a good vintage will be one of the great wines of the Médoc. It is common in Bordeaux to compare Montrose with Château Latour in nearby Pauillac, al-

though Latour is probably a better balanced wine in most years. Montrose needs at least a decade to reach maturity and shows great character after 20 years of age.

☆☆☆☆/☆☆☆☆☆

$$$

Morey-Saint-Denis.

Toward the northern end of the Côte de Nuits in the French Burgundy country the wines become more robust and fleshy, and require more aging before they reach the proper maturity for drinking. But when they reach their summit of perfection, they have few peers. One of the important *communes* producing these wines is Morey-Saint-Denis, which lies between Gevrey-Chambertin on the north and Chambolle-Musigny on the south. Unlike some of the other Burgundian *communes,* three of the four greatest wines of Morey-Saint-Denis do not share parts of the *commune* name and therefore do not confuse nonexperts. The *grands crus* of Morey are Bonnes-Mares, Clos de la Roche, Clos de Tart, and Clos Saint-Denis. Bonnes Mares lies partly in Chambolle-Musigny and is a superbly feminine wine with a bouquet redolent of violets and a seductive softness unique among the great Burgundies. Clos de Tart, a *monopole* of the house of Mommessin, is more delicate but displays the same aromatic bouquet. Clos de la Roche is equally sensuous and can be very long-lived. A bottle of the 1928 vintage, uncorked and decanted in Bronxville, New York, 48 years later in 1976, was fruity and full-bodied, with a full bouquet, although it soon dissipated. Morey-Saint-Denis also has more than two dozen *premiers crus* vineyards, of which the most famous is Clos des Lambrays. Good *commune* wines, labeled simply Morey-Saint-Denis, are also widely available. (*See also*

Côte de Nuits, Bonnes Mares, Clos de la Roche, etc.)

☆☆☆☆

$$/$$$

Morocco.

Morocco lies just west of Algeria in North Africa and shares with that country a common problem: the loss of the French market. When Algeria won independence from France in 1962 the export of wines from North Africa was reduced from hundreds of millions of gallons a year to a mere trickle. Many vineyards are no longer producing, although some very pleasant table wines are still made in Morocco. The best are the supple reds and crisp rosés; the whites in general are mediocre.

J. W. Morris Port Works.

The name of this winemaking enterprise in Emeryville, California, is misleading, for Port now accounts for only a small portion of its production, and premium varietal table wines are its main business. J. W. Morris does make good Port—about 4000 cases a year, partly vintage Port and partly what it calls Founder's Port. The vintage Port spends 20 months in barrels and then is bottled to preserve its freshness and fruit flavor, which require years to develop fully. The Founder's Port is barrel-aged for fully three years, although the cooperage is basically neutral, having been used for other wines, so little wood flavor is imparted. The two styles contain 20 percent alcohol and are best with cheese after a meal. Morris also produces some 40,000 cases a year of premium varietals, including two bottlings of Chardonnay, two Zinfandels, a Sauvignon Blanc, and a Pinot Noir, plus a generic red and a generic white called, simply, Private Reserve, a misleading name in view of the practice of many other wineries using the same designation for their very best wines.

J. W. Morris was founded by James W. Morris in 1975. The first bottlings came in 1977, initially all Port. The enterprise is a family business, with Morris's son-in-law Jim Olsen, a former wine retailer, active along with his wife, Terrill Olsen, and two other partners. The winery buys 100 percent of its grapes from outside growers.

☆/☆☆☆☆
$/$$

Moscadello di Montalcino.

The same Tuscan village that produces the great Brunello di Montalcino also produces a fruity white wine vinified mostly from the Moscatello grape. It is called Moscadello di Montalcino and has an earthily sweet taste that can be quite beguiling, in contrast to many of Italy's other semisweet wines.

☆/☆☆
$

Moscato.

This is the Italian name for the Muscat grape, which yields white wines that are often, though not always, sweet and heavy. Sometimes they are also sparkling and the name of a region or town is often attached, as in Moscato d'Asti, Moscata d'Elba, Moscato dell'Oltrepo' Pavese, etc.

☆/☆☆
$

Moscato d'Asti.

Asti Spumante is Italy's best-known sparkling wine, but Moscato d'Asti is also quite well known within Italy. It is not quite as fresh and charming as Asti Spumante and sometimes displays a sweet heaviness that seems overwhelming. Both Asti Spumante and Moscato d'Asti are produced in and near Asti in the Piedmont region in northern Italy.

☆
$

Mosel, Moselle.

One of the major wine regions of Germany and certainly one of the best white-wine producing areas of the world. The scenery in the Mosel River valley is breathtaking, for the river twists and turns back on its course frequently and lies at the bottom of a deep gorge cut into the natural slate and chalky soil that prevails in that part of Germany. The sides of the gorge facing south are hundreds of feet high and are where the best grapes grow, somehow clinging to slopes that are so steep that the pickers must be lowered from the top on ropes during the harvest. The steepness catches and holds the rays of the sun and the slate stones that cover the vineyards reflect it onto the grapes, enabling them to become riper than the grapes grown in the lowlands. Because the river twists and turns so frequently, both the left and right banks often face south in contortions which you must see to believe.

Unlike most other wine-growing areas in Germany, the great Riesling grape is dominant in the Mosel, producing wines of great elegance and character—perhaps somewhat more delicate than the bigger Rhine wines, but exhibiting an extraordinary finesse that is unique among the white wines of the world. The color is a greenish light gold and the bouquet is flowery and strong, pervading the cellars and tasting rooms of the region. One of the most appropriate words to describe the taste of a Mosel is "peachy," because the Riesling provides a fruity taste that almost resembles that of a very ripe peach.

The vines that bear the Riesling and occasionally the Müller-Thurgau and other grapes of the area are tied to stakes on the gorge sides in heart-shaped formations before they branch out later in the growing season. The long rows of stakes line the valley walls and signify that the Mosel economy is almost all wine. Years ago the river level was raised and the flow was slowed down when locks were installed to make the Mosel navigable for the ships carrying goods out of the Lorraine industrial area. The Mosel vineyards benefited. The higher and slower water in the river created a higher average temperature in the valley and extended the growing season, giving the grapes more time to ripen and produce better wines.

Automation will come to Mosel grape-growing only with great difficulty due to the steepness of the vineyard slopes. The stakes for each vine, the slate stones and earth that wash away in the winter storms, fertilizer to feed the vines, chemicals to spray them for protection against pests—everything must be carried up or down the slopes by hand, sometimes over distances of 700 feet and more. But the people of the Mosel have been doing it for many generations and it is their way of life.

Under the 1971 German wine law, the designation *Mosel-Saar-Ruwer* is given to the wines of the Mosel and the Saar and the Ruwer, reflecting the traditional inclusion of the wines from the Saar and Ruwer valleys branching from the southern reaches of the Mosel. Many non-Germans use a French word, *Moselle,* with the accent on the second syllable, for these wines, but the German word is *Mosel,* with the accent on the first syllable, and the German word should be used to refer to the wine from that country. The French spelling is not recognized under the 1971 law. Its use by the English and Americans probably became popular because of the habit of certain wine companies years ago of putting French names on virtually all wines on the theory that they would be more readily accepted. It is true that the Mosel River itself rises in the Vosges Mountains of eastern France, where it could logically be called *La Moselle,* but

most of the river is in Germany and the great German wines produced along its sides are called *Mosels.*

All of the wines of the Mosel-Saar-Ruwer region come in green bottles, whereas the wines from the various parts of the Rhine and Nahe areas come in brown bottles.

The best of the Mosel wines come from a portion of the river valley informally called the *Mittelmosel,* or central Mosel, which extends roughly from just north of the town of Trier on the south up through some world-famous villages to the area around Traben-Trarbach on the north. The most renowned vineyard is the Bernkasteler Doktor at Bernkastel, but the Wehlener Sonnenuhr at Wehlen, the Piesporter Goldtröpfchen at Piesport and the Erdener Treppchen at Erden are also very well known for the magnificent Riesling wines they produce. (Individual Mosel vineyards are listed under the alphabetized entries for each wine, e.g., Bernkasteler, Piesporter.)

☆/☆☆☆

$/$$$

Moselblümchen.

This is a German white wine theoretically from the Mosel River region but widely blended with up to one-third wines from other regions. Some Moselblümchens are interesting light wines, but most are very ordinary, because the name is virtually meaningless in terms of geography. Literally, it means "little flower of the Mosel" and sometimes—but rarely—the classic Riesling bouquet common to the great Mosel wines may be evident. But the fact is that growers who are proud of their wines and who want to obtain the highest prices for them will not bottle them as Moselblümchen if they are good enough to merit a more specific identification. Moselblümchens will usually have sugar added to increase their naturally low alcoholic content and sometimes will display a cloying sweetness that is sufficient to alienate the public from German wines in general. A Moselblümchen, although its price may be very low, should never be regarded as typical of the quality levels that Germany can achieve. It is a Mosel equivalent to Liebfraumilch, which also has evolved into a generic term meaning very little more than white Rhine wine, although some Liebfraumilch is made to fairly high standards and is far superior to the most ambitious Moselblümchen you are likely to encounter. Moselblümchen does have its uses—as the base for a wine punch, perhaps, or as a cheap picnic wine to wash down sandwiches.

☆

$

Mount Eden Vineyards.

Superb wines have been made at Mount Eden Vineyards since the enterprise split off from Martin Ray Vineyards in 1971. The estate is located high in the Santa Cruz Mountains of Santa Clara County, where 12 acres of grapes are cultivated under arduous mountain conditions. Mount Eden is owned by a group of about 25 shareholders headed by Robert Nikkel, a Sacramento lumberman who owns about 20 percent of the stock and was one of the original shareholders in Martin Ray. In recent years Mount Eden has been managed by Richard Graff and Phil Woodward, the driving forces behind Chalone Vineyard in Monterey County. The first Mountain Eden Vineyards wines were made in the 1972 vintage, and production now totals about 3000 cases of Cabernet Sauvignon, Chardonnay, and Pinot Noir under the Mount Eden label plus another 1000 cases under a second label, MEV. The grapes for MEV are purchased from other growers, including Doug Meador of Ventana Vineyards, whose grapes are

responsible for the balanced MEV Chardonnay.

☆/☆☆☆

$$

Mount Veeder Winery.

Michael and Arlene Bernstein produced mostly Cabernet Sauvignon of great texture and intense fruit at their 46-acre estate high on Mount Veeder in the Mayacamas Range that overlooks the Napa Valley from the west. Originally the vineyard consisted of 22 acres, but additional land has been purchased and part of it is being planted. The two Bernsteins were the dominant principals in the partnership that owned the business, but they sold out in 1983 to a Florida family after agreeing to remain active in management for three more years. The new owners are Henry and

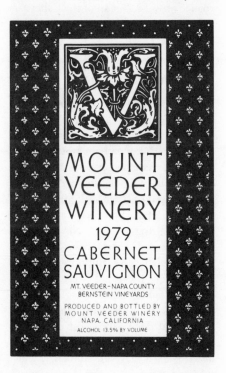

Lisille Matheson, who moved to Mount Veeder from Coral Gables after spotting an ad for a California winery for sale in *The Wall Street Journal*. The style of

wines made by Mount Veeder was not expected to change drastically, although production increases were planned.

The Bernsteins bought the initial piece of their estate on Mount Veeder in 1963, when it was a prune ranch. They began planting vines in 1965 and built their winery in 1973. During the intervening years they made wines basically for their own consumption prior to the first commercial vintage in 1973. Case production remains modest at 4500 to 5500 per year. Cabernet has accounted for 70 percent of production, but the winery also makes a small amount of Zinfandel and experiments with other varietals from year to year. It produces a branded wine called Sidehill Blanc which is a blend of Chenin Blanc and Pinot Blanc. Mount Veeder buys from 15 to 20 percent of its grapes from outside growers, but all of the Cabernet is from its own property.

☆/☆☆☆☆

$/$$

Mountain House Winery.

This Mendocino County winery in California was named after a stagecoach stop and inn that were built in the last century to accommodate travelers between the redwood forests that provided the basis for the lumber industry and northern California's booming metropolis, San Francisco. Mountain House, built by a transplanted New Yorker named Alexander McDonald, became a prominent landmark. But no stagecoach has run since the 1920s, and the property was fading into oblivion until it was acquired in 1979 by Ron Lipp, a Chicago attorney, who had worked the 1974 vintage at Mayacamas Vineyards in the Napa Valley and studied viticulture and oenology at the University of California at Davis. He considered more than 200 properties in several states before settling on the former Mountain House site and establishing Mountain

House Winery. The property has five acres of Chardonnay vines, but most of the grapes for Mountain House wines are purchased. Besides Chardonnay, the winery produces a Cabernet Sauvignon, a late-harvested Zinfandel, and a proprietary white called Mendocino Gold. About 4000 cases in all were made in 1981.

☆/☆☆☆

$/$$

Mountain Wines.

California generic labels often read "Mountain" Burgundy, "Mountain" Red or White, "Mountain" Rosé, etc. Though it is not yet a universally accepted term, it does indicate that the wine used in such blends comes mostly from grapes grown on hills or mountainsides, generally considered to produce better grapes than those from flatter terrain.

Château Mouton-Baronne-Philippe.

In 1951 the name of Château Mouton-d'Armailhacq was changed to Château Mouton-Baron-Philippe, after Baron Philippe de Rothschild, whose principal Bordeaux estate is the celebrated Château Mouton Rothschild lying adjacent to Mouton-Baron-Philippe. Still later, the name was changed to Château Mouton-Baronne-Philippe, in memory of Baron Philippe's late wife, Pauline. The baron bought the estate during the depths of the Depression, in 1933, and it consistently produces good wines there, although not up to the caliber of Mouton Rothschild itself. Like Mouton Rothschild, Mouton-Baronne-Philippe is vinified predominantly from Cabernet Sauvignon grapes, but the wine tends to lack the depth and fullness of its more famous neighbor. It is a credit to Philippe de Rothschild that he never yielded to the temptation to merge the two vineyards and call the entire production Mouton Rothschild, as he could have under the French wine laws. Mouton-d'Armailhacq was ranked a *cinquième cru,* or fifth growth, in the Bordeaux classification of 1855, and the estate naturally retains that status, despite the change in name. It would probably be elevated in any reclassification of the Bordeaux wines. Some of the production is understood to flow into Mouton-Cadet, the bulk wine that is produced by the Baron de Rothschild in his effort to cover the low-priced end of the market. (*See* Château Mouton Rothschild.)

☆☆☆☆

$$$

Château Mouton Rothschild.

Among the great red wines of the world, those produced by Baron Philippe de

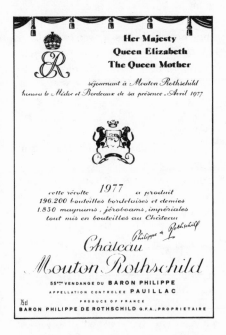

Rothschild at Château Mouton Rothschild have ranked near the top for generations. They are the biggest and fullest of all the Bordeaux reds, made almost entirely from the Cabernet Sauvignon grape, which traditionally produces the most robust of noble red wines. Yet in

1855, when the Médoc area on the peninsula north of Bordeaux was classified at an exposition in Paris, Mouton was ranked a second growth, or *deuxième cru classé,* behind four first growths: Châteaux Margaux, Latour, Haut-Brion, and Lafite-Rothschild, which is owned by Baron Philippe's cousins, the banking Rothschilds of Paris. That Mouton should have remained a second growth for more than a century, despite its acknowledged quality, demonstrated the fallibility of the 1855 classification.

Through four generations of ownership since 1853 by the Barons de Rothschild—Nathaniel, James, Henri, and now the great-grandson, Philippe—the family refused to accept Mouton's second-growth classification, even though it ranked the château among the best of the Bordeaux region. This rejection of second-growth status was exemplified in Mouton's motto on its coat of arms: "Premier ne puis, Second ne daigne, Mouton suis!" which translates as "First, I cannot be. Second, I do not deign to be. Mouton I am!" Baron Philippe struggled for a half-century after he took charge of the château in 1922 to have Mouton elevated in rank, and his efforts finally paid off in 1973, when the French Ministry of Agriculture raised Mouton Rothschild to *premier grand cru* status in the only revision of the 1855 classification that was ever made. It was a great personal triumph for Baron Philippe and, in honor of the event, he held a celebration at the château for his vineyard workers, serving a jeroboam of Mouton Rothschild 1923—the first vintage after he took over as the proprietor.

The Baron immediately changed Mouton's motto to: "First I am, second I was, but Mouton does not change." Mouton changes only with the weather conditions prevalent in each vintage and, like the nearby Château Latour, has a reputation for producing superior wines even in off years, when most other classified châteaux either do not bottle under their own labels or else turn out substandard wines. It is the bigness of Mouton, partly due to the predominance of Cabernet Sauvignon, that enables it to excel in poor vintages. But this same bigness sometimes means that Mouton lacks the elegance of some other great wines of the Pauillac *commune,* including Lafite, which is blended with less Cabernet. It is a question of style, with some connoisseurs preferring bigger, more robust wines and others opting for subtler, more elegant wines.

Mouton's elevation in rank occurred after the French Minister of Agriculture instructed the Bordeaux Chamber of Commerce to conduct a test of the *premiers grands crus* in 1971. Twelve judges held comparison testings of ten consecutive vintages of the leading Bordeaux reds, including at least nine of the 13 châteaux ranked *deuxième* at that time with Mouton. The evaluations were held under conditions of tight security, and only Mouton was raised to *premier cru,* although some of the other *deuxièmes* clearly merited similar elevations, in the view of many Bordelais experts. One factor that could not be ignored in the decision, however, was that only Mouton among the second growths had consistently brought prices equal or superior to the prices of the first growths—a condition which had existed for some years. Because price was an important consideration in the original 1855 classification, it was no doubt given weight in the adjustment of 1973, although the details of that judging still have not been fully disclosed. The public market, reflecting the evaluation of connoisseurs the world over, had already accorded Mouton first-growth status.

The château itself, sitting amid 175 acres of the best Pauillac vines, not only houses expansive *chais* and production facilities, but also one of the world's great wine museums, with ancient wine artifacts from all over the globe that only the Rothschild fortune could have collected. The construction of the museum, which was partly underground, was accomplished in great secrecy and, when it was ceremoniously opened in 1962 for viewing by the other Bordelais, it came as a surprise to many in the trade who thought they knew all that took place in their community. The contents, assembled with the knowledgeable assistance of Baron Philippe's wife, Pauline, include paintings, tapestries, pottery, and virtually every kind of wine receptacle imaginable, some fabricated of solid gold and silver set with gems.

Baron Philippe's flair for oenological showmanship extends even to the labels on his bottles. Each year is different, bearing a design commissioned from a leading artist. The 1970, for example, was done by Marc Chagall, and others have been the work of Salvador Dali, Dufy, Braque, Cocteau, and Miró. Each label is individually numbered and indicates how many bottles of each size, from halves up to imperials, were produced in each vintage. The rarest bottles of all, numbering some 80,000 and dating back to 1797, are marked "R.C.," for *réserve du château,* and are not for sale. If one should turn up at an auction, it would have left the château as a gift from Baron Philippe.

Many theories exist as to how the château got its name, but it obviously came from the French word for "sheep," which is *mouton.* Baron Philippe suggests that the name came from the topography, which consists of small rounded hills similar to the backs of sheep. In old French the land was called Mouton. Another explanation is that the designation simply refers to the fact that sheep once grazed in the area.

No matter, the wine made at Mouton Rothschild is superb, although the un-initiated should not confuse Château Mouton Rothschild itself with the other wines produced by Baron Philippe. These include Mouton-Cadet, a blend that claims to be the largest-selling Bor-deaux wine produced, Château Mouton-Baronne-Philippe, a fifth-growth Pauillac in the 1855 classification that was called Château Mouton-d'Armail-hacq until 1951, and Château Clerc-Milon, another fifth-growth Pauillac. These are all well-made wines from well-tended vineyards, although the price of Mouton-Cadet reflects to some extent the cost of heavy advertising, and better wines from *petits châteaux* can be found for less money.

☆☆☆☆/☆☆☆☆☆

$$$/$$$$

Müller-Thurgau.

Among the hybrid German grape va-rieties, the Müller-Thurgau is seen in-creasingly. It is a cross between the high-yielding Sylvaner and the less gen-erous but more distinguished Riesling. It produces wines with some of the qualities of each, but generally not up to the standards of the noble Riesling itself. (*See* Riesling.)

Château Musar.

The wines of Lebanon are little known in Europe and North America, but one of them, Château Musar, has begun to establish an international reputation be-cause of its high quality. The proprietor is Gaston Hochar, a Lebanese, whose son Serge is general manager and wine-maker. Serge Hochar was educated at the University of Bordeaux and then trained with Ronald Barton at Château Léoville-Barton and Château Langoa-Barton, two of the leading estates of the

Bordeaux Médoc. He has applied his considerable skill to producing Caber-net Sauvignon grapes in an ideal mi-croclimate at an elevation of 3300 feet on the slopes of Mount Lebanon, some 20 miles north of Beirut. Château Musar is mostly Cabernet Sauvignon, with small amounts of Merlot, Syrah, and Cinsault blended in. The result is a fully flavored, rich, balanced wine of great texture and elegance. Its one drawback is that there are fluctuations in quality from vintage to vintage, and obtaining vintage reports from Lebanon is not always a simple task. But even in poor vintages, Musar is good wine, demon-strating that France and California are not the only locations for growing good Cabernet.

☆☆/☆☆☆☆

$$/$$$

Muscadet.

When the big and famous white Bur-gundies of France became so popular in the late 1960s and 70s that their prices soared out of the reach of all but the wealthiest wine drinkers, a modest little wine from the westernmost portion of the Loire River Valley shot into the gap in the market. Muscadet, which had never been taken seriously by connois-seurs, suddenly achieved the renown it deserved as a crisp and fresh white that is delightful with the fish dishes that originated in nearby Brittany. It is produced in the area around Nantes, just before the Loire flows into the Atlantic Ocean, and, if it has any fault worth mentioning, Muscadet never seems to reach quite the level of elegance of, say, a Chablis *grand cru* or a big Meursault or Puligny. As the name implies, it has an almost musky taste. Nevertheless, it has found a secure place with many lovers of dry white wines and it has remained rel-atively inexpensive despite growing demand.

The best wines come from Sèvre-et-Maine, directly east of Nantes and south of the Loire. Their bouquet is flowery and their taste is soft and fruity. Like fresh Beaujolais, they must be drunk young, within two years of harvesting, to be tasted at their best. They are labeled Muscadet de Sèvre-et-Maine and sometimes carry a château name as well. Wines of greater longevity and fuller body but perhaps slightly less charm come from the Coteaux de la Loire north and east of Sèvre-et-Maine. They too may be found with specific vineyard names that signify superiority. Secondary wines of the area around Nantes include Gros Plant, a white, and Coteaux d'Ancenis, a red made with the Gamay grape of Beaujolais. Gros Plant and Coteaux d'Ancenis are V.D.Q.S. wines—*vins délimités de qualité supérieure*, the French designation for good local wines that have not merited *appellation contrôleé* status.

☆/☆☆

$/$$

Musigny.

No Burgundy wine displays as much finesse as Le Musigny, often called Les Musigny, which comes from the heart of the Burgundian Côte de Nuits. The vineyard is adjacent to Clos de Vougeot, where great wines are also made, but not as consistently as in Musigny. Whereas the robust wines of Chambertin are described as masculine, Musigny is feminine and seductive, with a perfumy bouquet redolent of honeysuckle and fresh lilacs and a depth of flavor rivaled by only two or three other red Burgundies. The vineyard lies in the *commune* of Chambolle-Musigny, where some other great wines are made, but none is as superb as Le Musigny itself. The best portion of the Musigny vineyard is owned by Comte Georges de Vogüé, whose 1934 vintage remained extraordinary into the 1970s. At a special dinner of the Wine and Food Society of New York in 1972, the members supplied rare old bottles from their own cellars, and the Musigny de Vogüé '34 was unanimously awarded top honors, above such treasures of Bordeaux as Châteaux Haut-Brion, Margaux, Mouton Rothschild, and Latour of the 1929 vintage; Lafite-Rothschild of the 1945 and '49 vintages; and Mouton Rothschild '45. The Society members present for the occasion would normally have a Bordeaux bias, so the unanimous victory of the Musigny was even more significant. The Musigny vineyard is obviously incapable of producing such superb wines every year, but its record is among the best in Burgundy. The Comte de Vogüé turns out a special bottling which he calls Vieilles Vignes, from old vines that yield only miserly amounts of grape juice, but the resulting wine is of extraordinary quality. Other owners that produce Musigny of great finesse are the Mugnier family, Roumier, Hudelot, and Prieur. Wines labeled Chambolle-Musigny, produced in the surrounding area, can be very pleasant, but they rarely measure up to Le (Les) Musigny itself.

☆☆☆☆

$$$/$$$$

· N ·

Nackenheimer.

German white wine produced in Nackenheim, which is one of the best winemaking villages in the Rheinhessen on the west bank of the Rhine River before it turns west at Mainz. Nackenheimers are few in number and the acreage planted in vines is small, but they are regarded highly by the experts. They have great finesse and tend to be a bit softer than the big whites of the Rheingau to the northwest. Because of the relatively small production, Nackenheimers have never achieved the renown of Niersteiners produced a short distance to the south, but many of them are just as elegant. The vineyard generally regarded as the best is called Nackenheimer Rothenberg, for "red hill," where the soil is a deep rust color, the same as in the Niersteiner ridge overlooking the Rhine.

The better-known vineyards are the following:

Nackenheimer Engelsberg*
Nackenheimer Fenchelberg
Nackenheimer Fritzenhöll
Nackenheimer Kapelle
Nackenheimer Kirchberg

Nackenheimer Rheinhahl
Nackenheimer Rothenberg*
Nackenheimer Sommerwinn
Nackenheimer Spitzenberg
Nackenheimer Stiehl

The vineyards marked with an asterisk (*) are among those that retained their identities, if not their shapes, in the revision of the German wine law in 1971. In general the law eliminated smaller vineyard names by merging them into larger ones to simplify identification. Some—for example, Spiegelberg—were made into *Grosslage,* or large vineyard areas, to take in fairly large chunks of the Rheinhessen.
☆/☆☆☆
$/$$

Nahe.

One of the principal wine-growing districts of Germany, named after the narrow river that rises in the Hunsrück Mountains to the south. The river meanders like a trout stream through green valleys with hardwoods and pines mingling on their flanks. The mountains protect the wine-growing area on the north and west. The earth is less rocky than in the Mosel and some other areas, and it often has a pinkish-red color, almost like modeling clay. Even the shoulders of the road that follows the treacherous course of the river are pink. Slate is more evident in other parts of the region, and the variation in the soil accounts for the broad variety among Nahe wines, which can be among the greatest produced in Germany.

Because the Nahe lies roughly between the Mosel on the west and the southern extension of the Rhine Valley on the east, its wines are sometimes described as being a sort of crossbreed between Mosels and Rhines. Although this no doubt is true in some instances, the Nahe wines in general have their own style and character. If they resemble any others, it would be the ones produced in the Rheinhessen immediately to the east, rather than the lighter and more delicate Mosels. The Rheinhessen town of Bingen, with its formidable Scharlachberg vineyard, lies at the junction of the Nahe with the Rhine, attesting to the geographical proximity of the two districts.

The main wine towns of the Nahe are Schloss Böckelheim and Bad Kreuznach, and the best wines tend to come from the portion of the area that lies between the two, roughly in the middle of the district, although good wines are produced in a number of other villages along the twisting river valley and some small tributaries. The quality level in general is high, but for a reason that remains unexplained Nahe wines are not very popular in the United States. This probably reflects the way the German export market is structured, rather than any active dislike of the wines by Americans. Nahe bottlings no doubt will increasingly find their way to the United States as Americans become better educated about fine German wines.

☆/☆☆☆

$/$$

Château Nairac.

Luscious sweet wines are made at this château in Barsac, in southern Bordeaux. The property, ranked as a *second cru* in the Sauternes classification of 1855, is owned by Thomas and Nicole Heeter-Tari. Tom Heeter is an American from Dayton, Ohio, who married Nicole Tari, of the Taris who own Château Giscours in Margaux. They are raising their family and tending the vines at the splendid Château Nairac.

☆☆/☆☆☆☆

$$

Napa.

In only a few short years the Napa Valley, clearly California's foremost wine district and the best in the United States, has established a worldwide reputation for producing fine wines from premium varietal grapes that originated in the vineyards of France, Germany, and Italy. Scarcely an hour's drive north of San Francisco, the region is now fairly bursting with vineyards, many of them planted or revived in the decade of the 1970s, when California wines came of age. The greatest number of fine wineries is concentrated here, the larger ones strung out along Highway 29, which cuts north through the heart of the valley and is often referred to as "Wine Way" because of the famous names that pop up one after another: Mondavi, Inglenook, Beaulieu, Louis Martini, Beringer, Christian Brothers, Charles Krug, Hanns Kornell. Smaller but no less prestigious ones sprinkle the mountainsides on either side of the valley. The first settlers were Indians who named the valley *Napa*, their word for "plenty." The most fertile trough of land is not large—it runs a distance of a little over seven miles from end to end.

Situated directly north of San Francisco Bay, the Napa Valley begins just below the town of Napa and swings north in a gentle arc that curves slightly to the west at its upper boundary, the town of Calistoga and the towering Mount St. Helena. The mountain long ago was an active volcano; inactive now, it still foments enough to provide hot springs and geysers for the thermal baths and spas in Calistoga. The valley is bounded east and west by mountain ranges, the western Mayacamas Range separating Napa and Sonoma being the most famous. Some of the small wineries tucked into hilltops have spectacular views of the valley below. Creeks run down the mountainsides and the Napa River runs the length of the valley before emptying into the Bay. The Silverado Trail, immortalized in the stories of Robert Louis Stevenson at the turn of the century, runs up the eastern side of the valley paralleling Highway 29. Other towns are spaced along the highway: Yountville, Oakville, Rutherford, and the most famous of them, St. Helena.

At one time there were 142 wineries in the Napa Valley. Prior to the recent wine boom the number had sunk to fewer than 50, with most of the others abandoned during Prohibition and never restarted. But heavy consumer demand in the late 1970s and early 1980s fostered a major revival, and the number of operating wineries in the Napa region has once again climbed past a hundred. Prime vineyard land has become extremely expensive, and most of the best sites have been acquired and planted. Not only Americans but Europeans as well have invested in the abundant potential of the Napa.

Wineries to some extent still come and go. The last ten years or so have seen many more coming than going, however, with new wineries such as Clos du Val and Grgich Hills starting from scratch, and others, such as Schramsberg, revived after a period of dormancy.

Napa Valley consists mostly of the agricultural growing regions designated I and II, which are the coolest in the state, with a smattering of Region III. (*See* California.) By far the most successful grape is Cabernet Sauvignon, but Chardonnay, Pinot Noir, Gamay varieties, Zinfandel, Johannisberg Riesling, and Chenin Blanc do extremely well here. Lesser amounts of other premium wine grapes—Gewürztraminer, Sauvignon Blanc, Sémillon, and Barbera—also thrive. The climate here is excellent for wine grapes, with mild winters, warm dry summers, hazy with fog during the day which shields the vines from excessive sun. One of the few climatic worries is spring frost. If it comes late when the vines are flowering, it can be disastrous, so the vineyards are staked out with heaters, fans made of old airplane engines and permanent irrigation systems equipped with water sprayers. Severe damage from frost does not occur often, but even once a decade is cause for concern, since recovery is slow and costly.

About 25,000 acres are under cultivation in the Napa Valley. With the increased demand for wine, new vineyard areas are constantly sought out. One of the areas that is being more fully developed, Carneros Creek, is situated in the tidewaters above San Pablo Bay. Los Carneros ("the sheep"), crisscrossed by creeks, air currents, and fog banks from the Bay, is a cool Region I area and is especially favorable to Pinot Noir, Chardonnay, and Riesling varieties that ripen later here. The extra time on the vine gives them more character and a better balance of sugar and fruit acid. Region I embraces vineyards all the way to Oakville. The middle section of the valley, from Oakville to St. Helena, is mostly Region II. The northern end of the valley is the warmest and is designated Region III. Microclimates, however, are scattered throughout. Due to drainage, exposure, and temperature they often approximate conditions in other growing regions. Researchers from the University of California at Davis have been diligent in isolating more and more of these "little climates," as have individual Napa growers, and they are being replanted with the most suitable vines for maximum response. Dozens of Napa Valley wineries have their own alphabetical listings. Many small, excellent wineries dot the valley and hillsides, most specializing in only three or four types of wine. Many are new, with their first wines just now becoming available, and then only in California.

Visitors throng the Napa Valley each year, not only for the warm welcome they receive at most of the wineries, furnished with tasting facilities and salesrooms, but to enjoy the scenic beauty of the valley itself.

Napa Creek Winery.

Napa Creek Winery in St. Helena, California, was established in 1980 by Jack Schulze and grew rapidly, producing some 25,000 cases of wine by 1981. All of the grapes are purchased from Napa County growers and are vinified in the former abattoir that is now the winery. The product array includes Cabernet Sauvignon, Riesling, Sauvignon Blanc, Chardonnay, Chenin Blanc, and Gewürztraminer.

☆/☆☆☆
$$

Nebbiolo.

The noblest grape of Italy is the Nebbiolo, widely cultivated in the northern Piedmont region, which produces that country's greatest red wines. The Nebbiolo is responsible for Barolo, Barbaresco, Gattinara, and Ghemme, among others. These are wines of great intensity, with full body, rich flavor, and a

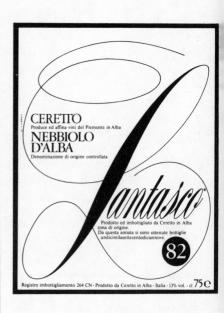

texture sometimes described as chewy. Around the town of Gattinara the local name for the Nebbiolo grape is the Spanna, and bottles simply labeled Spanna are available in the export markets. These are often the best buys from Italy. (*See also* Barolo, Gattinara, etc.)

Château Nénin.

Adjacent to Château La Pointe in the Pomerol District east of Bordeaux is Château Nénin, second only to Château de Sales in its volume of production of Pomerol wines. Nénin sometimes can rise to great peaks on the quality scale if the growing conditions are just right, but generally it does not rank on a par with the best growths of Pomerol. If Pomerol estates were classified according to quality, Nénin probably would rank in the middle one-third, equivalent to a fourth or fifth growth of the Médoc.

☆☆☆/☆☆☆☆
$$/$$$

New Jersey.

New Jersey grape growers were relieved of an onerous legislated burden in 1981 when the state legislature passed a new farm winery bill that made commercial wineries on a small scale more economically viable. Until then the number of New Jersey wineries was restricted to one per million residents, wineries were limited to production of 5000 gallons a year, and tastings were not permitted at the wineries. Licensing fees also were high. Now the license fees have been cut to as little as $50 in some cases, and the production limit has been raised substantially to 50,000 gallons annually. Tasting and selling at wineries are also permitted now. At Tewksbury Cellars in Lebanon, founded in 1979, Dan Vernon has planted such European varietals as Gamay Beaujolais, Chardonnay, Riesling, and Gewürztraminer, along with such European-American hybrids as Rayon d'Or and Chambourcin. Fennelley Farm Vineyards in Glen Gardner, owned by Don and Betty Fennelly, has acreage planted in Chardonnay, Riesling, and some hybrids. Del Vista Vineyards near Frenchtown has planted small amounts of three German varietals, Riesling, Sylvaner, and Gewürztraminer, as well as such other European varietals as Cabernet Sauvignon, Zinfandel, Pinot Noir, and Chardonnay. Other new plantings are taking place around the state, especially in Hunterdon County, and quantities should become significant by the late 1980s.

New York State.

New York State is the second-largest producer of wine in the United States. Though it produces less than a tenth as much as the leading state, California, its wines are widely known and are distributed throughout the country. New York's most famous wine is Champagne and for many years the larger New York companies—Great Western, Gold Seal, and Taylor—sold the greatest quantity of the festive bubbly to American consumers. The tremendous surge in wine-drinking in the United States in recent years has given the New York wine industry a setback in terms of sales, because as American palates become more experienced they preferred the taste of the European grape family, *Vitis vinifera,* the grape cultivated in California. The lag is likely to be only temporary, however, as New York's winemakers turn to French-American hybrid grapes. The wines from these grapes have a more familiar taste with a wider appeal. Some more adventurous souls are experimenting with Vinifera varieties such as Johannisberg Riesling, Cabernet Sauvignon, Merlot, Pinot Noir, and Chardonnay—and are getting surprisingly good results.

The wine industry of New York State was built upon native grape families, mostly *Vitis labrusca,* some Riparia and Rotundifolia, notably from grapes like Catawba, Delaware, Niagara, Concord, Isabella, Elvira, Missouri Riesling, Dutchess, Diamond, and others. The taste of wines from these grapes is distinctly different from that of any other wine grape; it is often described as "foxy." This rather meaningless term most probably arose from comparisons of the Labrusca with the taste of wild grapes, often called fox grapes, and denotes the sort of "wild grape" flavor so pronounced in the wines. While there are a good many people who favor this "foxiness" of flavor, drinkers more accustomed to European wines often find it odd or distasteful. One reason that New York's wine industry was so late in getting under way—after all, grapes grew all over the northeast as far north as Newfoundland, leading Leif Ericson to christen the New World Vineland—was that the first settlers were European and disliked the taste of the native grape. The European vines they imported quickly succumbed to the severe winter climate or to pests and disease. Though several attempts were made to nurture them, they all failed.

In 1829, the Reverend William Bostwick planted a vineyard in the rectory garden of the Episcopal Church at Hammondsport, near Lake Keuka in the Finger Lakes District, and later distributed cuttings to neighbors and parishioners. In the next few decades, an influx of European immigrants gradually increased vineyard acreage, and they began making wines out of native grapes for their own tables. The first commercial operation in the Finger Lakes Region was the Pleasant Valley Winery, which opened in Hammondsport in 1860. Wineries had operated earlier elsewhere in the state, in the Hudson River Valley above Newburgh, for example, as early as 1839. By the 1880s, however, the major wine-producing region was the Finger Lakes District, centered mostly around the southern shores of Lakes Keuka and Canandaigua. Several of the earliest winemakers specialized in Champagne and soon were winning medals for their wines at the Paris Exposition. Just as the industry was beginning to burgeon, the temperance campaign began, culminating finally in Prohibition. Fortunately for New York State growers, most of the vineyards were maintained, for many of the native grape varieties proved delightful to eat fresh and made delicious fruit juices, jams, and jellies. Some wineries obtained permission to make sacramental and medicinal wines and thus continued to operate, but the effects of the dry era were about as disastrous for the wine industry in New York as everywhere else. After repeal, New York State legislation did little to promote the regrowth of the industry. Temperance sentiment still ran high in the northern part of the state and licensing fees for wineries were set exorbitantly high, making it extremely difficult for small wineries to operate. Few, in fact, have existed at all until recently, when new

legislation cut the costs and some of the red tape for small producers. A handful of venturesome and enterprising people have been making admirable efforts on a small scale at such places as Benmarl, Glenora, Château Esperanza, Herron Hill, Clinton Vineyards, Wagner Vineyards, Hargrave Vineyard, Johnson Estate, and Vinifera. These wineries have had an influence on the New York State wine industry out of all proportion to their size. They are the ones that are attempting to make wines that can compete with California and Europe. They have pioneered with varieties other than the native Labrusca and their success has brought new attention to New York wines. The late Charles Fournier, Gold Seal's winemaker from the Champagne District of France, introduced the first French hybrids to the Finger Lakes District in the 1940s, initially using them in blends of Champagne. Everett Crosby planted them at High Tor in Rockland County in 1949. Johnson Estate, Benmarl, and Bully Hill planted them in the 60s and 70s. Gradually but steadily the hybrids have gained ground until now they make up a substantial portion of vineyards in every part of the state and are used to some extent by virtually every producer.

The French hybrids were developed in France and named for those who developed them, men with names like Baco, Seibel, Seyve-Villard, and others, with an identifying number for each variety. For most of them, alternate names have been derived to benefit the consumer. The leading white wines are Seyval Blanc, Aurora, and Villard Blanc; the reds bear names like Baco Noir, Chelois, Chancellor Noir, Cascade, Maréchal Foch, and Villard Noir. Occasionally one sees a name and number, such as Boordy Vineyards' Five-Two-Seven-Six, made from Seyve-Villard 5276. We are likely to see many more wines with names like these in years to come.

In the mid-1970s a major thrust toward producing European varietals took place, and some very good Chardonnays, Rieslings, Gewürztraminers and even some Cabernet Sauvignons were produced at a handful of small wineries. But many of the vines were wiped out with the disastrous 1981 vintage that suffered from a freeze at Christmas 1980, causing some producers to have second thoughts about producing *Vitis vinifera* grapes in the state. Nevertheless, most remained committed, and the setback was only temporary.

New York State wines are grown mainly in four regions, the largest being the Finger Lakes District. The others are Chautauqua, around Lake Chautauqua just east of Lake Erie, the Hudson River Valley and Niagara, along the Niagara River between Lake Erie and Lake Ontario. A few vineyards are beginning to appear in other places, too, such as Long Island.

FINGER LAKES

Early Indians believed that these elongated, glacier-gouged bodies of water were the handprint of the Great Spirit. Looking at them on a map or from high in the air it is easy to see how they drew such a conclusion, appearing as they do like the outstretched fingers of a giant hand. The steep and rolling hills surrounding the sky-blue waters make the Finger Lakes at all seasons one of the most attractive and picturesque wine districts in the world. Vineyards and wineries are clustered mainly around Lakes Keuka and Canandaigua, with lesser numbers at Seneca and Cayuga. The town of Hammondsport at the southern end of Keuka is headquarters for most of the large producers, e.g., Taylor, Gold Seal, and Great Western.

But it is also the home of smaller outfits such as Bully Hill and Vinifera. Widmer's Wine Cellars is located at Naples on Canandaigua Lake.

Champagne is the most famous product of the Finger Lakes District. Table wines are blended mostly from native grapes and American hybrids such as Catawba, Concord, Delaware, Dutchess, and others, but the wineries generally soften the Labrusca flavor of the wines by blending in California wine, which is imported in bulk. French hybrids are gaining importance among some producers in response to the market trend and public taste. Small producers such as Walter Taylor of Bully Hill have done much to encourage the use of French hybrids. Dr. Konstantin Frank and the late Charles Fournier have proven that even the Vinifera grape can be successfully grown in the region.

The lakes modify the severe climate to some extent, protecting the vines from killing frosts in autumn and spring and allowing a growing season of 150 days. Temperatures in winter still drop a good 20 degrees or more lower than the northernmost vineyards of Germany and France—cold enough to damage European vines until Dr. Frank developed vines grafted onto hardier rootstocks. It will probably be some time before the big companies can be persuaded to plant large quantities of Vinifera, if ever, but many smaller wineries are experimenting with Vinifera vines. Research continues, and the pioneer efforts of Frank, Fournier, and others will eventually result in better wines—and more of them.

CHAUTAUQUA

The Chautauqua-Erie Region was for years known more for its grape juice (Welch's) than for its wines, even though the earliest vines in the region were planted in 1818, again by a local man of the cloth, Deacon Elijah Fay. His son Joseph founded the first commercial winery in Brocton in 1859, a year before the Pleasant Valley Winery opened in Hammondsport. Today there are more than 20,000 acres of wine grape varieties. Dr. Charles Welch, a dentist, did his best to root out every variety but the Concord grape used in his world-famed juices, jams, and jellies, but in 1960 something happened to turn the tide. Frederick S. Johnson, who had inherited 70 acres of Concord from his father, decided to rip them out and plant grapes that would yield the kind of wine he had grown used to drinking in his travels around the world. Johnson Estate Wines are mostly dry, attractive, and well made. They include Seyval Blanc, Chancellor Noir, Cascade Rouge, Aurora Blanc, Delaware, and house blends of dry white, red and rosé. Other growers have planted French hybrids in Chautauqua and are finding ready buyers.

HUDSON RIVER VALLEY

This region lies mostly in Ulster and Orange Counties above Newburgh, west of the Hudson River. It was once a thriving fruitland, full of apple orchards and grapevines. Today only a few wineries of any size operate here—Brotherhood Winery, Royal Winery (makers of kosher wines), Marlboro Industries, Hudson River Valley Company, Benmarl, and High Tor. Of these, only the last three produce estate-bottled wines and all three grow French-American hybrids, plus some European varietals. Hudson River Valley also grows Labrusca varieties and Benmarl has several acres of Chardonnay, Riesling, Pinot Noir, and even Cabernet. The climate here is tempered by the Hudson River, which moderates the severity of winter and extends the warmer summers with

a growing season three weeks longer than upstate districts. Mark Miller of Benmarl deeply believes that the Hudson River Valley can be one of the nation's great wine districts. His interesting wines indicate that indeed it may be so. The Miller family has formed an organization to encourage further planting of vineyards in the valley and give local farmers a viable alternative to ailing and unprofitable apple orchards that now inhabit much of the land.

NIAGARA

The benign climate that exists in this patch of land between Lake Erie and Ontario makes it one of the best for growing wine grapes, including hybrids and Vinifera varieties, in the state. Grapes grow along both sides of the Niagara River. Peaches and cherries also flourish in the region. One of the wineries in this small district is Niagara Falls Wine Cellar, operated by Richard Vine, formerly of Taylor Wine Company. He grows hybrids and native varieties like Catawba and Dutchess and Chardonnay, all of which are labeled as varietal wines. Fewer than 2000 acres of vines grow at present in Niagara, but the area could become more important in the future.

LONG ISLAND

As they are everywhere else in America, new vineyards are springing up in Long Island in spots that never knew the vine before. In the early years of the country, vineyards were planted on Long Island, but they eventually faded into oblivion. Today, however, new possibilities are emerging. Out near the end of Long Island at Cutchogue, the Hargrave family planted 40 acres of *Vitis vinifera,* including Cabernet Sauvignon and Pinot Noir, which came into bearing in 1975. A unique microclimate allows the vineyard 210 growing days, comparable to the Napa Valley. Flanked by Long Island Sound and Great Peconic Bay, it is thus "not far from the *bord d'eaux*" and enjoys more sun than vineyards upstate because of 20 percent less cloud cover during summer. It is virtually frost-free during the entire growing season. The European varietals of Hargrave Vineyard have attracted a wide following in recent years because they are well made.

Newlan Vineyards & Winery.

Newlan is a small Napa Valley winery established in 1981 by Bruce Newland, a grape grower since 1968. A new winery building was planned in time for the crush of 1983, when production was expected to surpass 3000 cases of Cabernet Sauvignon, Pinot Noir, Chardonnay, and late-harvest Johannisberg Riesling. The first wines released by Newlan were a 1981 Chardonnay, a 1980 Pinot Noir, and a 1980 red table wine.
☆/☆☆
$/$$

Nichelini Vineyard.

This family-owned winemaking business near St. Helena in the Napa Valley of California was established in 1890 by Anton Nichelini, an intrepid vineyardist who continued making wine during Prohibition, got caught, served a six-month sentence, and was fined $500 as well. According to family lore, he served out his brief term in a hotel across the street from the jail. The business was revived after repeal in 1933 by his son William Anton Nichelini, and the present proprietor, Jim Nichelini, grew up on the estate, which now has 200 acres planted in vines and produces 8000 to 10,000 cases a year of estate-bottled wines. The vineyard also sells grapes under contract to such producers as Charles Krug, Louis Martini, the Napa Valley Cooperative, and others. Nichelini's roster of premium varietals includes Cabernet Sauvignon, Zinfandel,

Napa Gamay, Carnelian (a hybrid), Petite Sirah, Gamay Rose, Chenin Blanc, Sémillon, and a wine called Sauvignon Vert. The wines have been low-priced.
☆/☆☆
$/$$

Niebaum-Coppola Estate.

This winery represents another aspect of the Hollywood invasion of the California wine business. The proprietor is Francis Ford Coppola, the film producer, who bought the old mansion of Gustave Niebaum, the Finnish sea captain who settled in the Napa Valley town of Rutherford in 1879 and founded Inglenook Vineyards. Coppola also acquired the 90-acre vineyard adjacent to the mansion and announced plans to produce one wine made primarily from Cabernet Sauvignon grapes and another one from Chardonnay. The first wine, a red made in the 1978 vintage and scheduled for release in 1983, was 60 percent Cabernet Sauvignon, 38 percent Cabernet Franc, and 2 percent Merlot. Some 1500 cases were made. Production rose to 4000 cases in the 1979 and '80 vintages and to 6000 cases by 1983. Initial plans were to call it simply Red Table Wine. When tasted in 1981 it was medium ruby in color and exuded an intense bouquet of berries and cedarwood. There were raspberries and cedarwood in the flavor, but the wine was too young to be judged accurately.
☆☆☆
$$$

Niersteiner.

German white wine produced in Nierstein, one of the top villages in the Rheinhessen, which lies on the west bank of the Rhine River before it turns west at Mainz. Niersteiners are soft and elegant, the best in Hessia. They rival the big wines of the Rheingau to the

RHEINHESSEN

1959er
Niersteiner Rehbach
Riesling feinste Auslese

Produce of Germany
Weingut Franz Karl Schmitt, Nierstein a. Rhein

northwest in quality, and some connoisseurs contend they are the best in Germany. Many ordinary Niersteiners are produced and some of them are bottled as Liebfraumilch, which has evolved into a generic term for mostly undistinguished blends.

The best Niersteiners carry the names of specific vineyards and are made from grapes produced from the famous reddish soil on a ridge overlooking the Rhine. As in most other parts of Germany, the Riesling grape is responsible for the superior wines, although the Sylvaner accounts for the bulk of the production in the area and produces some excellent ones. Among the producers and bottlers who are most renowned are Franz Karl Schmitt, Rheinhold Senfter, Freiherr Heyl zu Herrnsheim, Louis Guntrum, and the Staatsweingutt, or state-owned business, but there are around 300 others whose name may appear on a label or whose wines are bottled by the local *Winzergenossenschaft,* or cooperative, which has extensive facilities, including five huge centrifuge presses, each with a capacity of 8000 kilograms. The cooperative produces about 600,000 gallons of wine a year. More than half is made from Sylvaner grapes, less than a third from Müller-Thurgau, and around 10 percent from Riesling, the noblest of them all.

Over the years certain specific vineyards have traditionally turned out the best wines. Connoisseurs tend to have their favorites; here are some of the best:

Niersteiner Auflangen*
Niersteiner Brudersberg
Niersteiner Flächenhahl
Niersteiner Floss
Niersteiner Fockenberg
Niersteiner Fuchsloch
Niersteiner Glöck*
Niersteiner Gutes Domtal*
Niersteiner Heiligenbaum*
Niersteiner Hipping
Niersteiner Hölle*
Neirsteiner Kehr
Niersteiner Kranzberg*
Niersteiner Oelberg*
Niersteiner Orbel*
Niersteiner Pettenthal
Niersteiner Rehbach
Niersteiner Rohr
Niersteiner St. Kiliansberg
Niersteiner Schnappenberg
Niersteiner Spiegelberg*
Niersteiner Streng

The vineyards marked with an asterisk (*) are among those that retained their names, if not their former configurations, in the revision of the German wine law in 1971. Auflangen, Gutes Domtal, and Spiegelberg were made *Grosslage,* or large vineyard areas, and are blends from a fairly large section around Nierstein. In general, small vineyards were merged into larger ones to simplify identification and some new vineyard names were created to encompass some of the old sites.
☆/☆☆☆
$/$$

noble rot, Botrytis cinerea.

The mold that afflicts grapes when they are left on the vines late in the autumn, when the combination of sunshine and humidity in the atmosphere is just right, is known in France as *pourriture noble,* or the noble rot. In Germany it is called *Edelfäule;* in Italy it is *muffa nobile.* The Latin species name is *Botrytis cinerea.* It imparts a special taste that is much sought in sweet white dessert wines, as well as in some of the more robust white Burgundies. It is also found in some parts of northern Italy, especially the Veneto, where it occasionally is evident in a red wine, the delicious Amarone. It has been successfully cultivated in California as well.

It is called "rot" because of its ugly appearance on the surface of the grape skins as they hang from the vines in the low autumn sun. In seeking a heavy sugar content, the growers in the Sauternes District of France and in the Rhine and Mosel Valleys of Germany wait until the latest possible moment in the autumn to harvest their grapes. Under the proper conditions, the noble rot will attack the grapes, penetrating the skins, so that the water in the grape juice can more readily evaporate, leaving behind highly concentrated, ultrasweet fluid.

According to legend, the beneficial aspects of the noble rot were discovered in 1847, when the Marquis de Lur-Saluces, the owner of Château d'Yquem in Sauternes, returned from a trip to Russia so late in the year that the grapes were overripe and totally contaminated with the mold. Nevertheless, he ordered the harvest to get under way, and the resulting wine became world-famous. Since then, late-harvesting in Sauternes has become standard and the best châteaux nowadays harvest only grapes that have been attacked by the marvelous, ugly parasite. (*See also* Sauternes, Château d'Yquem, Trockenbeerenauslese.)

North Salem Vineyard.

Crisp, clean Seyval Blancs are made by Dr. George Naumberg at this winery in northern Westchester County, New York. Naumburg, a Manhattan psychiatrist, also produces a Maréchal Foch that is light and dry. The first plantings

here were in 1965, but production remains modest.

☆

$

Novitiate Winery.

Novitiate, with a winery in Los Gatos in California's Santa Clara County, is owned and operated by the California Province of the Society of Jesus. The winery was founded by the Jesuits in 1888 and is one of the oldest in continuous operation in California. The first Jesuit winemaking operation was at the order's Santa Clara Mission in the 1850s, and the Novitiate Winery was founded by Jesuits from that mission. Whereas Novitiate at one time was an extensive grower of grapes to supply its winery, most of the vineyards have been sold off or leased out and the winery now relies almost entirely on grapes purchased from outside growers. Novitiate built up a reputation for good dessert wines at a time when dessert wines were popular, but they have long since been eclipsed by table wines in consumer preference, so Novitiate is attempting to turn out a line of improved table wines in response to the American wine boom. Novitiate also continues to make altar wines. The winery's total production runs 35,000 to 50,000 cases a year.

☆/☆☆

$

Nuits-Saint-Georges.

The namesake and principal *commune* of the Côte de Nuits in the French Burgundy country is Nuits-Saint-Georges. More wines are produced under this name than any other in the Côte de Nuits. The *commune* wines simply named Nuits-Saint-Georges can be very good value, but they can also be rather ordinary red Burgundies, so it is important to rely on a good *négociant,* or shipper, or else move up a step on the

quality scale and choose one of the *premiers crus* of Nuits. (A listing of these appears under the entry for Côte de Nuits.) These wines are usually good full-bodied Burgundies with a bit more character than some of the *premiers crus* of the Côte de Beaune just a few miles to the south. The better-known *premiers* of Nuits-Saint-Georges are Les Saint-Georges, Les Vaucrains, and Les Porets, as well as Clos de la Maréchale, which actually lies in neighboring Prémeaux but is marketed as a Nuits-Saint-Georges. As with all Burgundy *premiers crus,* the name of the *commune* will appear first on the label, followed by the name of the vineyard, e.g., Nuits-Saint-Georges-Les Saint-Georges or Nuits-Saint-Georges-Les Vaucrains. (*See also* Côte de Nuits, Prémeaux.)

☆☆☆/☆☆☆☆
$$/$$$

Numano Sake.

The Numano Sake Company began brewing rice wine in Berkeley, California, in 1978, and production soon reached more than one million bottles a year. Besides Sake, Numano also produces a plum wine. The company's brand names are Numano and Koshu. The products are distributed from coast to coast.

☆
$

· O ·

Oak Knoll Winery.

Oak Knoll, located in Hillsboro, Oregon, is mainly a fruit wine operation, but the winery also produces Pinot Noir, Chardonnay, Riesling, Sauvignon Blanc, and Cabernet Sauvignon, mainly from purchased grapes. Its Pinot Noirs tend to be peppery and spicy in bouquet, with spicy accents on the palate. Production is limited. The winery has been in operation since 1970, and expansion is planned from the current 5000 cases a year of grape wines and up to 10,000 more of fruit wines.
☆/☆☆☆
$/$$

Oakencroft Vineyard.

The first plantings at this small winery three miles from Charlottesville, Virginia, took place in 1978 in a section of the polled hereford farm owned by John B. and Felicia Warburg Rogan. An Oakencroft Chardonnay and a Seyval Blanc were released early in 1984, and Cabernet Sauvignon and Merlot were planned for the late 1980s. The vineyard, initially seven acres, was to be expanded to 12 acres by 1985.
☆
$$

Ockfener.

The Saar section of the Mosel-Saar-Ruwer region of Germany produces a handful of superior wines, and Ockfeners, produced at Ockfen, which is south of the more famous Wiltingen, are among the best. They can rank among the better German wines in the best vintage years, but in mediocre years they often fall below the quality levels achieved by the wines of the central Mosel Valley to the north. Ockfeners are more popular than the nearby Saarburgers and Serrigers, which produce great wines more sporadically. The best Ockfener vineyards are the Bockstein, Geisberg, Heppenstein, Herrenberg, Oberherrenberg, and St. Irminer. The names of vineyards that can legally be used following the revision of the German wine law in 1971 are Scharzberg, Heppenstein, Bockstein, Kupp, Herrenberg, and Geisberg.
☆/☆☆☆
$/$$

Oenology.

The science of viticulture is oenology, sometimes spelled enology and in both cases pronounced ee-nology. The term refers to all that goes into the creation of wine from grape juice. People who practice the science of oenology are oenologists, whereas people who simply grow grapes are viniculturists. An oenologist differs from a connoisseur in that the connoisseur's knowledge relates to the end product—the wine—whereas the oenologist's knowledge relates to how it was produced. From the same Greek derivation comes the oenophile, who is a lover of wine. Anybody with an abiding passion for wine is entitled to call himself an oenophile, but he must have considerable knowledge before he can be considered an oenologist. It is safe to say that the world is full of oenophiles but that only a tiny percentage qualify as oenologists.

Oestricher.

The villages of the famous Rheingau region of Germany are situated either along the northern bank of the Rhine River or else up in the hills above the river. Oestrich is one of the hillside towns and it produces more white wine than any other Rheingau section, with well over 700 acres planted in vines. Oestrichers tend to be somewhat earthy and soft, very pleasant in good vintages when the weather has been warm and sunny, but displaying a heavy quality in lesser years. Because so much Oestricher is produced, however, it is not difficult to find in the export markets and will cost somewhat less than the more expensive and elegant Schloss Johannisbergers or Marcobrunners from nearby Rheingau villages. The Lenchen and Doosberg vineyards are best known to connoisseurs, but any of the Oestrichers can be good value under the right conditions.

Among the better vineyards at Oestrich are the following:

Oestricher Deez
Oestricher Doosberg*
Oestricher Eiserberg
Oestricher Gottesthal*

Oestricher Hölle
Oestricher Kellerberg
Oestricher Kerbesberg
Oestricher Klosterberg*
Oestricher Klostergarten
Oestricher Lenchen*
Oestricher Magdalenengarten
Oestricher Mühlberg
Oestricher Pfaffenberg
Oestricher Pflanzer
Oestricher Raucherberg
Oestricher Rosengarten

An asterisk (*) indicates vineyard names that survived or that were created in the revision of the German wine law of 1971. The Gottesthal is now a *Grosslage,* or large vineyard area, similar to a generic wine of Oestrich.

☆/☆☆
$/$$

Ohio.

In 1850 thousands of acres were planted on the hillsides above the Ohio River, giving it the look of Germany's Rhine. Steamboats coursed along the wide waterway carrying cargoes of Nicholas Longworth's sparkling Catawba wine to St. Louis and New Orleans, whence they were carried to points east and west. In the mid-nineteenth century Ohio was the country's largest producer, with half a million gallons of wine yearly. Longworth was a lawyer who, upon tasting his first Catawba wines, abandoned his law practice and built a huge winery in Cincinnati. Their fame spread far and wide, praised in song and immortalized in verse by Longfellow. Sadly, Longworth saw his beautiful dream fade within the space of a few decades. Black rot and powdery mildew struck the vines, wiping out thousands of acres. By the time of his death in 1863 most of the vines were dead, and the winery went out of business a few years later. As the vineyards in the southern part of the state withered, new ones began to spring up in the northern part, along the shores of Lake Erie east of Toledo and on the Bass Islands off Sandusky. The most famous name in Ohio winemaking today is Meiers, whose wineries in Sandusky and Silverton near Cincinnati turn out vast amounts of wine from Catawba, Delaware, French hybrids, and a few Vinifera varieties. Henry Sonneman bought Meiers wine cellars in 1928 and later, in 1941, bought vineyards on Isle St. George, more or less taking up where Longworth had left off. Sonneman encouraged the regrowth of the wine industry in Ohio and the state is on its way to prominence once again.

Olarra, Bodegas Olarra.

The reds of Bodegas Olarra, one of the leading producers of the Rioja District of Spain, have built up a worldwide following. They tend to be soft, fruity, and less woody than some of the other Riojas. Olarra's Blanco Seco also is a pleasant wine.

☆/☆☆☆
$/$$

Old Creek Ranch Winery.

Old Creek is a producer of premium varietal wines in Ventura County, California. It was established in 1981 on the premises of an old winery built in the late 1800s and abandoned about 1940. The new owners have undertaken modest vineyard planting and had not yet produced 1000 cases of wine as of the 1981 vintage.

☆/☆☆
$$

Château Olivier.

One of the best-known white wines of the Graves District south and west of Bordeaux is produced at Château Olivier, which was accorded grand cru status for both its reds and whites in the Graves classification of 1959. Its production of dry white wines is larger than any other Graves estate, and many wine lovers all over the world equate white Graves with Château Olivier. The reds can also be quite good, although produced in only small quantities. The estate lies in the commune of Léognan, also the home of Château Haut-Bailly and Domaine de Chevalier. Olivier reds reach maturity in eight to ten years, while the whites should be drunk young—within four years of the harvest.

☆/☆☆☆
$$

Oltrepo' Pavese.

This is a productive wine district in the Lombardy region of northern Italy, with many wines that have qualified for recognition under the Italian D.O.C. law. Generally they bear varietal names, such as Oltrepo' Pavese Barbera, Bonarda, or Cortese.

☆/☆☆☆
$/$$

Oppenheimer.

German white wine produced in Oppenheim, which is one of the top villages in the Rheinhessen on the left bank of the Rhine River before it bends west at Mainz. Oppenheimers do not quite measure up to the nearby Niersteiners, but some are excellent and classy wines. The area planted in grapes is somewhat smaller than in Nierstein and thus the wines are less plentiful. As in other parts of Germany, the best wines are made from Riesling grapes, but most of the Oppenheimers are made from Sylvaner. Some of the production is pressed and bottled at the Winzergenossenschaft, or cooperative, in Nierstein, although it retains its Oppenheimer name.

Opinions vary among connoisseurs as to the best vineyards. Among those traditionally ranked among the top are the following:

Oppenheimer Daubhaus*
Oppenheimer Goldberg
Oppenheimer Guldenmorgen
Oppenheimer Herrenberg*
Oppenheimer Herrenweiher
Oppenheimer Kehrweg
Oppenheimer Kreuz*
Oppenheimer Kröttenbrunnen*
Oppenheimer Reisekahr
Oppenheimer Sackträger*
Oppenheimer Schlossberg*
Oppenheimer Steig
Oppenheimer Zuckerberg*

The vineyards marked with an asterisk (*) are among those that retained their identities, if not their shapes, in the revision of the German wine law in 1971. In general, the smaller vineyards were merged into larger ones to simplify identification. Gueldenmorgen and Kröttenbrunnen became *Grosslage,* or large vineyard areas, encompassing wine from a fairly large section.
☆/☆☆
$/$$

Oregon.

The vineyards of Oregon are clustered mainly in the northern part of the state in an arc that curves around Portland. A few are also located in the south near the California border. The state's fledgling wine industry is tiny but has a promising outlook. The climate is similar to that of northern Europe, closest in some places to Alsace. Consequently such varieties as Chardonnay, Johannisberg Riesling, and Pinot Noir stand a good chance of being successfully cultivated here. All of the vineyards are tiny, but they make up for their smallness with their prodigious efforts and quality wines. The Eyrie Vineyard, with a red-tailed hawk gracing its label, has produced a Pinot Noir aged in Limousin oak that exhibits good finish and complexity. Hillcrest Vineyard and Tualatin

Vineyards are making worthy efforts, as are the southern Oregon wineries of Bjelland and Jonicole. Oregon is a veritable fruitland and, not surprisingly, there are a fair number of "wines" made from pears, plums, raspberries, and even one from dry rhubarb.

Orvieto.

Italy is best known for her red wines, but Orvieto has established an international reputation as one of the country's best whites. More and more often these days it is vinified dry, no doubt in response to public tastes, but the classic Orvieto is semisweet—*abboccato* or *amabile*—with a taste of fruit that is full and pleasant. The wine comes from the city of Orvieto in Umbria, a region in central Italy north of Rome. The city is carved into a rocky outcropping, and the caves that run through the cliffside have been used for aging the local wines for many years. Orvieto is made mostly from the Trebbiano grape, with some Verdello and Malvasia blended in. The sweeter varieties employ the process known as *muffa nobile,* the same noble rot that is important in the production of Sauternes in France and the better white wines of the Mosel and Rhine valleys in Germany.

☆/☆☆

$/$$

Ozeki San Benito.

Ozeki San Benito is a producer of Sake in Hollister, California. The concern is a joint venture, involving two American companies and two Japanese companies, that was founded in 1979. By 1981 some 150,000 gallons of Sake and Mirin (the sweet Sake used for cooking) were being produced annually. Sake and Mirin are marketed under the brand names Ozeki and Kikkoman. (*See* Sake.)

☆

$

· P ·

Château Palmer.

Although Château Palmer was ranked among the *troisièmes crus,* or third growths, in the Bordeaux classification of 1855, it is without question one of the two or three best estates of Margaux and deserves to be ranked on a par with the best *seconds crus.* The château itself, which appears on the wine's labels, is near the road that bisects the Médoc running north from Bordeaux. It is a picturesque, almost Victorian old building, used nowadays mainly for entertaining by Palmer's owners, who include the Sichel family that also owns the nearby Château d'Angludet. The estate obtained its name from General Palmer of England, who maintained it in the early nineteenth century. The wines of Château Palmer are rich and elegant, sometimes displaying a hardness more characteristic of Saint-Estèphe than of Margaux. But this gives them great longevity, which is unusual in that portion of the Médoc. A Palmer needs at least a decade to reach its peak.

☆☆☆☆
$$$

Papagni Vineyards.

Papagni is one of the older California winery operations, with enormous vineyard holdings and production capacity of more than one million cases a year. But the enterprise passed a milestone of sorts in 1973 with the construction of a new winery that enabled Angelo Papagni, the proprietor, to produce a line of premium varietals of sometimes superior quality at relatively moderate prices. New equipment was imported from Germany and elsewhere in Europe, plus new 60-gallon oak aging barrels from France and Yugoslavia. American, French, and Yugoslavian oak barrels are used for aging the Angelo Papagni estate-bottled varietals. Now production of these varietals runs about 100,000 cases a year. In addition, there are two other labels, Papagni Vineyards and Rancho Yerba Buena.

Angelo Papagni himself is a fourth-generation winemaker. His father, Demetrio, emigrated to the United States in 1912 from Bari, near Italy's Adriatic coast, and brought with him the winemaking skills that he had learned from his father and grandfather. In 1920 Demetrio Papagni planted his first 20 acres of vines in California's San Joaquin Val-

ley. After his son Angelo had become active in the business, there were further plantings on their Clovis Ranch west of the Sierra Nevada Mountains, and these vineyards continue to produce Barbera and Alicante Bouschet grapes. Later there were additional plantings in Madera County, where the winery is situated in the town of Madera. The product lineup is very broad and includes such standard premium varietals as Chenin Blanc, Chardonnay, Fumé Blanc, Barbera, Zinfandel, Gamay Rose, sparkling wines and sherries, as well as such semiexotic varietals or brands as Moscato d'Angelo, late-harvested Emerald Riesling, Spumante d'Angelo, Charbono, and a few others.
☆/☆☆☆
$/$$

Château Pape-Clément.

Among the better red-wine producers of the Graves District south of Bordeaux is Château Pape-Clément, owned by the church until the French Revolution. Its origins date back to the Middle Ages. It lies in Pessac, the same *commune* that is the home of the noble Château Haut-Brion, but Pape-Clément tends to be a slightly lighter wine. The estate's reputation suffered in the 1930s and 1940s, but it began producing good wines again in the 1950s, and nowadays it can be good value. It was ranked a *grand cru* in the Graves classification of 1959. It is best drunk after a decade or more of bottle-age.
☆☆☆☆
$$/$$$

Paradiso.

Paradiso is a very good red wine produced from Nebbiolo grapes in the Valtellina, an important sector of northern Italy's Lombardy region. The wine was named after a famous castle near Sondrio. It is fairly intensely flavored, tannic and coarse when young, best drunk no earlier than age six. It is not to be confused with the Paradiso brand of Picolit produced in the Friuli-Venezia Giulia region.
☆☆☆
$/$$

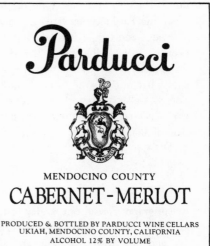

Parducci.

Parducci Wine Cellars of Mendocino County, run by brothers John and George Parducci, is located in Ukiah, a northern California town situated in an area formerly known more for its redwood lumber and pear orchards. That situation is slowly but surely being corrected by such wineries as Parducci. Plantings of superior varietal grapes over the past decade have produced a steady supply of quality wines. John Parducci is a popular and active figure in the California wine industry. Parducci wines, particularly the reds, are occasionally big and robust, because sometimes they are not filtered or fined, which leaves them vigorous and full-bodied.

The Parducci grape-growing business was established by John's father, Adolph, who acquired 100 acres of vineyards in a pioneering venture in Mendocino County in 1931, just prior to the end of Prohibition. The winery was begun the same year, although the business was heavily involved in bulk wines until the wine boom of the 1970s. The winery did not even have electric lights until 1939, and this is where John and his brothers grew up and got their experience. The property is known as the Home Ranch, which appears on Parducci labels to connote grape origins. The other Parducci vineyards are called Talmadge and Largo. Parducci has also been a strong influence in the rising prominence of Lake County wines. Superior batches of wine carry the notation "Cellar Master's Selection." Parducci's total production runs more than 50,000 cases a year.

☆/☆☆☆
$/$$

Passito.

Italian grapes spread out to dry in the sun after the harvest are known as *passito,* and this word also designates the dessert wines made from them. The name is often followed by the name of the region or district of production, e.g., Passito di Caluso from the Piedmont in the northern part of the country or Passito di Arco from the area near Lake Garda.

Paternina, Federico.

Federico Paternina is a major producer of red and white table wines in the Rioja District of northern Spain. The winery is represented in the United States with a half dozen different bottlings, and its *reserva* and *gran reserva* are superior in quality. (*See* Rioja.)

☆☆/☆☆☆☆
$/$$

Pauillac.

Among the major *communes,* or townships, of the Haut Médoc north of Bordeaux, Pauillac rightfully lays claim to being the greatest. Within its boundaries lie three of the five first growths, or *grands crus classés,* of Bordeaux: the

Châteaux Lafite-Rothschild, Latour, and Mouton Rothschild. For generations these have been among the most celebrated and expensive red wines produced anywhere in the world. In addition Pauillac has 15 other châteaux mentioned in the Bordeaux classification of 1855. The wines of Pauillac display great finesse and elegance. They are less supple than Margaux, not as robust as Saint-Estèphes, but more balanced than most other Bordeaux. Mature Pauillacs tend to exude an overwhelming bouquet that is reminiscent of fresh cedarwood, or violets or the pleasant aroma of hot tar from a newly patched highway. They reach maturity ahead of the Saint-Estèphes and later than the Margaux, and they have great longevity. Latour and Mouton Rothschild, especially, have good staying power, and well-kept bottles from the 1926 and '28 vintages display great fruit and richness even now. The wines recognized in the Bordeaux classification of 1855 are as follows:

Premiers Crus (First Growths)
Château Lafite-Rothschild
Château Latour
Château Mouton Rothschild

Seconds Crus (Second Growths)
Château Pichon-Longueville (Baron)
Château Pichon-Longueville
    (Comtesse de Lalande)

Quatrième Cru (Fourth Growth)
Château Duhart-Milon-Rothschild

Cinquièmes Crus (Fifth Growths)
Château Batailley
Château Haut-Batailley
Château Croizet-Bages
Château Clerc-Milon-Mondon
Château Grand-Puy-Ducasse
Château Grand-Puy-Lacoste
Château Haut-Bages-Libéral
Château Lynch-Bages
Château Lynch-Moussas

Château Mouton-Baron-Philíppe
   (Mouton d'Armailhacq)
Château Pédesclaux
Château Pontet-Canet

Château Mouton Rothschild was accorded *second cru* status in the 1855 classification, but was elevated to *premier cru* in 1973, because of its consistently great wines and the *premier cru* prices they had brought for decades. Some of the châteaux with fifth-growth rankings also would rank higher in any reclassification. The best example is Château Lynch-Bages, whose dark and rich wines have achieved considerable fame for their intensity and elegance. Lynch-Bages usually brings prices comparable to most second growths. All of the other fifth growths of Pauillac are well known and high in quality, but because they are ranked no higher than fifth, some of them sell at bargain prices that do not reflect their true worth.

An old seaport on the Gironde still exists there, and it is the headquarters town for the Commanderie du Bontemps du Médoc et des Graves, the organization of Bordeaux growers and their friends who gather periodically for good wine and good times. The group's offices are housed, appropriately, in La Maison du Vin on the docks of Pauillac overlooking the Gironde, where pirates once came ashore to raid the local citizenry.
☆☆☆/☆☆☆☆☆
$/$$$$

Château Pavie.

Château Pavie is one of the largest producers in Saint-Emilion, the important district near Libourne 20 miles east of Bordeaux. The estate consists of an ideally steep hillside with chalk outcroppings breaking through the greenery of the vines. Because of its location, it is one of the *côtes,* or hillside, vineyards,

as opposed to the *graves* vineyards, which are on the flatlands surrounding the medieval village of Saint-Emilion. Pavie, which should not be confused with Châteaux Pavie-Macquin or Pavie-Decesse, was ranked a *premier grand cru classé* in the Saint-Emilion classification of 1955. The other two were ranked as *grands crus classés.*
☆☆☆/☆☆☆☆☆
$$

Robert Pecota Winery.

The Robert Pecota Winery is one of many established in California in the late 1970s. Its namesake is the owner and winemaker, and he has established himself as a producer of excellent Sauvignon Blanc and superb Gamay Beaujolais. Pecota also produces Cabernet Sauvignon, French Colombard, and Muscat. The winery is in Calistoga, in the northern Napa Valley, amid 45 acres of vineyard. Production is moving toward 5000 cases a year.
☆/☆☆☆
$$

Pedrizzetti Winery.

The Pedrizzetti Winery was built, starting in 1913, by Camillo Colambano, an immigrant from the Piedmont District of Northern Italy. The business was acquired by John Pedrizzetti—coincidentally, also from the Piedmont—from the Colambano family in 1945, and it is now owned by Ed and Phyllis Pedrizzetti, a husband-and-wife team who share the management as well as the winemaking. A modernization and upgrading program has been under way since 1968. The open wooden fermenting tanks have been replaced with modern stainless steel, temperature-controlled fermenters, a new bottling line has been installed, and quality standards have been improved. Sixteen acres are planted in vines, but Pedrizzetti still buys 95 percent of its grapes from outside producers in San Luis Obispo, Santa Maria, Monterey, and Amador counties. Production has been running 60,000 cases a year, including about 5000 cases of jug-style wines. The winery turns out a broad array of varietals, including Petite Sirah, Barbera, Zinfandel, Cabernet Sauvignon, Pinot Noir, Chenin Blanc, French Colombard, Gewürztraminer, Johannisberg Riesling, Chardonnay, Green Hungarian, and Zinfandel Rosé. The production facility is in Morgan Hill, in Santa Clara County.

☆/☆☆☆

$/$$

J. Pedroncelli Winery.

The predecessor winery to J. Pedroncelli was founded in 1904 by John Canata, a San Francisco grocer who wanted wine to sell in his store. The operation was purchased in 1927 by the late John Pedroncelli, whose son John (he is not a Jr.) took over in 1957. During the Prohibition years the winery continued to operate, selling grapes to home winemakers, who made small quantities for their own consumption. Recently new fermenting tanks have been installed in a new building at the Guperville location in Sonoma County. For years Pedroncelli was a producer of bulk wines for other wineries, but now it also bottles under its own label. Production totals 125,000 cases a year, about 40 percent of which are in the jug-wine category. The enterprise owns 135 acres of vineyards but still buys two-thirds of its grape requirements from other growers, all in Sonoma County, and much of the total from the Dry Creek Valley. The present owners are John and Jim Pedroncelli, who are brothers. The Pedroncelli wines have established a reputation for good value, although prices have been climbing.

☆/☆☆

$/$$

Robert Pepi Winery.

Robert A. Pepi and Robert L. Pepi established their winery in the Napa Valley, near Oakville, in 1981 after buying vineyards as early as 1966, when the American wine boom was still a dream. Sauvignon Blanc is to be their primary wine, accounting for three-fourths of production, but Chardonnay and Cabernet Sauvignon also will be made. Production has already risen to 15,000 cases a year.

☆/☆☆

$$

Perelli-Minetti Winery.

The Perelli-Minetti Winery was the last member of the California Wine Association, which had originally been established in 1894 and absorbed 64 California wineries. It remained a powerful force in the California wine trade until Prohibition. The group went through another incarnation in the 1930s as Fruit Industries, then reverted to its old name, the California Wine Association, in 1950, when it had 11 wineries as members. All of these dropped out over a period of years, leaving only Perelli-Minetti. Thus Perelli-Minetti, once wholly owned by Antonio Perelli-Minetti, who emigrated to the United States from Italy at the turn of the century, now holds title to a number of

California brand names for wine, reflecting the former members of the association that have gone out of business. The winery is now in Delano, producing a line of varietal wines and brandies. Antonio Perelli-Minetti died in 1976 at age 95, after three sons had taken over the operation. But they are no longer associated with the winery, and its products generally are low-priced and lacking in character.

☆

$

Pernand-Vergelesses.

Lying on the hill above Aloxe-Corton and adjacent to the famous vineyards of Corton-Charlemagne is the rustic old village of Pernand, where some good red Burgundies of little renown are made. The wines of Pernand-Vergelesses are not ranked among the best of the Côte de Beaune in the French Burgundy country, and they are generally available at attractively low prices. The *premier cru* Vergelesses vineyard is shared with Savigny-les-Beaune, another nearby *commune* whose wines can also be good value. In Savigny the vineyard is called Vergelesses or Aux Vergelesses, and in Pernand it is called Ile des Vergelesses. Pernand has four other *premiers crus* which are rarely seen under their own names: Basses Vergelesses, Caradeux, Creux de la Net, and Les Fichots. Pernand-Vergelesses reaches it peak six to ten years after the harvest.

☆☆☆/☆☆☆☆
$$/$$$

Château Petit-Village.

The production of individual châteaux in Pomerol is modest in comparison with the output of the estates of the Médoc on the peninsula north of Bordeaux, and Château Petit-Village, with only about 6000 cases per year, is one of Pomerol's larger producers. The estate lies near Château La Conseillante and not far from the village of Catusseau, the principal town of the Pomerol District. Although no formal classification of Pomerol estates has been made. Petit-Village would rank with the fourth and fifth growths of the Médoc in any broad classification of Bordeaux wines.

☆☆☆/☆☆☆☆
$$/$$$

Petite Sirah.

A California grape that produces good varietal red wines is the Petite Sirah, which is believed to be a variation of the Syrah of the Rhône Valley of France. One theory is that the crusaders brought the grape to France from Syria in the thirteenth century, while another theory suggests that the Greeks carried it to the Rhône in the sixth century from the Greek Island of Syros or Syra. Some experts suggest that the California variety may be unrelated, but in any case it often produces dark, full-bodied and robust wines that should be aged at least a decade before consumption, although the vast majority of Petite Sirah is probably consumed within three years of the vintage. Most of the major California wineries produce it, and its style will vary according to the producer. When liberally blended with softer varieties, it can be pleasant at a fairly young age, but unfortunately most California producers do not indicate on their labels precisely what blend is involved. (*See* California.)

Château Pétrus.

The unchallenged king of Pomerol in the Bordeaux region of southwestern France is Château Pétrus, year after year one of the greatest red wines produced anywhere in the world. It is big and rich, but supple and elegant at the same time, reaching extraordinary peaks of finesse in good vintages. Bottles of this

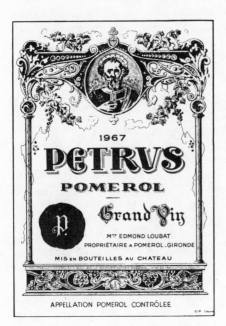

1967
PÉTRVS
POMEROL
Grand Vin
P.
Mme EDMOND LOUBAT
PROPRIÉTAIRE à POMEROL . GIRONDE
MIS en BOUTEILLES au CHATEAU

APPELLATION POMEROL CONTRÔLEE

great claret are to be treasured and consumed on special occasions, not casually quaffed for amusement, for the production of perhaps 4000 cases in a copious vintage is small compared to the output of other Bordeaux reds of comparable quality. (Château Latour produces at least six times as much, Lafite and Margaux five times as much.)

The Pétrus vineyard consists of about 30 acres of mostly flat terrain that is almost pure clay sprinkled with gravel, as opposed to the *cailloux,* or pebbles, that fill the soil in some nearby vineyards. (A small parcel was acquired from Château Gazin in the 1970s in a move that expanded the Pétrus vineyard by several acres.) The vines are 95 percent Merlot, a grape variety perfectly suited to the soil here, and they are old—the roots 60 to 80 years and the trunks 16 to 18. The choice not to replant with younger vines and to vinify in the traditional method has meant lower yields, but relatively high alcoholic content. The 1970 vintage averaged 13.5 percent and the '71 was 13.1 percent. One cask of

the '70 was measured at 14.5 percent. (The norm for the better Bordeaux is 12 to 12.5 percent.) The 1969 and 1972 vintages, in common with the rest of Bordeaux, were disappointing at Pétrus, but better than elsewhere. Some of the copious '70 is understood to have been blended with the '69 to "help" it, while the '72 was so light that the cellarmaster used old oak barrels from the 1970 vintage for aging, to avoid too much wood taste in the wine. (Oak increasingly loses its influence on the wine after each vintage.)

For many years Château Pétrus was owned by Madame Loubat, a leading Pomerol figure who actively managed her vineyard until well into her 80s. The Libourne firm of Jean Pierre Moueix now jointly owns Pétrus with Madame Loubat's heirs. But the Moueixes continue to make the wine in the traditional way and say they plan no changes. They have extensive interests in other châteaux in Pomerol and nearby Saint-Emilion, which enable them to satisfy any demands for wines of a different style than Pétrus. The name is Latin for Saint Peter, and the richly inscribed crimson label on Pétrus bottles tries to be Roman in style. Few wines made anywhere are more costly. Château Pétrus of recent vintages sells at the same prices as the first growths of the Médoc, or higher, whereas older vintages often are far more costly because of their extreme scarcity. Pétrus can be drunk as young as age ten, but is best several years older. (*See also* Pomerol.)
☆☆☆☆
$$$/$$$$

Château Peymartin.

Château Peymartin is, in effect, a secondary bottling of Château Gloria, the property of Henri Martin, mayor of the Bordeaux *commune* of Saint-Julien and former manager of Château Latour. The best grapes from the most mature vines of the Château Gloria vineyards are used to make the excellent red wines of Château Gloria. The remaining 35 to 40 percent of the grapes are used for Château Peymartin, or, if they do not meet even the standards for Peymartin, they are sold off to the Bordeaux trade to be bottled simply as Bordeaux *rouge*. The wines of Château Peymartin are never as supple and rich as those of Gloria itself, but they are always less expensive and can represent good value in exceptional vintages. (*See* Château Gloria.)

☆☆☆/☆☆☆☆
$$

Château de Pez.

Among the better Médoc estates not included in the Bordeaux classification of 1855 was Château de Pez, which produces good sturdy wines in Saint-Estèphe. It is a *cru bourgeois supérieur,* or better bourgeois growth, which can rank in quality on a par with some of the classified growths. Its origins date back more than five centuries. Like other wines of Saint-Estèphe, those of Château de Pez need plenty of bottle-age— at least a decade—before being consumed, and they often retain good fruit and balance for two to three decades. (*See also* Médoc, Saint-Estèphe.)

☆☆☆☆
$$

Château Phélan-Ségur.

Although Phélan-Ségur was not one of the 62 châteaux that won the status of *grand cru classé* in the Bordeaux classification of 1855, it is one of the leading estates of Saint-Estèphe and of the Médoc, partly because good wines are made there and partly because the production is fairly large. In recent years its prices have risen to classified fourth- and fifth-growth levels, reflecting the château's reputation among the better red wines of the celebrated Médoc north

of the city of Bordeaux. Phélan-Ségur needs at least eight years to reach maturity in good vintages. (*See also* Médoc, Saint-Estèphe.)

☆☆☆/☆☆☆☆
$$/$$$

Joseph Phelps Vineyards.

One of the top-ranking wineries in California is Joseph Phelps Vineyards, which consistently makes excellent white wines, especially late-harvested versions of Johannisberg Riesling and Gewürztraminer, as well as very good reds. The sole owner is Joseph Phelps, who founded a construction business, the Hensel Phelps Construction Company, in the mid-1950s and turned it into a major national concern. Phelps remains chairman and is the controlling stockholder. Joseph Phelps Vineyards was established in 1972, and the first Phelps wines were produced in '73, mainly on borrowed premises, including Heitz Cellars and Rutherford Hill. The Phelps winery was built between 1973 and 1975, and now it turns out 45,000 to 50,000 cases of premium varietals each year.

Phelps owns 210 acres of vineyards planted in Chardonnay, Cabernet Sauvignon, Gewürztraminer, Riesling, Sauvignon Blanc, true French Syrah, Zinfandel, and even a bit of Scheurebe, a German hybrid. Phelps also buys grapes from outside growers, who supply about 35 percent of the winery's needs in some vintages. The winemaker is Walter Schug, who grew up in the German Rheingau and took his degree from the Wine Institute at Geisenheim. Phelps produces Cabernet Sauvignon, Pinot Noir, Zinfandel, Syrah, Sauvignon Blanc, Chardonnay, Johannisberg Riesling, and Gewürztraminer. There are various bottlings of some varietals, with the source of the grapes identified on the labels. The late-harvested whites are eagerly sought by connoisseurs, who pay high prices for them and compare them with the better late-harvested wines of the German Rhine and Mosel. Careful handling is a byword at Phelps, where some 1500 oak barrels, nearly all French, are used for aging.

☆/☆☆☆☆

$$/$$$

Phylloxera.

Millions of acres of vineyards in Europe were destroyed in the second half of the last century by the Phylloxera vine blight, which apparently was imported to Europe on vine cuttings from the United States. *Phylloxera vastatrix* is a plant louse of the aphid family that burrows into the roots of vines, ultimately destroying them. No method has yet been devised to protect vines from it, other than to graft them onto Phylloxera-resistant American root systems. Virtually all European vineyards now grow on American roots and, because the roots actually are little more than conduits that carry nutrients and moisture from the soil to the grapes, there has been no significant impact on the quality of European wines. Some connoisseurs suggest that pre-Phylloxera wines were superior, and each year a few old bottles of claret from that era are auctioned at incredibly high prices in London. Some patches of pre-Phylloxera vineyard land also continue to exist in various parts of Europe, and the wines from these plots are always a curiosity, although the yield from these vineyards would be much greater if the vines had American root systems. Whether pre-Phylloxera wines or vines are actually superior is doubtful.

Château Pichon-Longueville (Baron).

In the middle of the nineteenth century, a split occurred in the Pichon family, and about 60 percent of the Pichon-Longueville vineyard went to the sisters of the Baron de Pichon, while 40 per-

cent remained with the baron himself. This latter portion is known as Pichon-Longueville (Baron) and it is one of the great wines of Pauillac in the Médoc peninsula north of Bordeaux. Pichon-Baron, as it is known for short in Bordeaux, was a *second cru,* or second growth, in the Bordeaux classification of 1855. The wines are well-balanced and elegant, displaying great character and finesse. They take ten to 15 years to reach maturity.

☆☆☆☆

$$$

Château Pichon-Longueville, Comtesse de Lalande.

When the celebrated Pichon-Longueville vineyard was divided up within the Pichon family in the mid-nineteenth century, some 60 percent went to the sisters of the Baron de Pichon, who were the Countess Sophie de Pichon, the Countess de Lalande, and the Vicountess de Lavaur. Today the wine is labeled either Pichon-Longueville-Lalande or Pichon-Longueville, Comtesse de Lalande. Like Pichon-Baron, Pichon-Lalande was a *second cru,* or second growth, in the Bordeaux classification of 1855. It is a typical Pauillac, displaying great fullness and finesse. The vineyards of the great Château Latour lie adjacent to those of Pichon-Lalande, and the two wines have much in common, although Pichon-Lalande is not quite as robust as Latour and tends to mature at a younger age, after about ten years.

☆☆☆☆

$$$

Picolit.

Every country seems to have one or more treasured and revered dessert wines, and Picolit is Italy's. It is frequently likened to the greatest Sauternes, Château d'Yquem, and to the Trockenbeerenauslesen of Germany, and

it tends to be almost as expensive. It is produced in Friuli-Venezia Giulia from Picolit grapes, which grow on vines that fell virtually into extinction because of disease. They have been going through a revival in recent years and probably are as vigorous now as at any time this century. Picolit is an intensely sweet wine made from *passito* grapes, or those that have been allowed to dry almost into raisins. It tends to be high in alcohol, sometimes running to 15 percent, and it is golden-hued and perfumed in bouquet. But it is not as sweet as Yquem or any other fine Sauternes, nor is it in the same exalted category as Germany's Trockenbeerenauslesen. But it is indeed complex, and the small amounts exported to the United States each year are eagerly snapped up by the few connoisseurs who appreciate it.
☆☆☆☆
$$$

Piedmont.

The Piedmont region of northern Italy is in the northwestern corner of the country, surrounded on three sides by the Swiss, French, and Italian Alps. Here is where the greatest Italian red wines are produced—the wines that rival the best of France and the United States. This is the home of the famous Barolo, the exquisite Gattinara, the charming Barbaresco, and the elegant Ghemme. The Nebbiolo grape, also known locally as the Spanna, is responsible for these great red wines that have won recognition among connoisseurs the world over. One of Italy's most famous white wines, Asti Spumante, with its sparkling richness, also comes from the Piedmont. Winemaking in this region dates at least as far back as the first century, when Pliny the Elder established vinicultural controls to try to maintain standards of high quality. (*See also* Barolo, Barbaresco, Gattinara, Amarone, etc.)

Piesporter.

German white wine produced in Piesport, one of the best vineyard towns of the Mosel River region. It is likely that more Piesporter is drunk outside Germany than any other Mosel wine, but it is also probable that some of it is not really Piesporter. So it is wise to insist on a label that specifies a vineyard, for example the famous Goldtröpfchen, and the name of the producer, and that indicates the producer bottled it himself. Imitations exist no doubt because authentic Piesporter is an elegant and fragrant wine typical of the best of the Mosel. The village lies south of Bernkastel and Brauneberg on one of the many horseshoe-shaped bends in the river. Among the better known vineyards at Piesport are the following:

Piesporter Bildchen
Piesporter Falkenberg
Piesporter Goldtröpfchen*
Piesporter Gräfenberg
Piesporter Güntherslay*
Piesporter Hohlweid
Piesporter Lay*
Piesporter Michelsberg*
Piesporter Olk
Piesporter Pichter
Piesporter Schubertslay*
Piesporter Taubengarten
Piesporter Treppchen*
Piesporter Wehr

The vineyard names marked with an asterisk (*) survived the revision of the German wine law in 1971 and now encompass some of the others. Examples of the others from pre-1971 vintages can still be found. The Michelsberg is now a *Grosslage,* or large vineyard area, similar to a generic term for wines from around Piesport.
☆/☆☆
$/$$

Pine Ridge Winery.

Pine Ridge lies just west of the Silverado Trail in the Stag's Leap area of the Napa Valley. It took its name from the stand of pines that borders the property and covers the top of a knoll that looms above the highway. The site was purchased in 1978 by Gary Andrus, who has made good Cabernet Sauvignons and Chardonnays there. A winery was built in time for the 1980 harvest. The property consists of 50 acres, some of it so steeply sloping that terracing was necessary to assure that the vines would not wash away in the winter rains. The site has a long history of winemaking dating back to pre-Prohibition times. Besides the grapes produced adjacent to the winery, Pine Ridge uses grapes purchased from other parts of the Napa Valley and has acquired vineyard parcels in several other locations. Production has climbed to 15,000 cases a year.
☆☆/☆☆☆
$$

Pinot Chardonnay.

The name Pinot Chardonnay is sometimes used to refer to the Chardonnay grape and to wines vinified from the Chardonnay grape, especially in California. But the usage is questionable, because the Chardonnay is not a member of the Pinot family. Nevertheless custom prevails in many parts of the world, and Pinot Chardonnay is still seen on labels for wines made from Chardonnay grapes. (*See* Chardonnay.)

Pinot Grigio.

Pinot Grigio is a variety of grape produced mostly in northern Italy, and the wines called Pinot Grigio are some of the best whites that Italy turns out. They tend to be full-bodied and fully flavored, with noticeable texture, wines that go well with all kinds of fish dishes and with the more subtly flavored poul-try and pasta dishes. Many are now available in the United States, Britain, and other export markets. They are best drunk within four years of the vintage.
☆/☆☆
$/$$

Pinot Noir.

The grape variety Pinot Noir makes some of the world's noblest wines, the great reds of Burgundy's Côte d'Or—Chambertin, Musigny, Romanée-Conti, Corton—as well as French Champagne. Two-thirds of the vineyards in the Champagne District of France are planted in Pinot Noir and its close relative Pinot Meunier. As one of the premium varietals of California, the Pinot Noir generally makes a good wine, often similar to lesser Burgundies, but it has never quite achieved the glory in the United States that it is capable of in France. There is a good deal of speculation as to why this is so. A shy bearer that ripens early, the vine does best in cooler growing regions where temperatures during the day do not fluctuate widely. In Burgundy cool summers render the situation extreme enough to warrant the addition of sugar to the grape must during fermentation. French law permits this practice, known as chaptalization. The additional sugar is sometimes partly responsible for the richness of flavor that gives French Burgundies some of their allure. The practice of adding sugar is not permitted or needed in California.

California Pinot Noir, while often good, is sometimes downright thin and uninteresting. Much experimentation is going on, however, by winemakers who feel it is worth the extra effort. Some vintners leave the juice with the grape skins longer to deepen color and extract the maximum varietal characteristics. Others omit the filtering process which removes flavor components along with sediment. Still others experiment with aging for varying lengths of time in different types of oak casks. Cooler growing regions of the California coastal counties look promising—the Carneros region of Napa Valley, for example, some of the mountainside vineyards in Mendocino and favorable exposures in Monterey. Recent plantings have taken advantage of these discoveries and the search for microclimates actively continues. Certain producers, among them Beaulieu, Robert Mondavi, Carneros Creek, Acacia, Hanzell, Chalone, and Freemark Abbey, consistently make good Pinot Noir. Special reserve bottlings from these wineries are often extremely well balanced wines with strong varietal nose and a good deal of complexity.

Piper Sonoma.

Piper Sonoma is a joint venture between Piper-Heidsieck, the big French Champagne house, and Sonoma Vineyards in Windsor, California. The first Piper Sonoma sparkling wines were from the 1980 vintage and were elegant and refined. The winemaker is Rodney D. Strong of Sonoma Vineyards, working in collaboration with Michel LaCroix, *chef de caves* of Piper-Heidsieck. Three vintage-dated wines are made—a *brut,* a Blanc de Noirs, and a *tête de cuvée.*
☆☆
$$/$$$

Château La Pointe.

One of the larger vineyards of the Pomerol District 20 miles east of Bordeaux is Château La Pointe, which has been among the most highly regarded Pomerols since the last century. The estate is said to have been so named because the vineyard makes a triangular-shaped point bordered by two roads that come together on the outskirts of Libourne, the city where the Pomerol and Saint-Emilion wine trade is centered. In recent vintages the wines of La Pointe have not been as big and intense as the

château's reputation would suggest, but this may be simply a passing phase. The estate would rank among the fourth or fifth growths in any broad classification that included the Médoc vineyards. La Pointe in recent vintages has brought prices comparable to the Médoc's fourths and fifths. It reaches maturity at about age ten and is best drunk before age 20.
☆☆☆☆
$$/$$$

Pomerol.

Among the greatest wine-producing *communes,* or townships, around Bordeaux in southwestern France is Pomerol, where robust red wines of great depth and intensity are made. So big are the Pomerols and so soft and supple at the same time that they are sometimes referred to as the "Burgundies of Bordeaux," although they are definitely Bordeaux in style and heritage. The Pomerol area is adjacent to Saint-Emilion near the city of Libourne some 20 miles east of Bordeaux. There is no village of Pomerol—it is strictly an agricultural area dotted with small châteaux and estates worked by men whose lifeblood is in the soil. The most important village is Catusseau, a tiny hamlet surrounded by vines.

The wines of Pomerol have never been officially classified, although the greatest *cru,* Château Pétrus, is acknowledged by wine lovers the world over to rank with the first growths of the Médoc. It often fetches even higher prices than Lafite or Latour, partly because only about one-tenth as much Pétrus is produced and the demand for this extraordinary wine is insatiable. It is made almost entirely (95 percent) from the Merlot grape, although a few Cabernet Sauvignon vines grow in the claylike soil of Pétrus's flat 30-acre vineyard. The vines are very old because the owners have refused to replant in order to increase the yield with younger stock. Although Pétrus is regarded as the unofficial *premier grand cru* of Pomerol, a number of other small estates produce exquisite wines that can occasionally be found at very reasonable prices in the export markets.

An unofficial and perhaps incomplete classification, based on what has been fairly regularly available in the United States and Britain, might be structured as follows:

Premier Grand Cru (First Great
    Growth)
Château Pétrus

Grands Crus (Great Growths)
Château Certan-de-May
Château Clinet
Château Gazin
Château La Conseillante
Château La Croix
Château La Croix de Gay
Château La Fleur
Château La Fleur-Pétrus
Château Lagrange
Château La Pointe
Château Latour à Pomerol
Château l'Eglise-Clinet
Château l'Evangile
Château Nénin
Château Petit-Village
Château Rouget
Château Trotanoy
Clos l'Eglise

Clos René
Vieux-Château-Certan

Other estates producing fine wines include Château de Sales, Château Beauregard, Domaine de l'Eglise, Château Le Gay, Château La Grave-Trigant-de-Boisset, Château Guillot, Château Certan-Giraud, Château Certan-Marzelle, Château Feytit-Clinet, Château l'Enclos, Château Moulinet, Château Gombaude-Guillot, Château Vraye-Croix-de-Gay, Château La Commanderie, Château Taillefer, Château Cantereau, Château Mazèyres. Greater distribution of some of these good *crus* no doubt would enhance their popularity abroad.

The leading family in the Pomerol trade in recent years has been that of Jean Pierre Moueix, who ran a wine-merchant business in Libourne for many years and owned a few small châteaux. After the war the Moueixes began entering the active ownership and management of vineyard properties more aggressively, and now they have a major interest in Château Pétrus, with the family of Madame Loubat, as well as in Châteaux La Fleur-Pétrus, Trotanoy, Lagrange, La Grave-Trigant-de-Boisset, La Tour-à-Pomerol, and Feytit-Clinet. In addition, the Moueix family markets the production of Château de Sales and Château Bourgneuf, among others. They also own Château Magdelaine in nearby Saint-Emilion. Their name in connection with a Pomerol is a sign of quality.

The better Pomerols have good staying power, although their suppleness makes them highly palatable at a very young age, and it is probable that most are consumed before they are a dozen years old. A Pétrus or Vieux-Château-Certan from a good vintage, however, needs at least 15 years of bottle-age, and will taste full, rich and elegant in its third decade. Generic wines labeled simply Pomerol without the name of a château or estate can represent some of the best values among Bordeaux, because of the charm that even the most modest of Pomerols tends to exude at a young age. Collectors who take an interest in the lesser known château-bottled Pomerols can also benefit from bargain prices and may find themselves with cellars full of treasure if an official classification of the district is ever accomplished. But the pressures for a more formal structure have been minimal over the years, and the people of the district are just as unpretentious and charming as their wines. Many Pomerol labels already say *premier cru* or *premier grand cru,* even though such designations do not officially exist there, and in general the quality level is so high that the use of such exalted terminology might even be justified—as long as consumers are aware that it's all strictly unofficial.

To the north of Pomerol itself, across the little River Barbanne, lie Lalande-de-Pomerol and Néac, which can be regarded as satellite *appellations* that produce some very good wines with characteristics quite comparable to their neighbors immediately to the south. Both use the *appellation* Lalande-de-Pomerol for their wines, which are rich and supple, if lacking some of the finesse of the better Pomerols. They also display some of the traits of Montagne-Saint-Emilion, the *commune* immediately to the east, because the soil is quite similar, sometimes gravelly, sometimes sandy and sometimes resembling clay. The grape varieties are also similar to both Saint-Emilion and Pomerol: lots of Merlot, plenty of Malbec and Cabernet, and occasionally some Petit Verdot.

The largest estates using the Lalande-de-Pomerol name are Château de Bel-Air, Château Perron, Château Sergant, Château des Annereaux, Château de la Commanderie, Château Tournefeuille, Château Belles-Graves, Château Moncets, Château Siraurac, Château Teys-son and Château Moulin-à-Vent (the last not to be confused with the Beaujolais similarly named). The area has dozens of proprietors who make only a few hundred cases of wine each year, although occasionally they may be found in overseas markets after an astute buyer has identified one with special character.

☆☆☆/☆☆☆☆☆

$$/$$$$

Pommard.

The vagaries of language are sometimes difficult to comprehend, but it is probable that Pommard has achieved worldwide renown because its name is easy to remember and simple for non-Gallic tongues to pronounce. The *commune* of Pommard lies in the heart of the Côte de Beaune in the Burgundy country of France, and it is true that some of the most charming red Burgundies are produced here. A Pommard is a luscious and pleasant wine, often displaying an intensity of character that is more typical of the more robust Burgundies of the Côte de Nuits a few miles to the north. Yet Pommard has been so widely imitated, and so much of this good wine has been "stretched" over the years with the addition of lesser wines from the Beaujolais or Mâconnais areas to the south that its reputation has suffered among connoisseurs. A Pommard should always be an elegant and pleasant wine, yet sometimes it is rather coarse—perhaps when it is not 100 percent Pommard. The *commune* lies between Beaune on the north and Volnay on the south, but the wines display more of the characteristics of Volnay than of Beune. Yet they tend to be more robust than Volnays and, when properly made, are typically good Burgundies. They should be drunk after reaching age ten. There are no *grands crus* Pommards. Among the better known *premiers crus* are the following:

Argillières
Arvelets
Boucherottes
Chanière
Clos de la Commaraine
Epenots, or Epenaux
Fremiers
Jarollières, or Garollières
Pézerolles
Platière
Rugiens-Bas
Rugiens-Haut

The Rugiens vineyards sometimes drop the "Bas" or "Haut" from their names. These, the Epenots and the Clos de la Commaraine, are often the best of Pommard.
☆☆☆/☆☆☆☆
$$/$$$

Château Pontet-Canet.

This château, ranked among the *cinquièmes crus,* or fifth growths, in the Bordeaux classification of 1855, is believed to have the highest production of any of the classified growths of the Médoc, running to 40,000 cases in copious vintages. The estate had been owned by the Cruse shipping firm since 1865 and the wines produced there were not château-bottled. Nevertheless, Château Pontet-Canet produces some very nice-tasting wines on a consistent basis. The property has been sold to Guy Tesseron, who also owns Château Lafon-Rochet in Saint-Estèphe and is a highly regarded proprietor in Bordeaux. The estate lies in Pauillac, not far from Mouton Rothschild, Lynch-Bages, and Grand-Puy-Lacoste. The area has a centuries-old record for producing fine wines. Pontet-Canet's cellars are held in high regard among the best in the Médoc. Older vintages of Pontet-Canet are especially esteemed, and the 1929 is one of the most celebrated of that excellent year. Pontet-Canet reaches maturity after about a decade in good vintages and usually starts fading by age 20. The vineyard is planted 60 percent in Cabernet Sauvignon, 28 percent in Merlot and 12 percent in Cabernet Franc.
☆☆☆☆
$$/$$$

Ponzi Vineyards.

Ponzi Vineyards was established in Beaverton, in northwestern Oregon, in 1970 and produces a line of European varietals of good quality, although the quantities are small. The proprietors are Dick and Nancy Ponzi, transplanted Californians, who also operate the winery. They produce Pinot Noir, Chardonnay, Pinot Gris, White Riesling, and a branded wine called Oregon Harvest Wine, which is mostly Pinot Blanc. The wines tend to be crisp and clean.
☆/☆☆
$/$$

Port, Porto.

The rich fortified red wine produced in the rugged vineyards above the Douro River in northern Portugal is called Port. This is probably the finest of all fortified wines and it is widely imitated in other parts of the world. In fact, so much "Port" is produced elsewhere, including in the United States, that the producers of true Port have undertaken an educational program to induce the public to call their wine Porto, but it is probable that connoisseurs, notably the British, will always call it Port and that the imitators will continue to use the name.

True Port is a luscious wine that is best consumed after dinner on a cold winter evening in front of a fireplace filled with blazing logs. Under Portuguese law it is fortified with Portuguese grape brandy up to a level of 20 percent alcohol. The fortification adds to its character and makes Port very long-lived. A vintage Port is best not consumed until it has aged for at least two decades, and some devotees of this great wine suggest that the ideal age is somewhere between 30 and 40 years. At proper maturity a vintage Port is a very robust, intense yet supple wine. Its texture is mouth-filling, and its subtle charm is difficult to resist. Once opened, a bottle is rarely left unconsumed at one sitting, even though moderation is especially advisable with all fortified wines.

Port is known as "the Englishman's wine." Although its history dates back to the Roman occupation of Portugal more than a century before the birth of Christ, it was a treaty between England and Portugal, signed in 1654, that granted English merchants special concessions in Portugal and led to the creation of a vast English market for Port wine. To this day the major Port firms in Oporto and nearby Vila Nova de Gaia, where the Douro River flows into the Atlantic, bear mostly English names and are run largely by English and English-Portuguese families. The British established a "factory"—precisely defined as a foreign trading station—in Oporto and soon began construction of their Factory House, the famous building that was the center of the Port trade, which was completed in 1790.

The Factory House, with its huge ballrooms and paneled meeting rooms for the British merchants, remains today a symbol of the British presence in Oporto. The Port shippers meet there every Wednesday for a luncheon in the third-floor dining salon whose mahogany table seats 38. Adjacent to this Lunch Room is the Dessert Room, where formal dinners are held on an identical table for the Port shippers, their wives and guests. The Ballroom, with its Wedgewood-like plasterwork and minstrel's gallery, is illuminated by seven huge Waterford chandeliers. Kings and queens of England have danced here and left mementoes of their visits that are now on display. The kitchen on the fourth floor is rarely used nowadays. Its huge iron stoves were carried by ship all the way from London, and the rusting old pots and pans and dusty pewterware create an atmosphere of time standing still.

In a hallway adjacent to the Map Room the names of the heads of the British Association of Oporto since 1811 are painted on wooden placards hung on the walls. The association has 13 member firms; individual members must be principals of the firms. The largest firms are the Companhia Velha (also known as the Royal Oporto Wine Co.), Sandeman, Cockburn, the Symington Group, the Barros Group, and Silva & Cousins. Mergers among the small firms that once dominated the business have occurred over the years. Britain's Allied Breweries owns Cockburn (pronounced "Coeburn"), and Dubonnet has a 20 percent interest in the Symington brands—Graham, Warre, and Dow. A nearly complete list of the existing Port brands would include these two-dozen names:

Calem
Cockburn
Croft
Delaforce

Dow
Ferreira
Feuerheed
Fonseca
Graham
Guimaraens
Gonzalez Byass
Kopke
Mackenzie
Morgan
Offley
Quarles Harris
Rebello Valente
Robertson
Sandeman
A. J. Silva
Smith Woodhouse
Taylor
Tuke Holdsworth
Warre

Each producer makes wines of varying styles. In addition, there are several basic categories of Port wine, reflecting different production methods.

Vintage Port: The wine held in highest regard by connoisseurs, the one that reaches the greatest level of quality, is vintage Port. As the name suggests, it is a wine entirely from a single vintage, and it is produced only from the very best grapes, which have achieved the greatest ripeness in the hot sun of the Douro Valley. Most firms declare a vintage only in the best years—when the weather conditions have been ideal and the majority of the grapes have fully ripened. The shipping firms usually agree in declaring which years will have vintage designations, but occasionally one or two shippers will declare a vintage when the rest do not. Such a declaration will be made only if the shipper is convinced he can bottle superior wines.

In general, perhaps three vintages are declared each decade, and the declaration occurs about 18 months after the harvest. There must be a plentitude of fruit evident in the wines, very dark

color, full body, and a strong tannin content. A vintage Port, in contrast to Ports with other designations, is aged only two years in wooden casks and then is bottled. As the wine ages in wood, it tends to lose its purple color and fruitiness, gradually turning tawny. Vintage Ports would rapidly lose their bigness and richness if permitted to mature longer in casks.

Twenty years is usually required for a vintage Port to reach the proper maturity for drinking, although each vintage will vary in style, and some mature earlier. The 1950 and '58 were lighter than most and drank well after 12 to 15 years. The 1970, which was extraordinarily robust, should reach its peak in about 1995, according to James Symington, whose firm produces the famous Graham's, Warre, and Dow. By his calculations, the 1960 vintage should be ready in the early 1980s, while the 1963 will not reach maturity until 1985 and then will probably hang on for a decade. Unlike table wines, Port will linger at its peak for a number of years before declining. The 1945 and '48, for example, were exquisite in the early 1970s and showed no signs of toppling from the summit when tasted in 1976 and again in 1981.

Port "of the vintage": Buyers of Port must be careful to distinguish between vintage Port and Port "of the vintage." They are not the same, and the Port Wine Institute, which by agreement governs the custom of declaring vintages, would best do away with the latter term, for it is misleading. Whereas a vintage Port is bottled after two years in wood, a Port "of the vintage" may spend 15 to 20 years in wood and most often will come from a year when no vintage is universally declared. The time spent in wood tends to extract the fruit from the wine and, in addition, rounds off the rough edges prematurely, creating a very smooth-tasting potion that lacks the character of vintage Port. It is a fine product, but not quite the same.

Crusted Port: The crust is the heavy sediment thrown off by a maturing wine, and is prevalent in vintage Port after it reaches its maturity. But some shippers produce a wine that they call Crusted or Crusting Port, mainly from off vintages blended together, aged an average of perhaps four years in wood and then laid down in bottles for four or five years more to enable the sediment to develop. Years ago, lead shot was shaken around inside the bottles to roughen the glass so that the sediment would be more likely to cling to the sides. Like mature vintage Port, crusted Port should be decanted before drinking. Sometimes a crusted Port will be "of the vintage," but rarely from the year of a general vintage declaration. It is often ready to drink when marketed, reflecting the fact that the wines blended to produce it have an average age of perhaps 10 years. Crusted Port is rarely seen nowadays.

"Late-bottled" vintage Port: Some shippers take wines from good but not great years, leave it in cask longer than the two years normal for vintage Port and then bottle it. Essentially, these wines are no more than very big and robust tawny Ports that come from years not generally regarded as worthy of a vintage declaration. The extra time in wood softens the wine and makes it pleasant for drinking at a relatively young age. It comes entirely from a single vintage and resembles a classic vintage Port that has matured at an unexpectedly early age.

Tawny Port: Wines blended from several vintages and permitted to age in casks for perhaps a decade or more, until they have lost the purple tinge of a young wine and turned brownish, are called Tawny Port. These are lighter and smoother wines that appeal to consumers who feel that the richness of a

vintage Port is overwhelming. Tawny Port is often produced through the same *solera* process used in making Sherry in Spain, whereby wines of varying ages are stacked in casks and systematically blended so that the wine in the lowest tiers contains the oldest mixture. Tawnies are produced in great volume, cost less than vintage or crusted Ports and can provide a good introduction to Port wine in general.

Ruby Port: This wine is aptly named, because it is ruby-colored and is made from very young wines blended from nonvintage years or from less favorably situated vineyards in vintage years. These are rich and fruity wines, displaying considerable sweetness. Although they would benefit from bottle-age, they are rarely laid down and are usually consumed "off the shelf." They are the least expensive Ports and lack the potential to achieve the character of vintage Ports. A serious student of wine will pass quickly from Ruby Port to the Tawnies, which are subtler and more balanced.

"Vintage-Character" Port: Reflecting the reluctance of consumers to buy vintage Port and lay it down in cellars for decades of aging, most of the top shipping firms have produced "Vintage-Character" Ports. These are comparable to aged Ruby Ports that have spent more time in the wood than the Rubies but less time than Port "of the vintage." They are dark, heavy, fruity wines that benefit from laying down. They are often marketed with such brand designations as "special reserve" or "special rare" and are quite similar to "late-bottled" vintage Ports, although they are usually blended from several vintages.

White Port: Debate has existed for many years over whether white Port, made entirely from white grapes, deserves to be categorized with the great reds. Because it is produced in the same region of Portugal that produces red Port, there really should be no argument over whether it merits the name. But in character it is somewhat different from the traditional red Port and is sometimes vinified fairly dry. It is customary to drink White Port in place of Sherry as an aperitif before lunch in the dining rooms of the lodges of Vila Nova de Gaia across the river from Oporto, and considerable quantities are exported to the Scandinavian countries. It is rarely seen in the United States and has even become difficult to find in the wine shops of England. It can be considered an interesting curiosity that really provides no competition for a well-made Sherry from Spain.

Single-Quinta Port: The term *quinta,* pronounced "kin-ta," is Portuguese for "agricultural property" or "parcel." In wine-growing areas like the Douro Valley, of course, it means vineyard. Virtually all Port is a blend from various vineyards but some firms market wines from a single *quinta,* or vineyard, contending that the Port from that vineyard is so great that it should not be blended. The best known of these is the Quinta do Noval produced by da Silva, one of the most elevated hillsides above the Douro not far from Pinhão. Some of the vines of Quinta do Noval date from the era preceding the arrival of Phylloxera, the vine blight, in the latter part of the nineteenth century. Whether this makes them truly capable of producing superior wines is debatable, but the Quinta do Noval is one of the most celebrated Port wines.

The vineyards, or *quintas,* where the grapes for Port wine are grown cling to the steep and rugged hillsides beyond the grimy town of Regua on the twisting Douro River about 50 miles inland and due east of Oporto and Vila Nova de Gaia. The countryside has a breathtaking, wild and primitive beauty that is unique among the world's major wine-producing areas. The vines grow on terraces cut into the hills, and some of them date back to the era before the vine blight, Phylloxera, swept through Europe in the latter part of the nineteenth century. The hilltops are rounded, as if worn down by eons of cruel winter winds, and there is little vegetation to be seen growing taller than the grape vines. The sun beats down unmercifully in the summer months, raising the daytime temperatures to well above 100 degrees Fahrenheit. Yet the winter weather is harsh and freezing, causing the wolves from even colder and wilder sections of Portugal to the north to slip down into the Douro region to forage.

Dams have halted the previously turbulent flow of the Douro and raised the water level. The river is now a wide, placid waterway, and old vines can be seen protruding from the surface near the banks in shallow areas. Fish hawks glide lazily along the shores above the white stucco vineyard houses owned by the shipping firms of Oporto. The walls of the buildings and sometimes their red and orange tiled roofs bear the names of the famous Port brands, but these facilities are virtually deserted for 10 months of the year. They stand idle except for the period around the autumn harvest, although some of the shippers maintain summer homes there.

Back in the primitive hill-towns are the growers and vineyard workers who cultivate the Tinta, Touriga, Alvarelhão, Souzão, Bastardo, and Mourisco grapes, as well as perhaps a half-dozen others that go into Port wine. Some of the vineyards are owned by the big shipping firms, but much of the production of the region is supplied by individual growers who make their own wines, adding brandy provided by the shippers for the necessary fortification. There has been an increasing trend for the shippers to buy the grapes themselves and vinify them in their facilities around picturesque little Douro villages like Pinhão several miles beyond Regua. The firms also keep representatives in each vineyard area to supervise the wine-making and assure that it is up to the proper standards.

The Douro is one of the last areas in the world where the pressing of the grapes is often accomplished by human feet. The grapes are dumped into big pressing tanks, and the men line up with arms linked and tread on the grapes, marching systematically back and forth, barefooted, for two-hour stretches. During rest intervals they drink brandy, which loosens tongues and inspires the singing of folk songs. The brandy—Bigaceira—is made from the pips and skins of grapes and is similar to the French Marc de Bourgogne or the Italian Grappa. The treading goes on until after midnight of the day of the picking and then resumes the next morning. Everything is fermented here; there is no separation of the grape juice from the seeds and stems, as in most other wine-producing areas of the world. The must is periodically stirred with big wooden devices that have blades like the spokes on a wheel.

The fermentation takes about three days, while the natural grape sugar is turning to alcohol, releasing huge amounts of carbon dioxide gas, the other principal by-product of fermentation. Grape brandy is added to halt the fermentation at around 6 or 7 percent, far below the level reached by a table wine, so that a fairly high sugar content is maintained. If the fermentation were allowed to continue, the sugar would be consumed and the natural sweetness of Port would be lost. Enough brandy is added not only to kill the yeasts that cause the fermentation but also to raise the alcohol level to the customary 20 percent for Port wine. Although the harvest occurs in September, the young wine is not drawn off its lees, or grape residue, until around the turn of the year.

Years ago the fresh wine was taken down the Douro to the Port lodges at Vila Nova de Gaia on sailing barges that somehow navigated the turbulent waters, but nowadays the wine is transported in big tank trucks and by rail to the same cellars and warehouses, where the equivalent of 150 million bottles of wine are stored in preparation for shipping to destinations all over the world. The natural harbor formed by the Douro estuary has been used for centuries, although the waters here are treacherous. The gray Atlantic pounds in at the sandbar, shifting the sand and uncovering new rocks in every storm. Hundreds of ships have been destroyed on the rocks here; even today the rusting hulks of modern vessels protrude from the choppy water at low tide, warning seamen to proceed with caution. Tons of Port in casks departing on the journey to England have gone to the bottom within sight of the Factory House on its steep hillside in Oporto.

Once the dominant market for Port, Great Britain now consumes much less, reflecting the changing tastes of the people, their steadily declining affluence and the increasing taxation of alcoholic beverages in the effort to pay the tab for the welfare programs of a succession of socialist governments. After-dinner wines have never been terribly popular in the United States, but a rising volume of Port is being shipped to northern European and Scandinavian countries that appreciate the value of a wine that can warm the body on the coldest and longest of winter nights. Talk of nationalizing the Port business has been heard since the Portuguese political upheaval of 1975, but such a move would jeopardize the biggest source of foreign exchange earnings that the country has. Some of the men who run the shipping firms in Vila Nova de Gaia fear that one day they will be forced to accept government "partners," but nobody suggests that the Port business will ever come to an end.

Vintage declarations occur perhaps only once every three or four years and vintage Ports display considerable variations in character, so it is prudent to be aware of the characteristics of each vintage that you are likely to encounter. Because Port ages so gracefully, great quantities of older vintages exist, especially in English cellars. They can be obtained through the periodic sales held by Christie, Manson & Woods, or Sotheby & Co. in London. Unlike older table wines whose storage may not have been proper, older Ports need not be considered in questionable condition when sold at auction. They are extremely durable.

The following vintage appraisals were furnished by James Symington of W. & J. Graham & Co. in Vila Nova de Gaia.

1945: A big, heavy, firm wine of magnificent bouquet. Still drinking nicely. One of the finest vintages of the century, it ranks with the 1912s and 1927s.

1947: A delicate, beautifully balanced vintage. Not as long-lasting as the 1945, it should be drunk sooner.

1948: A full, rich wine with particularly deep color. Not as great as the '45, but exceptionally attractive.

1950: A very hard wine and rather on the dry side. Not one of the finest vintages, but pleasant at its peak a few years ago.

1955: Luscious and full. An exceptionally well-balanced wine. Excellent drinking two decades after the harvest and beyond.

1958: An elegant vintage not unlike the 1947s. It developed quickly and has reached its peak.

1960: A very firm, dryish wine with plenty of character. Very pleasant, although not particularly dark in color. Ready for drinking in the late 1970s or early 1980s.

1963: A big, fat, luscious wine with a beautiful bouquet. It is undoubtedly the finest vintage of the sixties. At all stages of its development it has had a delightful, fruity nose. Unlikely to be at its best before 1980–1985.

1966: Not as big as the 1963, but particularly fresh and fruity. It will probably not be a great stayer. Perhaps drinkable from 1980.

1970: A superb Port. It has in full measure everything one can ask of a vintage—fruitiness, body, flavor and a magnificent bouquet. It will be surprising if it does not prove to be one of the great wines of this century. Too early to predict maturity, but certainly not before 1985.

1975: Not as good as the 1970s or the 1977, but very decent wines that have been overlooked by some connoisseurs. Lacking the intensity of the 1970s and not as dark-colored; best for drinking in 1987–89.

1977: Very fine, very tannic and big, like the 1963s. Will show great longevity. Lots of guts and structure. Intensely flavored, with a strong bouquet. Possibly not ready to drink until the end of the century!

☆☆☆☆☆

$$/$$$

Port (California).

Port-style wines have been made in California for a century, but not until the late 1970s was a serious effort undertaken to produce vintage Ports there in the style of true Port from Portugal. Now there are several producers making excellent California versions blended from such grapes as Zinfandel, Pinot Noir, Cabernet Sauvignon, and Petite Sirah. Among the leaders are Woodbury, Quady, J. W. Morris, Channing Rudd Cellars, Hacienda Wine Cellars, Prager Winery and Port Works, Shenandoah Vineyards, and Berkeley Wine Cellars. Ficklin Vineyards makes Port

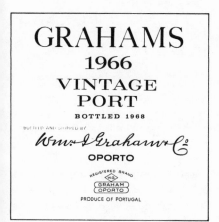

from grape varieties native to the Douro Region of Portugal but does not use vintage designations. (*See* entries for each California producer.)

☆☆☆/☆☆☆☆☆

$/$$$$

Portugal.

The best-known wine of Portugal is Mateus Rosé, although it is probable that many people who drink Mateus are unaware that it is Portuguese. For years, it was the largest-selling imported wine in the United States, but it is not representative of the best that Portugal has to offer. In fact, Portugal produces some of the world's truly great wines—wines that are taken much more seriously by connoisseurs than any rosé, Mateus included. Port, the fortified wine from the rugged Douro River Valley in the northern part of the country, has traditionally been regarded as the best wine of the Iberian Peninsula. It is a rich and velvety potion that benefits from many years of bottle-aging. Its biggest market has been England, reflecting the British involvement in developing the wine trade in the coastal city of Oporto, where the Douro flows into the Atlantic. But more and more Port has been flowing to the Scandinavian countries, where the

warmth it generates is especially suited to the climate.

Madeira, the other well-known fortified wine from Portugal, actually comes from the island of the same name lying in the Atlantic Ocean some 350 miles west of Africa. It was put under Portuguese control more than 500 years ago and, like the Port wine trade, the Madeira trade was developed by the British. No scientific evidence has been uncovered to support the reputed power of Madeira as an aphrodisiac.

Portugal also produces some excellent table wines. From the north-central region below the Douro River comes Dão, an excellent red wine whose bouquet can readily be mistaken for that of a good Bordeaux. Farther north, between the Douro and the Minho River Valley near the Spanish frontier, is the land of Vinho Verde, or green wine, that is not really green but can be either white or red. The best Vinho Verde is white, and it is very dry and light, often displaying a slight sparkle, or *pétillance,* as the French would describe it. It goes well with shellfish.

Yet the overseas image of Portuguese wines comes largely from the rosés, whose annual shipments abroad run high into the millions of bottles. Mateus, Lancers, Alianca and the others are light and pleasant, innocent and uncomplicated and have provided an introduction to imported wines for many an American and British wine-drinker. (*See* Dão, Lancers, Madeira, Mateus, Port, Vinho Verde.)

Pouilly-Fuissé.

South of the famous Côte d'Or portion of France's Burgundy District and just north of Beaujolais lies the Mâconnais, a hilly area whose white wines occasionally challenge the aristocratic Meursaults and Puligny-Montrachets from farther north. By far the best wine of the Mâconnais is Pouilly-Fuissé, which in good vintages can be full-bodied, rich and noble. Like all the better white Burgundies, it is made from the Chardonnay grape and displays some of the best Chardonnay traits. Only five small villages are entitled to the Pouilly-Fuissé name: Pouilly, Fuissé, Solutré-Pouilly, Chaintré, and Vergisson. Their total production is not large, and sharply escalating demand for their renowned white wine has meant that prices have gone up rapidly to levels that sometimes exceed the cost of a good Meursault or Chablis.

Pouilly-Fuissé tends to be slightly softer and earthier than other white Burgundies; it is excellent served with fish courses. It displays a bit more style and character than the other two white wines produced nearby: Pouilly-Vinzelles and Pouilly-Loché. None of these should be confused with the Pouilly Fumé, a different white wine from the upper Loire Valley. Pouilly-Fuissé is sometimes bottled under specific vineyard names, including Château de Fuissé, Château de Pouilly, Les Bouthières, Les Chailloux, Les Chanrue, Les Prâs, Les Peloux, Les Rinces, Le Clos, Clos de la Chapelle, Clos de Varambond, Menetrières, Les Perrières, Les Brûlets, Les Châtenets, Les Vignes-Blanches, and Les Versarmières. These single-vineyard wines are considered the best and must attain at least 12 percent alcoholic content, while simple Pouilly-Fuissé need reach only 11 percent. (*See* Mâconnais.)

☆/☆☆
$$/$$$

Pouilly Fumé.

One of the better-known white wines from the eastern portion of the Loire River Valley in France is Pouilly Fumé from the town of Pouilly-sur-Loire, not far from Sancerre. As the name implies, Pouilly Fumé has a slightly smoky taste and bouquet. It is not a subtle wine, but its earthiness can be quite charming.

It achieved great popularity in the United States in the late 1960s, when white Burgundy prices soared out of sight. The Ladoucette label became almost a trademark for good Pouilly Fumé. The suspicion also exists that part of this good wine's popularity is due to the similarity in name with Pouilly-Fuissé, which is another excellent wine produced in a different part of France, the Mâconnais. But other than their names and the fact that they are both good whites, the two have nothing in common.

Unlike Vouvray and some other Loire Valley wines, those from around Pouilly are made from the Sauvignon grape. It gives them a slightly green tint and a spicy taste that goes well with shellfish, although connoisseurs would probably prefer a good Chablis. Lesser wines from Pouilly are made with the Chasselas grape and are called simply Pouilly-sur-Loire after the full name of the town. The Sauvignon grape is a prerequisite for the Pouilly Fumé *appellation*. It produces wines of somewhat greater longevity, although not with the staying power of a big Vouvray from a good vintage. (*See also* Sancerre.)

☆/☆☆☆
$$/$$$

Pouilly-Loché, Pouilly-Vinzelles.

Besides Pouilly-Fuissé, two other Pouillys exist in the Mâconnais under the French *appellation contrôlée* laws—Pouilly-

Loché and Pouilly-Vinzelles. Both are produced from vineyards near Pouilly-Fuissé in the Mâconnais subregion of the French Burgundy country, but they lack the richness and depth of Pouilly-Fuissé at its best. Production is much smaller than for Pouilly-Fuissé, and prices are much lower, which means these two other Pouillys can be somewhat better value. Consumers should beware, however, of wine stewards and merchants who suggest that they are the same as Pouilly-Fuissé and try to obtain the same high prices for them. Like Pouilly-Fuissé, they are made from the Chardonnay grape and must achieve 11 percent alcohol to merit their appellations. But their quality rarely approaches that of a well-made Pouilly-Fuissé.

☆/☆☆

$/$$

Pousse-Rapière.

A Pousse-Rapière is a regional aperitif of Gascony, southeast of Bordeaux and the home of Armagnac, one of the great brandies of France. Fittingly, the Pousse-Rapière, or "rapier thrust," is a mixture of Armagnac and Champagne. The concoction, which is indeed potent and is capable of acting as a rapier thrust to the central nervous system, is best not consumed in large quantities. Moreover, it is questionable whether the mixture benefits either the Armagnac or the Champagne—or, for that matter, the consumer.

Prager Winery & Port Works.

Half of the production of the Prager Winery & Port Works in St. Helena, California, is in California vintage Port, a relatively new phenomenon for the state. Until Prager, Woodbury, and a few others got into the vintage Port business in recent years the Port-style wines made in California were mostly nonvintage and fairly mediocre—hardly competitive with genuine Port from Portugal. Prager was established in 1979 by Jim Prager, who had spent 22 years in the insurance business in southern California and was a collector of wines as well as books on wines.

Prager's first commercial harvest was the 1980, some of which was released in late 1981, although at least another decade of bottle-aging was needed for the wine to achieve the suppleness for which vintage Ports are noted. His 1980 was 100 percent Cabernet Sauvignon, and he is also experimenting with Pinot Noir, Zinfandel, and Petite Sirah blended with Cabernet, so subsequent vintages display a slightly different style. The Prager Ports contain only 5 percent residual sugar, which is low relative to other producers' Ports, and they contain 18 to 18½ percent alcohol.

Besides Port Prager produces such premium table wines as Cabernet Sauvignon, Zinfandel, Petite Sirah, and Chardonnay, all of which are aged in new and used American oak barrels of 50-gallon capacity. The Ports are aged in 60-gallon Limousin oak barrels from France. Prager buys all of its grapes from other growers. Production totals 3000 to 4000 cases a year.

☆/☆☆☆☆

$$

Prémeaux.

Near Nuits-Saint-Georges in the French Burgundy country is the *commune* of Prémeaux, where some good wines are made but are most often sold under the Nuits-Saint-Georges label, which is much better known. They reach maturity in six to ten years. The *commune* has no *grands crus,* but it has a number of *premiers crus* which are usually lumped together with the better *premiers* of Nuits-Saint-Georges. Among these are Clos des Corvées. Clos des Forêts, Clos des Grandes Vignes, and Clos de la Maréchale. In fact, almost any vineyard name including the word *clos* when marketed as a Nuits-Saint-Georges is in reality likely to be a Prémeaux. (*See also* Côte de Nuits, Nuits-Saint-Georges.)

☆☆☆/☆☆☆☆

$$/$$$

Premières Côtes de Bordeaux.

Upstream from Bordeaux and across the Garonne River from the district of Graves in southwestern France is an area called Premières Côtes de Bordeaux. Both red and white wines are produced here, but none of great quality, although the whites made in the villages of Cadillac, Langoiran, and Verdelais to the south not far from Sauternes sometimes can be quite pleasant. The reds should be drunk before they reach age ten.

☆/☆☆☆

$/$$

Premiat.

The only Rumanian wines marketed in the U.S. are imported by Monsieur Henri Wines Ltd. under the Premiat label. The Cabernet Sauvignon and Pinot Noir are the most successful varietals, and they are priced attractively. (*See* Rumania.)

☆/☆☆

$

Preston Vineyards.

Preston, just north of Healdsburg in California's Sonoma Valley, is the property of Louis Preston, a graduate of the Stanford University Business School who also studied oenology at the University of California at Davis. His family owned a dairy farm near Healdsburg, and he converted this to vines in the early 1970s. Then this property was sold and he bought 80 acres in the Dry Creek Valley of Sonoma in 1974. The first wines were made in 1975 after an old prune dehydrator was converted into a winery. The property also consisted partly of a prune orchard, which was replanted in vines. A new winery was built in time for the 1982 crush, when production was expected to total about 10,000 cases.

All of the 80 acres are now bearing, and Preston expects to continue to estate-bottle all of the Preston wines as well as sell a portion of his grapes to other producers. For example, he sells a good share of his Sauvignon Blanc to Dry Creek Vineyards. He believes this varietal is best suited to his estate, and he is emphasizing it in his production. Preston also makes Chenin Blanc, Zinfandel, and Cabernet Sauvignon, plus an occasional Petite Sirah or Gamay, depending on conditions. Basic red and white table wines are also produced.

☆/☆☆☆

$$

Château Prieuré-Lichine.

Château Prieuré-Lichine, formerly Château Le Prieuré, has been owned since 1952 by a group of Americans headed by Alexis Lichine, the author and wine exporter. It lies in Cantenac and, in common with others in this *commune,* has been entitled to the Margaux *appellation* since 1954. Le Prieuré was ranked a *quatrième cru,* or fourth growth, in the Bordeaux classification of 1855, but the Lichine group has considerably upgraded the estate through the acquisition of vineyard acreage from such other classified growths as Châteaux Palmer, Giscours, d'Issan, Kirwan, Boyd-Cantenac, and Ferrière among the third growths and Châteaux Brane-Cantenac and Durfort-Vivens among the seconds. Fairly extensive replantings were undertaken as well, and the winemaking procedures were upgraded— all in the hope of producing a superior wine. The vineyard is now more than 50 percent Cabernet Sauvignon, the noblest Bordeaux grape variety, and the wines produced there are of consistently high quality, with a soft fullness typical of Margaux. The wines of this château are widely available on the

American market. They often represent excellent value among the classified growths of the Médoc. They are best drunk between ages 10 and 15 years.
☆☆☆☆
$$/$$$

Primitivo.

The Primitivo is a grape variety cultivated in the hot and dry Puglia region of southern Italy, where it yields red wines of deep color, intense flavor, and high alcohol, routinely reaching 15 percent or more. The wine is chewy in texture, spicy, and leaves an impression of ripe berries in the mouth. Some grape historians have suggested that it is either closely related to or the same as the Zinfandel grape widely cultivated in California and in other states, and Puglia has been reported to be the long-sought home vineyard for the Zinfandel, whose origins have never been identified, although they are known to be European. Research has indicated that the Primitivo was established in Puglia, however, after the Zinfandel was established in California, which means they both probably came from somewhere else. Primitivo, not readily available outside Italy, shows great charm at an early age because of its high fruit level but also ages quite gracefully because of its high alcohol level.
☆☆☆/☆☆☆☆
$/$$

Privilegio del Rey Sancho.

Privilegio del Rey Sancho, most often simply called Privilegio, is the supple red and white wine produced in the Rioja District of northern Spain by the Pedro Domecq Company, which is better known for its dominant position in the Sherry business in the south of Spain. Privilegio is vinified from grapes produced in the Alavesa subregion of Rioja, and it was introduced in the United States in 1981 as a latecomer in the

Rioja boom after an early entry by Domecq, called Domecq Domaine, achieved very limited success. Privilegio red is produced only as a *reserva*, meaning that it undergoes more aging prior to its release than Riojas without the *reserva* designation. (*See* Rioja and Sherry.)
☆☆☆/☆☆☆☆
$$

Prosecco.

Prosecco is a charming white grape cultivated in Italy's Veneto region and also is the name of the wine made from that grape. In recent years the *spumante,* or sparkling, versions have begun to attract attention among connoisseurs, for they leave a lighter, more elegant impression on the palate than Italy's best-known sparkling wine, Asti Spumante. Prosecco Spumante may indeed be Italy's best sparkling wine when produced with the French *méthode champenoise*, but it still does not measure up to genuine Champagne. It is also somewhat less expensive.
☆☆
$$

Provence.

This is the sunny area encompassing the Riviera in southeastern France, where the resorts are much more famous than any of the wines produced nearby. A great quantity of rosé is made in the area, but it is not often as good as the Tavel rosé from just to the west at the bottom of the Rhône Valley. Some reds and whites are produced in Provence as well, but none of the wines from the area is exported in amounts large enough to have much of an impact. Names such as Cannes, Nice, and St.-Tropez are much better known than Provence's most important wines: Bandol, Bellet, Cassis, and Palette, each of which is entitled to its own place name under the French *appellation contrôlée* laws.

Bandol, from just east of Marseilles, produces rosés, reds, and whites from a surprisingly large number of grape varieties. To be entitled to the name, the wines must attain at least 11 percent in alcoholic content. The reds must be aged for at least 18 months in cask, the whites and rosés at least eight months. If these standards are not met, Bandol wines may simply be marketed locally as Côtes de Provence. The best Bandol reds come from Domaine Tempier, and mature bottlings, at least ten years old, are complex, elegant, and capable of rivaling fine Bordeaux, which they resemble in style, although the dominant grape variety is Mourvèdre.

Bellet, from the area around the famed resort town of Nice, also covers the spectrum of red, white, and rosé, but its production is only about one-tenth that of Bandol. The minimum alcoholic content is 10.5 percent. You are unlikely to encounter this wine anywhere but in a Riviera hotel or bistro.

Cassis, produced in the seaside town between Marseilles and Bandol, should not be confused with the black-currant liqueur of the same name. Cassis wines are mostly rosé and white—ideal partners for the fish stew, or *bouillabaisse,* that is the most famous food of the region. As in other parts of Provence, a number of grape varieties are permissible in wine production. To qualify

for the Cassis *appellation,* the wines must have at least 11 percent alcohol. But as with many of the other Provence wines, the hot sun and long summers tend to produce grapes of fairly high sugar content and, therefore, more alcoholic content.

Palette, producing good whites and reds, is the only important *appellation* of Provence that is not on the seacoast. It is up in the hills inland from Marseilles near Aix-en-Provence. Two dozen grape varieties are permissible in Palette wines, so they will vary according to the mixture of each grower. Like the other Provence wines, those of Palette are best drunk within five or six years of their birth and are not likely to be seen outside southern France.

Any visitor to the Mediterranean coast of France should avail himself of the opportunity to taste the better known local wines, but he should also experiment with the lesser wines of the area, which are usually bottled as Côtes de Provence, meaning that they have come from nearly anywhere within the district. They are only a notch below the others and their production is far greater, resulting in generally lower prices. In 1977, the Côtes de Provence wines were awarded *appellation contrôllée* status under the French wine law. One of the leading producers of Provence is Domaines Ott, based in Antibes, whose quality standards are high. Interestingly, some of the red wines of Provence actually seem to taste more like rosés, even though their color is somewhat darker than usual for a rosé. The saying "They do not travel well" may very well have been invented for these wines, which is why they rarely are found outside Provence or the nearby provinces.

Puligny-Montrachet.

The greatest white table wines produced anywhere in the world come from the vineyards of Puligny-Montrachet in the heart of the Côte de Beaune in the French Burgundy country. Puligny-Montrachet shares two of the most celebrated vineyards, Le Montrachet and Bâtard-Montrachet, with the neighboring *commune* of Chassagne-Montrachet. These wines are luscious and rich, with a creamy texture and full flavor evocative of herbs and spices, yet at the same time subtle and elegant. Le Montrachet

is regarded as the number-one white wine of France, but Bâtard-Montrachet often challenges it. These are both *grands crus* white Burgundies, and deservedly so. Two other *grands crus,* Chevalier-Montrachet and Bienvenues-Bâtard-Montrachet, are produced there in equally small quantities. These wines are always very expensive and are not easy to find. The extraordinary vineyard of Le Montrachet lies about equally in Puligny and Chassagne, but the ten acres in Puligny are said to be ever so slightly superior to the nine in Chassagne, possibly because they face slightly more to the east and catch the morning sun earlier.

The largest owner of Le Montrachet is the Marquis de Laguiche, and his wines are said to be the best, although comparisons of the wines from the different parts of the vineyard are difficult to make. The Domaine de la Romanée-Conti also owns a slice, on the theory that it must have the best white wine

to go with its reds, which are the most costly Burgundies of all. Baron Thénard, Bouchard Pére et Fils, Jacques Prieur, and Mme Bouillereault de Chauvigné also have important holdings. Bâtard-Montrachet, Chevalier-Montrachet, and Bienvenues-Bâtard-Montrachet are also magnificent wines, and the author recalls one occasion when a bottle of the 1970 Montrachet was rejected in a New York restaurant because it was good, but not good enough to merit its $35 price, whereas the 1969 Chevalier-Montrachet that was substituted was far superior.

Because of the fame of Le Montrachet itself, the simple *commune* wines bearing the name Puligny-Montrachet have become quite expensive—in fact more costly than they deserve to be. *Commune* wines from Meursault, which lies adjacent to Puligny, are usually better value nowadays. Nevertheless, even the lesser wines of Puligny are very good and must be taken seriously regardless of their price. Besides the four *grands crus,* the commune has a number of *premiers crus,* including the following:

Caillerets
Chalumeaux
Champ Canet
Clavoillons
Combettes
Folatières
Garenne
Hameau de Blagny
Pucelles
Referts
Sous le Puits

A very small quantity of red wine is produced in Puligny, and it is rarely seen under its own name.
☆/☆☆
$$/$$$

· Q ·

Quady Winery.

Andrew Quady became a pioneer in the California vintage Port field when he established his winery in Madera, in Madera County, California, in 1977. The concept of vintage Port in California, as opposed to the old nonvintage variety, which is quite different in style, was new. Quady uses mainly Amador County Zinfandel grapes as his raw material because of the intensity and concentration of flavor that they provide. He says that Amador and the Douro River region of Portugal, where true Port comes from, share many of the same climatic characteristics. Port, of course, is a fortified wine.

Quady allows his grapes to ferment until they contain about 12 percent residual sugar, or about half the level they contained at the harvest, prior to fermentation. At this point brandy is added to stop the fermentation by preventing the action of the yeasts. Thus the unfermented sugar remains, and the resulting wine contains 20 percent alcohol. This is the same way that Port is made in Portugal. Quady then barrel-ages his Port for 12 to 15 months before bottling. Any further barrel-aging would produce a ruby or tawny Port unsuitable to become vintage Port, for vintage Port must be given a chance to develop in the bottle. The best characteristics of vintage Port do not begin to become evident until after three or four years of bottle age. Andy Quady says his own vintage Ports age about twice as rapidly as those from Portugal, which means his are beginning to be drinkable from five to eight years after the vintage. His production is limited.
☆☆☆☆
$$

Quail Ridge.

From its inception in 1978, using leased premises for winemaking, Quail Ridge has made excellent Chardonnays in the style of the celebrated Montrachets of the Burgundian Côte de Beaune of France. Only 328 cases of the 1978 vintages were made, hardly enough to make a big reputation, but 1100 cases were produced in 1979 and now production is approaching 5000 cases, while the renown of Quail Ridge has grown. The wines are among the most expensive Chardonnays produced in California, but they also are of high quality. They are barrel-fermented and the first few vintages were made entirely from purchased grapes while the acreage planted in vines at the Quail Ridge property on Mount Veeder above the Napa Valley matured.

The prime mover behind Quail Ridge is Elaine Wellesley, who was born in Durban, South Africa, and came to the United States as a journalist and later worked as a Hollywood script editor. She and an associate, Jesse Corallo, became home winemakers in a garage in Los Angeles in the early 1970s, and later Elaine Wellesley got a degree in oenology from the University of California at Davis. She and Corallo, a television advertising producer and director, decided to make a major commitment to the wine business and established Quail Ridge on the mountain above St. Helena in 1978. They leased the former Hedgeside Distillery in the Silverado area of Napa for making their wines, and success followed. A French Colombard and a Cabernet Sauvignon were added to the Quail Ridge line, but the Chardonnays continued to be the main attraction. Corallo died in 1981, and Wellesley continued as winemaker, hiring Leon Santoro away from Stag's Leap Wine Cellars to be her general manager. Wellesley remains the sole owner of Quail Ridge.
☆☆
$$$

Qualitätswein.

German for "quality wine," which is the next level above *Tafelwein,* or "table wine," under the German wine law of 1971. Quality wine must be produced from one of the approved grape varieties, and must come from one of the 11 regions specified for quality wines: Ahr, Baden, Franken, Hessische, Mittelrhein, Mosel-Saar-Ruwer, Nahe, Rheingau, Rheinhessen, Rheinpfalz, or Württemberg. Control numbers are awarded by the German government, guaranteeing that these wines have been tasted and analyzed and meet the standards required. Quality wine may be labeled only according to the region where it was produced, or according to smaller and more specific designations such as vineyard name, but only if at least 85 percent of the wine comes from the smallest area named. The grape type—for example, Riesling, Sylvaner, Müller-Thurgau, etc.—may be specified if at least 85 percent of the wine comes from that variety. A vineyard must contain 12 to 25 acres for its name to be mentioned on the label. As a result, some of the confusion was removed from German labels starting in 1971, because many German vineyards were too small to qualify.

Qualitätswein mit Prädikat.

German for "quality wine with special attributes," the highest category of German wines following the revision of the German wine laws in 1971. These wines must be made from approved grape varieties and must achieve 10 percent natural alcohol. The government specified certain attributes, or *Prädikats*, which also appear on the labels: Cabinet or Kabinett, Spätlese, Auslese, Beerenauslese, or Trockenbeerenauslese. These terms (which are defined under their alphabetical listings) refer to the degree of natural sweetness and method of harvesting. Quality controls are rigid and the wines are tasted and analyzed by a government agency before being awarded control numbers which are intended to guarantee a consistent high level of quality. The designation, if it appeared by happenstance prior to the 1971 vintage, had no legal standing.

Quincy.

One of the tributaries of the Loire River in France is the Cher, where some good white wines are produced. Quincy is one of these, and it is dry and earthy, but its earthiness is spicy and charming, rather than coarse and acrid as in some other Loire Valley whites. It is made from the Sauvignon Blanc grape, which is also used to make dry white Graves and sweet Sauternes. Quincy is pronounced "kan-see." (*See* Loire Valley.)
☆/☆☆
$/$$

Quinta.

Quinta (pronounced *kin*-tuh) is the Portuguese term for an agricultural property or parcel, and in such wine-producing regions as the Douro River Valley in the northern part of the country it means "vineyard." Nearly all Port is a blend of wines from various vineyards, or *quintas,* but there are some single-*quinta* Ports. The best known is Quinta do Noval. (*See* Port.)

· R ·

Ratafia.

Ratafia is an aperitif produced in France's Champagne district from the second and third pressings of the grapes used to make Champagne. It is made by blending unfermented grape juice with distilled wine spirits to yield an alcohol level of about 18 percent. The addition of the spirits inhibits the fermentation of the grape juice, leaving residual sugar that may run upward of 10 percent. This fortified wine, rarely exported, may be aged in wooden barrels for a year or more, developing a tawny-yellow hue.

Rauenthaler.

Occasionally the wines of a particular vineyard area win high regard strictly among connoisseurs, and the Rauenthalers are in this category. In the best vintages they have consistently achieved the distinction of being the highest-priced wines in all of Germany, even more costly than such famous Rheingau neighbors as Schloss Johannisberger and Schloss Vollrads. Rauenthal is one of the hillside villages lying north of Eltville in the heart of the Rheingau, which is Germany's most highly regarded wine region. It benefits from a combination of factors, including excellent southern exposure in that brief stretch of the Rhine Valley where the river flows roughly east to west. Some sections of the Rauenthal vineyards are classified as the most valuable agricultural land in Germany, reflecting the high prices their produce attains. It would be highly subjective to argue that the extraordinary Rauenthaler Baiken is greater than the Steinberger, the Marcobrunner, Schloss Vollrads, or Schloss Johannisberger, but certainly all are in the same supreme category among the world's leading white wines.

The German State Domain (Staatsweingut) is one of the major owners of the Baiken, and the Graf Eltz and the Freiherr Langwerth von Simmern also have substantial Rauenthaler properties. The quantity of acreage planted in vine is somewhat less than in other Rheingau villages, which helps explain the high prices. Wines have been produced in the area since the thirteenth century. Nowadays Rauenthalers display astonishing balance and finesse combined with a full-bodied intensity that represents the summit of achievement for the Riesling grape. They are less consistent in mediocre years, when some of the other Rheingau wines usually represent much better value.

Among the better vineyards at Rauenthal are the following:

Rauenthaler Baiken*
Rauenthaler Burggraben
Rauenthaler Gehrn*
Rauenthaler Grossenstück
Rauenthaler Herberg
Rauenthaler Hilpitzberg
Rauenthaler Hühnerberg
Rauenthaler Langenstück*
Rauenthaler Maasborn
Rauenthaler Nonnenberg*
Rauenthaler Pfaffenberg
Rauenthaler Rothenberg*
Rauenthaler Steinmächer*
Rauenthaler Weishell
Rauenthaler Wülfen*

An asterisk (*) indicates vineyard names that survived or that were created in the revision of the German wine law of 1971. The Steinmächer is now a *Grosslage,* or large vineyard area, similar to a generic wine.
☆/☆☆☆
$$/$$$

Château Rausan-Ségla.

This château in Margaux produces big and rich wines of great depth and intensity requiring at least a decade of bottle-aging before drinking. Rausan-Ségla, once joined with the neighboring Château Rauzan-Gassies, was ranked a second growth in the Bordeaux classification of 1855 and continues to merit this status.
☆☆☆☆
$$/$$$

Château Rauzan-Gassies.

Ranked a second growth in the Bordeaux classification of 1855, this estate in Margaux is not one of the better producers among the *seconds crus.* Its wines tend to be less full-bodied than those of the neighboring Château Rausan-Ségla, with which it once was joined. Rauzan-Gassies is especially to be avoided in light vintages, although it produces good wines in the best years. It reaches maturity between the ages of eight and 12 years.
☆☆☆/☆☆☆☆
$$

Martin Ray Vineyards.

The late Martin Ray was in the vanguard of California boutique wineries with his Santa Clara County facility established on top of Mount Eden near Saratoga in 1946. He had owned and operated Paul Masson Champagne Company (now owned by Seagram's) from 1935 to 1943, and then decided to go into production of premium varietals. He specialized in the production of small amounts of Cabernet Sauvignon, Pinot Noir, Chardonnay, White Riesling, and sparkling wines that were sometimes very good, sometimes not well made, and usually very expensive. Occasionally he would produce a Cabernet that would resemble a fine Bordeaux, and he did so in 1953. It won several blind tastings in New York against the likes of Château Latour and Château Mouton-Rothschild. In the late 1970s Martin Ray Vineyards went briefly into eclipse following the proprietor's death in 1976, but his son Peter Martin Ray, a university professor, took over, and Martin Ray wines are once more on the shelves, although in limited amounts. The winery now produces a sometimes excellent Chardonnay, an often indifferent Pinot Noir and a Cabernet Sauvignon, Merlot, Riesling, and sparkling wines made with the *méthode champenoise.* A second brand, La Montana, is also produced.
☆/☆☆☆☆
$$/$$$

Raymond Vineyard and Cellar.

Raymond is a family winery located in St. Helena in California's Napa Valley.

Roy Raymond, Sr., worked at Beringer as a winemaker until 1970, when Beringer was sold to Nestlé. He and his wife, the former Martha Jane Beringer, then bought their 90 acres near St. Helena and began planting them in vines in 1971. A winery was built in 1974, the first year that wines appeared under the Raymond label, and production expanded quickly with the help of Roy, Sr.'s sons, Walter, the winemaker, and Roy, Jr., the vineyard manager. A new winery was completed in 1979, and production of the Raymond line of premium varietals has grown to more than 30,000 cases a year. Eighty acres are planted in vines, and all of the Raymond wines were estate-bottled until 1981, when some grapes were purchased from other growers for the first time. The Raymond Chardonnay and Johannisberg Riesling have established fine reputations nationally. The winery also produces Cabernet Sauvignon, Chenin Blanc, and Zinfandel in some vintages.
☆/☆☆☆
$$

Recioto della Valpolicella.

While most Valpolicella is light, dry, and uncomplicated, the Recioto della Valpolicella is a wine of substantial character. Both are made in Italy's Ve-

neto region from roughly the same blend of grapes: 55 to 70 percent Corvina, 25 to 30 percent Rondinella, 5 to 15 percent Molinara, and 10 percent other varieties. Recioto della Valpolicella is vinified sweet from raisined grapes that have been allowed to dry until their remaining juice is very concentrated. The term *recioto* comes from the Italian for "ears," which is *recie* or *recia,* depending on the dialect, and referring to the upper portions of the grape clusters that receive the most sun and therefore ripen the earliest. If the word "Amarone" is added, the wine is dry, a superb accompaniment to fully flavored meat or game, or to sharp cheeses. Amarone is so characterful, in fact, that it has an identity all its own and is often consumed without any knowledge that it is actually a type of Valpolicella. Both the dry and sweet versions have considerable longevity. (*See* Amarone.)
☆☆☆/☆☆☆☆
$$/$$$

Reuilly.

One of the many wine-producing parts of the Loire Valley of France is Reuilly, where some fairly decent whites are made from the Sauvignon Blanc grape. Not often found in foreign markets, Reuilly tends to be dry and earthy, resembling Quincy, which is produced not far away. (*See* Loire Valley.)
☆/☆☆
$/$$

Rheingau.

This is one of the greatest white-wine-producing areas in the world, the centerpiece of German wines, often copied in name but rarely if ever matched in quality. Some connoisseurs assert without reservation that the Rheingau has no peer in terms of the consistency of its big but elegant whites. Even the most ardent lovers of the wines made from the Chardonnay grape in the Burgundian Côte d'Or of France would have to concede that the Rheingau produces more great white wines than Burgundy could ever hope to produce. Whether Le Montrachet 1969 from the portion of the vineyard owned by the Marquis de Laguiche is superior to a Schloss Vollrads 1971 Auslese or a Schloss Johannisberger 1971 Beerenauslese—from two of the foremost vineyards of the Rheingau—is useless to argue, for the question must come down to personal taste when such noble vineyards are compared. Suffice it to say that the Rheingau is unmatched in the quantity of superior white wines that come out of its vineyards and only a few small patches of ground in France and California produce anything capable of challenging Rheingau character and finesse.

The Riesling grape, stingy in yield but generous in quality, achieves its highest level here, and the other grapes usually regarded as less noble—the Sylvaner, the Müller-Thurgau, even the spicy Traminer—somehow. rise to extraordinary heights when they are nurtured in Rheingau vineyards. The sun, soil, climate, and perhaps a mysterious "x" factor come together here to give birth to great white wines more often than anywhere else. The "x" factor may very well be the direction in which the Rhine River flows.

From its source at Lake Constance on the Swiss border in the south, the Rhine flows generally northwest toward Holland—except for the 20-mile stretch between Mainz on the east and the area just past Rüdesheim on the west, where it flows west and even slightly southwest. Great wines certainly are produced in the areas where the Rhine flows northwest, for example the Palatinate and Hessia, but in the Rheingau, where the river changes course for that brief 20-mile run, German wines achieve their highest levels. The fertile slopes

where the best vineyards lie are situated on the northern bank of the river here, where they catch direct sunlight throughout the day during the growing season. In contrast, the best slopes in Hessia and the Palatinate tend to face east or southeast, where they catch the full heat of the rising sun but perhaps miss some of the late afternoon brightness that southern vineyards receive.

The area encompassed by the Rheingau vineyards is somewhat smaller than the other principal wine-growing areas of Germany. It is surrounded on the northern slopes by the Taunus Mountains, which protect it from the inclement weather that sometimes blows down from Scandinavia. The soil varies somewhat and has been likened to that of the Burgundy District of France. In fact, the best red wine of Germany— albeit relatively mediocre compared to Burgundian reds—is the Assmannshauser just north of Rüdesheim, produced from the Spätburgunder grape, which is virtually the same as the Pinot Noir of Burgundy. Because the production of Rheingau wines is not large and the quality level is so high, they tend to be somewhat more costly than other German wines. The individual must decide for himself whether they are worth the price, but the connoisseur will happily pay extra for them. Of course, they tend to be sweet—like the other fine German wines—but their sweetness is natural and elegant and bears virtually no resemblance to the cloying artificiality displayed by the so-called "pop" wines of America that have given sweet wines in general a bad name. They are best drunk before a meal as an aperitif or with the starter course or, best of all, with dessert or ripe fruit.

Nearly all of the great Rheingau vineyards are divided among a fairly large number of producers, much as the vineyards of Burgundy have multiple ownership. There are only three important exceptions: Schloss Johannisberger, owned by the Metternich family, Schloss Vollrads, owned by the Graf Matuschka, and Steinberger, owned by the German State. These and Marcobrunner are the most famous of the Rheingaus, with perhaps one exception. The vineyards of Hochheim have achieved great renown outside Germany because of the British habit of referring to all German wine from anywhere in the Rhine Valley as "hock." Actually, Hochheim is only one of the superior wine towns of the Rheingau and it is classified a Rheingau only by agreement, because it lies above the Main River to the east. But Hochheimers are clearly representative of the best Rheingaus, so the somewhat indiscriminate use of the word "hock" is understandable.

The foremost wine-producing towns of the Rheingau number only a dozen, and they are discussed under the alphabetical listings for their wines: Eltviller, Erbacher, Geisenheimer, Hallgartener, Hattenheimer, Hochheimer, Johannisberger, Kiedricher, Oestricher, Rauenthaler, Rüdesheimer, Winkeler. Schloss Vollrads is discussed under Winkeler, Schloss Johannisberger under Johannisberger and Steinberg under Hattenheimer.

☆/☆☆☆
$/$$$

Rheinhessen, Hessia.

One of the outstanding wine regions of Germany, Hessia lies mostly on the west bank of the Rhine River just before it bends westward at Mainz. The Sylvaner grape is dominant, although Müller-Thurgau, Scheurebe, and Riesling are planted in large quantities as well. The best white wines come from the Riesling grape planted in the named vineyards of Nierstein. Oppenheim, Nackenheim, Bodenheim, and Bingen are the other principal wine towns of the Rheinhessen. The best wines clearly

rival those of the top Rheingau vineyards in style and finesse, and although they tend to be slightly softer, some have great character and elegance. Most of the lesser wines of the area tend to stay out of the export markets, except in the form of Liebfraumilch, the blended wine that is believed to have originated there. Among the most renowned vineyards of the Rheinhessen are the Niersteiner Rehbach and the Niersteiner Hipping, the Nackenheimer Rothenberg, and the Binger-Büdesheimer Scharlachberg. (Refer to the alphabetical entries for each town for a fuller description.)

Hessia is best known to Americans for its Hessians, the mercenary soldiers hired to help England in the American Revolution. Today it is a vital area to the German wine trade, partly because Mainz, the capital of the wine business, is one of its principal cities. The area of Hessia totals about 600 square miles and much of it is planted in vineyards. It extends to the Nahe River on the west and to the area around Worms on the south. (*See* Niersteiner, Oppenheimer, Nackenheimer.)

☆/☆☆☆
$/$$$

Rheinpfalz, Palatinate.

The southernmost of the major German wine-producing districts, lying below the Rheinhessen on the west bank of the Rhine as it flows from the Swiss border farther to the south. The area has been famed for its wine since the days of the Holy Roman Empire and the word *Pfalz* comes from an ancient Latin word for "palace." Climate plays an important role in the style and quality of any wine, and the climate in the Pfalz is the warmest of the major German wine areas. The Haardt Mountains protect the Pfalz along its western edge and give the area one of its secondary names, the Haardt. Indeed, the three principal subdivisions of the Pfalz are the Oberhaardt, or Upper Haardt, the Mittelhaardt, or Middle Haardt, where the most noble wines are made, and the Unterhaardt, or Lower Haardt. The Mittelhaardt wines are sought after by connoisseurs and tend to flow into export markets, whereas the others tend to stay home or be used for blending, because many have an intensely earthy taste that can shock a delicate palate.

The wines of the Mittelhaardt have made the Rheinpfalz famous. They are big and robust, with full bodies, more assertive than most other German wines, although perhaps less elegant than the Rheingaus and better Rheinhessens. In superior vintages, when the weather has been kind, and good quantities of Auslese, Beerenauslese, and Trockenbeerenauslese can be produced, the wines of the Mittelhaardt can rise above anything else produced in Germany. The best come from the Riesling grape, but even the more prolific Sylvaner sometimes produces a wine that challenges the Rieslings in class and finesse when all the conditions are perfect. Some interesting blends of Scheurebe, Müller-Thurgau, and even Gewürztraminer as well as hybrids are made in the area.

Through the center of the district runs the famous Deutsche Weinstrasse, or German wine road, wending its way among the picturesque villages where the great vines grow. The most famous are Wachenheim, Forst, Deidesheim, and Ruppertsberg, which cover some of the best vineyard areas in the world. Many of the vineyards are very small and there are dozens of different owners with various parcels of land. The center of the wine trade is at Deidesheim, where Dr. Ludwig Bassermann-Jordan makes excellent wines and keeps one of the world's most spectacular private wine museums beneath the cobbled streets of the village. His narrow, chilly passageways run for more than half a mile under other houses that have no cellars. He keeps 500,000 bottles in all, plus many artifacts related to wine. The 1706 vintage is the earliest he has and he keeps a total of about 10,000 bottles of collector's items that include every year from 1880 to the present. He uses only wooden casks for aging the wine that he sells and some of them have dates from the early eighteenth century hand-carved into their butts. In one section of the vast cellar is a tasting room with an arched stone ceiling built in 1554. It has amphorae raised from ancient sunken ships in the Mediterranean Sea positioned around the walls and the room has a seating capacity for 120 guests.

Dr. Bassermann-Jordan produced one of the greatest Trockenbeerenausleses ever made in his 1971 vintage at Forster-Jesuitengarten. He was able to capture only 300 litres of the precious wine, which the German government certified as having achieved a natural sugar content of 250 degrees on the Oechsle scale, the standard measure of sweetness. This was one of the highest levels ever recorded, 100 degrees above the minimum necessary for a Trockenbeerenauslese, attesting not only to the proprietor's skill as a winemaker, but also to the astonishing quality of the 1971 vintage. When tasted in 1973 the wine had an overwhelming bouquet of honey, a deep Cognac-like color and richness and intensity of taste that defy description. The grapes contained so much natural sugar that they began to ferment at the end of October as soon as they were harvested and the juice kept on fermenting until the end of February.

Although Bassermann-Jordan is a towering figure in the Pfalz, some other producers have even bigger vineyard holdings and are fully capable of making wines of comparable quality. Among the largest are Bürklin-Wolf, von Buhl, Deinhard, Pioth, Spindler, Georg Siben Erben, and Koch-Herzog Erben. There are many smaller producers who turn out their own wines, as well as some cooperatives that consist of producers who band together to offer their wines under a single cooperative label. Considerable quantities of Pfalz wines are also shipped in barrels to bulk bottling points as distant as Mainz. (*See* Deidesheimer, Forster, Ruppertsberger, Wachenheimer, Ungsteiner, Durkheimer, Königsbacher, and Kallstadter.) ☆/☆☆☆ $/$$$

Rhône Valley.

Some of the best red wines of France come from the 100-mile stretch of the Rhône River Valley running south of Lyon almost to Avignon, but over the years they have not developed the worldwide popularity of Burgundies from the Côte d'Or to the north or Bordeaux from far to the west. As a result, they can be good buys, although the best Rhônes need a great deal of bottle age to reach their peaks and it has become increasingly difficult to find properly mature examples. The wine-lover who lays down a few dozen in their youth will be rewarded with splendid bottles if he is patient enough to wait a decade.

The most famous Rhône is Châteauneuf-du-Pape, usually a big and robust red made from perhaps a dozen different grape varieties. It is dark-colored and full-bodied, and is produced under the most stringent legal controls anywhere in France. It comes from the area just north of Avignon and south of the Roman city of Orange and takes its name from the castle of the Pope built there in the fourteenth century when the papacy was based in Avignon instead of Rome.

Hermitage has been called the world's manliest wine, and it is vaguely similar to Châteauneuf-du-Pape, although connoisseurs contend that it is slightly more elegant. It comes from the area north of Valence around the town of Tain-l'Hermitage, which is 50 miles south of Lyon. It takes its name from a hermit who lived on the hillside above Tain in the thirteenth century and cultivated wines there. It needs at least a decade in the bottle. Crozes-Hermitage is a less robust wine produced just north of Hermitage. Substantial quantities of white Hermitage are also produced; they are big and earthy.

Côtes-du-Rhône is the name given to the wines produced anywhere in the Rhône Valley if they are not entitled to a more specific designation. Sometimes they can be very ordinary, but occasionally they rise to great quality peaks and the one sold in the United States as La Vieille Ferme is excellent—almost as fruity as a Beaujolais but displaying more depth and character in the best vintages. Many of the Côtes-du-Rhônes are similar to Beaujolais, but they usually cost less and represent very good value when they come from the better shippers.

The Côte Rôtie in the northernmost portion of the district on the west bank of the Rhône produces wines with more depth and class than those called simply Côtes-du-Rhône but not as much character and staying power as Hermitage or Châteauneuf-du-Pape. A Côte Rôtie should not be as expensive, either, but it will display a certain robust elegance and charm after less bottle-age than is required for a Hermitage. The name means "roasted hillside" and refers to the slope where Côte Rôtie is produced.

Less well known but occasionally just as high on the quality scale are the reds known as Cornas, St. Joseph, and Gigondas. They tend to lack the finesse of the other big Rhônes. Tavel and Lirac are the vineyard areas that produce excellent rosé wine just north of Avignon and not far from Châteauneuf-du-Pape. Quantities of white Rhône wines are also produced, and perhaps the most renowned is the Château Grillet made from the Viognier grape at Condrieu adjacent to the Côte Rôtie. This grape produces a dry and earthy white that is sometimes blended with the Syrah, the region's predominant red grape, to relieve the harshness that may be evident in a young Côte Rôtie. Whites produced outside the Château Grillet vineyards but within Condrieu are bottled under the Condrieu name. (*See also* Châteauneuf-du-Pape, Condrieu, Côte Rôtie, Hermitage, Tavel.)

☆/☆☆☆☆
$/$$$

Richebourg.

The Domaine de la Romanée-Conti is one of the principal owners of this extraordinary Burgundian vineyard of only 20 acres, where some of the best red wines of the world are produced. It has been accorded *grand cru* status, the highest category of Burgundy estates, because of its consistently balanced, full-bodied, luscious, and velvety wines. Besides the Domaine, there are half a dozen other owners, including Charles Noëllat and Louis Gros. Richebourg lies in the *commune* of Vosne-Romanée in the heart of the Côte d'Or, or Golden Slope of Burgundy. (*See also* Romanée-Conti, Vosne-Romanée, Côte de Nuits.)

☆☆☆☆
$$$/$$$$

Ridge Vineyards.

Ridge Vineyards sits 2600 feet above the town of Cupertino in Santa Clara County, California. Ridge was started as a hobby in 1959, by four Stanford Ph.D.s who worked in the vineyards and the winery on weekends with their families. The first wine, a Cabernet Sauvignon, was so good, however, that they began to get more serious about it, especially David Bennion, who left Stanford in 1967 to devote full time to winemaking activities on Monte Bello Ridge. Ridge is constantly searching out mountain vineyards for grapes of sufficient intensity to make wines in the big style that it is known for. Ridge has made its reputation with Zinfandel and it produces a number of them from various vineyards. The names are always stated on the labels; thus one sees Zinfandel Monte Bello or Occidental or Lytton Springs. All are slightly different, with a *goût de terroir* of their own. Ridge fans have their particular favorites. One of the most popular was Lytton Springs 1973. Like most Ridge wines, it was big and full-flavored with enormous complexity. The Occidental of the same vintage was similarly big. Ridge Cabernet is every bit as big as the Zinfandels— sometimes it is said that Ridge wines are *too* big and lack finesse and elegance, but they simply require long aging and most people are not used to waiting that long for California wines. As with a number of wineries, Ridge eschews the filtering process, allowing the wines to settle naturally, then racking carefully. This is a major reason that the wines are so robust, but at Ridge they also cite the stressed mountain grapes of lower yield but more concentrated flavor. Paul Draper is the winemaker at Ridge, and the winery also produces Chardonnay, Petite Sirah, Cabernet Rosé, and Gamay. Aging is entirely in French and American oak.

Production runs some 35,000 cases a year, more than half of which is Zinfandel purchased from outside growers that Bennion and Draper have identified as superior producers. Production of Cabernet Sauvignon from the home Monte Bello vineyard runs about 4000 cases a year and from York Creek runs about 5000 cases. Cabernets from other sources amount to some 3000 cases a year, and there are about 3000 additional cases annually of Chardonnay, Petite Sirah, and Ruby Cabernet. The vineyard at Monte Bello produces only about 20 percent of Ridge's total requirements.

The Monte Bello Cabernet is a superb wine, and this was clearly demonstrated in a vertical blind tasting against Château Latour in 1981. The Ridge Monte Bello 1964 and the Latour 1962 tied for first place, and none of the older Ridge wines was readily identifiable as being from California. The Ridge '64 was clearly superior to the Latour '64, and the Ridge '62 still needed more time to mature. The tasting provided a rare opportunity to demonstrate that older California Cabernets can compete on a quality level with the best of Bordeaux.

☆☆/☆☆☆☆
$$/$$$

Riesling.

In the vineyards of Germany's Mosel and Rhine River Valleys the Riesling is the noblest grape, creating some of the world's finest white wines. Nearly all of the best German estates strive to produce wines dominated by the Riesling, and it is widely cultivated in the United States, Austria, Yugoslavia, Chile, Alsace, Switzerland, and Italy. In California it is often called the Johannisberg Riesling, a name derived from one of the greatest vineyard areas of the German Rheingau, but the so-called Grey Riesling and others using the name often are not true Rieslings at all.

The Riesling is not a copious producer, yielding rather modest quantities of juice. But when the soil and climatic conditions are proper, it produces wines of extraordinary finesse, with a flowery bouquet, delicate fruitiness, and full body. In the Mosel Valley the Riesling taste

and bouquet are not unlike the taste of ripe peaches, a fruit that the wine complements beautifully. German producers try their best to produce wines of great sweetness that are best drunk as aperitifs or with dessert. But the sweetness is natural and delights the unbiased palate. It comes from ripeness—the riper the grapes, the greater the natural sugar content. Thus, the grapes are left on the vines as late as possible in the autumn to enable them to benefit from the sun as long as they can without fear of frost, rain, or hail. Under ideal conditions, the grapes are permitted to ripen to the point where they actually begin to shrivel into raisins that contain extremely concentrated juice capable of producing wines of magnificent depth and intensity. The wine made from Riesling grapes in Germany is often blended with other varieties, such as the Sylvaner or Müller-Thurgau because of their higher yield or greater durability, but the Riesling itself is acknowledged to be the greatest of the German whites. (*See also* Germany, Mosel, Rheingau, etc.)

Rioja.

The greatest red table wine produced in Spain comes from the area known as the Rioja Valley that stretches across the northern part of the country. The region's principal river is the Ebro, and one of its tributaries is the Rio Oja, whence the name Rioja. Rioja reds can be full-bodied, robust, and complex, although many that flow into the export markets are not representative of the best that the region can produce. Spaniards themselves serve Rioja at their tables when they wish to please their foreign guests, however, and careful selection can produce good values in foreign markets. According to legend, there is a very good reason for the high quality of some of the Riojas: when the Phylloxera blight swept the French vineyards in the nineteenth century, an army of French vintners migrated across the Pyrenees Mountains into northern Spain and settled in the first region they met that seemed suited for their style of viniculture. This was the Rioja Valley, and it thus may be the only place in the world that actually benefited from Phylloxera, which wiped out millions upon millions of vines all over Europe. The blight eventually found its way to the Rioja, and the French itinerants fled back to their native country, but they left behind a legacy of winemaking expertise.

The center of the Rioja trade is the village of Haro in the Rioja Alta, or Upper Valley. Both reds and whites are produced here, but the whites are usually undistinguished. Prior to the 1970s both the reds and whites of Rioja spent many years aging in wooden casks and barrels, sometimes losing much of their character because of the extensive wood aging. But the classification system was changed starting in 1981, and now the Riojas taste fresher and cleaner. There are four main categories. The commonest is Rioja Sin Crianza, or "without breeding," which can be released a year after it is made and need spend no time aging in wood. Then there is Rioja Crianza, or "with breeding," which is the standard bottling and must spend one year in large fermenting tanks and one year in barrels. Rioja Reserva must be at least four years old prior to release and must spend a combination of three years in barrels and bottles after the initial year in fermenting tanks. Rioja Gran Reserva must be at least six years and sometimes eight years old before release, including a combination of years in barrels and bottles—for example, two years in barrels plus five years in bottles, or four years in barrels plus one year in bottles, following the initial year in fermenting tanks. The varying require-

ments enable producers to adjust for the different characteristics of each vintage. Old bottles of Rioja occasionally come on the market, and they can provide interesting taste experiences, although most experts continue to suggest that Spanish vintage dates cannot be trusted due to the absence of a strong national wine law.

Several Riojas have stood far above the others on the quality scale for a number of years, including the Marqués de Riscal and the Marqués de Murrieta, both of which make excellent dry red wines. These are wines of balance and charm in most vintages; they tend to be somewhat lighter in off years, but weather conditions are not as variable in the Rioja as in the Médoc. Wines of the Marqués de Riscal, in their Bordeaux-shaped bottles, are fairly widely available in the United States and Britain, and those of the Marqués de Murrieta can also be found in many retail outlets.

A dozen or more grape varieties go into Rioja wines, yet apparently none is a direct descendant of any of the noble grapes of Bordeaux or Burgundy, despite the influx of French winemakers late in the last century. The Rioja grapes include the Graciano, Garnacha, Tinto, Maturana Tinta, Mazuelo, Miguel del Arco, Monastrel, Tempranillo, and Turrantés. Some are related to other European varieties, but they have unique personalities in the Rioja. The wines made largely from the Tempranillo grape often are the most complex and textured.

Besides the Marqués de Riscal and the Marqués de Murrieta, which were widely available on the American market long before the Rioja boom of the 1970s, excellent Riojas are now available from the following producers: Bodegas R. Lopez de Heredia, Bodegas Berberana, Bodegas Palacio, Pedro Domecq, Federico Paternina, Bodegas

Campo Viejo de Savin, Bodegas Muerza, Bodegas Marqués de Cáceres, Bodegas Carlos Serres, Bodegas Olarra, Bodegas Velazquez, Bodegas Perez de Albéniz, Bodegas Lan, Age Bodegas Unidas (Siglo), Bodegas Bilbainas, Bodegas Franco-Españolas, and Compania Vinicola del Norte de España (CUNE). All of these as well as several other producers make wines of almost uniformly high quality, which is one of the unusual traits of the Rioja District.
☆☆/☆☆☆☆
$/$$

Château Ripeau.

More than 60 estates were ranked as *grands crus classés* in the Saint-Emilion classification of 1955, and Château Ripeau was one of them. The estate lies northwest of the village of Saint-Emilion in the same part of the district that produces the Corbin wines: Châteaux Corbin, Corbin-Michotte, Grand Corbin Despagne, etc. The area consists of the *graves*, or gravelly flatlands, as opposed to the *côtes*, or hillside vineyards, immediately surrounding the ancient village of Saint-Emilion itself. A magnificent old house stands at Ripeau, with colorful angels and cherubs painted on the ceiling of its rather tired, turn-of-the-century salon. In one outbuilding an intriguing small museum of old keys and locks has been assembled, and it doubles as a tasting room for visitors. Ripeau produces mellow and attractive wines that mature relatively early. They should be drunk starting about age ten. They have achieved a following in the United States.
☆☆☆☆
$$

River Oaks Vineyards.

River Oaks is a member of that minority of California producers that can claim to make wines only from its own vineyards. It is owned by a partnership of growers with 600 acres in the Alexander Valley of Sonoma County. The first vineyards were planted in 1964, but the first wine made under the River Oaks name was the 1977. The array of products is broad, and the production is fairly large, running to 50,000 cases in a copious vintage. Vinification takes place at several different facilities. Frank M. Woods, who also is the proprietor of Clos du Bois, heads the partnership that owns River Oaks, and Tom Hobart is the winemaker at both.
☆/☆☆☆
$/$$

Riviera del Garda Bresciano.

Despite its name, the wines of Riviera del Garda Bresciano have nothing to do with the Italian Riviera in the region of Liguria along the northern Mediterranean coast. Rather, these are the wines produced near Lake Garda in the inland region of Lombardy, and they are charming rosés and reds that have won recognition under the D.O.C. law. The Chiaretto, a rosé, is sometimes vinified sweet and should be served chilled. The Rosso is also fairly light and should not be aged more than about five years.
☆/☆☆
$

Riunite.

This lightly sparkling Lambrusco is the largest-selling brand of imported wine in the United States, with sales running into the millions of cases annually. It is not a connoisseur's wine and apparently is consumed almost entirely in the so-called "youth market," but there is no gainsaying its success or the role it has played in introducing consumers to wine in general.
☆
$

Romanée, La.

Lying just up the hillside from Romanée-Conti is La Romanée, with a vineyard area barely surpassing two acres. This is the smallest of the *grands crus* of the *commune* of Vosne-Romanée, one of the greatest vineyard areas of the Burgundian Côte d'Or in France. The luscious red wines of La Romanée display the same velvety texture, rich flavor, extraordinary balance, and flowery bouquet of the other *grands crus* of Vosne-Romanée, but sometimes they do not have quite the same depth of character. A bottle of the off-vintage La Romanée 1950, sampled in New York in 1972, was astonishing in its youth and vigor. It retained plenty of fruit and a redolent bouquet. La Romanée is best drunk at about age ten. Production of this tiny parcel of land is fewer than 200 cases per year; the wine is very difficult to find and very expensive. (*See also* Romanée-Conti, Vosne-Romanée, Côte de Nuits.)

☆☆☆☆

$$$/$$$$

Romanée-Conti.

The Domaine de la Romanée-Conti owns the most important collection of vineyards in the Burgundy country of France and perhaps in the world. The Romanée-Conti vineyard itself contains only four and a half acres of vines and consistently produces the most expensive wines made anywhere. The ownership of this one vineyard would give the Domaine a special prominence in the universe of wine, but it also owns all of La Tâche and portions of Richebourg, Romanée-Saint-Vivant, Grands Echézeaux, and Echézeaux, as well as a slice of the greatest white wine vineyard of France, Le Montrachet, in the *commune* of Puligny. If the wine of the tiny Romanée-Conti vineyard is not the greatest of all the red Burgundies, it certainly ranks close to the top. The same can be said of La Tâche, Richebourg, and portions of Romanée-Saint-Vivant, Grands Echézeaux, and Echézeaux. These are *grands crus* vineyards of the *commune* of Vosne-Romanée in the Burgundian Côte d'Or, or Golden Slope, and they each produce wines of great finesse and elegance, with flowery bouquets and extraordinary balance. They are challenged only by wines from a few neighboring vineyards, Les Musigny, Chambertin, Chambertin-Clos de Bèze and Bonnes-Mares.

Finding the Romanée-Conti cellars in Vosne is not easy, even though the village is barely a crossroads on the Route des Grands Crus that runs through the Burgundy vineyards. They lie close to the ground behind a large wooden gate, with the hillside vineyards looking down upon them. In the subterranean *caves* lie 400,000 bottles worth perhaps $40 million at retail and possibly much more, depending on economic conditions. The Comte de Villaine presides over this hoard, shipping bottles out when they have reached the proper maturity and taking in the new wines after each harvest. The *régisseur*, or cellarmaster, is André Noblet, now in his 60s, who has worked there since he was sixteen.

Noblet is a rustic Burgundian, a hulk of a man in a greenish sweater and canvas shoes with no socks, who was weaned on the wines of the Romanée-Conti Domaine. "It is my tonic," he said. "I am never sick." Deep in the cellars are row upon row of oaken casks where the young wines of the Domaine are aged. A chalk inscription on the butt of each identifies which vineyard it came from. The Comte de Villaine draws out a sampling of La Tâche, pours it into glasses and relates a village maxim: "After having a baby, the mother is told by her doctor to drink La Tâche each evening for warmth and health." After tasting, one does not pour out the wine remaining in his glass, as in other Burgundian cellars. The glass is carefully returned to the Comte, who pours the remainder back into its cask. After all, its value can be measured in dollars per ounce. Besides the younger wines in casks, there are the older ones in bottles lying on their sides, dating back many years. But it is difficult to taste too many vintages, because each year involves six different wines of the Domaine: Romanée-Conti, La Tâche, Richebourg, Romanée-Saint-Vivant, Grands Echézeaux, and Echézeaux.

Some fortunate connoisseurs claim to have favorites among the six, to be able to say that Romanée-Conti is more refined and elegant than Romanée-Saint-Vivant on a consistent basis over the years, that La Tâche is the most feminine of the Domaine's wines, and that Grands Echézeaux is best in off-vintages, like the 1958. But how many people, no matter how great their enthusiasm and wealth, can drink the wines of Romanée-Conti regularly? Suffice it to say that a mystique has built up around the Domaine over the years, and its wines have been elevated almost to deity status. They are certainly magnificent, but not immune to challenge from other great Burgundies. And it is valid to question whether they are worth the sums that are charged for them. (*See also* Vosne-Romanée, Côte de Nuits, etc.)
☆☆☆☆
$$$$

Romanée-Saint-Vivant.

The largest of the seven *grands crus* vineyards of the *commune* of Vosne-Romanée in the Burgundian Côte d'Or is Romanée-Saint-Vivant, whose 24 acres of vines lie just below Romanée-Conti outside the village of Vosne. Very good bottlings of this magnificent wine are made by the Domaine de la Romanée-Conti, among others, and the 1955 from Marey-Monge was a classic. Generally

these wines are best drunk between the ages of ten and 15. Romanée-Saint-Vivant is big and robust, yet displays a velvety texture and great depth of flavor typical of the best wines of Vosne-Romanée. (*See also* Romanée-Conti, Vosne-Romanée, Côte de Nuits.)
☆☆☆☆
$$$/$$$$

Rosé.

Although it is possible to make rosé, or pink wine, by blending white wine with red, this is not the classic method and it is not the best method. Rosé wines are produced naturally in many parts of the world from red grapes cultivated under climatic and geographical conditions that forestall the production of fully red wines. The redness of a wine comes from the grape skins. The juice is white, but it turns red as the natural grape sugar ferments into alcohol that breaks down the skins, drawing out the pigmentation. In regions where viniculture is difficult and the grapes do not completely ripen and lack pigmentation, the alcohol level of the wine tends to be lower, which means it is more difficult to make wines that are completely red. Thus rosé.

Pink wines are also intentionally made in regions that would permit vinification into completely red wines, when the resulting reds are inferior. A rosé that displays great charm and lightness is preferable, after all, to a coarse or unpleasant red. Simply by filtering out the grape skins partway through the fermentation, a skillful producer can make a rosé wine. The best rosés come from Tavel, in the southern Rhône Valley of France, and Anjou, in the Loire Valley. Very pleasant rosés are also produced in Portugal. In fact, two of the largest-selling wines in the world, Mateus and Lancers, are Portuguese rosés. Good rosés are also produced in California, often from the Grenache grape. But rosé wines are rarely produced in the world's best wine regions. All rosés are best served well chilled as aperitifs, although they can be taken during a meal. Generally they do not benefit from bottle-aging. (*See also* Anjou, Lancers, Mateus, Tavel.)

☆/☆☆
$/$$

Rosso Conero.

This is a pleasing red wine produced in Italy's Marches region, mostly from Montepulciano grapes, with some Sangiovese in the blend. The wine is named after Monte Conero, where some of the vineyards lie, and it has been accorded recognition under the Italian D.O.C. law.

☆☆
$

Rosso Piceno.

Rosso Piceno is a textured red wine from the Marches region of Italy, made from 60 percent Sangiovese grapes, the same grapes that dominate most Chiantis. Most of the rest of the blend is Montepulciano grapes. The wines tend to be full-bodied, although lacking in firmness, and do not merit lengthy aging in cellars. They have been accorded recognition under the Italian D.O.C. law.

☆☆
$

Roudon-Smith Vineyards.

Roudon-Smith is a family-owned and family-operated winemaking operation in Santa Cruz County, south of San Francisco, whose proprietors are Bob and Annamaria Roudon and Jim and June Smith. They established the enterprise in 1972 with production of a grand total of 400 cases, but now produce more than 10,000 cases a year of very good Cabernet Sauvignon, Zinfandel, and Chardonnay, as well as Petite

Sirah. A new winery was built in 1978, facilitating a large increase in production. The wines are aged in 50-gallon French and American oak barrels, which provide a degree of complexity to the finished wines without overwhelming them with wood aromas and flavors. Annamaria Roudon designs the labels and manages the books and June Smith is in charge of public relations. The four Smith children are also active with such chores as bottling and labeling. Bob Roudon is the winemaker. All of the grapes for Roudon-Smith are purchased from other growers in various parts of California.

☆/☆☆☆
$$

Château Rouget.

Château Rouget is one of the largest producers in the Pomerol District east of Bordeaux and adjacent to Saint-Emilion, but the estate's annual output of some 8000 cases is fairly modest in comparison to the production at the big estates of the Médoc peninsula north of Bordeaux. The Rouget '47 was especially good, as the vintage was for most Pomerol estates. In any broad classification that included both the Médoc and Pomerol, Rouget would probably rank with the fourth or fifth growths of the Médoc. It is best drunk after it reaches ten years of age and before it reaches 25.

☆☆☆☆
$$/$$$

Round Hill Vineyards.

Round Hill Vineyards is a purchaser of bulk wines and grapes with facilities five miles north of St. Helena in California's Napa Valley. The business was established in 1975 and initially relied entirely on bulk wines, which it bottled and sold under the Round Hill label. Some of these were very good, including a Zinfandel and a Cabernet Sauvignon of the 1974 vintage that helped give Round Hill a national reputation. The stone winery building was erected in the early 1900s and has recently undergone modernization. Although Round Hill continues to buy and bottle bulk wines in fairly substantial quantities, it has also begun to produce its own wines from grapes purchased largely from growers who are also Round Hill stockholders. The reds are aged in 60-gallon French oak barrels. Round Hill now turns out some 80,000 cases of wine each year, most of it made from bulk wines acquired from other producers with excess supplies but some produced in Round Hill's own winery. Besides the Zinfandel and Cabernet Sauvignon, there are Chardonnay, Sauvignon Blanc, Johannisberg Riesling, Chenin Blanc, French Colombard, Gewürztraminer, Gamay Rosé, and Napa Gamay. The winery also bottles under the Rutherford Ranch brand.

☆/☆☆☆

$/$$

Rüdesheimer.

At the western end of the Rheingau, just as the Rhine River begins turning north again after its 20-mile east-west run through Germany's most renowned wine region, is the Rüdesheimer Berg, a steeply sloping hillside where some of the world's greatest whites are produced. The best vineyards are located on the Berg itself and have used "Berg" in their names to connote their preeminent position. Because the drainage here is better than that of more gently sloping vineyard sites, good wines are often produced in rainy years. In the best vintages, however, when the weather is drier and sun shines brightly, the Rüdesheim vineyards not situated on the Berg itself tend to produce the better wines, while the Berg vineyards suffer from their superior drainage.

Rüdesheim is a resort town that lies a short way upstream from the Berg, on the last patch of level ground before the Rhine plunges through the gorge known as the Bingen Hole, named after the town across the river near where the Nahe adds its flow and helps create the turbulence that has cut the Rhine deeply into the valley. Car ferries ply between Rüdesheim and Bingen, tourist steamers put in there regularly during the summer months, and a cable car carries visitors up the mountain to the Ehrenfels Castle. The terraced vineyards are something like those of the Mosel Valley, although the wines they produce are bigger and richer, with fuller bodies and greater intensity. They tend to be less elegant than some of the other wines of the Rheingau, but connoisseurs of big and robust whites hold them in the highest regard. The complex and often heavily subdivided list of Rüdesheim vineyards has been simplified in recent years, but some examples from before the 1971 vintage remain available, showing remarkable staying power.

Among the better vineyards at Rüdesheim are the following:

Rüdesheimer Berg Bronnen
Rüdesheimer Berg Burgweg*
Rüdesheimer Berg Dickerstein
Rüdesheimer Berg Eiseninger
Rüdesheimer Berg Helpfad
Rüdesheimer Berg Katerloch
Rüdesheimer Berg Kronest
Rüdesheimer Berg Lay
Rüdesheimer Berg Mühlstein
Rüdesheimer Berg Paares
Rüdesheimer Berg Platz
Rüdesheimer Berg Ramstein
Rüdesheimer Berg Roseneck*
Rüdesheimer Berg Rottland*
Rüdesheimer Berg Stoll
Rüdesheimer Berg Stumpfenort
Rüdesheimer Berg Zollhaus
Rüdesheimer Bischofsberg*

Rüdesheimer Drachenstein*
Rüdesheimer Engerweg
Rüdesheimer Hasenläufer
Rüdesheimer Häuserweg
Rüdesheimer Hinterhaus
Rüdesheimer Kirchenpfad*
Rüdesheimer Klosterberg*
Rüdesheimer Klosterkiesel*
Rüdesheimer Klosterlay*
Rüdesheimer Linngrub
Rüdesheimer Magdalenenkreuz*
Rüdesheimer Rosengarten*
Rüdesheimer Wilgert

An asterisk (*) indicates vineyards whose names survived or which were created in the revision of the German wine law of 1971. In some cases the survival of the name does not necessarily indicate that precisely the same vineyard boundaries have been maintained, since a principal goal of the new law was to simplify German wine names and eliminate confusion. The Burgweg is now a *Grosslage,* or large vineyard area, similar to a generic wine from Rüdesheim.

☆/☆☆☆
$/$$

Ruffino.

Among the Italian Chiantis with wide foreign distribution is Ruffino, whose huge main plant is located in Pontassieve, a picturesque village about ten miles from Florence, the capital of the Chianti country. The company has been owned by the Folonari family since the early 1900s. Ruffino is Italy's largest Chianti exporter, and the wine is available in many restaurants all over the United States. Ruffino has cultivated relationships with numerous small grapegrowers in the hills of Tuscany since the firm's founding in 1877. It buys their production, trucks it to the cellars in Pontassieve or one of the satellite wineries in Monte Masso or Zano, and

pumps it into glass-lined concrete vats, where it rests for six months before it is piped through a set of filters and

bottled. The wicker for the *fiaschi,* or flasklike bottles, is handwoven by Tuscan women, who can turn out 300 a day, although the use of this type of container is dying out throughout the Chianti business because it is becoming too expensive. Besides Chianti, Ruffino produces several other wines, including Ruffino Rosatello, a rosé, Toscano Bianco, a white, Galestro, another Tuscan white, Ruffino Orvieto, a white from Umbria, the region just south of Tuscany, and a highly successful line of Veronese wines that include some Bardolino and Valpolicella. The Ruffino Riserva Ducale is the firm's premium Chianti and it ranks among the better Chiantis in the export markets. It needs ten years of bottle-age. The Riserva Ducale Gold Label is one of Italy's finest reds. Two other Chiantis now produced by Ruffino are Aziano, a Classico, and Torgaio, made with the *governo* process to achieve early maturity and suppleness. There is also Il Magnifico, a simple and inexpensive table red. (*See also* Chianti.)

☆/☆☆☆☆

$/$$$

Rully.

Just south of the southern tip of the Burgundian Côte d'Or in France lies the village of Rully, whose vineyards produce white, red, and red sparkling wines. This is the beginning of the Côte Chalonnaise as the Saône River runs south, and the justification for halting the Côte d'Or farther upstream is evident in the style of Rully wines. Although they are produced from the same premium grapes that make the best Burgundies, they have a different style. A Rully red or white will be more earthy and less elegant than a good Burgundy from the Côte d'Or, although in the best vintages Rully can rival the wines from the nearby Côte de Beaune. Rully red is best drunk three to seven years after the vintage, and the white should be drunk younger. (*See* Chalonnais.)

☆/☆☆

$/$$

Rumania.

Like other East European countries, Rumania is a major producer of wines, but much of the country's production for export goes to other communist countries and little flows to the United States or Great Britain. What does come into the United States is imported exclusively under the highly successful Premiat label, via Monsieur Henri Wines Ltd., a subsidiary of PepsiCo that also imports the Trakia line from another eastern European country, Bulgaria. The Premiat Cabernet Sauvignon, Pinot Noir, Tarnave Castle Riesling, Valea Blanc Riesling and sparkling wine appear to be well made, pleasant-tasting, and attractively priced at around $3 a bottle, which is perhaps the primary factor in their popularity. These wines lack distinctive varietal characteristics, but display considerable charm.

Rumania lies on the Balkan Peninsula, surrounded by Russia and the Black Sea to the north and east, by Bulgaria to the south, and by Yugoslavia and Hungary to the west. Rumania has a Latin heritage, however, and has always been the dominant wine-producing country in the Balkans. The country's most recent wine law, adopted in 1971, established three levels of quality: VS for superior wines; VSO, for superior wines with appellation of origin; and VSOC, for superior wines with appellation of origin and quality grades. The latter category is further subdivided according to degrees of sweetness: grapes harvested at full maturity, grapes attacked by *Botrytis cinerea,* and fully botrytised grapes reduced to the berry state. The Premiat wines brought into the U.S. all carry the VSOC designation. (*See* Botrytis cinerea, noble rot.)

Ruppertsberger.

German white and red wine produced in Ruppertsberg, one of the better wine towns in the center of the Rheinpfalz, or Palatinate, the country's southernmost region for superior table wines. The red wines are mediocre at best and generally do not flow into the export markets. But the whites of Ruppertsberg are rated among the best in the Pfalz, which is a very high rating indeed. Only the neighboring Deidesheim and the nearby Forst are considered better, and some Ruppertsbergers will challenge them in certain years. Only a minority of Ruppertsbergers are made with the great Riesling, although Sylvaners and other grape varieties produce excellent wines.

Because Ruppertsbergers lack the

world renown of the Forsters and Deidesheimers, they are sometimes overlooked. But they can represent excellent value. Among the better known vineyards are the following:

Ruppertsberger Achtmorgen
Ruppertsberger Bildstöckl
Ruppertsberger Gaisböhl*
Ruppertsberger Goldschmid
Ruppertsberger Grund
Ruppertsberger Hofstück*
Ruppertsberger Hoheburg
Ruppertsberger Kieselberg
Ruppertsberger Kreuz
Ruppertsberger Linsenbusch*
Ruppertsberger Mandelacker
Ruppertsberger Mandelgarten
Ruppertsberger Nussbien
Ruppertsberger Reiterpfad*
Ruppertsberger Spiess*
Ruppertsberger Weisslich

The vineyards marked with an asterisk (*) are among those that retained their identities, if not their former shapes, in the revision of the German wine law in 1971. The others were merged and consolidated to simplify identification. The law also made provision for Ruppertsberger Hubbien. Hofstück has become a *Grosslage,* or large vineyard area, and is virtually a generic term.
☆/☆☆
$/$$

Russia. *(See* Soviet Union.)

Rutherford Hill Winery.

The people behind the Rutherford Hill Winery in St. Helena in California's Napa Valley are the same people who own and operate Freemark Abbey, also in St. Helena. Bill Jaeger and Chuck Carpy are the managing partners of Rutherford Hill and are the top-ranking partners in Freemark Abbey. But they are following a slightly different and more expansive philosophy at Rutherford Hill, where production now runs more than 100,000 cases a year and is still growing, while production at Freemark Abbey has remained in the boutique category at 20,000 to 25,000 cases a year for some time.

Rutherford Hill was constructed in 1972 as a new site for the Souverain Winery, owned by Pillsbury. It was bought by the Jaeger-Carpy partnership in 1976. Rutherford Hill now produces wine almost entirely from grapes grown in vineyards owned by the partners but managed independently of the winery operation. These include Jaeger's 300-acre Curtis Ranches vineyards that grow just north of the city limits of Napa as well as the Freemark-Carpy-Frank Wood ranches in Rutherford, amounting to another 300 acres. Rutherford Hill also buys Zinfandel grapes from the Mead Ranch on Atlas Mountain above Napa to the east. The winery's products include Cabernet Sauvignon, Merlot, Pinot Noir, Zinfandel, Chardonnay, Gewürztraminer, and Johannisberg Riesling.
☆/☆☆☆
$$

Rutherford Vintners.

Rutherford Vintners had its origins while Bernard L. Skoda was working for Louis M. Martini, the big California winemaking concern. Skoda bought a 25-acre tract in Rutherford in the central Napa Valley in 1967 and planted this acreage in 1968 entirely with Cabernet Sauvignon vines. Another, smaller plot nearby was acquired in 1972 and was planted with Johannisberg Riesling. Skoda retired as vice-president of the Martini organization in 1976 and immediately began construction of his own winery on the smaller plot at Rutherford. The facility was completed in 1977, when Rutherford Vintners became operational. Annual production has now reached roughly 15,000 cases of Cabernet Sauvignon, Pinot Noir, Chardonnay, and Johannisberg Riesling. The Riesling, especially, has shown promise, and Skoda is fond of comparing it with the Rieslings produced in his native Alsace and in Germany.

☆/☆☆☆

$$

Ruwer.

The Ruwer River Valley is one of the three contributors to the German regional designation Mosel-Saar-Ruwer, the other two being the Mosel and Saar areas nearby. The production in the Ruwer is very small and the river itself more closely resembles a meandering trout stream than what might be expected in one of the better-known German wine areas. Ruwer wines are similar to those of the Saar in many ways. In the best years, when the weather conditions have been ideal, with warm temperatures in the spring flowering season and sunshine well into the autumn, Ruwer wines rise to extraordinary quality levels. Some connoisseurs say they can be among the best in Germany in such vintages, with a steely elegance and delicate richness that the experts can always identify in blind tastings. Like the Saar wines, however, those from the Ruwer tend to be sharp and unyielding in all but the best years, displaying an almost metallic taste and thinness that detract from their quality. These are among the lightest wines of Germany, with an alcoholic content that sometimes may be only around 9 percent. The best-known wine of the Ruwer is the Maximin Grünhäuser with its picturesque label. The only other Ruwer wines of consequence are the Eitelsbachers, Kaselers, and Waldrachers, all of which can represent good value when they appear in the export markets. But their production is not large and they are unlikely to be seen outside Germany in any but superior vintage years comparable to the 1971.

Among the better known vineyards of the Ruwer are the following:

Eitelsbacher Karthäuserhofberger
    Burgberg*
Eitelsbacher Karthäuserhofberger
    Kronenberg*
Eitelsbacher Karthäuserhofberger
    Sang*
Eitelsbacher Marienholz*
Eitelsbacher Sonnenberg
Kaseler Herrenberg*
Kaseler Hitzlay*
Kaseler Hocht
Kaseler Käulchen
Kaseler Kernagel*
Kaseler Timpert*
Kaseler Niesgen*
Kaseler Steiniger
Kaseler Taubenberg
Maximin Grünhäuser*
Waldracher Laurentiusberg*
Waldracher Hubertusberg*
Waldracher Jesuitengarten*
Waldracher Sonnenberg*
Waldracher Krone*

An asterisk (*) indicates a vineyard name that survived in the revision of the German wine law of 1971.

☆/☆☆☆

$/$$

· S ·

Saar.

The Saar River Valley is at the southern part of the Mosel-Saar-Ruwer region of Germany. In the best years, when the weather conditions are ideal, Saar wines are of superior quality, but in the mediocre years they tend to be inferior to the wines of the central Mosel Valley to the north. When the weather is chilly and damp, the wines display a hardness, which some connoisseurs liken to a metallic taste, such as steel. In these years they tend to be used for blending elsewhere in Germany, where they lose their Saar identities in such sparkling wines as Sekt. A few oenophiles profess to find superior qualities in the *stahlig,* or steely taste, while others prefer to call it sour. In the good vintages, Saar wines are elegant and rich, with great character and assertiveness approaching the best of the Rheingau. The most renowned Saar wine is Scharzhofberger, produced at Wiltingen, the best wine town of the valley, but good wines are also made at Ayl and Ockfen. (The wines from these areas are discussed under their alphabetical entries.)
☆/☆☆☆
$/$$

St. Clement Vineyards.

St. Clement Vineyards stands high above the floor of the Napa Valley overlooking St. Helena on the eastern slope of Spring Mountain. The handsomely restored Victorian home above the St. Clement cellars was built in 1876 and is now a local landmark and appears on the winery's label. The first wines of Spring Mountain Vineyards were made here, and the property was purchased in 1975 from Mike and Shirly Robbins, owners of Spring Mountain Vineyards, by Dr. William J. Casey, a San Francisco eye surgeon. Chuck Ortman joined St. Clement as winemaker after eight years as winemaker at the Spring Mountain Winery and was later succeeded by Dennis Johns. From the outset the St. Clement wines have been very good, and production has risen to around 10,000 cases of Chardonnay, Cabernet Sauvignon, and Sauvignon Blanc. The Chardonnay won an immediate following as a rich, complex, creamy wine filled with fruit.
☆/☆☆☆
$$

Saint-Emilion.

Across the River Garonne and eastward from Bordeaux in the hills above the meandering course of the Dordogne in southwestern France lies the medieval village of Saint-Emilion, named after a hermit who went on a retreat there around the third century A.D. and liked the peaceful countryside so much that he decided to stay. He lived in a grotto and attracted followers who worshiped his reclusive virtues and built up a community on the nearby hilltop. Over the centuries the grotto was deepened and extended, and became a monolithic church that attracts pilgrims to this day. The Romans planted vines there and Ausonius, the fourth-century poet, was a landowner and vineyard-keeper on the neighboring slopes.

Nowadays the big and soft reds of Saint-Emilion (no whites are made there) are among the greatest wines of Bordeaux, although sometimes they lack the breeding and aristocratic finesse of the best Médocs. The premier Saint-Emilion, Chateau Cheval Blanc, fetches prices comparable to such *premier grands crus* of the Médoc as Châteaux Latour and Margaux. Château Ausone, named after the Roman poet, is equally celebrated and has resumed its exalted position after a period of decline in the 1960s and early '70s. Both Cheval Blanc and Ausone are members in good standing of Bordeaux's most exclusive club, the so-called "Big Eight," consisting of Châteaux Lafite-Rothschild, Latour, Margaux and Mouton Rothschild of the Médoc, Chateau Haut-Brion of Graves and Chateau Pétrus of Pomerol, as well as the two *premiers grands crus* of Saint-Emilion.

Château Figeac, whose vineyards are adjacent to Cheval Blanc, is the largest Saint-Emilion producer, ranking in quality with the best second growths of the Médoc and sometimes challenging the firsts. Thierry Manoncourt, the proprietor of Figeac, is a leading spokesman of Saint-Emilion and probably knows more about making Bordeaux wines than all the Médoc's absentee landlords put together. Like others in Saint-Emilion, Manoncourt divides the *commune,* or parish, into two distinct vineyard categories whose wines display contrasting styles. These are the *côtes* and the *graves*. The *côtes* vineyards are on the sloping terrain around the village itself, whereas the *graves* area is the plateau or flatland, with its gravelly soil that holds and reflects the heat of the sun. The differences between the two styles are subtle, but experts can distinguish them.

The *côtes* wines, which come from vines growing from highly alkaline, chalky soil in which fossilized shellfish remnants are evident, tend to be very full but not as rich and fruity as the Graves wines, which grow in soil composed of siliceous pebbles mixed with sand. In Saint-Emilion it is said the shellfish fossils in the soil are 300 million years old, and at Château Beauséjour a well and washing basin have been constructed from them. In the summer sun the soil virtually shimmers in the heat, creating an almost desertlike atmosphere with its sandy yellow color. The entire region rests on a huge layer of limestone, and in the *côtes* area around the village itself cellars for wine storage are cut deep underground. The *caves* at Beauséjour extend hundreds of yards beneath the vineyards and are linked with those of Château Canon and Clos Fourtet.

Saint-Emilion was totally ignored in the Bordeaux classification of 1855, partly because the area is some 20 miles due east of Bordeaux and the wines from a district so far afield were not trusted as to authenticity. It is true that many wines adopted the Saint-Emilion name without legal authority or geographic reason in the early centuries of its viniculture, so the attitude of the Bordelais was, to some extent, justified. At the same time, however, competitive considerations also played a role, and keeping Saint-Emilion wines off the Bordeaux market meant more business for the producers of the Médoc, Graves, and other areas near the city.

For many years the so-called "east bank" wines, mainly from Saint-Emilion and neighboring Pomerol, were not permitted to come to market at the Bordeaux seaport each season until all of the Médocs, Graves, Sauternes, etc., had been sold. This presented a special hardship in the early years when the youngest wines were the most prized and storage for long periods was difficult because the use of cork seals in bottles was relatively unknown. Even today, when relations between the east bank and the west bank of the Gironde are cordial, very few Saint-Emilion vineyards or shipping houses are owned by the Bordelais. Much of the Saint-Emilion and Pomerol trade is handled in Libourne, a bustling town at the junction of the Dordogne and l'Isle Rivers whose suburbs abut the Pomerol vineyards. It was named after Roger Leyburn, seneschal to Edward I of England in the thirteenth century, when Britain dominated the area and consumed most of its wines.

Not until 1954 did Saint-Emilion receive an official classification, although today it is regarded as perhaps the most valid rating system in Bordeaux. Ratified in 1955, the system established four levels of appellation: premier grand cru classé, grand cru classé, grand cru, and, simply, Saint-Emilion, without further notation. A notably appropriate aspect of the original decree was that it should be reviewed every ten years to assure its continuing validity. A by-product of this provision is that the vineyard owners cannot become complacent once they have achieved grand cru classé or premier grand cru classé status, lest they lose the designation at the next review. To merit the grand cru or higher appellation, the wine must be at least 11.5 percent alcohol, whereas 11 percent is the minimum required to use the basic Saint-Emilion name. Minimum natural sugar content in the must, or freshly pressed grape juice, is also specified.

Within the highest, or premier grand cru classé, category, Château Ausone and Château Cheval Blanc received special recognition in a subdivision of their own above the rest. They comprise an "a" group, while the ten other premiers grands crus classés make up a "b" group. Sixty-two châteaux are included in the grand cru classé category, while all the other vineyards in the district are entitled to the designation grand cru or, simply, Saint-Emilion. Thus, the word classé is extremely important in recognizing those châteaux of superior status. The designation grand cru in Saint-Emilion means little, whereas a wine with grand cru classé on its label is one of the better products of the area. The word classé means that the château or cru has been "classified." Also noteworthy is that each grouping is arranged alphabetically, which means no conclusions about quality can be drawn from the fact that Château l'Angelus is first on the list of grands crus classés and Château Yon-Figeac is last.

Besides the crus that have received classé status, there are numerous châteaux that produce excellent wine that may occasionally come on the export markets and can represent good value. At the same time, a château's appearance on the list cannot be regarded as a guarantee of good quality. Weather conditions and production standards can vary from vintage to vintage. As a general rule, however, the crus classés tend to be better wines. Here is a listing of the classified growths of Saint-Emilion:

Premiers Grands Crus Classés (First Great
   Growths)
"a" Château Ausone
     Château Cheval Blanc
"b" Château Beauséjour (Duffau)
     Château Beauséjour (Fagouet)
     Château Belair
     Château Canon
     Château Figeac
     Clos Fourtet
     Château La Gaffelière
     Château Magdelaine
     Château Pavie
     Château Trottevieille

Grands Crus Classés (Great Growths)
     Château l'Angelus
     Château l'Arrosée
     Château Balestard-la-Tonnelle
     Château Bellevue
     Château Bergat
     Château Cadet Bon
     Château Cadet Piolat
     Château Canon-La Gaffelière
     Château Cap-de-Mourlin
     Château Chapelle-Madeleine
     Château Chauvin
     Château Corbin (Gonaud)
     Château Corbin (Michotte)
     Château Coutet
     Château Croque-Michotte
     Château Curé-Bon
     Château Fonplégade
     Château Fonroque
     Château Franc-Mayne
     Château Grand Barrail
        Lamarzelle Figeac
     Château Grand Corbin
     Château Grand Corbin Despagne
     Château Grand Mayne
     Château Grand Pontet
     Château Grandes Murailles
     Château Guadet Saint Julien
     Clos des Jacobins
     Château Jean Faure
     Château La Carte
     Château La Clotte
     Château La Cluzière

Château La Couspaude
Château La Dominique
Clos La Madeleine
Château Lamarzelle
Château Larcis Ducasse
Château Larmande
Château Laroze
Château La Serre
Château La Tour du Pin Figeac
Château La Tour Figeac
Château Le Chatelet
Château Le Couvent
Château Le Prieuré
Château Mauvezin
Château Moulin-du-Cadet
Château Pavie-Décesse
Château Pavie-Macquin
Château Pavillon Cadet
Château Petit Faurie de
   Souchard
Château Petit Faurie de Soutard
Château Ripeau
Château Saint Georges Côte-
   Pavie
Clos Saint Martin
Château Sansonnet
Château Soutard
Château Tertre-Daugay
Château Trimoulet
Château Trois-Moulins
Château Troplong-Mondot
Château Villemaurine
Château Yon-Figeac

(Note: As in the Médoc and Graves,
it is common to refer to a vineyard area
as a "château," even if there is no castle
or large house on the estate. Some Saint-
Emilion estates, however, use the term
"clos" in place of "château." The term
"clos" means "enclosure" or "field" in
this context and should not be inter-
preted to indicate that no château exists
on the property. For example, at Clos
Fourtet, one of the *premiers grands crus
classés,* a large château and storage *chais*
stand above extensive cellars carved into
the subterranean limestone, and the wine

is *mis en bouteilles au château* in the strictest sense of the term.)

Besides the area immediately surrounding the village of Saint-Emilion itself, vineyards entitled to the Saint-Emilion name extend to seven other *communes:* Saint-Christophe-des-Bardes, Saint-Etienne-de-Lisse, Saint-Hippolyte, Saint-Laurent-des-Combes, Saint-Pey-d'Armens, Saint-Sulpice-de-Faleyrens, and Vignonet. In addition, a number of other nearby communities, mostly beyond the Barbanne River to the north and northeast, are permitted to add their names to the Saint-Emilion name as satellite *appellations.* These include Montagne-Saint-Emilion, Saint-Georges-Saint-Emilion, Parsac-Saint-Emilion, Puisseguin-Saint-Emilion, and Lussac-Saint-Emilion. Although there are no *grands crus classés* in any of these parishes, some first-rate wines are produced there and occasionally seen, but its vineyards have been diminishing under urban encroachments from Labourne.

In all there are some 700 *crus,* or individual land parcels, in the roughly 20,000-acre surface area in the total Saint-Emilion *appellation.* Of the 20,000 acres, about 12,500 are planted in vines. Obviously, many of the estates are very small and perhaps should not even be referred to as estates. In these cases, the term *cru* becomes especially appropriate. The Cabernet Sauvignon grape is less dominant in Saint-Emilion than in the Médoc or Graves, while the Cabernet Franc and the Merlot, which yield softer wines, are in greater use. The Malbec and the Bouchet, which is a Cabernet variety, are also cultivated in Saint-Emilion. Each grower has his own blend, which may vary from year to year according to the weather, because certain grapes thrive in conditions that thwart other grapes. As a rule, a Saint-Emilion will reach its summit of perfection in less time than a good Médoc,

perhaps in only six or seven years, although the robust 1966 Saint-Emilions remained in their adolescence for a decade or more.

☆☆/☆☆☆☆
$/$$$$

Saint-Estèphe.

Among the four great *communes* of the Médoc above Bordeaux in southwestern France, Saint-Estèphe is the northernmost and borders on the upper area of the Bordeaux peninsula once known as the Bas-Médoc. The big red wines of Saint-Estèphe are harder than those of Pauillac, Margaux, and Saint-Julien to the south, and sometimes lack the finesse of the others. Yet the three most famous estates of Saint-Estèphe—Château Cos d'Estournel, Château Montrose, and Château Calon-Ségur—are acknowledged to rank among the best red wines of the Bordeaux region. They are robust and full, often needing two decades in the bottle to reach maturity when produced in a good vintage. Château Lafon-Rochet and Château Cos-Labory also make excellent wines that are sought by connoisseurs the world over. The *commune* has only five vineyards that won *cru classé* status in the Bordeaux classification of 1855. They are as follows:

Seconds Crus (Second Growths)
Château Cos d'Estournel
Château Montrose

Troisième Cru (Third Growth)
Château Calon-Ségur

Quatrième Cru (Fourth Growth)
Château Lafon-Rochet

Cinquième Cru (Fifth Growth)
Château Cos-Labory

Besides the classified growths, there are many other châteaux in Saint-Estèphe producing excellent wines, although generally without the consistency of the five best-known estates. Among these are Châteaux Beauséjour, Beau Site, Canteloup, Capbern, Haut-Marbuzet, Marbuzet, Meyney, Les Ormes-de-Pez, de Pez, Phélan-Ségur, and Tronquoy-Lalande. Château Meyney is owned by the Cordier shipping firm and produces consistently good wines. Château Phélan-Ségur also makes very good wines and deserves to be ranked among the classified growths, as does Château de Pez.

☆☆☆☆
$$/$$$

St. Francis Vineyards.

St. Francis Vineyards was originally planted in the early 1900s by Will Behler, whose family ceased production in 1922 because of Prohibition. The property is near Kenwood in the Sonoma Valley and consists of 100 acres in vines, now planted in *Vitis vinifera* vines by Joseph Martin, who acquired St. Francis in 1972. Chardonnay, Gewürztraminer, Johannisberg Riesling, Merlot, and Pinot Noir were put in to take advantage of the loamy, gravelly soil. Initially the grapes were sold to Château St. Jean, Buena Vista, and Grand Cru Vineyards, among others. In 1979 Joe Martin joined with Mike Richmond and Brad Webb to install a new winery and began bottling estate wines in limited quantities. Production has risen to 20,000 cases a year.

☆/☆☆
$$

Saint Georges-Saint-Emilion.

Several satellite areas near the city of Libourne outside of urban Bordeaux in southwestern France are entitled to attach their names to that of Saint-Emilion, one of the most renowned *communes* of the region. Among these are Saint Georges-Saint-Emilion, where some very palatable red wines are produced. (*See also* Saint-Emilion.)

☆☆☆
$/$$

Château Saint Jean.

One of the most successful new winemaking enterprises in California is Château Saint Jean, located near Kenwood in the Sonoma growing area. The estate, with about 100 acres planted in vines, was purchased in 1973 by a group of investors that included Robert and Edward Merzoian, Kenneth Sheffield, and Allan Hemphill. The winemaker, Richard Arrowood, previously worked at Sonoma Vineyards, Korbel, and Italian Swiss Colony and is now regarded as one of the leading members of his profession in California.

Construction of the winery was begun in 1975 after initial production from purchased grapes had taken place in borrowed premises. The winery was finished in 1977, but then a major expansion occurred in 1979–80, involving new storage facilities and enclosing the fermentation tanks, some of which had been outdoors. Saint Jean has more than 100 such tanks, a huge number for a winery of its size, but the purpose is to accommodate and keep separate the various batches of grapes that come from a variety of sources. As a result, Saint Jean at one time was boasting that it produced more than three dozen bottlings a year in nine different varietals. Many of these bottlings bear the name of individual vineyards on their labels.

Saint Jean has important relationships with some of the best grape growers of the Sonoma Valley, including Robert Young, whose name appears on Saint Jean Chardonnays and Rieslings. Dick Arrowood acknowledges that Saint Jean itself will probably always buy grapes from other producers because of the high quality that can be found from outside sources like Robert Young.

Nearly all of these outside grapes come from within 35 miles of the Saint Jean winery, however, and they are crushed as soon as they arrive. It is not unusual for crushing to occur at midnight or two o'clock in the morning during the harvest season.

Besides its temperature-controlled stainless steel fermenting tanks, Saint Jean maintains nearly 1000 barrels made of three kinds of French oak as well as American oak. It is the careful aging in these barrels that adds complexity to the Saint Jean wines. The expansion of the winery included a new bottling room, whose floors are rinsed down with iodine water before the bottling starts. The neck of each bottle is heated under a gas flame to kill bacteria. Sulphur dioxide gas also is injected into the bottles to complete the sterilizing process.

Among the numerous bottlings of Saint Jean Chardonnay are those whose labels identify the source of the grapes as the Robert Young Vineyard, Belle Terre Vineyard, Wildwood Vineyard, and others. Devotees of Saint Jean wines have their favorites. The Saint Jean Rieslings are especially sought by connoisseurs of dessert wines. Arrowood produced one in 1978 from grapes that contained an enormous 51.3 percent residual sugar at harvest and $37\frac{1}{2}$ percent after fermentation, close to the level of honey made by bees. The winery at first called these wines "individually dried bunch selected late harvest" Rieslings, but the name has been simplified. They are very expensive. Besides excellent Chardonnays and Rieslings, Saint Jean has made very good Gewürztraminers, Sauvignon Blancs, Pinot Blancs, Cabernet Sauvignons, and sparkling wines. The production is about 100,000 cases a year, and as of 1982 it was 100 percent white, mostly Chardonnay and Sauvignon Blanc.
☆/☆☆☆
$$/$$$

Saint-Julien.

The Médoc peninsula north of the city of Bordeaux in France is broken down into four *communes,* or townships, that include most of the great red-wine estates of the area, for the purpose of geographical identification. Saint-Julien is one of them, lying just south of Pauillac and just north of Margaux. The remaining *commune,* Saint-Estèphe, is north of Pauillac. The wines of Saint-Julien more closely approximate the supple and elegant reds of Margaux than they do the full and elegant Pauillacs. They are not noted for their longevity, although the better vineyards of Saint-Julien produce wines that do not reach their peaks for perhaps two decades. In this category would be the great Château Beychevelle, ranked a fourth growth in the Bordeaux classification of 1855, and Château Ducru-Beaucaillou, ranked as a second growth. They consistently bring prices comparable to the best second growths. All of the famous Léovilles are in Saint-Julien, and they, too, are held in high regard. The estates classified in 1855 are as follows:

Seconds Crus (Second Growths)
Château Léoville-Las-Cases
Château Léoville-Poyferré
Château Léoville-Barton
Château Gruaud-Larose
Château Ducru-Beaucaillou

Troisièmes Crus (Third Growths)
Château Lagrange
Château Langoa-Barton

Quatrièmes Crus (Fourth Growths)
Château Saint-Pierre
Château Talbot
Château Branaire-Ducru
Château Beychevelle

There are several good vineyards that were not classified in 1855, including Château Gloria, Château Moulin-Riche, and Château des Ormes. Château Gloria has wide distribution and is owned by Henri Martin, mayor of Saint-Julien and one of the leading figures in Bordeaux, who also managed Château Latour. Château Gloria produces soft and supple wines that tend to mature at an early age, but they are capable of showing great finesse in some vintages. This château clearly merits status as a classified growth, as the prices it brings demonstrate. Moreover, the Gloria vineyards include parcels from several nearby classified growths, and some of the château's production facilities once were part of Château Saint-Pierre, a fourth growth.

☆☆☆/☆☆☆☆

$$/$$$

GRAND CRU CLASSÉ EN 1855

CHATEAU SAINT-PIERRE
MIS EN BOUTEILLES   1982   NUNC PLURIBUS
AU CHATEAU   SAINT-JULIEN   IMPAR
APPELLATION SAINT-JULIEN CONTRÔLÉE

S.C.DOMAINES HENRI MARTIN
PROPRIÉTAIRE A SAINT-JULIEN BEYCHEVELLE.GIRONDE 33250   75cl
PRODUCE OF FRANCE

Château Saint-Pierre.

The name of this château in the Bordeaux Médoc *commune* of Saint-Julien used to be Saint-Pierre-Sevaistre, and the last word still appears in smaller type on old labels. A separate part of the vineyard was once called Saint-Pierre-Bontemps. The estate was ranked as a *quatriéme cru,* or fourth growth, in the Bordeaux classification of 1855. It lies between Château Talbot and Château Gruaud-Larose, but Saint-Pierre produces lighter wines than either of these other two estates. The 1971 vintage Saint-Pierre was one of the earliest Médocs of that year to reach maturity; it was pleasant and balanced when tasted in 1976, but seemed to have little future. Other vintages have shown a similar lack of distinction.

Henri Martin, mayor of Saint-Julien and proprietor of Château Gloria, bought the property in time for the 1982 harvest and can be expected to improve the wines, with the help of his son-in-law, Jean-Louis Triaud, general manager. The château itself is being renovated as the new Martin residence.

☆☆/☆☆☆☆

$$

Saint-Romain.

Far up in the hills above Meursault and Auxey-Duresses lies the tiny *commune* of Saint-Romain, with a total of 350 acres under cultivation. Traditionally, these wines, both red and white, have been sold as Côte de Beaune-Villages, but recently Roland Thévenin, one of the leading shippers of the French Burgundy country, has been marketing what he calls "Saint-Romain mon Village" at modest prices. Monsieur Thévenin, besides being active in the Burgundy trade, was also the mayor of Saint-Romain, and he has literally put the *commune* back on the Burgundy map through his marketing efforts. His Saint-Romain is a white that resembles Meursault, although it is somewhat earthier and displays less balance.

☆/☆☆☆

$$

Saint-Véran.

Saint-Véran is a crisp, dry yet fruity white wine produced in the Mâconnais District of France not far from the celebrated vineyards of Pouilly-Fuissé. In fact, were it not for the popularity of

Pouilly-Fuissé, especially among Americans, it is probable that nobody would be drinking Saint-Véran very far from its region of production, for it was the soaring price of Pouilly-Fuissé that caused consumers to seek other wines from the same region. Saint-Véran was one of these. Like Pouilly-Fuissé, it is vinified from the noble Chardonnay grape, but it rarely achieves the creamy richness or finesse of a well-made Pouilly-Fuissé. At the same time, so many Pouilly-Fuissés seem to lack their traditional quality these days that a good Saint-Véran can be a far more reliable wine, at no more than half the price. It tends to be superior to the two other so-called satellites of Pouilly-Fuissé—the Pouilly-Vinzelles and Pouilly-Loché—and often is roughly on a par with Mâcon-Lugny, which means it is pleasant to drink and of high quality in exceptional vintages. The *appellation* is relatively new, having become official with the 1971 vintage, just as Pouilly-Fuissé's popularity was rising sharply.

☆/☆☆

$$

Ste. Chapelle.

A highly successful winery was established at Sunny Slope, Idaho, near Caldwell, about 25 miles northwest of Boise, in 1976 by Bill Broich, who first made wine in 1970 when somebody gave him a home winemaking kit. The area had long been prominent in fruit-growing, with major crops of apples and pears, so grape-growing seemed natural enough. The results since then have been promising, and now Ste. Chapelle turns out more than 50,000 cases a year of premium varietals that sometimes challenge the best from Europe and California. The vineyards are at an elevation of 2700 feet above sea level, which places them among the highest in the country. The soil is similar to the German Rheingau's, and the vineyards are at about the same latitude, so it is not surprising that Riesling is one of Ste. Chapelle's prime products.

Initially grapes were purchased from growers in Washington as well as Idaho, as the Ste. Chapelle plantings matured. The product lineup also includes Gewürztraminer vinified both dry and sweet, as well as Chenin Blanc, Cabernet Sauvignon, Merlot, Rosé of Pinot Noir and Rosé of Cabernet. Winter temperatures can be fiercely frigid in the area, so Ste. Chapelle probably will find itself purchasing grapes frequently from growers in other areas to maintain production levels while its own vines undergo recovery periods. The goal is to raise production eventually to 100,000 cases a year, most of which will be white varietals. Ste. Chapelle's Chardonnays and Rieslings are of especially fine quality and have received accolades from connoisseurs.

☆/☆☆☆

$$

Sainte-Croix-du-Mont.

On the east bank of the Garonne River directly across from Sauternes south of Bordeaux in southwestern France is a small subdivision of Entre-Deux-Mers called Sainte-Croix-du-Mont. Some decent white dessert wines are produced here in modest quantities, and they can sometimes compete with a good Sauternes or Barsac.

☆/☆☆

$/$$

Sainte-Foy-Bordeaux.

In the large vinicultural region known as Entre-Deux-Mers near Bordeaux in southwestern France is a subdivision entitled to its own *appellation,* Sainte-Foy-Bordeaux. Both red and white wines are produced here, but the best are the whites. These are sweet or semisweet, however, and lack the finesse of the luscious whites produced in Sauternes and Barsac some 20 miles to the west. The principal town of the area is Sainte-Foy-la-Grande.

☆☆

$

STE. MICHELLE
CHATEAU RESERVE

WASHINGTON STATE
CABERNET SAUVIGNON
1976

PRODUCED AND BOTTLED BY CHATEAU STE. MICHELLE ® B.W.#8
WOODINVILLE, WASHINGTON ALCOHOL 12½% BY VOLUME

Ste. Michelle Vineyards.

Many good wines made from European varietal grapes are now produced in the State of Washington, and the largest producer there is Ste. Michelle Vineyards, owned by the United States Tobacco Company. The winery operation was established after the repeal of Prohibition in the mid-1930s, but the first harvest under the Ste. Michelle name did not take place until 1967, with André Tchelistcheff consulting. He has been associated with the operation on a consulting basis ever since, adding to his far-reaching reputation as one of the fathers of modern West Coast viticulture.

Ste. Michelle owns some 2000 acres of Washington vineyards in all, or a substantial percentage of the state's total acreage planted in *Vitis vinifera* vines. Total production runs upward of 300,000 cases a year, which requires Ste. Michelle to purchase 20 to 30 percent of its grape requirements from outside growers. Of the 300,000 cases, about

50,000 cases are generic red, white, and rosé sold in 1.5-litre jugs, mainly within Washington State. The balance are premium varietals—Chardonnay and Fumé Blanc aged in French oak barrels, plus Johannisberg Riesling, Chenin Blanc, Gewürztraminer, Sémillon, Muscat of Alexandria, Grenache Rosé, Cabernet Sauvignon, and Merlot. A small quantity of sparkling Pinot Noir Blanc also is made. The Chardonnay is Ste. Michelle's best known wine among connoisseurs—a complex wine that sometimes challenges the best of California. But all of the Ste. Michelle wines are well made, demonstrating that California is not the only state producing fine table wines.

☆/☆☆☆☆

$/$$

Sake.

Sake is Japanese rice wine, made from fermented rice. The Japanese usually serve it warm in porcelain cups. The cups are tiny and are often refilled, making it difficult to keep track of how much is being consumed. Sake runs as high as 16 percent alcohol, however, which means that keeping track of consumption is important. Several California facilities have been established by Japanese interests to produce the potion for the American market. (*See* Numano Sake Company, Ozeki San Benito.)

☆

$

Sakonnet Vineyards.

Sakonnet, founded in 1975 by Jim and Lolly Mitchell, is the first commercial vineyard and winery to be established in Rhode Island since Prohibition. Besides French-American hybrids, the Mitchells are cultivating Chardonnay, Johannisberg Riesling, and Pinot Noir on their 40 acres of vineyards near the seaside town of Little Compton. Production has climbed to about 10,000

cases a year, and the product array has included a botrytised Vidal Reserve, a crisp Seyval Blanc, and Delaware and Aurora among local varieties. Sakonnet also makes several branded blends, including America's Cup White, Rhode Island Red, and Light House Red.
☆/☆☆
$/$$

Château de Sales.

Only one estate in the Pomerol District east of the city of Bordeaux challenges the big châteaus of the Médoc in terms of the quantity of production, and that one is Château de Sales, which in a copious vintage is capable of producing 20,000 cases of full-bodied, earthy red wine. Consequently de Sales is fairly widely available in the United States and has provided an introduction to Pomerol for many American wine lovers. Because de Sales lies in the northwestern corner of the district, rather distant from such great estates as Châteaux Pétrus and Vieux-Certan, it is not as highly regarded on a quality basis. But some excellent wines of great depth and intensity are made at Château de Sales, and they deserve to be taken seriously. They are best drunk between ages ten and 15. The entire production is purchased and marketed by Jean Pierre Moueix, the Libourne shipper and Pomerol estate-owner, who owns 50 percent of Château Pétrus and all of Château Trotanoy.
☆☆☆☆
$$/$$$

Sancerre.

In the eastern part of the Loire Valley of France after it has curved toward the south from Orléans lie two important wine-growing villages, Sancerre and Pouilly-sur-Loire. Pouilly Fumé from the eastern bank of the river is perhaps slightly better known than Sancerre from the western bank, but the two are quite similar with their smoky taste that can be a bit overwhelming in poor vintages. In good vintages, Sancerre can be soft and mellow and is a perfect accompaniment to shellfish and other seafood, although purists might prefer a Chablis Grand Cru. Sancerre gets its smoky flavor and "gun-flint" bouquet from the Sauvignon grape and from the limestone soil where the vines are nurtured. It needs a couple of years of bottle-age to soften, but it is not a wine for laying down. (*See also* Pouilly Fumé.)
☆/☆☆
$$

Sanford & Benedict Vineyards.

Mike Benedict, a former research botanist with the University of California at Santa Barbara, is proving that the southern part of the state can produce good wines. He purchased 700 acres of land in 1972 and planted 113 of these in Pinot Noir, Cabernet Sauvignon, Merlot, Chardonnay, and White Riesling. The winery was built in 1976 at Lompoc, in Santa Barbara County, and the first vintage for Sanford & Benedict was the same year. Benedict's original partner, J. Richard Sanford, dropped out in 1980, and now Benedict is the sole proprietor. Production totals 8000 to 10,000 cases a year, and the quality of the varietals, especially the Chardonnay and the Pinot Noir, has been high. The Chardonnay is fermented in French oak barrels, and the red wines are fermented in wooden tanks ranging in size from 1100 to 1400 gallons. The winery has sufficient vineyard acreage to produce only estate-bottled wines.
☆/☆☆☆
$$

Sangiovese.

The principal grape of the Chianti wine produced in Tuscany is the Sangiovese.

According to a formula developed by Baron Bettino Ricasoli in the mid-1800s, the best Chianti is vinified from 50 to 80 percent Sangiovese, 10 to 30 percent Cannaiolo and 10 to 30 percent Trebbiano or Malvasia. This is one of the superior grapes of Italy. (*See* Chianti.)

Sangría.

For years the Spanish have been mixing their red wines with the juices of sweet Andalusian oranges and lemons to make Sangría, a pleasant drink for a hot summer's day. Bottled Sangría from several producers has become popular in the American market, but making your own mixture is a relatively simple matter. Almost any inexpensive red wine can be used. Simply pour it into a large pitcher, add small amounts of fresh lemon and orange juice and garnish with fruit slices. Some mixers add a quantity of brandy, which can produce devastating results if the drinkers aren't warned of its presence. Sangría should always be served well chilled or else on the rocks. It can be made with white wine as well as red, or a mixture of the two. Some people refrigerate their leftover wines and save them for this purpose.

☆

$

San Martin Winery.

San Martin is a major producer of premium varietals as well as jug-style wines, with facilities in San Martin in California's Santa Clara County. San Martin was established in 1906 as a cooperative owned by grape growers who provided the grapes for the San Martin wines until Prohibition. The Felice family bought San Martin in 1932 and expanded the vineyard holdings in the post-Prohibition era. The winery went through another ownership change in 1973 when it was bought by the Southdown Corporation of Houston. Somerset Wine Company bought the business in 1977, but the vineyards have been sold off and the winery now purchases all of its grapes from outside growers. Under the direction of Ed Friedrich, a native of Trier, Germany, who has since left the company, the San Martin operation was modernized and expanded. It produces some 340,000 cases a year, including about 180,000 cases of premium varietals. The rest consists of vintage-dated jug-style wines. San Martin has attracted considerable attention with its superpremium line of wines that bear special labels with the "select vintage" designation. These initially included a Cabernet Sauvignon 1977 from San Luis Obispo County as well as a Chardonnay 1979 from Santa Barbara County. They were vinified with special care and displayed good quality. The San Martin product lineup includes such other premium varietals as Chenin Blanc, Fumé Blanc, Johannisberg Riesling, and a Zinfandel made from Amador County grapes. San Martin also pioneered with low-alcohol wines when it released its so-called "soft" line of varietals ranging from 7 to 9 percent in alcoholic content.

☆/☆☆☆

$/$$

Santa Chiara.

Santa Chiara is a reliable red wine produced in Italy's Piedmont region. It is made from the Nebbiolo grape that is responsible for Barolo, Barbaresco, and Gattinara, among others, that have made the Piedmont famous for its red wines. Santa Chiara lacks D.O.C. status under the Italian wine law because it is a branded wine without specific geographical origins, although it is made by Mario Antoniolo, a major Gattinara producer.

☆☆/☆☆☆

$

Santa Clara-Santa Cruz-San Benito.

As in neighboring Livermore, wine-makers in the Central Coast counties of the Santa Clara and Santa Cruz Valleys, south of San Francisco, are finding themselves crowded out by population explosion and urban sprawl. This area, however, is one of the oldest and best-known California wine districts with three of California's leading quality producers headquartered there—Paul Masson at Saratoga, Mirassou at San Jose, and Almadén at Los Gatos. Each has established important and extensive vineyards farther south in San Benito County where virus-resistant vines such as Chardonnay, Pinot Noir, Cabernet, Johannisberg Riesling, and Gewürz-traminer are growing on their own rootstocks. The wines from these vineyards have been of excellent quality so far and, as predicted by the experts at the University of California at Davis, San Benito will be a district to reckon with in the future.

There are a number of other wineries in the Santa Clara Valley, but most of them are small and not well known outside California. Two of the best are Ridge and David Bruce, both producing wines that are greatly sought after by connoisseurs, and deservedly so. The Novitiate of Los Gatos is run by a group of Jesuit fathers and novices, specializing in altar wines but also producing wines for the public.

Santenay.

The southernmost of the best wine-producing *communes* of the Côte de Beaune in the heart of the Burgundy country of France is Santenay, where excellent red Burgundies of flowery bouquet and great charm are produced. Several other communities just to the south of Santenay, e.g., Sampigny, Cheilly, and Dezize, also produce good wines, but Santenay is the first *commune* of importance heading north toward the ancient city of Beaune. Its wines are not as robust and full-bodied as those from Pommard only a few miles to the north, but they display classic Burgundian characteristics when properly made. The *commune* has no *grands crus,* and some of its production is blended and sold as Côte de Beaune-Villages. The seven *premiers crus* of Santenay that are widely recognized are:

Beauregard
Beaurepaire
Clos des Tavannes
Comme
Gravières
Maladière
Passe Temps

These wines are identified with the word "Santenay" first, followed by the vineyard name—for example, Santenay-Les Gravières. Wines produced on vineyard areas anywhere in the *commune* are called simply Santenay.
☆☆☆/☆☆☆☆☆
$$/$$$

Sarah's Vineyard.

Sarah's Vineyard is a tiny producer of excellent Chardonnay and Cabernet Sauvignon in the Hecker Pass area of Santa Clara County, California. Marilyn and John Otteman, the proprietors, have planted a small amount of Chardonnay, but the early bottlings of Sarah's Vineyard were from purchased grapes. The wines have varietal intensity and tend to be expensive, reflecting the small production and growing recognition. By 1981 production had not yet surpassed 1800 cases a year, but the wines were available in selected stores and restaurants in 12 states, including New York.
☆☆/☆☆☆☆☆
$$

Sassella.

One of the best wines of Lombardy in northern Italy is Sassella, which lies in the region's mountainous Valtellina District. Sassella is made mostly from the Nebbiolo grape, which is the superior red grape of the Piedmont as well. It is a robust, earthy wine that reaches a velvety softness after perhaps five years of aging. It is considered the most balanced of the four top Valtellina wines: Grumello, Inferno, and Valgella as well as Sassella.

☆☆/☆☆☆
$/$$

Sassicaia.

Sassicaia is a brand of red wine made entirely from Cabernet Sauvignon grapes in Tuscany, the region of Italy best known for Chianti, which is dominated by another grape variety, the Sangiovese. The property is owned by the heirs of the late Marchese Mario Incisa della Rochetta and lies at Bolghieri. The wines are bottled at the Antinori cellars, and Piero and Lodovico Antinori, Incisa's nephews, have been responsible for much of the marketing of Sassicaia. The 1972 vintage swept the field in a widely publicized Cabernet tasting in London sponsored by *Decanter Magazine* in 1978. Because it is a brand of wine without a geographical designation, it lacks recognition under the D.O.C. law of Italy, but Sassicaia has won ample public recognition on its own.

☆☆☆/☆☆☆☆☆
$$

Saumur.

One of the major wine-producing areas of the Loire Valley in France is Saumur, lying in the province of Anjou, which is famed for its rosés. Reds, whites, and rosés are all made under the Saumur name, and some are quite pleasant, although the whites, made from the Chenin Blanc grape, are somewhat earthy in taste. The reds and rosés are made from the Cabernet Franc, which is also cultivated extensively in Saint-Emilion. The reds are best drunk within three to five years of the vintage, although they can last longer. They can be served slightly chilled or at room temperature. Sometimes the name of one of the villages of Saumur is appended on labels, as in Saumur-Champigny. The area also produces a considerable volume of sparkling wine that can be very pleasant, if not as fine as true Champagne. (*See also* Loire Valley.)

☆/☆☆
$/$$

Sauternes and Barsac.

Once upon a time, before dryness in beverage tastes became the paramount requisite for a successful marketing program, Sauternes reigned as a king among the world's great wines. This was in the bygone days when the public judged a wine strictly on its merits, instead of in response to the publicity machines of the big import-export houses which seem to have convinced much of the drinking world that anything sweet is cheap and inferior. The trend reached its nadir a few years ago in the abortive effort to swamp the public in "white whiskey." Sauternes is sweet, but it is neither cheap nor inferior. When it is properly made in and around the area of southern Bordeaux in France that is entitled to the Sauternes name, it is a truly majestic wine that pleases unprejudiced palates and astonishes open-minded tasters who sample its richness for the first time.

Sauternes and the wines from nearby Barsac that are sometimes called Sauternes are big and luscious, with an intense, rich texture, flowery bouquet, and elegance matched only by the rare Trockenbeerenauslese of Germany. They are meant to be drunk as aperitifs or with fresh *foie gras* (not *pâté de foie gras*), or with such desserts as ripe fruit, creamy cheesecake, or even sharp cheeses. Like sweet German wines, they are best not served with the main courses of a meal, though some Sauternes-lovers are known to serve the wine from drier vintages with certain full-flavored fish courses. It is a wine that stands on its own and that needs no apologies for its sweetness, which is achieved only at great expense and difficulty.

Unfortunately, Sauternes is also a widely imitated wine, in name at least, if not in style or character. Like Champagne, which really should come only from the Champagne District of France, Sauternes should come only from in and near the geographical area in France that is designated Sauternes. But the name is used just as widely as Champagne in other parts of the world. Most often, a Sauternes produced elsewhere will be an artificially sweetened wine made by the least expensive method possible and marketed in cut-rate stores whose clientele's main objective is high alcoholic content at minimal cost. The only resemblance to true Sauternes will be that it is vaguely white and that it is wet. Sometimes even the name is changed, so that the final "s" is dropped to avoid confusing people who are unaware that the French word has an "s" on the end of the singular form. Whenever you see the word "Sauterne" on a label or a wine list, it is time to start wondering about the product. You may rarely encounter a "Sauterne" of non-French origin that turns out to be a fairly well-made wine, but it is a shame that it cannot be given a name of its own.

The unusual process by which Sauternes is produced is one of the most expensive and time-consuming in France. It can be employed only in years when the weather has been favorable, enabling the Sémillon and Sauvignon grapes grown in the area to reach a high degree of ripeness and then to contract *pourriture noble,* or the noble rot, a mold or fungus that also goes by its Latin name, *Botrytis cinerea.* This ugly mold forms on the skins of the grapes during the late autumn and penetrates without noticeably breaking the surface, enabling the water inside to evaporate. The grapes slowly shrivel almost into raisins and the juice that is left behind is extremely concentrated—almost like nectar in its intensity. At the same time, the mold seems to impart a special taste to the juice, a taste that is pleasant and readily identifiable in other sweet wines as well, including the better German wines and the Tokay of Hungary. The high degree of sweetness comes from the concentration of the natural sugar in each grape, not from any artificial means employed later in the production process.

The mold does not attack every grape or even every bunch at the same time, of course, so each vineyard must be harvested perhaps six or eight times each autumn. The ripest grapes with the ugliest appearance are culled individually, and the process continues until very late in the year. The *vignerons* must exercise great skill and an extraordinary sense of timing. Even then, they are at the mercy of the elements, for as the autumn wears on the chance of storm increases, and a major portion of a crop can be wiped out just as the noble rot is bringing the grapes to the perfect state. But when all conditions are right, the wine that results is rich and golden, with a thick texture that makes it seem to flow more slowly when it is poured and leave "sheets" and "legs" running slowly down the sides of a glass when the luscious wine is swirled around inside.

Sauternes is one of the few white wines that benefits from bottle-age. Its natural sugar content tends to act as a preservative, as does the relatively high level of alcohol attained in good vintages. A Sauternes that reaches 16 or 17 percent alcohol is not unusual. As it ages, the wine darkens and slowly reaches the color of caramel, but the fruit in the bouquet and taste seems to remain, displaying an elegant balance after ten or 15 years of proper storage. Today, the 1955 vintage is drinking nicely and older ones, if you can find them, are still showing well. The fantastic 1921, regarded by many connoisseurs as the vintage of the century, was still alive and well in 1973. Sauternes vintages, of course, are not necessarily the same in terms of quality as other Bordeaux vintages, because the weather can be quite different some 35 miles south of the Médoc. During the 1960s, for example, good Sauternes were produced in 1961, 1962, 1967, and 1969, and the best years are generally agreed to have been the 1962 and the 1967. In the Médoc, however, excellent wines were also produced in 1966 and 1964, while 1967 was good but not great. The temptation is to assume that Sauternes vintages are the same and, with this in mind, some restaurateurs will display 1964s and '66s on their wine lists at prices just as high as those of the '62s and '67s. In the lesser vintages, some very decent Sauternes is made, but it will lack the finesse and richness of the best years.

Like the Médoc, the Sauternes District was classified in connection with the Paris Exposition of 1855. This ranking system was based on earlier systems as well as on the prices fetched for the wines of each château at that time. Obviously, quality levels from château to château will vary over a century and a quarter, but the 1855 classification has held up fairly well, perhaps partly because it is self-fulfilling: wines ranked higher tend to obtain better prices, enabling the château owner to invest more in his vineyards. In any event, few experts would argue that Château d'Yquem, ranked above the others in a class by itself in 1855, is not today the reigning monarch of the district. All of the attributes of great Sauternes were to come together in this 220-acre vineyard, and Count Alexandre de Lur-Saluces, the proprietor, insists on maintaining the same high standards practiced by his family at Yquem for well over a century. It is always the most expensive Sauternes, reflecting its worldwide reputation, and sometimes a few of the lesser growths will represent better value because of their lower prices.

The best way to taste Château d'Yquem—albeit a way that most wine lovers will not have an opportunity to experience—is at the lovely château itself on its extraordinarily valuable hilltop in the center of the Sauternes District. Count Lur-Saluces has been known to conduct impromptu browsing, through his *chais,* pulling a sample from this cask or that, or uncorking an occasional bottle of an older vintage for a visitor. The château has been the scene of festivities in the annual Bordeaux music festival, and the author recalls one very special evening there in the spring of 1973, when hors d'oeuvres of seemingly unlimited variety were served at midnight following a musical presentation attended by several hundred Bordelais and their guests in the courtyard. Yquem of the 1966 vintage, not quite as sweet as the '67 or the '62, was poured unstintingly for hours and hundreds of bottles were served. For variety, one could also choose an ice-cold Pommery et Greno Champagne, but the extraordinary aspect of the evening was that Yquem itself could be drunk without restriction. The music, the soft spring air, the spotlit château and the elegantly attired Bordeaux nobility produced a memorable Old-World, prerecession atmosphere that could not be duplicated anywhere. The '66 vintage seemed perfect—just light enough to savor, yet displaying the classic Yquem traits to perfection. Older vintages of this splendid wine, of course, can provide outstanding taste experiences, and it is no wonder that they obtain very high prices at the wine auctions at Sotheby & Co. and Christie's in London. It is said of the Yquem 1921 that you can place a glassful under the nose of a dead man, and he will revive immediately with a smile on his face, drink down the luscious nectar and then lapse into an eternal sleep filled with dreams of all that is pleasant. Château d'Yquem also produces a drier wine called Château Y but it does not compare with the elegantly sweet Yquem itself.

Ranked just beneath Yquem in the classification of 1855 are eleven other growths that sometimes challenge the *premier grand cru.* Among those that are not difficult to find in export markets are the Château La Tour Blanche, owned by the French government since 1907 and the site of an important viticultural college, Château de Suduiraut, Château de Rayne-Vigneau, Château Coutet, Château Climens, Château Guiraud, and Château Rieussec. These are First Growths, or *premiers crus,* and another dozen *seconds crus* follow these, the best known being Châteaux Doisy-Daëne, Doisy-Védrines, and Filhot. The Sauternes District has five different *communes:* Bommes, Preignac, and Fargues, as well as Sauternes itself and Barsac, which can call its wines either Sauternes or Barsac. The principal grape is the Sémillon, but most wines from the area also have quantities of Sauvignon and a bit of Muscadelle blended in. Because of the complex harvesting process, the grapes picked later are usually better and the production from any one château will vary somewhat in each vintage. Wines that do not measure up to the highest quality standards are sold off to the Bordeaux wine trade and are bottled simply as Sauternes without the château name.

Between the classified growths and the regional Sauternes are a number of other châteaux that sometimes produce excellent wines at very reasonable prices. But they do not find their ways readily into the export markets because the prices for the classified châteaux tend to be so low (Yquem excepted, of course) that little room is left for the unclassified châteaux to be exported profitably. Now and then, however, one can be found. The Château du Pick 1962, from Preignac, was sold in the United States for about two dollars a bottle and was largely responsible for turning the author into a Sauternes lover. The sharp-eyed bargain hunter should be alert for these lesser known wines from good vintages.

THE SAUTERNES CLASSIFICATION OF 1855

Premier Grand Cru:
Château d'Yquem

Premiers Crus:
Château La Tour Blanche
Château Lafaurie-Peyraguey
Clos Haut-Peyraguey
Château de Rayne-Vigneau
Château de Suduiraut
Château Coutet
Château Climens
Château Guiraud
Château Rieussec
Château Rabaud-Promis
Château Sigalas-Rabaud

Seconds Crus:
Château Myrat
Château Doisy-Daëne
Château Doisy-Dubroca
Château Doisy-Védrines
Château d'Arche
Château Filhot
Château Broustet

Château Nairac
Château Caillou
Château Suau
Château de Malle
Château Romer
Château Lamothe
(*See also* Château d'Yquem.)
☆☆/☆☆☆☆
$$/$$$$

Savigny-les-Beaune.

Due north of the Burgundian wine capital of Beaune lies the *commune* of Savigny, which has added Beaune to its name. Although the wines of Savigny are held not to be the equals of the better wines of the famous Côte de Beaune, they are often quite good and can represent excellent value in favorable vintages. Because Savigny is one of the northernmost *communes* before the Côte de Beaune stops and the Côte de Nuits begins, its wines sometimes are sturdy and robust, although lacking the finesse of the better red Burgundies. Part of the Vergelesses vineyard usually associated with Pernand lies in Savigny, and part of the Marconnets vineyard associated with Beaune also extends into this *commune*. Savigny-Vergelesses and Savigny-Marconnets are very good *premiers crus* vineyards whose quality belies the reputation of Savigny wines for lightness and lack of character. Les Lavières is another Savigny *premier cru* sometimes found on foreign markets, and two other *premiers,* Jarrons and Dominode, exist there, but much of the production is blended to be sold as Côte de Beaune-Villages. A good Savigny will be at its best after six to eight years of age, although some last much longer without fading. (*See also* Côte de Beaune.)
☆☆☆/☆☆☆☆☆
$$/$$$

Scharffenberger Cellars.

Scharffenberger Cellars, founded in 1981, specializes in sparkling wines made in Mendocino County, California. The first wines, made using the Champagne method, were not to be released until late 1983 or 1984. Production has already risen past 15,000 cases annually, and the wines are expected to be high in quality when they reach the market.
☆☆
$$

Scharzhofberger.

This is one of the few wines of the Mosel-Saar-Ruwer region of Germany that traditionally did not bear the name of the village, Wiltingen, where it was produced. The fame of Scharzhofberger was so great and its quality in good years so high that it stood on its own. It is clearly one of the best wines of the Saar River, although it has the shortcoming of all other Saar wines—in poor years the quality level drops well below that of the Mosels. Still, in the best vintages it can compete with the elegant Bernkastelers, Wehleners, and Piesporters of the central Mosel. Its taste tends to be slightly steely, in some ways like a Chablis from France, but this steeliness turns into a hardness that is not to everyone's liking in poor vintages, which seem to occur more often in the Saar Valley because the weather conditions there are not quite so favorable as in the central Mosel. Scharzhofberger should not be confused with Scharzberger, which is another wine produced in neighboring Saar vineyards and which sometimes appears without the name of the town Wiltingen. Dom Scharzhofberger is the name given to the Scharzhofberger wine produced by the Cathedral of Trier. The best-known producer is Egon Müller, owner of the old manor house, or Scharzhof, which is responsible for the name of the wine. Under the German wine law of 1971, Scharzberger became a sort of generic name for Saar wines and can be used with the production of a number of Saar villages. Scharzhofberger, on the other hand, retained its individuality, although since 1971 it has been used with the name of the town, Wiltingen. (*See also* Saar, Wiltingen.)

☆/☆☆☆

$$

Schramsberg.

In the hillside at the northern end of California's Napa Valley near the town of Calistoga are cool storage cellars carved out of the earth by Jacob Schramm's Chinese laborers 100 years ago. Once they provided storage for red and white table wines, highly acclaimed both here and in Europe. Robert Louis Stevenson, visiting the Schramm family with his new bride in 1880, also praised them in *Silverado Squatters,* set in the Napa Valley. Today thousands of bottles of Champagne repose in the cool recesses where rough walls are gray with age and damp to touch. Jack Davies, a West Coast businessman, bought and restored the winery, which had been closed down half a century after Schramm's death in 1905, with only brief and unsuccessful attempts at revival. Davies' aim was to create wines of unique excellence and he set about his task with singleminded purpose.

Champagne is the only wine made at Schramsberg. As a medium-sized operation—about 50,000 cases produced annually—Davies feels the best role is to specialize, "to find something you can do well and then try to get as good at it as you can."

Every operation at Schramsberg is modeled faithfully after the traditional method for making Champagne in Reims and Epernay (*see* Champagne), beginning with the use of the same grape varieties—Pinot Noir, Pinot Chardonnay, and Pinot Blanc, grown on hillsides that Davies feels are particularly suited to these varieties because of the cooler climate and elevation. Schramsberg now

owns about 40 acres of vineyards. The new lots of wine are blended by Davies himself, then bottled and set aside to await second fermentation and the subsequent series of steps that create the costly and distinctive effervescence that results.

During a walk through the winery one hears the thumping rhythm of *rémuage,* the quarter-turn of the bottles, neck-down in riddling racks, that shakes the yeast sediment down on top of the temporary cork before disgorgement and *dosage.* It is an expensive process and one that takes time; neither is slighted at Schramsberg and the superb crisp wines attest to it. Several sparkling wines are made: a dry Blanc de Blancs, made mostly from Chardonnay and a lesser amount of Pinot Blanc; a Blanc de Noirs, the most like traditional Champagne, made from the free-run juice of Pinot Noir pressed apart from the skins, with Chardonnay added in the blend; Cuvée de Pinot, a blend of free-run Napa Gamay and Pinot Noir, left just long enough with the grape skins to pick up a delicate salmon color; and Cremant, a *demi-sec* dessert Champagne. A Blanc de Blancs Reserve Cuvée, made from a selected portion of the vintage and aged longer with the yeasts to develop character, is available in limited quantities.

☆☆

$$$

Sebastiani.

When Samuele Sebastiani came over from Italy in 1893 his first job was hauling cobblestones out of Sonoma to pave the streets of San Francisco. Sebastiani's real trade, however, was winemaking. Raised in the Tuscan hills of Italy where he learned from his father how to tend vines and make wines, Sebastiani started making wine at Sonoma as soon as he could afford a grape crusher and a 500-gallon cask. Shortly after the turn of the century he acquired his first vineyard on land originally planted in 1825 when the Franciscan fathers established the Sonoma Mission of San Francisco de Solano. Today the Sebastiani winery is still a family operation. But the mantle of responsibility for the Sebastiani affairs has now passed to Sam J. Sebastiani, grandson of Samuele and son of the late August Sebastiani, who became a familiar figure to generations of Sebastiani devotees with the bibbed overalls that he habitually wore and the down-to-earth attitude that he espoused. When he died in 1980, it was widely assumed that the business would be sold, for many large companies had already made tempting offers for it. But the speculation has proven wrong, for young Sam has taken over with a strong hand and in general has been upgrading the quality of the Sebastiani line. The upgrading process has been costly in terms of sales, and the company has lost market share in recent years as Sam has tried to reposition some of his brands. It is his signature that is now above the "Proprietor's Reserve" notation on the labels, and the wines have been improving, although they were always high in quality.

The Sebastiani winery is located right in the town of Sonoma. The original crusher and cask that Samuele first used are still there for visitors to see as they tour the winery. It is a colorful place to visit, with its huge redwood vats, two of them holding 60,000 gallons, dark brown with age and trimmed with red hoops. Many of the oak casks depict scenes of the Franciscan fathers making wine at Sonoma mission, hand-carved by Earle Brown, a retired sign-maker who revived the art of carving wine casks begun centuries ago in European cellars. Back of the old winery is a new fermentation cellar with stainless steel tanks to handle temperature-controlled fermentation and for storing wines that have spent their prescribed time in oak but are not yet ready for bottling.

The wine that first brought attention to Sebastiani was Barbera and it still is considered one of their best, robust and hearty, fruitier and deeper-flavored than the Italian version. It also keeps well, though it does not improve in bottle. Sebastiani reds are generally bold and vigorous, earthy wines like the Zinfandel and Gamay Beaujolais. The nonvintage Cabernet Sauvignon (in fifths) is especially attractive and the Mountain Burgundy, a blend of Zinfandel and Petite Sirah, makes pleasant drinking at a good price. Sebastiani is best known for and perhaps more successful with its red wines, although the Green Hungarian, a semi-dry white, is popular. The Chardonnay is fruity, well-balanced, very lightly oaked, as is generally the case with Sebastiani wines. A limited amount of the new Gamay Beaujolais is bottled immediately after fermentation each fall and released as Nouveau Beaujolais.

Total sales of Sebastiani wines, including the "Mountain" wines that have been among the most popular in the jug category, has fallen from a peak of 4.2 million cases a year to about 2.7 million in 1983. Sebastiani wines are available throughout the American market and are sold in two dozen foreign countries.

☆/☆☆☆

$/$$

Sekt.

Immense quantities of sparkling wine are produced and consumed by the Germans—so much, in fact, that the majority of the basic wine used to produce it must be imported. The rest comes from Germany's secondary vineyards as well as from some of the better vineyards in poor years. It is generally called Sekt and tastes more like California "Champagne" than French Champagne. Part of its popularity no doubt derives from its relatively low cost, which not only reflects highly efficient German productivity but also the much lower tax imposed there on sparkling wines. A fairly large percentage of the white wine imported for Sekt comes from France's Charente District, where the same wines are used to produce Cognac and other brandies. To be called Sekt, the wine must have nine months' storage in bottle during the second fermentation in a process similar to the *méthode champenoise* used in the Champagne District of France. If the wine is produced using the bulk process, in which the second fermentation does not occur in the bottle, it is called Schaumwein.

Some of the better German sparkling wines are entitled to more specific place names if 85 percent of the grapes come from the named area—for example, Sparkling Mosel or Rheingau Sekt. Red versions are also made and they taste something like Sparkling Burgundies. The production lines at the big German sparkling wine firms are extremely efficient, producing well made wines whose only fault is that superior grapes are usually not used in them. It is no coincidence that the same technology is used in Champagne, where a number of the leading French firms have German origins and some have German-sounding names: Heidsieck, Mumm, Roederer, Taittinger. Sparkling Liebfraumilch from Germany—actually Sekt with a brand name—has achieved some popularity in the United States in recent years, partly because it is less costly than Champagne and partly because it benefits from the American familiarity with the Liebfraumilch name. Sometimes it is superior to the cheaper American "Champagnes."

☆/☆☆

$$

Seyssel.

One of the sparkling wines of France that comes from outside the Champagne District is Seyssel, from the Haute-Savoie, southwest of Geneva. It is a white that lacks great character but that can be very pleasant and inexpensive. Not much is exported.

☆/☆☆

$

Shafer Vineyards.

John and Elizabeth Shafer and their four children are partners in Shafer Vineyards, established in 1972 when the family purchased an old vineyard in the Stag's Leap area of the Napa Valley of California. They spent seven years clearing and replanting the property and now have 40 acres in bearing and 17 more are being planted. The first vintage under the Shafer label was the 1978 Cabernet Sauvignon, which was crushed at Round Hill Vineyards. The 1979 Shafer vintage, consisting of Cabernet Sauvignon and Zinfandel, was crushed at Rutherford Hill. Shafer's own winery on the Silverado Trail in Napa was completed in time for the 1980 crush. Initially, most of the Shafer grapes were purchased from other growers, but the percentage has declined to a minority as their own vineyards have come into bearing. Production totals about 12,000 cases of Cabernet Sauvignon, Zinfandel, and Chardonnay. The wines are well made.

☆/☆☆☆

$$

Charles F. Shaw Vineyard and Winery.

Some of the best Beaujolais-style wines made in California come out of the winery of Chuck and Lucy Shaw in St. Helena on the west bank of the Napa River, where they grow Napa Gamay grapes, the same grapes that are used to produce the fruity wines of Beaujolais in France. Shaw, a former international banker based in Paris, uses carbonic maceraction, the time-honored Beaujolais method of winemaking. Under this method, the grapes are dumped into fermenting tanks with the clusters intact, and the fermentation is allowed to proceed spontaneously. The carbon dioxide gas given off as a natural by-product of fermentation blankets the grapes in the tank, forcing out the oxygen and forestalling oxidation. The result is freshness, with a soft and spicy flavor.

Shaw grows his grapes mostly in the vineyard adjacent to his winery and also purchases grapes from a few vineyards on Spring Mountain and Pritchard Hill. Shaw also makes small amounts of Chardonnay, Fumé Blanc, and Zinfandel. His first vineyard purchase, on Howell Mountain east of St. Helena, took place in 1974 while he and his wife were still in Paris. In 1978 they bought another vineyard north of St. Helena that was planted in Napa Gamay and some Zinfandel. The Shaws moved to St. Helena in 1978 and finished the restoration and expansion of a turn-of-the-century farmhouse amid their vines and built a new winery nearby. Production totals about 15,000 cases a year. The Shaw Napa Gamay wines benefit from two to three years of bottle-age at most, but they are not meant to be drunk within the first year of production as are many true Beaujolais from France.
☆
$$

Shenandoah Vineyards.

Lee and Shirley Sobon, coproprietors of Shenandoah Vineyards, made wine in their basement in Los Altos while Lee was an engineer working for Lockheed and Hewlett-Packard. Lee developed a serious interest in wine in the early 1970s,

and the family moved to Amador County, which was beginning to develop a reputation for its fully flavored and robust Zinfandels. They bought their land and established Shenandoah Vineyards near the town of Plymouth in 1977, making their first wines from purchased grapes provided by other Amador growers. Now production totals about 7000 cases a year, mostly of Zinfandel but also of Cabernet Sauvignon, Chenin Blanc, and Black Muscat. The Chenin Blanc is purchased from El Dorado County, just north of Amador. Shenandoah Vineyards also produces a Port from Zinfandel grapes and a Cream Sherry. The Sobons have been planting vines on their property, but still buy the majority of their grapes.
☆/☆☆☆☆
$$

Sherry.

The drive south from Seville to Jerez de la Frontera in the south of Spain is not long, perhaps 50 miles, but the heat intensifies all along the way until you approach the capital of the Sherry country, where an occasional breeze washes in from the sea to provide relief. This is Andalusia, a sleepy land of vines that yield some of the world's finest fortified wines. It is the home of Sherry and, no matter that similar wines borrowing the Sherry name are made in California, Cyprus, South Africa, and elsewhere, the only real Sherry comes from this part of Spain. The soil is chalky, as it is in the French Champagne District, and it provides the nutrients for the Palomino and Pedro Ximénez grapes that thrive in the hot climate. The hills where the grapes grow are rolling and gently rounded, stretching out mile after mile and catching the direct sun at varying times of the day. Little vegetation taller than the vines grows here, and other agricultural crops are not much in evidence. Here and there a *bodega* with tiled roof and whitewashed walls rises among the vines, but you have the feeling that the grape is everything and that life in this part of Spain would not continue without it. The grape and the vine seem immune to change, and it is probable that the lay of the land and the vines were little different when viniculture was first practiced here a thousand years before the birth of Christ.

The name "Sherry" is a bastardized form of the name of the town, Jerez, deriving from the Spanish pronunciation of *J* as *H* and reflecting the evolution of the town's name through various occupations: "Ceret" under the Romans, "Shera" under the Greeks, "Seret" under the Visigoths, and "Scherich" under the Arabs. It is called Jerez de la Frontera because it was on the frontier between the warring Moslem and Christian worlds until late in the thirteenth century.

Nowadays the names of the big Sherry-producing companies are painted in huge letters on the sides of the *bodegas:* Domecq, Duff Gordon, Gonzalez Byass, Terry, Garvey, Sandeman, etc. Although the names are different, there has been intermarriage over the years among the Sherry families and rare indeed is the Sherry producer who does not have cousins or in-laws in most of the other firms. The dusty streets, simple cafes, pottery shops, leather-goods stores, motorized bicycles, and sleepy atmosphere seem to mask the fact that Jerez is a town of extraordinary upper-class wealth. The life-style of the Sherry barons, as they are known, is matched for sheer opulence only in the oil sheikdoms of the Middle East.

Not long ago, Henry Ford II happened to be the guest of José Ignacio Domecq, patriarch of the Pedro Domecq empire, and was heard to remark: "I have more money than you, but you have a better way of life." One of the Domecqs later commented: "He was a bit wrong when he talked about himself being richer." The Domecq family business, one of the biggest in Jerez and probably one of the biggest private companies anywhere, is said to bring in upwards of $200 million a year for the family members. Don José and the other patriarchs of Jerez know that they are manning the last bastion of eighteenth-century aristocracy and are proud of their heritage. Yet at the same time they are curiously unpretentious. Don José works in a small, sparsely furnished cubicle adjacent to a laboratory at the huge Domecq plant and used to drive himself around in a ten-year-old American Ford sedan with a stick shift. His home is magnificent, but it is tucked back in an alley and is hard for a stranger to locate. The children learn English from their Irish nannies almost before they know Spanish, and then are educated at the best colleges and universities of England. The Sherry families get their recreation from polo, a sport they dominate in southern Spain, and from such other pastimes as automobile racing and tennis. They breed polo ponies, racehorses and fighting bulls—and manage to produce some very fine wine.

In common with the other leading fortified wines of the world—Port, Madeira and Marsala—Sherry's market was developed by the English, and they still consume the lion's share of the production. Sherry remains *the* aperitif of the British Isles and in many of the outposts of the former British Empire. No British household would be without a bottle when guests are expected on a Sunday afternoon, and no merchant bank in London's financial district would fail to offer Sherry prior to a luncheon meeting. This pleasant wine has never proven as captivating to American drinkers, possibly because there are so many American imitations that fail to measure up to the real thing from Spain.

In Andalusia, however, everybody

drinks it. One of the rare taste combinations of modern civilization is a well-chilled Fino drunk with freshly shelled prawns from the Bay of Cádiz at a roadside cafe in Puerto de Santa Maria, the seaside town just south of Jerez. Chilled dry Sherry, in fact, is good company with nearly all seafood, and it is probable that Americans would agree if only they would learn to chill it. All other Sherries can be taken chilled or on ice, although purists would object to a Cream or Amoroso Sherry at any but room temperature. A glass or two of Sherry taken before a meal is much healthier than a cocktail, moreover, and will not produce a negative reaction with the table wines consumed during the meal.

Considerable confusion exists over the various categories of true Sherry, possibly due to misnaming by imitators in other countries but also because of the proliferation of brand names dreamed up by the producers themselves. Many lovers of Harveys Bristol Cream are surprised to discover that this luscious sweet Sherry actually comes from Spain, where it is produced according to the specifications of John Harvey & Sons of Bristol, England. All true Sherries initially are one of only two types: Fino or Oloroso. Later they may be refined and blended into whatever the producers want, but they have no control over that first stage when the young wine drifts on its own toward the Fino or Oloroso style.

Fino is light and dry, the ideal aperitif. It is created when the *flor*, a floating layer of yeasts, is present on the surface of the wine, extracting any sugar left over from fermentation. The *flor* ("flower" in Spanish) feeds on the young wine and leaves behind a pale golden potion with a slightly woody bouquet and taste. Fino is made entirely from the Palomino grape and is held in the highest regard by the Spanish. It tends to come from vineyards that are older, have more *al-*

bariza (chalk) in the soil and grow closer to the sea. The drier the weather in a particular year, the more Fino will be produced, and also the cooler the autumn weather, the more Fino as well. For local consumption in Spain, it runs about 16 percent alcohol; for export it is at least 18 and sometimes 20 percent.

Manzanilla is a Fino that is produced in Sanlúcar de Barrameda, a dozen miles west of Jerez and directly on the Atlantic Ocean. It is sometimes not categorized as a Sherry. The sea breezes wafting through the *bodegas*, or high-ceilinged warehouses, of Sanlúcar impart a special tang that cannot be imitated in Jerez or the other main Sherry town, Puerto de Santa Maria. Manzanilla does not travel to export markets as dependably as other Sherries.

Palo Cortado is a rare type of Sherry from the Oloroso family. Similar in style to Amontillado, it tends to be lighter and more elegant, although not quite as light as Fino. It is seldom seen outside Spain.

Amontillado starts out as Fino, but then the *flor* mysteriously subsides and stops feeding on the wine. The result is a darker-colored, more complex Sherry with a pronounced nutty taste. In its natural state it is quite dry, but it is usually sweetened for export.

Oloroso is, with Fino, one of the two basic types of Sherry. It is a darker, more full-bodied, richer, and earthier wine in which the *flor* has not developed. It is very dry in its natural state—just as dry as Fino, but the versions seen in foreign markets have usually been sweetened. For example, Amorosos and Cream Sherries are sweetened Olorosos. An Oloroso may be aged ten to fifteen years in butts, or wooden casks, before bottling.

Amoroso is basically a sweetened Oloroso designed for the British market. It is similar to Cream Sherry.

Cream Sherry is a sweetened Oloroso

with a rich brown color and luscious taste. It is best consumed as a dessert wine or after a meal, although many people drink it as an aperitif.

Brown Sherry is another sweetened Oloroso designed for the British market.

The grape used for sweetening Sherries is the Pedro Ximénez, which grows in the lowlands on sandier, less calciferous soil. These are tougher grapes, with a lower yield than the Palomino. After picking they are set out to dry on large asbestos sheets and are protected from rain and dew by sheets of clear plastic laid on top. They turn almost into raisins with highly concentrated juice. If they were allowed to ferment completely, they would produce wines of 14 percent or more alcohol, but the fermentation is stopped at about 12 percent, leaving a substantial amount of sugar in the wine. The fermentation is always halted through the addition of grape brandy to the must; the brandy kills the yeasts that are the agents of fermentation. A pure old Pedro Ximénez Sherry (usually called a P.X.) is very thick and rich, almost like honey. Its extremely dark color and consistency make it look like unrefined petroleum in a glass, yet it can be very pleasant-tasting.

The blending of the various Sherries to create consistency of style is accomplished through the *solera* system, a process widely emulated in other parts of the world. Butts of Sherries of varying ages are arranged in tiers in the *bodegas* of Jerez and the other nearby towns where the wine is produced, and the newer wines are blended over time with older wines in casks lower in the tiers until the desired product is produced. The producers determine by tasting whether a Sherry of a different style should be piped into the *solera* to assure the consistency of the end product. Even

the fresh and young-tasting Finos (e.g., Tio Pepe of Gonzales Byass or La Ina of Domecq) will have aged an average of three to eight years before bottling.

The method of tasting from the big Sherry butts is centuries old, but it is as efficient for experts as it is picturesque. A *venencia*—a test-tubelike silver cup on the end of a flexible three-foot rod—is plunged through the *flor* into the wine and is then extracted. The expert next swings the *venencia* in a swift arc until it hangs somewhere above his head and pours out the Sherry in a narrow, four-feet-long stream that lands unerringly in the glass held in his other hand. Amateurs who try it invariably splatter Sherry on their wrists, sleeves, and trousers.

☆/☆☆☆☆

$/$$

Shown & Sons Vineyards.

The Shown & Sons vineyard in Rutherford in California's Napa Valley was planted in 1971, and some 77 acres are now bearing grapes, enabling all of the enterprise's wines since 1978 to be estate-bottled. The first wine under the Shown label was a Cabernet Sauvignon 1978 that was vinified on borrowed premises, and the Shown winery was completed in 1979. Earlier, Shown sold grapes to other wineries, including Château Montelena, Conn Creek, and Grgich Hills. The property is owned by a family partnership headed by Dick Shown and his wife, Suzanne. Production totals 15,000 to 21,000 cases a year of Cabernet Sauvignon, Johannisberg Riesling, and Chenin Blanc. The Shown vineyards also produce Zinfandel, which will be sold under contract to another winery until the contract expires, after which Shown will add this varietal to its estate-bottled roster.

☆/☆☆☆

$$

Siglo.

Siglo is the brand name of the soft and velvety Rioja wine produced in Spain by AGE Bodegas Unidas, perennially one of the largest exporters of wines from the Rioja region, with a 10 to 15 percent share of the worldwide Rioja market. Siglo is available as a white and as a rosé, but it is the Siglo red that is most popular and that has attracted the attention of consumers in many countries. Besides its soft flavor, one reason for Siglo's success is the burlap sheath that covers each bottle. Consumers who are unable to remember the wine's name at least do not forget its distinctive package. The Siglo red of the 1976 vintage won a gold medal at a Bordeaux wine competition in 1981.

☆/☆☆☆
$/$$

Silver Oak Cellars.

Justin Meyer, formerly of Christian Brothers, and Raymond Duncan of Denver established Silver Oak Cellars in 1972 as a superpremium winery and sideline to their principal enterprise, Franciscan Vineyards. When Franciscan was sold in 1979 to a German company, the two former Franciscan partners retained ownership of Silver Oak, with facilities in Oakville in the Napa Valley. Silver Oak produces only Cabernet Sauvignon, and each vintage is aged in oak casks and is not released for sale until five years after the harvest. The wines are expensive, but they are very well made and display a silky elegance. The Silver Oak Cabernets are what the trade calls "restaurant" wines, meaning that they are fairly mature and do not require extensive additional bottle-aging when released for sale. (Thus restaurants can list them immediately after

they buy them.) Only 14,000 cases a year are produced.

☆☆☆☆
$$$

Silverado Vineyards.

The family of the late Walt Disney found the California wine country irresistible, so they decided to establish a presence in the Napa Valley and set up Silverado Vineyards in 1981 on a knoll on the west side of the Silverado Trail in the southern portion of the valley. The three partners in the venture are Lillian Disney, Walt's widow, and his daughter and son-in-law, Diane and Ronald Miller. They hired Jack Stuart, formerly of Durney Vineyard and Robert Mondavi, to be general manager and winemaker, and his first efforts were wines of substantial character, not bashful or conservative wines that consumers will soon forget. The winery has the most modern, state-of-the-art equipment that money can buy, and it has access to the grapes of the former Retlaw Vineyards and See Vineyards, 300 acres in all, which were purchased by the Disney interests. (About half of that acreage was bearing grapes as of 1982.) In 1981 only about 8000 cases of wine were made, but the total rose to about 18,000 cases in 1982, with a goal of 40,000 cases or more achievable by the mid-1980s. All of the cooperage, including the upright tanks, was manufactured in France, and the first wines of Silverado Cellars have displayed a pronounced flavor of French oak along with the intense fruitiness to be expected from prime vineyards on the floor of the Napa Valley.

☆☆/☆☆☆
$$

Simi Winery.

Simi Winery was founded in 1876 by a pair of Italian brothers, Giuseppe and Pietro Simi, at Healdsburg in northern

SIMI

SINCE 1876

MENDOCINO COUNTY
CHARDONNAY
1980

Alcohol 14% by Vol.

Produced and Bottled by SIMI Winery, Healdsburg, California, U.S.A.

Sonoma Country, California. They were quality producers who made some excellent wines. Nothing attests to that fact more impressively than their 1935 Cabernet Sauvignon, still very much alive when last tried in 1980. During more recent decades the winery declined somewhat, until Russell Green acquired it in order to do something with all the grapes he had planted around his summer home in the Alexander Valley. Once again, good varietals under the Simi label began to appear, notably Cabernet Sauvignon, a particularly rich and pleasing Zinfandel, and Carignane, a variety generally used for fleshing out other reds but here an interesting departure as a varietal. Simi itself produces no grapes and buys from four growers under long-term contracts. The first whites were produced from the 1974 vintage and became immediately recognized for their quality—Johannisberg Riesling, Chenin Blanc, and chablis.

Russ Green and his oenologist, Mary Ann Graf, not only put Simi back on its feet but made it a worthy contender among the best Sonoma has to offer. In recent years the winery has been sold several times, and Zelma Long has re-

placed Mary Ann Graf as winemaker. Michael Dixon bought Simi in 1974, then sold out to Schieffelin & Company, an importer based in New York, in 1976, although Dixon remained as president. When Schieffelin was acquired by Moët-Hennessy of France in 1980, the Champagne and Cognac concern, Moët-Hennessy also took over Simi.

A major expansion project took place in 1980, when the annual capacity of the winery was raised from 95,000 cases to 135,000, half red and half white. A fermenting cellar with 14,000 square feet of capacity was built, and the barrel-aging capacity was raised from 2000 barrels to 6500. New fermenting tanks were installed in varying sizes so that each grower's grapes could be fermented separately to retain varietal integrity. Six premium varietals are produced: Cabernet Sauvignon, Zinfandel, Pinot Noir, Chardonnay, Sauvignon Blanc, Chenin Blanc, and Gewürztraminer. Simi occasionally bottles a Reserve Cabernet of surpassing quality, and its Chardonnay also rises to excellent quality in certain vintages.

☆/☆☆☆☆

$$

Smith and Hook.

Excellent Cabernet Sauvignons, and only these, are produced by Smith and Hook, a small Monterey County winery that opened in 1980. The devotion exclusively to red wine is unusual at a time when the optimum formula for the product mix of a new American wine enterprise would be something like 80 percent white to 20 percent red. But their early efforts were successful, resulting in Cabernets of character and intensity that lacked the herbaceous quality of so many other Monterey wines. Production was about 11,000 cases in the 1981 vintage. The winery is at Gonzales.

☆☆☆/☆☆☆☆☆

$$

Château Smith-Haut-Lafitte.

Both red and white wines are produced on this estate in the *commune* of Martillac, south of Bordeaux in the district of Graves, and the output of red is by far the largest of any of the vineyards ranked as *grands crus* in the Graves classification of 1959. Château Smith-Haut-Lafitte is owned by the Bordeaux firm of Louis Eschenauer, which gives the wine full distribution in the United States and Great Britain. Sommeliers have been known to serve Smith-Haut-Lafitte as Château Lafite-Rothschild. Not only are the names different but the vineyards are entirely different as well and there is no relationship between them. Château Smith-Haut-Lafitte reds are good but generally not on a par with Château Haut-Bailly, Domaine de Chevalier, Château La Mission-Haut-Brion and Château Haut-Brion itself among the leading red Graves. Smith-Haut-Lafitte reaches maturity after eight to ten years of age and is best drunk before age 20.
☆/☆☆☆
$/$$

Smith-Madrone Vineyards.

On Spring Mountain, at an elevation of 1700 feet above sea level, high above St. Helena overlooking California's Napa Valley, is Smith-Madrone Vineyards, which produces modest quantities of good Chardonnay, Johannisberg Riesling, Cabernet Sauvignon, and Pinot Noir. Production totals only about 5000 cases a year, but it is growing. Smith-Madrone, owned and run by Stuart Smith and his wife, Susan, was launched in 1971 with the purchase of 200 acres of what turned out to be a long-abandoned vineyard then overgrown with trees on Spring Mountain. A nineteenth-century wine cave dug 90 feet into the hillside also was unearthed nearby. Planting began in 1972, with the four varietals in about equal amounts, on 20 acres that had been cleared. Plantings have doubled since then. Further clearing and planting is under way, with a goal of 50 acres of vineyard in mind. The winery itself has a sod roof.
☆/☆☆☆
$$

Smothers Wines.

One of the Smothers Brothers, Dick, and his wife, Linda, bought a house in Santa Cruz, California, in 1974, and there was a small vineyard nearby that was owned by Ridge, a well known producer of quality Zinfandels and Cabernet Sauvignons. Ridge decided to sell the vineyard, and Dick Smothers bought it in 1976, thereby leaping into the wine business. He had built a four-car garage adjacent to his house, and he expanded the garage to accommodate a new winery. Now the Smothers wine enterprise was born, and the initial crops from the 11½ acres in Santa Cruz were Chardonnay and Riesling, bottled under the Vine Hill appellation. (The corporate name of the Smothers wine business is Vine Hill Wines Inc.) The first wines under the Smothers label were produced with the 1977 vintage. Since then a Gewürztraminer, a Zinfandel, and a Cabernet Sauvignon have been added to the Chardonnay and White Riesling to round out the product lineup. (A Pinot Noir was produced in 1978, avowedly the first and last for Smothers.)

Meanwhile the other Smothers brother, Tom, had bought property in the Sonoma Valley far to the north of Santa Cruz and had planted vines there. This meant the Smothers Brothers were not only a comedy act but a wine act as well, although the two wine enterprises remained separate. Production of Smothers wines at Santa Cruz remained modest, at 3500 cases a year, but getting it to customers was difficult because of the narrow, twisting driveway leading to the winery, a driveway that trucks could not negotiate. So Dick and Linda Smothers decided to move their winemaking operation to Tom's property in the Sonoma Valley. The move was scheduled for 1983.

About 80 percent of the Smothers wines have been made from purchased grapes, but this percentage is expected to decline under the new arrangement near Glen Ellen in the Sonoma Valley, where the Smothers Brothers expect to practice estate-bottling. Thus a transformation in the Smothers wines is expected once they are made from Sonoma grapes. The Vine Hill Vineyard was expected to be sold, and the Smothers expected to continue to purchase grapes from other growers even after the move, to fill their production needs. Initially the Smothers whites were superior to the reds, but obviously the operation was evolving rapidly, and new personalities could be expected in all of the Smothers vintages after 1981 or '82.

☆/☆☆☆

$$

Soave.

Perhaps the best-known white wine of Italy and certainly one of the best known in the world is Soave, which is pleasant and dry and comes from the Veneto region in the northeastern part of the country. Soave sometimes displays the same greenish-straw glint evident in Chablis, and the two wines are often compared. In fact, it is probable that some of the white carafe wines served in the fish houses of London under the Chablis name are in reality Soave. The wine has an almost almondlike flavor and is usually quite dry. It should never be laid down for bottle-aging and is best served well chilled. It is made mostly from the Garganega grape, with a blend of 10 to 30 percent Trebbiano. Soave does not stand up well in direct comparisons with the best white wines of France and Germany, but it has a light-hearted charm that is entirely appropriate when dining on seafood in a cafe in Venice. The leading brands available in the U.S. include Santa Sofia, Tomonasi, Folonari, Bolla, Bertani, Anselmi, Barbella, Della Scala, Petternella, Antinori, and Barberini. Through intelligent marketing, Soave Bolla has spearheaded the Soave invasion of the American market, and many consumers are uncertain whether the name of the wine is Soave or Bolla

☆

$/$$

Sokol Blosser Winery.

Sokol Blosser was established when Bill and Susan Blosser bought property and began planting grapes in 1970 in Dundee, in northwestern Oregon. Initially they sold their grapes to other nearby wineries, then began making their own wines after building a winery on the property in 1977. Production grew rapidly, and now Sokol Blosser is one of the larger operations in the area, with upward of 20,000 cases a year of Pinot Noir, Riesling, Chardonnay, and Merlot, among other varietals. By 1978 the winery was turning out creamy, rich, Burgundian Chardonnays that were beginning to win a national reputation.

☆/☆☆☆

$/$$

Sommelier.

A sommelier is a wine waiter, or wine steward, in a French restaurant. Such an individual should be knowledgeable about all of the wines on the restaurant's list and should be able to advise customers on the best choices to accompany the foods that they order. Some sommeliers are highly knowledgeable and professional. Some are not. In the U.S. in recent years the level of sophistication in the sommelier trade has risen substantially, but unfortunately there are many individuals practicing who are not qualified to do so.

Sonoma County.

Some of the best wines made in California, and therefore in the United States, come from Sonoma County, an important member of the triumvirate that make up the North Coast Counties of California in the United States (Napa, Sonoma, and Mendocino). The region lies due north of San Francisco, running parallel to the famed Napa Valley and extending northward along the Russian River to the county line of Mendocino. It is bounded on the east by the Mayacamas Range and on the west by the Pacific Ocean where, in climate too cool and fogbound for grapevines, stately redwoods grow. Sonoma County has several place-names that are important. Foremost is Sonoma Valley, named "valley of the moons" by the Indians because of the way the moon appeared successively between the peaks of the Mayacamas Mountains during its nightly course. The beautiful verdant valley and the picturesque town of Sonoma attracted writer Jack London, who popularized the name Valley of the Moons. Sonoma still has the look of frontier California and is one of the state's most charming towns, with friendly townfolk, good restaurants, and, of course, excellent wines.

Vineyards are also located around the town of Santa Rosa, the county seat, in the Russian River Valley below Guerneville, northward in Alexander Valley (near Healdsburg and Geyserville). Vineyards near the northernmost towns of Asti and Cloverdale are a little warmer in climate and are designated as California Region III, similar to the upper Rhône Valley in southern France. Most of Sonoma County consists of Region I and Region II. (*See* California.) The cool climate is similar to that of Burgundy, and the finest Sonoma wines equal those of Napa. Many Napa wineries in fact have vineyards in Sonoma which produce superb wines from the Cabernet, Chardonnay, and Pinot Noir grape varieties. Sonoma Zinfandels are often big, tannic red wines that require ten years to hit their peak, developing a depth and finesse similar to those of Cabernet. Johannisberg Riesling is sometimes picked late and allowed to develop Botrytis, the noble mold that attacks the ripe grape and concentrates sweetness. A number of other premium varietals grow well here too, among them Barbera, Chenin Blanc, Green Hungarian, French Colombard, and the Gamays.

Next to the Napa Valley, Sonoma is California's prime vineyard region, and the number of wineries operating there has grown from fewer than 50 in the mid-1970s to more than 80. Some of this growth has occurred partly because of the virtual saturation of the Napa Valley, but Sonoma should not be regarded as a secondary region. (*See* individual entries for Sonoma wineries.)

Sonoma Vineyards.

Sonoma Vineyards Inc. was founded in 1959 by Rodney D. Strong, who then called the enterprise Windsor Vineyards. He purchased wine in bulk and bottled it at Tiburon, just across the Golden Gate Bridge from San Francisco. The Tiburon tasting room is there to this day. Windsor Vineyards still exists as a mail-order wine business under the corporate umbrella of Sonoma Vineyards, but vast changes have taken place in the intervening years, and Sonoma Vineyards has grown into a diversified conglomerate through acquisitions outside the wine field. Now wine accounts for less than one-third of the company's annual sales volume, which runs into many millions of dollars. Rod Strong, the founder, who was once a successful dancer and choreographer, is chairman of Sonoma's Wine Division and today is a minority shareholder in the parent company. Nearly half of the stock in the parent company is owned by Renfield Importers, an importer and distributor of wines based in New York. The stock is publicly traded.

Strong moved his fledgling business to the town of Windsor in the Sonoma Valley in 1962, but the operation did not become Sonoma Vineyards until 1970, when it went public with a stock offering. Much of the business was still via mail order, using the Windsor Vineyards name. Then came the California grape glut of the early 1970s, just as Sonoma Vineyards was bearing major expenses in an effort to move into national distribution. By 1975 Sonoma's distributor in New York, Renfield, had bought 18 percent of the equity by infusing needed capital into the enterprise. Later Kenneth Kwit and Alin Gruber also bought into the company, providing still more needed capital, and now Sonoma Vineyards owns several mail-order tool companies, a printing and advertising company, and some other businesses, acquired through acquisitions.

Meanwhile the wine business was beginning to thrive again, and Sonoma Vineyards began establishing a national reputation for fine Cabernet Sauvignon with its Alexander's Crown, starting with the superb 1974 vintage, which was not released until 1977. Sonoma's River West Old Vines Zinfandel 1976 was rich, spicy, and intensely flavored, and its Chalk Hill and River West Chardonnays established a string of successful vintages. By the late 1970s Sonoma Vineyards had recovered from its adversity, and most of its offerings were held in high regard.

The annual production of Sonoma Vineyards has soared far beyond the few bottles that once were marketed through Tiburon Vintners and now totals in excess of 600,000 cases. The company owns 1300 acres in the Sonoma Valley and 300 acres in Mendocino County, although it still purchases about 60 percent of its grapes from outside growers. The Windsor Vineyards direct-sales business has expanded into New York State with the purchase of Marlboro Winery, about 60 miles up the Hudson River from New York City, which now markets New York State wines under the Marlboro name as well as California wines under the Windsor name.

In 1980 Sonoma Vineyards, Renfield, and the Piper-Heidsieck Champagne house of France announced a three-way corporate venture to produce vintage sparkling wines in California, with Rod Strong as the winemaker. The new venture is called Piper-Sonoma, and its first releases came in the fall of 1982. There were three different bottlings: Brut, Tête de Cuvée, and Blanc de Noirs—some 30,000 cases in all from the 1980 vintage, followed by 50,000 more from the 1981 vintage. Meanwhile Sonoma Vineyards continues to market a broad line of premium varietals which include all of the important members of the *Vitis vinifera* family. In 1983, Strong announced plans to change the name of the enterprise to Rodney D. Strong Vineyards because it was felt that Sonoma Vineyards sounded too much like a generic name for all Sonoma wines.
☆/☆☆☆
$/$$

South Africa.

Winemaking in South Africa dates back more than 300 years to the day in 1655 when Jan van Riebeek of the Dutch East India Company planted the first vines in the garden of the company's resident director at Protea, in the lower slopes of Table Mountain not far from Cape Town. The vines apparently had been shipped from Holland and probably had been cultivated in the Rhineland. Now, some three centuries later, the South African wine industry is a big business, despite setbacks from the Phylloxera vine blight and the interruption of shipping in two world wars. Good table wines, both red and white, are produced from European grape varieties under strict supervision of the Cooperative Wine Growers' Association of

South Africa Ltd., known as the K.W.V., which is empowered by law to set production limits and fix prices. Table wines are usually named after the grape varieties used to produce them. They tend to be comparable in style to good California wines, which means they sometimes—but not with any regularity—measure up to French and German wines.

South Africa's dessert wines and fortified wines, on the other hand, are rather special. Palomino grapes have been imported from Spain to produce Sherry-type wines from the *solera* system used in Andalusia, the Spanish Sherry country, and these wines are fortified only with grape brandy, as in Spain. They now account for the bulk of South Africa's wine exports, along with such other sweet wines as Port types, made from Portuguese grapes, and Muscats and Muscadels. It is to the credit of the South African producers that they have traditionally not stolen the names Sherry or Port, which rightfully belong to Spain and Portugal. Brand names are used instead. The availability of these wines is limited in the United States, partly reflecting the cost of the long journey from the Cape of Good Hope.

Souverain Cellars.

Souverain Cellars was established in 1943 by J. Leland Stewart with a vineyard on top of Howell Mountain off the Silverado Trail in California's Napa Valley. Stewart had retired from his executive position with Armour & Company and went to the Napa Valley to begin a second career as a writer. Writing turned out not to be sufficiently remunerative, so he began making wines in an unused winery on his property. The first vintage bottled under the Souverain label was in 1945, and the winery's production began winning awards in state fairs. In 1972 the Pillsbury Company bought Souverain, and in 1973 the company began building a larger winery in Gey-serville in the Sonoma Valley. Thus Souverain for a time was one of the few winemaking enterprises with wineries in California's two most celebrated wine regions.

The Napa facility, in Rutherford, was sold to a group of investors associated with Freemark Abbey in 1976, and they established the Rutherford Hill Winery there. The Souverain wine inventory at Rutherford, all rights to produce Souverain wines, plus the winery in Geyserville were purchased at the same time by North Coast Cellars, a cooperative consisting of some 300 grape growers in Napa, Sonoma, and Mendocino counties. Thus wines bearing the Souverain label are now produced by the cooperative and have multiple sources. All Souverain premium varietals are vintage-dated, some are aged in oak, and some are aged in the bottle for up to three years prior to release. The best wines from any above-average harvest are bottled under a "Vintage Selection" Souverain label and tend to be superior. The total production of North Coast Cellars at Souverain is some 500,000 cases a year; this amount includes private label bottlings. The products include some 17 varietals.

☆/☆☆☆

$/$$

Soviet Union.

In the early 1970s, PepsiCo Inc. signed a trade agreement with the Soviet Union under which soft drinks and soft-drink technology were to be provided by PepsiCo in return for the right to distribute Soviet wines in the United States through PepsiCo's wine subsidiary, Monsieur Henri. It appeared that suddenly American consumers would be exposed to a broad array of wines from behind the Iron Curtain, and some Americans awaited this development with great anticipation and curiosity. A few

Soviet wines are now being marketed in the United States by Monsieur Henri, but public demand turned out to be less than expected and the availability of Soviet wines suitable for the American palate has been minimal. The wines of the Soviet Union have a reputation for sweetness, and certainly those tasted by the author have been either quite sweet or else overwhelmingly harsh and tannic.

Soviet Champagne is produced in substantial quantities and some of it is flowing abroad. However, it is not inexpensive and is viewed more as a curiosity than as an actual competitor for real champagne from France and the sparkling wines of California and New York State. A good deal of fortified wine, sometimes bearing the names of fortified wines from other countries, is also produced in the Soviet Union. No doubt as East-West trade continues to develop and the Soviet Union becomes more exposed to Western winemaking technology, her wines will improve.

Spain.

From her sun-baked vineyards to her redolent mountains Spain is a country that lives by the vine. From Jerez de la Frontera near the Atlantic Ocean in the south to Rioja in the north and Catalonia in the east Spain produces all of the basic varieties—usually at lower cost than any other wine country. Only two other countries, Italy and France, produce more wine, and neither does it so inexpensively and with so little effort. Perhaps it is because the grape grows so naturally in Spain that most of her wines are taken less seriously than those of some other countries. Indeed, were it not for the prominence of Sherry among the world's fine fortified wines, Spain's place among the major wine-producing countries would be less distinguished.

Yet it would be a gross injustice to

suggest that some of Spain's table wines do not rank with the greatest in the world. In the Rioja Valley, stretching across the northern part of the country 70 to 80 miles below the French border, some red wines of great character are produced. Because of a lack of public awareness they are not in great demand in foreign markets, where they would be able to compete at a cost advantage. Some table wine producers have made strong showings in the American market, and the most successful has been Miguel Torres of Penedés, who ships more than 100,000 cases a year to the U.S. and many more to some 85 other countries. Part of the Torres success derives from the ready charm of the Penedés wines, which are more appealing to the average consumer than are the Riojas, which are more complex and structured. The winemaking heritage of the Rioja District owes much to the French, who brought their expertise when they fled south across the Pyrenees in the 1870s after the Phylloxera vine blight had begun to wipe out the French vineyards. Some similarities can still be perceived between a well-made Rioja and good French Bordeaux. Spain produces charming Montilla white wines in her south, but her most celebrated whites are her Sherries.

Widely imitated in many parts of the world but rarely equaled, Spanish Sherry is the only true Sherry. The word itself derives from the name of the capital of the Sherry region, Jerez de la Frontera, which lies not far from the Bay of Cádiz in the southernmost part of the country. The British, with their highly cultivated wine tastes, have consumed the lion's share of Spanish Sherry for many generations, but this pleasant fortified wine has developed a strong following in many other countries as well. Sherry has been less popular in the United States, where the hour of the aperitif before dining has traditionally been the cocktail hour. The American awakening to wine in recent years should enhance Sherry's popularity, although the market is fairly well saturated with cheap American imitations.

A large segment of Spain's wine production is not even bottled in the country of its origin. Rather, it is shipped to France, Germany, Italy, and other countries in big tank trucks or in the holds of ships and is used for blending to make *vin ordinaire* or else as a base for Vermouths and cordials. Some of the Spanish wine so treated deserves a better fate, but it is probable that most of it would be rather coarse and acidic on the palate if drunk in its natural form. On the other hand, travelers through Spain will come across excellent local wines that are never even bottled, much less exported. These can be surprisingly good—just as surprising as Spain's better known wines. (*See also* Sherry, Rioja, Montilla-Moriles, Catalonia, La Mancha.)

Spätlese.

This is one of the categories of wine with special attributes produced in Germany as *Qualitätswein mit Prädikat*. It usually is sweeter than a Kabinett wine but lower on the sweetness scale than Auslese, Beerenauslese, or Trockenbeerenauslese. The term "Spätlese" means "late-selected" or "late-harvested," indicating that the grapes have been picked later than the normal harvest after additional ripeness has been achieved. Because this is a style or category of wine, it may be produced in almost any good vineyard in Germany under the appropriate weather conditions. Its sweetness is natural and elegant and only remotely resembles the cheap, artificially sweetened wines produced in the United States and some other countries. It should be drunk with a sweet dessert or ripe fruit after the meal or perhaps as an aperitif. Usually it will be more expensive than a Kabinett wine but less costly than an Auslese or one of the other sweeter categories. (*See also* Germany, Auslese, etc.)

Spanna.

The local name for the Nebbiolo grape around the town of Gattinara in Italy's Piedmont region is Spanna. Whereas Gattinara is a rich, velvety red wine that deserves a place among the great reds produced anywhere and is therefore difficult to find, Spanna is more readily available and usually is less costly. Because it means, basically, Nebbiolo, it is a very good dry red wine of great depth and intensity. The Nebbiolo is the superior grape of Italy, producing most of its greatest red wines, except for Chianti, which is made mostly from the Sangiovese grape. Spanna can be one of the best buys from Italy. It should not be drunk before its tenth birthday and should remain in good condition beyond age 20. (*See also* Gattinara.)

☆☆☆/☆☆☆☆

$$

Spring Mountain Vineyards.

Spring Mountain Vineyards has been a producer of high-quality wines almost since its founding in 1968 on Spring Mountain above St. Helena in California's Napa Valley. Mike Robbins, a Naval Academy graduate and former naval officer, who has a law degree from the University of San Francisco and was in the real estate business, is the founder and controlling partner. In 1976 the original Spring Mountain property was sold to St. Clement Vineyards, and Mike Robbins moved up the mountain, where he bought a large estate that held the potential for expansion. The first harvest under the Spring Mountain label was the Cabernet Sauvignon 1968, which was blended with the 1969 and not released as a vintage wine. A Chardonnay produced in 1968 was sold off in bulk.

Robbins has 258 acres on Spring Mountain, but only a small percentage of these are planted. He also owns 105 acres on the Silverado Trail in Napa, which contribute grapes to his production. The winemaker, John Williams, is a graduate of the University of California at Davis and of Cornell University who worked at Glenora Wine Cellars, a leading vineyard in New York's Finger Lakes area, before moving to Spring Mountain in 1980. Three other Davis graduates are on the Spring Mountain payroll. The team produces Cabernet Sauvignon and Chardonnay, which together account for 85 percent of production, plus some Sauvignon Blanc and a small quantity of Pinot Noir that sometimes contains a blending of Chardonnay. Occasionally Spring Mountain still produces a blended wine without a vintage, such as the Trois Cuvées that contained the 1975, 1976, and 1977 vintages of Cabernet Sauvignon.

☆/☆☆☆

$$

Spritzer.

A spritzer is a mixture of white wine, preferably German white wine, and club soda or seltzer. It is a light, refreshing drink in summertime and is ideal as an aperitif for consumers who wish to keep their alcohol intake to a minimum. Classically, it should be half wine and half sparkling water, and it is most often served over ice.

Spumante Brut.

Among the better sparkling wines of Italy are those called Spumante Brut, generally produced in the Friuli-Venezia Giulia, Trentino-Alto Adige, and Veneto regions from Pinot Bianco or Chardonnay grapes, which separates them decisively from the Asti Spumantes made from Moscato grapes. The Spumante Bruts come closer to genuine Champagne than any other category of Italian sparkling wines and usually are made using the *metodo champenois,* involving fermentation inside the bottles. These wines are usually sold under brand names of the producers, and one of the best is Ferrari, with vineyards near Trento and a reputation that challenges the best Champagnes of France. Other good producers in the same area include Equipe 5 and Cavit; Gancia has built a strong reputation for its Brut from Lombardy. Many others are now making excellent dry sparkling wines in Italy in response to the Italians' own thirst for Champagne-style beverages as well as the insatiable thirst of American consumers.

☆/☆☆
$$/$$$

Stags' Leap Vineyard.

The winery at Stags' Leap was built in the early 1900s and was revived by a new ownership group headed by Carl Doumani, a former Los Angeles restaurateur and real estate man, in 1973. The wines were crushed at the Souverain Cellars (now Rutherford Hill) Napa Valley facility, starting with the 1972 vintage and extending through the 1979, while the old winery was being rebuilt and modernized. Stags' Leap Vineyard has more than 100 acres planted in vines and sells grapes to other wineries besides filling all of its own needs. Production totals roughly 10,000 cases a year of Cabernet Sauvignon, Petite Sirah, Merlot, Chenin Blanc, an occasional Pinot Noir, and an occasional generic burgundy that is a blend of Petite Sirah and Pinot Noir. The wines generally are not quite as high in quality as those of Stag's Leap Wine Cellars, although the Petite Sirah is one of the best made in the United States and has won a large following among connoisseurs of robust reds. Carl Doumani and Warren Winiarski, proprietor of the nearby Stag's Leap Wine Cellars, have been involved in litigation over the use of the name.
☆/☆☆☆☆
$$

Stag's Leap Wine Cellars.

The Cabernet Sauvignons of Stag's Leap Wine Cellars have been rich and complex ever since the winery was established on the Silverado Trail near Napa, California, in 1972. It was the 1973 vintage Cabernet from this enterprise that helped bring world attention to the rising quality of California wines. The Stag's Leap 1973 took first prize in a widely publicized blind tasting in Paris in 1976, finishing ahead of Château Mouton-Rothschild 1970, Château Haut-Brion 1970, and Château Montrose 1970, among other great French Bordeaux. The 1970 vintage from Bordeaux may have been passing through an awkward stage in its evolution at that moment, but this did not detract from the Stag's Leap victory, and suddenly the offerings from this small winery in Napa had established an international reputation.

The winery was founded in 1972 by Warren and Barbara Winiarski. Warren Winiarski had worked for Robert Mondavi and Souverain Cellars and before that had been a lecturer in political philosophy at the University of Chicago. His ability to produce such exquisite wines in the Napa Valley attested not only to his own skill but also to the basic soundness of the area. Stag's Leap now has 40 acres in Merlot and Cabernet Sauvignon which were planted in 1970, and production has expanded to the 15,000-to-20,000-case level. Besides Cabernet, the winery produces Merlot, Gamay Beaujolais, Chardonnay, White Riesling, and Petite Sirah. From 50 to 70 percent of its grape requirements are purchased from other growers in the Napa Valley. The winery should not be confused with the Stags' Leap Vineyard, a Napa winery nearby that produces good wines.

☆/☆☆☆☆
$$/$$$

Robert Stemmler Winery.

Robert Stemmler and his partner, Trumbull Kelly, established their enterprise in Healdsburg, in California's Sonoma Valley, in 1977. They have four acres of Chardonnay in the Dry Creek area and buy additional grapes, including more Chardonnay, Sauvignon Blanc, and Cabernet Sauvignon, from other local growers. Stemmler was born in Germany and received his initial training in oenology at the German agricultural college at Bad Kreuznach in the Nahe Valley. His Chardonnays are aged in Limousin oak barrels for up to ten months, and they are toasty with oak flavor as a result. His Cabernets are graceful. The winery's total output has reached 5000 cases, with a goal of 8000.

☆☆/☆☆☆☆
$$

STERLING VINEYARDS

ESTATE BOTTLED

1979

STERLING RESERVE

Cabernet Sauvignon

NAPA VALLEY

GROWN, PRODUCED AND BOTTLED BY
STERLING VINEYARDS
CALISTOGA, NAPA VALLEY, CALIF. ALCOHOL 12.5% BY VOLUME

Sterling Vineyards.

This sparkling white citadel, set on a wooded knoll at the northern end of California's Napa Valley, looks as if it has been transported from the sun-washed shores of the Mediterranean, an illusion reinforced at intervals by the sound of Swiss-made bells that peal out over the valley from three rounded bell towers. The structure was specifically designed to attract visitors, for the original plan was to distribute the wines solely at the winery.

Visitors' access to the winery and tasting rooms is by aerial tramway, and the little yellow gondolas take about three minutes to reach their destination, affording along the way a superb view of the valley. Once inside, visitors can tour the winery by themselves. An upper-level walkway looks down on all winemaking operations and storage facilities. The handsomely appointed tasting rooms are housed in a separate building. Fireplaces adorn the inside rooms, and on summer days visitors can sit outside on decks overlooking the valley.

The winery was owned by Sterling International, a paper company based in San Francisco. Sterling's Peter Newton and Michael Stone first acquired vineyard land in Napa Valley in 1964 and bought 400 acres surrounding the winery, which opened in 1973. Richard Forman, a graduate of the University of California at Davis with a master's degree in oenology, was the winemaker, an open-minded young man whose willingness to experiment was fully in line with Sterling's forward-looking spirit.

In 1977 Sterling was sold to the Coca-Cola Company of Atlanta as part of a major diversification into wine by the soft-drink concern. Coca-Cola also bought the Taylor Wine Company of New York and the Monterey Vineyard of California, where the Taylor California Cellars wines are now made. But Sterling remained Coca-Cola's entry in the premium-wine business, and the company provided infusions of capital to assure that high-quality standards were maintained. Forman left in 1978 to establish his own vineyards, and Sterling hired Theo Rosenbrand, who had spent 22 years at Beaulieu Vineyards. His assistant was Dr. Sergio Traverso, who left in 1981 to join Concannon.

Mike Stone left in 1982 as the Sterling president, and other changes have taken place. Coca-Cola sold all of its wine operations to Seagram's in 1983, abandoning the diversification effort begun only six years earlier. Now only four varietals are made—Cabernet Sauvignon, Merlot, Chardonnay, and Sauvignon Blanc. The Cabernet usually has about 10 percent Merlot and the Sauvignon Blanc about 20 percent Sémillon. Sterling has 520 acres of vineyards under its control, including the new Diamond Mountain Ranch across the Napa Valley, and plans to limit total production to 100,000 cases a year. The Sterling Reserve Cabernet, first produced in 1973, is an exceptional wine that has won plaudits from many connoisseurs. It too is blended with some Merlot and is a rich and textured wine that is best drunk after about a decade.

Despite gainsayers who predicted that the quality standards at Sterling would decline under big corporate ownership, the opposite has been the case. If anything, the wines are better than ever as more and more devotion and expertise are used to make them. The purchase of the Diamond Mountain Ranch on Diamond Mountain was an example. It is one of the steepest vineyards in the Napa Valley, with a grade of 60 percent in places, and growing grapes there is extremely difficult. But Sterling believes the benefits in terms of concentrated flavors and complexity resulting from stressed vines are worth the extra cost and effort. The 120-acre tract has been planted in Chardonnay (a section that has already partly washed away at least once), Sauvignon Blanc, Cabernet Sauvignon, Merlot, and some Cabernet Franc. The elevation is about 1500 feet above sea level on the western slopes of the Napa Valley. Reservoirs had to be built to provide water for drip irrigation. Gophers and raccoons gnaw on the irrigation lines and dig among the vine roots. The vineyard vehicles are military surplus cannon carriers with four-wheel drive. Initial grape yields from the Diamond Mountain vineyard were only about one-quarter of a ton per acre, or a fraction of the normal volume.

All of the Sterling wines are well made, and some devotees say they prefer the regular Cabernet Sauvignon to the Reserve. The Sauvignon Blanc, with its liberal blending of Sémillon, also has a big following. It is rich and mellow, although lacking residual sugar. The Chardonnay is balanced yet complex, and the Merlot is one of the better examples of this varietal produced in California.

☆/☆☆☆☆

$/$$$

Stevenot Vineyards.

The vineyards of Stevenot were planted in 1974 in the Sierra Nevada foothills 130 miles east of San Francisco, in Calaveras County, the scene of intensive gold prospecting in the last century. Fifteen acres initially were planted in Cabernet Sauvignon, Zinfandel, and Chenin Blanc, and 12 more acres of Chardonnay were added later. Stevenot also buys grapes from other producers in California. The winery, built in 1978, was established by Barden Stevenot, a fifth-generation member of a pioneering family that homesteaded in Calaveras County. Production has grown from 2200 cases in 1978 to more than 15,000. The goal is 30,000.

☆☆/☆☆☆☆

$$

Stonegate Winery.

Near Calistoga in the northern sector of the Napa Valley's prime growing area in California is Stonegate Winery, the property of Jim and Barbara Spaulding, whose son David is the winemaker. Jim Spaulding was a medical-affairs writer for the Milwaukee *Journal* for 20 years before moving to California in 1969 to become a lecturer at the communications school at the University of California at Berkeley. That year the Spauldings bought 29 acres of land on a hill above Calistoga for a reported price of $52,500,

a modest sum compared to today's Napa prices. The land had been used for prunes and walnuts, but the Spauldings tore out the other crops and planted Chardonnay, among other grapes.

They became partners in a winery on the floor of the Napa Valley in 1973 and have been producing Cabernet Sauvignon, Chenin Blanc, and Sauvignon Blanc, along with Chardonnay, since then. Initially their production was 70 percent red wine, reflecting the taste preference of many California producers in those days. Eventually, like many other producers, however, they had to shift their focus to white wines, and they began grafting white vines onto their red rootstocks. More recently the output has been 80 percent white, in a direct response to the booming consumer demand for white wines all across the country. Production totals around 14,000 cases per year, depending on the vintage, which places Stonegate firmly in the so-called boutique category.

The Stonegate wines have achieved popularity across the country through a careful marketing program intended to assure that they are not sold entirely in California. Stonegate has climbed into the top category of boutique producers, although its wines sometimes lack balance. The Sauvignon Blanc, especially, has won followers, and the Cabernet Sauvignon has proved consistent. The Chardonnay tends to be a big wine of great charm.

☆/☆☆☆☆

$$

Stony Hill.

Stony Hill, tucked into a curving hilltop of the Mayacamas Range in Napa County, California, produces three of the finest white wines to be found in the country: Chardonnay, Johannisberg Riesling, and

Gewürztraminer. When the late Fred McCrea and his wife, Eleanor, purchased this spectacular site as a summer home and place for growing children in 1943, they wanted to raise something and were advised that the land was good only for goats or grapes. They chose grapes, not surprisingly, since a stroll along the crest of their hilltop affords a spectacular view of the Napa Valley stretching below, with grapevines spreading from end to end and up the slopes that embrace the valley. They knew nothing about winemaking at the time. But with help from valley vintners they were soon making wine for their own table—wine that turned out to be so good that friends urged them to make more and sell it. In 1951 the winery was established. Fred retired from the advertising business, and within a decade Stony Hill wines were piling up accolades right and left.

The 29 acres consist of all white varieties, mainly Chardonnay, Riesling, and Gewürztraminer, and smaller amounts of Sémillon. The small stone winery sits within a stone's throw of the swimming pool on a hillside below the house. Inside are a wooden hand press, a small stainless steel fermenter, and oak barrels of various sizes, the largest holding 5000 gallons. When one compares it to the bigger producers, growing by leaps and bounds in the valley below, it is fascinating to see a miniature operation such as Stony Hill. Only 4000 cases of Chardonnay, Riesling, Gewürztraminer, and some Sémillon are made each year. The only way to obtain the wines is to be on the mailing list, an exclusive register that rarely has openings for new names. A few choice restaurants and retail outlets in San Francisco and New York receive a few bottles from time to time.
☆/☆☆
$$

Stony Ridge Winery.

The former Ruby Hill Winery, which produced its first vintage in 1887 after a 13-year construction period, was taken over by a small group of new owners in 1975. The winery is said to have been in continuous production since its inception, but the output had fallen to a mere trickle when the most recent ownership change took place. Since then the winery has been upgraded, the name has been changed, and production has risen to 30,000 cases a year of various premium varietals, most carrying individual vineyard or geographical designations. The property is in the southwest corner of the Livermore Valley near Pleasanton in Alameda County. The adjacent vineyard is leased, and grapes are purchased from a fairly diverse area. The vines from the adjacent estate were planted some 50 years ago in Chardonnay, Sémillon, Malvasia Blanca, Zinfandel, and Barbera.

Early offerings of Zinfandel under the Stony Ridge label from the home vineyard were spicy and intense. A late-harvest Zinfandel produced in a small quantity in 1977 was 17.2 percent alcohol and attracted attention. Other offerings have included Cabernet Sauvignon from Bergstrom Vineyard, Petite Sirah from Ventana Vineyards, Pinot Noir from Monterey and San Luis Obispo counties, a Chardonnay identified as "Young Vines Home Vineyard Lot II," another Chardonnay, identified as "Monterey County Lot I," and a third, described as "La Reina Monterey County." Stony Ridge also produces Pinot Blanc, Fumé Blanc, Chenin Blanc, Sémillon, Barbera, Pinot Noir, and Malvasia.
☆/☆☆☆
$/$$

Story Vineyard.

Story Vineyard is one of a handful of Zinfandel producers in Amador County, where many Zinfandel devotees feel the best examples of this varietal are made. Story has 28 acres planted in the 1920s in Zinfandel vines, and it began commercial production in the early 1970s after the winery had been run as a hobby. The Story Zinfandels are typical of Amador—intensely flavored, long-lived, and robust. Story produces a vintage-dated wine, one blended from two or more vintages which matures earlier, and another that is not aged in oak barrels, is thereby lacking in tannin and becomes soft and supple at a young age. Production totals only about 6000 cases a year, but the wines are in national distribution.

☆/☆☆☆☆
$$

Sutter Home Winery.

Devotees of California Zinfandels have long been followers of the intensely flavored, robust wines made by Sutter Home at its extensive facilities in St. Helena, in the prime growing area of the Napa Valley. But Sutter Home's grapes come mostly from vineyards in El Dorado County and Amador County, where the best Zinfandels of all are produced, largely because of the superior ripeness achieved in the hot, dry climate in the area southeast of Sacramento.

The winery in St. Helena was built in 1874 and was purchased by the Sutter family at the turn of the century. In 1946 the Trinchero family, with six generations of winemaking experience and origins in the Italian district of Asti, bought Sutter Home. Today the winemaker and general manager is Louis "Bob" Trinchero, and three generations of Trincheros work there. Zinfandel accounts for 85 percent of production, most of it from El Dorado and Amador counties. (Connoisseurs are convinced that the ones from Amador are still superior.)

Sutter Home also makes a white Zin-

fandel by removing the dark skins from the juice of the grapes immediately after the crush, and this wine is best as an aperitif or served with fully flavored fish or poultry dishes. There is also a Moscato Amabile (sweet Muscat), made from Muscat of Alexandria grapes. It is best with dessert or as an aperitif. Production of Sutter Home wines is around 150,000 cases a year, and prices have stayed within reach of the average consumer, which seems to be a company policy. Visitors to the winery in St. Helena also should not miss the opportunity to buy some of Sutter Home's wine vinegar made from Zinfandel grapes.

☆/☆☆☆☆
$/$$

Switzerland.

Switzerland's enviable position is unique among wine-producing countries. Not only does she produce good wines of her own but her close proximity to France, Germany, and Italy provides access to many of the greatest vineyards of the world. Moreover, she has great wealth as a banking nation and traditionally has printed the most stable reserve currency in the world—the Swiss franc tends to rise in value while other currencies fall, a relationship that makes foreign wines cheap for Swiss buyers. So the Swiss are great connoisseurs, and the cellars in Geneva, Zurich, and Basel hold some of the greatest vinous treasures from neighboring countries. Individual collections of 10,000 or more bottles are not uncommon, and the Swiss are continually adding to their inventories by purchasing directly from the best vineyards of Europe and buying at the London wine auctions, where their francs have great acquisitive power when converted into British pounds.

With all this in their favor, it would seem unnecessary for the Swiss to be involved in viniculture. Yet some very creditable white wines and some good reds come from the steeply sloping vineyards of this Alpine country. Not many are exported, but it would be unthinkable not to drink Aigle, the fresh and fruity Swiss white, when dining on fresh perch on a hillside above Lake Geneva. Nor should you forsake a bottle of the red Dôle with your cheese course in Zurich. These are everyday drinking wines in the serious cellars of Switzerland, yet they merit respect. When found in export markets, Swiss wines should not, generally, be expensive, nor should they be expected to measure up to their French, German, and Italian cousins.

Just as in France and the other European countries, the wine names of Switzerland are geographical. Many of the best Swiss wines come from the sloping vineyards above the Rhône River and above Lake Geneva (Lac Léman), which is really just a gigantic bulge in the Rhône as it rushes from the Swiss Alps toward its union with the Saône at Lyon, the gastronomic capital of France. Here are the major wine designations from this part of Switzerland:

Vaud: The area on the north shore of Lake Geneva produces white wines from the Chasselas grape, sometimes called the Vaud Dorin, and some modest reds.

Valais: East of Lake Geneva along the Rhône the Chasselas also produces good whites, but here they are called Fendant, with the name of the local town or parish added—e.g., Sion, Sierre, Conthey, Vétroz. Whites are also made here from the Sylvaner and Malvoisie, or Pinot Gris. Dôle is the best known red wine of Valais and perhaps of Switzerland. It is a mixture of Pinot Noir and Gamay Grapes.

Chablais: Not to be confused with Chablis, the French white Burgundy, Chablais lies between the Vaud and Valais and is the home of Aigle, named after the village of Aigle on the Rhône.

Lavaux: This is the eastern hillside above Lake Geneva, between Lausanne and Montreux, where excellent whites are produced in such villages as Epesses, Chardonne, Lutry, and Villette.

Geneva: Vineyards stretch up the hillsides from Geneva on the French border, but they produce modest wines. Just across the border in France, Crépy is made from the Chasselas grape.

Vines grow everywhere in Switzerland, but the only wines that seem to turn up in foreign countries, besides those mentioned above, come from the vineyards around Lake Neuchâtel, toward the northwest border with France, where good reds and whites are made. They are called Neuchâtel and are widely available abroad.

Sylvaner.

The Sylvaner is the most widely planted grape in Germany, yielding vast quantities of white wine that often is quite good, although the Riesling is the greatest of all the German grapes. The Sylvaner produces good wines in the Palatinate and better wines in Franconia, where few other grape varieties are cultivated. It is also cultivated in Austria, where it may have originated, and in Alsace, Switzerland, Chile, and California. Sylvaner wines generally are not as long-lived as Rieslings and rarely achieve great finesse, but they can approach greatness under ideal growing conditions. (*See also* Germany, Riesling.)

· T ·

La Tâche.

This magnificent Burgundy vineyard is wholly owned by the Domaine de la Romanée-Conti and ranks second only to Romanée-Conti itself among the six vineyards in which the Domaine has interests. La Tâche lies in the *commune* of Vosne-Romanée in the Burgundian Côte d'Or, or Golden Slope, between two *premiers crus* vineyards, Les Malconsorts and La Grande Rue. The vineyard area of La Tâche is a modest 15 acres, and the property is one of seven *grands crus* of Vosne-Romanée. In good vintages La Tâche will challenge Romanée-Conti with its refined richness, flowery bouquet of violets and lilacs, and its extraordinary balance. It is undisputedly one of the greatest Burgundies of France and one of the world's best red wines. (*See also* Romanée-Conti, Vosne-Romanée, Côte de Nuits.)

☆☆☆☆

$$$/$$$$

Tafelwein.

German term for table wine that assumed legal status with the German wine law of 1971. These wines are comparable to the *vin ordinaire* of France. They are light and simple and are consumed mostly within Germany. They must be made from one of the approved grape varieties in one of the five *Tafelwein* regions: Mosel, Rhein, Main, Neckar, or Oberrhein, which now has two parts. If the name of the region appears on the label, 85 percent of the wine in the bottle must be made from the named grape grown in the specified area. If the label carries the name of a smaller community or subdivision of one of the six regions, 85 percent of the wine must have come from that community. Specific vineyard names are not permitted on *Tafelwein* labels. If a vintage is specified, 85 percent of the wine must come from grapes harvested in that year. (*See also* Germany.)

Château Talbot.

This is one of many estates in the Bordeaux region that carries an Anglo-Saxon name, reflecting the substantial British interests that have existed in southwestern France for centuries. Although Talbot, named after the British military leader who died in France in 1453, was ranked a *quatrième cru,* or fourth growth, in the Bordeaux classification of 1855, it is one of the best estates of the entire

CONTENTS
1 Pt 8 Fl. OZ.

RED FRENCH
TABLE WINE

GRAND CRU CLASSÉ

CHÂTEAU

TALBOT

Ancien Domaine
DU CONNÉTABLE TALBOT
GOUVERNEUR DE GUYENNE
· 1400 · 1453 ·

MÉDOC

APPELLATION St JULIEN CONTRÔLÉE

1961

MISE EN BOUTEILLES
AU CHÂTEAU

Georges Cordier
Propriétaire

PRODUCE OF FRJ   EXPORTATION STRICTEMENT RÉSERVÉE   IMPRIMÉ EN FRANCE

and then in chestnut casks. In special cases, when vintage conditions are very favorable and superior grapes are available from exceptional vineyard sites, some Taurasi is chosen for four years of wood-aging and merits the *riserva* designation. Taurasi from a good vintage normally requires at least a decade of aging before drinking. At maturity it displays a black-cherry scent combined with earthiness. One of the leading producers, Mastroberardino, describes the bouquet of his mature Taurasi as "the smell in the forest after the rain."

☆☆☆/☆☆☆☆

$$

Tavel.

Many rosé, or pink, wines are produced all over the world, but few have attained the fame of Tavel, which is produced at the southern end of the Rhône River District of France, just north of Avignon and not far from the most famous red-wine area of the district, Châteauneuf-du-Pape. Tavel rosés have more character than most other pink wines and often are less sweet. If any rosé is capable of living up to the outmoded cliché that pink wines go well with all foods, it would probably be Tavel. It is made from the Grenache grape and has a light, refreshing taste. It should be served well chilled and is best drunk as an aperitif. (*See also* Rosé.)

☆/☆☆

$/$$

Taylor California Cellars.

Taylor California Cellars is a brand of California wines introduced after the Coca-Cola Company bought the Taylor Wine Company of New York State in early 1977. Until the Coca-Cola acquisition Taylor produced only New York State wines, although occasionally California wines were transported east in bulk for blending into Taylor products.

Médoc and deserves to be upgraded in any reclassification. It consistently brings prices equal to the best second growths. The estate lies in the *commune* of Saint-Julien and is operated by the Cordier family, who also operate the neighboring Château Gruaud-Larose. Talbot is a wine of great intensity and depth that can be overpowering in its youth, but it mellows with the passage of time, requiring at least 15 years and perhaps 20 to reach its peak of perfection. The 1926 continued to display a wealth of fruit, a big and elegant bouquet, and great charm when tasted a half century later.

☆☆☆☆

$$/$$$

Taurasi.

Taurasi is an excellent red wine made in the Campania region of southwestern Italy, near Naples. The grape is the Aglianico, which is sometimes used exclusively and sometimes blended with portions of Piedirosso, Sangiovese, and Barbera, although Aglianico must make up at least 70 percent of the blend. After fermentation the wine is normally aged first in large Yugoslavian oak casks

The Taylor California Cellars brand was introduced in the fall of 1978. The winemaker has been Richard Peterson, also the winemaker at Monterey Vineyard, another Coca-Cola property, and the Taylor California wines initially were produced at the Monterey Vineyard facilities in Gonzales, in California's upper Monterey County. Plans for a separate new facility in Gonzales for the California Cellars brand were announced in 1981, largely because of the enormous growth in sales of the brand—from about 500,000 cases in the final four months of 1978 to a rate of more than four million a year in 1982.

Using Coca-Cola's well-known marketing muscle as well as the widespread brand identification with the Taylor name, Taylor California Cellars initially produced generic Rhine, chablis, rosé, and burgundy. They are made from grapes purchased from six California regions. Following the generics came a line of six premium varietals: Chardonnay, Chenin Blanc, Sauvignon Blanc, Riesling, Cabernet Sauvignon, and Zinfandel. This line was marketed in an effort to satisfy consumers who wanted to move up from the California Cellars generics. The Cabernet Sauvignon, Zinfandel, Chardonnay, and Sauvignon Blanc all receive some aging in small oak barrels. Adding to the product array, a so-called light chablis, with 25 percent fewer calories, was introduced in 1981, and a "dry white wine" and a "dry red wine" were introduced the same year at the same relatively low prices as the California Cellars generics. In another move aimed at securing a larger share of the market, California Cellars chablis and burgundy in aluminum cans were marketed to airlines to enable them to save weight, starting in 1980. All of the California Cellars wines are well made and tend to rank with the highest quality in their price category, although the superior wines marketed under the aegis of Coca-Cola came from Monterey Vineyard and Sterling Vineyards, which also were acquired by the big soft-drink producer in the 1970s. In 1983, all of the Coca-Cola wine operations, including California Cellars, were sold to Seagram's, which meant that the Taylor and Paul Masson lines, formerly competitors, were now under the same corporate umbrella.

☆

$

Taylor Wine Company.

Taylor Wine Company of Hammondsport, New York, is the largest New York State producer, incorporating the Pleasant Valley Wine Company, which makes wine under another well-known label, Great Western. Total cooperage capacity at Taylor is 31 million gallons, and the company's 60 products include aperitifs, dessert wines, table wines, and some 800,000 cases per year of the company's most famous product, Champagne. Taylor wines are made from blends of native grape varieties, a few French-American hybrids, and some California hybrids. One best-selling line is the Lake Country family: red, white, pink, and the latest addition, Lake Country gold, a sweet white. The taste of the native Labrusca is quite discernible in most Taylor products. In some wines the Labrusca flavor is modified by the addition of French-American hybrids developed by Seibel, Seyve-Villard, and others.

Taylor acquired the Pleasant Valley Wine Company in 1962. It operates as a separate company (but on property adjacent to Taylor) and retains the old and well-known Great Western name on its table and dessert wines and Champagne. The name Great Western on a New York State wine is a bit confusing, but it was so named after a connoisseur, sampling one of the company's earliest Champagnes, exclaimed, "Truly, this will be the great Champagne of the West!"—meaning at that time, 1870, the Western world and the continent of America. The Pleasant Valley Wine Company was founded in 1860 by Charles Champlin, who recognized that the climate was similar to that of Champagne in France. He felt that the region could become the Champagne District of America and began producing Champagnes that won prizes in Europe.

The Taylor Wine Company was acquired by the Coca-Cola Company of Atlanta in January 1977 as part of the big soft-drink concern's major diversification into the wine field. Taylor became part of Coca-Cola's Wine Spectrum, and it has experienced strong growth since then. Market-research studies showed that Taylor's name was considered by consumers to be second only to Gallo in terms of recognition and that it was high in prestige. Coca-Cola also found that Taylor had an excellent distribution network, not only for its Champagnes but for its table wines as well.

Taylor's Lake Country brand of table wines was a strong franchise, and Coca-Cola continued to put heavy emphasis on this category. A line of "soft"—meaning low-alcohol—Lake Country table wines was introduced in 1981. The entire Lake Country line is blended from native and hybrid grapes, including grapes produced in California which account for a minor percentage of the blend.

In 1983 Coca-Cola sold its Wine Spectrum to Seagram's, the big wine and spirits conglomerate that also owns Paul Masson and Gold Seal Vineyards, previously an arch-rival of Taylor's in Hammondsport. Plans were being made to merge the various entities into an efficient corporate structure, although it was assumed that the various brands would retain their identities.
☆/☆☆☆
$/$$

Terlano.

Excellent white wines are produced from the vineyards surrounding the town of Terlano in Italy's Trentino-Alto Adige region, and several have qualified for recognition under the D.O.C. law, including the one that is called by the town's name. Labels that say only Terlano indicate that the wine is half Pinot Bianco, with the rest consisting of Riesling, Sauvignon, and perhaps some Sylvaner grapes. The wine tends to be soft and clean, with a charming personality. All of the other D.O.C. wines of Terlano are varietals, meaning that they bear the name of the grape—e.g., Terlano Pinot Bianco, which is 90 percent that variety, Terlano-Riesling Italico, Terlano Riesling Renano, Terlano Sauvignon, Terlano Sylvaner, Terlano Müller-Thurgau.
☆/☆☆
$

Tignanello.

Italy is a country of history and tradition, and its wines date back many centuries, so it is unusual when a new wine is born and emerges suddenly among the ranks of the world's best. Such is the case with Tignanello, produced in Tuscany by the Marchesi Piero and Lodovico Antinori, a wine first introduced with the 1971 vintage. Tignanello is composed mostly of Sangiovese, the dominant red grape of Chianti, but it also contains Canaiolo and, since 1975, about 10 percent of Cabernet Sauvignon, which seems to add a complexity absent from most other Tuscan reds. The wine is made only in superior vintages: 1971, 1975, 1977, 1978, 1979. The first vintage, 1971, contained some

Malvasia, a white grape that belongs to the Muscat family, but the Antinoris decided that it gave their Tignanello a tendency to oxidize prematurely, so the wine has been made entirely from red grapes since then. The Tignanello vineyard, which lies in the Chianti Classico district of Tuscany, receives the best southern exposure in the entire Antinori Santa Cristina estate. Tignanello is aged in small Yugoslavian oak barrels for two years and then is further bottle-aged for at least 18 months before being marketed. At maturity Tignanello is silky and elegant, with great complexity and internal structure and an exquisite residue of mature fruit that charms the palate. It is also expensive.

☆☆☆/☆☆☆☆☆

$$/$$$

Tokay, Tokaji.

One of the world's greatest sweet dessert wines is the Tokay of Hungary, which takes its name from the village of Tokaj, not far from the Russian border in the northeastern corner of the country. This is a wine of great depth and intensity, made from the white Furmint and Hárslevelü grapes, although the wine's color is usually reddish-brown or almost tawny. Its name on labels is always Tokaji, which means it comes from the town of Tokaj, and it is usually followed by the words "Aszu" or "Szamorodni" and sometimes by the name of the grape—e.g., Furmint.

The greatest is Tokaji Aszu, made from late-picked grapes that have contracted *Botrytis cinerea,* the noble rot that causes water in the grape juice to evaporate through the skins, leaving behind a highly concentrated nectar. The ripest, or Aszu, grapes are set aside and crushed separately into a pulp, which is then added to the fermenting juice in specific proportions called *puttonyos,* or *puttonos.* In a great year, when large quantities of Aszu grapes are harvested, Tokaji Aszu 5 *puttonyos* can be made. This designation means that the wine is entirely vinified from Aszu grapes. Gradations from one to four *puttonyos* are also made; the fewer the number of *puttonyos,* the less sweet the wine. Tokaji Szamorodni is the driest, because no *puttonyos* of Aszu grapes have been added, although a Szamorodni may be fairly sweet when produced in an especially good year.

Considerable confusion exists about the sweetest of all Tokajis, the Essence or Eszencia, that carry no *puttonyos* designations on their labels. These are produced only in special years, and there is said to be a difference between the Aszu Eszencia and the Essence, although it is possible that something was lost in the translation. The ripest grapes are used, and the juice that trickles down naturally without being pressed when the grapes are stored in the tanks is the essence of Eszencia. Some of the Aszu Eszencia 1964 was on the market in the U.S. in the early 1980s at around $50 a bottle, but this was a rarity.

Tokaji Aszu, on the other hand, is widely available in its squat bottle with the narrow neck, and it has many devotees the world over. In comparison tastings with Sauternes from good vintages and German Rhines and Mosels of at least the Beerenauslese degree of sweetness, however, even an Aszu of five *puttonyos* will rarely match the others. Tokaji is not quite as soft and velvety, perhaps because the Hungarian government now pasteurizes it to stabilize it for shipping. In addition, the German Trockenbeerenauslese designation has begun cropping up on Tokaji Aszu labels, though it is doubtful that it has quite the same meaning in Hungary. (*See also* Hungary, Sauternes, Beerenauslese, Trockenbeerenauslese.)

☆/☆☆☆☆

$$/$$$

Tonneau.

This is the standard volume measure for Bordeaux wines, meaning four barrels of 225 liters each, or 900 liters in all. A *tonneau* is equal to 96 cases, or 1,152 standard bottles of wine. Bordeaux wines are priced initially according to the *tonneau* at the château. In a less specific sense, *tonneau* is also sometimes used simply to mean "cask" or "large barrel."

Torgiano.

The village of Torgiano lies in Umbria, in central Italy, and it is dominated by one firm, Cantine Giorgio Lungarotti, which makes all of the Torgiano wine that ever sees commercial channels. Its best known brand names are Rubesco, for its red Torgiano, and Torre di Giano, for the white. The Rubesco is structured similarly to Chianti, with Sangiovese accounting for 50 to 70 percent of the blend, Canaiolo at 15 to 30 percent, Trebbiano at 10 percent, and small amounts of other red grapes. Rubesco tends to be somewhat more austere and elegant than the other big reds of Italy, but it also exudes complexity. The Rubesco Riserva, which represents the best that Giorgio Lungarotti can make, is usually aged at least four years in oak barrels and then spends two more years in bottles before being marketed.

☆☆☆/☆☆☆☆
$$/$$$

Torre Quarto.

Torre Quarto is the brand name used by the family of Cirillo Farrusi in the Puglia region of southern Italy for excellent red and white wines made at their estate in Quarto. The Rosso is very unusual for Italy in that it is made mostly from Malbec grapes, one of the varieties used for blending in Bordeaux reds. This becomes less unusual when it is realized that the Farrusi estate was established by the French noble family of La Rochefoucauld more than a century ago. The Torre Quarto Rosso is an intensely flavored red of grace and complexity that should not be drunk before age eight. The Bianco and Rosato are less complex but are very well made.

☆/☆☆☆☆
$/$$

Miguel Torres.

The leading exporter of Spanish table wines to the U.S. is Miguel Torres, based in Penedés. It is a family business, and a daughter, Marimar Torres, has led the thrust into the American market. The Torres wines are well made and moderately priced. The Gran Coronas Black Label, which is 90 percent Cabernet Sauvignon, is an excellent wine regardless of price.

☆/☆☆☆☆
$/$$

Château La Tour-Haut-Brion.

This small vineyard in Talence in the Graves District south of Bordeaux achieved its fame under the late Henri Woltner, who also owned the nearby Château La Mission-Haut-Brion. La

Tour-Haut-Brion is vinified in the same cellars as La Mission and is similar in many ways. Like La Mission, it is about two-thirds Cabernet Sauvignon, with most of the rest Merlot. La Tour-Haut-Brion rarely achieves the finesse of La Mission and is less good in off vintages, but it displays many characteristics in common with La Mission. Production is little more than 10 percent as large as the output at La Mission. La Tour-Haut-Brion needs about ten years of aging to reach maturity. (*See also* Château La Mission-Haut-Brion.)

☆☆☆☆

$$/$$$

Château La Tour-Martillac.

Montesquieu is said to have cultivated some of his best vines here in the eighteenth century, when his vineyards covered part of the estate that is now Château La Tour-Martillac, one of the better producers of red and white Graves in the *commune* of Martillac, south of Bordeaux. Montesquieu's Château de la Brède estate at one time covered many of today's Graves vineyards, although it is no longer an important wine-producing estate in its own right and the château itself, surrounded by a moat, is mainly of historical interest. Château La Tour-Martillac, covering part of the old Montesquieu domain, produces excellent wines under the tutelage of Jean Kressmann, a leading figure in the Bordeaux wine trade. Some of the vines on this estate actually were grafted onto American roots in 1884, when the Phylloxera blight was sweeping through Bordeaux and killing vines by the millions, and have not been replanted since then. As a result, the yield of white wines, especially, is very small, but they are quite good—typically dry, with the almost steely taste common to Graves. The *commune* of Martillac is farther south in Graves than most of the other major producing *communes*. La Tour-Martillac

was accorded *grand cru* ranking in the Graves classification of 1959 for both its white and red wines. The reds need ten to 12 years to reach maturity, for the best drinking.

☆/☆☆☆☆

$$/$$$

Touraine.

One of the major subdivisions of the Loire River Valley of France is the Touraine, centered around the city of Tours, a major tourist jumping-off point for the famous château country. Most of the wines entitled to the Touraine or Côteaux de Touraine name are rather ordinary and white, although some reds and rosés are produced. They can be somewhat heavy and flabby, with a pronounced earthiness that is not always pleasant. Two different white Touraines ordered one spring afternoon in a small hotel in Amboise, a picturesque town with a castle east of Tours, had to be turned into *vin blanc cassis* by adding Cassis, the black-currant liqueur, before they were palatable. Substantial quantities of sparkling Touraine are also produced and these can be quite pleasant. They are referred to as *vins mousseux* and are made with the Champagne process. The principal white grape is the Chenin Blanc.

The better-known subdivisions of the Touraine are Vouvray, Chinon, and Bourgueil. Vouvray is one of the more elegant whites of the Loire Valley producing balanced, fruity wines of good character in the better vintages. Chinon is best-known for its reds, made from the Cabernet Franc grape of Bordeaux, although some rosés and whites are grown there as well. Bourgueil and Saint-Nicolas-de-Bourgueil produce only red and rosé wines entitled to their place names and are unique in the Loire Valley in this respect. The Cabernet Franc is the only permissible grape variety, and it produces wines that are softer,

fruitier, and less elegant than red Bordeaux. Some white wines are produced around Bourgueil, but they are entitled only to be called Touraine. (*See also* Vouvray.)
☆/☆☆
$/$$

Trakia.

Most of the Bulgarian wines that enter the U.S. are imported under the Trakia label by Monsieur Henri Wines Ltd., a PepsiCo subsidiary. Trakia means "Thracian," from the ancient name for the part of eastern Europe that is now Bulgaria. The Cabernet Sauvignon and Merlot are charming, modest wines that have been priced attractively and represent good value. A Chardonnay and a Blanc de Blancs, made from the Misket grape, are also imported. (*See* Bulgaria.)
☆/☆☆
$

Trarbacher.

This German white wine comes from the right bank of the Mosel River at the important wine town of Traben-Trarbach, one of the more northern, or downstream, parts of the central Mosel region. Actually, two towns exist there, with Traben on the river's left bank, but they are connected by a bridge and are always referred to as one. The wines from the Trarbach side are held in higher regard, but neither is listed among the top Mosels. The town is important partly because its vineyard area is large and partly because it is a center for the Mosel wine trade and for tourists. It has several good hotels and is a logical place to stay if you are making a leisurely trip through the area. Trarbachers lack some of the character and body of the nearby Graachers and Erdeners and do not seem to be as popular in the export trade. But they can represent good value when they appear.

Among the better-known vineyards at Traben-Trarbach are the following:

Trarbacher Halsberg
Trarbacher Hühnersberg*
Trarbacher Königsberg*
Trarbacher Liebeskummer
Trarbacher Schlossberg*
Trarbacher Ungsberg*

An asterisk (*) indicates a vineyard name that survived the revision of the German wine law of 1971. The law also made provision for these other Traben-Trarbach vineyard names: Gaispfad, Kräuterhaus, Kreuzberg, Taubenhaus, Wurzgarten, and Zollturm.
☆/☆☆
$/$$

Trebbiano.

The Trebbiano grape variety is used in a number of Italian white wines and is a constituent of Soave, among others. It has also been bottled increasingly as a varietal under its own name in recent years, often by major Soave producers, who cannot seem to make enough Soave to satisfy the enormous demand in the United States and other foreign markets. The grape is said to have originated in the Trebbia Valley of Emilia-Romagna, but it is much more widely cultivated today. Often the name Trebbiano on a label will be followed by the name of the area of production, as in Trebbiano d'Abruzzo, Trebbiano di Romagna, or Trebbiano di Sicilia.
☆/☆☆
$

Trefethen Vineyards.

A winery can strike it rich with one superb bottling, as Trefethen Vineyards did with its Chardonnay 1976, a superb example of the quality heights that a California wine can reach when conditions are optimum. The wine was rich, creamy, buttery, complex, aromatic yet balanced and elegant, without overwhelming woodiness and intensity. It captured top honors in blind tastings in the United States and abroad, and suddenly Trefethen Vineyards had established an international reputation.

Trefethen is one of the few Napa Valley wineries that lists the city of Napa as its address. The winery occupies the premises of the former Eshcol Vineyards, a handsome wooden building that was constructed in 1886 by Hamden McIntyre, a prominent winery architect of that era. It was named Eshcol after the biblical reference to the Brook of Eshcol, in which Joshua and Caleb cut down a vine branch on instructions from Moses. No wine had been made at Eshcol for 27 years when Gene Trefethen bought it and the surrounding vineyard in 1968. A family company, headed by his son John and John's wife, Janet, now runs the operation, consistently producing excellent wines under the Trefethen label.

The vineyard is substantial—600 acres—and began producing under the Trefethen name in 1973. Besides Chardonnay, it makes Cabernet Sauvignon and White Riesling and has revived the Eshcol brand for white and red table wines without varietal names. All of the Trefethen wines are made 100 percent from Trefethen grapes, and production now totals some 40,000 cases a year. Trefethen also was an early supplier of grapes to Domaine Chandon, whose sparkling wines have won a large following.
☆/☆☆
$$

Trentadue Winery.

Trentadue, established in 1969, is a family winemaking business located three miles south of Geyserville in the Sonoma Valley of California. It is operated by Leo and Evelyn Trentadue and their son Victor, who not only produce wines under the Trentadue label but also sell grapes to Ridge Vineyards and other wineries. Production totals 25,000 cases a year of such varietals as Chardonnay, Chenin Blanc, Johannisberg Riesling, Sémillon, French Colombard, White Zinfandel, Cabernet Sauvignon, Gamay, Merlot, Petite Sirah, and Zinfandel. Trentadue also makes a generic burgundy. The wines generally have been low priced for premium varietals and have lacked concentration and balance.
☆/☆☆
$/$$

Trentino.

Ten wines have qualified for D.O.C. recognition under the Italian wine law under the Trentino denomination. They come from the region of northeastern Italy called Trentino-Alto Adige, north of Verona, an area of spectacularly rugged beauty. The wines are varietally named—e.g., Trentino Cabernet (made from either Cabernet Franc or Cabernet Sauvignon), Trentino Lagrein, Trentino Marzemino, Trentino Merlot, Trentino Moscato, Trentino Pinot (half Pinot Bianco, half Pinot Grigio), Trentino Pinot Nero, Trentino Riesling, Trentino Traminer Aromatico (Gewürztraminer), Trentino Vin Santo. The wines share a certain austerity of style that pleases palates unaccustomed to the richness or even heaviness of many other Italian wines.
☆/☆☆☆
$/$$

Trentino-Alto Adige.

This is Italy's northernmost region, bordering on Austria and the Alps and sometimes called the South Tyrol. The term "Südtirol" sometimes appears on wine labels from the region, and as much German is spoken in some sectors as Italian. Many of the wines are varietal, and the German influence is evident, with such names as Sylvaner, Riesling, and Traminer Aromatico (Gewürztraminer) frequently appearing on labels.

Trittenheimer.

German white wine produced at Trittenheim, the southernmost wine town of the Middle Mosel in the Mosel River region, just upstream from Neumagen, Dhron, and Wintrich. Trittenheimers are fresh and zesty, with a clean finish, but they tend to be less elegant and full than the Piesporters, Bernkastelers, and Wehleners farther north on the river as it winds circuitously toward the Rhine. In years when the weather conditions are ideal, Trittenheimers can rise to extraordinary peaks and often represent excellent value.

Among the better known vineyards at Trittenheim are the following:

Trittenheimer Altärchen
Trittenheimer Apotheke
Trittenheimer Clemensberg
Trittenheimer Falkenberg
Trittenheimer Laurentiusberg
Trittenheimer Neuberg
Trittenheimer Olk
Trittenheimer Sonnenberg
Trittenheimer Sonnteil
Trittenheimer Weierbach

Only the Altärchen and Apotheke vineyard names survived the revision of the German wine law in 1971, but examples from the other vineyards from vintages prior to 1971 can still be found.
☆/☆☆
$/$$

Trockenbeerenauslese.

This is the rare and expensive supersweet wine most revered by German connoisseurs. The word often is abbreviated to "T.B.A." by English-speaking wine-lovers reluctant to grapple with the German pronunciation. It means, literally, "selected dried berries." If the weather has been favorable, with sunshine until late in the autumn, certain grapes are left to shrivel on the vines until they turn virtually into raisins, or berries with highly concentrated juice. Under ideal conditions, the grapes will contract the noble rot, a fungus called *Edelfäule* in German and *Botrytis cinerea* in Latin. This parasite is sought in the production of Sauternes and Monbazillac, among others, in France, Tokay in Hungary and most German white wines. In attacking the grapes, the fungus penetrates the skins, permitting the water in the juice to evaporate and leaving behind an extremely concentrated nectarlike fluid that tastes uniquely of the fungus itself as well as of the grape variety. Because the quantities of juice available from each dried grape are so minute and because the grapes must be harvested by hand, the production costs of this wine are extremely high and only devout connoisseurs can afford to drink it.

Trockenbeerenauslese is one of the categories of wine produced as *Qualitätswein mit Prädikat*. Thus it can be made almost anywhere in Germany and you may encounter a Bernkasteler Doktor T.B.A. from the Mosel River District or perhaps a Niersteiner Rehbach T.B.A. from the Rheinhessen or a T.B.A. from any of the other better vineyard areas of the country. Most experts prefer to drink these wines with fruit at the end of a meal. A perfect combination is a very ripe pear or peach eaten between sips. To savor the taste fully, the taste of the fruit should be allowed to mingle with that of the wine. Another interesting combination is T.B.A. with fresh *foie gras,* which tastes much more appropriate than might be anticipated. The most important point to remember is that this type of wine is to be savored only on special occasions with friends or guests who will fully appreciate it.

Château Troplong-Mondot.

Of the 62 estates that were accorded *grand cru classé* status in the Saint-Emilion classification of 1955, Château Troplong-Mondot is one of the best-known on foreign dining tables because its pro-

GRAND CRU CLASSÉ

CHÂTEAU TROPLONG MONDOT

SAINT-EMILION

1966   Claude et Alain Valette
MISE AU CHÂTEAU   PROPRIÉTAIRES A SAINT-ÉMILION (GIRONDE)

APPELLATION St EMILION GRAND CRU CLASSÉ CONTROLÉE

duction, more than 12,000 cases in a good vintage, is quite large for this important district east of Bordeaux. Only Château l'Angelus, another *grand cru classé,* produces more wine among the *grand crus,* although Châteaux Cheval Blanc, Figeac, and Pavie among the *premiers grands crus* also have higher production. Troplong-Mondot is one of the *côtes,* or hillside vineyards, of Saint-Emilion, lying just east of the ancient hilltop village and not far from Château Pavie. Its good red wines are consistently among the better wines produced in the district. They are soft and early-maturing, with a richness typical of the area, and are best drunk between the ages of eight and 12.
☆☆☆/☆☆☆☆
$$/$$$

Château Trotanoy.

Among the châteaus of Pomerol that would be accorded *grand cru,* or great growth, status in any classification of this important district east of Bordeaux is Château Trotanoy, which makes velvety and robust wines of considerable style. The estate is owned by Jean Pierre Moueix, one of the leading figures of Pomerol and the Libourne wine trade that services both Pomerol and the nearby Saint-Emilion. The supple reds of Trotanoy exude a great bouquet reminiscent of truffles. The wine is generally more esteemed than the neighboring Château Gombaude-Guillot and Château La Violette. Trotanoy would rank among the second growths in any broad classification that included the Médoc. It reaches maturity between ages ten and 12.
☆☆☆☆
$$$

Château Trottevieille.

The balanced red wines of Château Trottevieille were accorded *premier grand cru classé* status in the Saint-Emilion classification of 1955. The estate lies due east of the ancient village of Saint-Emilion and is on the *côtes,* or hillside portions of the district, as opposed to the *graves,* which is the gravelly flatland. The *côtes* vineyards are held in higher regard in general, and ten of the twelve *premier grand cru* estates are on the *côtes.* The production of Château Trottevieille is not large, yet the wines are widely recognized for their quality—which means the price has gone up. Next to Châteaux Cheval Blanc, Ausone, and Figeac, Château Trottevieille is probably the most expensive Saint-Emilion. The wines of this estate have an earthy fullness and richness virtually unique to the district. They are best drunk after they reach the age of ten and before age 20.
☆☆☆☆
$$/$$$

Tualatin Vineyards.

One of the leading winemaking operations in Oregon is Tualatin Vineyards near the town of Forest Grove in the Willamette Valley, about 40 miles west of Portland and 60 miles east of the Pacific Ocean. The microclimate there is a result of the sheltering influence of the Coast Range Mountains on the west and the Cascade Range on the east. Tualatin, with production approaching 20,000 cases, is owned by Bill Malkmus and Bill Fuller, with Fuller as the winemaker. Fuller spent eight years with Louis Martini in California before join-ing with Malkmus in the purchase of the Tualatin property in 1972. They planted vines in 1973 and '74 and made wine from purchased grapes as early as 1973. The vineyard is about 40 percent Riesling, with the rest divided among Pinot Noir, Chardonnay, and Gewürz-traminer. Some grapes are purchased from growers in the state of Washington.

☆/☆☆☆

$/$$

· U ·

Umbria.

Umbria is an important region in central Italy, the source of many wines consumed in Roman cafes and restaurants, including Orvieto and Torgiano.

Ungsteiner.

German white and red wine produced in Ungstein, one of the better wine towns in the Rheinpfalz, or Palatinate, the country's southernmost region for superior table wines. Much of the wine produced in the Ungsteiner vineyards is mediocre red, but the whites made from the Riesling grape rank high among all German wines in terms of quality. They are full-bodied and rich, with a big bouquet in the best vintages, although sometimes a pungent earthiness creeps into the wines not made from the Riesling grape.

Ungsteiners are less renowned than the Forsters and Deidesheimers farther south in the Pfalz. Among the better-known vineyards are the following:

Ungsteiner Herrenberg*
Ungsteiner Honigsachel*
Ungsteiner Kreuz
Ungsteiner Michelsberg*
Ungsteiner Roterd
Ungsteiner Spielberg

The Herrenberg and Honigsachel vineyard names are among those that continued to exist after the revision of the German wine law in 1971, although Honigsachel became a *Grosslage,* or large vineyard virtually synonymous with generic Ungsteiner. Most small vineyards were merged into larger ones to simplify identification. The asterisk (*) indicates vineyard names that survived the German wine law revisions of 1971.
☆/☆☆
$/$$

United States.

The wild grapes that the explorers found growing all over America foretold a great future in winemaking that is only just now beginning to be realized. In the nineteenth century, especially the second half, the United States seemed to be headed for greatness among the world's wine-producing nations. Wines from all over—New York, California, Missouri and Ohio—were winning prizes in European competitions.

Winemaking in the New World was started by the earliest settlers. European monarchs encouraged their colonists in viticulture. The English from Massachusetts Bay to Virginia, the Carolinas and Georgia, the Swedes of Delaware, and the French Huguenots in the Middle-Atlantic States all attempted to grow European grapes. Everywhere the vines failed, lacking durability and resistance to the diseases and pests of the New World. The founding fathers also strongly supported the growth of a wine industry, particularly after the Revolution. George Washington grew grapes at Mount Vernon, as did Jefferson at Monticello. Jefferson was particularly keen on developing wine in America, hoping to substitute wine as a national beverage in place of the hard liquor that his countrymen favored. "No nation is drunken where wine is cheap," he wrote. But he felt that the wine also had to be good. The wild and unfamiliar taste of native grape varieties, the only ones that seemed to thrive, was slow to develop a following.

The first domesticated native grape was called the Alexander, cultivated by the gardener of Pennsylvania's Lieutenant Governor, John Penn, but it still had the rough taste of the wild grape. Soon, through the efforts of grape breeders and hybridizers, better varieties began to appear—the Catawba, the Elvira, the Concord, the Isabella. Plantings spread throughout the Northeast and into Midwestern and Southern states such as Ohio, Michigan, Illinois, Missouri, Tennessee, Arkansas, even Mississippi. The wines still had that wild, "foxy" flavor but they were beginning to satisfy more wine drinkers. In California, meanwhile, the Mission grape, a Vinifera variety, had been planted since the mid-1700s, moving progressively northward with the Franciscan missions. European immigrants a hundred years later quickly discovered that European wine grapes were equally well suited to California, and its sunny climate warmly welcomed the new ar-

rivals. In all parts of the country winemaking flourished. Enormous quantities were made and shipped all over the globe.

Prohibition halted the momentum, wiped out viniculture completely in some regions and necessitated a start from scratch nearly everywhere after it was over. This involved replacing rusted machinery and finding long-gone winemakers, replanting vineyards that had withered or grown unmanageable or were planted in thick-skinned varieties for table use, and establishing marketing organizations and procedures. At last, with nearly half a century lapsed, vineyards again are thriving as they did before. New ones are growing on the gravesites of those that flourished a century ago; others are sprouting in heretofore unlikely places. New technology and new knowledge about viticulture and its techniques have improved the wines of existing wineries and lured surprising numbers of would-be winemakers and vineyardists away from desk jobs to start operations of their own. Scientists at such institutions as the University of California at Davis, Fresno State College, the University of Arkansas, Mississippi State University, the Missouri School of Mines, Syracuse and Cornell Universities in New York are responsible for many of the new developments that are making it possible.

Commercial wineries now operate in more than half of the 50 states. The states and wineries with a substantial output have their own entries alphabetically listed.

Ürziger, Uerziger.

German white wine produced at Ürzig, one of the better wine towns of the Mosel River region. Ürzigers tend to display a spicy character all their own, sometimes accompanied by a touch of *spritzig,* or tendency to sparkle. Although the town lies just north of Wehlen, its wines tend to be harder than the elegant Wehleners, reflecting a different type of soil. The Ürziger vineyards are especially rocky, climbing up the left-hand or northwest side of the river. The vineyard area is relatively small and production is substantially lower than in Zeltingen or Bernkastel. As a result, Ürzigers can be fairly costly in good vintages when top-quality wines of the Auslese or sweeter categories are produced.

Among the better-known vineyards at Ürzig are the following:

Ürziger Kranklay
Ürziger Lay
Ürziger Schwarzlay

Ürziger Urglück
Ürziger Würzgarten

Only the Würzgarten and Schwarzlay vineyard names survived the revision of the German wine law in 1971, which means some of the other wines are now bottled under these names. Examples of the others from vintages prior to the excellent 1971 will diminish in availability.

☆/☆☆☆
$/$$

uva.

Uva is the Italian word for "grapes." "A bunch of grapes" is *un grappolo d'uva.*

· V ·

Valdadige.

Valdadige is a subregion within the Trentino-Alto Adige region which borders on Austria in northern Italy. The area is called Etschaler in German, which is the second language there. The Bianco and Rosso produced there, along the Adige River Valley, are simple and charming.

☆/☆☆

$

Valdepeñas.

The most popular red carafe wine of Spain is Valdepeñas, which is produced in La Mancha, a large region southeast of Madrid. It is named after the town of Valdepeñas, where the wine trade is centered. (*See also* La Mancha.)

☆

$

Valgella.

One of the very good wines produced in northern Italy is Valgella, which comes from the mountainous Valtellina subdivision of Lombardy. It is made mostly from the Nebbiolo grape, which is the noble red variety of northern Italy that also produces Barolo, Gattinara, and Ghemme, among others, in the Piedmont region just to the west. Valgella is lighter and earlier maturing than some of the other Valtellina wines, reaching maturity after four or five years.

☆☆

$/$$

Valle Isarco.

Valle Isarco is the northeastern portion of the Trentino-Alto Adige region that borders on Austria in northern Italy. The German word "Eisacktaler" for the region appears on many labels, and much of the wine is marketed in Germany, Austria, and Switzerland. The wines are varietally named—e.g., Müller-Thurgau della Valle Isarco, Pinot Grigio della Valle Isarco, Sylvaner della Valle Isarco, Traminer Aromatico della Valle Isarco, Veltliner della Valle Isarco.

☆/☆☆

$/$$

Valpantena.

One of the light red wines of the Veneto region of northeastern Italy is Valpantena, which is quite similar to Valpolicella. It is a fresh dry wine not meant for laying down in cellars and is best consumed young and slightly chilled.

☆

$

Valpolicella.

Next to Chianti, Valpolicella is probably the best known Italian red wine. It is a light and fresh wine produced in the province of Verona in the Veneto region of northeastern Italy. It is made from the Corvina, Rondinella, and Molinara grapes and is very similar in style to Bardolino, which comes from the same region. Valpolicella has slightly more character than Bardolino, however, although it cannot be placed in the same category as the robust reds of the Piedmont region farther to the west. Valpolicella is best consumed when it is young and fresh and slightly chilled, although some of its devotees contend that it benefits from three to five years of laying down. Valpolicella Classico comes from a small section of the region and is supposed to be superior. Recioto della Valpolicella is a semisweet wine made partially from dried grapes that provide great intensity and an alcohol level upward of 14 percent. An Amarone is also produced, and it is similar to the Recioto, although drier. (*See* Amarone.)

☆/☆☆☆☆
$/$$$

Varietal wines.

The term "varietal" applies to wines that are predominately made from a single grape variety, such as Cabernet Sauvignon, Pinot Noir, or Chenin Blanc. It is used primarily in California and other parts of the United States to designate better-quality wines, though the practice is increasingly used in Latin America and also in France. French wines with varietal names can be quite good, but *commune* names and individual vineyard names regulated by *appellation contrôlée* laws denote the best wines and limit their geographical usage. Switzerland, Austria, and Alsace also use varietal names. The premium varietals,

along with the three mentioned above, include Johannisberg Riesling, Chardonnay (sometimes called Pinot Chardonnay, but not a true Pinot), Zinfandel, the Gamays, Gewürztraminer, Sauvignon Blanc, Sémillon, Pinot Blanc, Sylvaner, Grenache, Petite Sirah. Several lesser varietals are appearing more frequently, among them French Colombard, Ruby Cabernet (a cross between Cabernet Sauvignon and Carignane), Barbera, Folle Blanche, Merlot, and others.

Veedercrest Vineyards.

Good late-harvested white wines are produced from vineyards planted on Mount Veeder by Veedercrest Vineyards, whose winery was established in 1972 in the basement of the home of Alfred Baxter in Berkeley in 1972, the first vintage that appeared under the Veedercrest label. A new winery was established in an existing building in Emeryville in Alameda County in 1975. Baxter, the Veedercrest founder, was a financial and engineering consultant with his own firm in Berkeley before entering the wine business. He heads a partnership that includes Ronald Fenolio and Ringsbridge Vintners, a family corporation of the Ring family. About 60 acres have been planted on Mount Veeder above the Napa Valley and about 50 more are plantable. The business ran into financial trouble in 1982, when large quantities of Veedercrest wines were liquidated at cut-rate prices, and its future remains in doubt. Production has been curtailed, but Veedercrest is capable of producing excellent wines.

☆/☆☆☆
$/$$

Vega Sicilia.

This is the most celebrated wine of Spain, a legendary red that comes from a 150-acre vineyard in Valbueña de Duero, near Valladolid, in the central part of the country northwest of Madrid. The property was replanted following the Phylloxera blight of the nineteenth century, and Bordeaux methods and barrels are used there, as in the Rioja District to the north. The precise blend of grape varieties is unknown, but cuttings were brought from France about a hundred years ago. Vega Sicilia undergoes at least five years of aging before being sold. It is rarely seen outside Spain, and it is expensive.

☆☆☆☆

$$$

Vendange Tardive.

Vendange tardive is the term used in the Alsatian region of eastern France for white wines made from late-harvested grapes achieving a high level of natural sweetness roughly equivalent to a German Auslese. Grape sugars must reach at least 24.5° on the Brix scale, which is fairly high. (*See* Brix.) If the grapes achieve an average of 29° Brix, they are entitled to be called *sélection des grains nobles*. These approach the sweetness level of German Beerenauslese. Such Alsatian wines are rare and expensive and are best consumed with *foie gras* at the beginning of a meal or with a sweet dessert.

Veneto.

Some of the best-known wines of Italy are produced in the region known as the Veneto, which lies in the northeastern part of the country on the Adriatic Sea. Here is where Bardolino, Valpolicella, and Soave come from, and although these wines are not as highly regarded as the best wines of Tuscany or the Piedmont, they are produced in great volume and display a pleasing charm reflective of Italy's lighthearted national disposition. Sipping a slightly chilled Bardolino in a cafe in Venice on a sleepy afternoon in May can be a glorious experience. A robust Barolo or an elegant Gattinara would not be nearly so appropriate on such an occasion as the pleasant Bardolino produced not far away in the Veneto. Soave, which literally means "suave," is an equally pleasant if unassuming white wine that has achieved considerable fame throughout the world. It is light and charming and should never be compared with the better white wines of France, Germany, or the United States. Valpolicella is the foremost wine of the Veneto, although it is a rather light-colored red that is best consumed within five or six years of the harvest. In general, the wines of the Veneto are not meant for laying down. (*See also* Bardolino, Valpantena, Valpolicella, Soave.)

☆/☆☆☆☆

$/$$$

Ventana Vineyards.

Ventana takes its name from the Ventana Wilderness area of the Santa Lucia Mountain Range in California, just to the west of the Ventana plantings in the Salinas Valley of Monterey County, not far from Soledad. The proprietor, Doug Meador, has been producing excellent Chardonnay since the winery was established, amid 300 acres of vines, in a converted Swiss-style dairy barn in 1978. Ventana also turns out Pinot Blanc, Chenin Blanc, White Riesling, Gamay Noir, Gamay Blanc, Zinfandel, White Zinfandel, botrytised Sauvignon Blanc, dry Sauvignon Blanc, Cabernet Sauvignon, Merlot, and several other varietals, some on an experimental basis. A portion of Ventana's annual grape production is sold to other wineries, which happily indicate Ventana's name as the source on their labels. Ventana's production totals about 30,000 cases a year. In 1979 Doug Meador won five gold medals after entering only seven wines from his first vintage in the Los Angeles County Fair.

☆/☆☆☆

$$

Verdicchio.

One of the best white wines of Italy is Verdicchio, which is produced in the region of the Marches on the Adriatic Sea in the east-central part of the country. Verdicchio is a more assertive wine than Soave, displaying more of the taste of the grape used to make it, the Verdicchio. The best wine is the Verdicchio dei Castelli di Jesi, produced in the Esino River Valley that runs into the Adriatic. A sparkling version of this wine is also made. Verdicchio di Matelica is a similar wine from the provinces of Ancona and Macerata, also in the region of the Marches. Verdicchio comes in a green bottle sometimes shaped like a fish standing on its tail, a needless affectation suggesting that the wine is best consumed with seafood. The suggestion is accurate.

☆/☆☆
$/$$

Vermouth.

One of the more ubiquitous aperitif wines is vermouth, which has been produced traditionally in Italy and France but nowadays is also produced in the United States and a number of other countries. The word "vermouth" comes from the German *Wermut,* or wormwood, whose flowers are used in producing the end product. Vermouth in itself is not a variety of wine. Rather, it is a wine that has been treated in a certain way, usually through the addition of distilled alcohol and various herbs and spices. Each producer is likely to have his own formula, but all formulas are supposed to involve the use of flowers from the wormwood shrub. Leaves from the same plant are an important ingredient in absinthe, the powerful spirit that has been banned in many countries because of the deleterious impact it is supposed to have on the central nervous system. Vermouth is either red or white and dry or sweet. Dry white vermouth is used in making the American Martini cocktail; sweet red vermouth is used in the Manhattan cocktail. Vermouth by itself is a widely used aperitif in Europe; American tourists may be surprised to receive a glass of vermouth when they order a Martini.

☆
$/$$

Vernaccia.

Vernaccia is an Italian white grape variety that yields wines of very different characters in different parts of the country. In fact, there is considerable doubt that all of the Vernaccias of Italy even belong to the same viticultural family. The best is probably the Vernaccia di San Gimignano of Tuscany, but there are also Vernaccia di Cannara of Umbria, Vernaccia di Corniglia of Liguria, Vernaccia di Oristano of the island of Sardinia, Vernaccia di Serrapetrona of the Marches, which is a sparkling red wine often vinified sweet.

☆/☆☆
$/$$

Vernaccia di San Gimignano.

Among the better dry white wines of Tuscany is Vernaccia di San Gimignano, produced from the Vernaccia grape in the province of Siena. It is best after about two years of bottle-age and is made under the supervision of the Chianti Colli Senesi Consorzio, which also oversees Chianti production in this area of Tuscany.

☆
$/$$

Vesuvio.

Italian wines bearing the Vesuvio name come from grapes grown around Mount Vesuvius, the volcano near Naples in the Campania region. The best known wine of Vesuvio is probably Lacrima Christi del Vesuvio, but there are also

Vesuvio Bianco, Rosato, and Rosso. The wines generally are pleasant but not long-lived.
☆/☆☆
$

Vichon Winery.

The new Vichon winery in California, on a steep bend in the Oakville Grade that links the central Napa and Sonoma valleys across the Mayacamas Mountain Range, opened in 1982 after the business was established in 1980, with the first two vintages being handled at another winery, in St. Helena. George Vierra, the winemaker, spent nine years at Charles Krug and Robert Mondavi before joining the Vichon venture, which produces Chardonnay, Cabernet Sauvignon, and a blended table white called Chevrier Blanc, which is made from Sauvignon Blanc and Sémillon. Vichon's early Chardonnays were crisp and clean, displaying the austere style of Mâcon Blanc. Production climbed rapidly past 25,000 cases in the 1981 vintage and was expected to reach 40,000 cases annually within a few years.
☆☆/☆☆☆
$$

Vieux-Château-Certan.

In the Pomerol District east of Bordeaux and adjacent to Saint-Emilion the estates are relatively small and less well known than in the other major Bordeaux subdivisions, possibly because Pomerol was never formally classified. Château Pétrus is the acknowledged king of the Pomerols, and until recent years few would argue that Vieux-Château-Certan was not a close second, perhaps worthy of being called the crown prince. Vieux-Certan consistently sells at prices well above the other Pomerols, reflecting its worldwide following among connoisseurs. It is often a full-bodied yet supple wine of great richness and intensity that achieves considerable elegance when consumed at maturity—about 15 years of age. Some recent vintages from this château have been disappointing because of a lack of intensity and richness, but its reputation has suffered little.
☆☆☆☆
$$$

Villa Mt. Eden Winery.

Jim and Anne McWilliams bought property near Oakville in the Napa Valley in California in 1970, where a winery had existed since 1881. They originally purchased the tract as a summer home, but by 1973 they had revived and modernized the winery and began ripping out old vines from the 87-acre vineyard. Now it is half Cabernet Sauvignon, with the balance in Pinot Noir, Chardonnay, and Gewürztraminer. There will be no more Gamay produced there, because all of the Gamay vines were grafted over to Cabernet and Chardonnay. Production now totals 13,000 to 15,000 cases a year, all from grapes grown entirely on the Villa Mt. Eden estate. Jim McWilliams still operates an investment firm called McWilliams & Company in San Francisco which he started in 1967. Before that he worked for another investment concern. Anne McWilliams is the granddaughter of A. P. Giannini, who founded the Bank of America in San Francisco, now the nation's largest bank. The first commercial harvest at Villa Mt. Eden was the 1974, a fine vintage over most of California, and quality standards have remained high.
☆/☆☆☆
$$

vin ordinaire.

The French term for ordinary wine is vin ordinaire. It usually refers to the local wines in a particular region or district that are unlikely to be exported from that region and may not even be bottled. Sometimes a *vin ordinaire* may be quite pleasant, but often it will be precisely what the term implies.

vin du pays.

Vin du pays means, literally, "wine of the country," indicating that it was produced in the part of France where it is being consumed. It is the local *vin ordinaire* in many cases, although theoretically a *vin du pays* should actually come from the area, whereas a *vin ordinaire* might be a blend of wines from as far away as Algeria, Italy, or Spain.

Los Viñeros Winery.

Los Viñeros is a producer of wines under several labels in Santa Barbara County, California. Established in 1980, the venture did not have its own winery until the following year, when Cabernet Sauvignon in both red and white versions was made. The grapes come from vineyards in both Santa Barbara and San Luis Obispo counties, and the wines are sold almost entirely in California under the Los Viñeros, Coastal Cellars, Central Coast Cellars, and Central Cellars labels.

☆/☆☆☆
$/$$

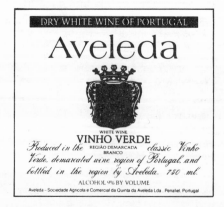

DRY WHITE WINE OF PORTUGAL

Aveleda

WHITE WINE
VINHO VERDE
Produced in the REGIÃO DEMARCADA *classic Vinho*
BRANCO
Verde, demarcated wine region of Portugal, and
bottled in the region by Aveleda. 750 ml.
ALCOHOL 9% BY VOLUME
Aveleda - Sociedade Agrícola e Comercial da Quinta da Aveleda Lda . Penafiel. Portugal

Vinho Verde.

Northern Portugal produces some light, pleasant table wines, and one of these is Vinho Verde which, literally, translated, means "green wine." However, the wine is not green, but can be either white or red. The use of the word *verde,* "green," reflects the youth and freshness of Vinho Verde—the taste of the fruit and acidity evident in most young wines. It comes from vineyards lying north of the Douro River, where Port is made, and stretching up to the Minho River on the Spanish frontier. In fact, similar wines are made just over the border in Spain, demonstrating that winemaking does not respect national boundaries. The vines for Vinho Verde grow everywhere, right up to the roadsides, and are trained along wooden or metal racks that hold them eight to ten feet above the ground. Some vines can even be seen growing up trees, and the grapes from them must be harvested by ladder. This elevation, away from the soil that reflects the sun's heat, prevents the grapes from becoming as ripe as they would if trained closer to the ground in the traditional manner. And it is this lack of ripeness that gives Vinho Verde its distinctive quality. It tends to be slightly sparkling and very dry, almost astringent in taste. The white is a perfect accompaniment to the shellfish that can be found in restaurants along the Atlantic coast of Portugal. The red is a very hard wine not often seen in the export markets. Both the red and the white are best drunk well chilled. (*See also* Portugal.)

☆/☆☆
$/$$

Vinifera Wine Cellars.

Vinifera Wine Cellars Ltd. of Hammondsport, New York, is owned and operated by Dr. Konstantin Frank, one of the most important and influential figures in American wine. Dr. Frank was born in 1899 to German parents living in Russia, where after many years of extensive training he became viticulturist and supervisor of 2000 acres of Riesling grapes in the Ukraine. In 1950 Dr. Frank immigrated to the United States and applied to the experimental agricultural station at Geneva, New York, for a job utilizing his knowledge and expertise. Despite his training and experience, he was given only menial work. Frank was convinced that *Vitis vinifera* varieties such as Riesling and Chardonnay could grow in the Finger Lakes Region which, though colder than European wine regions, was not as cold as the subzero Ukraine. Charles Fournier, the French winemaker at Gold Seal, became intrigued with the idea and hired Frank to experiment with a plot of European vines. Their success with Chardonnay and Riesling was so gratifying to Dr. Frank that he left after the first vintage received its acclaim in 1961 and started his own vineyards and winery in Hammondsport.

Dr. Frank is strong in his conviction that Vinifera grape varieties should be planted in the Finger Lakes District instead of the hybrids that most New York wineries are turning to. His wines, Chardonnay, Johannisberg Riesling, and Pinot Noir, certainly attest to the degree of success that is possible. Although the larger producers are as yet unwilling to risk extensive replanting in Vinifera varieties, Dr. Frank's success has encouraged some of the smaller wineries to experiment with them. Dr. Frank grows more Riesling than anything else, all of which is Spätlese (late-picked). He makes small quantities of very expensive Trockenbeerenauslese in certain years. In addition, he makes a Gewürztraminer and a sweet, fortified Muscat Ottonel.

In more recent vintages, the quality of the Frank wines appears to have fallen off, and excess acidity and other imbalances have occasionally been evident. Sometimes his wines seem to have received too much oak-aging or bottle-aging, but then Dr. Frank proves himself anew with another exceptional vintage that seems to silence the gainsayers. ☆/☆☆☆
$$

Vini del Piave.

The Piave denomination signifies that a wine comes from the Piave River area of the Veneto region of northeastern Italy. The better local wines are varietally named—e.g., Cabernet del Piave, Merlot del Piave, Tocai del Piave, Verduzzo del Piave, all of which have been recognized under the Italian D.O.C. law. Merlot, originally a basic grape of red Bordeaux, is widely cultivated here, yielding soft wines often lacking in character but pleasant to drink. The Cabernet, made either from Cabernet Franc or Cabernet Sauvignon, tends to display more backbone, and the *riserva* versions have complexity. ☆/☆☆☆
$/$$

Vino Nobile di Montepulciano.

Quite similar to Chianti but longer-lasting and more elegant, the Vino Nobile di Montepulciano is sometimes compared with the great Brunello di Montalcino, perhaps Italy's most magnificent red wine. Besides using the classic Sangiovese red grape of Chianti, Vino Nobile di Montepulciano uses about 25 percent white grapes and begins to turn a slightly tawny color after about seven years of age. In general, it reaches maturity far sooner than Brunello. The ordinary wines of this district are simply called Montepulciano, so the Nobile designation on the label is important. It is produced in the Tuscan province of Siena and is best in its *riserva* and *riserva speciale* versions that benefit from additional aging in casks.

☆☆☆☆

$$/$$$

vino da tavola.

Vino da tavola is the Italian term for table wine, which under the D.O.C. law means that the wine has not qualified for D.O.C. recognition for geographical origin, grape variety, or production method. Most such wines are simple and short-lived, but there are also many brand-name wines from major producers that do not qualify for D.O.C. recognition yet are of very high quality.

vintage.

The vintage is the annual harvest of grapes that takes place in September and October in the northern hemisphere and February and March in the southern hemisphere, as well as the wine produced from that harvest. A "vintage" wine is one produced in a particular year, as opposed to blended wines that come from a number of vintages. The term "vintage" has taken on a favorable connotation, but actually there are good vintages and bad, and every year in which a harvest occurs there is a vintage. In two areas, the Champagne District of France and the Douro Valley of Portugal, vintage years are attached to the wines only if the quality is sufficiently high. Thus a vintage Champagne or a vintage Port is made only in good vintages. But vintage wines are made every year in every other winegrowing region of the world, so the fact that a year appears on a label does not mean it is automatically a good wine. Some vintages—for example 1965 and '68 in France—yielded wines of quite poor quality. The factor that accounts for variations among vintages is the weather. Favorable weather results in fully ripe grapes and superior wines.

vins délimités de qualité supérieure.

On a quality level below the French wines entitled to an *appellation contrôlée* are those recognized by the government as *vins délimités de qualité supérieure,* more often referred to as V.D.Q.S. wines. They have won government recognition for "superior quality," yet they are not on a par with the best French wines. V.D.Q.S. wines are not often seen in the export markets, but when they are, they can be good value at a fraction of the cost of a wine with an *appellation contrôlée.* (*See also* appellation contrôlée.)

Vitis vinifera.

Vitis vinifera is the species of vine from which nearly all good wine is made. It is cultivated extensively in Europe, South America, and California, and with less success in the eastern United States and Canada. The grape varieties widely acknowledged as the best for premium wine production are all *Vitis vinifera.* Cabernet Sauvignon, Pinot Noir, Chardonnay, Sémillon, Sauvignon Blanc, Gamay, Riesling, Sylvaner, etc.

Volnay.

Lying adjacent to Pommard and just above Meursault in the Côte de Beaune

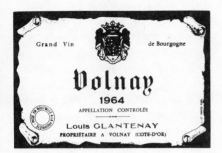

of Burgundy is Volnay, where some of the best red Burgundies of delicacy and lightness are produced. They have a flowery bouquet and a special charm that is extremely appealing to the wine-lover who is not in the mood for one of the more complex and robust red Burgundies produced farther to the north in the Côte de Nuits. A Volnay will not be quite as big as a Pommard, even though the two vineyard areas are separated only by a stone wall, but it will not be quite as costly, either, and usually will be just as well made. Volnay wines have a peculiar elegance that is almost romantic, if not aphrodisiac, and it is easy to understand why they have been sought for centuries by connoisseurs the world over. It is often said that a Volnay should be drunk before it reaches ten years of age, but the author has kept bottles for much longer in his cellar and found them fresh and seductive when sampled after 20 years. However, it is true that Volnays are not as long-lived as most other good Burgundies, and perhaps partly for this reason the *commune* has no recognized *grands crus.* Among the *premiers crus* are the following:

Angles
Barre
Brouillards
Caillerets
Caillerets Dessus

Champans
Santenots
Clos des Chênes
Clos des Ducs
Fremiets
Ormeau
Pousse d'Or
Robardelle

The red wines of nearby Meursault are usually bottled as Volnay, and the whites of Volnay are usually sold as Meursault. Although a Volnay-Caillerets or Volnay-Champans will display great breeding, the wines simply named Volnay, from anywhere in the *commune,* can be excellent.

☆☆☆/☆☆☆☆
$$/$$$

Vosne-Romanée.

Connoisseurs of the world's greatest red wines know that the *commune,* or township, of Vosne-Romanée in the Burgundian Côte de'Or of France produces several that rank at or near the very top. This is the home of the celebrated Domaine de la Romanée-Conti, where wines far more costly than even the *premiers grands crus classés* of Bordeaux are made. The production of the tiny Romanée-Conti vineyard, a scant four and a half acres in size, amounts to only 600 to 700 cases annually—compared to the 12,000 or more cases, for example, of Château Lafite-Rothschild. The other wines produced by La Domaine, while not as costly as Romanée-Conti itself, are still very expensive and are made in relatively modest quantities. These are La Tâche, Richebourg, Romanée-Saint-Vivant, Grands Echézeaux, and Echézeaux.

The *commune* wines, called simply Vosne-Romanée, are among the best and most reliable *commune* wines of Burgundy. These are usually blends from any vineyards lying within the geographic boundaries of Vosne-Romanée and the neighboring Flagey-Echézeaux, which are usually marketed as Vosne-Romanée. A Vosne-Romanée will generally be superior, for example, to a Nuits-Saint-Georges *commune* wine or a similar wine from Morey-Saint-Denis, another part of the Côte de Nuits section of the Côte d'Or, or Golden Slope of Burgundy. The village of Vosne-Romanée is scarcely a crossroads in the hills above Route 74 as it runs between Vougeot and Nuits-Saint-Georges. Besides the Domaine de la Romanée-Conti, the *commune* has a number of other growers producing excellent wines. Such *premiers crus* vineyards as La Grande Rue, Les Malconsorts, and Les Beaux Monts produce such refined and elegant Burgundies with such extraordinarily perfumed bouquets that they would probably be *grands crus* in almost any other *commune* of Burgundy.

In general, the wines of Vosne-Romanée are not quite as robust as those of Gevrey-Chambertin, Nuits-Saint-Georges, and Morey-Saint-Denis, yet they are not fast-maturing either, requiring at least five or six years of aging before they approach maturity. The *grands* and *premiers crus* are best after a decade and will last two or three times that long when properly stored. A La Romanée 1950, not a great vintage, retained plenty of fruit and body along with a flowery bouquet when sampled in New York in 1972. Although the quality level of the wines of Vosne-Romanée is very high, buyers must be careful to avoid confusion due to the similarity of their names. The *grands crus,* e.g., La Romanée and Romanée-Conti, do not carry the name Vosne, whereas the words Vosne-Romanée will always precede the vineyard names of the *premiers crus,* e.g., Vosne-Romanée-Les Suchots or Beaumonts. (*See also* Côte de Nuits, Romanée-Conti.)

☆☆☆☆

$$/$$$$

Vougeot (*See* Clos de Vougeot.)

Vouvray.

In the heart of the Loire Valley's famed château country just east of Tours is the town of Vouvray on the river's north bank. Some great white wines are produced there, but not every year, because the weather is not always favorable in this part of France that is somewhat farther north than most of the other major wine-growing areas. Vouvray can be big and rich, as it was in the 1959 vintage, with a fullness and ripeness that is extraordinary. Or it can be fairly dry, as it often is. Some sparkling Vouvray is produced, especially in years when the weather has been unkind and the wine seems too acid. Vouvray with a slight prickle is sometimes even produced by mistake, when unfermented sugar reacts anew after bottling. This quality, called *pétillant,* can be very pleasant and often seems to occur in Loire Valley wines.

Diagonally across from Vouvray on the south side of the Loire is Montlouis-sur-Loire, where wines quite similar to Vouvray are bottled under the Montlouis *appellation.* Like Vouvray, Montlouis is made from the Chenin Blanc grape and often is produced as a sparkling wine using the champagne process. Only 9.5 percent alcoholic content is required of the Montlouis and Vouvray sparkling wines; still Montlouis must attain 10 percent alcohol and still Vouvray must reach 11 percent. The content can run higher in good vintages after plenty of warm sunshine. (*See* Touraine.)

☆/☆☆☆

$/$$

· W ·

Wachenheimer.

German white and red wine produced in Wachenheim, one of the better wine towns in the middle of the Rheinpfalz, or Palatinate, the country's southernmost region for superior table wines. Only small quantities of red wine are produced; it is inferior to the reds of France and Italy and generally is not exported. But the whites of Wachenheim are among the best in the Pfalz, equivalent to the best Ruppertsbergers and just a notch below the Forsters and Deidesheimers on the historical quality scale. They are rich and full-bodied, with a flowery aroma in good vintages, when Trockenbeerenauslese is made. Wachenheim is the northernmost of the four most important wine towns of the Pfalz, just above Forst.

Wachenheim has a number of outstanding vineyards whose names appear on labels in the export trade, including the following:

Wachenheimer Altenburg*
Wachenheimer Bachel
Wachenheimer Böhlig*
Wachenheimer Dreispitz
Wachenheimer Fuchsmantel
Wachenheimer Gerümpel*

Wachenheimer Goldbächel*
Wachenheimer Hagel
Wachenheimer Langenbachel
Wachenheimer Luginsland
Wachenheimer Rechbachel*
Wachenheimer Schenkenbohl
Wachenheimer Sussbuckel
Wachenheimer Wolfsdarm

The vineyards marked with an asterisk (*) are among those that retained their identities, if not their former shapes, in the revision of the German wine law in 1971. The new law also made provision for Wachenheimer Belz. Examples of the other vineyard wines from pre-1971 vintages can still be found. ☆/☆☆☆
$/$$$

Wagner Vineyards.

Wagner Vineyards is a small New York State producer mostly of European-American hybrid wines, with 112 acres planted in grapes on the eastern slope above Seneca Lake, in the Finger Lakes District in the central part of the state, the heart of New York's most important wine region, not far from the town of Lodi. The proximity of the lake provides a microclimate that moderates the winter temperatures—which can be fiercely cold—and that protects the grapes from frosts in the spring and fall. The western-facing slopes are steep, providing good drainage. Proprietor Bill Wagner has been growing grapes for more than 30 years, but ground was not broken for his winery until early 1976, and the winery did not open for business until 1979. The Wagner products include Delaware, Aurora, Seyval Blanc, de Chaunac and Rougeon among the hybrids and Chardonnay, Riesling, and Gewürztraminer among the European varietals. From only two acres of Chardonnay grapes Wagner produces an extraordinary oak-aged Chardonnay wine that rivals some of the Chardonnays from California in terms of depth and complexity when the weather conditions permit, which means not in every vintage. Total production of Wagner Vineyards runs about 25,000 cases in favorable vintages.

☆/☆☆☆
$/$$

Washington.

The excellent wines that have come out of Washington's Yakima Valley have inspired some experts to proclaim that this region one day will be America's greatest. Although the state's vines were primarily Concord used for grape juice and Cold Duck until the mid-60s, substantial plots of Vinifera varieties are now thriving in Yakima, in the Columbia Basin to the southeast, and along the shores of the Columbia River itself. Climatic conditions are similar to those of northern France. The research station at Prosser started in about 1965 and since that time, with the help and expertise of California's esteemed oenologist André Tchelistcheff, vineyard acreage has increased by leaps and bounds. It has been estimated that there is room in eastern Washington for 250,000 acres of vines, a quantity that could make Washington the second largest wine district in the country. Ste. Michelle Vineyards is the foremost producer, the first to get into large-scale production of varietal wines. Intense varietal character marks these wines and they have scored impressively in blind tastings by panels of experts. The Chardonnay and Cabernet Sauvignon are especially impressive.

Wehlener.

German white wine produced in Wehlen, one of the best vineyard towns of the Mosel River region. The Wehlener Sonnenuhr (for sundial) is the vineyard that has made the town famous, often approaching the Bernkasteler Doktor, produced just to the south, on a quality level. Many connoisseurs prefer the Wehlener Sonnenuhr to all other Mosels because of its freshness and delicate yet assertive character. Its price reflects its quality and popularity; next to the Doktor at Bernkastel, it tends to be the most expensive Mosel wine. You know you are at Wehlen while driving north along the Mosel Valley when you can see a big sundial fashioned in rock in the middle of the Sonnenuhr vineyard on the right-hand side of the river. Several other Wehlen vineyards approach the Sonnenuhr in quality, and nearly all of these are owned by the Prüm family, whose name on a label from that part of the Mosel is an accurate guide to the better wines.

Among the better-known vineyards at Wehlen are the following:

Wehlener Abtei
Wehlener Feinter
Wehlener Klosterlay
Wehlener Lay
Wehlener Michelsberg
Wehlener Munzlay
Wehlener Nonnenberg
Wehlener Rosenberg
Wehlener Sonnenuhr
Wehlener Wertspitz

Only the Sonnenuhr and Nonnen-berg vineyard names survived the re-vision of the German wine law in 1971. There is also a Klosterberg. The others were merged, but examples from pre-1971 vintages can still be found.

☆/☆☆☆

$$/$$$

Weibel.

The Weibel family of Swiss heritage founded Weibel Champagne Vineyards in 1945 on the site of the old Leland Stanford winery near Mission San Jose in Santa Clara County, California. Char-donnay Champagne Brut, an excellent dry bottle-fermented Champagne, is perhaps their best-known wine, but as a specialist in Champagne-making Wei-bel has also made great quantities under private label for stores and hotels all over California. Its other wines, pre-mium varietals including Chardonnay, Cabernet Sauvignon, Pinot Noir, Chenin Blanc, Johannisberg Riesling, and Green Hungarian, are generally quite good but not as well known. Weibel now owns several hundred acres in the North Coast Counties of Sonoma and Mendocino. Most of the table wines are made at their winery in Ukiah. Weibel also makes several dessert wines, including *soiera* Sherries and Ports and a rich Cream of Muscat. Total production is large—more than 900,000 cases a year.

☆/☆☆

$/$$

Wente Bros.

The green label of Wente Brothers, winemakers of California's Livermore Valley, south of San Francisco Bay, is familiar to anyone who has ever sought fine wines from California. The whites from Wente have been widely available in the United States for nearly a cen-tury. Wente and Louis Martini have shared the same distributor for years and wherever the white wines of Wente could be found, the reds of Louis M. Martini were sure to be there, too. The arrangement has worked nicely for both, though in actual fact each makes both red and white wines.

The founder of Wente Brothers em-igrated from Hanover, Germany, in 1880 and learned the art of winemaking from Charles Krug, a fellow countryman al-ready well established in the Napa Val-ley. In 1883 Carl Wente acquired his first vineyards in Livermore and pur-chased cuttings of Sauvignon Blanc and Sémillon that the owner of Cresta Blanca had brought over from Château d'Yquem, the incomparable *premier grand cru* of Sauternes, in France. Perhaps it is the illustrious heritage of these cuttings and their descendants that gives Wente's Sauvignon Blanc its silkiness and spice; some say it is the gravelly soil and par-ticular climate of Livermore Valley. No matter, it was an auspicious beginning and the Wentes soon began to excel with other whites, notably Dry Sémil-lon, the ever-popular Grey Riesling, and Chardonnay. Chardonnay was pro-duced by Wente long before it became prominent elsewhere in California, and though more heavily oaked versions are currently in vogue, this wine has a loyal following. Much of the quality came from the skill of the vintner.

Herman Wente, Carl's son, was one of California's most esteemed wine-makers. He and his brother Ernest ran the winery until Herman's death in 1961 when Ernest's son Karl became the winemaker. Karl's sons, Eric and Philip, have both earned degrees in oenology and viticulture and are carrying on the family tradition. Several other members of the Wente family are actively in-volved in the winery's management. Er-nest Wente, the other member of the original pair, died in 1981. The family vineyards have been gradually expanded with new plantings in the Livermore Valley and in the Monterey region. Annual production now totals more than 1.5 million gallons.

Wente's Blanc de Blancs is a popular wine introduced in the late 60s; it is a lightly sweet blend of Ugni Blanc and Chenin Blanc (a French variety increasingly seen here). In recent vintages Wente has made a Riesling Auslese from overripe grapes that developed *Botrytis cinerea.* This dusty mold works through the skin of the grape, allowing the moisture to evaporate and leaving a residue of sweetness that, if properly handled, results in a luscious wine. (*See Botrytis cinerea.*)

☆/☆☆☆
$/$$

Whitehall Lane Winery.

This modern winery was erected in 1980 just off the west side of the St. Helena Highway in the heart of California's Napa Valley. About 25 acres of vineyards surround the winery. Production is mostly white wine, including a stylish Chardonnay. A Cabernet Sauvignon is also made.

☆/☆☆☆
$$

Widmer's.

John Jacob Widmer immigrated to the United States from Switzerland in 1882 and settled in Naples, New York, at the southern end of the westernmost of the Finger Lakes, Canandaigua. As soon as he could borrow some money, he bought land and planted grapes, producing his first vintage in 1888. But it was his son William who firmly established the reputation of Widmer wines. Will was sent to school in Germany where, at the viticultural school in Geisenheim on the Rhine, he learned the finest techniques in grape-growing and winemaking. Through his influence Widmer established itself as one of the few New York State producers specializing in wines with varietal labels. Using native Labrusca varieties such as Niagara, Delaware, Catawba, and Elvira, he marketed them under the grape name, often with vintage dates.

Widmer is now owned by the R. T. French Company, a food-processing firm, but it has continued, with Will's help, to make Widmer wines in the tradition of the Widmer family. The white varietal Lake Niagara, for example, is still one of their most popular and appealing wines. The Labrusca flavor is immediately discernible in the aroma but surprisingly little in the taste. It is soft and fruity, medium sweet but quite fresh and rather delightful. 1970 marked another enterprising departure for Widmer when the company purchased 400 acres in the Alexander Valley of Sonoma County, California, where they are producing varietals such as Cabernet Sauvignon and other Vinifera wines.

In New York, Widmer also uses the Spanish *solera* system in producing some very fine Sherries which age in 50-gallon white oak barrels on top of the winery roof in Naples, where they are supposed to benefit from exposure to the weather. The unusual sight of its "cellars on the roof" is a drawing card for tourists and a must on the list for visitors to the Finger Lakes District.

☆/☆☆
$/$$

Hermann J. Wiemer Vineyard.

Hermann J. Wiemer, formerly the chief winemaker at Bully Hill Vineyards in Hammondsport, New York, established his own winery on 140 acres of land at Dundee on Seneca Lake in the heart of the New York Finger Lakes district a few years before leaving Bully Hill at the end of 1980. He found a ramshackle house built in 1790, with an adjacent barn built by the Mennonites in the early 1900s, and bought the entire property in 1973. It took time and money to acquire the stainless steel fermenting tanks and oak barrels that he needed and to begin planting his own grapes, but by 1979 he was producing Chardonnay and Riesling of excellent quality, so his parting of the ways with Walter S. Taylor, proprietor of Bully Hill, came as no surprise.

Initially he used purchased grapes from other growers as his own vines matured, but his 1980 harvest yielded excellent grapes. The wines are crisp, clean, and dry, even the Riesling, which is so often slightly cloying when made by other producers. As of 1981 a total of 30 acres of vines had been planted on his property, just in time for the disastrous winter kill that all but wiped out the crop for many New York growers in 1981.

Wiemer's hometown was Bernkastel, the famous wine village on the Mosel River in Germany, where his father ran the vine-grafting institute. Hermann studied oenology at the wine schools in Geisenheim and Neustadt and is now applying all of his knowledge to making superior products in Dundee, New York.
☆/☆☆
$$

Wilson Daniels Ltd.

Wilson Daniels Ltd. is primarily a wine-marketing and sales organization based in St. Helena, California. It takes responsibility for the products of individual wineries and markets them around the United States, as well as abroad if quantities are sufficient. Wilson Daniels also has begun to market wines under its own label. These wines are usually made at the facilities of the Wilson Daniels clients, but carry only the Wilson Daniels name. For example, the Wilson Daniels Cabernet Sauvignon 1978 was vinified at the winery of St. Clement Vineyards in St. Helena, and the Wilson Daniels Sauvignon Blanc 1980 was made at Napa Wine Cellars in Yountville. Production of these wines is small, but they are distributed nationally in selected markets.
☆/☆☆
$$

Wiltinger.

Perhaps the best wine town of the Saar River, which flows into the Mosel at its southern end, is Wiltingen, where Wiltinger wines are produced. The most renowned of the Wiltingers, however, do not carry the town's name. These are Scharzhofberg and, sometimes, Scharzberg. Although the Saar and the Ruwer were lumped together with the Mosel under the German wine law of 1971 to form the region called Mosel-Saar-Ruwer, Saar wines are quite distinctive and the Wiltingers are among the best examples. They tend to be harder, with an almost metallic taste in poor years, but they are big, rich, and assertive wines in the best years. Some connoisseurs rank them with the Bernkastelers and Wehleners of the Mosel Valley to the north, while others contend that they never quite reach those peaks. Wiltingers overshadow the nearby Kanzemers, Wawerners, Oberemmelers, and Niedermenningers, although these can be excellent value in good years.

Among the better-known vineyards at Wiltingen are the following:

Wiltinger Braune Kupp*
Wiltinger Braunfels*
Wiltinger Dohr
Wiltinger Gottesfuss*
Wiltinger Grawels
Wiltinger Klosterberg*
Wiltinger Kupp*
Wiltinger Rosenberg*
Wiltinger Sandberg*
Scharzberg* or
    Wiltinger Scharzberg
Scharzhofberg*

An asterisk (*) indicates a vineyard name that survived the revision of the German wine law of 1971. Other Wiltinger vineyard names for which provision was made in the law include Hölle, Schlangengraben and Schlossberg. Scharzberg is now a *Grosslage,* or large vineyard area, encompassing many other vineyards that previously had their own identities. It can be regarded as a generic term for Saar wines.
☆/☆☆☆
$$

Wine and the People.

Peter Brehm, once a participant in the Peace Corps and later a lobster fisherman in Connecticut and Florida, opened a store selling supplies for home winemakers and beer makers in Berkeley, California, in 1970. He called it Wine and the People, to invoke an image of everyday drinking instead of the image of wine as an almost regal, aloof product reserved for the affluent. A winery was established in time for the crush of 1975, and since then Wine and the People has been producing bulk wines, which it sells mainly to hobbyists for home bottling, as well as a line of premium varietals. Some of the latter group are sold under the name Berkeley Wine Cellars in an effort to achieve greater acceptability among consumers beyond the immediate Berkeley market. Brehm now heads a corporation with about 25 shareholders who own the Wine and the People operation. Production has risen to the equivalent of about 20,000 cases of bulk wine sold mainly to hobbyists, plus 1250 to 1500 cases a year of premium varietals, including Zinfandel, Pinot Noir, and Chardonnay. A vintage Port of good quality is made in some years when the Zinfandel grapes achieve unusually high sugar levels, leading to high alcohol levels after fermentation. Wine and the People owns

no vineyards and buys all of its grapes as well as some wines in bulk for resale.
☆/☆☆☆
$/$$

Winkeler.

The Rheingau region of Germany consistently produces the country's finest wines, and the town of Winkel is clearly one of the Rheingau's foremost. Winkelers are big and elegant, with great natural finesse, and are made almost entirely from the superior Riesling grape, the best of Germany. The most renowned Winkeler of all is Schloss Vollrads, one of the few vineyards in Germany under single ownership. The late Graf Matuschka-Greiffenklau, a leading figure in German wines, was the proprietor, and for many years he and his family closely watched over the previous vineyard of 81 acres and the manor house with its nearby watchtower surrounded by a moat where ducks and swans nest. The property is in the hills above Winkel and is the largest privately owned estate of the Rheingau.

The Graf Matuschka traditionally bottled Schloss Vollrads under his own rating system involving the use of capsules of various colors. (The capsule is the lead or plastic covering over the upper neck and cork of the bottle.) The system is rather complex, because six different quality levels of Schloss Vollrads are marketed, and each has its own subdivisions. The *Qualitätswein* has a green or a red capsule, Kabinett wines have a blue capsule, Spätlese wines have a pink capsule, Auslese wines have a white capsule, Beerenauslese wines have a gold capsule and Trockenbeerenauslese wines have a gold capsule as well as a distinctive neck label. The addition of gold or silver stripes to the capsule is used as a further indication of quality within each category. For example, a Schloss Vollrads Auslese with gold stripes on its white capsule would theoretically be superior to one without the gold stripes, although the nuances of the two wines might be difficult for anyone but an expert to differentiate. The use of different capsules to connote various quality levels existed long before the passage of the German wine law of 1971 and complies with that law because the capsules technically are not labels. Less sophisticated wine lovers need to know little more than that Schloss Vollrads is one of the greatest wines of Germany and that almost any bottle, regardless of the color of its capsule, should be superior. Under the 1971 law Schloss Vollrads became a suburb of Winkel, so that it would continue to be entitled to its traditional name. If this technical change had not been made, it would have become Winkeler Schloss Vollrads or something similar.

The village of Winkel on the north bank of the Rhine River near Johannisberg has a number of smaller vineyards divided among about a dozen owners who produce excellent wines that can approach Schloss Vollrads in quality if not in fame. Most of them lie between Schloss Vollrads and Schloss Johannisberg, another renowned vineyard, and usually represent excellent value.

Among the better-known vineyards at Winkel are the following:

Schloss Vollrads*
Winkeler Ansbach
Winkeler Bienengarten
Winkeler Dachsberg*
Winkeler Gutenberg*
Winkeler Hasensprung*
Winkeler Honigberg*
Winkeler Jesuitengarten*
Winkeler Klaus
Winkeler Klauserweg
Winkeler Oberberg
Winkeler Rheingarten
Winkeler Schlossberg*

An asterisk (*) indicates vineyard names that survived or that were created in the revision of the German wine law of 1971. The Honigberg is now a *Grosslage,* or large vineyard area, similar to a generic wine from Winkel.
☆/☆☆☆
$/$$$

Woodbury Vineyards.

Not to be confused with Woodbury Winery, a producer of Port in California, Woodbury Vineyards is a small New York State winery in Chatauqua County in the western part of the state. Woodbury Vineyards first planted Chardonnay and Riesling vines in 1971, and added to these plantings over the years, but the grapes were sold to other small wineries in the Northeast. Woodbury's first harvest of wines to be bottled under its own label occurred in 1979, and in the fall of 1980 it released the first commercial Chardonnay produced in the Chatauqua region. Gewürztraminer was harvested by Woodbury in 1980. The winery is quite small.
☆/☆☆
$/$$

Woodbury Winery.

One of the leaders in the California vintage Port revival is Russell Woodbury of Woodbury Winery in San Rafael, near San Francisco. Woodbury founded his business in 1977, when he made the '77 vintage at the facilities of Wine and the People in Berkeley. He did the same with his '78 vintage before moving into his own new winery in San Rafael in time for the 1979 crush. He produces only Port and uses four grape varieties: Pinot Noir, Cabernet Sauvignon, Zinfandel, and Petite Sirah. The blend can change from vintage to vintage, depending on grape quality, but all of the grapes come from 50-year-old vineyards in the Alexander Valley of Sonoma County. His wines achieve greater flavor concentration because of the lower yield of the old vines. All of his grapes are purchased under contracts with growers in that area.

Russ Woodbury worked at Cresta Blanca before setting up his own Port works. He has a master's degree in business administration from the University of Southern California and a bachelor's degree from the same institution. All Woodbury's Ports are fortified with 145 proof pot-stilled brandy that he has been buying from Cresta Blanca, which has one of the few pot stills still operable in California. The Woodbury Ports run 19 to 20 percent in alcoholic content and normally contain about 10 percent residual sugar, or close to the makeup of true vintage Port from Portugal. His Ports are aged in neutral barrels made of American oak. They spend 18 to 22 months in the wood, depending on the vintage, and then are bottled. Another ten years of bottle-age is advisable before drinking, but it is probable that most of the Woodbury Ports are drunk when much younger because of the impatience of consumers to sample them. Production runs 4000 cases a year. Woodbury also produces a 100 percent pot-stilled brandy, the only one of its kind in California.

☆☆☆☆

$$

· Y ·

SAUTERNES-APPELLATION CONTRÔLÉE

Château d'Yquem

Lur-Saluces

1961

MIS EN BOUTEILLE AU CHÂTEAU

Château D'Yquem.

The richest, fullest, most luscious dessert wines in the world are made at Château d'Yquem, the greatest of the Sauternes châteaux and the only one accorded the status of *premier grand cru,* or first great growth, at the Paris Exposition of 1855. Although other châteaux in Sauternes and the surrounding vineyard areas may occasionally surpass Yquem, and sometimes the great sweet whites of Germany may achieve more richness and elegance, none is as consistent as Yquem. The château's vineyards are situated on and around a hill overlooking the Garonne River south of Bordeaux, exposing the grapes to bright sunshine for full ripening and encour-

aging the humid atmosphere that helps cultivate the *pourriture noble,* or noble rot, that makes a good Sauternes unique. At Château d'Yquem, in fact, only grapes afflicted by the extraordinary parasite are used to make wine for bottling under the Yquem label. In vintages with inadequate noble rot or too low a sugar content due to poor autumn weather no Château d'Yquem is bottled. This was the case in 1964, 1952, 1951, and 1930.

The château itself is built on the site of a fortress dating back to the twelfth century and retains a fortresslike appearance, with turreted walls enclosing an inner courtyard, where part of the Bordeaux music festival takes place each May. The château and vineyards have been owned by the Lur-Saluces family since 1786, and the current proprietor, the Comte Alexandre de Lur-Saluces, is actively involved in the vineyard's management on a day-to-day basis. The estate covers 430 acres, with some 300 acres entitled to the Yquem name. Of this total, 250 acres make up the Yquem vineyard, but the continuous process of replacing old vines means that only 214 acres—or about half the total estate—ever produce Château d'Yquem wine in any one vintage.

According to the Comte, a convivial and hospitable member of the Bordeaux aristocracy, each harvest of Yquem actually involves ten vintages, because the vineyards usually undergo ten pickings each autumn. The vineyard workers are taught to pick only the ripest grapes that have been attacked by the beneficial parasite, *Botrytis cinerea,* leaving the less ripe grapes to be harvested a day, a week, or perhaps even a month later, when they have achieved the proper maturity. According to legend, it was an early Marquis de Lur-Saluces who, upon his return from a trip to Russia late in the autumn of 1847, found his vineyard completely contaminated with Botrytis. But he ordered the harvest to get under way, and the resulting wine attracted worldwide acclaim because of its highly concentrated sweetness and unique flavor. The parasite came to be known as *pourriture noble,* and its appearance is eagerly awaited each autumn.

Because the Botrytis causes the grapes to shrivel almost into raisins and makes the skins porous, facilitating the evaporation of the water in the juice, the yield from the Sémillon and Sauvignon grapes at Yquem is minuscule—about 75 gallons per acres, compared to 400 to 500 gallons under normal conditions of wine production. It is estimated that each bottle of Château d'Yquem contains the output of six or seven vines— or one glass of wine per year from each plant. The harvest may last two months or more if the weather conditions are suitable. The 1972 vintage got under way on October 4 and did not conclude until December 14, the latest ever. In the *chai,* or storage building, each barrel bears the date of the picking and pressing of the wine inside it. (The pressing always occurs on the same day as the picking, because the grapes start to ferment as soon as they are removed from the vines.)

Château d'Yquem has only three presses, one crusher, and a modest amount of other equipment for production, reflecting the slowness of the harvest. On some days as little as one *barrique,* containing about 50 gallons, is gathered. The fermentation takes several days and produces wines of extraordinarily high alcoholic levels because of the great natural sugar content of the grapes. Fourteen or 15 percent alcohol is not uncommon in Yquem, and in some years the percentage has risen above 17. It all takes place naturally, without any alcohol not produced by the fermenting grape juice itself. The wine is kept in new oak casks for three years before bottling, and only the best merits the Yquem name. The rest is sold off to be bottled as generic Sauternes without any hint that it came from Château d'Yquem, or else, in years of especially low sugar content, it is used to make Château Y, pronounced *ee-grék,* the dry white wine of Château d'Yquem that is much less costly than the noble Yquem itself. An average of 82,500 bottles of Yquem are made each year—a tiny production compared to the 200,000 bottles produced on somewhat less acreage by a *premier grand cru* Médoc such as Château Latour.

Château d'Yquem is the costliest wine to produce in the entire Bordeaux District of France, reflecting the need for multiple harvesting in combination with the tiny yield from each vine. It fetches prices comparable to the first growths of the Médoc, and old vintages are eagerly sought when they become available from private collectors at the auctions held in London by Sotheby & Co. and Christie, Manson & Woods. The 1921 is considered the greatest ever made and was still showing well in the 1970s on those rare occasions when a bottle was available for tasting. Occasionally another Sauternes or Barsac will rise to Yquem's level, but none is so consistently exquisite. (*See also* Sauternes, noble rot.)

☆☆☆/☆☆☆☆

$$$/$$$$

Yugoslavia.

Substantial quantities of red and white wine are produced in Yugoslavia, and they are increasingly visible in the export markets. The best come from Slovenia and Croatia in the north, but there are vineyards everywhere, even on the rocky islands of the Dalmatian coast. The Riesling, Traminer, Sauvignon, Sémillon, and Furmint white grapes are cultivated, along with the Pinot Noir, Gamay, Prokupac, Skadarka, and Zacinak, among the reds. The whites seem to be the most visible abroad, and a Yugoslavian Riesling can be a pleasant wine, although it will be somewhat earthier than German or Austrian Rieslings. The Yugoslavian wines that are available overseas are often identified primarily by the grape variety and secondarily by the district of production. Much of the exported wine of this country is bottled by large cooperatives. The wines of small, local vineyard owners rarely go abroad.

· Z ·

Zaca Mesa Winery.

Zaca Mesa belongs to the new generation of California wineries that came into being along with the American wine boom that began in the 1970s. The vineyards of Zaca Mesa were planted in 1973 and the business was established in 1975, but the winery itself was not finished until 1978. For the three previous vintages, borrowed premises were used, and the wines were inconsistent. The winery is in Los Olivos in the Santa Ynez Valley of Santa Barbara County. A nearby hillside vineyard consisting of 220 acres supplies the grapes for estate-bottled Chardonnay, Johannisberg Riesling, Sauvignon Blanc, Cabernet Sauvignon, Zinfandel, and Pinot Noir. In 1981 the proprietor, Marshall Ream, announced a major expansion program intended to raise production from 20,000 cases a year to 60,000. New winery equipment was installed, along with small oak barrels for aging. In 1983 control of Zaca Mesa passed into the hands of a Wall Street group as part of a major refinancing.
☆/☆☆☆
$$

ZD Wines.

ZD Wines, with facilities on the Silverado Trail in California's Napa Valley, derives its name from the two partners who founded the enterprise in 1969, Gino Zepponi and Norman De Leuze. Initially they made their wines at a small winery in Sonoma, but they built the new facility in 1979 in Napa. They purchase grapes from all over California, and the wines are surprisingly true in varietal character, often displaying an intensity and richness that challenge the wines produced by better-known wineries. Production totals upward of 10,000 cases a year of such premium varietals as Cabernet Sauvignon, Zinfandel, Merlot, Chardonnay, White Riesling and, occasionally, Gewürztraminer. The Chardonnay, Zinfandel, and Cabernet are especially noteworthy.
☆/☆☆☆
$$

Zeller Schwarze Katz.

In some parts of the world the name and label design on a bottle achieve a great deal more fame than the wine that is inside the bottle. Such is the case with the wines of Zell, a town on the lower Mosel River in the Mosel-Saar-

Ruwer region of Germany. In this case "lower" means farther north, as the Mosel flows toward its junction with the Rhine. The wines from this area also tend to be lower in quality than those of the central Mosel area to the south, although in good vintages they may represent attractive value. The fame of the Zeller Schwarze Katz comes from the picture of the black cat on the label. Virtually all of the wines of Zell are bottled as Schwarze Katz, a name that is said to date back a century. Individual vineyards within Zell thus lose their identities. The Schwarze Katz can be good wine, but a connoisseur will usually opt for something with more breeding from farther south in the Mosel Valley or from the Saar or Ruwer tributaries. Like virtually all of the other wines from the area, the Zeller Schwarze Katz is white and slightly to moderately sweet.
☆/☆☆
$

Zeltinger.

German white wine produced at Zeltingen, one of the leading wine towns of the Mosel River region. The wine production at this town is the largest of the district and some of it rivals the best of Wehlen and Bernkastel, although much of it falls short of the best quality levels. Zeltingers, especially those from the Himmelreich and the Schlossberg vineyards, are big and assertive wines, perhaps lacking the elegance of some of the other great Mosels but always displaying plenty of character. Because the production is large, prices can be lower than for other good Mosels even though a Zeltinger's quality will be just as high. Part of the famous Sonnenuhr vineyard of Wehlen extends into neighboring Zeltingen, attesting to the quality of the wines produced there, and the Prüm family that dominates Wehlen also has interests in Zeltingen.

Among the better-known vineyards at Zeltingen are the following:

Zeltinger Bickert
Zeltinger Himmelreich*
Zeltinger Kirchenpfad
Zeltinger Rotlay
Zeltinger Schlossberg*
Zeltinger Schwarzlay
Zeltinger Sonnenuhr*
Zeltinger Steinmauer
Zeltinger Stephanslay

Those vineyard names marked with an asterisk (*) survived the revision of the German wine law in 1971. The new law also made provision for another Zeltinger vineyard name, Deutschherrenberg.
☆/☆☆
$/$$

Zinfandel.

Zinfandel is the most widely planted varietal grape in California, with nearly 30,000 acres spread through every growing region of the state and producing mostly red wine, occasionally rosé. The Zinfandel grape is unique to California and its origins are shrouded in mystery and controversy. Whether or not it was one of the hundred thousand or so cuttings brought back from Europe by Count Agoston Haraszthy in 1862 is still a matter of speculation. It is definitely a variety of Vitis vinifera, the premium European wine grape species. Professors A. J. Winkler and Harold P. Olmo of the University of California at Davis studied the vine minutely, trying to determine its closest relative. For a long time it was believed to be a scion of the Austrian Zierfandler grape, but latest research relates it to Italian grape varieties from Puglia and Tuscany. Whether this proves to be so, only time can tell; the research continues.

So many different styles of Zinfandel are made in California that any taste preference can be satisfied. By far the greatest quantity is a light, soft red of medium body, rather fruity and not particularly distinguished but a cut or so above the usual *vin ordinaire* elsewhere. Most comes from the warmer growing areas of the Central Valley or southern California. In the cooler climates of northern regions the wine is of better quality and, depending on its vinification, possesses varying degrees of complexity. In the north-coast counties (Napa, Sonoma, and Mendocino), and in Santa Clara, San Benito, or Monterey it ranges from a round mellow wine, pleasant for everyday drinking, to something quite glorious and unique. It can be deep and powerful like those made by Ridge or Mayacamas or it can display the elegance of Simi or Clos du Val, capable of aging and developing in bottle for many years. It can be youthful and fresh, its fruit reminiscent of wild raspberries or black currants, a wine to enjoy at a moment's notice from makers such as Paul Masson, Christian Brothers or Almadén. In recent years, some of the most concentrated, stylish Zinfandels have come from Amador and El Dorado Counties, east of Sacramento. (*See* Amador County.)

The late-harvest Zinfandel made by Mayacamas, Mount Veeder, Calera, Sutter Home, David Bruce, and Mirassou, among others, is a spectacular wine that has attracted wide attention. The grapes are left longer on the vines in the autumn to develop maximum sugar, and the result, a lusciously concentrated wine of enormous depth and body, offers an extraordinary experience. With as much as 17 percent alcohol in some cases, it can sometimes be too overpowering to serve with a meal. Such a wine is better enjoyed with a good cheese and sipped slowly to allow every nuance of its complexity to come forth, just as vintage Port would be savored.

Some excellent rosé is now made from Zinfandel. Most Zinfandels are best at around age five, but some need a decade or more to mature.

Index